# The Ultimate

# BAR

## BOOK

André Dominé

# The Ultimate
# BAR
## BOOK

## The World of Spirits and Cocktails

**Photography**
Armin Faber
Thomas Pothmann

**Text**
André Dominé
Barbara E. Euler
Wolfgang Faßbender
Matthias Stelzig

**Editor**
Martina Schlagenhaufer

**Layout**
Christian Heße

h.f.ullmann

**Abbreviations:**

| | | | | | | |
|---|---|---|---|---|---|---|
| % vol. | = | volume percent | | ha | = | hectare |
| l | = | liter | | cl | = | centiliter |
| bsp | = | bar spoon | | tbsp | = | tablespoon |
| kg | = | kilogram | | g | = | gram |
| oz | = | ounce | | ABV | = | alcohol by volume |
| AOC | = | Appellation d'Origine Contrôlée | | | | |

It is advisable not to serve any drinks that contain raw egg to very young children, pregnant women, elderly people or anyone weakened by serious illness. If in any doubt consult your doctor. Be sure that all the eggs you use are as fresh as possible.

© 2008 Tandem Verlag GmbH
h.f.ullmann is an imprint of Tandem Verlag GmbH
Original title: *The Ultimate Bar Book: Die Welt der Spirituosen und Cocktails*
ISBN 978-3-8331-4802-6

© VG Bild-Kunst, Bonn 2008/Leonetto Cappiello: pp. 495, 531, 588
© VG Bild-Kunst, Bonn 2008/Marcello Dudovich: pp. 522, 588

All text by André Dominé except for:
Barbara E. Euler: Liqueurs
Wolfgang Faßbender: Pomace and pomace brandies
Matthias Stelzig: The bar; Behind the bar; Fruit brandies except for
calvados; Grain spirits; Ouzo and raki; Cocktails and other drinks

Graphic design: Martin Wellner
Layout: Christian Heße
Editor: Martina Schlagenhaufer
Editorial assistants: Kathrin Jurgenowski, Ursula Münden
Cartography: DuMont Reisekartografie GmbH
Project management: Isabel Weiler

© 2008 for the English edition: Tandem Verlag GmbH
h.f.ullmann is an imprint of Tandem Verlag GmbH

English translation: Ann Drummond, Rosemary Lawrey and Katherine Taylor
in association with First Edition Translations Ltd, Cambridge, UK
Editing: Jenny Knight in association with First Edition Translations Ltd, Cambridge, UK
Typesetting: The WriteIdea in association with First Edition Translations Ltd, UK

ISBN 978-3-8331-4803-3

Printed in China

10 9 8 7 6 5 4 3 2 1
X IX VIII VII VI V IV III II I

www.ullmann-publishing.com

# Contents

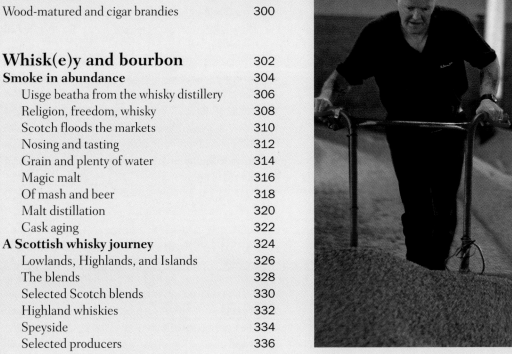

## Selected spirits at a glance

# From al-kuhl to cocktail

A small section of the range in Munich's Commercial Bar, where the array of spirits and cocktails is indeed extensive.

Page 12: A distilling plant comprising two heated stills, their long, winding spirit pipes being fed through a cooling system. (Title plate with subsequent coloring from: Hieronymus Brunschwig, *The Book of Distilling*, Strasbourg 1532)

# Condensed diversity

The world of spirits has never been as colorful and diverse, the range on the shelves of specialist retailers and supermarkets as rich and international, or the demand for top alcoholic products as great as is the case today. Never before have the menus in bars, pubs, cafes, restaurants, and discotheques featured so many cocktails and long drinks—nor have so many bartenders in so many countries been familiar with the art of mixing, and so many private individuals taken so much pleasure in serving drinks from a shaker at home. And in the same vein, it has never been more difficult to obtain a comprehensive overview.

Without doubt the internet offers countless pages on individual spirits as well as on whole categories of them. You can acquire mountains of books on whisk(e)y, rum, port, cognac, or cocktails, as well as specialist magazines. Works offering an overview, on the other hand, are less common—and are seldom comprehensive. A comprehensive overview is precisely what is at issue here. Of course, not all of the world's spirits and cocktails are listed in this book. That would be neither possible nor particularly meaningful. Instead, the different categories are presented here—relating to spirits on the one hand and cocktails on the other: how they are made, what characterizes them, and how they differ. To this end it has been beneficial to select typical examples in order to create an appropriate impression of the relevant groups, from the everyday brands through to the noble distillates, from classic mixed drinks through to innovative creations. If it is a question of determining what makes a specific bottled malt so special or how far back the tradition of flavored vodkas extends, then neither the last single cask bottling from Macallan nor the latest flavor from Absolut is really going to be of much help. Unfortunately, the many regional specialties would have extended beyond the scope of an overview focusing on specific drink categories.

Anyone wanting to learn more about a high-proof gift will find the detailed index in this book a quick way to obtain more information. Anyone interested in the history of a very special "fire water" will also find plenty of interesting reading matter. There is much to be learnt about the world of spirits as it has taken shape over the last 700 years or so, starting with the realization that the development of spirits is inseparable from that of medicine and culture, and of nations and societies. Ultimately, the interest in distillation had a medicinal motivation; even vermouth, bitters, and herbal liqueurs used to serve the purposes of convalescence and not indulgence.

Indulgence raises the issue of the more problematic aspects, be it the infamous trilateral trade between the Caribbean, Africa, and Europe or America; be it the health and social decline caused by gin in 18th-century England, or that caused by absinthe in France at the *fin de siècle*. Today all of the large spirits companies are committed to "responsible drinking," most especially to counter teenage alcoholism and drink driving effectively. This book explains how whisk(e)y or cognac, rum, tequila, vodka, and fruit schnapps are distilled and what determines their quality, so that the next time you go shopping you know what you need to pay attention to. Some distillates, such as whisk(e)y and cognac, only reach their optimal expression after many years of aging, while with others—particularly the fruit schnapps varieties—it is a question of capturing the fresh aroma of the selected fruit at its purest potency. Both examples give off an intense and complex aroma from the glass, and this is what constitutes the true miracle of high-quality schnapps, a miracle that connoisseurs have only really addressed in the last two decades and that has contributed to the very diverse range available today, albeit with the requisite restraint.

André Dominé

# For a special occasion

People have always found occasion to drink. In ancient cultures alcoholic intoxication provided a gateway to the gods, this being said of the ancient Egyptians as well as the ancient Greeks, and the same is alleged of the ancient Germanic peoples. Leaving out the reason for drinking, the deciding factor was that drinking took place in company—as is the case today. Drinking alone is still viewed as questionable. As drinking has a social significance, rules were soon put in place as to who was allowed to, or had to, drink what with whom.

Initially only beer, wine, and mead were worthy of any discussion. It was only in the 18th century that drinking customs were extended to spirits, particularly home-brewed spirits. Hence farmers greeted their guests with a home brew, drinking "to their health" as, in fact, it was not that long ago that schnapps had actually been administered as medicine.

A change in these customs came about in the 19th century with the flourishing of the economy, emerging industrialization, and spreading urbanization. This was accompanied by an increase in outlets: coffee houses and pubs, taverns, and ultimately bars were opened—places where people met for social interaction and to enjoy a drink together.

In the Mediterranean countries, where wine had always been seen more as a foodstuff, it remains almost exclusively a food accompaniment to this day and is not normally touched outside mealtimes. When people meet prior to the midday or evening meal, it is time for an aperitif. The drinks that were initially served as such were indeed appetite stimulants, many of them containing quinine and other stimulatory plants and herbs. Even absinthe, flavored predominantly with aniseed, was largely a stimulant first and foremost.

Pastis or other aniseed spirits remain the most popular aperitif throughout the Mediterranean region.

You don't only visit a bar for a drink after work; it can also be part of an evening program. (Edouard Manet, *A Bar at the Folies-Bergère*, 1881/2, London, Courtauld Institute Galleries)

## Before and after meals

Once the occasions became established, the producers moved on to developing drinks specifically for these occasions and even creating brands to suit them.

Today the aperitif or before-dinner drink is perhaps the most frequent of these occasions, deriving from the indispensable habit in the Mediterranean region of popping into the local bar before the midday or evening meal for a well-earned drink.

This is coupled with the worldwide custom of beginning every gathering, every party, and every celebration that usually involves a meal with at least one if not more introductory drinks. Depending on country, status, and preference, a wide variety of spirits can be served as cocktails or long drinks, or else sherry, white port, vermouth, or bitters, for example. It is not unusual for such preludes to take two hours. Bars, which are frequented less often before dinner, attract customers with Happy Hours at reduced prices. Then comes the phase after the meal, particularly the evening meal. First of all the various classics are offered as digestifs because alcohol aids digestion. This is the best moment for the great distillates, especially those that have aged for years in oak barrels, be it cognac, armagnac, brandy de Jerez, or calvados, or other aged apple or plum schnapps varieties such as vintage whiskies and rums, or well-aged tawnys, madeiras, sherrys, and banyuls.

Once night falls the stage is set for after-dinner cocktails. Thereafter it is time for the bars, clubs, or discotheques, and with them the full diversity of mixed drinks.

Cocktails have long since found their way into the arts. (Scene from the debut performance of the play *The Cocktail Party* by T.S. Eliot, 1949 in Edinburgh)

# Fine for a time

In a well-organized bar it is the colorful liqueurs that first attract attention from among the rows of very different bottles on the shelves, today taking up more and more space, while in the end your eyes are sure to linger on the elaborate bottles and carafes indicative of expensive distillates. The order is left to the barkeeper's discretion, but he does ensure that the spirits he uses the most are the ones that are quickest to hand.

The following chapters present spirits according to their categories, relate their histories, define their methods of production, explain their differences in quality, and demonstrate their possible uses with the help of recipes.

The classic breakdown of spirits and cocktails served in the world of gastronomy comprises aperitifs and digestifs—i.e. before-dinner and after-dinner drinks. Spirits themselves are often subject to such different categorization that it is difficult to allocate them to the two traditional groups of aperitifs and digestifs. The most consumed alcoholic drinks today, vodka and white rum, are characterized by their largely neutral flavor, making them ideal for mixing and a range of other uses, especially in light, refreshing drinks.

Neat high proof is not suitable prior to a meal, and that is why aperitifs initially include wine-based drinks, provided—to every rule there is an exception—that they are on the dry side. Hence vermouth, dry sherries, madeiras, white ports, and marsalas fall into this category. These are joined by

The barkeeper—as shown here at the Green Door Bar in Berlin—is less concerned with a spirit's category than with its easy accessibility.

those members of the complex category of liqueurs that can be mixed with mineral water, soft drinks, or juices, although these are usually the bitter liqueurs. Their advantage is their quick and easy preparation. Classic spirits such as gin, whisk(e)y, and cognac are admitted in their diluted form, most simply with soda or with other mixers in more sophisticated versions such as highballs, while the addition of lemon juice—as with gin—produces a refreshing result. The aniseed spirits play a special role, most of them being diluted with chilled water and being considered aperitifs *par excellence* due to their low alcohol content, their character, and the effect of the aniseed. If aperitifs are to be seen as a prelude to a good meal, then you should be sure to choose only drinks that do not compromise or anaesthetize the taste buds with too strong an aroma or too much alcohol.

As their name suggests, digestifs are intended to aid digestion, which they indeed do after a rich meal, thanks to the alcohol. The great classics in this category are of course the brandies as well as all of the brown spirits matured for a long time in barrels, be it whisk(e)y, rum, calvados, or some marcs. However the pale, aromatic distillates also put in an appearance here, primarily fruit schnapps—as well as grappa and aquavit. Herbal liqueurs and bitters maintain a fixed position under the digestifs, but this category does also include many other liqueurs ideally suited to harmonizing with the coffee served after a meal. Well-aged tawnys, amontillados, or banyuls are considered to be special digestifs whose outstanding aromas are better appreciated after rather than before the meal. Digestifs offer something for everyone's palate.

Intriguing before-dinner drinks, but anyone wanting to be able to appreciate the meal afterward ought to avoid combinations with too much alcohol and too much aroma.

# To your good health?

Opposite: "Drink no brandy, for it is poison." Colored chalk lithograph from Neuruppin Prints, around 1850.

Alcohol is a toxin that can be fatal at a blood concentration of 0.4–0.5%. You can easily observe the strong effect of alcohol yourself as just a small glass of high-proof spirits causes perceptible changes. You feel excited, more relaxed, and you start to become talkative. Double the quantity brings about a certain euphoria that is generally considered to be pleasant. However, just 0.05% slows your reactions and can lead to the misjudgment of risks that even at this stage can compromise your fitness to drive.

If the percentage of the ethanol—the scientific name for alcohol— in your blood rises, then a lack of physical coordination, a loss of balance, a tendency to aggression, increasing loss of self-control, and therefore significantly reduced physical and mental ability are the result; vomiting, inebriation, and loss of memory follow as of 0.2%. As of

0.3% there is a risk of coma, and even death. The way in which a person reacts to the intake of ethanol differs according to the individual and depends on a great many factors, including body weight, state of health, age, genes, and gender. Asians are less able to tolerate alcohol than western Europeans, women less than men. Anyone who has dined well on rich food can genuinely afford an extra glass.

## Absorption and breakdown

The absorption of alcohol into the body begins as soon as you take a sip, even if it is just a small amount, as it is absorbed via the oral mucosa.

Nine tenths of the alcohol reach the blood via the small intestines and is carried in the blood to the liver, which breaks it down. It takes from 30 minutes to 2 hours before the

Who can cope with how much alcohol largely depends on a number of individual factors.

## What is alcohol?

Alcohol or, scientifically, ethanol is a colorless liquid with an intense, penetrating smell. It comprises two carbon atoms, five hydrogen atoms and a hydroxyl group. Also known colloquially as spirits, ethanol has two distinct properties: firstly it is highly inflammable and burns with pale, blue flame, forming CO2 and water vapor; secondly, it is strongly water absorbent, hygroscopic, and therefore a strong, proven solvent. Ethanol is lighter than water with a density of 0.7913 g/cm3 and vaporizes earlier with a boiling point of just above 173 °F (78.3 °C). Ethanol occurs naturally through fermentation, in which yeast converts fructose into alcohol and carbon dioxide. This occurs automatically in ripe fruit as well as in other foodstuffs. For example, bread can contain up to 0.3% vol. ethanol, sauerkraut around 0.5% vol., and a ripe banana up to 1% vol.

alcohol you have drunk is absorbed by the body. The alcohol dehydrogenase enzyme performs the breaking down at a constant rate, amounting to at least 0.1 g alcohol per kg body weight. For someone weighing 165 lb (75 kg) this means about 4 fl oz (7.5 g) alcohol in one hour. It is therefore easy to calculate the amount of time your body requires to excrete the amount of alcohol you have drunk.

A hangover develops if the body has to break down too large an amount of alcohol, as this involves a great deal of water and dehydration causes headaches. The symptoms are intensified if the spirits consumed contained fusel oil, which form toxins when broken down. As a preventive measure, therefore, you should always drink a few glasses of water between alcoholic drinks, as well as several glasses of water at the end of the evening.

## Risks and commitment

Even though alcohol has played a medicinal role from the earliest times through to today, having been and still being used to extract the active agents from plants in order to administer them to patients, its abuse leads to addiction and thereby to a multitude of illnesses, often followed by an early death. There are two main categories of illness: one category comprises psychic and neurological conditions such as depression and hallucinations, dementia, and epilepsy; the other comprises the consequences of metabolic problems, including cirrhosis of the liver, impotence, cardiac insufficiency, various types of cancer, and a general weakening of the immune system.

No less serious are the social problems and irresponsible behavior caused by excessive alcohol consumption, not least among teenagers and among drivers. For a number of years now the manufacturers and producers of alcoholic drinks and their industry associations have been carrying out effective consumer education, particularly among those sectors of the population at risk—especially teenagers, with concrete results starting to become apparent.

In addition, the discussion as to whether moderate alcohol consumption is beneficial to health continues. It is interesting to note that recent studies carried out among older people show that low-level alcohol consumption and a good state of health are often related.

# Spirit and intellect: the distillation idea

Matthaeus Platearius compiled one of the key pharmaceutical works of the Middle Ages in Salerno in 1150, the *Circa instans*, or *De medicinis simplicibus*. (Illumination on parchment from: *Le Livre des simples médecines*, around 1500, Russian National Library, St. Petersburg)

You only need to bring water to the boil in a covered saucepan on the stove and to then remove the lid: the drops on the inside of the lid are an example of distillation. The water reaches its boiling point, rises as vapor, meets the cooler saucepan lid, and condenses to form water again. If you vaporize a mixed liquid, then the different components volatize out of the mixture in the order of their boiling points. So much for the physical side of things. The basic principle was known to the Sumerians back in the 13th century

B.C.—at least, the principle of distillation itself, not necessarily the distillation of alcohol. The first applications of this technology were for the purposes of beauty care and personal hygiene, being used to extract essential oils from plants. Once the plants are chopped up and the mixture heated in water, the water vapor "carries" the ephemeral agents with it. The oil then separates from the water in the resulting condensate— from *destillare*, meaning to drip. Around 1,000 years later Greek sailors used this principle in order to obtain drinking water from seawater while at sea, evaporating the water and collecting the condensate. The vessels used were constantly adapted to their purpose, and the ancient Egyptians designed a cap for the rounded lower part to which a pipe was attached, from which the distillate could drip. The Greeks adopted the model and called the cap *mastarion* because it was shaped like a breast. Although they knew that wine contained an inflammable substance (which they utilized in the Dionysian cult), there is no evidence of their having distilled alcohol.

## A cool head

The cap or helmet so important for efficient dripping was known as the *alanbiq* in Arabic, which the Romans adopted as the *alambicus*, an accepted term in many languages today. The *alembic* became the typical instrument of alchemists—motivated by the teachings of Aristotle—who endeavored to perfect metal and convert it into gold. Although they did not achieve this, they did make numerous discoveries regarding chemical elements, substances, and processes. It was for the extraction of rose water that distillation technology was largely perfected, rose water having become a lucrative trading commodity in the Middle East after 900.

There is still one decisive prerequisite for the distilling of alcohol: the distillation of substances with boiling points lower than that of water (geraniol, the main component in rose oil, boils at 446 °F/ 230 °C, alcohol at 173 °F / 78.3 °C). In order to be able to collect them, the heating has to be done carefully and the rising vapors cooled. This realization is ascribed to the Persian alchemist Abu Musar Dschabir Ibn Hajjan, while the physician Al Razi (Abu Bakr Mohammad Ibn Zakariya al-Razi, 865–925) was the first to record how substances with low boiling points are distilled. He is also said to have distilled wine, naming the result *al-kull*, the whole, and to have used it for medical treatment because of its sterilizing properties. In Arabic *al-kuhl* referred to eye makeup and it was only in Spain that the word became reinterpreted as spirits.

It was the Moors who brought alchemical skills to Europe, where alchemy, science, and philosophy underwent a significant upsurge in the 11th century. In Salerno the monks' hospital belonging to the Monte Cassino monastery became one of the first medical universities in Europe. It was here that a recipe was copied into Matthaeus Platearius' famous medicinal book *De medicinis simplicibus*, known as the *Circa instans* (after the first words of the introduction) in the mid 12th century. It contained instructions on how to produce *aqua ardens*, fire water, the common name for spirits throughout the Middle Ages. The distillation of alcohol in Europe had begun.

*Alembics* came to Andalusia with the Moors, but it was only centuries later that they were used for distilling wine. This is Gonzalez Byass' new distillery.

# Remedy and indulgence

Two physicians stand at the forefront of the modern art of distilling: the Italian Taddeo Alderotti and the Spaniard Arnaldus de Villanova. Alderotti (known in his writings as Thaddaeus Florentinus; ca. 1223–1303), was born in Florence, and taught medicine at the University of Bologna from 1260, where he began distilling wine a few years later. His work *De virtutibus aquae vite et eius operationibus* provides a detailed description of how high-proof spirits can be obtained through repeated distillation. Three to four runs were usual, but at least ten were required for an especially pure distillate, the *aqua vitae perfectissima* or *rectivicata*. These rectifications were made possible by an important new development: the *canale serpentinum*, a winding pipe housed in a cooling vessel kept cold with water, in which the vapors containing the alcohol condensed. This technology became widespread among alchemists and chemists at the end of the 13th century, and both Alderotti and his colleagues recognized that this distillate was ideally suited to medicinal purposes.

One of the most famous physicians of the age was the Knight Templar and alchemist Arnaldus de Villanova (ca. 1235–1311), personal physician to the king of Aragon. He distilled wine at Mas Deu, the headquarters of the Knights Templar near Perpignan, and in 1285 he discovered that the fermentation of wine can be halted by the addition of spirits, making the wine non-perishable on the one hand, and giving it a proportion of residual sugar on the other. This is still the way fortified wines are made today. He considered the *aqua vitae* to be a universal remedy, recommending its application in numerous works as well as that of a variety of flavored wines that he described in his *Liber de vinis*. While the laboriously produced *aqua vitae* was initially administered to the sick by the spoonful, an epidemic in the second half of the 14th century required a less restrained approach to spirits. Helpless in the face of the plague and death, people placed their faith, not entirely without justification, in the strength of the water of life—often acquiring a taste for it in the process. The first commercial distilleries with large stills were established in the centuries that followed. By this time it had already been established that not only was wine a suitable starting basis, but that alcohol was produced in all fermenting fruit.

The Strasbourg physician Hieronymus Brunschwig (ca. 1450–1513) provided such a detailed description of distilling in his widely circulated books that people were able to reproduce the process. The use of corn mash became widespread as of the mid 16th century, making alcohol affordable and available in larger quantities. The distillation process remained largely unchanged for

An old, hand-crafted column still at Florio in Marsala.

several centuries. In order to be able to separate as much water as possible from the alcohol, distilling had to be carried out several times, and this could only be done consecutively, the run taking place in the same direction, the liquid vaporizing, the vapor rising, turning to liquid, and dripping down. A first important further development, patented in 1801, can be attributed to the French chemist and physicist Jean-Edouard Adam (1768–1807), who arranged several vessels behind one another in which the alcohol vapors partially condensed, enabling him to produce a better yield. The decisive step toward today's column stills, however, came in 1808 from the Frenchman Jean-Baptiste Cellier-Blumenthal (1768–1840), who ran a sugar beet factory in Belgium. He was the first to use a column with several bell type trays on top of one another in order to concentrate the alcohol. In Scotland Robert Stein put together his still in 1826; it was perfected by the Irishman Aeneas Coffey and patented in 1831. His column device allowed for repeated, continual distilling without interruption in a kind of circulatory system, making it considerably more cost effective. It became the basic model not only for industrial stills but also for modern stills, with rectifier columns as used today by top-class distillers.

Old still from the historic corn distillery in Hilden, Fabry-Museum.

# Distillation: the classic method

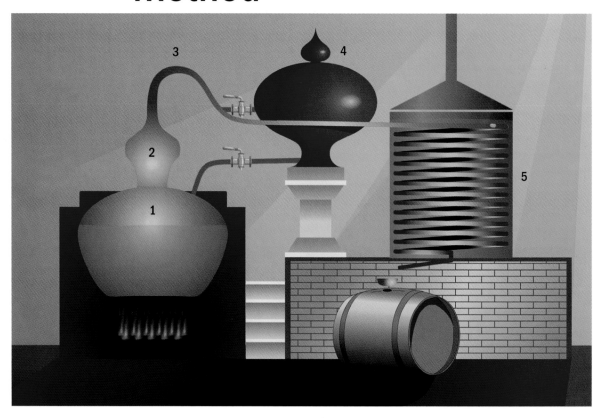

The famous model for batch distillation is the *alambic charentais* for cognac. Its special feature is a wine preheater fitted to the still, from where the alcoholic vapors rise up through the helmet and swan's neck to condense in the cooling pipe. Here the vapor loses heat so that the wine flowing into the still has a temperature of about 104 °F (40 °C).
1  Still
2  Helmet
3  Swan's neck (also the spirit pipe)
4  Wine preheater
5  Cooling pipe

When distilling spirits a slightly alcoholic liquid is extracted from the alcohol and collected separately. The liquid in question also has to be heated so that the alcohol, with a boiling point of 173 °F (78.3 °C), vaporizes before the water. This vapor is collected and allowed to condense, either using batch and/or coflow distillation, or by means of continual and/or counterflow distillation.

The principle behind the older, batch method—which remains in use today for the production of such famous spirits as cognac and malt whisk(e)y—underwent significant improvements by the physicians and alchemists of the 13th century. It is based on two aspects: on the one hand the rising alcohol vapors need to be cooled so that they then condense; on the other hand, repeated distilling is necessary in order to obtain a higher alcohol content and a purer distillate.

While, in the centuries gone by, three, four, and even 10–15 distilling runs were necessary, today two are sufficient when carried out perfectly.

Generations of distillers have sought to increase the efficiency of their distilling plants ever since the 13th century. The unit itself essentially comprised of an oven, with a pumpkin-shape still, and a pipe through which the rising alcohol vapors were fed off and cooled. A major improvement was the replacement of the glass still with a copper one, enabling an increase in volume. In the 15th century the next step was the placing of a helmet on top of the still with a winding spirit pipe, the swan's neck, through which the vapors slowly rose. Today we know that the shape of this helmet has a decisive influence on the character of the distillate.

## One after the other

Distilling begins with the filling of the still. The first batch comprises wine, beer, or the alcohol-containing mash, and is usually heated by gas today. In the first run this is distilled to a still slightly cloudy raw spirit with an alcohol content of between 25 and 35% vol. (depending on the starting substance). The raw spirit also contains aromatic agents such as ester, aldehyde, various alcohols and acids such as terpene, and acetals as well as the infamous fusel oils. All of the insoluble and non-volatile components, on the other hand, remain in the still. For the second batch the distiller collects enough raw spirit in order to refill the still—but not without having cleaned it thoroughly beforehand. With a second unit the process can be continued with no time loss. The distiller requires experience and expertise for the extraction of the refined spirit. He has to raise the temperature carefully in order to use the opportunity to separate the first runnings, the first part of the condensing distillate with undesired, slightly volatile substances such as methanol. This is followed by the middle runnings or the heart: he begins with an alcohol content of up to 80% vol. that then sinks gradually during the course of distillation. Depending on the starting material, the distiller lets it sink down to 55–45% vol. before drawing off the end runnings that contain the fusel oils. The sooner the middle runnings are ended, the purer the distillate, but a small proportion of fusel oils can ensure greater complexity and more character in spirits aged in barrels for many years. The alcohol content of the refined spirit, which amounts to about one third of the quantity of raw spirit, varies between 60 and 75% vol.

Modern versions of the *alambic charentais* at Cognac Frapin, clearly showing that the basic design has been retained.

# Distillation: the modern methods

Batch distilling, or coflow distillation, is a complex method that is both time consuming and cost intensive, but that produces outstanding results because it enables the precise separation of the first and last runnings. An alcohol value of a maximum of 75% vol. is achieved with double distilled spirits. Continual and/or counterflow distillation is quicker and more cost effective, producing a higher alcohol concentration, albeit at the expense of the aroma agents. During the first decades of the 19th century a number of inventors in different countries busied themselves with the technical improvement of distillation. The first continual distilling unit to be built was developed by the Frenchman Jean-Baptiste Cellier-Blumenthal and was patented in 1808. The German distiller Johann Heinrich Leberecht Pistorius patented his two still apparatus with mash preheater in 1817. The Scotsman Robert Stein experimented with his notion of more rational distillation in the 1820s, a concept that was then perfected by the Irishman Aeneas Coffey as the highly complex continual patent still that was patented in 1831 and that bears his name. The basic principle behind continual and/or counterflow distillation requires that the liquid to be distilled flows constantly and the alcohol contained therein is vaporized, condensed, and continually fed off. This occurs by means of one or several rectifier columns comprising several bell-like separating layers functioning as small stills. The liquid is poured into the column from above and flows downward through the perforated separating layers. In the process it encounters the vapor rising from the bottom of the column that heats it, vaporizing the alcohol contained therein, so that it begins to rise. From layer to layer, condensing in part at each level and dripping down again, the alcohol leaves other liquid substances behind, becoming more and more concentrated until it reaches the condenser via the spirit pipe. The alcohol-free liquid is then fed out of the column. Today the majority of spirits are distilled using the continual method, be it vodka, rum, bourbon, or grain whisk(e)y.

Left: The Cellier-Blumenthal apparatus (patent 1808); the wine is added from the top right.

Right: Coffey's patent still— patent 1831 (graphics based on: Meyers *Großes Konversations-Lexikon,* Leipzig 1905–9, volume 4)

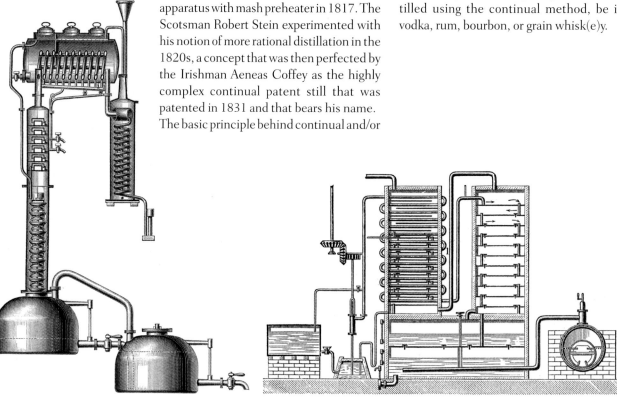

1  Catalyzer
2  Dephlegmator
3  Coolant collector tank
4  Fine distillate column
5  Cooling tube
6  Agitator
7  Still
8  Mash and pomace
   outlet
9  Heating unit
10  Water bath

## Top of the range distillation unit

The development of the column devices ultimately gave blacksmiths the idea of combining conventional stills with a column to enable top-class distillers to complete batch distillation in one distilling process, in which the distillate is simultaneously rectified and/or cleansed and concentrated. (The example comes from Arnold Holstein, a producer from Lake Constance in Germany specialized in distillation technology.)

The **still** (7), made from tempered copper, is filled from the side. It is heated in the **water bath** (10), which avoids any risk of scorching. An **agitator** (6) is integrated for more viscous mashes.

A variety of layers can be fitted individually in the **fine distillate column** (4). Using the dephlegmator (2), which condenses vapors by means of targeted cooling and feeds them back into the column, the middle runnings produce a very high concentration of aroma components.

The **catalyzer** (1) ensures the reduction of undesired acids. At the top of the catalyzer the vapors are fed through a pipe to the actual **cooling tube** (5), the distillate emerging from its lower end. These perfected distilling units and the fact that top-class distillers now focus on the highest quality mean that distillates of an unprecedented clarity and finesse are now being produced.

# Panacea and commodity

The old well and an ancient, disused alembic (in the background) in a yard in Cognac stand as testimony to the century-old tradition.

The alchemists who engaged in distillation were in fact searching for the philosopher's stone. Initially said to be a miracle substance capable of turning inexpensive metals into gold, they soon interpreted it to be a kind of universal medicine believed to grant health, strength, eternal youth, and wisdom. Once knowledge of the processes behind the technology of distillation became more widespread with the first publications about it, more and more physicians, chemists, and alchemists managed to produce colorless, slightly inflammable spirits. They did not find the philosopher's stone but they did discover the *quinta essential*, the quintessence of life. They were fascinated by this liquid substance that completely disappeared as soon as they set it alight and that therefore contradicted the teachings on the four non-transformable elements, which formed the very basis of the Aristotelian worldview. They discovered that this substance had further astounding properties aside from its flammability, particularly from a medicinal perspective. It was its decay prohibiting and disinfecting properties that made the use of pure alcohol a blessing. What's more, it absorbed the active agents from other plants in previously unknown concentrations. The fact that, like wine, it affected the psyche—but much faster—and that it stimulated, exhilarated, and intoxicated did not go unnoticed either.

However, it took an immense amount of effort to obtain just a small quantity of this water of life, and so it remained a precious panacea for a long time. It was the monasteries, in particular, that took up its production, thereby obtaining a multitude of tinctures—the predecessors of liqueurs—

the most bitter of which were sweetened with honey. The more progress the monks made in perfecting this art and the more palatable their health elixirs became, the more the production of pure medicines was left to the chemists, who had been granted professional recognition with a decree from Emperor Friedrich II, patron of Salerno university, as early as 1241.

## Spirits bring profits

The consumption of spirits gradually spread throughout Europe, but remained a local affair initially until Dutch merchants discovered its benefits in the 16th century. When The Netherlands rose to become the greatest trading power in the 17th century, *brandewijn* became one of the most lucrative trading commodities. To start with, the Dutch bought wine in the harbors of the French Atlantic coast, then sold it at home or in the Baltic countries. There were large quantities available in the Charente in particular, but the quality was poor. The Dutch merchants showed considerable interest in the distillation of wine that began there in the mid 16th century as, unlike wine, spirits were non-perishable and required only a fraction of the space for transportation. Like

wine, spirits were not considered a luxury but simply as a thirst quenching drink, the crystal clear distillate being mixed with what was at that time often polluted water.

The Dutch obtained their spirits from the Cognac region, via Bayonne harbor, as well as later from Armagnac. Like wine, the spirits were transported in barrels, and it was soon discovered that this improved them and that they took on an attractive color after a while. The customers in London in particular—England was the principal brandy customer—noticed significant differences in quality depending on the origin and the type of barrel. Accordingly, toward the end of the 17th century the upper classes began to make specific demands for specific brandies, particularly the brandy from Cognac, for which they were willing to pay higher prices. This made cognac a forerunner of a development that only took hold in other regions and countries in the 19th century, namely the development of high-quality spirits.

Left: Not a lot seems to have changed in the cellar at Chateau de Salles since the first successes with armagnac.

Right: Paradise at Hennessy with some of the cognacs dating back to the previous century.

# Everyday alcohol

The emergence of modern spirits as we know them today is inseparable from the development of western society. The Industrial Revolution was the most important factor in this process, bringing with it increased urbanization as well as completely new work and income structures. The influence of the nobility declined while the middle class—who now were able to play a decisive role in economic, political, and cultural life—grew in significance.

France provided the most striking example of these changes. Antoine Beauvilliers, former quartermaster to the counts of Provence, opened the first upmarket restaurant in Paris in 1782. A number of others

Byrrh, originally introduced as a tonic, also successfully developed its appeal for the well-to-do middle class.

followed his example but in the year of the revolution, 1789, there were not even 50 restaurants in Paris. One of the farreaching consequences of the revolution was that the nobility's kitchen staff lost their jobs. What solution was more obvious for them than to set up a location where people could "revitalize" themselves? As a result, by 1820 there were already some 3,000 restaurants established in Paris.

The gastronomical expansion was one prerequisite for the later success of beverage brands, but there was also another: new mealtimes. In the towns the main meal used to be eaten between 2 and 4 o'clock, with people going to the theatre as of 5 o'clock and then enjoying a light supper at 9 o'clock. This rhythm was broken by the meetings of the National Assembly: the members of the assembly, who drafted the new constitution, began work at 1 o'clock. They developed the habit of eating beforehand and, because those working in administration and in government departments were soon working from 9 a.m. to 4 p.m., they followed this example, eating at around 12 o'clock and then taking their main meal at about 7 o'clock in the evening. All amusement activities were postponed until later in the evening. All of a sudden there was a time span in the late afternoon that was ideally suited to visiting one of the large boulevard cafes and to enjoy a drink, an aperitif.

## The thirsty bourgeoisie

The development of a well-to-do middle class brought with it potential consumers for branded beverages. At the start of the 19th century the evolution had already begun in Turin and Milan, where the drinking of vermouth was met with much enthusiasm. As the manufacturers ensured vigorous competition for one another, each of them tried to gain exposure for their brand. One example was Cinzano, taking part in the second World Exhibition in London in 1862 in order to present their own vermouth

MARTINI

VERMOUTH·MARTINI & ROSSI-TORINO

Above: Spirits became brands that were portrayed by famous poster artists (this one by Giorgio Muggiani) wanting to establish a name for themselves.

Below: Even back then the modern trend showed a clear preference for addressing women.

MARSALA FLORIO

CASA FONDATA NEL 1833

brand, and of course using the gold medal they won there as a sales pitch.

The *belle époque* era was the real boom time, with Europe not only experiencing a further wave of industrialization toward the end of the 19th century, but also a comparatively long period of peace. Cafes and coffee houses developed into society meeting places, the frequenting of which was seen as a lifestyle expression. The bars provided the scope for casual exchanges as well as giving rise to entirely now consumer behavior at the same time. People met to enjoy a drink together and the industry reacted with a constant range of new and intriguing drinks: *apéritifs à base de vin*, vermouth, bitters, absinthe, liqueurs. Anyone having trouble deciding between the wealth of options could refer to the new but already widespread advertising media such as calendar posters, water fountains, and placards. Branded drinks were here to stay.

# Prohibition

Alcohol continues to provoke lively debate as to its uses and dangers. Towns, regions, and provinces have been confronted with the consequences of inebriation since the very early history of alcohol consumption, reacting with bans and other measures. Price increases proved to be a clever move in many respects. For example, it was with higher taxation that the English were able to control the excesses of the gin craze in the 18th century, gin becoming unaffordable for the poor who sought oblivion under its influence.

The authorities realized very early on that the public's appetite for alcohol was too great to be able to deter them entirely with taxes, which is why this is a pleasingly reliable source of income. The authorities' relationship to alcoholic beverages has been an ambivalent one ever since. On the one hand, they can see the damage caused by excessive consumption, which they therefore want to stop but, on the other hand, they pocket the tax millions deriving from the

As in the 19th century: the atmosphere at Jack Daniel's in Tennessee.

consumption of alcohol with no noticeable signs of reluctance.

Prohibition in the United States proved just how ineffective a ban is in dealing with the problem of alcoholism. Beer and bourbon consumption having reached sizeable proportions by the beginning of the 19th century, opposition to the demonic substance alcohol increased, especially in religious circles. A ban on alcohol was imposed in the state of Maine as early as 1851, covering both production and consumption. It was initially the conservative southern states that were determined to become "dry," while the northern states were not prepared to have moral behavior dictated to them.

It was women in particular who took up arms against alcohol, and the Women's Christian Temperance Union founded in 1873 became one of the most influential organizations. They and the Prohibition Party were superseded by the Anti-Saloon League, who used a polished strategy and religious fervor

to fight for a nationwide alcohol ban. And this with success, the Prohibition passed by Congress coming into force in 1920.

## Health and immorality

Prohibition was a success in that alcohol consumption in general saw a significant decrease, and this did bring distinctly positive results at least in terms of the diseases directly related to alcoholism such as cirrhosis of the liver. In many families there was also less aggressive behavior caused by drunkenness than had been the case previously. However, not only did Prohibition bring about the collapse of thousands of smaller, previously legal breweries, wine makers, distilleries, spirits merchants, and saloons, but it also created a vacuum that was filled by organized crime. For although the demand for alcohol declined due to the ban, it still remained a significant factor—not every citizen became a teetotaler on the orders of the state. The secret bars, known as speakeasies, and the black market moonshine flourished, as did smuggling from Canada, Cuba, and Mexico. Al Capone and

Johnny Torrio became rich and powerful as a result of Prohibition. Criminality rose dramatically during the 13 years of the alcohol ban and the American mafia developed into a permanent feature.

These negative effects, the ever present protest against the alcohol ban, and the economic crisis of 1929 ultimately led to Prohibition being lifted in 1933. The smaller, traditional distilleries had not survived this dry period. Anyone who, like Jim Beam, had the courage and the skills to start again afterward was able to build the basis for an international concern.

Alcohol bans were also imposed outside the USA, in the Soviet Union (1914–25), Norway (1916–27), and Finland (1919–32), for example. Prohibition has never been able to assert itself in western countries since then, however, although the antialcohol lobbies are gaining influence again.

Confiscation of distilling apparatus used to produce moonshine in New York in around 1920.

# Modern style

Opposite: Sketch in London, a potpourri of bars, restaurants, and an art gallery, is extravagant and the smart cocktails match its ambiance.

When Jerry Thomas published the world's first cocktail book in 1862 with his *Bar-Tender's Guide or How to Mix Drinks*, he himself was able to look back on several years' experience gained in various hotels and saloons; he had earned the nickname "Professor" not only with his artistic drinks, but also with his show-time acts. His book, which was expanded several times, presented a wealth of different drinks, thus demonstrating how widespread and how popular mixed drinks were in the United States at the time. The cocktail's popularity actually increased during Prohibition because it served as a disguise on the one hand, and its non-alcoholic ingredients often helped to cover up the objectionable taste of the illegally brewed or smuggled fusel alcohol. This extensive source of inspiration became an enduring enrichment to the bartender's recipe repertoire.

It was with envy that the world of the 1950s viewed the Americans and their American way of life, a life in which the bar was an institution—one that subsequently spread internationally, together with the knowledge of and creative skills with spirits. Even though new ones were constantly being added, recipes still focused on gin, rum, and whisk(e)y and, like the legendary martini, were often bristling with alcoholic content. When vodka appeared in the 1970s as a noncommunist, neutral-tasting spirit, it took over the alcohol proportion of many mixed drinks as well as gaining first place in the popularity stakes a decade later, way ahead of all its competitors.

The recipes have since become ever richer in ingredients and the world of cocktails (now the prevalent umbrella term) is all the more colorful, exotic, and playful. Modern bar patrons have "slim," "sporty," and "healthy" as their ideals and expect drinks to match. The awareness that excess alcohol is damaging to health has led to the establishment of the "less but better" trend and to an increase in demand for high-quality spirits. Distilleries with genuine tradition, distinct origins, and inspirational quality have suddenly become the focus of attention. The world of spirits has never been as fascinating as it is today.

## Spirits stipulations

It goes without saying that legislators have paid detailed attention to the production and sale of spirits. Apart from the protection aimed at teenagers in particular, legislation is primarily concerned with the concept definition, designation, packaging, and labeling of spirits, as well as with the protection of geographic indications. Regulation no. 110/2008 passed by the European Parliament and the Council of Europe has been in force within the European Union since May 2008 and is available for review in the internet in all of the community's languages. "The measures applicable to the spirit drinks sector should contribute to the attainment of a high level of consumer protection, the prevention of deceptive practices and the attainment of market transparency and fair competition," says the regulation. This is not intended to oppose innovation, but the latter must serve "to improve quality, without affecting the traditional character of the spirit drinks concerned." It is emphasized that the production of spirits constitutes an important market opportunity for agricultural products from within the Community. In order to safeguard diversity the member states have the right to impose stricter regulations within their own territory. Detailed appendices to the regulation provide details of technical concept definitions and conditions, define the numerous categories, and list those spirits that may declare themselves to be of a specific geographic origin. In the USA it is the ATF—the Bureau of Alcohol, Tobacco, and Firearms and Explosives—that concerns itself with these matters, and that also determines the rules governing the advertising of alcohol, in cooperation with the Federal Trade Commission.

# Location

# bar

- Passing trade and regulars
- Barely respectable
- Old expatriate bars
- Exotically seductive
- Unmistakably Cuban
- Obviously famous
- Exclusive bars
- Ever changing bars
- Very cool bars
- By no means cold
- Philippe Starck's bars

The Embryo in Bucharest takes its inspiration from the design of forms and structures in the human body, all in warm tones and soft textures.

Opposite: In the Cuckoo Club in London everything is in shades of violet.

Page 38: The King Kamehameha Club has established itself in the former boiler house of a Frankfurt beer factory, and its design and corporate identity have become famous.

# Passing trade and regulars

People have sat down, chatted, celebrated, and drunk together since time immemorial. But they didn't need taverns just for that. Merchants and pilgrims who left home for long periods were grateful to find a place where, ideally, they could not only rest their weary bones, but find sustenance to satisfy their hunger and quench their thirst when they were far from home. There was a long, if not predestined, way to go, however, before the first perfectly stirred martini. A combination of good company, exchanges of information, and the catering trade was destined for global success. We now know it by the name of "bar."

Large-scale global business is nothing new. We have evidence that it was going on at least 3,000 years before our time, with operators shifting large quantities—eventually truckloads—of goods. Such transport required logistics, well-rested draft animals, food, and somewhere to sleep. In the time of the Roman Empire relay posts where travelers could obtain provisions grew up at major crossroads. Drinks were initially served as an extra.

In time taverns and public houses became popular with the locals too, who would call in to such establishments even if they were not traveling through. Innkeepers became content to forego unpredictable passing trade, preferring to serve the local inhabitants. Their taprooms over the centuries would become meeting places for simple folk. Rich citizens and the higher earners—where such existed—expected more sophisticated fare in a more genteel atmosphere. They would find it in the homes of noblemen running their own personalized gastronomic service. Different social strata did not sit down together at the same table and the nature of the hospitality reflected the social position of the clientele. Until the Industrial Revolution the catering trade became established in various forms for the various classes of society. Laborers would frequent simple taverns serving simple drink. The well-to-do stopped off at exclusive hotels with equally fine dining where the concept of bars quickly caught on, some of these rapidly achieving fame. It was not until the 20th century that a degree of democratization entered the trade. Many bars ceased to exclude certain sectors of the population categorically, but did deliberately appeal to specific interest groups. In the 1960s bars adapted to a wide range of different tastes started to open. There were Caribbean bars, coffee bars, singles bars, milk bars, dance bars, cigar bars, wine bars—which meant that virtually every preference was catered for.

Nowadays almost anyone can go for a drink in almost any bar, with the exception perhaps of those highly exclusive ones that not everyone can afford, and clubs that not just anyone can enter. Whether everyone will feel comfortable there is another matter. In many bars the atmosphere is inextricably linked with the regular clientele that frequent it, forming a unique microcosm. People go to the Western bar in their cowboy outfits, the bikers' bar in leathers, and the tango bar in slightly faded elegance. When you enter such settings you leave your daily life behind you at the door. For many customers the appeal of the institutions we call bars lies in that very fact.

# Barely respectable

The early settlers to the North American continent didn't have it easy. They worked hard morning till evening and many families lived an isolated existence on their farms. Any shopping trip into the next "town" would have been a welcome change. The local store sold everything a settler could need and some things he didn't actually need, among them alcohol, probably whiskey, on tap. Whether such establishments took the form of general stores or drugstores is the subject of much speculation. One thing is certain: there were as yet no bars even though the name is said to have had its origins in that era. Cautious shop owners are said to have barricaded fragile goods against vandalism from brawling alcohol consumers, hence the word "bar."

Alcohol on tap was in high demand. The Swedish cleric Israel Acrelius traveled around the British colonies of North America between 1749 and 1756, and noted 45 different mixed drinks available over the counter. The alcohol was topped up, among other things, with lemon juice, milk, and sweetened vinegar.

About 1800 the name "saloon" came into common use for establishments other than grocery stores that sold alcoholic drinks across the counter. It probably derives from the Italian word *salone*. Depending on the location these were initially tents or booths where whiskeys that gloried in brand names such as Tarantula Juice or Coffin Varnish were dispensed. As time went by the buildings became more robust and investments were made in the furnishings, which went from the rough and ready rustic to the bourgeois and ostentatious. Food was rarely available at saloons, but gambling games and musical entertainment were on offer in many establishments. Their customers were almost exclusively men. No respectable woman would have been seen in a saloon.

This changed in the bars of the 19th century. Opened near to or even inside the better

The clients in the Wild West could be somewhat unruly, so the host had to erect a barricade (the bar is therefore actually a divider). Here cowboys in Texas stand at a bar in 1910. No respectable woman would have joined them there.

hotels in prosperous cities, bars quickly became the expression of a new attitude to life. There were hardly any social reservations concerning the display of wealth. Bars became a public forum where those with private riches were able to live it up. William Grimes, a restaurant critic for the *New York Times*, saw in these establishments a distinctively American phenomenon. US citizens who were bent on success were looking for fast, multiple contacts that would benefit them financially.

The first bar book, the *Bartender's Guide*, was published in 1862 by American bar keeper Jerry Thomas. In addition to rules of conduct for the bartender toward their customers, there is a handy selection of recipes. In 1869 the best barkeepers in the USA competed with one another in a mixing championship held in Chicago. By the turn of the century the bar had become a fixed point in the American way of life. In the "golden age of American drinking," according to society critic Henry Louis Mencken, the basis had been created for the fame of manhattans, martinis, old fashioneds, and cobblers, all

served with ice delivered to the door, in those days, by the ice man on his horse-drawn cart. Prohibition between 1920 and 1933 drastically restricted alcohol consumption in the USA. Substances such as hair lotion and antifreeze were used in the illicit production of spirits, and such "poison" was best mixed and diluted. Nevertheless, by the end of the dry period a fund of cocktail knowledge had been lost. American journalist Wayne Curtis joked that this had been as devastating for the American drinking culture as the burning of the library of Alexandria for the ancients.

Nowadays the "bar" is so anchored in our minds that even fictional bars such as Humphrey Bogart's, or rather Rick Blaine's, Rick's Café Américain in *Casablanca* are more alive to many of us than any real building in the next street. The sitcom *Cheers*, which made do with just a bar as a backdrop for its 11-year success story between 1982 and 1993, reaped more than two dozen Emmy awards.

Mata Hari (Greta Garbo) among her adoring fans at the Paris bar. Although the movie was set in 1914, the bar is more in the style of the period in which it was made, 1931, which also applies to the clothes of the customer in the foreground.

# Old expatriate bars

Opposite top: Harry's Bar in Venice, opened in 1931, had many imitators.

Opposite bottom: Harry's New York Bar in Berlin is reminiscent of a 1970s style bar.

On Vienna's Kärntner Durchgang, architect Adolf Loos designed this tiny American bar in 1908.

As is so often the case the bright idea is attributed to the Romans. It was the Romans that set up a network of inns across Europe. Throughout their sphere of influence and beyond, their concept found innumerable imitators that adapted the successful formula to their own country's customs. But an inn wasn't quite yet a bar, so the Old World needed a helping hand from the New World. Many of the now legendary first bars in Europe took their inspiration from America or benefited from American assistance. And with this American influence the myth of the bar was propagated.

Americans who in the 20th century, for whatever reasons, found themselves temporarily in the land of their forebears would find a little piece of their own culture in the bars that had grown up there, where they could feel at home. Cafes full of expatriate Americans and American bars became hot spots. Harry's Bar in Venice, the Bar Vendôme at the Paris Ritz, and the Viennese Loos American Bar—built by genius architect and artist Adolf Loos in 1908 after travels in the United States—were small exclaves of ordinary American culture. Occupying soldiers and exiled literati, stragglers, and refugees all stopped there to experience a little piece of home and a sense of belonging. The Paris cafes, for example, were constant meeting points for so many authors and artists that expatriate Americans in Paris in the 1920s created their own literary genre.

One anecdote from the long history of Harry's Bar in Venice illustrates just how important bars were as contact points. Giuseppe Cipriani, who opened his establishment in 1931 and made a good name for himself, could not always choose his customers. In 1942 he is said to have had an encounter with Joseph Goebbels, and Cipriani must have wondered if it would not be better to close. He served his last Bellini when the Italian fascists commandeered the bar as a canteen for naval forces. When in 1946 the Allies put an end to the specter of fascism, Cipriani was running a small hostelry on the island of Torcello off Venice. There he was summonsed by the American military command, only to be showered with reproaches. An American officer rebuked him severely, saying that he could not be a good Italian because he had not yet reopened Harry's Bar.

Cipriani didn't need to be asked twice and quickly set about reopening his old business. A few months later Harry's Bar, named after

Cipriani's former partner Harold Pickering, was once more an (almost) permanent institution near to St. Mark's Square.

You can still enjoy a Bellini at Harry's Bar and a daiquiri in the Paris Hemingway Bar. However, the old clientele who came here to forget their foreign status temporarily are no longer to be found. Instead you will encounter tourists with colorful shorts and digital cameras, all in pursuit of a myth, a reminder of what American bars once meant to European culture. But for a furnished room with atmosphere to become a bar, you also need the right kind of people having the right kind of conversations.

# Exotically seductive

The Singapore Sling (top) was invented in the Long Bar of the Raffles Hotel (bottom).

Opposite: The Ara Bar in the Taj Tashi Hotel in Bhutan (top) and the bar of Raffles in Dubai (bottom) are exclusive venues.

With its spices, fabrics, and teas, South East Asia has long been a major trading destination for European merchants. But the route there was long and arduous, and daily life in the hot, humid topics was strange and stressful. How refreshing to escape the hurrying throngs and the rickshaw drivers threading their way through the crowds, to enjoy a cool, reviving drink in a quiet atmosphere.

Bars grew up from India to China as consoling refuges. Their clients were thousands of miles from home, in the middle of a culture the customs and habits of which were almost as incomprehensible to them as the languages spoken. For a long time the colonialists and merchants, many of them certainly quite deliberately, remained outsiders in Asia and led there the lives of a privileged fringe group.

This distancing was quite helpful in staving off the sense of culture shock. Where could it be more pleasantly conquered than in a bar that was a mixture of the best of several civilizations: colonial tastefulness and British character with exotic foods and beverages. The colonial style—with its rattan chairs, carved furniture, and hunting trophies such as elephant tusks—could hardly find a more suitable setting than in the Far Eastern hotel bars.

Some of them earned their reputation for more than just catering. When the Raffles Hotel in Singapore—named after Sir Thomas Stamford Raffles, founder of the new Singapore—opened its doors for the first time on December 1, 1887, 1 Beach Road immediately became one of the top addresses in the city and the establishment's fame rose just as steadily as the number of its building extensions. The myth that the last of Singapore's tigers was shot here in 1902 was hardly needed to enhance its rep-

utation. It was its luxury and distinguished style that brought it fame.

The hotel was acclaimed too for its Long Bar. Some time between 1910 and 1915—even the people at the venerable old hotel itself aren't sure exactly when—the first Singapore Sling was mixed. The ingredients its creator Ngiam Tong Boon selected for it remained his secret as the original recipe has been lost. Despite various versions that are now to be found on bar menus throughout the world, professionals agree that gin, cherry brandy, and Benedictine should be used. To avoid any further confusion the recipe has now been listed as an "official drink" by the IBA, the International Bartenders Association.

Whatever the Singapore Sling contains—and whatever it costs—knowing that you are drinking it in the Long Bar of the Raffles where it was first created may well increase its thrill. Many illustrious clients at this hotel have savored its delights, among them Charlie Chaplin and Jean Harlow, representatives of the old Hollywood, and George Bush Senior and Rudy Giuliani, representatives of the late 20th-century political scene. But the Raffles isn't just a showcase for personal dramas. Dramas of a theatrical kind have taken place there too. Short stories and movies have been set at the Raffles. Joseph Conrad and Rudyard Kipling, who both spent a large portion of their lives in South East Asia, put up here. They incorporated their experiences at the Raffles into their works, sometimes written while actually staying at the hotel. For Somerset Maugham, the influential author and chronicler of the end of the colonial period in South East Asia, the Raffles became a symbol of "all the fables of the exotic East."

Nowadays the Raffles is recognized as a national monument. It is one of the few hotels in which guests enjoy up-to-the-minute service and modern luxury furnishings but can still visit a museum with souvenirs of the history of the establishment—in a side wing.

# Unmistakably Cuban

Pirates, smugglers, and Englishmen have all had a significant influence on Cuba's history. All had designs on the favorable harbor and the legendary treasures of what is now Cuba's capital. And they all drank rum. Lots of rum. Together with the slave trade, rum was long a major cornerstone of the infamous trade triangle between the Caribbean, Africa, Europe, and north America.

Havana's harbor districts have seethed with life for centuries. Seafarers and travelers were hungry for entertainment and the landlords could always count on a steady stream of customers. In 1817 an initially unimpressive new establishment was added. The Piña de Plata soon renamed itself the La Florida and finally La Floridita. This old harborside pub is now approaching its 200th anniversary, it maintains its own web page, and in the 20th century it was the recipient of awards for being one of the seven most famous bars in the world, the best of the best five star diamond bars, and king of the daiquiris. Strictly speaking it owes its enduring fame to a vexation. It seems that in 1932 a young writer named Ernest Hemingway was finding it hard to cope with his new-found fame. After the success of *Death in the Afternoon*, he could hardly escape well-meaning visits by friends and those who would have liked to be his friends to his house on Whitehead Street, Key West, Florida. The solitary leisure essential to a writer was gone. Without ado he took the ferry to neighboring Havana and rented some quiet rooms there. In the creative peace of the fourth floor of the Ambos Mundos, he quickly started a new literary project. His work went so well that he was able to explore the district in the afternoons. Apart from deep sea fishing, he was attracted to the bars—of which there is a more than ample supply in Havana.

Prohibition in the neighboring USA had guaranteed the city a constant stream of tourists for the past 12 years. Thirsty *gringos* landed on the island in droves, eager for a drink. Rum, which since the old colonial days had scraped a shadowy existence in the USA, became a society drink.

The Floridita proudly calls itself the birthplace of the daiquiri as here its bar-keeper Constante once mixed a high-proof Special for Ernest Hemingway.

An essential feature of the Havana bars are the cigars no less appreciated by Cuban women than by the *aficionados*.

Hemingway, in the well-run bars of the old harbor city, discovered a love for daiquiris which he enjoyed most in the Floridita. The atmosphere of the bar and the care that his favorite bartender Constante devoted to his work fascinated him. Hemingway would later also become famous for his alcoholic escapades, and his favorite bars—the Floridita and La Bodeguita del Medio—have become destinations of pilgrimage. Nowadays literati and cocktail fans alike pay painfully high prices there, but in the alleys of the neoclassical old quarter of Havana, a World Cultural Heritage site, there are plenty other bars and good rum—as indeed there are throughout the Caribbean.

The superlative success of rum exports dates back to the Bacardi company, which opened a bottling plant in Barcelona as early as 1910 and set up a branch in New York immediately after the end of Prohibition, before it was driven out of Cuba after the socialist revolution, finally moving its headquarters in 1965 to the Bahamas. But even if the rums of the other Caribbean islands cannot keep up with the large-scale producers in terms of quantity, they are still the source of many outstanding spirits. Each prides itself on its own style, from the fine French-oak-matured Haiti rums through to luxury Jamaica rum. Straight or as a cocktail, rum is available in every bar, and over recent years Caribbean bars have been in vogue, not least thanks to Cuban music.

Hemingway had his favorite bars in which to drink mojitos or daiquiris, as documented here in La Bodeguita del Medio.

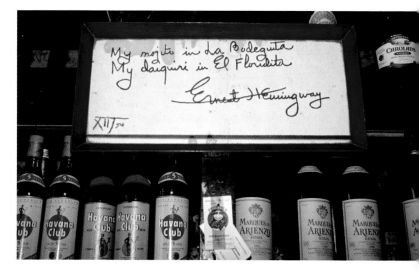

# Obviously famous

There are bars that bear his name and bars that sport his bust. He made some famous with his preferences for drinks, others into tourist attractions—such as Sloppy Joe's bar in Key West. At least one cocktail bearing his name has a fixed place in bar books and on bar lists. Of all the stars that have drunk at bars, Ernest Hemingway has certainly exerted the most influence on bar culture, being both an enthusiastic and reckless drinker. But he was not the only one.

In particular in the first half of the 20th century men of letters were accustomed to lingering in bars because at this time cafes and bars were vital artistic meeting points. Here creative people could converse and exchange ideas and inspiration with their own kind. By contrast with painters and sculptors, authors were able to practice a great deal of their art on location actually sitting at the bar. All they needed was a pen and a supply of paper. William Faulkner, F. Scott Fitzgerald, John Steinbeck, Jack Kerouac, and Malcolm Lowry, or Dylan Thomas and Eugene O'Neill, not only wrote about alcohol, but were under its influence.

Some gave the life of the bar a new spark and preached their opinions or a specific form or unique perspective on life. The surrealist moviemaker Luis Buñuel, who claimed never to miss his aperitif, saw a clear difference between the bars and cafes of his Spanish home. The latter were for him an institution that you use when you have a particular requirement. In a bar, however, the client acquires a certain state. For Buñuel the ideal bar was a school of solitude, which above all had to be quiet, as somber as possible, and very comfortable. "All music… is taboo… at the most a dozen tables, if possible only regular customers who should be as incommunicative as possible."

Many would drink too much at some point and would then indeed lose some of their mystique. For some that would be the point at which they gained it. At the forefront of these was Charles Bukowski, who regarded alcohol as a means of research (which

Left: The effervescent Josephine Baker had fun in bars such as this one in Venice.

Middle: Hemingway in 1954 with Spencer Tracy, his wife, and friends in La Floridita in Havana.

brought him to the edge of self-dissolution). Bukowski's uncompromising drinking behavior was immortalized in the 1987 movie *Barfly*, for which Bukowski himself wrote the script. Mickey Rourke played the role of Henri Chinaski. And Bukowski "signed" the film with a walkon part as an aging drinker.

Countless musicians—not just obliging pianists—garnered their first stage experience in bars. Perhaps some of them for that very reason felt most at home there when they were long famous and filling concert halls. Perhaps however it is because of the type of music associated with bars. In particular jazz is so closely related to bar culture that the borderline between bar and jazz club is often a very fluid one. However seldom have bars stamped the lives and work of any musician so lastingly as was the case with Tom Waits. At the beginning of his career he scraped a living performing in shabby bars and in his songs from the 1970s he repeatedly sings of social outcasts, whose ways inevitably lead to bars—not scene bars of the jet set, but gathering places of the hopeless. For actors too bars become a stage. If they are famous they can expect, even in the gloomiest establishment, to have their every movements recorded by press and fans. And it is usually the embarrassing moments that fill the pages of the scandal sheets. And yet when stars from Liz Taylor through Paris Hilton suffer such disasters, there is always the hint of a suspicion that they have been merely carefully calculated stunts in an undignified game of publicity.

Humphrey Bogart's most famous role was largely played out in Rick's Café Américain in Casablanca. The portrayal of a man whose disappointment turns him into a cynic, but who in the end stands by his ideals, made him immortal. In real life as well Bogart spent a lot of time in restaurants and bars without ever achieving the outward serenity of Rick Blaine. "Up to half-past eleven at night he was completely normal," the owner of his favorite bar once described him, "but then he would start to think he was Humphrey Bogart."

In the movie *Casablanca* Humphrey Bogart played the owner of Rick's Café Américain, where expatriates and displaced persons meet. Bogart was also frequently to be found in bars in his own private life.

# Exclusive bars

Opposite: Perfectly converted—Campbell Apartment, the former offices of the rail magnate John W. Campbell in New York's Grand Central Terminal, is one of the best bars in the US.

In luxury London hotel The Berkeley, the designer David Collins created the Blue Bar and made the breathtaking blue color a focal feature.

The first bars focused only on selling alcohol. But the more time the clients had on their hands, the more important inviting surroundings became. Bar owners soon realized that alcoholic drink was seldom a sufficient attraction by itself to encourage customers to come back. The staff played a vital part, as did the decor, especially if a competitor had invested in furniture, decoration, and ambience. Finally these three aspects had to fit together. Entertainment, atmosphere, and enticing drinks together would have to give the customer sufficient reason to return. The right clientele in many bars constitute an added attraction in their own right, and also, so to speak, a living asset. To gain customers' favor bartenders strove for perfection in two respects. Barmen began to offer increasingly better drinks from ever more exotic ingredients, and interiors became ever more luxurious. This applied in particular to the magnificent American bars of the 19th century and their successors in the Old World. In large hotels the elegant bar became an object of prestige. Even if such bars have seen their heyday, almost all hotels still maintain a bar in keeping with the style of the hotel.

# Ever changing bars

Underground bars of the 1970s and 1980s turned their backs on design mania. Famous addresses such as Studio 54 in New York, the London Ministry of Sound, and countless punk clubs of later years demonstrably denied the question of decor and set new trends. The minimalist modern bars of today have developed this heritage still further.

Bars soon began to be created around the desires of a particular clientele. The now typical form with musical entertainment was largely a product of Prohibition, when illegal speakeasies made efforts to distract attention from prohibited spirits with beautiful sounds. Particularly after World War II,

clubs became established in which music was a major factor, although this tended to be recorded rather than live. The first were known as discotheques.

Bars and clubs—the borderline between these has always been a fluid one—are no longer places of entertainment serving a single purpose. The classic American bar, living off its tranquility and expensive handmade cocktails, has more or less died out. Multifunctional establishments have replaced them, serving morning breakfast and turning themselves into lounges in the afternoon and dance clubs in the evening. Bernard Khoury perfected this concept in

The Morimoto in New York combines ultramodern design, a cool bar feeling, and inspired Japanese cuisine.

the B018. The tables in this Beirut club can be turned into dance surfaces. The underground bunker becomes an open-air dance floor with a retractable roof. The bar, the counter that was once a necessary barricade, is still there. But at the bar at times cappuccinos are ordered, then aperitifs and light meals, as well as tropical drinks throughout the night.

The hotel bar is now in a category of its own. It has almost lost its previous significance, but some remarkable examples do exist because hoteliers consider the bar to be part of their overall concept. Designer Philippe Starck has been doing some pioneering work in this field from Mexico to Moscow. Bars create a select ambience which in many cases is one of their main purposes. Design dominated bars do not strive after gastronomic values such as coziness, rapid service, or a private atmosphere. Design is often placed above function. And some are deliberately nothing but design.

The facilities represent both leisure area and stage setting at the same time. Philippe Starck used this concept in his designs, treating the clients as actors. He created hotels and bars that are not only somewhere to stay at the place of one's destination, but the destination itself.

At the multifunctional B018 in Beirut, dancing is sometimes under cover, and sometimes in the open air.

# Very cool bars

Top: Every six months the Absolute Ice Bar Tokyo is redesigned, always at 23 °F (–5 °C). The ice comes from the river Torne in Sweden, so that customers can drink authentic Vodka "on the rocks."

Bottom: Dramatic use of lighting and steel walls give Club Camellia in Hiroshima an almost sacred atmosphere.

Opposite: In the Bed Supperclub in Bangkok first-class drinks are served in a cool interior.

# By no means cold

Top: The exclusive NASA bar in Copenhagen creates its space-age atmosphere in white and neon.

Bottom: Behind the bar at the Pat Club, Bucharest, the idiosyncratic drinks wall draws attention to itself with bottles that are sunk into the lights.

Opposite: T-o 12, pronounced "Teo zwoelf," is a black-and-white bar and party venue in central Stuttgart. The name alludes to former German president Theodor Heuss.

# Philippe Starck's bars

Opposite top: The Oyster Bar at the Lan Club, Beijing (2006).

Opposite bottom: VOLAR, Shanghai (December 2006).

The S Bar in Los Angeles (2007).

Without him the international bar scene would be missing some of its most thrilling and original creations. Philippe Starck, 1949 vintage. In the studio of his father, an aircraft inventor, Philippe began to pull things apart and put them back together again in a new way, and he is now the most influential and inspired designer of our times. His designs have ranged from the Juicy Salif lemon press through to the Virgin Galactic space project, for which he is the creative director. It all began in 1976 with La Main Bleue in Montreuil. The theatrical Oyster Bar at the Lan Club in Beijing with its Meteorite counter underlines Starck's approach of "claiming no style except that of being free." The VOLAR in Shanghai with its spread eagle decor is a vibrant example, as is the S Bar in Los Angeles completed in 2007, with its surrealist ambiance and upside-down lamps.

# Behind
# the bar

The Caribbean Blue, made with white rum, b
curaçao, and a drop of angostura bitters, is
always a visual treat.
Opposite: Three variations, making it hard to
choose, from left to right: Daiquiri, Mango
Daiquiri, and Strawberry Daiquiri.

Page 62: Manhattan and Gin Fizz are bar
classics.

# The myth of the bartender

Women find him sexy. Men envy him. A good bartender has hundreds of cocktails in his head and keeps a constant eye on the joint. With a slight smile on his lips, he conjures up trendy drinks for the bar counter. A good bartender knows what his customers want: he is the illusionist in his own vaudeville act, the animal trainer in his circus, making everyone feel as if they are in safe hands. In a perfect scenario he serves everyone with just the right drink: maybe a Metropolitan for the stressed-out office worker; a Fallen Angel—sweet, yet with a melancholic hint of bitterness—for the mature blonde; or a Mojito for the Latin lover, dropping by while on their way to a night club.

In spite of all the cliches associated with the topic of bartenders, there is a certain appeal in swapping sides of the bar. Even Tom Cruise succumbed to this fascination when he dabbled with using a shaker himself in the 1988 movie *Cocktail*. Many dry, and not so dry, runs were needed for him to master all the right moves, which he finally managed by the end of it. It is hardly surprising, for extensive lines of bottles are stacked up behind a bartender. Professionals often have a few hundred ingredients on hand to create more and more new drinks, not to mention exotic juices and fresh fruit on the counter. The perfectionists spice up their concoctions with all sorts of added extras, finishing up with fruit.

And that is not all. The bartender spends nights on end listening. Often he knows more about the customers' worries than those of his own wife, and he would rather bite off his own tongue than reveal anything personal himself. As long as he is behind the bar, he is there for the folk in front of it, knowing what they need and when they have had enough—of speaking and of drinking. In lively Caribbean bars especially, any number of people are thrown together in a mood for celebration. But the party can only go on if everyone is still on their feet. Any bartender who watches while his guests get excessively drunk is doomed to failure.

Seasoned pros know that the job of bartender takes heart and soul. It is more a way of life than of earning a living. Given such sheer passion, it is debatable whether a practical budget version is an option. At least it seems to involve as much work as it does startup capital. Yet when seen in the cold light of day, the bartender's job is not really that complicated, provided a few basic concepts are mastered. In most mixed drinks, especially the immortal classics we know and love, a single spirit dominates. Often whole families of cocktails are named after this base drink. So, for example, a Red, White, Black, or Green Russian owes its "national affiliation" to vodka in each case. Coordinated liqueurs, juices, and sodas are then matched up to each spirit. From that point on it becomes just a question of personal taste, so individual creativity can be liberally applied.

# Getting started

By far the most important basics with a high alcohol content are whisk(e)y, gin, white rum, and vodka. While the last two of these have been rising in popularity for years, whisk(e)y and gin have been fighting against their association with open fires and graying temples. Another reason lies perhaps in the fact that they are mainly found in dry classics like Manhattans and martinis. Nearly all the popular exotic drinks that contain a high proportion of fruit are now based on vodka and rum, or their close relatives cachaça and tequila.

To start then, the four strong basics will suffice. Those with particular preferences and those who perhaps prefer fruity or sweet cocktails can manage quite well with just rum and vodka.

All that is missing are lower alcohol drinks that change the taste. These are known as "modifiers," such as vermouth which slightly varies the taste; "flavorings" intervene more obviously in the taste profile, even though angostura bitters and grenadine are only added in small amounts. The choice of syrups is amazing.

The rest of the selection is alcohol free, meaning that it does not always have a long shelf life. For this reason, it is best always to let your own palate guide you. Ginger ale, bit-ter lemon, and mineral water are very good for storing. A lot of drinks stand or fall, how-ever, with juices made from passion fruit, peach, or pineapple. It is then a matter of set-ting priorities. Lemons, limes, and oranges should always be in the house, for adding to the shaker really freshly squeezed.

So much for the software: now a little about the hardware, without which even the best Canadian whisky will not make a good Man-hattan. The bartender's main tool is the shaker, a two-part beaker for shaking that holds whatever is appropriate for the drink. Liquids are measured with a bar measure. Stronger components are apportioned with a bar spoon, which is like a long-handled teaspoon. A citrus juicer is in almost per-manent use, and for this reason an electric one is best. Fruits and peels for garnishing need to be cut with a sharp knife on a plas-tic chopping board.

Ice raises the next logistical problem. Firstly, how much: an ice-cube tray from the freezer compartment will not go very far. A gener-ous supply of very cold ice must always be on hand, so a complete drawer in the freezer devoted to ice cubes is a minimum require-ment. The ultimate, but expensive, next step up would be an ice-making machine.

Fast cooled by expert shaking, the finished drink flows through a special bar strainer into the appropriate glass. A few basic shapes should be available as its visual appearance is the making of every cocktail. A Bronx cuts quite a figure in a simple cocktail glass, and a Sazerac tastes different when drunk from a lovely rocks glass than from an empty mus-tard jar.

All in all, a touch of style does no harm. Even the trendiest cocktail is killed by empty potato chip packets and dirty plates. By con-trast, an elegant tray can provide a fitting entrance for cocktail glasses. And anyone who wants to perform it all in perfect sequence must not lose hope: bar schools now offer the self-taught bartender exhaus-tive training camps.

This impressive range should not cause alarm, as it can all be acquired gradually.

# The tools of the trade

**For opening**

A crown bottle opener (7) should either sit comfortably in the hand or be fixed to the wall with a catch tray under it. At peak times this saves valuable seconds. A corkscrew must always be on hand as well. Many bar workers swear by the waiter's friend (2) with autofoiler. Longer corks can be pulled easily with a two-stage model such as the one illustrated. An additional foil cutter is another practical item (1). Champagne tongs (6) remove the wire from sparkling wine first of all, before helping to twist the cork out with leverage. And a can opener is an absolute must (5).

**For closing**

Opened bottles of wine and sparkling wine can be sealed with thick stoppers (8). The shelf life of still wines can be extended by using a vacuum pump (4) to remove the air from the partially empty bottle. Using a pressure sealer for sparkling wine (9) pumps air into the bottle to aerate the wine. This will be enough to last one night. Leftovers that have been in the fridge for a few days are best used in cooking.

**For pouring**

Bottles that the bartender reaches for dozens of times, night after night, in order to measure out small amounts require a pourer (3). Some models measure exactly, but they are seen as a sign of meanness, or an indication that the person behind the bar lacks flair. Syrup bottles with pourers sit underneath the counter, ready to whisk up to the work surface, but stay out of sight of the customer.

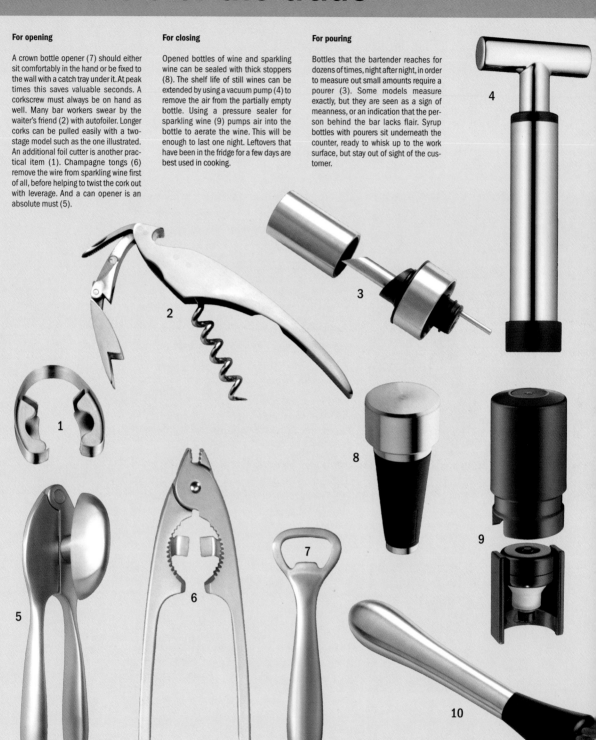

## Citrus juicer and muddler

Fresh citrus fruits make the difference in many drinks. Squeezing by hand is a laborious business and will result in impatient customers. An electric citrus juicer (15) is a mainstay, and it should be a sturdy model with a powerful motor, capable of withstanding heavy use. The moving parts at least should be metal and easy to clean; otherwise holdups are bound to occur. Mashing is the next activity for a bartender: the most important tool for making a caipirinha is a muddler (10).

## Swizzle sticks, picks, etc.

A set of little helpers is essential for the final finishing touches. Drinks that are to be mixed directly in the glass can be swirled (14) or stirred (12). Picks (11) and cocktail forks (13) are responsible for holding the decorations perfectly in place.

11

12

13

14

15

# Measuring out

### Measuring

In bars not only are the measuring units regulated by law, but the proportions must be correct. For this purpose, calibrated bar measures are used for fluid ounces (fl. oz; 9) or for centiliters (cl; 8, 4). 1 US fl. oz = 29.5 cm³. Larger amounts are measured in the shaker glass (5), while the long-handled bar spoon measuring about ⅙ oz (0.5 cl) is used for smaller quantities (10), when it is not stirring, swirling, or crushing. With a twisted stem and a scoop on the end, it can be turned over to layer spirits neatly into the serving glass. For dashes and drops there are special bar bottles with fine pourers (1, 3).

### Chilling and stirring

Ice is scooped (12) out of a machine or a separate bucket (7). Larger quantities of liquid are mixed in a measuring jug with pouring spout (2). Some drinks are only stirred in the shaker glass (5)—for example the classic Vodka Martini, which has regrettably been shaken, not stirred, by generations of James Bonds.

### Shaking

An indispensable tool for the bartender is a shaker with a separate strainer. This container is used to create the majority of classic drinks. And it is without doubt the most stylish way to make a mixed drink. The Boston shaker (5, 6) consists of an adjustable stainless steel beaker and a mixing glass, preferably with a measuring scale. The ingredients are put into the glass part, and then both halves are clicked together to make one tight container that is reopened by giving it a light tap on the edge of the work surface. The finished drink is then poured out of the metal beaker through a Hawthorn strainer (11), which fits several sizes of openings, and into the prepared glass. All parts can be cleaned without (almost) any effort.

# Mixing and shaking

### Electric cocktail mixers

The measuring beaker can be clasped firmly onto the mixer (1), and as it is going through the beating or fast-whipping functions the bartender can be getting on with the next task. This makes his job much easier. Thick drinks with a milk component, which are based on milk-shake recipes, are whipped up in an electric cocktail mixer. It is a traditional part of American cocktail culture.

### Electric blenders

The electric blender (2, 4) is a kind of multipurpose tool for the bartender. The specially shaped, stainless steel blades not only puree any type of fruit, but also even chop ice into a homogeneous mass. Smoothies and frozen drinks like Strawberry Margaritas, with their puree-style consistency, would be unthinkable without this equipment. Good blenders are heavy in order to stand up to the powerful mixing. A good motor achieves 20,000 rotations per minute and must be able to run for several minutes at the high-speed setting without damage. It is not worth having more than two different speeds and a pulse action to allow the motor to stop and start repeatedly. Professional machines turn off automatically when the lid disengages. The special shape of the jug with cloverleaf grooves constantly channels the contents evenly down to the blades. The electric blender is a classic mainstay of the American bar, but its design makes it great for use anywhere.

### Hand-held mixers

Basically a hand-held mixer (3) fulfills the same functions as the electric blender, but can also be used directly in a glass. Modern versions are impressive and powerful, but never cut ingredients quite as evenly as the electric blender's blades.

1

2

## All-in-one processors

An expensive, but efficient, solution for small bars and personal use is the all-in-one processor (4). Within one space-saving single item are a citrus juicer, blender, and "shaver" (for fine slices and shaved ice). The motor driving all three parts is extremely powerful, producing a higher yield from squeezed oranges, faster crushed ice, and silky smooth frozen drinks. The metal rod beside the beaker is a safety feature to allow the mixer to run unattended. If it loses electrical contact with the lid, the cutting mechanism automatically shuts down.

3

4

# Glasses

A bar needs a wide range of different glasses, as nearly every drink more or less matches up with a specific type of glass. Cocktails and many short drinks are served in stem glasses (2, 3, 4, 8), and champagne-based drinks in long-stemmed flutes (6). Fancy drinks require a pretty glass (10), usually footed and with a welled or flower-shape goblet. Some drinks look good in red (5) and white (7) wine glasses. Long drinks are presented in tall, straight glasses (11) or an Old Fashioned glass (12). Tumblers are good for medium drinks and for bourbon on ice. Malt whiskies and spirits like cognac, armagnac, other brandies, and calvados are sipped from a cordial glass (1), a bit bigger than a sherry glass (8). Tall, slim glasses (9) are the classic glasses for sours, and heat-resistant beakers (14) are for hot drinks. Shot glasses (15) mean rapid consumption of the contents. Glasses should always match the style of the bar as well. In a Caribbean bar ones with brightly colored stems are called for, while an exclusive hotel bar prefers to use crystal.

5    6          7      8      9          10

14

11

15

# Ice for the bar

An ice bucket for wine or champagne bottles is an indispensable bar item.

Chilling drinks goes back to Greek and Roman times: they added snow and ice, especially to their wine. The advantages of a great empire that encompassed plenty of glaciers were enjoyed only by the small elite that could afford to transport the cold goods for miles to their Mediterranean homes.

Accounts dating back to the 17th century exist of the summer use of naturally frozen water kept in specially constructed cold cellars. Then, in the 19th century, ice cupboards in middle class kitchens were more manageable: well-insulated cupboards for bars of ice which the iceman brought to the house entrance by horse-drawn cart on a regular basis. Once it began to melt, it was removed through a small faucet on the kitchen floor. The USA was the first country to chill on a grand scale, firstly without and then with electricity. Electrically operated refrigerators became widespread in households in the early 20th century. The first ice-cube trays for freezer compartments

appeared in the 1920s, making ice-cold drinks a permanent feature of life, as they still are today.

Although they are referred to as "cubes," the cooling elements rarely drop into the glass in the same shape and size. Squares, spheres, and cylinders, usually hollowed out on one of the flat sides, are the shapes most widely encountered. The scooped-out form originates from industrial production, where ice cubes are frozen from inside outward over cooling pins. At the end of the process the rods are briefly heated and the clear piece of ice drops off. Relatively clear ice is also produced by slowly chilling boiled water. In a refrigerator ice cubes freeze quickly from the outside inward, thus incorporating microscopic gas bubbles. This makes the cubes cloudy, and when they melt limestone sediment can be seen floating about—harmless, but unsightly.

In chemical terms ice cubes do not chill their environment, but instead draw its heat. They

use this to release hydrogen bridges and assume liquid form. The energy needs associated with this process depend on the temperature of the ice cube. At 4 °F (–20 °C) it chills more effectively than a cube of the same size that is also frozen, but only at 30 °F (–1 °C).

Large ice cubes chill for longer, so they are found in long drinks. The bigger the ice surface, the faster the liquid will become cold. Crushed ice cools more quickly than an ice cube. Cobbler or shaved ice, produced mechanically, is even finer. Also water can be atomized industrially at 30 to 32 °F (–1 to 0 °C), and in the form of ice snow it has the fastest, but shortest lived, cooling effect. As a general rule, 5–7 oz (150–200 g) of ice cubes should be allowed for each drink, aiming for the upper limit if using crushed ice. In order to chill larger quantities of bottles, calculate 66–132 lb (30–60 kg) of ice in a bathtub. Dry ice is the coldest form of ice at –108 °F (–78 °C), a temperature at which bottles crack because the contents are frozen instantly. Dry ice is pure, solid carbon dioxide and is unsuitable for chilling in a bar, but is excellent for creating "fog" effects. Long blocks of ice, like those used in the old ice cupboards, make fancy decorations when used for walls and counters. Colored ice cubes and ice glasses can also be introduced as gimmicks with a wow factor. Fruits and leaves can be frozen into cubes, as well as colorful ice cubes made from fruit juices.

An ice-making machine is a must for the professional bar. The bartender can then help himself using ice tongs or an ice shovel. Never the hands! Ice cubes are a foodstuff, yet tests in the catering trade have regularly revealed significant levels of bacteria such as *E. coli* and streptococci in them. For this reason in the US they prefer to use prefilled one-way ice containers, while in India ice cubes are seen as a health risk. For ice that has stuck together there are ice picks—reduced to small pieces it makes its way into vacuum-insulated ice buckets or champagne coolers.

Large and angular, round and hollow, crushed or shaved: all ice is not the same. An ice crusher like the one illustrated on the right involves a lot of manual labor, but is reliable. By contrast, readymade crushed ice is usually too fine: it cools things down quickly, but does not last long enough.

# Fruit juices

Fruit juices—that is, drinks that come under the category of "mixers"—constitute by far the largest ingredient in many mixed drinks. As well as their ubiquitous sweetness, they give the drink the fruity taste component that often integrates with the alcoholic strength of the spirits. The perfect balance between juice and alcohol is achieved when the fruity flavors are strengthened by the alcohol, while the taste of the alcohol is tempered. A Screwdriver is a clear example of this: mixed to perfection, the vodka and orange taste distinctly better together than they do individually.

Given their importance, it is evident that the fruit juices used should be top quality, though the huge variation makes it a risky business. In the case of orange juice, the quality ranges from 100% fruit content to 6% in "fruit drink" in a carton. Pure fruit juice consists of 100% fruit, but may sometimes contain additional sweetening, even in so-called "natural" juice. Many juices are vacuum evaporated in the country of origin, removing 50–80% of the liquid to minimize transportation costs. The concentrate is then watered down at a later stage, and is called "fruit juice made from concentrates." "Freshly squeezed juice" is pasteurized, frozen, defrosted, and pasteurized once again, making it at best a relatively fresh product.

"Nectars" contain a proportion of 25–50% fruit, depending on the type. Down at the bottom of the proportion list are the "fruit juice drinks," which are made from bottled water and sugar, with added fruit juice, composite or concentrate, giving it a fruit content of between 6% and 30%. As many types of fruit do not contain much liquid, they appear in stores only as lightly concentrated juice in the form of nectar. Hence extracts from bananas or passion fruits have to be liberally topped up with water. With nectars up to 20% sugar may also be added, which barely conceals the poor quality of cheaper juices and adulterates every mixed drink. Juices from fruits that are high in acidity, like pineapple, are turned into dull candy water by adding sugar. Pineapple juice should only be allowed in the bar in unsweetened form. The most sensible thing to do is to pay a visit to a delicatessen, a health food store, or an organic store. There you will find some juices that do not contain any fruit at all. Tomato juice is the reviving ingredient in the hangover cure Bloody Mary. Here too, a high proportion of fruit or vegetable is important. Presalted or spiced vegetable juices nearly always mask poor quality. Purists use high-grade bottled tomatoes and puree them in a blender. Even in the case of common fruits like oranges, the premium quality juices are, justifiably, very expensive. The bartender should always compare the price with an equivalent amount of fresh oranges. The better the juice is, the smaller the difference in price. In season, freshly squeezed orange juice can even be cheaper than bought juice, and it is invariably better.

An intensely fruity taste is the real kick in many mixed drinks. High-quality or freshly squeezed juice, especially from exotic fruits, can transform a simple combination into an unforgettable mixed drink. Citrus juices are absolute essentials for the bar. Their acidity gives the majority of mixtures the initial, vital freshness. The strikingly distinctive flavor of passion fruit juice puts the "good taste" into recipes like a Hurricane.

# Fruit juices

Exotics such as pineapple, mango, and papaya are intensely fruity and give many tropical drinks their complex aroma. As they go well with many spirits—especially rum, tequila, and vodka—they are perfect for experimenting with new combinations. The more common, local fruits should not be ignored, however. As well as their fruity taste, peaches and apricots add a velvety consistency that gives many drinks their elegant texture. Some of these fruits take a lot of squeezing with juicers. With readymade products the fruit content is the decisive factor.

Juice from berries, such as blackcurrants, adds a characteristic note to many drinks. White grape juice replaces wine in non-alcoholic drinks, and even in alcoholic ones it would often have been a better choice with its rounded, grape flavor. Grapes go equally as well with tropical and common fruits such as cherries, but they should not be combined with tomatoes as the latter's stronger juice is rarely found in sweet mixtures. Tomato juice demands salt, pepper, and seasoning, and helps hangover victims back onto their feet, thanks to its vitamins and nutrients.

# Soft drinks and waters

Soft drinks and carbonated waters have always been ingredients in a mixed drink. They are usually one or two, or three at most, components, as in gin and tonic, where they also appear in the name of the drink itself and make it a long drink. Nearly all soft drinks are made of flavored water, a lot of sugar, and carbon dioxide, and sometimes enhanced with drugs like quinine and caffeine. A German, Johann Jacob Schweppe, patented a process in 1783 that made it possible to carbonate water. Not long after, Schweppes

soda water began its unexpectedly meteoric career. Schweppes is also responsible for the ingenious idea of transforming quinine, the bitter malaria medicine, into a pleasant drink called tonic water by adding sugar, lemon juice, and soda water: it was administered to British soldiers in India in the 1870s as quinine could be used in malaria prevention at this concentration. Military personnel had to swig it back on a daily basis as protection against the inevitable scurvy of sailors and the many infections encountered in occupied tropical zones.

To be completely effective these beverages had a considerably higher proportion of quinine in those days. The bitter taste was correspondingly powerful, so additives to take the edge off were advisable. It is no real surprise that in classics—like highballs with ginger ale, or vodka with bitter lemon—many of the original active ingredients have been immortalized. At any rate, it is conceivable that the cocktail culture graduated from its pilot stage onboard warships.

Around the same time as the introduction of tonic water, Schweppes also incorporated ginger ale into its range, though the ginger soda only reached the peak of its popularity in the mid 20th century.

By this time Coca-Cola had long since become part of the American way of life,

even though the cocaine of the original recipe—brewed by the apothecary John Stith Pemberton in 1886 in the hope of overcoming his morphine addiction—was no longer in evidence.

In contrast to sodas, mineral waters are mostly neutral in flavor, and this means they do not date. Often they assume the role of the subservient vehicle for carbon dioxide. Cocktail families like Collinses, fizzes, and highballs are mainly defined by water and, not without reason, mineral water is still known as Club Soda to this day. Water has, however, established itself as a serious soft drink, so any good bar should offer a range of qualities, both sparkling and still. A well-appointed water list can prevent abstainers from alcohol from seeming like party poopers too early in the evening.

In the past ten years new readymade soft drinks and juices have kept appearing on the market, only to disappear just as quickly. Perhaps this is why hardly any of them have made it onto the ingredient list of any fashionable mixed drink. Even Sprite, which was developed in the 1960s, can only be ordered in a bar au naturel.

Johann Jacob Schweppe
(1740–1821)

John Stith Pemberton
(1831–1888)

## Wine and beer in the bar

If a customer is looking for something other than a mixed drink, beer is usually offered in bars in the form of the latest premium brand in bottles. Bars renowned for their beers are often in the habit of offering local specialties.

Following the drop in beer consumption in the traditional beer-drinking nations over past years, beers with added flavorings and readymade mixed drinks with beer in the style of alcopops have been replacing unadulterated beer, especially in clubs. In this indirect way beer has also started to become popular as a mixer in cocktails, with many bartenders developing their own recipes.

Wine is mainly poured by the glass in a bar. It should be accessible and correspond to general international expecta-

tions, but on no account should it taste ordinary. It is advisable to have a selective, well-thought-out range, for which two white and three red wines can be sufficient. For white wine there should be a fruity one, and one that is more full bodied and oak aged. The red wines should all be mature: a fruity, Beaujolais-style red, a medium-bodied one like a Sangiovese, and a third rich and full-bodied one like an Australian Shiraz. The demand for wine for tastings in bars is not high, unless the bartender has built up his own special clientele. Even then it is best to concentrate on a few vintage wines and perhaps a theme-based selection. Champagnes occupy a special position as they are presented freely in a wide range of qualities on the wine list.

# Sugar, syrup, and other extras

Sugar is found in almost every mixed drink. On the one hand it softens the harshness of the alcohol, and on the other it takes the edge off the acidity of many fruit juices. In its natural form it is usually processed as powdered or granulated sugar—the finer it is, of course, the faster it dissolves when cold. For the traditional ritual involved in an absinthe, it has to be a sugar cube. Unrefined cane and palm sugars add their own particular note, which is eminently suited to tropical drinks. Normally the sugar is dissolved in water in advance however, and then used in liquid form. Bartenders often produce this "sugar syrup" themselves, giving them control of the sugar concentration. Whether in the bar or at home, syrups have a special significance, most notably simple sugar syrup made from sugar cane, which gives drinks with young rum their sweetness without affecting the clarity. Even in cases where only a hint of added sweetness is required, it is indispensable.

## Sugar syrup, or inverted sugar

Sugar that is heated with water to 216 °F (102 °C) and boiled for 2 minutes is known as inverted sugar. As it is heated the sugar solution begins to foam up, allowing any impurities to be removed with the foam. Usually the sugar and water are mixed in a 1:1 solution, but the proportion of sugar can be higher. The higher the sugar content, the better the preservative qualities, but the sugar is then prone to crystallization as the solution cools. To prevent this happening, up to 3/100 oz (1 g) of citric or ascorbic acid is added, causing the sucrose to split into the simple sugars glucose and fructose. The solution is heated to 167 °F (75 °C) and maintained at this temperature for up to 90 minutes, then strained into bottles. Sugar syrup can be used in any application where the texture of sugar crystals would be inappropriate.

## Syrups

Fruit syrups provide a variety of additional flavors. A classic is grenadine, which was originally made from pomegranates but now contains only traces of the original main ingredient and all sorts of other flavorings instead. As a rule not all syrups are as natural as they seem, and their fruit content fluctuates between 10% and 38%. Some of the standard selection in the bar include strawberry, raspberry, orgeat (made from almonds), and coconut syrups, as well as Rose's Lemon and Lime juice.

The product range of syrups has expanded enormously with the trend toward flavored coffees and the new-found popularity of tropical drinks. Fancy tastes are now catered for in products featuring sea buckthorn, elderflower, hazelnut, and sangria. The combination possibilities for mixed drinks are far from exhausted yet, so look out for more to come.

## Milk, cream, eggs, and ice cream

Flips, eggnogs, and coffee-based drinks require milk products. In modern versions of coladas the coconut taste is refined with cream. Many syrups go well with milk. And of course milk, cream, eggs, and ice cream form the basis of non-alcoholic drinks like milk shakes. These ingredients, with the exception of ice cream, are relatively perishable, so for this reason many bars stock long-life milks and cream. Pity the cocktails made with them. High-grade fresh milk lasts longer than you might think, as does cream, and they can make an ordinary milk-based drink into a real bar specialty. It goes without saying that eggs from battery hens should not be inflicted on customers. The only effort involved in milk mixes is the preparation as they have to be shaken for some time, but not too hard, and then served immediately as the ingredients may separate.

# Garnishes

Fresh fruit is to the cocktail what the "Flying Lady" is to a Rolls-Royce. Every well-stocked bar has lemons, limes, and oranges, primarily for making freshly squeezed juice. The emphasis here is on "fresh." Juices and fruit purees should always be made on the spot, otherwise they lose all their nutritional value. In the case of a freshly squeezed orange, the vitamins begin to degrade after just ten minutes.

Some of the citrus fruits should be organic, so that the peel can be used. Their highly aromatic, essential oils add a touch of class to many cocktails. The peel also makes a very good garnish: a long, thin strip wound over the top of the glass is eye catching.

Some fruits can be used as fresh purees in drinks, so a blender is a great help. Peach puree (remember to take the skin off) is the distinguishing feature of a Bellini. And the pureed flesh of raspberries or passion fruit forms the flavorsome basis of champagne cocktails. In the profession, catering suppliers will deliver these products fresh and direct to your door.

Even if it is only to be used for decoration, a bartender should not skimp on fruit. Exotic fruit in particular can boost the visual appearance as well as the taste of a drink, as long as it is ripe. A piece of pineapple should not be sour but aromatic, just like a strawberry or banana slice. Customers will be more satisfied if the appetizing look of the garnish also delivers in terms of taste. A huge selection is available: seasonal berries, cape gooseberries, melons, mango, papaya... Slices of lemon or star fruit are more pleasing on the eye than the palate, but then of course no one expects to be able to eat them. Fresh mint is essential for a Mojito, but it must be the right kind, without too much menthol to dull the taste buds. Suitable types are either Cuban mint (*Mentha nemorosa*) or spearmint.

Candied fruits are a simple answer to the issue of freshness. While lurid red Maraschino cherries with their cloying sweetness should remain a tribute to the 1960s, candied ginger, banana slices, and limes can prove quite successful in terms of experimentation. Dry classics like a Vodka Gibson or Martini are best accompanied by pickled vegetables—olives (in brine, not stuffed with peppers), gherkins, or pearl onions. Then there is cayenne pepper for

Whether as an ingredient or a garnish, fruits are mainly—but not exclusively—deployed. Vegetables, spices, and herbs can also provide an interesting touch.

cocktails with fresh cream, nutmeg for flips, cloves for mulled wine, and cinnamon sticks for punch. Salt, pepper, celery salt, and Tabasco and Worcestershire sauces liven up hangover drinks like the Bloody Mary.
If drinks have a classic garnish, like a piece of pineapple for a Piña Colada, think twice whether any change is necessary: a garnish that fits the contents of the drink makes sense, and that's that. You can give free rein to the imagination, on the other hand, when it comes to the loose interplay of a number of fruits, as in Cobblers, Fancies, and Smoothies.

# Basic techniques

The best way to mix a drink depends on the type of liquid that is being used. The result should simply be the technically perfect mixture at the right temperature for every drink. And as different drinks have different needs in this respect, there are four basic techniques that can be distinguished when it comes to mixing.

## Building in a glass

Mixing a drink in the glass out of which it will be consumed must be the oldest way of making a cocktail. It is a simple, yet effective method. It is mainly used when the ingredients blend well together, that is when their gravitational weight is similar and any more intensive stirring or shaking would be superfluous. Usually these involve recipes that consist of two strong spirits or of a spirit and a juice. In terms of a glass, the best one to choose is a wide beaker type that allows plenty of room for stirring. The ingredients are stirred together with ice in the glass and, depending on the recipe, they can be topped up with champagne or soda. Solid ingredients like sugar, lime, and mint are muddled in the empty glass, then topped with crushed ice and white rum in the case of a Mojito. Layered cocktails occupy a special place among the built drinks: liquids of different density (and preferably different colors) are carefully poured so they lie separately on top of each other, and therefore on no account should they be stirred.

## Stirring in a mixing glass

Drinks to be served ice cold, preferably in an iced glass, or even with ice, should be stirred in a mixing glass that is big enough to hold enough ice cubes to chill the drink quickly, without melting too much. Liquids that need to be blended together only very lightly are also best

in a mixing glass, especially if they are clear and would rapidly become cloudy in a shaker. Stirring should be done with a bar spoon for 20–30 seconds, using circular movements from the bottom of the glass upward, then strain through a Hawthorn sieve into the prepared glass. Of course, the ice from the mixing glass is then discarded.

## Shaking in a shaker

Brandies, syrups, liqueurs, milk, and cream all have different gravitational weights and have to be mixed more energetically, so this is best done in a shaker. Carbonated drinks should, however, never be put in a shaker. Put the ingredients for at most three (two for a Boston shaker) drinks into the (glass) beaker with ice, seal on the metal part of the shaker, and then shake firmly for 10 seconds, or 20 for thicker juices or cream. It does not matter whether the shaking is horizontal or vertical: the most important thing is not to point it in the direction of the customer. Finally, the well-chilled drink can be strained through the bar sieve into the prepared glass.

## Mixing with a blender

Drinks with ice cream, egg yolk, or fresh fruit are best processed with an electric blender. Pour the measured ingredients onto ice cubes in the blender attachment. Again, in this case do not add carbonated liquids until after blending. Start slowly, increase the speed until the mixture is completely integrated, and then pour it into prepared glasses. When using an electric blender, especially for frozen drinks with a sorbet consistency, a little more sweetening is normally required.

# Garnishing and serving

Do not overestimate (or underestimate) the finishing touches. Useful tools are scoops, sharp knives, zesters, and fluting knives.

Each mixed drink is a minor work of art. The contents of the glass should be a tasty surprise and show true inspiration, for anyone ordering a drink in a bar does not expect a glass of just any old thing. What appears should catch the attention, not by cheap gimmicks but through the skilled composition of the individual parts. In doing so, less is usually more. As with ingredients, the purely decorative aspects of the fruit should concentrate on two to three features that enhance the basic expression of the drink.

The correct tools are needed to create the final touches. A plastic chopping board is required in the catering industry for cutting fresh fruit, though it is not ideal for the sharpness of the knives. Serrated knives are not as badly affected. Zesters and fluting knives tear strips of different thicknesses from citrus fruit peel, which then twirl decoratively over or in the glass. Scoops are used for soft, fleshy fruit.

Unless hung on the edge of the glass as a decoration, most garnishes are lined up against the glass on wooden or plastic cocktail sticks. Empty sticks are also useful for chasing olives and pearl onions around the glass.

Garnishes are pretty add-ons, which above all must be in proportion. Too small is just as inappropriate as too big. Drinking straws are a must for drinks with crushed ice: they should be thick but not too long, and brightly colored. An excessive amount of fruit garnish is dubious enough, but the discomfiture level can easily increase when there are umbrellas, national flags, tinsel, or sparklers. What is justified cause for celebration on a child's birthday can sometimes ruin a visit to a bar. Crustas, which are standard for some drinks, are purely a matter of taste as sugar and salt crystals or desiccated coconut on the rim of a glass can affect every sip. The crusta (sugared rim) is created by moistening the rim of the glass with a piece of citrus fruit, and then dipping the glass into the particular garnish. If blue curaçao or cassis is used for this, the edge becomes brightly colored.

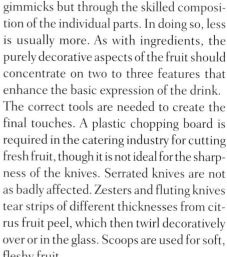

## The *mise-en-place*

Mixing the perfect, tasty drink is a demanding job that entails quite a few maneuvers: all the more important, then, to prepare everything in advance, especially if several guests are to be served quickly. Virtually no one will use all of the things listed on the previous pages at the same time. Whether an amateur or a professional, each person can choose what to offer and make a note of everything required before shopping for the ingredients.

Once all the tools and ingredients are present, they have to be put into a meaningful order. The exact detail is up to the individual, but a few basic ground rules should be followed. Firstly, unnecessary journeys should be avoided, so everything should be within reach. Make sure shakers, measuring jugs, and chopping board are to hand. The electric blender and ingredients for garnishing should be on the work surface behind the bar.

The bottles can be problematic. They need to follow a logical order, grouped either by the type of drink or by the type of drink it goes into. Everyone will develop their own system here too, but the main thing is to be able to find all the important bottles without even looking. Ice, fruit juices, and sodas should also be within reach of the workstation, ideally in a refrigerator under the work surface.

All that remains are the glasses. In many bars they hang on a glass rail above the bartender's head. In addition, a selection of cocktail glasses should be kept in the freezer compartment as shorts stay cold in these for longer.

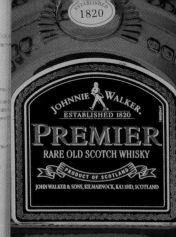

# The world's spirits

Sugar cane forms the basis of alcohol production in many countries, not only in the Caribbean and Brazil, but in Asia in particular.

Opposite: In many countries such as here in Brazil, local spirits are produced by the smallest of distilleries.

# The triumph of the national drink

The diverse range of spirits available in supermarkets, drugstores, and duty free shops is just one aspect of high-proof alcoholic beverages and one that belies the fact that spirits of whatever variety are today still primarily a very local pastime. The spirit brands we know are of less significance worldwide when it comes to their consumption than we in the west might assume, as is evidenced by a glance at the spirits hit list. First place among the ten most important brands is occupied by a name completely unknown to the majority of Europeans and Americans: Jinro. With about 185 million gallons (700 million liters) annually, the Korean Soju, a clear spirit, is the undoubted leader in the world rankings.

It is estimated that around 13.2 billion gallons (50 billion liters) of spirits are produced annually worldwide. Only around 8 billion gallons (31 billion liters) of these appear in the official statistics because, in many countries, alcoholic drinks are produced at home or in village communities. Of course, this applies primarily to fermented drinks. In the less developed regions of Africa and Asia in particular, but also in South America, there are countless traditions for fermenting beer-like brews from grain or other starchy plants or for using fruit as the basic raw material. These home-made drinks are often the only alcohol produced in a given region or that is affordable for the majority of the population. In these regions home distilling serves not least as a means of making these home-made brews capable of being stored. Made with rudimentary equipment, there is a risk of the spirits containing methanol or other toxic substances. In rural areas home-made beers or spirits are also often used as an income supplement.

Private distilling is widespread in eastern Europe and in parts of Asia. In the Balkan countries the readily available fruit, especially plums, are usually used for the purpose. Home-brewed vodka has as lengthy a tradition in the Russian Federation as it has in Poland, Lithuania, Latvia, Estonia, Belarus, and the Ukraine. However, in China and other Asian countries too, rice or millet is made into *baijiu*, white alcohol, distilled privately in 30,000 small distilleries whose production is seldom officially registered. A similar situation applies to the pisco derived from Muscatel grapes in Peru and to a significant proportion of Brazilian cachaça, which is often distilled in primitive home-made stills in just one run, resulting in a somewhat dubious quality.

Brazil is a clear example of the fact that the internationally known spirits constitute only the tip of the actual production iceberg. There are some 30,000 distilleries producing cachaça in Brazil, most of which are very small operators. Overall production is estimated to amount to about 3 million gallons (1.3 billion liters). Although there are some 5,000 brands, only a small proportion of these are distributed nationwide and only a fraction of what is produced is exported. Nevertheless, three cachaça brands have made it into the top 50 spirits in the world, an indication of the fact that the local spirits from populous countries are gaining in significance.

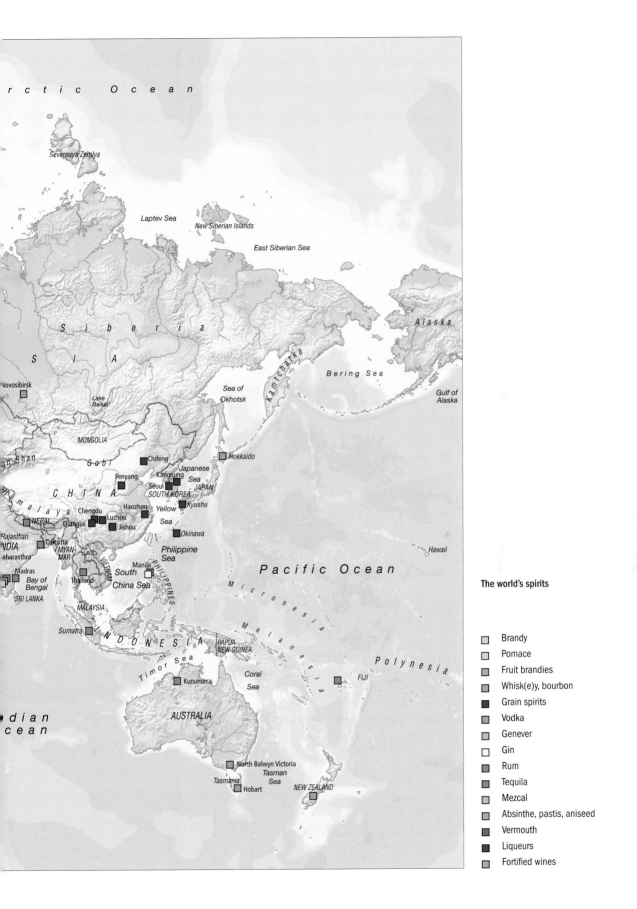

Arctic Ocean

Severnaya Zemlya

Laptev Sea

New Siberian Islands

East Siberian Sea

S i b e r i a

Alaska

S      I     A

Novosibirsk

Lake Baikal

Kamchatka

Bering Sea

Gulf of Alaska

Sea of Okhotsk

MONGOLIA

Gobi

an Shan

Chifeng

Hokkaido

CHINA

Fenyang

Japanese Sea

Kangnung

Seoul

SOUTH KOREA

JAPAN

Chengdu

Haozhou

Luzhou

Yellow

Kyushu

NEPAL

Qionglai

Jishou

Sea

m a l a y a

Rajasthan

Calcutta

Okinawa

NDIA

MYAN-MAR

Philippine Sea

Hawaii

aharasthra

LAOS

VIETNAM

Pacific Ocean

Madras

Manila

Bay of Bengal

Thailand

South China Sea

PHILIPPINES

SRI LANKA

M i c r o n e s i a

MALAYSIA

M e l a n e s i a

Sumatra

I N D O N E S I A

P o l y n e s i a

PAPUA NEW GUINEA

Timor Sea

FIJI

Coral Sea

Kununurra

dian cean

AUSTRALIA

North Balwyn Victoria

Tasman Sea

Tasmania

Hobart

NEW ZEALAND

**The world's spirits**

- ☐ Brandy
- ☐ Pomace
- ☐ Fruit brandies
- ☐ Whisk(e)y, bourbon
- ■ Grain spirits
- ☐ Vodka
- ☐ Genever
- ☐ Gin
- ☐ Rum
- ☐ Tequila
- ☐ Mezcal
- ☐ Absinthe, pastis, aniseed
- ☐ Vermouth
- ■ Liqueurs
- ☐ Fortified wines

# Distilled champions

A glance at the spirits industry's top ten worldwide brings some surprises. The top positions are actually occupied by brands and drinks that hardly anyone outside the industry has heard of, and the list features countries that it was assumed would not have any notable—or even significant—spirits production.

However, it is the national drinks that determine this hit list, as is evidenced by Jinro, which has occupied first place unchallenged for a number of years. It has increased its volume to 182 million gallons (694 million liters), surpassing second place cachaça by an impressive 129 million gallons (489 million liters). Jinro is a *soju*, a clear South Korean grain spirit with an alcohol content of just 20–5% vol. The 49 million South Koreans, with a pro capita consumption of up to 7 gallons (25 liters), have the highest spirit consumption in the world after the inhabitants of the US Virgin Islands, and drink over 3 billion bottles of it annually. Hence Kyongwal and Kumbokju have also made it into the top ten, with daesun, muhak, and bohae following in positions 12, 13, and 20.

Closely related to soju is the Japanese shochu, with Jun Legend from Takara Shuzo (7) being the leading brand albeit there are five other brands among the top 50, even though the Japanese drink significantly less than their neighbors with a pro capita consumption of 2½ gallons (9.6 liters).

## The Philippines and India

The fact that Pirassununga (Cachaça 51) has reached second position in the world rankings is indicative of the significance of cachaça, the Brazilian sugar-cane spirit that is the third largest spirit worldwide in terms of quantity, because it is the national drink of 182.5 million inhabitants. Pitu at 18 and Ypioca at 37 have also increased in turnover. Their close relative rum also maintains its top ranking, especially Bacardi, one of only three internationally distributed spirits under the ten best. The inhabitants of the Caribbean are among contemporaries drinking the most alcohol but, with the exception of Captain Morgan at no. 25, the other big rum brands now come from Asia: Tanduay (11), from the Philippines, Old Monk (24) and Celebration Rum (31) from India, as well as Sang Som from Thailand (38).

With the exception of Tanduay, the Philippine distilleries are among the largest in the industry, especially San Miguel with gin (5) and Gran Matador Brandy (49), as well as the Consolidates Distillers with Emperador Brandy (23). No less conspicuous are the developments in India, where the United Breweries Group in particular is showing significant growth with Bagpiper Whisky (8) and McDowell Brandy (30), in addition to rum. The fact that the current top ten spirits include only one American vodka, Smirnoff, and yet no Russian vodka, is due to the restructuring of the Russian industry as vodka remains the most widely drunk spirit in the world with around 1.2 million gallons (4.6 billion liters).

This is based on its dual significance as the national drink of the Russians, the Poles,

## The ten most produced spirits in the world

Annual production in million gallons (million liters).
Status 2006; Source: IWSR

| | |
|---|---|
| Jinro | 182 (694) |
| Pirassununga | 54 (205) |
| Smirnoff | 51 (193) |
| Bacardi | 46 (176) |
| Ginebra San Miguel | 43 (162) |
| Kyongwal | 42 (159) |
| Jun Legend | 35 (131) |
| Bagpiper | 32 (121) |
| Johnnie Walker | 31 (119) |
| Kumbokju | 29 (110) |

## Spirit consumption worldwide

*Figures in pints (liters). Finished products per capita; selection from 118 countries surveyed. Status 2006; Source: IWSR/BSI*

| | | |
|---|---|---|
| 1. Virgin Islands (USA) 57 (27.1) | 31. Poland 15 (7.2) | 61. Belgium/Luxembourg 7 (3.5) |
| 2. South Korea 53 (25.3) | 33. Spain 14 (6.7) | 63. China 7 (3.4) |
| 3. Russian Federation 42 (19.9) | 34. Hungary 14 (6.6) | 64. Denmark 7 (3.4) |
| 4. Virgin Islands (GB) 42 (19.8) | 35. Finland 13 (6.3) | 68. Austria 7 (3.2) |
| 5. Estonia 39 (18.6) | 36. Cyprus 13 (6.3) | 71. Portugal 6 (3.0) |
| 6. Aruba 32 (15.3) | 43. Brazil 12 (5.6) | 72. Slovenia 6 (3.0) |
| 7. St. Lucia 32 (15.3) | 44. Germany 12 (5.5) | 74. Norway 6 (2.9) |
| 8. Grenada 30 (14.0) | 45. France 12 (5.5) | 76. Switzerland 6 (2.8) |
| 9. St Kitts 30 (14.0) | 46. Greece 11 (5.4) | 77. Australia 6 (2.7) |
| 10. Bermuda 29 (13.8) | 47. The Philippines 11 (5.4) | 81. Italy 5 (2.6) |
| 15. Bulgaria 23 (10.7) | 48. Serbia 11 (5.4) | 83. Israel 5 (2.5) |
| 18. Belarus 21 (10.0) | 49. Ireland 11 (5.3) | 87. South Africa 5 (2.4) |
| 20. Japan 20 (9.6) | 50. USA 11 (5.1) | 90. New Zealand 5 (2.3) |
| 22. Czech Republic 19 (9.0) | 53. Croatia 10 (4.5) | 91. Sweden 5 (2.3) |
| 24. Slovakia 17 (8.2) | 54. Canada 9 (4.4) | 101. Argentina 2 (1.0) |
| 27. Lithuania 17 (7.9) | 56. Chile 9 (4.2) | 105. Turkey 2 (0.9) |
| 28. Romania 17 (7.8) | 57. Great Britain 9 (4.1) | 106. India 1¾ (0.8) |
| 29. Latvia 16 (7.6) | 59. The Netherlands 9 (4.1) | 115. Morocco 3 fl oz (0.1) |

and other nations on the one hand, and as an international mixing spirit on the other. The Swedish brand Absolut (15) is followed initially by the Ukrainian Nemiroff (19), ahead of the Russians. Stolichnaya, ranked second in 2002, has since lost significant ground to be placed at 47 and is still sinking. Like vodka, whisky continues to do good business with 10 products (including 3 from India) among the top 50. The indefatigable Johnny Walker is still way ahead of all its international competitors (9), while Jack Daniel's makes it to position 17. Overall the spirit brands have managed substantial increases in volume, even though 11 of the 50 biggest brands have at times had to accept disappointing losses.

## The world's 20 largest spirits concerns

*Annual production in million gallons (million liters) Status 2006, source: IWSR*

| | | | |
|---|---|---|---|
| Diageo | 222 (840) | Kyongwal | 42 (159) |
| Hite Brewery | 183 (694) | Takara Shuzo | 40 (152) |
| Pernod Ricard | 179 (677) | V & S Group | 38 (143) |
| U. B. India | 145 (547) | Constellation Brands | 36 (138) |
| Bacardi-Martini | 83 (314) | Campari | 30 (115) |
| Beam Global | 247 (65) | Asahi | 29 (111) |
| Muller De Bebidas | 60 (227) | Kumbokju | 29 (110) |
| San Miguel Group | 54 (206) | Tanduay | 28 (108) |
| Brown-Forman | 45 (170) | Belvedere SA | 27 (101) |
| Suntory | 44 (168) | Daesun | 25 (95) |

# Global players

The world of spirits is showing the increasing effects of globalization. Distribution is everything. The company that succeeds in establishing and expanding its presence in the most important consumer countries in good time has the best deck of cards in the great "Who is swallowing who?" game. In the background is an ongoing process during the course of which tightly managed, visionary companies were able to reinforce their portfolios, capacities, and thereby their positions in times of crisis. In the second phase the industry's big names considered merger to be the best move. Space does not allow a comprehensive discussion of these here, but further details can be found in the individual spirits sections.

The following thumbnail sketches focus on those western concerns constituting the giants of the spirits industry in terms of turnover. They are intended to serve as examples illustrating just how far advanced the concentration of internationally relevant brands is—and new mergers and takeovers are taking place all the time. This is in no way a comprehensive list of all the major groups, the main issue being the quality of the distillates and not who belongs to who.

Baileys is no. 11 among the internationally distributed brands.

## Diageo

The world's largest beverage concern was formed in 1997 when the British companies Grand Metropolitan and Guinness merged. They both brought with them a substantial portfolio of brands, while their two spirits companies International Distillers & Vintners IDV and United Distillers UD merged to form United Distillers & Vintners UDV, which were then integrated into Diageo in 2002. The name, a combination of *dia* (day) and *geo* (world), is intended to symbolize the fact that Diageo products are present all over the world every day.

Their most famous brands include: Smirnoff, Johnny Walker, Baileys, Captain Morgan, J&B, Gordon's Gin, Crown Royal, Bell's, Tanqueray, and Cacique.

Bacardi, also often drunk as Mojito, is one of the biggest spirits brands in the world.

## Pernod Ricard

The largest pastis competitors merged in 1975 in order to conquer the export markets together, creating a worldwide distribution network between 1985 and 1993. The key acquisitions began in 1988 with Irish Distillers, reaching their culmination in 2001 with a holding in Seagrams and in 2005 with a holding in Allied Domecq. The concern focused on its 15 main brands at the same time, namely Ballantine's, Chivas Regal, Malibu, Havana Club, Beefeater, Kahlúa, Jameson, Martell, and of course Ricard. In 2008 Patrick Ricard was able to assert himself against three rivals and took over the Swedish V&S Group, which produces Absolut Vodka (15th place among the most produced and 4th place among the internationally distributed spirits) for 5.6 billion euros. The group also owns Aalborg and Malteserkreuz Aquavit, Gammel Dansk, Cruzan Rum, and Plymouth Gin.

## Bacardi-Martini

The light, aromatic rum style developed by the company's Catalan founder, Facundo

Bacardi Massó, after 1862 in Santiago de Cuba provided the basis for the sensational international success of the private company after 1975, the company having emigrated to the USA following the Cuban revolution. Having become a high turnover concern by 1992, Bacardi was able to acquire Martini & Rossi as well as a variety of other brands including Bombay Sapphire, Bénédictine, Tequila Cazadores, Eristoff, and seven whisky brands, of which Dewar's and William Lawsons are the most well known.

With clever marketing and modern design, Absolut Vodka has today risen to become one of the most popular internationally distributed spirits.

## Beam Global

Its initial success having been based on America's most successful bourbon, the group belonging to Fortune Brands is today one of the largest spirits concerns in the world and, since the takeover in 2005 of more than 25 brands that had belonged to Allied Domecq, has consolidated its international position significantly. Apart from Jim Beam, the company also owns Canadian Club, Courvoisier, Laphroaig, Sauza Tequila, Larios Gin, Makers Mark, Whisky DYC, and Teacher's.

## Brown-Forman

This concern now represented in 135 countries dates back to George Garvin Brown, who was the first to market his Old Forester Kentucky Straight Bourbon Whisky in bottles in Louisville, Kentucky, in 1870. Today the company's portfolio comprises no less than 35 wine and spirit brands, including first and foremost Jack Daniel's, Canadian Mist, Southern Comfort, Woodford Reserve, and Finlandia.

## LVMH

Louis Vuitton Moët Hennessy, worldwide leader in luxury goods, owns more than 60 top brands. In addition to champagne and wine, Hennessy Cognac is one of the most lucrative spirit brands there is and is the concern's hallmark. However, the concern also owns Glenmorangie and Ardbeg, as well as the Belvedere and Chopin vodkas.

## William Grant & Sons

Founded by William Grant in 1886, Scotland's third largest whisky company is still family owned. While Glenfiddich is definitely no. 1 among the malts, Grant's is one of the most widely sold blends worldwide. Balvenie, Hendrick's Gin, and a range of other whiskies, rums, and the premium vodka Reyka are among its brands.

## The Edrington Group

This Scottish whisky company dates back to William A. Robertson in 1860 and is run today by the charity The Robertson Trust. It launched the Cutty Sark blend in 1936 and took over Highland Distillers in 1999. The group owns five distilleries and produces the famous brands The Macallan, Highland Park, and The Famous Grouse, amongst others.

Together with Black 55 and Matroschka, Smirnoff now forms part of the ongoing trend toward upmarket vodkas.

## Rémy Cointreau

The French group derives from the famous Rémy Martin cognac house founded in 1724 on the one hand and from the Cointreau liqueur developed in Angers in 1849 on the other, having been formed in 1990/1. Rémy Martin had decided to develop its own distribution within the premium sector as of 1965. The champagne companies Charles Heidsieck and Piper-Heidsieck were taken over in order to expand the range, as were international spirits such as Galliano, Mount Gay Rum, Metaxa, Izarra, and recently Ponche Kuba.

# Cognac, armagnac, and other brandies

Left: Hieronymus Brunschwig, *Liber de arte distillandi de simplicibus*, Strasbourg 1505 (detail).

Page 102:
The famous brandy of Gascony owes its distinctive character to the *alembic armagnaçais*, a column still for continuous distillation.

# The spirit of wine

Of all the spirits, those distilled from wine still enjoy a special cachet. This cannot just be explained by the fact that as they were the first high-percentage distillates to be used for medicinal purposes—and in general terms they had to become more palatable to take over from other drinks—they developed into pure luxury products, consumed for their own sake. In the early days they were called *brandewij*, for Dutch seafarers and merchants were the ones who successfully distributed them in Europe and beyond. The rise of brandies became meteoric when two significant factors came into play: origin and aging. To this day, they determine the quality and the price.

In terms of volume, the global leader in brandy is McDowell No. 1, which is made in Bangalore, India. The Philippines appears right at the top of the list of confirmed brandy consumers, and in the USA more than one in three empty brandy bottles has been imported from the Cognac region. Brandy is appreciated more than you might think in many other countries across the world, as well as being produced in far more countries than you might expect. Although it is no exaggeration to describe brandy as one of the leading international drinks, its most famous and prestigious representatives continue to come from the countries that were most important in its history: France and Spain. This history of brandies made from wine can be divided into four main phases. Around the year 800, reference to distilling equipment and the medicinal use of alcohol begin to occur in various Arabic sources, and while wine is not explicitly mentioned, it is obviously the source product. In the second half of the 13th century, Arnaldus de Villanova—a doctor and academic who worked in Valencia and Catalonia and had experience of the Orient—was experimenting with the spirit of wine, while at the same time Thaddaeus Florentinus (Taddeo Alderotti, 1223–1303) wrote his famous treatise *De virtutibus aque vite et eius operationibus* in Bologna, Italy. For the first time, it gave a detailed enough description of the art of distillation for it to be visualized, and in this way he promoted and spread the process of brandy production.

From the end of the 16th century, on account of their country's growth as a maritime and trading power, Dutch ships docked regularly in European ports. Among the goods traded were brandies, which promised ample profits and went on to establish a flourishing line of business—especially in the Jerez triangle, and in the Armagnac and Cognac regions—thanks to soaring demand. These clear, rough, and fiery wine distillates—initially produced to overcome the technical problems of transporting wine—were certainly not intended to be consumed neat, but to be mixed together with water, wine, or herbal extracts.

The third episode of the brandy story began in the 17th century, when it was noticed (presumably in many cellars about the same time) that storing the young, colorless distillate produced a completely transformed product: a milder brandy, gleaming gold with a fragrant scent of sweet spices, dried fruits, and smoky aromas. The first to catch on was cognac, or "coniack" brandy, followed by armagnac, and then eventually Jerez brandy, trailing behind at the end of the 19th century.

Now nothing stood in the way of success for the three individual official appellations of brandy, each of which displays a distinctive and recognizable character, thanks to the peculiarities of their respective region. Each of them experienced highs and lows in the next and fourth period of brandy history, which continues into the present day. In the process, however, a solid knowledge base was developed relating to the factors that determine quality. While ordinary brandies play a leading role in the ensemble that goes to make up many trendy cocktails, topping the scale in terms of quality are the solo artists: cognacs, armagnacs, and Solera Gran Reservas from Jerez help the connoisseur to find the most subtle sensory experiences at a sublime intellectual level.

# Wine—the raw material

"Brandy" is a generic term that prevents any conclusions being drawn about the source product, and a throwback to the early days of distillation when the focus was on the alcohol, which was practically revered as a mystical elixir of life. In the context used here, "brandy" is used exclusively to describe brandies that are made from wine, or more precisely from grape wine.

Towards the end of the 17th century it was initially innkeepers and their customers in London who discovered certain brandies from Cognac tasted better than those from other sources. Local traders in the Charente were the first to notice that the brandies from their own area were distinguished by more intensive flavors. Then it did not take long to work out that chalky soil yielded the best quality brandies. In this way at first, unofficial classification of the locations emerged. The storage and maturation of the brandies in wood also attracted a great deal of attention, which over the years provided reliable knowledge about the qualities, loca-

tions, and individual communities. The development of armagnac followed a very similar course.

## Bringing glamour to something dull

For the Dutch trading ships, wine was a lucrative commodity but not altogether unproblematic. They obtained wines from the Charente region, in the hinterland of their usual ports like La Rochelle or Rochefort, but they turned out to be mostly weak and acidic rather than sweetly pleasant, and they were all too quick to turn to vinegar. Easily perishable as it was, the wine could be transported by ship with greater stability as a distillate, and this also saved on space: in the destination harbor it could then be watered back down into wine. It was soon established that the tart white wines were best suited to distillation.

Before the grape phylloxera disaster in the 19th century, the most cultivated grape variety on the French Atlantic coast was Folle

The star grape varieties that are particularly suitable for distillation: the hybrid Baco (left), a specialty of Armagnac; and Colombard, prized especially in the New World (right).

Blanche, known as Gros-Plant in the Muscadet region, where distillation was also popular. When it came to replanting, the Cognac region decided against the variety that was awkward to cultivate and difficult to process, and opted for Ugni Blanc instead. A grape variety from Italy, where it goes by the name Trebbiano, Ugni Blanc is one of—if not the—best in the world in terms of yield. The vine had arrived in Provence by the time of the Avignon popes, and it then progressed through Gascony to the Charente. Easy to grow, it gave high yields of light, acidic wine that were ideal for distilling.

So the most impressive wine-based spirits are produced from these rather bland, unexciting white wines with low alcohol content and a high level of acidity. In much the same way the Palomino variety in Andalucia and Airén in La Mancha is used predominantly by the sherry houses and is without doubt the most widely cultivated vine in the world. In the Charente and Armagnac regions there is one other grape variety from which wine for distillation is produced: Colombard.

Colombard too has a good acidic content, and even intense flavors if vinified carefully,

though it does develop too much alcohol for the liking of many a French distiller. This is not such a problem in the USA, South Africa, and Israel, where Colombard has certainly proved its worth.

Baco Blanc occupies a special place in Gascony in particular, though it is the only hybrid permitted in an appellation. It too has proved itself to be resistant to grape phylloxera, and its unpalatable drinking wines produce excellent, full-bodied eaux-de-vie with long-aging potential.

In recent decades wine growers have most notably tried to create special brandies with high-quality vine varieties, and with considerable success: the examples of Riesling and Grüner Veltliner prove the point. Yet the classic profile of a cognac, armagnac, or brandy de Jerez is marked by the flavors produced through aging, which develops a relatively unostentatious but well-structured spirit made from bland wine over a period of years and decades, through the interplay with the evolving character of the cask.

The once dominant Folle Blanche (left) is now being honored again, though it will not threaten the supremacy of the Ugni Blanc or Trebbiano (right) in France and Italy.

# Cognac is cool

It has a new image. Instead of being served in pretentious cognac balloons, it is now poured liberally into a shaker, and Boston or Chicago barkeepers mix it with trendy liqueurs like Alizé or Hypnotiq, using all their artistic skills before sliding it across the counter as a Pink Love or an Incredible Hulk to hip-hop or rap fans. Brandy from the west of France is eminently suitable for mixing, thanks to its incomparable range of flavors. But connoisseurs are not diverted for long: they continue to bring their noses carefully to tulip-shape glasses and relax into sipping decades-old cognac in the here and now.

"Grape spirits against grain spirits" runs the motto of African Americans, who in recent years have turned their backs increasingly on the evil white man's drink, whisky. Instead of that they are consuming cognac with growing enthusiasm: a relatively gentle protest. Hip-hop artists love to flaunt it when they make the big time. The words of their songs have been embellished by the obligatory status symbols for some time now. Cognac had its moment of fame in 2001 in the song "Pass the Courvoisier" by hip-hop musicians P. Diddy and Busta Rhymes, singing "Give me the Henny, you can give me the Cris. You can pass me the Remy, but pass the Courvoisier." Whether Hennessy, Rémy Martin, or Courvoisier, sales rocketed in the USA from 2002 onward. This happened at a time when the staying power of the Charente wine growers had reached an all-time low. The main cause of this was the economic crisis in Asia in 1997, which resulted in a drastic collapse in demand. "Brown" brandies like the cognac family were out of fashion in other markets as it was, while clear schnapps with a high mixability factor were definitely "in." The hip-hop artists were responsible for turning the tide.

All of a sudden brand names were literally being hailed in rap songs. The "American Brandstand" website trawled through the Billboard Top Singles Chart in 2003 and found brand names in 43 out of 111 top hits, including Mercedes (first place), Cristal Roederer champagne (seventh), and Hennessy (eighth place). The next year Cadillac was top of the list, followed by Hennessy, which managed to keep sixth place even in 2005. In the meantime more and more songs have featured "shout-outs" of brands, and the bug has even spread to rhythm & blues and pop music.

As a result of all this, Hennessy has assumed the unrivalled top spot in terms of African American taste. As "Henn," "Henny," "Henn-roc," or "Henn Dog"—in Eminem's "Just Lose It"—or in songs by the Ying Yang Twins or Lil John & the East Side Boyz, Hennessy has now been glorified in over a hundred titles and clips. The house could not have wished for better publicity. Cognac has become part of a new lifestyle, enjoyed without constraint and with refreshing inventiveness, preferably at V.S. and V.S.O.P. level. There is a yawning gap stretching miles between the Charente wine growers and the rap scene, but it can hardly be any wider than the one that existed in the 18th century between the producers and the London clubs.

Brown spirits in general have come back into fashion in the meantime, and the number of aficionados of premium quality grades has once more reached gratifying levels. Connoisseurs in Asia, Russia, and the European markets have been learning the art of tasting, thanks to wine and malt whisky, and they are going back to the roots of cognac as a luxury product with a history spanning 400 years.

It is a precious, and often expensive, experience for someone to enjoy a cognac that was distilled when they were still in diapers, and that was then quietly able to mature for decades, oblivious to all the turmoil of history, developing ever more complex and elegant characteristics. The wine growers and cellar masters in the Cognac region have long been conscious of this heritage, and are now storing brandies that will be tasted only by the next generation. As an up-and-coming young cellar master states emphatically, "It is vital to preserve the taste, otherwise your heart goes out of it."

# Raise a glass to sea salt

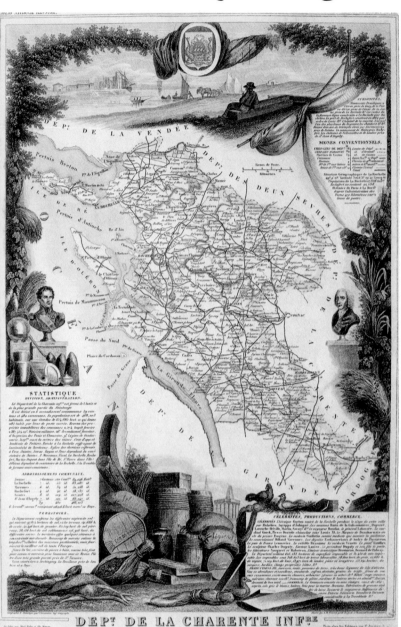

STATISTIQUE

DEPT. DE LA CHARENTE INFRE.

The *département* of Lower Charente from the *Atlas National illustré*, Paris 1852

Page 108: Juillac-le-Coq with its Romanesque church of Saint-Martin lies nearly 4 miles (about 6 km) southwest of Segonzac.

Strange as it may sound, cognac owes its development in a fundamental sense to sea salt. Without the salt ships of the Hanseatic League that loaded the essential food preservative in the 11th century in the harbors of what is now Charente-Maritime, thereby boosting the salt trade, the wine produced by the local population in the hinterland (initially for its own consumption) might never have come to the attention of shipowners thirsty for trade.

When the Dutch began to trade in wine in the 13th century, viticulture experienced a welcome upturn and the vineyards spread into the interior of the region. The white wines that thrived on the gentle chalky slopes around Cognac and Segonzac soon gained a good reputation, especially the fine sweet Borderies pressed from Colombard grapes. By contrast the growing wine production in Aunis near La Rochelle was offering worsening quality. The low percentage content of many casks did not survive the journey northward without becoming acidic (acescence). Once they reached The Netherlands, many cargoes could only be distilled into "brandewijn" in the newly created stills. Soon the Charente wine bought by the Dutch could be sold directly as wine only in exceptional circumstances, and by far the greater part was destined for the distilleries from the outset. Then it was only a question of time until the first traders had the lucrative idea of setting up stills in the Charente, and undertaking the distillation locally. The records of the first four shipped casks of *eau-de-vie*, or distilled water of life, are dated 1549 in La Rochelle.

## Coniack brandy

From a commercial point of view, the advantages of brandy were perfectly obvious: it took up a fraction of the space; it kept indefinitely, and it could be thinned down to drinking strength at its destination. The rise of cognac really took hold when producers realized that the region's wine needed to be distilled only twice in order to obtain a clear, clean spirit. In those days "wines" from other fruits and sources of origin had to be rectified several times at considerable cost. What is more, the ideally suited, acidic Charente base wines lent to the cognac a pleasantly fruity flavor that was absent from other types of schnapps.

Like most liquids, alcohol was transported in casks in those days. As there were constant delays involved in transporting goods by ship, it was discovered that eau-de-vie improved when stored in oak casks and could be enjoyed neat—in no time at all, cognac was born. Its quality began to gain a reputation, with the result that *coniack* (a mispronunciation of the French word) brandy had enough followers in London by the end of the 17th century that were prepared to pay more for it than any other brandy. The term appeared for the first time in 1678 in the *London Gazette*.

Cognac became a commodity that was in much demand, and heavily taxed. After the siege of La Rochelle came to an end in 1628 with the defeat of the Huguenots and their British allies, the Dutch expanded their position in the cognac export market. As before, it was the English aristocracy to whom they supplied the best cognac. The necessary infrastructure developed in order to meet the demand. Branches opened in all the larger towns in the region, where brandy was collected for shipping. Young men from The Netherlands, Britain, Ireland, or Scandinavia took care of trade and contacts abroad and settled in the local community through marriage. Many of the families involved in the cognac trade were still Huguenots. It was only when Louis XIV repealed the edict of Nantes in 1685 that most of them emigrated, though they often maintained their business links with their native country, which promoted the cognac trade even more. Cognac was first and foremost an export product, both then and now.

Chests destined for export are loaded onto a *gabare* (one of the standard cargo ships) on the quayside in Cognac (ca. 1920).

# Aged cognac

The oldest trading house specializing in cognac was founded in 1643 by Philippe Augier, whose marriage to a Dutchwoman guaranteed him excellent contacts in her native country. The oldest of the great brands, Martell, goes back to the year 1715, followed by Rémy Martin in 1724. Louis Gautier, whose grandfather had married a wine grower's daughter in 1644, was given permission to set up a cognac company in Aigre in 1755. The famous house of Delamain began in 1759, when the Irishman

In 1765 Richard Hennessy (1724–1800) founded what is now the leading cognac company.

James Delamain went into business with Jean-Isaac Ranson, who came from the Charente and would later become his father-in-law. Hennessy started up in 1765.

Until the French Revolution several families were active in the cognac trade without any of them gaining the upper hand, but the situation was to change fundamentally during the revolution. In the 1790s Martell and Hennessy were able to seize the opportunity afforded by the new government in order to secure more markets for themselves. They dominated the business for the next 150 years—hand in hand, so to speak, for there had been many occasions when hands in marriage were requested and given—and set the supply price according to the prevailing economic situation. At the same time a few dozen smaller companies emerged in the 19th century that were able to secure a share of the business for themselves. England maintained its position as the most important market until well into the 20th century, quaffing four fifths of all cognac exported for many years.

## Young, clear brandy

In the first three centuries of its existence, cognac bore scarcely any similarity to the product we enjoy today, other than its origins. It was mostly young, clear brandy that was marketed to the wider public, who drank it diluted with water—not so much because the cognac could not be taken neat, but because the water was undrinkable. Cognac was classed as old when it had been in the cask for a year. Even though aged cognac could command higher prices in 1720, it was rare to find quality brandy aged three years or over. The companies themselves did not undertake much in the way of storage and elaboration, as they bought quantities from wine growers according to demand, and in this way the growers bore the brunt of what were at times quite unpredictable fluctuations in the market. Even by the mid 19th century the leading companies' stocks consisted

predominantly of young brandies barely two years old. Only a very small quantity was left to mature for five or more years. Many a wine grower that did its own distilling speculated by holding back casks, as is still the case today. At that time nearly all the old eaux-de-vie were to be found in the cellars of the producers. Cognac may originally have been sold exclusively in casks, but the houses then began to move over to using smaller units, spawning a diverse supply industry that produced and supplied the bottles, corks, chests, and labels.

Increasing demand in the 19th century induced the growers to plant more and more vines, a serious mistake that culminated in overproduction and a consequent collapse in prices. The all-time high, or low, was reached in 1877 with a registration of about 690,000 acres (over 280,000 ha).

The vault where the oldest brandies of a cognac house are kept securely in demijohns is known as "paradise."

Left: Accompanying document from Cognac in 1763 for collection of a 317-gallon (1,200-liter) consignment of schnapps. Right: Contract between Connelly and Hennessy dated September 10, 1765: the founding document of the company.

# A rude awakening

In the last quarter of the 19th century Cognac was one of the regions ravaged by the phylloxera plague. When it hit the Charente vineyards it was initially seen as a solution to overproduction. But the extent of its effect was enormous. In the next 16 years the insects destroyed more than 85% of the cultivation area. It took the region two decades to recover from the catastrophe and replant a quarter of the previous vines with resistant American stock. In doing so they concentrated on the best locations around the town of Cognac and gave preference to the reliable, if rather bland, Ugni Blanc variety over its predecessor, Folle Blanche, which had more character but was more delicate.

It was only when the new vineyards produced yields and cognac came back onto the market that the companies became aware of the damage that had been caused in the interim by forgers, who were selling potato spirit as cognac in many countries. It became evident that clear definitions and protective regulations were needed. These were formulated for the first time in 1909 and ratified in 1936 as *Appellation d'Origine Controlée*. Before World War I cognac won England back as its main market, followed by the French colonies and other countries including Argentina, India, and Egypt.

The interwar years proved to be difficult ones. As in so many other countries, high taxation hampered turnover in France as well, and the French resorted to less expensive, wine-based aperitifs such as Byrrh or Dubonnet.

Careful sampling of the cognacs and their blending, as seen here in the 1930s, has always been a priority for cellar masters.

The German occupying forces in World War II made free with the companies' stocks that had been built up in the meantime, while the wine growers were able to expand and age their stock of eaux-de-vie unhindered, with the result that cognac was well equipped to face the future after the Liberation.

## Golden days

The end of the war saw the start of a boom in France that lasted nearly 30 years and brought cognac a golden period as well. In the early part of this era the Bureau National Interprofessionel du Cognac, or B.N.I.C., was formed, the joint professional body set up by wine growers and companies to safeguard and boost the quality and reputation of cognac. B.N.I.C. defined the different quality grades, for which registration, control, and certification relating to age and origin are essential, an unprecedented guarantee of quality in the world of spirits. Its success meant that cognac was not protected from the economic rules of the market game. Elaborating their own stock demanded a higher level of business acumen and flair on the part of the companies, one that did not always come naturally. At the same time foreign investors were registering a growing interest. As a consequence very few of the houses have survived under family ownership. Once again the boom tempted the growers to overextend their planting so that in 1976 the cultivated area had expanded to over 270,000 acres (110,000 ha), clearly more than the market could bear. A new crisis loomed that lasted beyond the millennium and led to grim predictions on the part of industry experts.

The cognacs of the Hennessy house were bottled and prepared for shipping in this warehouse around 1920.

# The rules of the game

As the 20th century drew to an end, cognac producers found themselves in a changed situation. Three out of four companies had disappeared from the market. The Big Four—Hennessy, Rémy Martin, Martell, and Courvoisier—are now parts of multinational groups with extremely efficient international distribution systems: they sell over 70% of a total production of 160 million bottles, of which 95% are exported.

In terms of production little has changed. The companies that dominate the market do not own their own vineyards. They have to buy young eaux-de-vie from 4,500 wine growers with their own distilleries, the "bouilleurs du cru," or from professional distillers that process the wines from the 1,500 wine growers who only grow grapes. This division of tasks that has existed since time immemorial separates the wine growers from the markets, consumers, and trends. If business is going well, the companies try to secure their supply through agreements—Rémy Martin set up a cooperative with a membership of 2,000 wine growers—but in times of crisis the wine growers always bear the brunt. It has been a long time since the fortunes of cognac were determined in Cognac, and the heads of the four leading brands are no longer Charente residents.

What is left over by the four giants is shared, according to the B.N.I.C. register, by 217 direct sales wine growers, three cooperatives, and another 141 firms: the numbers of the last named are swollen by the established domains whose status as traders

Bottle labeling and preparation for sale at Hennessy, ca. 1920

allows them greater freedom of action. Barely 30 financially strong trading companies are still in existence.

## A fresh wind

Today the estates handling their own sales, most of which did not take the leap into independence until after 1945, are experiencing growth brought by a new, cosmopolitan, and critical generation. They harness the potential of modern communication to present their product in the proper light. In terms of production they distinguish themselves by dealing confidently with traditions and are developing a style that tends to be more modern, emphasizing the geographical origins even if this is not in Grande Champagne. They work their vineyards more conscientiously than ever before in the region's history. Their cognacs are often single vintage brandies and for elaboration they often prefer fine-grained durmast oak from Allier to the coarser grained pedunculate oak from Limousin. In this way their cognacs have lower oxidation, which gives them a more elegant, sweeter flavor.

Cognac, even though it is not immediately evident, is also picking up in the Charente.

The future looks bright again. After their parents had taken to cognac back in the 1970s, young black people in America, predominantly rappers and hip-hop artists, made "yak" into their cult drink. Suddenly sales of cognac are booming once more. In recent years demand has also been growing for premium quality cognacs, especially in Asia, where the economy is on the upturn after the crash of 1997. How long will the feverish desire to make a fortune last this time?

Château de Beaulon in Saint-Dizant-du-Gua is an example of an estate that has made a name for itself through personal initiative and its own marketing.

An invitation to visit the great houses in the little town of Cognac.

# The terroirs of Cognac

The source of the Charente river is in neighboring Limousin, which is well known for its oaks. It then meanders across the former provinces of Angoumois and Saintonge, and circumnavigates Rochefort to the south before finally flowing into the Atlantic opposite the Ile d'Oléron. It represents the artery of the Cognac region, which owes its geological formation, as well as the capricious climate and favorable transport routes, to the river. In the gently undulating landscape to the south of its banks between Cognac and Jarnac, vines rise up the slopes, trained on wire frames in precise rows. They grow in pale, chalky soil for, as in the Champagne region, chalk marks out the best locations, which in this case are called Grande and Petite Champagne.

Two French *départements* are named after the river: Charente and Charente-Maritime. They encompass the whole Cognac region with the exception of two small enclaves in the Dordogne and Deux-Sèvres. The total cultivation area comprises 42 square miles (110 sq km), of which nearly 200,000 acres (80,000 ha) are grape-yielding land. The main concentration is in the almost square central zone where chalk and limestone permeate the soil.

The climate is equally as important for the quality of cognac. The region is a crossroads for north, south, Atlantic, and continental climatic conditions, leading to a variety of microclimates in places and to a myriad nuances in the wines and distillates.

There are six different terroirs that were defined for the first time in the decree of 1909 and then confirmed by the Appellation d'Origine Contrôlée awarded in 1936.

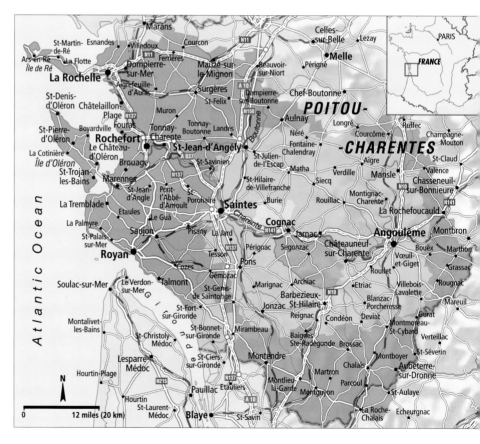

The growth areas, or crus,
of Cognac Appellation

- Grande Champagne
- Petite Champagne
- Borderies
- Fins Bois
- Bons Bois
- Bois Ordinaires

## Grande Champagne

Around Segonzac, as far as the town of Cognac and then to Jarnac, where the climate is at its steadiest, the soils are characterized by chalk and porous limestone excellent for drainage while storing water like a sponge. Cognacs from this area have an astonishing aging potential and develop a complex bouquet and the greatest finesse. Growth area: over 32,000 acres (13,000 ha); the figures relate only to cognac production.

## Petite Champagne

It embraces Grande Champagne in a semicircle whose northern boundary is formed by the Charente. Although their soils are similar (apart from the chalk being less porous and lying deeper) and the climate is only slightly more maritime or continental, the cognacs are lighter on the palate and have a more restrained finesse. Growth area: 40,000 acres (16,000 ha). Fine Champagne is a blend of a maximum of 50% Petite and a minimum of 50% Grande Champagne.

## Borderies

The smallest and most enclosed terroir to the north of Cognac has chalky soil containing clay and stronger Atlantic influences, giving smooth, aromatic, and interesting brandies that are faster aging and have a characteristic scent of violets. Mostly used for blending. Growth area: 9,900 acres (4,000 ha).

## Fins Bois

This extensive terroir covered in woods and meadows surrounds the crus of Grande Champagne, Petite Champagne, and Borderies. It is famed for its early aging and its pleasant and accessible cognacs. The area known as Fins Bois de Jarnac and the enclave near Mirambeau on the Gironde produce some delightful quality cognacs which also age well. Growth area: 81,500 acres (33,000 ha).

## Bons Bois

The largest terroir encircles the first four, boasting a diversity in terms of both its soil and climate, which is reflected in its fast-aging brandies: less distinguished, these are often used to make Pineau des Charentes, the liqueur of the region. Growth area: 30,000 acres (12,000 ha).

## Bois Ordinaires

(now renamed Bois à Terroir) The extensive cultivated area on the coastal plain took its current form back in the 19th century. In this not very exceptional terroir they concentrate mainly on the production of dry white wines. Spirits with a more distinctive character are more readily found in the terroirs of the Ile d'Oléron and the Ile de Ré, with their maritime location and gravelly soil. Growth area: 4,200 acres (1,700 ha).

The wine landscapes of the Charente: terroirs with their special soil characteristics and microclimate create the basis for the cognac's quality.

# Charentais distillation

Once the first wines have completely fermented in November, an unmistakable aroma begins to permeate the villages of Grande and Petite Champagne in particular—the scent of freshly distilled eaux-de-vie, the cognacs of the future. It lies heavily in the air until March 31 at the latest, although the *bouilleurs de cru* (wine growers who do their own distilling), the professional *bouilleurs* (companies with their own distillation facilities), and the professional distilleries and cooperatives are all anxious to start work quickly—the fresher the wine, the cleaner the spirit. The wine should ideally have an alcohol content of 8–9% and be very acidic, clean, straightforward, and typical, and should also have completed the fermentation process. "We don't need anything fancy, just a sound and fruity product," explains Jean-Pierre Vidal, the head distiller at Hennessy. The distillation process is what produces the concentration of flavors, and it takes 2–3 gallons (8–10 liters) of wine to make a bottle of cognac.

## Charentais pot still

The Charentais pot still, or alembic, is the classic type for batch distillation. The principle remained the same for centuries, only the capacity changed. Although wine growers do still operate smaller versions, the large distilleries have stills for producing brandy with which they have the capacity, and permission, to distill 660 gallons (2,500 liters). The most important part of the copper still is the still-head, in which the concentration takes place. From there the vapors pass over into the swan neck and on into the condenser unit.

The alembic must be heated on an open flame. In the past this was done with wood in daytime and with coal at night—an exhausting and stressful process—but it is now done by gas so that the required temperature can be easily regulated. An energy-saving wine warmer is usually attached to the still: it preheats the base wine to 104 °F (40 °C) before it goes into the boiler and is heated over the gas flames. At 172.9 °F (78.3 °C) the alcohol and other volatile substances rise up in the form of vapors and then condense when cooled down. This distillation process takes 12 hours.

During the first distillation, *brouillis*, a slightly cloudy raw distillate like pomace with an alcohol content of 28–30%, is collected first of all, and this liquid contains all the characteristics of the final spirit. The second distillation, known as the *bonne chauffe*, sees a further concentration to 70–72% vol. at the very most. This batch distillation gives the distiller controlled access to the heads and tails (*têtes* and *secondes*). He decides when they should be separated from the rest in order to collect only the *coeur* or heart, which flows out of the condenser into the cask as a clear spirit with an intense aroma.

## The delicate tails

The "heads" consisting of alcohol at too high a percentage play a fairly subsidiary role, but the "tails" make all the difference. These are heavy, aromatic substances, some of which are harmful. For this reason, the distiller will remove them completely from spirits used for young cognac, while leaving some of them for longer-aging ones. This decision-making freedom distinguishes double distillation from continuous distillation. The heads and tails are reused by the distiller. If flavor and complexity are required, he adds the tails to the next batch of brouillis, and if he wants the brandy to have a less distinctive flavor, he adds it to the next batch of base wine. Base wines with or without lees give added nuances. "Distillation using lees is the traditional method," stresses Pascal Fillioux, the owner of Cognac Jean Fillioux. "In Grande Champagne in particular, this gives more pronounced expression to the flavors of the terroir and you get smoother eaux-de-vie that are bursting with complexity."

Opposite: The classic Charentais pot still consists of a boiler and still-head with a swan neck, and a cylindrical condenser unit (from which the spirit flows into the cask). The large bulbous container is the wine pre-warmer, through which the hot vapors pass on the way to the condenser: it preheats the wine to be distilled in the next cycle. Aerometers measure the alcohol content.

# Without oak, no cognac

Cognac was born at the very moment it was discovered that brandy develops completely different and more sophisticated flavors when aged in oak casks. The oak wood that has always been used in the Charente for this purpose comes from nearby Limousin. It is mainly pedunculate oak that grows there, and its wood is ideally suited to the aging of cognac over many years. In the fertile Limousin soil the oaks grow more strongly in spring than in summer. The result is larger intervals in the annual ring of the tree and a correspondingly coarser grain structure, which means a higher level of phenolic compounds. The fine-grained, less porous wood from the durmast oak found in the Allier—the most famous from the Tronçais region in northern Auvergne—is used for younger cognacs on account of its wealth of aromatic essences like vanillin, or chosen by producers looking for a more distinctive, unmistakable signature of the terroir.

In addition to oak wood, the tools needed by the cooper to make a cask are a hammer, wedge, drawknife, plane, lever, and compasses.

**How a cask is made, from top left to bottom right:**

The cut wood is fed through the band saw to give the staves equal width and length from the very start.

The cooper joins the curved staves together using a metal ring to hold them firmly in place.

Once the circular shape of the cask is complete, the cooper hammers a second and then third hoop over it to keep the staves in position.

The staves at the other end of the cask are still splayed, so they have to be made more pliable by heating over an open flame. The intensity with which the cask is burned has a crucial effect on the flavors it later imparts to the cognac.

A metal sling is placed round the cask and the cooper applies a lever action to tighten it progressively, while he moistens the outside of the staves.

Finally the staves form a completely closed circle at the other end and it can be finished off with a ring.

The cask still does not have a side opening, so the cooper drills a bunghole in the oak wood, and mills it to the required size.

The heads have yet to be put in place, but the outside of the cask is already being given the final touch.

# The mysteries of the chais

Cognac ages in casks with a capacity of around 106 gallons (400 liters) made from French oak. The vats are used for the *assemblage*, or blending (left: Camus). Some casks are used for decades (right: Ragnaud-Sabourin).

Jarnac, a sleepy little town, is the second most important brandy producer in the region. The typical scent of casks wafts permanently up the alleys that lead onto the river Charente and the walls display the characteristic black fungus *Torula cognaciensis* that thrives on evaporated alcohol.

The river is never far from the places where cognac is stored. The location may originally have been chosen for its transportation options, but it turned out that the air humidity near water is conducive to a gentle aging process and natural way of reducing the spirit that starts out at about 70% volume. At the same time the humidity cuts down the evaporation. Evaporation increases in a dry *chai* (above-ground cellar for casks), and the distillate does not sacrifice much of its alcohol content, though it does lose more water and, with it, volume. Those who have access to both storage options know how to make best use of them to age their cognacs. Moreover, in every chai in summer a singular aroma permeates the air as a hallmark of diversity.

If distillation represents the first concentration of the flavors in the eau-de-vie, then evaporation is the second. Without it there would be no development and aging of the cognac. Evaporation exerts its own influence, depending on the properties of the oak wood (harder from the Limousin forests, softer from the Tronçais region), the character of the chai (mellower in a humid one, more distinctive in a dry one), and the size of the cask (the bigger it is, the less it loses). Each year around 23 million bottles of cognac—known as the "angels' share"—evaporate. On average, producers allow for 3% annually, which means that over a period of ten years, for every 26 gallons (100 liters), 7 (26) have disappeared into the air!

## Theories about casks

When it comes to casks—92 gallons (350 liters) is the most popular size—opinions are divided among the Cognaçais. "You certainly wouldn't store old cognac in new wood, or young in old: there are rules that have to be

respected," a point made emphatically by Olivier Paultes, the cellar master of Frapin. There are three different types of cask.

*Fûts neufs*: casks are classed as new in the first five years; they contain a lot of tannins, but also flavors like vanillin, and are used only for freshly distilled eaux-de-vie.

*Fûts roux*: casks that are 5–15 years old, 20 at most; they no longer contain many tannins, and are used for cognacs that are mostly intended to undergo further oxidation.

*Vieux fûts*: 15–20 years old and above; they have no tannins, but they are soaked in cognac and suitable for refining the oldest vintages. Before the cellar master decides on the cask, he assesses the new eau-de-vie. What is the potential of the distillate? The young brandies with the most flavor are destined for the youngest quality cognac, while more closed types long to be developed and are elaborated into the older cognacs. The tasting always determines the future development. The elaboration begins in new casks—toasted to a greater or lesser degree from inside during their production—that are vital for enriching the cognac with tannins, color, and flavor.

The length of time is crucial. At Raymond Ragnaud they stick to 6–8 months, while Frapin leaves it for a maximum of 12. Hennessy secretly feels that fine eaux-de-vie should not be kept for too long in new wood. On the other hand, Jean Fillioux keeps young brandies of 18–24 months in new casks, and vintage cognacs are kept in their new cask for the whole maturation period. All producers agree that the notes of the wood are harsh and bitter to begin with, and that it takes years of oxidation for the desired flavors to develop: of vanilla, then of preserved fruit such as apricot and orange as well as almonds and nuts, and finally the intensely complex flavor known as "rancio."

Cognacs have reached their peak of maturation after 60 years, or 70 at most. They are then poured into demijohns in order to prevent further oxidation and, above all, any further evaporation.

The Delamain cellar master (left) takes a sample from an old cask. Spiders' webs are welcomed in chais as they are natural fly traps and signs of a healthy cellar atmosphere.

# The finishing touch

The great art of cognac lies in the assemblage, or blending. It is only in recent years that the still rare vintage, or even single cask, bottlings have been available. Irrespective of the quality level—whether V.S., V.S.O.P., X.O., or considerably older reserves—cognac houses and domains are mainly concerned with having a balanced and harmonious product, the quality and style of which remain unchanged and homogeneous from one bottling to the next and over a period of many years. For this reason, younger blends often combine eaux-de-vie from different sources. Basically, one cask will never be exactly the same as another one.

Cognac changes with age, acquiring ever more complex flavors and transforming from being crystal clear to a dark mahogany color.

And with the often large quantities that have to be blended in such a way as to preserve their signature intact, it is difficult to imagine a more delicate process. As a rule the cellar masters carry out a meticulous inventory each year between April and September in the form of an ongoing preassemblage process, which moves maturation on step by step and ideally creates greater harmony. Gradually they carry out further cuts, which, depending on the size of the brand, can sometimes involve between 100 and 150 different brandies.

The higher and older the quality, the more subtle and appealing are the constituent

parts of varying ages. "This is when the cellar master is in demand, when he can prove himself, giving free rein to his talent and inspiration. "The only thing he must not do is make a mistake," stresses Patrick Peyrelongue, who runs Delamain. "It's not a simple matter to compose a product that manages to achieve a perfect balance of finesse, elegance, distinction, subtlety, freshness, punch, soft sweetness, directness, and purity while maintaining a powerful signature." For this a substantial stock which has the greatest possible variety of nuances is required.

## Drinking strength and color

The highest degree of instinctive flair is equally expected of the cellar masters when it comes to reduction. Young cognac flows out of the condenser with an alcohol content of about 70% volume, whereas it clearly has less when it finally reaches retail outlets. In order to reduce its strength to the maximum legal limit of 45% volume, it must be "broken down" with demineralized or distilled water. This is not quite as simple as it sounds, for if it is done too abruptly the cognac will later smell of soap and taste flat and watered down. It has to be carried out in careful stages, leaving plenty of time even with a three-year-old V.S. For reduction, the experts in vintage blends use *vieilles faibles*, a 15% volume mixture of watered down old cognac that has matured in casks for up to two years.

The color is determined by the addition of caramel and the taste by the option of adding up to ¾ oz per 2½ gallons (20 g per 10 liters) of sugar or syrup. Before bottling, cognacs are normally stabilized and filtered at a sub-zero temperature so that they sparkle in the glass in all geographical climates. Very few houses and wine growers oppose this procedure, which suppresses elements of the flavor.

## Qualities

The age of cognac is officially controlled and counted: 00 represents a cognac from harvest to March 31 the following year, at which point the number changes to 0. From April 1 each year that follows, the number increases by 1. The highest official registration of age is 10.

V.S. (Very Special) or ✴✴✴: the youngest cognac allowed on the market must be at least two and a half years old, the reference date being October 1 of the wine harvest year.

V.S.O.P. (Very Superior Old Pale), V.O. (Very Old) or Réserve: minimum age of four and a half years.

Napoléon, X.O. (Extra Old), Extra or Hors d'Age: minimum age of six and a half years.

Often cellar masters use cognac for their blends that far exceed the minimum age.

Millésime, or vintage, cognac may be bottled in France after the 1988 vintage, while older ones are the "early landed" cognacs aged and bottled in England or quite special quantities, controlled by the B.N.I.C. and kept under lock and key.

# The big four

## Hennessy

Hennessy is the heavyweight of the four giant cognac companies. Although the founder Richard Hennessy still figures prominently as a hero, it was under his son James during the French Revolution that the company attained the priority position that it continues to defend successfully today, now as part of the L.V.M.H. group (Louis Vuitton—Moët Hennessy). Right from the outset it focused on exports to England, followed later by the United States, Australia, and Asia, attaining the top position in many countries. Branding policy and advertising similarly contributed to this success, as Hennessy recognized their importance early on. Today the company owns over 440 acres (180 ha) of vines, administers another 540 acres (220 ha), and works with around 1,700 suppliers. Their Grande Champagne is mainly distilled in house in the Distillerie du Peu. The style and quality of the house is defined by the Fillioux family, cellar masters for over two hundred years. The full-bodied, rounded, and spicy X.O. with its sweet fruity notes is typical of the house style, while the Paradis captivates the palate with its elegant rancio and extraordinary finesse.

## Rémy Martin

Rémy Martin, a wine grower and the son-in-law of a merchant, founded his cognac company in 1724. Its success was built up over three generations, until Paul Rémy Martin proved incapable of overcoming a series of contemporary crises and his own megalomania. The company was saved in 1910 by André Renaud, a qualified lawyer who grew up in Grande Champagne. In 1927 he created the Fine Champagne V.S.O.P. by linking the old term with the top terroir, blending longer aged brandies to give it a spicy, full-bodied, and fruity character. Inspired by Renaud's son-in-law André Hériard Dubreuil, Rémy Martin put only Fine Champagne onto the market from 1948, and the V.S.O.P. became one of the most successful cognacs to this day. He helped to make a medium-size company into second in the league of giants, merging in 1990 with Cointreau. In order to secure supplies Rémy Martin concluded the first deals with wine growers as early as 1965, which led eventually to the Alliance Fine Champagne in 2005, a cooperative with 2,000 members.

## Martell

Founded in 1715, Martell is the oldest cognac company of the quartet. At that time 21-year-old Jean Martell settled in Cognac. He came from the island of Jersey, which at that time was an important, if not quite legal, place for turning goods round, and where his family was based. His first attempts in the cognac business failed, but then he married into one of the main families, the Lallemand, and from that moment on his cognac trade began to flourish, especially with London and Dublin. Martell rose quickly to become the leading cognac company, a position it managed to maintain until 1985. The Hennessys, related by marriage, occupied second place. Following a decade in decline under Seagram's management, Martell (which has been part of the Pernod Ricard group since 2002) has caught up with Rémy Martin. It has 700 acres (283 ha) of cultivation area at its disposal (for 3% of production) and owns the largest distillery in the region. Its flagship cognac continues to be the Cordon Bleu in its 1912 bottle design. It owes its nutty flavor to Borderies brandies and its sweet spicy notes and dry smoothness to maturation in Tronçais oak.

## Courvoisier

Courvoisier has always been the outsider of the Big Four. Emmanuel Courvoisier was a wine merchant in the Parisian district of Bercy who supplied cognac to Napoleon Bonaparte. In 1843 his son Félix decided to form his own cognac company in Jarnac. It was sold in 1909 to the Simon family from England, who knew how to build Courvoisier into a brand. They deliberately focused on the old imperial connection, presenting their cognac as "The Brandy of Napoleon." Today the Napoleon is still a smooth, full-bodied, and spicy Fine Champagne that lingers on the palate, the jewel in the company's crown. Courvoisier buys in cognacs according to need rather than building up its own stock, a policy that initially proved very advantageous. But when cognac became scarce after the frost of 1956, the company did not have enough capital to secure their supply. In 1964 Hiram Walker stepped in, the first international group to invest in cognac. Today the house—which now has a stock of 14.8 million gallons (56 million liters) and fixed contracts with 1,100 wine growers—is one of the main brands of Beam Global Spirits and Wine.

# Houses with class

### Delamain

Delamain, one of the great names in cognac, was founded in Jarnac in 1762 by the Irishman James Delamain, and rose to become what was certainly the biggest company at the time. Since then, the Delamain and their descendants have used Grande Champagne exclusively and market only old cognacs. The range starts confidently with the elegantly fruity Pale & Dry X.O. and culminates in Très Vénérable, a cognac of great finesse and fresh subtlety, and the outstanding Très Vieille Réserve de la Famille.

### Hine

In 1791 Thomas Hine from Dorset in England sought his fortune in Jarnac. Specializing in early landed vintages, cognacs aged in Bristol, the Hines also reserved great vintages of Grande Champagne in Jarnac. They offer an exquisite selection that includes the 1957 vintage (rich and robust with a very long finish) and the wonderfully elegant and well-rounded 1960 vintage. Hine also produces excellent blends, like the superbly complex Triomphe with its subtle rancio note and Antique, which demonstrates what a true X.O. should be like.

### A. E. Dor

This small cognac house in Jarnac was founded in 1858 and taken over in 1981 by Jacques Rivière and his wife Odile. Its fame is based on a priceless collection of ancient eaux-de-vie dating from 1805 to 1893 and on the range of cognacs on offer, numbered from 6 to 11. These are mainly made with Grande Champagne—such as the very elegant No. 7 with its subtle notes suggesting wood, leather, and oak, or the extremely long and complex No. 8 with its superb rancio. An elegant X.O. is also available.

### Camus

Established in 1863, the company is now headed by Cyril Camus and sits in fifth place in the league of cognac houses. At one time its main market was czarist Russia, then later the duty-free one. The house owns 310 acres (125 ha) of cultivation area in the Borderies cru, which gives the X.O. its full, nutty flavor. There is a floral, fruity V.S.O.P. in the Elégance range. The innovative Fine Island Cognac from the Ile de Ré reveals inventive salty, marine notes with a subtle spiciness. The Extra delivers mellowness and structure.

## Louis Royer

In 1853 cellar master Louis Royer formed his own company in Jarnac and developed a close relationship with the distillers of the Cognac terroirs whose cognacs appealed most to him. Under Suntory management since 1989, the traditional range has been expanded, especially with the Distilleries Collection—five cognacs from five distilleries in the five best terroirs. Distinctive from each other in style, the Fins Bois with its fruity, raisin tones and the velvety smooth Grande Champagne with its rancio note are particularly palatable.

## Pierre Ferrand

Founded in 1989 by Jean-Dominique Andreu and Alexandre Gabriel, the Cognac Ferrand company has at its heart the Domaine du Logis d'Angeac in the center of Grande Champagne. It has over 185 acres (75 ha) of vineyards, a modern cellar, and ten alembic stills. Its impressive premiers crus cover a wide range: the fruity, elegant Ambre; the spicy, floral Reserve; the very aromatic Réserve des Dieux with its sweet note of plums, leather, and tobacco; the outstanding Abel and Ancestrale; and the rare, great vintage selection.

## H. Mounier

In 1858 Captain Henri Mounier began his wholesale trade in cognac. In 1874 he founded Henri Mounier & Co., later renamed H. Mounier, and then he took up bottling and distribution at home and abroad. Taken over by Unicoop, the powerful cooperative of five hundred wine growers, the company markets its cognacs primarily under the brand name Prince Hubert de Polignac. Its sweet and mellow Grande Champagne, Extra—with intense notes of fruit, spice, and oak, as well as a rancio of walnuts, leather, and tobacco—is a cognac of merit.

## Leopold Gourmel

Launched in 1961 by Olivier Blanc's father-in-law, Gourmel has introduced a refreshingly no-nonsense style, based on premier cru wines from Fins Bois, "oily" distillation and aging in fine-grained Allier oak. The cognacs are bottled by vintage and are named after their character, so there is Age du fruit (elegant, with citrus notes), Age des fleurs (more complexity, delightful), Age des épices (very spicy and multilayered), and Quintessence (surprisingly complex and a lasting finish). Very classy.

# Estate cognacs

### Pierre Frapin

Château de Fontpinot in Segonzac plays a leading role among the few chateaux in the Cognac region. With 778 acres (315 ha), it represents the largest estate in the entire region and it distills, ages, and distributes its own harvest. The house of Frapin to which it belongs goes back to 1270 in a direct line from Geneviève Renaud, the wife of Max Cointreau. The famous creator of Gargantua, François Rabelais, numbers among its members. The X.O., matured in a dry chai for a very long time, has developed the hint of vanilla from the oak, combined with a pronounced bouquet of dried apricots and candied orange, and overlaid by an elegant note of rancio.

### Jean Fillioux

Pascal and Monique Fillioux have run the estate of La Pouyade in the little community of Juillac Le Coq since 1982. Their vineyards, covering 54 acres (22 ha), are in the best locations in Grande Champagne. Pascal Fillioux represents the fourth generation of the family since the house was founded during 1894. Of his cognacs, matured to different ages, the Très Vieux (blended from the four vintages from 1975 to 1979) is the most representative example of Grande Champagne. Characterized by intensely fruity notes dominated by vanilla and the pronounced flavor of orange marmalade, it is mellow and harmonious, its sweet fruitiness combining with spice and a hint of rancio.

### Guy Lhéraud

In 1971 Guy Lhéraud began to market the cognac from his family estate independently, after previously supplying the big companies. As far back as 1680 a certain Alexandre Lhéraud owned a vineyard in the hamlet of Lasdoux near Angeac in Petite Champagne, and since then it has grown to 173 acres (70 ha). Guy Lhéraud and his son Laurent distill their wines themselves in two alembic stills. They do not cut cognacs of different ages, nor do they add sugar or coloring. Their Cuvée 20 is very impressive—intensely fruity and velvety smooth—and the excellent X.O. Eugénie, which has aged for 30 years, pushes back all the boundaries with its spicy, nutty notes.

### Ragnaud Sabourin

The La Voûte estate near Ambleville has been run by women for three generations. One reason for its outstanding reputation lies in the 114 acres (46 ha) of vineyards in Grande Champagne, but it is primarily based on the great old cognacs that have been passed down from one generation to the next. Even though they do offer younger cognacs—one of which is the elegant, delicately aromatic 20-year-old Réserve Spéciale—the real quality cognacs are revealed upward of the Grande Réserve Fontvieille, matured for 35 years in Limousin oak casks to become a Grande Champagne of incredible complexity—with notes of plums, cigar boxes, and rancio, and a delightfully dry finish.

### Daniel Bouju

Wine has been produced by Daniel Bouju's family in Saint-Preuil in the heart of Grande Champagne for eight generations. He represents the descendants with a range of about 20 different cognacs, made from base wines from 62 acres (25 ha) of vines. Age, and sometimes the reduction, differentiates the different cognacs. From the time of Napoleon onward the old eaux-de-vie reveal a wonderful concentration of sweet dried fruit combined with the notes of old oak casks. Drawn directly from the cask, the unfiltered Très Vieux Brut du Fût has a truly great intensity and dense complexity that culminates in subtle tobacco notes.

### François Voyer

Even though Voyer now buys in from other producers, the heart of the company consists of 82 acres (33 ha) of vineyards in the villages of Verrières and Ambleville, in the justifiably famous belt of land in Grande Champagne. Starting with the V.S.O.P., the cognacs display elegance and balance. The extremely complex X.O. is a top-quality cognac, with flavors ranging from vanilla through dried fruit to nuts, oak, and blond tobacco. But with its wonderful finesse and most elegant of rancios, the exceptionally rare Lot 6 Ancestral (only 222 bottles were filled) represents simply one of the most outstanding cognacs available on the market today.

### Louis Bouron

These cognacs have been produced since 1832 in Château de la Grange, a magnificent castle with two medieval turrets situated 19 miles (30 km) northwest of Cognac. It owns 220 acres (90 ha) of vineyards, whose cultivation areas are spread across three of the six terroirs (Fins Bois, Borderies, and Petite Champagne)—which is extremely unusual. With its 20 wine growers, the estate is run by Monique Parias, the great-granddaughter of the founder, Louis Bouron. She offers a broad palette of cognacs of different ages, which she blends from the three crus: among these is the tantalizingly complex, spicy, and full-bodied Très Vieille Réserve.

### Château de Beaulon

The imposing castle dating back to 1480 is located in Saint-Dizant-du-Gua, not far from the Gironde. The influence of Bordeaux, whose archbishops administered it in the 17th century, manifests itself in the grape varieties—Semillon, Sauvignon, Merlot, and Cabernet—which are used for the excellent pineaus; while the cognac is mainly distilled from Folle Blanche, Colombard, and Montil grapes. Four small alembics in neighboring Lorignac are used for distillation. The X.O. Vintage 1971 is very impressive, with its intense ripe fruit; notes of vanilla, curry, nuts, and tobacco; and subtly sweet floral aroma that has a very long finish.

### Bernard Boutinet

At Brissoneau, which lies in the Fins Bois near Bréville, there are 67 acres (27 ha) of vines that were planted for the first time over a century ago on deep but light soils. Typically for the Fins Bois cru, they produce fruity eaux-de-vie with a distinctive flavor of fresh and preserved grapes, which age comparatively quickly. Thirty years ago Bernard Boutinet decided to market the domain's output under his own name. His well-balanced X.O. with honey and gingerbread tones is a blend made up 50:50 of a 15- and a 20-year-old cognac.

### Roland Seguin

Roland and Claudette Seguin, who have been involved in organic production since 1982 on their farm in the village of Villars-les-Bois, just 12 miles (20 km) northeast of Cognac, have planted 7 acres (3 ha) with vines. They distill cognac from the grapes, as well as making pineau, Vin de Pays Charentais, and a blackcurrant liqueur. Their vineyards lie in the Borderies cru, whose clay soil is famous for producing particularly aromatic and fast-aging cognacs. This is evident in the lovely dark color of the V.S.O.P. that the Seguins allowed to mature for ten years, and it is also tasted in its well-rounded, harmonious character and hazelnut notes.

# Red-hot armagnac

What is thought to be the oldest "spiritus vini gallici" to be drunk for pleasure rather than for medicinal purposes has kept its fiery soul. It is deeply rooted in its homeland of Gascony, renowned as much for its legendary swashbucklers, the musketeers, as its hearty cuisine. Foie gras and confit of duck are common indulgences, often well beyond the hundredth birthday, and armagnac has its part to play in this longevity. Anyone seeking the genuine article will find heaven on earth in Gascony, and the elixir of life in armagnac.

Documents proving the existence of armagnac go back to the 15th century, when it was used for a range of medical purposes. In *Recettes Alchimiques* (alchemist recipes), a manuscript dated 1441 and held in the town archives of Auch, its beneficial effects on general well-being are described: it was reputed to stimulate the appetite, boost the memory, keep the person young, and bestow joy and happiness. The next step from medicinal applications to enjoyment was a small one. Although armagnac was affected by Dutch trade interests as much as cognac, and was shipped abroad in large quantities, it has remained first and foremost the schnapps of peasants. This explains why the oak cask filled with armagnac is a permanent feature of household provisions in many country cellars.

At the end of the 1960s gastronomy in general experienced an unexpected upturn, and armagnac too had its moment of glory. It was a time when rows of armagnac bottles of varying vintages and from different producers festooned the well-stocked digestif trolleys in top restaurants. Single vintages were in fact blossoming into the real specialty of the region.

Opinions diverge, however, when it comes to vintage armagnacs. The producing companies, with four times the market impact of the domains, emphasize their experience of aging, blending, and reduction, stressing the importance of the blends. After all, it was blends that made armagnac available to consumers internationally through large-scale distribution and provided the guarantee of standardized quality. The "bouilleurs de cru" that do their own bottling, especially in the famous Bas-Armagnac region, emphasize the uniqueness of their cask-conditioned spirits, which are bottled according to year, and see themselves as the true guardians of tradition and quality.

Although stubborn Gascons on both sides of the argument are vociferous, they do exist side by side in peaceful, albeit modest, fashion—for in terms of quantities, armagnac makes up only a twentieth of cognac's capacity. What is certain is that when the business carried more weight in the past, things were considerably better for all the Armagnac wine growers.

However Gascons do not give up easily. They have won the official seal of approval for their white Armagnac—that floral, fruity, and clear eau-de-vie used as a *trou gascon*, which is ice-cold schnapps served in the middle of a rich meal to aid digestion. It is also excellent for making sorbets or mixing. They helped their old brandies to link up with Cuba too, causing quite a sensation: experts in Havana award an annual prize for the most successful combination of Havana cigars and armagnac. With a revival in interest in dark spirits, the Gascon brandies bursting with character are once more taking center stage—and high time too.

# Spiritual fortification

Page 134: An unusual insight: an old cellar door was replaced by glass in the Château de Laubade. Page 135: A typical landscape in Bas-Armagnac, where they prefer to make casks out of local oak. Opposite: Often large wooden vats are used in a chai for younger brandies and for blending, just as small casks are used for longer aging.

Château Busca-Maniban, homestead of the oldest armagnac distillery.

Armagnac is France's oldest eau-de-vie or "firewater." Based on the earliest documented reference in 1411 in Toulouse, brandy was distilled legally in Gascony about 100 years before the fruit schnapps of Alsace, and as much as 200 years before cognac. Although the southwest region remained untouched by the historic transport routes, the three basic prerequisites for brandy production were established there early on: vines from the Romans, stills from the Moors, and casks from the Celts. It can be verified that the first barrels of *aygordent* (burning water) were put on sale in 1461 at Saint-Sever market in the Landes *département*. From there, the art of distillation spread in Gascony, a process for which the citizens of Bordeaux bore an element of responsibility.

## The advantages of distillation

Aquitaine had been linked to England by marriage since 1152, and the English market was the main consumer of its wines. From Bordeaux it was not just the sought-after, bright red clarets that were shipped out, but all the wines of the hinterland from Cahors to Bergerac. This competition was a thorn in the side of the Bordeaux citizens, who set up a wine police that only allowed the other regions onto their "quais" after the important winter market was over for the year. They clearly had brandy in mind in enforcing this regulation.

The Gascons used this to their own advantage. They could only transport their goods with difficulty to Bordeaux anyway, by wagon and then in flat barges on the Garonne river. This is where wine distillation offered them definite benefits: it reduced the volume and weight of the cargo, and also preserved the end product. As early as the 16th century an unnamed spirit was shipped from Gascony to England, The Netherlands and northern France. Only 100 years later, after the name "Armagnac" first appeared on a map in 1595, did they begin to name the "wine spirit" after its place of origin.

Demand soared in the 17th century thanks to the Dutch. As the leading trading power of the age, they supplied the whole of northern Europe with wine, which they fortified with the spirit to preserve it. In order to safeguard their needs the Dutch merchants persuaded the wine growers around Eauze and Nogaro to distill their wines.

In 1649 Thomas de Maniban, the leader of the Toulouse parliament, built his fabulous Château de Busca south of Condom, where he also set up the first efficient distillery in the region. His example quickly took on, and all the great estates equipped themselves with their own stills.

It was not long before they discovered that armagnac improved when stored in casks, and Gascons took every opportunity to boast about their old eaux-de-vie. By the 18th century at the latest they had become established at court. As was the case with cognac, the introduction of bottling ensured a further upturn. The armagnac business was lucrative for wine growers, distillers, and traders, and the link to the rail network in the 1850s promised a golden future. But all expectations were dashed in 1878 with the grape phylloxera. Armagnac was never to regain the glory days of its early successes.

# A continuous process

An old wooden tank for blending.

Wine growers who do their own distilling, and most of the companies selling it, insist that true armagnac should be distilled in an "alembic armagnaçais." This is the unique way it develops its typical character, though this realization has been reached fairly late in the game. In the early days of the distillation art in Gascony, they managed by using simple pot stills, distilling wine as many times as necessary to create a satisfactory eau-de-vie. By refining the equipment and becoming more experienced in its handling, the *double chauffe* (double distillation) of the Charente was found to be adequate. It has been licensed again since 1972 in Armagnac and is deployed occasionally for younger brandies.

The simpler, faster, energy-efficient, and therefore more cost-effective process known as continuous distillation was introduced to the Armagnac region by Antoine de Mellet, Marquis de Bonas. The marquis, a man of science and progress, acquired a still invented by Jean-Edouard Adam in 1801 in Montpellier, and it was patented in 1818. He used it to show that a distillate with an alcohol content of 52–62% vol. could be achieved in one cycle, and he even developed a system that fed fresh, base wine into the alembic continuously.

More and more estate owners and distillers followed his example during the 1820s. Smaller wine growers employed mobile stills that distilled wine onsite in a wood-fired, column system on wheels. These have become quite rare, for wine can now be transported easily, while on the other hand the fragile distilling equipment is best left in place. Distillation usually begins in early November and, while the official finishing date used to be March 31, the boilers are now often shut down as early as January 31 because of an insufficient quantity of wine. Most armagnac producers have long since agreed that their eau-de-vie owes its distinctive character in no small part to their special type of alembic. After all, it produces a spirit with a 20% lower alcohol volume than cognac, that contains a correspondingly higher proportion of tails made up of heavy, flavorsome substances, and that only reaches maturation after many years of aging into particularly complex and original spirits.

Left: A typical continuous still made of copper.
Right: Bubble cap trays dismantled for cleaning.

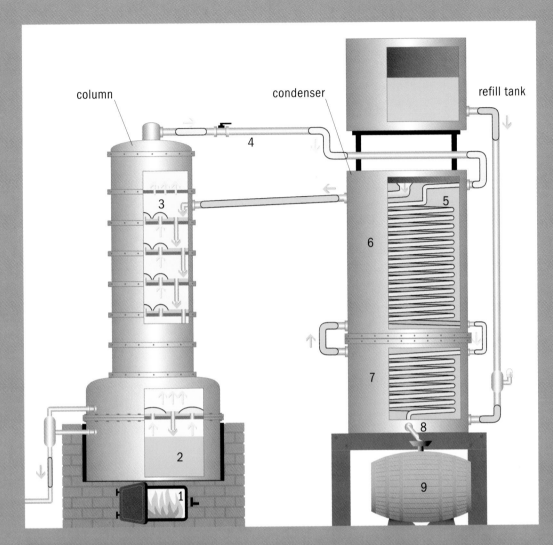

column     condenser     refill tank

## The alembic armagnaçais

The armagnac still—which consists of two main parts, the column [left] and the condenser [right]—carries out a continuous distillation in the form of a more or less circular flow. Above the fire box [1] the wine [shown in yellow] is heated in the boiler [2], producing vapors [blue] that rise up the column through the bubble cap trays [3], passing through the swan's neck [4] until they reach the two-tier condenser with cooling coil [5]. They wind their way through the wine prewarmer [6] in the upper part of the condenser. As the alcoholic vapors condense, they transmit their heat to the wine, which acts as a cooling agent here and in the lower part of the condenser in the cooling tank [7] and flows freely out of the

tails tank. The warmest wine rises and moves over into the column and down through the trays. In doing so it comes in contact with the constantly rising alcohol vapors, which bubble through the wine and then become infused with aromatic substances. They condense in the coil, at the end of which the clear spirit is collected [8], usually with an alcohol content of between 52% and 60% vol. It is still raw spirit, but has an aromatic intensity redolent of fruits like grapes and plums, or of vine or lime blossom. The aging in oak casks [9] is what gives it smoothness, balance, and complexity.

# Soils and grapes

The cultivation area of Armagnac is divided into three very different zones that were defined by decree in 1909 and authorized in 1936 as an *Appellation d'Origine Controlée*. Bas-Armagnac, with its capital Eauze, has clayey, pale red, sandy soil known as *sables fauves*, and extends over the Gers and Landes *départements*. Ténarèze (main town, Condom) stretches into Lot-et-Garonne and has clay and limestone soils, while Haut-Armagnac (to the east and south of the town of Auch) is made up of chalky hills. In terms of climate Bas-Armagnac is determined by the damp, mild weather of the Landes region, Haut-Armagnac on the other hand is influenced by the drier Mediterranean climate, and both of these influences converge in the Ténarèze region.

Significant differences can be discerned in the eaux-de-vie of the three different regions: in Bas-Armagnac they are very fruity and elegant; in Ténarèze more robust and full-bodied, if slightly more acidic; and in Haut-Armagnac, whose wines are less well suited to distillation, the eaux-de-vie are distinctly harsher.

## Baco wins out

Only four of the ten grape varieties that are allowed to be used for armagnac are of any significance: Ugni Blanc, Folle Blanche, Baco Blanc, and Colombard. The last of these is not particularly favored by most distillers as its pleasantly dry white wine has too high an alcohol content for distillation.

As is the case with cognac, Ugni Blanc is by far the leading variety, yielding the most suitable base wines—rather bland, low in alcohol, and very acidic. Folle Blanche is experiencing something of a renaissance: it dominated under the name "Piquepoult" before the grape phylloxera, and produces elegantly floral spirits with a long aftertaste. It is impressive in the form of Blanche d'Armagnac (white armagnac) or brandies that have aged for only a few years.

**The cultivation areas of the Armagnac appellation**

- Haut-Armagnac
- Ténarèze
- Bas-Armagnac

## Facts and figures about Armagnac

34,600 acres (14,000 ha) cultivation area

31,700 gallons/2.5 acres (120,000 liters/ha) base wine

6–8 million bottles of armagnac annually

4,000 wine growers

Over 1,000 owners of armagnac casks

250 producers who sell armagnac in bottles

40 companies

45% export sales

132 countries importing armagnac

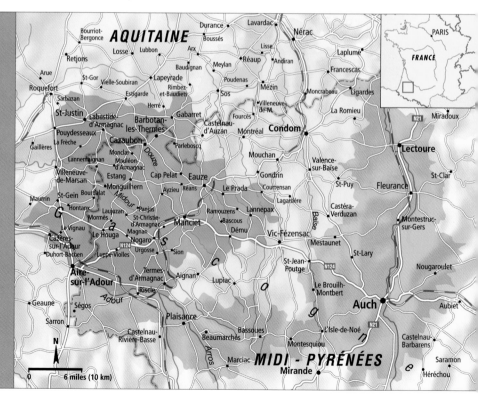

Baco Blanc, whose proper name is Baco 22A, is a hybrid created from Folle Blanche and Noah in 1909. Its resistance to phylloxera and its high yields saved Bas-Armagnac after the devastation caused by the disease. It is the only hybrid permitted in an A.O.C., a worthy tribute to the vine's qualities. On the sandy soils of Bas-Armagnac, it produces full-bodied and robust spirits that need long aging in casks to reveal their truly great smoothness and aromas of ripe fruit. They form the backbone of many blends. The grapes for distillation are harvested in October, and pressed and fermented naturally, without the addition of sulphur. The base wines are normally very acidic and have a low alcohol content of just 7–9% vol. Nowadays the emphasis is on impeccable, fresh, and aromatic wines that are distilled as soon as possible—distillation concentrates the good, as well as the bad, properties.

The vines used for armagnac are trained on high cordons that protect them from both frost and damp, encouraging acidity in the grapes.

Pierre Laberdolive is an avid fan of the Baco variety and knows how to handle it with great expertise.

# The tears of maturity

Apart from the clear, "blanche" version, armagnac acquires its aromas, complexity, balance, and finesse from aging in oak casks, as do cognac and other brandies. As cellar master Yvan Auban emphasizes, "Really impressive aging can only take place in casks with a capacity of 106–10 gallons (400–20 liters). That is the perfect size. The wood is important, and the way it is handled and dried out properly is most important of all. The oak must be able to age naturally in the open air for three to five years." Young armagnac is put into new casks until the cellar master decides that enough tannins and oak flavors have been absorbed. He then transfers it to older casks which are already "seasoned" and allow the spirit to oxidize slowly, lose alcohol, and become concentrated through evaporation. "The long aging process makes the armagnac 'oily,' producing 'tears' on the glass," as Bernard Domecq, the cellar master with Ryst-Dupeyron in Condom explains. "This is when you get the highest level of scents such as prunes, vanilla, quince, honey, and lime blossom. The longer the armagnac matures, the more it evolves the rancio with flavors of roasted nuts, as well as liquorice, chocolate, and tobacco."

## A valuable tradition

Armagnac's heyday was during the 19th century, when the cultivation area expanded to 267,000 acres (108,000 ha). It has now dropped to less than an eighth of that level, partly because the banks, still reeling from the oil crisis, decided to stop financing the risky business of armagnac in 1992. Fortunately very few Gascons make their living solely from armagnac: they are involved in agriculture and specialist poultry farming, or else produce table wines. In spite of all this, they feel responsible for guarding the tradition of armagnac. "You really cannot have good armagnacs without aging," according to Pierre Laberdolive. "Time is essential, and we have to think of future generations. If my great-grandfather had not begun to build up the stock now established today, and on

Bernard Domecq, cellar master with Ryst-Dupeyron in Condom, demonstrates the aging process of armagnac.

Armagnacs reach the end of their maturation period in the chai of the Château de Salles.

The "tears" left on the glass are a sign of armagnac's richness in natural glycerol, alcohol, residual sugar—as well as having aromas and complexity.

which we rely, we would not be in a position to finance the work here. In a sense it is a threefold continuity: of place, resources, and technique. For me, the key word is 'remembering': the people, the chais, and the work."

## All about labels

The quality of armagnac is linked to the length of time it ages in the oak casks. For the youngest armagnac used for blending, it is a minimum of the following:

| | |
|---|---|
| Three stars | 2 years |
| V.S.O.P. | 5 years |
| X.O. | 6 years |
| Hors d'Age | 10 years |
| Specified age | e.g. 15, 21, or 30 years |
| Millésime | at least 10 years |

In the case of millésimes, the vintage spirits, the year of harvest is specified, but the decisive factor is how many years the armagnac in question has been aging in casks before being bottled. For this reason serious producers also state this date.

Simplified labels:

| | |
|---|---|
| Armagnac | less than 6 years in cask |
| Vieil Armagnac | over 6 years in cask |
| Blanche d'Armagnac | no cask aging |

# Vintage or blend

Unlike cognac, which began bottling single vintages barely 20 years ago—except for the very rare, early landed cognacs aged in England—the domains that do their own distilling issue their armagnacs almost exclusively as millésimes. They are quite happy to leave the blends to the bigger companies that offer a range of grades according to age, some of which supplement the selection with premium blends, 21-year-olds for instance, as well as selected vintages. This is confirmed by Arnaud Papelorey of Larressingle: "Blending is the guarantee of consistent quality. Distilling is a mechanical process, and not much can be done in terms of the aging, but you need expertise to blend the products from the different crus, terroirs, and communities. We have been buying the same terroirs since 1837, but there are still no set routines, just experience." In terms of reducing to an alcohol content of at least 40% vol., a process is carried out using *petits eaux*, a mixture of distilled water and armagnac that is matured for several months to prevent any kind of deviation in tone. There are some outstanding armagnac blends of great complexity and finesse. Many of the well-known Bas-Armagnac producers have rejected the contrived image

A selection of the best armagnacs, aged for a long time in oak casks

of brandies of different ages. They swear by years, although for armagnac this means something different from a wine vintage. In the case of an armagnac that specifies a year, the consumer gets an eau-de-vie aged for ten years or more—provided that the date of bottling is noted, for maturation stops when the spirit is in the bottle. As Yvan Auban explains, "We distill eau-de-vie at an alcohol content of 52–53% vol. and allow it to age naturally without anything being added. Our eau-de-vie is not broken down to drinking strength, so its alcohol content is in relation to the length of aging. There are two main ways of creating a product, the commercial and the artisan way, and we have chosen the latter." Without artificial reduction, the alcohol content of armagnac drops to about 46% after 25 years of maturation in a cask, giving a generally well-integrated product. As a rule, the quality of armagnac increases with age. Each batch provides only a very limited number of armagnacs that are full of character and individuality. This may not be very lucrative, but it is worthwhile.

# Selected producers

### Domaine Boingnères

In 1953 Léon Lafitte married into the Domaine Boingnères, founded in 1807 as the Domaine Labastide-d'Armagnac. He replanted the cultivation areas with Ugni Blanc and Colombard, but was highly enthusiastic about Folle Blanche. His daughter Martine expanded the growth area to 54 acres (22 ha) and helped put the single-variety Folle Blanche back on the world map. The 1984 vintage presents an impressive example of pronounced spice and fruit, with great balance and length. The 1972 is outstanding—floral, nutty, and elegant.

### Domaine de Jouanda

Founded in 1855, the estate of Baron de Poyferré de Cère in Grand Bas-Armagnac, the most famous region in the *département*, comprises 395 acres (160 ha). Of this land, 43 miles (70 km) from the Atlantic, 21 acres (8.5 ha) are planted with vines. Taken over by Jacques de Poyferré in 1960, regular distilling has been underway, and the vintages are aging in three different chais. The oldest armagnac dates back to 1893. The 1979 vintage (May 2006) exhibits a spicy complexity with elegant rancio and tobacco. Recommended: 1980, 1985, 1990.

### Laberdolive

In four generations the Laberdolives have brought together several domains with a total of 106 acres (43 ha), whose grapes are ideal for distilling. Only the amount required for distillation is vinified. For Pierre Laberdolive the vintages are of prime importance, producing complex armagnacs of distinction. A dozen of the large stocks of old eaux-de-vie are on sale. The youngest is 15 years old, and the oldest 85. The robust 1976 vintage with its distinctive rancio is excellent, as is the smooth 1942 with its lovely violet notes.

### Les Alambics du Bas-Armagnac

Yvan Auban, a fourth generation distiller, built his new distillery in Estang, near Labastide d'Armagnac, in 1990. In addition to the yields of the 23 acres (9.5 ha) of vineyards, the family also distills for a range of wine growers in Bas-Armagnac. They represent a strictly traditional way of working, with careful elaboration and frequent recasking. They offer a fascinating range of vintages, especially the sensational 1964 with the most elegant rancio and wonderful balance, as well as the excellent, classic 1979 vintage.

## Château du Busca-Maniban

When Thomas de Maniban built the chateau in 1649, he also installed the region's first still. Both were taken over in 1803 by Dr Rizon. Today, the 494 acre (200 ha) estate is run by Floriane de Ferron, along with 15 acres (6 ha) of vines in the Ténarèze area. She distills Ugni Blanc into eaux-de-vie with an alcohol content of 56.5–59% vol., giving their armagnacs the intensity of the majestic 1974 vintage that won the 2006 trophy in Havana. The rare 1946 vintage has great balance, and the 1985 is very well structured, with a subtle rancio.

## Château de Laubade

The largest estate in the business, 260 acres (105 ha), has been owned by the Lesgourgues family for three generations. Over 70 vintages from 1888 to 1991 lie in one of the largest stocks of old armagnac. Distilling is undertaken in house, each of the four types separately, and some 2,800 x 106-gallon (400-liter) casks age in seven chais. A proportion is blended, such as the Intemporel range with No. 3, No. 5, and the complex No. 7, with its elegant rancio. The 1969 vintage has a distinctive rancio, and the 1941 is a headstrong, but charming, vintage.

## Château du Tariquet

The chateau by Eauze, the main town of Bas-Armagnac, dates back to 1683. Pierre and Hélène Grassa made a name with their armagnac, and their children Maïté and Yves with Cotes de Gascogne white wines. Along with unreduced vintages, they concentrate on armagnacs made with Folle Blanche (aged 4, 8, and 12 years with an alcohol content of 45% vol.), on blends with 40% vol., and more recently on premium bottlings such as the X.O. 54.9% vol. fût No. 6, bursting with toasted notes, plums, and vanilla with a well-integrated alcohol content.

## Château de Ravignan

The oldest wing in this chateau in the style of Louis XIII dates back to 1663; since 1732 it has been a family property. Today the 49 acre (200 ha) estate in Bas-Armagnac is run by Arnaud de Ravignan, who can look back on nearly 300 years of distillation and elaboration in casks made from their own oaks. Each year they bring out half a dozen vintages with naturally reduced alcohol content, aged between 12 and 30 years. A very elegant 1978 commends itself, with a pronounced aroma of plums and a refined palate of sweet spiciness.

# Spanish brandy—the mark of the bull and solera

Spanish brandies, Brandy de Jerez in particular, are favored by aficionados of Spain and holidaymakers returning full of enthusiasm from the Costa de la Luz, Costa del Sol, or Costa Brava. Tourists may have been content in times past with bottles of cheap Solera brandy, but for some time now travelers to Spain have been more interested in the premium quality Solera Gran Reservas. At the same time brandy consumption has been on the decline for years in the country itself, and Spanish gentlemen swirling their generously filled brandy glasses after a substantial meal as a quiet digestif are almost a thing of the past.

Wherever you go in Spain, there is a greeting from a bull. In May 1957 its first likeness appeared on the Madrid–Burgos freeway, 23 feet (7 meters) high and made of wood. In the intervening years 93 locations have seen bulls towering up into the sky, forged out of solid metal and now twice the height, with an area of 2,150 square feet (200 sq m). It was devised by the designer Manolo Prieto as an advertisement for Osborne's Brandy Veterano. This was the beginning of Brandy de Jerez's heyday, as it became extremely popular at home and remained the Spaniard's favorite spirit for decades to come. The bull was responsible for Osborne's scoring success abroad as well. When the Spanish government condemned advertising boards on freeways in 1988, it took a national furor to save the bull. Unburdened by any logo, it now rises up with pride as the image of Spain and has the highest approval in the land to do so, for a ruling of the highest court in Spain in 1997 decreed that it was an "essential part of the Spanish landscape."

Yet the effectiveness of advertising lies in the eye of the beholder, so irrespective of its unparalleled career as a brand name, the bull will continue to be associated with the company from Puerto de Santa Maria, which along with Jerez de la Frontera and Sanlúcar de Barrameda is one of the three sources prescribed by law for Brandy de Jerez. Nine out of ten bottles of brandy come from the "sherry triangle," whose points are marked out by the three aforementioned towns. Sherry itself is also responsible for giving brandy its unique identity, winning the same recognition for Brandy de Jerez as cognac and armagnac, the official appellation designation as a guarantee of origin among brandies. Unlike those of its French counterparts, the Brandy de Jerez appellation is not related to the origin of the grapes, but to their elaboration. It is so special that it deserves this honor. The brandy must age in casks that have previously contained sherry, so it owes a great deal of its character to sherries, and is dependent on them for the type of aroma they impart to the casks—whether it is a fino, amontillado, oloroso, or Pedro Ximénez. The result is brandies that distinguish themselves by their smoothness and sweetness, or as they are in the habit of saying in Andalusia, "fire on the tongue, velvet in the throat and warmth in the stomach."

# Great-grandfather's forgotten holandas

Like so many other things, Spain has the Moors, who conquered Andalusia in 711, to thank for brandy. They were familiar with the principle of distillation and from about 900 they used the wines produced in the occupied territories since Roman times to distill alcohol for medicinal and cosmetic purposes. After the "reconquista" of Jerez by Alfonso X and by 1254 at the latest, the Spaniards had gained enough of an insight into this art to strengthen the regional wines with spirits, thus both preserving them and helping to make sherry a remarkable success story.

A reference to *aguardiente* (high-grade wine spirit) is first noted, however, in a document dated January 16, 1580, in which the taxes it raised were designated for building a Jesuit college. The Dutch—whose trade routes extended the length of the Atlantic coast and, from the end of the 16th century, into the Mediterranean—were also interested in Andalusian brandy. During the 18th and 19th centuries especially, trade with young wine distillates flourished, making the production of *holandas* (low-strength wine spirit) an important line of business.

## The founding brandy

Many of the sherry houses also traded in holandas, and here too it can be assumed that many a cellar master "forgot" brandy in casks, which then turned into the coveted specialty. The official debut of Brandy de Jerez took place in 1874. The legend is recounted by Beltran Domecq: "My great-grandfather, Pedro Domecq Loustau, had received an order from a Dutchman for over 66,000 gallons (250,000 liters) of holandas, our name for our spirit. For whatever reason, he ended up not being able to take this amount, and my great-grandfather did not know what on earth he should do with it. He had this Bodega de la Luz, where the sherry

casks had just been emptied, so he spontaneously decided to fill the empty casks with the holandas. When he had a look a few years later, he found that the holandas had transformed into a very flavorsome brandy. So he decided to launch the Fundador brandy. The year was 1874, the year of the first Spanish brandy." During the ensuing decade other sherry houses followed suit with their own brandies.

Marketed in bottles under the name "coñac," the brandy was an immediate hit that soon posed a serious problem for the bodegas. They did not have enough base wines as the production curve of sherry was also rising steeply, and the capacities of their own Palo-mino grapes were exhausted. Another base wine suitable for holandas had to be found, and without delay. They struck gold in Huelva, Extremadura, Valencia, and La Mancha, with the town of Tomelloso acting as the trading base. The choice fell on Airén, the most cultivated vine in Spain. To this day, the trade in the clear distillate produced from it is handled from Tomelloso. It is only in the sherry regions, however, that Brandy de Jerez is made using the prescribed, traditional *solera* method, in casks that previously contained sherry.

The most popular brands of Brandy de Jerez.
Opposite top: Consumers enjoy the 20–30-year-old brandies.
Opposite bottom: Brandy de Jerez also ages using the famous solera system.

Page 148: One of the Bodegas Barbardillo gates in Sanlúcar de Barrameda.
Page 149: The bull, once a symbol of brandy and now a national emblem, marks the Spanish landscape.

# The art of enjoyment

In 1987 the Consejo Regulador de la Denominacion Especifica del Brandy de Jerez, the regulatory body for Spanish brandy, was set up. Its purpose is to control, oversee, and protect the production of Brandy de Jerez, as well as enhancing its international reputation. The Consejo has defined the production areas, the distillate used, the aging process, and the three different quality grades; and it monitors the producers, stock levels, brand names, and products on offer.

Among the many campaigns undertaken by the Consejo on behalf of Brandy de Jerez, one in particular deserves special mention: the commission, given in the first instance to 12 Spanish artists in 1992, to dedicate a work to Brandy de Jerez. The organizers took a liberal attitude to the art project, approaching artists working in painting, illustration, graphic design, comic art, and photomontage. Each participant was given a different aspect of enjoying Brandy de Jerez. Reflecting the artistic diversity of Spain, they created 12 works initially (others have followed) that deal with an important "spirit" in Spanish life.

The spectator is introduced to Brandy de Jerez: consumed neat, or as a shot in coffee; a *carajillo* (brandy and coffee); as a digestif with coffee and cigars; and on ice, or cradled in the hand and savored warm. They can appreciate its role in sangria, as a long drink with cola or orange juice, and as *leche panther* (panther milk) with fresh milk and cinnamon. They see it in elegant mode, as a julep with mint, sugar, and lemon on crushed ice; as a *lumumba* mixed with chocolate milk shake; and, really ringing the changes, with fresh fruit and sweet sherry on ice. Each artist has created an individual world for Brandy de Jerez, and dipping into it is sheer pleasure.

# Return of the alembic

When Gonzalez Byass inaugurated its new distillery in 2005, it opened a new chapter in the history of brandy in Jerez de la Frontera. Equipped with alembics, pot stills from Cognac, it is used exclusively to distill wines from Palomino grapes using the batch distillation method: this produces elegant and very fruity holandas with an alcohol content of up to 70% vol., which is reserved for Solera Gran Reserva Lepanto. What is remarkable about this, apart from its being the first new distillery in Jerez in over 100 years, is that wine from the sherry region is being used as it is now available for distilling following a number of crises in sales.

The holandas, which are comparatively low in alcohol, are the best raw material for brandy as they contain the largest proportion of aromatic substances and are aged mainly for Solera Gran Reserva. For Solera and Solera Reserva, which are not aged for as long, they are going back to *destilados*, wine spirit distilled in continuous stills, which is either medium strength at 70–86% vol., or strong at 86–94.8% vol. The base wines reach an alcohol content of 10.5–13%.

## Dynamic aging

Holandas and destilados are brought to the three brandy towns in tankers. For the younger brandies, the high percentage spirit is broken down before it is put into casks for aging. These 130–160-gallon (500–600-liter) casks must have contained sherry for at least four years, one of the basic prerequisites for Brandy de Jerez. Many producers would rather use casks that have been soaked in Oloroso Dulce or Pedro Ximénez because they value the sweetness they impart to the brandy.

Bottom left: The new Gonzalez Byass brandy distillery in Jerez de la Frontera. Bottom right: The spirit is crystal clear when it flows out of the condenser. Opposite: A "venencia" is used to sample brandy (left) in order to assess the colors and flavors (right).

Depending on the desired quality, the young spirits are put into the appropriate soleras. Like sherries, brandies must undergo this special process of "dynamic" aging, which is another essential condition. Each solera consists of a number of *criaderas*, rows of casks originally stacked on top of one another, each containing brandies at an incremental stage of aging. When it comes to bottling, a proportion is taken from the solera, from the bottom row with the oldest brandy. It is replaced by an equivalent amount from the row above, and the topmost row is replenished with young brandy. In this way the character of the particular brandy is successfully maintained from one bottling to the next. They age in the famous bodegas of the region, which provide perfect conditions for maturation, thanks to their height, and to the cooling winds that blow in from the Atlantic and sweep through the windows unimpeded.

## Conditions laid down for the three qualities of Brandy de Jerez:

| | |
|---|---|
| Solera | must age for at least 6 months in casks, but mostly matures for 12. |
| Solera Reserva | must age for at least 12 months in casks, but mostly matures for 30. |
| Solera Gran Reserva | must age for at least 3 years in casks, but often matures for 8, 12, or more years. |

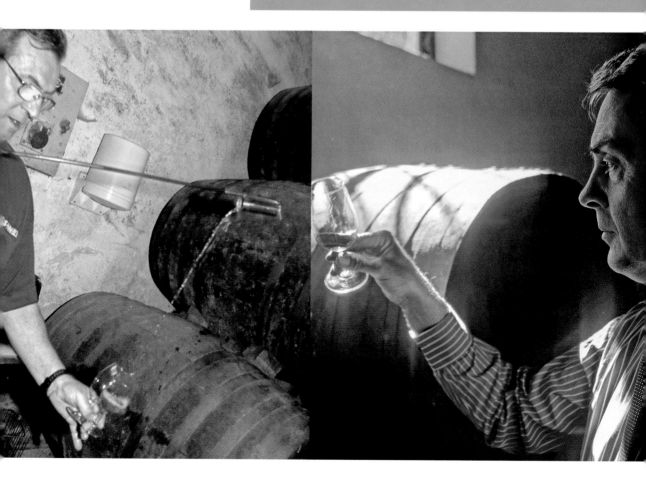

# Solera Gran Reserva

The Solera Gran Reservas represent the pinnacle of Brandy de Jerez quality, and great pains are taken in their production. Even for the Solera grades, which age for 6–12 months in the various soleras, the brandy is composed of as many as 15 different components. The Solera Gran Reservas also benefit from this high art form, only their constituent parts are incomparably more matured and complex. Every company swears by its in-house recipe. Lepanto from Gonzalez Byass and Fernando de Castillo use nothing but batch distilled

holandas and start the aging process in new casks made from American and French oak. There is a general preference for American oak in the Jerez region, even for brandies. The young spirits remain in the new casks for up to two years and then they are brought to the soleras. Some houses put the young spirits into the soleras immediately, and many have reduced the alcohol content to 40–44% vol. beforehand. Brandies are sold with an alcohol content of 36–45% vol. The sherry casks used for the maturation exert the greatest influence on the future

The best Solera Gran Reservas on a *finca* (villa) in the Jerez region, against the dazzling white, chalky Albariza soils.

taste of the Solera Gran Reserva. The classic Lepanto, the driest of the top brandies, is elaborated exclusively in casks that previously contained Tio Pepe fino. Other houses use casks that are infused with different types of sherry. Carlos I from Domecq is aged in amontillado casks, while for Cardenal Mendoza, they stick to Pedro Ximénez (P.X.). After 2 years of static aging the brandy is transferred to a seven-tier solera with P.X. casks for 15 years, giving this dark brandy its sweet aroma with elegant hints of the Orient. Dried fruits and nuts are also added during maceration—legally, though it is not something that is widely broadcast—in order to give a particular brandy a more complex character.

Recent tendencies take account of the trend toward exclusivity and a greater artisan quality. There are the first single-cask bottlings, or bottlings from one single solera, without cutting, coloring, sweeteners, clarification, or cold filtration.

# Beyond Jerez

Nine out of ten bottles of brandy sold in Spain contain Brandy de Jerez. The contents of the tenth bottle represent the energetic brandy production in the rest of the country. The bodegas of the sherry-producing area created competition for themselves by having wine spirits distilled in other regions. In this way they "contaminated" Condado de Huelva, Montilla-Moriles, and Malaga, where there is a long tradition of sweet wines fortified with wine spirit, and hence experience of working with distillates. In La Mancha too, however, a few distilleries decided not to sell all of their wine spirit to the Jerezanos, but instead to age brandy themselves. The Bodegas Centro Españolas are a famous example, offering a brandy from a solera that is over 100 years old—their Casajuana Solera Gran Reserva 1892.

Interest in brandy also began to grow in Penedès in Catalonia. In 1928 the Torres family set up a distillery there, and rose to become one of the best-known brandy producers in Spain. Narcisco Mascaró, who equipped himself with a charentais pot still, followed their example in 1945. A few of the bodegas in Majorca took up distilling as well: one of these, Bodegas Suau, gained a very good reputation for its brandy.

Torres in Penedès has been distilling wine for 80 years now, and produces one of the best-known brandies in Spain.

# Other Spanish brandies

### Torres 20

Torres, an estate-owning family going back to the 17th century, has good reason to be proud of its Imperial Brandy. It was voted the best brandy in the world in the Wine & Spirit Competition for the first time in 1977, an accolade it then won again in 1997, 2006, and 2007. The base wine is made from a blend of two grape varieties, the Catalonian Parellada and Ugni Blanc. It is double distilled in copper pot stills and put into new casks made of French Limousin oak. It is transferred to older oak after a year, where its oldest parts mature for up to 20 years. Its bouquet is characterized by dried fruit, nuts, and subtle spices, and it exhibits an elegance and balance on the palate, with mellow sweetness and a lovely velvety texture.

### Antonio Mascaró Ego

In 1966 Antonio Mascaró took over the family business in Villafranca de Penedès from his father, including the wineries of Mas Miquel and El Castell. The company has made a name for itself for producing brandies, as well as wine and cava. They are made from the Catalonian grapes, Macabeu, Parellada, and Xarello, following the cognac process of double distillation. The elaboration is carried out in casks made of Limousin oak, with the X.O. quality Ego aging for a minimum of eight years. It is only during this time that it develops its fine vanilla aromas and the smooth finesse of its long finish.

### Bodegas Suau
### Reserva Privada

There is a long-standing tradition of distilling and preparing various types of liqueur on Majorca. Even though Suau Bodegas y Destilerías de Mallorca are part of this heritage, the company has been in existence for a relatively short time. Frederic Suau, who started out as a seafarer, founded the Bodegas in Pont d'Inca, near Palma, in 1951. Production still remains at an artisan level of 30,000 bottles. Suau ages his brandies in casks made from American and French oak, using the solera system. Even the exceptionally light, younger brandies are excellent, but the Reserva Privada, bottled after 50 years of maturation, is the peak of the distillery's achievement. Dried fruit notes form a perfect harmony with the flavors of decades of cask aging, creating balanced aromas of toast, coffee, and tobacco.

### Pérez Barquero
### Monte Cristo Gran Reserva

Founded in 1905 in Montilla, south of Córdoba, Pérez Barquero has specialized in wines made from the Pedro Ximénez grape. From these they develop finos, amontillados, and olorosos, which are aged in soleras. This gives Pérez Barquero casks like those in Jerez, soaked in aromatic wines (in the case of oloroso, sweet ones) and ideal for the maturation of brandy. The brandy solera is constructed out of extremely old casks, in which the Gran Reserva develops its mahogany tone and exceptionally rich, sweet aromas over a 35-year period at least. Redolent of dried fruit and nuts, it has a long, sweet finish.

### Esdor

This novice among Spanish brandies comes from the wine-growing area of Ribera del Duero, where the famous bodega group Matarromera opened the Destilerías del Duero in San Bernardo. The idea was to harness the ancient tradition of the Cistercian monks, who produced schnapps and liqueurs in the neighboring Santa Maria de Valbuena monastery. The only distillery in Ribera obtains wine from the Tinta del País grape, known locally as Tempranillo, to make their brandy. The base wine is distilled in copper pot stills with a capacity of 80 or 130 gallons (300 or 500 liters). Esdor is aged for 32 months in casks made from American and French oak, each type imparting its aromas; one is more pronounced in vanilla and coffee, and the other with more cinnamon and coconut. These are well balanced with notes of ripe berries and blossoms, lingering long on the palate.

# Portuguese aguardente

Most of the wine distillate in Portugal is used to fortify port wine. At the same time, a few regions, especially Vinho Verde in the north and Lourinhã, northwest of Lisbon, have managed to make a name for themselves with their brandies known as "aguardente."

For over 200 years port houses favored the young brandies from Lourinhã to fortify their wines, and this led to the product gaining a reputation in its own right. The area—part of the Estremadura region of Portugal, the tract of land historically known simply as "oeste" (west)—extends along a 19-mile (30 km) wide strip of the Atlantic coast. It is famous for its reasonably priced, light white wines, products of the Atlantic climate and the heterogeneous, partially sandy soil. These wines are low in alcohol (now limited by law to a maximum of 10% vol.) and ideally suited to distillation. As in the rest of Portugal, a wide range of different grapes thrives in Lourinhã, though the white varieties Malvasia Rei (Seminário) and Tália (Douradinha) and the red Cabinda tend to be most popular.

While the spirit was traditionally batch distilled twice in copper pot stills to an alcohol content of around 70% vol., distillers in Lourinhã have now nearly all changed over to the continuous distillation process, establishing the alcohol content at a maximum level of 78% vol. Wine growers and distillers had the confidence to obtain the status of DOC (Denominação de Origem Controlada) for their region in 1992, thus making them the fourth official wine region for brandy production alongside Cognac, Armagnac, and Jerez. Aguardente is aged in oak or chestnut casks with a maximum capacity of about 210 gallons (800 liters). In the Vinho Verde region wine growers use grapes from particularly rich harvests to distill their brandy, which has been officially recognized since 1984. The low percentage, white base wines fulfill all the prerequisites for good distillation. The best-quality brandies are distilled twice. Aguardente vínica matures for at least 6 months, aguardente (vínica) velha for a minimum of 12 months, and better brands for even longer periods.

## Cavipor · Centúria

Established in 1918, the winery Caves Monteiros in Penafiel (to the east of the city of Porto) merged with Caves Vinicolas de Portugal under the name Cavipor. Their portfolio is made up of wines from all over the country. Its flagship brandy is the 17-year-old Centúria. With intense aromas of dried fruits (apricots) and notes of cocoa, tobacco, and caramel, it is well balanced and long on the palate.

## Quinta do Tamariz Aguardente velhissima X.O.

The estate acquired in 1939 by the Vinagre family is part of their company in Barcelos, Quinta de Santa Maria. Since 1951 aguardente has been made using the double distillation method with Loureiro, Arinto, and Alvarinho grape varieties, and a little red wine. It is aged in 66-gallon (250-liter) casks made of Limousin oak—for over 20 years in the case of their excellent X.O. It is complex in character, with floral, spicy notes and hints of blond tobacco. Fruity, well balanced, and elegant, it has a refined rancio.

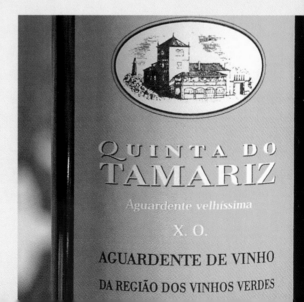

## Ferreirinha · Aguardente velha

A.A. Ferreira was founded in Vila Nova de Gaia in 1751 and is now part of the Sogrape group. It became famous under Dona Antónia Adelaide Ferreira, who developed viticulture significantly in the Duoro Valley during the 19th century and used her wealth to support a range of social projects. "Ferreirinha" (little Ferreira) became the company's domestic brand name. This blend of aguardentes aged from 5 to 30 years is impressive—with notes of spice, fruit, and oak; plenty of finesse; and a subtle rancio.

## Casa d'Avelleda · Adega velha

This outstanding aguardente is made by the Quinta da Aveleda company, which is a leading producer of vinho verde under the wine label Casal Garcia. The historical estate and its beautiful park have belonged to the Guedes family since 1947. Distilled in a charentais pot still, this brandy is aged for at least 12 years in the estate's old wine cellar, hence the name. The aromas of vanilla, ripe fruit, and cocoa combine on the palate with notes of raisins and nuts to give a fine, spicy, and rich velvety finish.

## Vinhos Campelo · Prestige X.O.

This brandy—long aged judging from its color—is advertised as Aguardente Vínica Velhissima Fine, Old & Rare. Pleasant and smooth, the aguardente is fruity (plums) with a subtle note of caramel. The three brothers who now run Vinhos Campelo are continuing the work of their father, Joaquim M. Campelo, who established the winery in 1951. It mainly concentrates on producing vinho verde wines, especially bagacieras (grape marc) made from pomace.

## José Maria da Fonseca Velha Reserva 1964

Born in 1804 in the Dão region, José Maria da Fonseca was one of the great forerunners of viticulture and the wine trade in Portugal. His descendants have carried on his pioneer spirit and now manage vineyards of 1,600 acres (650 ha) and one of the most modern wineries in the land, near Setubal. This rich, golden aguardente, distilled from vinho verde and aged for 34 years in oak, is highly recommended due to its elegant, floral aromas laced with apricot, its lovely spiciness, and its finesse.

# Italian arzente

One of the pioneers in the art of distillation was the Italian physician Taddeo Alderotti (1223–1303), better known as Thaddaeus Florentinus. A professor at the University of Bologna, he wrote the well-regarded tract *De virtutibus aque vite et eius operationibus* (On the properties of waters of life and their uses; ca. 1280). In it he describes the equipment and elaborate distilling techniques he used to produce drinkable brandy, and even highly pure alcohol, through repeated rectification. As a medical practitioner he was able to apply both products in a range of different ways. His work influenced the art of distillation not only in Italy, but also in neighboring countries, contributing a great deal to the widespread production of brandies.

The real period of *arzente*, the generic name in Italian for cognac-style wine spirits, was initiated by the Frenchman Jean Bouton, who opened one of the first steam-operated distilleries in Bologna in 1820. Under the name Giovanni Buton, his products were remarkably successful and widely imitated. Buton benefited from the fact that the Romagna region was able to supply his company with sufficient wine. On the fertile plains Trebbiano (which became the local grape of the Cognac region, known as Ugni Blanche) is the dominant variety, yielding high volumes of low-alcohol, acidic wine that is perfect for distilling. In 1939 Buton's descendants were able to provide just what the public wanted with their new product Vecchia Romagna. As the huge cask store had miraculously survived the upheavals of war without suffering any damage, the opportunity to conquer the international markets at the beginning of the postwar period was very propitious.

It was not long before Vecchia Romagna had risen to become one of the leading names in brandy, even outside Italy. The other great name in Italian brandy began when 18-year-old Lionello Stock was watching as wine was being loaded for France on the docks in his native city of Trieste. Since the disaster of the grape phylloxera, France had experienced a shortage of base wines for distillation. Fired by the idea that it would be better to distill Italian wine in Italy, he founded his own brandy-producing company along with his friend Carlo Camis in the Trieste suburb of Barcola. It was soon a flourishing concern. Stock took over sole control of the company in 1906, and when tariff barriers made exports difficult he decided to establish branches of the company abroad. In the 1920s he brought out Stock 84, which has remained the mainstay of the company.

Much as the Italians cherish their arzente, they tend to stick to standard qualities. Both main brands together represent more than two thirds of sales. Longer aged brandies, often produced as specialties by grappa distilleries, are the exception.

Stravecchio is blended in Milan in the largest brandy cask in the world, which has been empty only once since 1892, during a relocation.

# Selected Italian brandies

### Vecchia Romana Riserva

By 1830, ten years after it was founded, Giovanni Buton's spirit manufacturing business had grown to such an extent that he built a bigger, more up-to-date distillery. In the following decades the company established itself as one of the leading producers in Italy. In the spirit of the Belle Epoque, it tried to enhance its brand name with high-quality advertising using art posters. Vecchia Romagna brandy was able to build on this reputation before and after World War II. Even its unconventional bottle with the emblem of the young Bacchus helped the company to make its mark both nationally and internationally. It soon became one of Italy's favorite spirits, as it still is today. While the Etichetta Nera (Black Label) ages for three years in casks made from Limousin oak, the Riserva takes at least ten years, which is well expressed in its elegant balance and complexity.

### Villa Zarri Brandy, 16 Anni di Vino Trebbiano Toscano e Romagnaio

Though Villa Zarri does in fact go back to the year 1578, its present site in the middle of a great park is actually the result of extensive renovation works in the 18th century. Leonida Zarri helped to give the property a facelift. Only Trebbiano grapes from the Tuscan and Emilia-Romagna hillsides 490–2,300 ft (150–700 m) high are selected for their brandy: they produce the light, acidic base wines required for double distillation using the charentais pot still. The young spirit is put in new 92-gallon (350-liter) casks made from French oak. As it ages it is transferred to older casks, and the alcohol content drops slowly to the 42–4% that Guido Fini believes is perfect. Only the very best wines from a vintage stand a chance of being chosen for this excellent, high-quality 16-year-old brandy.

### Mazzetti d'Altavilla Brandy Opera Prima

Filippo Mazzetti began distilling grappa in Monferrato in Piedmont in 1846, at a time when pomace was regarded as no more than the byproduct of pressing. He and his son Luigi scoured the whole of Monferrato for the highest quality base products for their distillery, so that they could transform them into exceptionally distinctive spirits. Father and son moved to Altavilla with their distillery, where first Felice and then Franco Mazzetti kept refining their craft throughout the 20th century, building an ever increasing reputation for their grappa. Brandy was, and is, the second passion of the Mazzettis. They use copper pot stills for distilling their brandy, and age it for 20 years in casks made from Slovenian oak. They then select the best casks for the impressive, velvety Opera Prima.

### Jacopo Poli Arzente

In 1898 in Schiavon near Bassano del Grappa in the heart of Veneto—the most typical region for grappa production—Jacopo Poli's great-grandfather began his craft as a *grappaioli* with a small mobile still. Jacopo's grandfather was a very different sort of person, a patriarch open to progress. To make his fixed still, he modified the wood-fired steam engine of a locomotive. In 1956 Jacopo's father Toni introduced marked improvements and the equipment has stayed the same to this day, unlike the products. The Polis have created a whole range of classic grappas, and also an arzente, a 10-year-old, oak-aged brandy distilled from Trebbiano di Soave. With intense aromas of vanilla, tea, and nuts, it is full bodied, balanced, and elegant on the palate.

> "Finally, here I am, born in a still, hoping to be able to honor my ancestors. Together with my siblings, Giampaolo, Barbara, and Andrea, I am carrying on the tradition, with one specific aim in mind: to convey all the hard work and dedication, and especially love, that is contained in a bottle of grappa. It is a profound love for our own art, and our own world, a love without which nothing worthwhile would ever be possible."
> **Jacopo Poli**

# Greek brandy

Metaxa is not a pure wine spirit, although it is based on it. Aging in large oak casks does, however, play an important part in its development.

The top position attained by Metaxa is one enjoyed by only a few in the spirits business. It is regarded as the ultimate Greek brandy, and strictly speaking it is not really a brandy at all.

Spyros Metaxa, a wine grower from the island of Kefalonia, moved to Piraus in 1880 with his brothers and acquired extensive vineyards in southern Attica. He began to experiment with his wines, mixing them and distilling them in his own still. He then fiddled around some more until he had concocted an elixir from brandies and wines that appealed to him. He bottled it, gave it a vivid label, called it simply Metaxa, and brought it onto the market in 1888. During con-

struction of the first manufacturing plant, an ancient coin with the portrait of a warrior from the battle of Salamis was found. Spyros Metaxa took this to be a good omen and chose it as the brand image of his company. Today it can still be seen on every label and has brought good luck to Metaxa.

## An unusual formula

Metaxa is now produced in a hi-tech plant in Kifissia, Athens, and follows the old established recipe unchanged. The base wines consist of the grape varieties Sabbatiano (the basis of retsina), Soultanina (often used to make raisins or as dessert grapes), and Black Corinthian (mainly used to make currants). The pressed base wines from each are then processed separately to make Metaxa. Wine spirit is used to strengthen it to 18–24% vol., and this mixture is distilled to produce wine spirits with quite different bouquets. Depending on the distillation system used—continuous or batch—they reach an alcohol content of between 52 and 86% vol. Many years of experience are needed to blend the spirits perfectly before they are put into casks made of Limousin oak. Depending on the particular type of Metaxa being produced, the wine spirits have to age for between 5 and 30 years in the wooden casks, giving them a progressively darker color and greater smoothness.

After the first maturation period, the process developed by Spyros Metaxa is applied. Six months before bottling the traditional brandies pass through a filtration layer on their way to the blending vats: it is a secret formula made from herbs and spices, including rose petals. This gives the brandies additional aromas and complexity, before they are fused with ripe Muscat wines from Limnos and Samos and then "married" in huge wooden tuns until they are ready for bottling.

## Grades of Metaxa

| | |
|---|---|
| **3 stars** | Aged for three years; only distributed in Greece; light, fruity sweetness |
| **5 stars** | Aged for five years; international market; mild, honey-color classic with smooth caramel flavor; also suitable for long drinks |
| **7 stars** | Aged for seven years; sold in amphora-shape bottle; mid golden color, mellow and round with fruit and spice notes; neat or on the rocks |
| **Grande Fine** | Aged for at least 15 years; sold in porcelain carafe; amber tones, velvety with fruity sweetness, and long on the palate; enjoy it neat |
| **Private Reserve** | Aged for up to 30 years; until recently available only in a glass carafe in Greece; dark amber, very complex, spicy-sweet aromas, full bodied, and long finish |

# The brandy of Georgia

## Armenia

Armenian brandy was, and still is, especially popular in the former Soviet Union. Now it is beginning to gain respect once more on the international market. The most important producer is the Yerevan Brandy Company (founded in 1887), now part of the Pernod Ricard group. The company sells brandies aged for 3 to 18 years under its brand name Ararat. After the end of the Soviet Union, a few of the former wine growers decided to set up their own distilleries. Production is regulated to a certain extent, so for instance only wines from five grape varieties are permitted: Rkatsiteli, Mskhali, Garan Dmak, Kangun, and Voskehat. Armenian brandies are usually aged in casks that are made from Caucasian oak.

The oldest archeological finds, which bear witness to viticulture in Georgia, are around 7,000 years old: they are tools used in wine growing and, later, jewelry with grape and vine leaf motifs. By far the most important wine region in the country is the Caucasus responsible for over two thirds of total wine and brandy production. The region lies in the southeast of the country and descends in two valleys to the Azerbaijani border. This is where the extremely resistant white grape Rkatsiteli flourishes, one of the oldest and most cultivated varieties in the world. Not only light table wines and heavy port wines are pressed from it, but also the base wines for brandy; these are freshly acidic, with an alcohol content of about 12% vol.

Professional distilleries did not become established until the second part of the 19th century. The founding father of Georgian brandy is considered to be David Saradjishvili (1848–1911). A doctor of chemistry and philosophy, he learned distillation techniques in France and established the Tbilisi Brandy Factory in the Georgian capital in 1884. Back in 1945 in Yalta, Stalin and Winston Churchill were said to have been impressed by their best-known brand Eniseli, a 17-year-old brandy distilled from wines of the east Georgian regions of Shilda and Eniseli. The founder of the company Saradjishvili, is still admired today for his socially progressive business policy. The current distillery was built in 1954, but has been modernized in the last decade and brought up to international standards. It has always used the double distillation method for cognac, which produces a first raw spirit at 34%, and then a clear 70% wine spirit after the second distillation. This distillate is put into 106-gallon (400-liter) casks, for which mainly locally grown Iberian oak is used, as well as oak from Bulgaria and Cyprus. The Saradjishvili Company stores 18,000 casks in 17 cellars, where a constant temperature of 63–4 °F (17–18 °C) and a 70% humidity level are maintained.

A total of 15 different types of brandy is produced, classified as follows: standard, aged for three to five years; vintage brandies, aged for six to eight years; and old vintages, starting with the 9-year-old Gremi. Base wines from other regions of Georgia are also distilled. During the elaboration process a range of old spirits from various sources is blended together, reduced, and enriched with up to 2 oz. per gallon (15 g per liter) of sugar. The firm, which sells roughly four fifths of Georgia's brandy output, is justifiably proud of its special edition XX Century, a blend of 17 brandies dating from 1905 to 1993, and its Saradjishvili-155 (to mark the 155th anniversary of the company's founder), made from brandies that were distilled by David Saradjishvili personally between 1893 and 1905. Both are proof of the noble culture of brandy in Georgia.

Portrait of company founder, David Saradjishvili.

# German brandy

The German economic miracle of the 1950s and 1960s saw a similar rise in the fortunes of the country's brandy, which asserted itself as the Germans' favorite spirit. It was able to expand its position quantitatively until after reunification, only to end up losing all its bounce in the face of the onslaught from fashionable drinks, vodka and whisky in particular. Yet German brandy continues to have an important role to play, and strenuous steps are being taken to liven up its image.

In terms of taste, it does much to accommodate the brandy aficionado: it is mellow and velvety, subtly sweet with aromas of vanilla and caramel, dried fruit, and nuts, and often incorporating toasted notes from the wood aging. Throughout the successful decades it developed a very typical, appealing, and harmonious profile. But just how German is the brandy in fact?

All the brandies presented so far, irrespective of their country of origin, have been based on home-grown grapes. This is not the case in Germany, with a few exceptions. All of the bigger brands buy in their distilling wines from abroad in the cultivation year, mainly from France and Italy. In Germany this practice means base wines that have been fortified with wine spirit to give them an alcohol content of 18–24% vol. They are then distilled a second time in Germany, and finally are left to age in oak casks for at least 12 months or a minimum of 6 months if they are stored in casks with a capacity lower than 265 gallons (1,000 liters).

With falling demand, the magic words "cost optimization" are becoming ever louder. Readymade double distilled spirits are being bought in, sometimes even fully aged, retaining only the essential part: blending together the company's own brandy from various spirits—differing in origin, elaboration, and character—with the traditional additives permitted by law. As well as caramel, a wine spirit mash of dried fruit, nuts, and their shells is used. The final brandy is left for another few months to allow the tastes to harmonize before bottling takes place.

## What's in a name?

Throughout Europe spirits distilled from wine bore the name "cognac" until well into the 20th century. (In addition, the term *Franzbranntwein* is used in Germany to describe an alcohol-based product sold in drugstores as a liniment.)

Hugo Asbach learned the art of distillation in France, and set up his own distillery in Rüdesheim in 1892. By 1896 he was using the term *Weinbrand* (brandy) as well as "cognac," and stopped using the French name completely after 1911. He was ahead of his time in this respect, for eight years later German producers were banned from using the term "cognac" though the name Weinbrand was only protected in law in 1971.

Asbach Uralt pursues a special policy even today: the company keeps a stock of 21,000 x 80-gallon (300-liter) casks of Limousin oak in Ottersweier, far from the Rhine. Aged for a period of up to 50 years, these old brandies allow the company to create new, high-

Though German brandy is mainly represented by the big-name brands, small-scale artisan production and aging of specialist editions—as seen here at Gerhard Gutzler—is arousing greater interest and enthusiasm.

quality products from their own reserves. There is a niche market for brandies from smaller distilleries concentrating on premium quality, or brandies aged for many years from wine growers who are mostly subcontracted to distill their own grapes. Really special ones with distinctive character can be found among these selected products.

Top left: Rheingau wine grower Hans Lang ages his X.O. made from Riesling for six years in the cask.

Top right: Gerhard Gutzler, a wine grower from Rheinhessen, is one of the best distillers in Germany.

### Asbach Selection 21-year-old

This top brandy came onto the market in 1989. Its long cask aging is evident in the very complex aromas, with floral, spicy, nutty notes, as well as the striking roasted hints of cocoa and coffee.

### Wilde Wasser 1999

A brandy cask-aged for six years that distillers Thomas Helferich and Gerhard Gutzler selected for their "Wilde Wasser" (Wild Water) collection. They offer exquisite and rare brandies from small distilleries working with traditional methods.

### Chantré Cuvée Rouge

Market leader Chantré, whose very mild brandy took the company to the top in Germany soon after it was founded in 1953, also offers this fruity specialty made from red wines.

# South African brandies

In choosing the national drink of South Africa, brandy would stand a good chance of coming out top of the list, even though it would probably be with cola. With roots going back over 300 years and its own production regulations, which are quite different from those of other brandies, it is certainly worth careful consideration. While it used to be a business dominated by big companies, fresh impetus has been brought to brandy in the last few years, thanks to small artisan producers.

The recent upturn is reflected in the statistics: each year, roughly 45 million South Africans consume around 12 million gallons (45 million liters) of brandy. This makes it by far the number one spirit, accounting for almost half of total sales of alcoholic beverages. Vodka and whisky, which have replaced traditional spirits in other countries to a large extent, have been relegated to a lower placing. South Africa is proud of its leading brandy, as well as of its wine. Those enjoying the economic boom (and fortunately this includes increasing numbers of people) choose an old brandy such as Van Ryn or Oude Molen from K.W.V. (Kooperatieve Wijnbouwers Vereniging van Zuid-Afrika) instead of whisky or a Bordeaux.

Jan van Riebeeck, who founded Cape Town in 1652, is said to have brought brandy from the Charente to South Africa. Brandy was, after all, a lucrative commodity for the United East India Company, quite apart from the fact that Dutch sailors appreciated it themselves. As viticulture began to flourish (the first grapes were pressed in 1659), brandy production could not be far away. Whether it was for his own needs or for the purposes of demonstrating the pot still he had brought back with him, the ship's cook of the schooner *De Pilj* distilled the first South African brandy on May 19, 1672. Before long brandy sat fairly high up the shopping list of the stores masters on the ships that stopped at the Cape en route to India and Indonesia. At first the *dopbrandewijn* distilled from pomace was said to have taken the breath away, but also rendered the stale water on long sea journeys less injurious to health. To this day, *dop* in Afrikaans means a schnapps glass full.

The quality of the brandy improved immediately with the British annexation in 1806. One of the first to make a name with brandy was the immigrant Philippus Bernardus Wolvaart, who was allocated an estate in the Paarl Valley in 1791. At Nederburg, as he christened his property and where he planted 63,000 vines, he distilled roughly 700 gallons (2,600 liters) of brandy per annum. And he was certainly not the only one.

A new chapter in brandy's history was written in 1918 by K.W.V., a private cooperative founded with a mandate to stabilize the wine industry and raise the quality of wine and brandy. Brandy grew to be a mass product consumed as the drink of preference by the black population, which did not exactly help to solve the social problems. Alcohol misuse does still continue to be an issue, though brandy is probably less to blame nowadays, given the changes in the range of products and purchasing habits. South African brandy records its growth rate in the premium sector, and it is black citizens who value the prestigious brands like Martell V.O., Klipdrift Premium, Oude Molen 100, and K.W.V. 10 Years Old.

# Cape style

Page 170: K.W.V. House of Brandy in Worcester offers a very good guided tour.

Page 171: Distilling is done the traditional way in the Louiesenhof winery near Stellenbosch, in a pot still from Stuttgart made in 1930.

Opposite:
In the biggest brandy distillery in the world, the K.W.V. House of Brandy, 120 hand-regulated, small South African pot stills are used (right), along with the alembic charentais (on the left).

Worcester's extensive vineyards provide a large proportion of the base wines for brandy production.

In Stellenbosch, if visitors inquire about brandy grapes, wine growers send them to the other side of the mountain as the grapes in their own sites are in too much demand and too expensive. Crossing the Du-Toitskloof Pass leads to the main cultivation area for brandy grapes. This is located in Worcester and Robertson near the Breede river. Mainly Colombard and Chenin Blanc grapes are cultivated for this purpose, and wine growers aim to produce healthy grapes with high acidity and an alcohol content of 10–11% vol. Grapes grown in South Africa at the standard French strength of 8–9% vol. would not be aromatic enough. The very high yields do not have a negative effect as distillation is of course a process of concentration, with 1–1½ gallons (5–6 liters) of wine allowed for each 3 gallons (11 liters) of brandy.

Moreover, until the 1980s 80% of grape varieties in South Africa were white and were mainly used for distillation. The varieties mentioned have stood the test of time, but distillers also use others like Cinsault or Pinotage to make the spirit fruitier. Most base wines for distillation are pressed by wine cooperatives according to the instructions of the brandy companies, K.W.V. in particular, which has the biggest pot still in the world in Worcester and needs an average of 77 million lb (35 million kg) of grapes each year.

Since the restrictions on smaller companies were lifted in 1990 and 1993, more and more estates are now distilling their own wines.

## Distilling, South African style

"We are looking for fruity base wines with typical aromas of banana, guava, and green grass," K.W.V. brandy master Kobus Gelderblom explains. "We only rack the wine once, as we want to retain the lees. It contains many fatty acids and that is also why we use pot stills made of copper: this material reacts with the alcohol, or ethanol, to form the esters with their wonderful aromas, and that is what matters to us."

The distillation hall at K.W.V. is impressive. It has 120 pot stills, manufactured by coppersmith David Benjamin Woudberg in Wellington, arranged in two rows for batch

distillation. Each of the steam-heated pot stills holds about 260 gallons (1,000 liters). As Kobus explains, "In the first run, we distill to an alcohol content of 31% vol. which increases to 70% vol. with the second distillation, at which point the heads and tails are removed."

The clear brandy from the pot still is then put into casks of French oak, the capacity of which must be less than 90 gallons (340 liters) by law. And there it must stay for three years. "We prefer to use French oak rather than South African, as our summers are too hot and the trees grow too quickly, making the wood soft and porous. Too much brandy would be lost through evaporation. Even as things are, we lose 2 gallons (9 liters) per cask each year."

The best South African brandies are those distilled naturally in pot stills and aged for a minimum of three, often five, and not infrequently ten or more years. With entry level grades of brandy, as with the higher vintage category, brandy masters turn to pure wine spirit (which has been column distilled and rectified) for their blends, a practice which does not conform to international conventions. In addition, brandies can be sweetened with up to 2 oz. per gallon (15 g per liter) of sugar, caramel, dessert wine, honey, or must concentrate, or natural plant aromas.

## South African brandy types

### Standard or blended brandy
Minimum 30% brandy from pot stills, aged in casks for at least three years, rectified with neutral, non-aged wine spirit; minimum 43% vol. alcohol content (40% vol. for export quality); used in mixed drinks.

### Pot still brandy
Minimum 90% pot still brandy, cask aged for at least three years, and bottled at alcohol content of 38% vol. minimum; best drunk neat.

### Vintage brandy
A blend of at least 30% pot still brandy with a maximum of 60% wine spirit made in a column still, each aged for at least eight years. It is rectified with neutral wine spirit and bottled at alcohol content of 38% vol. minimum; pronounced wood notes; drink neat or with soda.

# On the brandy routes

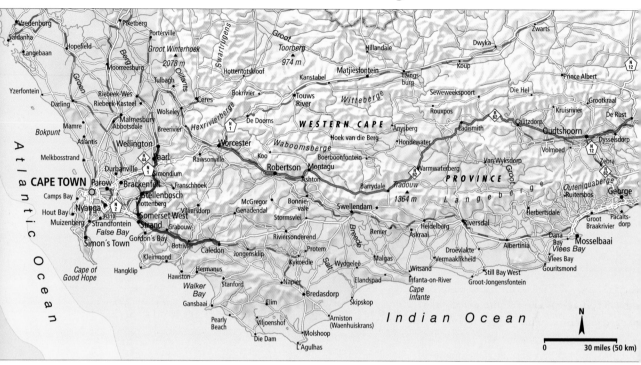

The Western Cape Brandy Route was opened on May 19, 1997, exactly 325 years after the first brandy was distilled in South Africa. It is believed to be the first of its kind in the world. Starting in the south, the first stop is in the Elgin Valley, the up-and-coming wine region with a cool climate located an hour by automobile southwest of Cape Town. This is now home to the brand Oude Molen from the family-owned Edward Snell & Company, which has a completely renovated distillery built originally in 1942. It is a tribute to Rene Santhagen, the founder of the brand, who is also known as the "father of South African brandy" and was famous for his lavish parties around 1900.

The Van Ryn distillery near Vlottenberg, where Distell distills and ages its top-quality products, is very impressive. At Louiesenhof a small pot still that was manufactured in Germany in 1930 is in operation. Near Backberg, south of Paarl, Michael Back was able to afford an alembic charentais from Cognac, while on their neat 300-year-old Gut De Compagnie estate near Wellington

attorney Johann Loubser and his wife—Afrikaans writer Riana Scheepers—distill their brandy in a pot still first activated in 1849. Not far from there Edmund Oerttlé makes his very fruity brandies from organically grown grapes.

What might be called the epicenter of South African brandy, the House of Brandy of the international company K.W.V., is located in the small town of Worcester. It offers a guided tour with an excellent commentary, and is the official end point of the Western Cape Brandy Route. It is also the start of the second brandy route, which follows the R62 freeway. It runs across the tranquil, spectacular landscape of the Klein Karoo, where the cooperative in the pretty town of Barrydale continues to use old Woudberg pot stills. Via the pleasant staging post of Ladysmith the road reaches Calitzdorp, the stronghold of South African port wine. Its fortification has always required good brandy, and for this reason the family-run business Boplass has exported its brandy since 1880. Carel Nel produced the first

estate brandy in 1994. The final stop is in Van der Riet Street, in the rambling little town of Oudtshoorn, where the visitor can

sample the excellent Hanepoot brandy made from Muscat grapes in the new Kango Wijnhuis distillery.

Wine and brandy are produced on the Avontuur estate, against the fabulous backdrop of the Helderberg mountains. Race horses are also bred there.

## Western Cape Brandy Route

**Oude Molen Distillery**
near Grabouw
Tip: Oude Molen V.O.V.

**Avontuur Wine Estate**
between Somerset West and Stellenbosch
Tip: 10 Year Old

**Tokara**
top of the Helshoogte Pass (R310), 3 miles (5 km) from Stellenbosch.
Tip: 5 Year Old Pot Still Brandy

**Van Ryn Brandy Distillers**
near Vlottenberg, 5 miles (8 km) from Stellenbosch
Tip: 20 Year Old

**Louiesenhof**
on the Koelenhof Road (R304), 2½ miles (4 km) from Stellenbosch
Tip: Marbonne Pot Still Brandy

**Uitkyk**
on the R44 between Stellenbosch and Paarl
Tip: 10 Year Old Estate Brandy

**Backsberg**
in Suider Paarl near Klapmuts
Tip: 10 Year Old

**Laborie Estate**
Taillerfer Street in Paarl
Tip: Laborie Alambic Brandy

**Nederburg**
near Paarl
Tip: Nederburg Pot Stilled Solera Brandy

**De Compagnie**
near Wellington
Tip: De Compagnie Pot Still Brandy

**Oude Wellington Estate**
on the R301 between Wellington and Bain's Kloof
Tip: Dr. Schumacher's Estate Brandy

**Upland Organic Estate**
on the Blouvlei Road outside Wellington
Tip: Upland Pure Pot Still Brandy

## R62 Brandy Route

**KWV House of Brandy**
in Worcester
Tip: Imoya V.S.O.P.

**Rietriver Wine Cellar**
on the R62 between Montagu and Barrydale
Tip: John Montagu 5 Year Brandy

**Barrydale Wine and Brandy Cellar**
in Barrydale
Tip: Joseph Barry Cape Pot Still Brandy

**Boplaas**
in Calitzdorp
Tip: Boplaas Pot Still Brandy 7 Year Old

**Grundheim**
just outside Oudtshoorn on the R62
Tip: Grundheim Pot Still Brandy

**Kango Wijnhuis**
in Oudtshoorn
Tip: Kango Hanepoot Brandy

# Finest brandies from the Cape

A representative selection of the 50 or so branded South African brandies is lined up in front of the old Oude Wellington farmhouse. The spectrum is wide: from the oldest and highest quality spirits from the large producer K.W.V. (fourth from right) and Van Ryn (third from right), each of which matures for 20 years in 80-gallon (300-liter) casks; to the Louiesenhof's 16-year-old Marbonne (second from left); to younger estate brandies. Savignac de Versailles—the only estate in South Africa specializing solely in brandy—produces artisan pot still brandies like this 10-year-old from 1994 (first on left) while Tokara (third from left) stands out in its use of top-quality wines. Younger brandies from Oude Wellington (fourth from left) and Upland (second from right) are very convincing, intensely fruity with elegant vanilla notes, while the mellowness of the De Compagnie brandy (first on right), distilled in 1996 and aged for seven years, is impressive.

# Estate brandies

The liberalization of South African wine production also affected brandy, allowing independent wine-growing estates to do their own distillation. With their artisan brandies often produced in historical pot stills, these newcomers revived an interest in high-quality products, and the larger companies producing predominantly standard quality brandy also benefited from it. In recent years sophisticated spirits are the ones showing the highest growth rate.

At Oude Wellington Dr. Rolf Schumacher and his wife Vanessa pamper their old alembic to keep it from expiring permanently. Rolf Schumacher has a great deal of experience when it comes to aging brandy. "Age

big brands will taste exactly the same in three years' time as it does now. By contrast, our brandies are capable of evolving. Of course, I put my own stamp on it as well, but essentially one of our brandies is full of floral aromas and flavors after three years, with the nutty aromas only developing at a later stage. The longer it is kept in the cask, the stronger the wood notes will become, while there is a corresponding loss of fruit. Then it develops the aromas and flavors of walnuts and hazelnuts. Many houses are actually trying to revive the fruit notes by blending the different ages."

All of the small distillers try to give their brandies an individual expression, which is influenced as much by the grapes as by the

should not always be equated with quality, for brandy passes through different stages as it matures. Grapes react to their environment, so every brandy tastes differently from one year to the next. The large commercial houses take great pains to give their brandies a consistent taste profile over decades if at all possible. A fine cognac from one of the

pot still. Without the personal philosophy of the distiller, getting to know the brandies of South Africa would be far less appealing and diverse.

Left: Oude Wellington's old pot still distills 530 gallons (2,000 liters) of brandy each year.
Right: Tasting the 16-year-old Marbonne at the Loueisenhof distillery.

# Brandies from other lands

Wherever grapes grow, brandy is always distilled as well, especially if the grapes are plentiful and the wine produced from them is less than impressive. A textbook example of this is the Thompson Seedless table grape, also used to make raisins and known as the "Sultana" variety. In Mexico and the USA the base wines from this grape are used to make brandy. As they pass through the pot still and condenser, they transform into the mass Mexican brands, Presidente and Don Pedro, which together sell over 110 million bottles—far more than tequila. Similarly, the leading brand names in terms of quantity in the US—such as Gallo's E&J, Christian Brothers, P. Masson's Grande Amber, and Korbel—are also distilled from it. Yet a new trend is emerging globally. In precisely those places where they now know how to produce first-rate wines, wine growers and distillers are aiming for a comparable quality with spirits, and are making inroads into niche markets. In the US, Germain Robin distills brandy made from Pinot Noir rosé, which is often served as a digestif in the White House. Austria provides a host of equally impressive examples, and the connoisseur can find exquisite brandies in Switzerland as well. A small selection of brands from different countries is assembled here to illustrate the astonishing range in the world of brandy.

### Domäne Wachau
### Cigar Reserve X.A.
### 25-year-old

Under the label Domäne Wachau, the Freien Weingärtner Wachau cooperative offers its premium wines and brandies with the distinctive mark of the terroir and the grape varieties. Back in 1965 long-standing head of the company Willi Schwengler began to distill brandies from Grüner Veltliner and set up one of the biggest distillation plants in Austria. When harvested early Grüner Veltliner is well suited to producing complex spirits as the low sugar gradation results in brandies rich in extracts, with good fruit concentration and integrated alcohol. Over the years a large stock of mature spirits has been built up in this way; with some batches dating back to the 1960s, it represents a real treasure trove. From this wine growers are now composing their unreduced, completely unadulterated Veltliner brandies: the complex Cigar Reserve, with its elegant toasted notes and mature spiciness, represents the pinnacle of their achievement.

### Donatsch
### Malans brandy

The Donatsch family runs the Zum Ochsen wine tavern and a wine estate of 11 acres (4.5 ha) in Malans, the southernmost village in the Bündner Herrschaft region of eastern Switzerland. For decades they have cultivated their plot of land according to integrated farming principles, and during this time they have planted grape varieties that are best suited to growing on the land. Thomas Donatsch and his son Martin are famous for their high-quality appellation wines, especially their range of Pinot Noirs. Their brandy is also based on Pinot Noir—on the gleanings of the grapes in fact, which are immediately pressed and fermented. After distillation the spirit ages for at least eight years in casks of Allier oak, which were previously used for Pinot Noir and are then stored in the centuries-old vaulted cellars of the Ochsen tavern. Pinot Noir gives the brandy its lovely fruitiness and nicely rounded character, while the oak casks contribute the elegant spicy notes.

# Selected brandies

**McDowell's No. 1 Brandy**

This brandy is produced by the Indian U.B. Group: its top brand is Kingfisher beer, which is sold in 52 countries and enjoys a 50% share of the market in India alone. McDowell's brandy is one of the 13 spirit brands of the group, and sells over a million cases per year, making it the largest selling brandy in the world. U.B.'s biotechnologists discovered that black grapes from western India were the most suitable for it. The wine, fermented under extremely hygienic conditions, is double distilled and aged in wood casks. To get the finished product, it is then cut with extra neutral alcohol that is obtained from a five-column continuous still, as well as with caramel. The brandy, with its grape, honey, and toffee aromas, tastes pleasantly mild and smooth, and has a sweet flavor reminiscent of honey.

**Carmel XO 100**

The Carmel winery was founded in 1882 by Baron Edmond de Rothschild, the owner of Château Lafite. In 1898 they produced their first brandy from surplus grapes. The distillery itself was set up in 1930 in the Rishon Le Zion winery south of Tel Aviv, where Carmel operates four pot and two column stills. The brandy is made from base wines, mainly from Colombard grapes, and the spirit ages in small French casks that have previously been used to mature wine. They are stored in a 115-year-old cask cellar that still has its original wooden roof. Carmel 100 was created to mark the hundredth anniversary: it is a nine-year-old brandy with a high proportion of pot still spirits from the popular three-year-old Carmel 777. An after-dinner brandy with rich aromas of dried fruit, it is pleasantly warm and long on the palate. (Michael Ben-Joseph)

**Germain Robin Mendocino County Brandy**

In the summer of 1981 Ansley Coale picked up a hitchhiker that happened to be French, and from an old cognac dynasty. A year later Hubert Germain-Robin shipped an old alembic over to Mendocino County in California, where they began to distill together on Coale's remote ranch—using rosé made from Pinot Noir grapes. The result was proof in itself. In 1987 they produced their first brandy, followed in 1994 by the Select Barrel X.O. and the Anno Domini in 1999, which was set alongside the best cognacs in a competition. They tried out 19 grape varieties, but Pinot Noir, Colombard, and Sémillon turned out to be the best. Even the entry level brandy shows the style of these two distillers: an intense, elegantly sweet spiciness, with pronounced fruit and toasted notes—round, long, and balanced.

**Hardys XO**

Thomas Hardy from Devon in England emigrated to Australia in 1850, where he opened a winery in Adelaide barely three years later. It was not until the end of the 19th century that he turned to distilling wine, mainly in order to fortify the port wines that were much in demand. In 1941 Hardys (now part of Constellation Brands with an annual turnover of over 100 million bottles of wine in 80 countries) produced its first premium brandy, V.S.O.P. Since 1995 it has been known as X.O. and is a blend of 15–30-year-old vintage brandies. Today Trebbiano and Colombard are used for the base wines, which are double distilled in copper pot stills and then aged in French oak casks. With its distinctive vanilla and oak notes, the X.O. proves to be very smooth and elegant on the palate, finishing on a cocoa note.

**Gran Pisco Control**

Hardly a day goes by in Chile or Peru without a Pisco Sour, the cocktail made from aromatic, light brandy, lime juice, and ice. The name means "flying bird" in Quechuan. While they use many grape varieties in Peru—subsequently differentiating the types (aromatic and non-aromatic) and distilling them only once—it is primarily the exceptionally aromatic Muscat d'Alexandrie that is used in Chile. It is grown in designated areas and high valleys (Elqui is the best known) 310 miles (500 km) north of Santiago de Chile. After distillation the Pisco Control is allowed time to refine in oak casks. In Chile piscos are designated according to alcohol content: the Gran Pisco must contain at least 43% vol. The unmistakable, intense aroma of ripe Muscat grapes characterizes both its scent and its mild taste, though it is very rarely consumed neat.

# How to savor brandies

Since the 18th century cognac has managed to establish itself as the digestif par excellence, and for many cognac aficionados it is a sacrilege to enjoy it any other way. This has not stopped bartenders from using it, of course. A number of now legendary cocktails, such as the Sidecar, Alexander, Between the Sheets, and Champagne Cocktail, would be unthinkable without cognac. Cognac and soda and cognac highballs were popular drinks decades ago, before almost slipping into oblivion, but recently the American hip-hop culture has gone back to an unashamed association with brandy from the Charente—and with some justification, at least as far as the young V.S. and most V.S.O.P. brandies are concerned.

In other countries and cultures they have been less concerned about French etiquette. In Scandinavia ice-cold cognac is served with fish, and in Asia it is also popular with food as it is extremely compatible with sweet and sour dishes. Elsewhere, other charming matches have been tried out, such as X.O. with Parmesan, mature Gouda, or Stilton, while finest bitter chocolate is highly recommended with the oldest cognac vintages. And, saving the best for last, there is frosted cognac from the freezer cabinet with sushi. Really old cognacs still give the greatest pleasure if you enter the tasting process with dedication. The right glass is needed for this—a tulip-shape one made from clear, fine crystal, or a balloon glass with a constricted mouth. Cognac needs a little time to unfold in its glass.

## An orgy of scents

The nose should be brought to the glass without swirling it, otherwise it releases mostly alcohol. Cognac will unfold its aromas very gradually, and there will always be new ones to discover. "Nosing," as malt whisky experts call it, is a wonderful experience for the

Today cognac is a versatile treat, whether enjoyed on the rocks, in a tulip-shape nosing glass, or in an atmospheric bar as a component of a fabulous cocktail.

senses. The palette of aromas is multifaceted: it ranges from floral to fresh, dried and candied fruits; from vanilla, cinnamon, and other spices to caramel and honey; from nuts, through toasted aromas like coffee and tobacco, to notes of wood, wax, resin, leather; and finally to the unmistakable scent of vintage cognac, the legendary rancio. A leisurely approach is needed to appreciate this rich diversity. Small sips should be taken, rolling them in the mouth as they create a comforting glow, and relaxing in the thought of all the decades wafting up before you like a perfume. Magical.

## Delicious experiences

What is good for cognac also holds true for armagnac and brandy. The older a brandy, the more leisurely the attention it deserves and the greater its complexity, developed over the years of aging in an oak cask. Each one has its own special character worth figuring out. As far as the younger spirits are concerned, a distinction should be made between the standard qualities (which are better for mixing than enjoying neat, as they are one dimensional and often harsher) and the artisan-crafted distillates. The latter come mainly from wineries where the wine growers select the grapes with special care, often from just one particular variety: for them, distillation is all about capturing their essence. That said, the young, intense aromas can be just as fascinating as the more mature spirits. Younger spirits, with their primary aromas, which are good for serving chilled, make a good accompaniment for food, especially smoked fish, ham, or gourmet sausages, as well as desserts with citrus fruits.

Unlike neutral spirits, cognac, armagnac, and other brandies always have distinctive aromas. If you are not inclined to enjoy them for their own sake, then a little flair is needed when using them, whether in the bar, at the table, or in the kitchen. In the right amounts they will reward you with incomparably delicious experiences. Fortunately the rather uptight reverence of previous years has now given way to an unbridled joy in experimenting. This is where brandies from all corners of the globe offer truly undreamt-of possibilities.

# Pomace

# and

# pomace

# brandies

It was the Italians who first gave pomace, the pulp from pressed grapes, the credit it deserved, using it in the distillation of choice grappas.

Opposite: Fruit and pomace distillates mature in vaulted cellars at the premises of celebrated Austrian distiller Alois Gölles.

Page 182: Grappa, marc, and pomace brandy have now caught up with the more refined distillates and are often presented to consumers in magnificent style.

# Refined residues

By contrast with cognac or armagnac, for example, pomace brandy had to get by for a long time without prestige product status. It was considered to be a rather low-brow little spirit for rustic folk, and confined within very strict geographical limits. Even Italian grappa has had access to international markets for only a few decades. However, it soon drew attention to itself when it did. Anyone today who speaks of Trester, Treberschnaps, marc, grappa, or tsipouro, or of Spanish orujo or Portuguese bagaceira, will no doubt be thinking too of hefebrands and pomace brandies in general, all of which are now upwardly mobile.

Some brandy producers may look down their noses at the upstarts. After all, pomace brandy is produced from the wastes of wine production. Yet in terms of quality, grappa, marc, and co.—at least over the past 30 years—have gained greatly in quality. Indeed, they have even set new standards for spirits in general both in terms of aroma and finesse.

Spirits made from wine (including brandy, cognac, and armagnac) and from grape pomace are closely related to one another. All are made from the same raw material, the grape, and can look back over an equally long history. Anyone who knew how to distill wine would certainly quickly have grasped the fact that there remain in the residues from wine preparation enough sugar and aromas to make them worth distilling. Moreover, in the old days most people couldn't afford to waste anything. In the Middle Ages (and even into the 20th century), pomace brandies were a cheap rustic product. They were made as informally as they were consumed. In almost all European wine-growing areas it was a familiar way of using up residues that, as such, would hardly have had a chance to grace any nobleman's or well-to-do citizen's table, or indeed later those of the star marked restaurants. It was not until the 1970s that the contempt for pomace brandies come to an end, when the spirit of the times and inspired producers brought Italian grappa cult status within just a few years. Poured into futuristic designer bottles, grappas in the 1980s and 1990s won their place in the gourmets' temples. Even if this trend has now passed its peak, grappa remains popular. In 2004 Austrian celebrity cook Heinz Hanner, for example, set up the world's first grappa bar devoted entirely to producer Romano Levi in his restaurant near Vienna. Pomace brandies from a venerable distillery with old fashioned charm, it would seem, form an excellent partnership with molecular cuisine.

Awareness of high-quality pomace spirits has increased even outside Italy over recent years. For instance Marc de Bourgogne is now an essential part of French gastronomic culture. An illustrious circle of aficionados now wax lyrical over Austrian, German, and Swiss noble pomace brandies. Nevertheless, these products—despite their often outstanding quality—have not as yet achieved worldwide popularity. Restaurateurs too have been reluctant to embrace a spirit made from stalks, skins, and sometimes even stems. On the one hand restaurants boast an exclusive grappa selection, but on the other hand they seldom trouble to serve it in glasses that would do it justice. In bars pomace brandies are hardly to be found at all. Cocktail recipes with grappa or marc are few and far between. Nevertheless, cooks appreciate the aromatic potential of marc and co. and use it in desserts, pralines, and fish and meat dishes.

The residues from pressing for fruit wine or fruit must are also distilled. Pomace brandies from other fruits such as pears, for example, are covered in the "Fruit Spirits" chapter of this book.

# Rise of a disreputable spirit

At Romano Levi the distillation equipment is fired using dried pomace residues left over from the previous year.

Nobody knows exactly when the first pomace brandies were produced, but one thing is more or less certain: it was the wine growers who discovered that not only could wine be distilled to make brandy, but the apparently less attractive residues of grape pressing could be used to make spirits too. As knowledge and expertise in distillation (generally considered to have originated in Arabia, where it was primarily used to produce cosmetics and fragrances) is assumed to have started in Europe at the earliest shortly before the turn of the first millennium, pomace brandy production must be younger.

After wine growers learned how to distill, it was not long before they learned how to make pomace brandies too. The residues of wine preparation have by no means been wasted from the beginning of wine cultivation until far into the 20th century, but have always been considered a valuable basic commodity. Pomace wine, the slightly alcoholic liquid obtained from pomace supplemented with water and then pressed a second time, was for a long time the house drink of wine growers, wine being produced exclusively to be sold.

Of course it could not be expected that a miracle drink would emerge from stalks, skins, stems, and seeds, distilled together with some fruit flesh and yeast residues. It would largely have been treated as an unpretentious, rough and ready spirit, presumably often clouded by various unintentional offnotes, such as is still the case in some parts of Europe. Grappa, marc, and trester were kept after distillation in large glass bottles or in barrels and largely consumed by the producers themselves.

In Distilleria Sibona at Piobesi d'Alba the pomace is heated in a water bath so that it is not burned.

## Pomace brandy is best distilled cold

It is easy to conclude that such rustic spirits would hardly travel beyond the boundaries of their districts of origin. And in the case of pomace brandies, this district was the wine-producing region itself, although not all wine-growing areas developed a real distilling tradition of their own. As grape residues are highly susceptible to infection and oxidation, those districts that had a cool climate in fall were favored above all. The further north you are, the more safely could grape residues be kept from attack by cold sensitive acetobacter bacteria or mildew. Condensing the distilled alcohol too was easier the lower the outside temperatures were, and the colder the water used for cooling. By contrast with spirits such as cognac, calvados, rum, or whisky, pomace brandies did not become branded goods for a long time. Over the centuries marc and grappa were occasionally smuggled, but only rarely officially exported.

If grappa and other pomace spirits have finally emancipated themselves from their rustic origins, this has been due to improvements in distillation methods. Gone are the days of direct-fired pot stills in which pomace brandies all too often became burnt. Another contributing factor was a change in drinking habits in the second half of the 20th century. The distinct trend toward more refined wining and dining has swept spirits and grape pomaces along with it.

In the imposing underground barrel cellar of the Distilleria Berta at Casalotto di Mombaruzzo, grappa matures into an extraordinarily complex spirit.

# Selected grapes

Nowadays nobody would claim that it does not matter which grapes you use because they are all the same when it comes to making pomace brandy. Word has gone round that a well-made grappa or a first-rate marc may very well express its district of origin and that you can certainly taste the grape varieties used. The more care that is invested in the processing, the more primary aromas are present in the finished spirit. However if the pomace is stored for weeks or months under unfavorable conditions, in the best cases faintly oxidative aromas will be discerned after the distillation process, and in others a penetrating raisiny tone, or—even worse—the tainted whiffs of mildew and acetobacter bacteria appear.

The careful selection of aromatic varieties and the distillation of each separately are innovations of the most recent past. For a long time the pomace brandy distillers gave no consideration to the grape varieties they used and simply took as the basis of their spirit whatever was available. Until the vine pest catastrophe in the 19th century, many vineyards were stocked with mixed varieties but later, too, even quality conscious distillers scooped up all available pomaces together after wine preparation.

Even in the past, however, where material was available in surplus, aromatic varieties were preferred—in particular in those areas of Europe in which the light colored non-cask matured brandies were popular. Grape varieties with high proportions of the terpenes responsible for the aromas remain first choice even today, and for some decades their names have been proudly displayed on

The south Tyrolese grape varieties Lagrein (left) as well as Schiava Grossa alias Trollinger (middle) and Müller-Thurgau (right) provide excellent bases for pomace brandies.

abels. Gewürztraminers and the various Muscatel varieties in Alsace and in Baden, southern Tyrol, and Austria are some of the most popular pomace sources.

## Many are called…

Müller-Thurgau or Sauvignon Blanc, Kerner pomace from these varieties of grape is available in Germany, southern Tyrol, and Trentino), and of course Riesling are some of the preferred grape varieties. More neutral spirits are produced for example from Chardonnay, Silvaner, and Pinot Blanc. In Piedmont it is mostly Barbera and Nebbiolo that are processed from among the strong and spicy red grape varieties, and in Tuscany it is mainly Sangiovese and its variants. Some specialists among the distillers deliberately seek out rare, indigenous grape varieties: the famous Nero d'Avola from Sicily, the Lagrein from south Tyrol, or the Aglianco from Campania. In particular Trentino,

Friuli, Veneto, and Piedmont have made a name for themselves in this respect, giving, for instance, Schiava, Brachetto, Teroldego, and Prosecco new life as grappa.

Pomace brandies from overripe botrytized or raisined grapes have one peculiarity. A distinctive grape aroma rises to the nose even as the pomace brandy is poured out. Examples are the dried grape spirits from Weinlaubenhof Alois Kracher and the Tuscan Grappe di Vin Santo. Whether the willingness of distillers to experiment, egged on by rising demand for noble pomace brandies, is always a good idea is debatable because not every grape variety proves punchy enough for distillation.

Beloved among distillers of noble spirits are the particularly aromatic varieties such as Morio Muscat (left) and Muscat Ottonel (middle), while Prosecco (right) with its natural acidity is also highly suitable.

# Grappa gains respectability

With grappa the Italians have shown us how to stylize a simple spirit into a prestige brandy. Hardly any distillate has developed as rapidly as grappa from a drink with no name to the darling of international gastronomy. If in the 1950s pomace brandies from Trentino or Piedmont were still exclusively drinks restricted to their region of origin, some 20 years later connoisseurs were already celebrating a grappa cult. Although the meteoric rise of the grappa in the 1980s has slowed down, Italian producers are still the pioneers when it comes to distilled pomaces.

Together with Guinness & co., the Irish honor whiskey as their national drink; the Americans rave about bourbon; and the French will not admit that anything compares with cognac, armagnac, and calvados. The Italians have always been somewhat more idiosyncratic. Each region has its own traditional spirits. Brandy was esteemed as highly as sambuca or grappa. None of the regional pomace brandies has achieved national popularity in Italy. No city or province has its name inextricably linked with any spirit drink which has been produced in a certain way.

When you consider the long history of grappa production, this is quite astonishing. The first literary source that expressly mentions grappa stems from as early as 1451. In Friuli the notary Everardo da Cividale, in the inventory of an estate, listed a pot still for the production of "acqua-vitem," which elsewhere in the text was defined as "grape." In the region it is commonly claimed that this was pomace brandy and not distilled wine.

The name grappa, derived from the Italian *grappolo* or grape, took a long time to become established. Up to the end of the 19th century the term *acquavite* or more precisely *acquavite di vinaccia* was generally used—i.e. spirits from grape residues. When Italian author Vittorio Imbrani expressly wrote about grappa in one of his novels in 1876, he was one of the first to introduce this rather colloquial word into standard Italian.

For a long time grappa was understood to be a pomace brandy produced in northern Italy. In particular farmers in the remote valleys of Friui, Trentino, Piedmont, Lombardy, and Veneto produced a spirit from grape seeds, skins, and stalks. It was bartered, smuggled over borders, and of course even drunk. Because hardly anyone had the necessary equipment for distilling, from September to December travelling distillers journeyed with horse and cart carrying simple pot stills across the country. In primitive apparatus over an open fire, any solid materials burnt easily. Undesirable taints in the spirits they produced were commonplace.

No individual producer can boast of being the first in the history of modern grappa. The process of refining the strong—and by today's standards barely drinkable—pomace brandy took centuries. Bortolo Nardini, the founding father of the distillery that still exists, made efforts to improve quality toward the end of the 18th century. Acquavite Nardini then became a household name, and nowadays the legendary Osteria sul Ponte on the bank of the river Brenta is considered by connoisseurs as the grappa Mecca. But it would take further decades until in 1973 a breakthrough was made. The Nonino family produced the first single variety grappa in history—and nothing stood in the way of the rise of grappa to a cult drink.

Nowadays major industrial distilleries operate side by side with medium-size companies and artisanal distillers. Some wine producers themselves distill. Others let the major distilleries do the job for them. They are all concerned to protect the term "grappa" and make this protection official. Outside Italy grappa only exists in the Swiss canton of Ticino and in Italian speaking regions of Graubünden—and overseas, for instance in California and in South Africa.

# Italy's major grappa regions

Page 190: As in Trentino many wine producers of northern Italy use the pomace from their grapes to produce grappa.

Opposite: The grapes maturing in the hills of the Asti region—shown here near Canelli—produce outstanding grappas.

**Italy's grappa regions**

- Piedmont
- Lombardy
- Trentino
- Southern Tyrol
- Friuli—Venezia—Giulia
- Veneto
- Tuscany
- Sicily
- Sardinia

☐ Grappa centers

Grappa is now produced throughout Italy. Even if the north is traditionally more favored and has a higher density of distilleries, in recent years ever more vineyards—even in the central and southern regions of the country—have begun to include a grappa from their own pomaces in their ranges. High-quality grappas for example come from the Marches, from Umbria, and also from the Val d'Aosta, from Lombardy and Liguria, and Sardinia—not forgetting Sicily, where a grappa culture became established among the Arabs in the 10th century.

In the meantime protected designations of origin for grappas have been set up. Currently these are Grappa lombarda (Grappa di Lombardia), Grappa di Barolo, Grappa piemontese (Grappa del Piemonte), Südtiroler Grappa (Grappa dell'Alto Adige), Grappa trentina (Grappa del Trentino), Grappa friulana (Grappa del Friuli), Grappa veneta (Grappa del Veneto), Grappa Sarda (Fil'e Ferru), Grappa siciliana (Grappa di Sicilia), and Grappa di Marsala.

## Trentino—southern Tyrol (Alto Adige)

Trentino is considered to be one of the most traditional grappa regions in Italy and is also one of the most innovative. Among the protected designations of origin, Grappa trentina is particularly well renowned. Bertagnolli, Pilzer, and Pojer & Sandri are some of the major producers.

## Friuli—Venezia—Giulia

Without the producers of Friuli, Italian grappa would not be what it is today. Grappa di Picolit from the Nonino distillery was the first single variety Italian grappa that quickly acquired a female following. Among the many indigenous grape varieties of the region, collectors here will find an unusual richness of flavors, among them the rare Grappa di Ribolla Gialla.

## Veneto

The Grapperia Nardini in Bassano del Grappa is considered to be a starting point for the modern Veneto culture of Acquavite di Vinaccia. Nowadays famous producers such as Piave and Bolla are also established here, as are small traditional operations. Grappa di Amarone and the Grappa di Torcolato produced by Jacopo Poli are considered to be particularly typical of the region.

## Piedmont

Piedmont grappa is considered to be one of the oldest. However, with few exceptions, production remained rural here until well into the second half of the 20th century. Nowadays Moscato pomace brandies (Gran Moscato from Bocchino) are produced here, as are the pomace brandies of Nebbiolo (Grappa di Barolo) and Barbera. No other

egion can compare to Piedmont if you are
liscovering grappa.

## ■uscany

Although the grappa tradition of the Tuscan
producers cannot quite compare with that
of their colleagues in Trentino or Veneto,
over the last 30 years the pomace scene has
been experiencing a steady boom. Many
vineyards have started to have their grappa
produced by reputable distilleries. Grappa
li Ornellaia, for instance, has gained cult sta-
us in this way. Grappa di Vin Santo is one
of the specialties of the region.

## Aromatized and sweetened grappas

Anyone who talks of grappa today generally has in mind the clear or
more or less golden variants of pomace brandy that have been cask
matured. But there still exists a traditional form of grappa that can be
primarily found on the Italian market, *grappa aromatizzata*. In the past
grappas supplemented with herbs, juniper berries, mint, cinnamon, or
other plant essences were considered to be medicinal. A bottle of such
a spirit would in olden times have had its place in every good Italian
household. Particularly Grappa alla ruta, containing a sprig of bitter
rue, was and still is a favorite. After distilling, however, many "ordinary"
grappas have their flavor altered and it is permitted to round them off
with a maximum of 3 oz per gallon of sugar (20 g per liter) of alcohol.
The practice is controversial: an increasing number of consumers are
asking for pure, unadulterated grappa.

# How grappa is made

Grappa production starts with the wine harvest. It is then that the distillers collect the basic material for their product—the residues from pressing. For the quality of the finished grappa, as for pomace brandies in general, another decisive factor is how fresh these residues are when processed, as they are highly susceptible to bacteria and the formation of mildew. Pomace usually contains—in addition to skins, seeds, and a little grape must—fruit flesh residues and yeast, as well as stems and stalks. Because the grapes are increasingly stripped for wine preparation—i.e. processed without any stems and stalks—the vegetable aromas they create have also disappeared from pomace brandies.

For grappa only the solid components of grapes selected in Italy are used, as prescribed by law. The more aromatic the grapes, the higher the quality of the wine produced from them and the higher quality the pomace as in this case the grapes have been stripped and gently pressed. Only pomace from the "first pressing" is permitted for grappa production. The residual moisture is restricted by law. The leaching of the pressing residues with water, which is common in some other countries, is not permitted in Italy if it is intended to market the end product as grappa.

A distinction is made between raw—i.e. non-fermented and semifermented, and fully fermented pomace. The last of these originates in red wine production (as the color is only in the skins and is very slowly dissolved into the juice), already contains alcohol, and can be distilled as it is (which means that it is not as susceptible to infection and therefore is the kind of pomace that keeps best).

Raw pomace is the residues of white wine production and contains sugar that has first to be fermented with yeast into alcohol before being distilled.

Semifermented pomace, such as that from the production of rosé or light red wines, contains both sugar and alcohol, and it is up

Left: Pomace, preserved in safe food containers, is emptied into a hopper.

Right: The quality of the grappa that will be produced largely depends on clean storage and fermentation of the pomace.

o the distiller's discretion whether he thinks the alcohol content is indeed sufficient or whether the residual sugar should be fermented further.

If pomace cannot be distilled immediately after pressing, it must be stored it in an airtight container, and it should be ensured that no air bubbles are trapped in the container by stamping down the highly inhomogeneous mass into the storage containers.

## Distillation and storage

The yield from 220 lb (100 kg) of pomace is approximately 3 gallons (10 liters) of pure alcohol, and the figure can be considerably lower the more discriminating the distiller. At Jacopo Poli, for example, the yield is just 2.5 gallons per 100 lb (2.7 liters per 100 kg). All traditional distillers work in batches. The pomace is heated in copper pot stills using water vapor (as at Berta) or in a water bath (*bagna vapore*) that condenses any alcohol escaping, and then the heads and tails are removed. Many grappas are only distilled once, others twice or even three times.

The raw spirit may have a maximum of 86% alcohol. However, as this limit is often not used by the best distillers, it is often just 80% by volume or less. Grappa with a minimum alcohol content of 37.5% by volume is sold. A distinction is made between *grappa bianca* (not cask matured but aged in stainless steel or carboys) and the golden variants that have been matured for a shorter or longer period of time in large barrels or *barriques*. Berta has an impressive, naturally insulated storage cellar with about 1,900 barrels. Some of them are new, and some of them were previously used to contain port, sherry, or Moscato di Pantelleria. As well as oak barrels, some producers also use chestnut, cherrywood, or acacia casks. Grappas that have been matured for 12 months (including 6 months in wood) may be designated *invecchiata*. Those grappas matured for a minimum of 18 months may be referred to as *riserva* or *stravecchia*.

The residues left over from grappa production are also used, as fertilizer for the vineyards, as animal feed (the skins), or as basic materials for the production of grape seed oil (seeds only).

Left: In modern, steam heated columns, alcohol and aromatic substances are extracted from the pomace.

Right: After maturation comes bottling. This grappa has been matured in wood barrels, as the golden color shows.

# Grappa is a people drink

Grappa connoisseurs like to think that the character of the producer expresses itself in grappa as in no other spirits drink. In this respect grappas from Friuli, Piedmont, and Sicily are distinct from armagnac, cognac, and whisky. In France or Scotland it is house style that has characterized the type of product for decades and that relies on the skillful composition of various elements by a master distiller—who generally remains anonymous and is known at most to insiders.

The situation is quite different among most small grappa distillers, where the spirits reflect the personality of the distiller surprisingly clearly. Admittedly, whether a grappa tastes mellow, sharp, or complex; whether it has a fine acidic structure; or whether it is harmoniously rounded naturally depends on the choice of raw materials, the type of distillation, the level of moisture in the pomace, the filtration, and the nature and length of maturation. Someone has to make all these decisions. In the small grappa distilleries it is the owner, using the best of his knowledge and personal taste. This is especially clear with a grappa such as Grappa Original Romano Levi. The primitive, idiosyncratic, sometimes sharply rustic spirits with their hand inscribed labels are inextricably bound up with the personality of their eccentric *padrone*. The grappas of the sophisticated, urbane Jacopo Poli, by contrast, leave a completely different impression. They are accessible, elegant, fragrant, and at the same time highly complex.

Regardless of the many different stylistic genres, over recent years there has been a tendency towards early mature, well-modulated variants. Demand for the harsher spirits is dwindling and, as a result, they are more difficult to find, whereas those grappas that have more in common with a well-made fruit brandy than a classical pomace spirit are coming into fashion. This development is welcomed by some, and by others it is derided as a trend toward quickly drinkable, sometimes sugared mass market products—though, to be honest, hardly anyone will really miss dubiously tainted spirits and those wood flavored grappas that have spent far too long aging in casks.

## Nonino

No other distillery in Italy has done so much for the development of grappa. Founded in 1897, in 1967 it caused a stir with its vintage grappas and later with pomace spirits. Nowadays Giannola and Benito Nonino, and their three daughters, guarantee top-quality products. Various grappas are now produced by batch distillation in pot stills, some clearer and finer than the others. Müller-Thurgau or Fragolino, for instance—typical of their variety—have a mellow, lively taste. Production quantities fluctuate according to the quality of the wine harvest.

## Marzadro

What was begun by Attillio Marzadro almost 60 years ago is now being continued by Andrea Marzadro. The particularly moist pomace is distilled immediately after the grape harvest. This results not only in the single variety Grappa di Prosecco: the original spicy Sgnapa de Cësa is the entry level Marzadro. The Riserva Ciliego matured in cherrywood casks has a lovely aroma of dried fruit, and Grappa Stravecchia Diciotto Lune is matured for 18 months in wood. In addition to a fine, vanilla fragrance, it has extraordinary length.

### Berta

Berta distills for producers throughout Italy, but the raw materials for the spirits bottled under its own label come exclusively from Piedmont. Decisive for the quality of the grappas are fresh, not too heavily pressed pomaces that are stored in 60-gallon (225-liter) airtight containers. Distillation is in batches in copper pot stills. Around 51,500 gallons (195,000 liters) of grappa are produced a year. The very best spirits mature for up to 20 years in casks and smell of cherries, sage, or vanilla.

### Jacopo Poli

When the company was founded in 1898, nobody would have dreamed that Poli, a hundred years later, would become the most famous grappa distillery in Veneto, and for a long time this seemed highly unlikely. It was not until the 1980s that major success came in thin walled, elegant bottles and an ambitious quality philosophy. The pomaces now are distilled as quickly as possible after harvest. The products range from young Grappa del Museo through to barrique matured specialties such as Sarpa Riserva.

### Bertagnolli

Among the many grappa distillers in Trentino, Livia and Beppe Bertagnolli are the most legendary, not least because of their long history. It began back in 1870, when Austrian landowner Giulia von Kreutzenberg married an apothecary from Bolzano by the name of Edoardo Bertagnolli. Nowadays about 600,000 bottles are produced a year. The impressive range includes some unique spirits such as Grappa Puris (Teroldego, Traminer, and Chardonnay) and Grappa di Marzemino.

### Romano Levi

Romano Levi is the uncontested but controversial cult figure of the Italian distillery scene, whose brewery in Neive in Piedmont has its own museum dedicated to the history of grappa, to which a ceaseless file of admiring pilgrims make their way to honor the spirits. The secret certainly lies in the historic production facilities. Nebbiolo, Dolcetto, and Barbera pomaces are distilled over an open fire, just as they were two centuries ago. In addition the hand painted labels make the bottles expensive collectors' items.

# Selected grappas

## Avignonesi
### Grappa da vinacce di Vin Santo

Only two varieties of grappa are produced at the wine estate in Montepulciano in Tuscany. Grappa di Vin Santo is distilled from the grape varieties Grechetto, Malvasia, and Trebbiano a few days after the dried grapes are pressed. After maturation in a barrique, the spirit develops a very complex bouquet with notes of almond, dried fruits, and spices. Grappa da Uve di Vino Nobile, which is only distilled from moderately pressed, comparatively moist grape residues of the Sangiovese variety, is more floral and lighter. The red wine character is clearly discernible.

## Branca/Candolini
### Sensèa
### Monovitigno di Prosecco

The modern style grappas that go by the name of Sensèa are produced by the Candolini distillery, a subsidiary of the Branca giant. Elegance is a priority in the Grappa di Moscato, di Chardonnay, and di Pinot, with a bottle design and taste clearly aimed at younger consumers. All varieties are light, elegant, and fruity, with hardly any yeasty pomace or raisiny aroma, just fruit. This also applies to Grappa di Prosecco, which has an impressively fine fruity aroma, a light floral fragrance, and a surprisingly fine acidic structure.

## Brancaia
### Grappa 2005

Swiss-born Brigitte and Bruno Widmer took over the vineyard at Castellina in Chianti in 1981. It is currently managed by Barbara and Martin Widmer-Kronenberg. The estate's own grappa has been produced since 2002. It is made in collaboration with the noble Piedmontese distillery Berta. Merlot, Sangiovese, and some Cabernet Sauvignon are distilled. The pomace, already fermented, is introduced into pot stills after transportation. Storage in used Brancaia barriques makes a significant contribution to the character of the grappa, which is nutty and redolent of vanilla and dried cherry.

## Capovilla
### Grappa di Torcolato

Although the Venetian born Vittorio Capovilla is approaching retirement age, he has no intention of stopping work. He himself is the secret of the company's success when it comes to single variety grappas. He is one of the few distillers in Italy also known for spirits distilled from other kinds of fruit, and even from beer (Bierbrand and eau de vie de bière). Grappa di Cabernet Sauvignon and Grappa di Recioto di Amarone are made only from top-quality pomaces as moist as the rules permit, which is reflected in the surprisingly fine fruitiness. Grappa di Torcolato has nutty and spicy aromas, a complex structure, and a great deal of sweet fruitiness.

## Casimiro Poli
### Casimiro Pica d'Oro
### Trentino Grappa

The wine-growing estate run by the son Bernardino Poli is now almost better known for its grappas than for its less alcoholic products. The small distillery in S. Massenza (just 15,000 bottles are produced per year) specializes in single variety spirits from the grapes typical of Trentino—with one exception: the cuvée made from several pomace varieties distilled just after the grape harvest goes by the name of Pica d'Oro. With its aggressively pomace aroma, it demonstrates the original character of a Trentino grappa and is both rustic and powerful in the best sense of the words, if slightly sharp.

**Domenis**
**Grappa Storica Nera**

This venerable old family run business was producing pomace brandies of various sorts, including grappa, in the first half of the 20th century. Later Pietro and Emilio Domenis surprised customers with their pomace brandies that had significantly higher alcohol content than usual. Storica Stravecchia, for example, batch distilled using the vapor method, distinguishes itself with 50% alcohol by volume and five years' maturation in oak casks. Every year 500,000 barrels are marketed, including distillates from organic pomaces or kosher grappas. Storica Nera, clear as water, has a crisp fruitiness with a rustic touch.

**Giovanni Poli**
**Grappa Vecchia Riserva**

The distillery with a wine estate attached to it in S. Massenza, Trentino, is quite wrongly in the shadow of its famous namesake Jacopo Poli. Nosiola, Marzemino, and Moscato are distilled in batches and have a distinctively mellow harmonious structure. This applies too to the silkily strong Vecchia Riserva, made from white and red pomace and matured in French barriques. In contrast with many other grappas, the wood-cask character is perfectly integrated. The distillate has a mellow, fruity style and is convincingly well balanced.

**Nardini**
**Aquavite Riserva**

Bortolo Nardini moved in 1779 to Bassano del Grappa, where he purchased the now famous Osteria sul Ponte on the bridge over the river Brenta. Most prestigious is the Riserva, aged for three years in Slavonian oak barrels—a golden, full-bodied, mellow grappa made from red and white wine pomace. The Grappa Nardini is the epitome of the grappa accessible at first sip, anything but sharp. Considerably stronger (for some connoisseurs actually too strong), characterized by the wood it has been aged in, is the 15-year-old grappa created to mark the company's 225th jubilee.

**Pojer & Sandri**
**Grappa di Traminer**

Since the beginning of the 1980s two wine growers, Fiorentino Sandri and Mario Pojer, have devoted as much attention to their grappa as to their wine. The pomace intended for distilling here is often more moist than elsewhere. Particular care is given to the acidity values, and not every grappa is produced every year. The spirits made from Müller-Thurgau pomace, the rare grappas from Schiava or Moscato Rosa, and Essenzia from the pressed residues of very late-harvested grapes have become legendary. The Traminer is the very model of a single variety grappa: rose scented and clear, with a mild spicy resonance.

**Stock**
**Grappa di Julia**
**Superiore**

Surely no other grappa is as widely distributed as this distillate from northeastern Italy, marketed in its characteristic pot-bellied bottles. It is said that every Italian household has at least one bottle of it, if only for emergencies. The company's history began when Lionello Stock came to Trieste in 1884. It is now the headquarters of the biggest spirits groups in Italy. Grappa di Julia, whether clear or barrel matured, and despite the industrial continuous distillation process, has a respectable quality—a straight, typical pomace brandy, fruity and highly accessible.

# Marc from France

It's a part of France like baguettes or Camembert cheese: marc—or more correctly eau de vie de marc de raisin—the water of life from grape residues. For centuries it has been made in almost all wine-growing regions of la Grande Nation. In many districts it is still very much a part of daily life. Marc de Bourgogne and Marc de Champagne in particular have made a name for themselves beyond their country's boundaries. But it is often the rarities from Provence, Languedoc, or even Lorraine that make a journey of discovery into France's pomace brandies such a thrill.

Marc by itself doesn't mean a great deal as in France they call coffee grounds by that name too (presumably this dates back to the old French *marcher*, meaning to crush). This almost legendary commodity can only be truly discovered in its context. Marc, French pomace brandy, was served even before the French Revolution as a digestif, but usually drunk by the wine growers themselves—after work, often even before it—and in the 19th century it was also frequently enjoyed as a fortifying addition to coffee, a breakfast-time custom that has largely dwindled into obscurity over the past 30 years.

Marc production, like the production of Italian grappa, is inextricably linked with wine making. However, pomace brandy often had to compete with brandy itself. Where this became popular, as in the Charente with cognac, marc lost ground. In rural wine-growing areas such as Burgundy pomace spirits were especially appreciated, being less popular in more feudal regions.

With the exception of Alsace and Lorraine, where clear marc from aromatic pomace was popular, most French pomace spirits were matured in wooden casks and often not bottled for years. Whatever the legal requirements, spirits bearing the predicates *vieux* or *très vieux* were actually almost always very old. Many producers mature their best spirits for 8–10 years and in very special cases for as many as 40 years or longer in used (rarely new) barriques or *tonneaux*. Another term that often appears on the labels of eaux de vie de marc is *égrappé*. It refers to the fact that the grapes are stripped of their stems and most of the stalks, so that the pomace, when distilled, consists only of skins, seeds and fruit flesh residues, yeast, and wine. This makes marc particularly mellow. Marc in France is traditionally not only drunk neat but also further processed. Macvin du Jura is an aperitif enjoyed not only in the Arbois district, consisting of a mixture of marc and grape juice, similar to Pineau des Charentes from the Cognac region. The ratafia made in Champagne and in Burgundy is also in this category of marc-based mistelles. Where such aperitifs are carefully produced and stored for several years in a barrel, high-quality, clearly unique products are the result. In French cuisine the aromatic quality of marc is also renowned. Visitors to Alsace will certainly encounter the Soufflé Glacé au Marc de Gewürztraminer. Elsewhere in the country marc is used flambéed in wild game dishes or to aromatize terrines. Finally, almost every French confectioner has marc de champagne chocolate truffles in his range—if only because of the delightful name.

# France's best marc regions

Page 256: Some outstanding crus, and marcs égrappés, originate in Vougeot and other wine-growing communities on the Côte d'Or.

Page 257: The pomace is introduced into a compartment of the modern pot still at the Alsatian Distillerie Gilbert Miclo.

**France's marc producing regions**

- Champagne
- Lorraine
- Alsace
- Burgundy
- Jura
- Beaujolais
- Savoy & Bugey
- Auvergne
- Provence
- Languedoc
- Aquitaine
- Centers of marc production

In the late Middle Ages the climate must have been milder on average than it was between the 16th and 20th centuries, as grape vines thrived even north of the Nantes–Paris line. It can be assumed therefore that pomace was distilled in those times almost throughout the country, although over the ages different customs developed. While Champagne is now one of the most prominent marc regions, you have to look hard for marc in Roussillon. The fact that the northern districts were at an advantage is obvious. Pomace with a certain degree of acidity and not too much alcohol gives a more elegant marc (and in cooler climates the grapes are not as sweet as those grown under constant sunshine). Using modern technology distillers in Languedoc and Provence have succeeded in producing some highly distinctive distillates. Aficionados appreciate marc from the Rhône (Châteauneuf du Pape is also legendary for

pomace) and those of the French Basque country. The rarest—and most expensive— marcs include those distilled from Mouton Rothschild pomace in the Bordelais area, and are marketed as Eau de Vie de Marc d'Aquitaine.

A large number of designations of origin have now been established and are protected for marc or eau de vie de marc. These include Marc originaire de Bugey, Marc d'Auvergne, Marc de Champagne, Marc de Bourgogne, Marc originaire de Provence, Marc de Lorraine, Marc de Savoie, Marc originaire de Franche-Comté, Marc d'Alsace de Gewürztraminer, and Marc du Languedoc.

## Burgundy

This is perhaps the region of France that has the richest marc tradition. Tens of thousands of wine growers once distilled for their own consumption, but small-scale producers have declined notably in recent decades. Large-scale marc production is now in the hands of a few major distillers. But many wine growers still distill Chardonnay and Pinot Noir pomace, and aging for several years in characteristic Burgundy *pièces* is the norm. Marc de Beaujolais is more of a rarity, but it can be outstanding.

## Champagne

Even if many great champagne houses offer their "own" marc, for a long time now not every pomace spirit has been home produced. As red wine production in the region is almost negligible, which means that the grapes can be pressed immediately, the raw material—from the grape varieties Pinot Noir, Pinot Meunier, and Chardonnay—is still unfermented when it is delivered to the distillery and still has to be mashed before distillation.

## Jura

The Jura is the secret weapon among French marc regions. Pomace from grape varieties Savagnin, Poulsard, and Trousseau—and also those from Chardonnay and Pinot Noir—are traditionally distilled. Production is largely small scale and rustic, as it was centuries ago. Often the marc is bottled at 50% by volume alcohol. Most producers also distill a *fine*, which is a cognac-like spirit made from wine, as well as producing the marc-based Macvin.

## Alsace and Lorraine

In particular Marc de Gewürztraminer and Marc de Muscat are considered the epitome of Alsatian pomace spirits. They are generally as clear as water when bottled. Marc de Riesling and Marc de Pinot Noir are of lesser significance. Producers such as Metté, Miclo, and Nusbaumer have become renowned across the regions, although some wine growers distill their own pomace. The elusive Marc de Lorraine can be an experience—as can the rare Alsace spirits distilled from overripe late-harvested pomace.

## Provence

Marc originaire de Provence is protected and has a significant tradition, but is produced nowadays by comparatively few distillers. The specialists include Domaine Ott and Domaines Bunan. On the Rhône marc production is little publicized. Here Château Mont-Redon with its Marc de Châteauneuf-du-Pape plays a special role.

The excellent Marc du Château de Mont-Redon comes from the extremely stony vineyards of Châteauneuf du Pape.

# Bouilleurs de cru and traveling distillers

Since olden times they have been seen and heard at work—the traveling distillers. Steaming, hissing, and puffing smoke, they take up their work in late fall in the villages of the Burgundy region. Little would seem to have changed over recent decades and the tradition of the traveling distiller goes back several generations. In the 19th century as well, they began their work when the wine growers had largely finished theirs. At the end of the harvest and often right through into February, even today specialist distillers relieve the grape producers of the laborious process of distilling—a process which requires a great deal of experience and expertise. Only for a very few growers is procuring their own distillery worthwhile. Closely linked with the tradition of the *bouilleur ambulant* is that of the *bouilleur de cru*, the house distiller. It was Napoleon who brought about a revival of the industry. The French emperor decreed that the bouilleur de cru could produce a small quantity of alcohol tax free provided that the spirits were distilled from home grown ingredients. Later this rule was modified. Its complete abolition is planned. Even today more than 100,000 French citizens are privileged house distillers—and many of them allow traveling experts to do the work for them.

Fine—stripped Pinot-Noir pomace consisting only of skins, residual fruit flesh, and grape seeds—is poured into the pot still.

# The art of the bouilleur

The often ancient distillation equipment usually consists of three alembics, copper pot stills, with which almost continuous distillation is possible. While one still is gently steam heated to produce alcohol, the others can be filled with pomace or cleaned of residual material. The residue of white grapes (in Burgundy in addition to Chardonnay, also Aligoté) and of red grapes (generally Pinot Noir) is distilled. While the white pomace

does not as yet contain any alcohol and has first to be fermented, the red grapes already contain significant amounts of alcohol and can be processed immediately. In the Burgundy region stripping of the grapes has become widespread so that the pomace contains no stems or stalks. Relatively moist pomace is favored, with a high must or wine content. Above all, the freshness of the pomace is the decisive factor for the finished product. Poorly stored material affected by acetobacter bacteria, rot, or mildew gives a poor-quality distillate. The pomace from the beginning and end of each batch is unusable anyway, and the distiller has to judge exactly the right moment for removing the heads and tails.

The young marc is either matured by the bouilleur de cru himself and then diluted to drinking strength and put on the market (or drunk), or sold to one of the major spirits companies. Used barrels are preferable for maturing. Only in exceptional cases are new casks used. A well-distilled traditional Marc de Bourgogne can have its own nostalgic charm. It is usually strong—50% by volume alcohol content as a rule—has a powerful taste, and is a little sharp. Once the house distiller has finished his work, or the traveling distiller leaves the premises after completing his smoky operations to set up camp elsewhere, there remain the residues of distillation, the *fumée*. Together with the grape stems and stalks they can be used as fertilizer in wine cultivation. Virtually nothing is wasted here!

The conveyor belt for pomace (left) feeds the pot stills (center left). The alcohol content is tested using an aerometer. After the distillation process the distillation residues must be removed from the equipment (right).

# Selected eaux de vie de Marc

**Château Mont-Redon**
**Vieux Marc du Châteauneuf-du-Pape**

This *vieux* marc from grapes of the Appellation Châteauneuf du Pape has become a classic and is famed beyond France's borders. At Château Mont-Redon the pomace from many different varieties of grape is distilled carefully in a partial vacuum. The young marc matures initially for eight years in new barriques, and then for a further two to four years in well-used casks. After this time it takes on a coppery hue, with mellow aromas of pomace, cask, and caramel; it is complex and has a discreet woody note in the finish.

**Distillerie La Catalane**
**Marc de Muscat**

Distillerie Cooperative Roussillon Alimentaire La Catalane, founded in 1975 near the city of Perpignan, markets an absolute rarity in this Marc de Muscat. This once highly popular spirit is now extremely hard to find. The Eau de Vie de Marc du Languedoc, to give it its correct title, is distilled from the residues of muscatelle grapes. It is as clear as water, and it has a subtle but acutely creamy marc muscat fragrance with a slight note of dried berries. The marc is fruity and has a piquant acidity.

**Domaines Bunan**
**Vieux Marc Egrappé de Provence**

Like the wines of the Domaines Bunan in Bandol known throughout Provence, their top-quality pomace brandies benefit from the attributes of old Mourvèdre vines. The comparatively moist stripped pomace is distilled with great care in small batches in an old fashioned looking pot still. Then the proportion that is to be sold as *vieux* marc is kept for more than 10 years in barriques. Reddish golden in color, it has a slightly toasty hazelnut bouquet and is fiery in the mouth, vibrant, and very idiosyncratic.

**Domaine Désiré Petit**
**Vieux Marc Egrappé**

In 1932 Désiré Petit founded the wine-growing estate in Pupillin that is now managed by his sons Gérard and Marcel. It covers about 50 acres (20 ha) about the community and on the Coteaux du Jura. The Petits have a very traditional operation and use the large number of wine styles of the Jura, but have long been distilling their Eau de Vie de Marc de Franche-Comté, an authentic and fiery marc that is allowed to mature in small old casks.

**Domaine Virgile Joly**
**Eau de Vie de Marc du Languedoc**

In the Languedoc pomace brandy is considered a rarity and really elegant, carefully crafted variants are especially scarce. Matthieu Frecon distills pomace from mixed white and red grapes commissioned by the organic wine grower Virgile Joly into clear, fruity Eau de Vie de Marc du Languedoc. The spirit is matured for at least three years in stainless steel containers, and has a delightful aroma of dried fruits, with a slightly smoky spiciness and a rather sharp character (45% by volume alcohol).

**Joseph Cartron**
**Très Vieux Marc de Bourgogne des Dames Huguette Égrappé**

For more than 100 years now the Cartron company at Nuits-Saint-Georges has been distilling pomace, using many different techniques. Distillation is traditional, in copper pot stills. Well-used oak casks in which the spirit will age for 10 years or more are used for maturation. The influence of the wood is clearly discernable but never strident. Cartron's Très Vieux Marc Egrappé has an intensive aroma of old armagnac and plums. It is spicy, has a hint of pomace, and has a ripe, plummy, nutty resonance.

**Michel Goujot**
**Marc de Lorraine**

Wines from Lorraine are rare nowadays. Even the once famous Marc de Lorraine is hardly to be found now. Up to the the pest disaster in the late 19th century the situation was completely different. In those days grapes were grown over great swathes of the region. organic wine grower Michel Goujot is one of the last champions of his region's marc. He istills it from pomace of the appellation Côtes de Toul, using white and red grape varieties. he water clear distillate has a rather unobtrusive bouquet, is aintly floral but nevertheless uoyant, with a piquant acidity.

**Maison Védrenne**
**1992 Eau de Vie de Marc Hospices de Beaune**

The distillery established in Nuits-Saint-Georges in 1919 has made a name for itself with traditional spirits ranging from Crème de Cassis and Fine de Bourgogne through to marc. Just as legendary is the 1992 Hospices de Beaune pomace brandy, aged for several years in used oak barrels, resulting in a decidedly amber coloration. It has a clear, subtle woody note and an elegant aroma of walnut, and it is decidedly spicy, multilayered, and very crisp. A terroir marc!

**Metté**
**1990 Marc d'Alsace Gewürztraminer Vendanges Tardives**

The Metté company has become the epitome of Alsatian pomace brandies. In Ribeauvillé the rather rare Marc de Sylvaner and Marc de Riesling, Pinot Noir, and Pinot Gris are double distilled and then matured for several months in stainless steel tanks. Among their notable specialties are Marc de Gewürztraminer 1990 Vendanges Tardives, distilled from the residues of very late harvested grapes. It is floral and ripe and cannot conceal a somewhat sharp pomace taste.

**Moutard-Diligent**
**Vieux Marc de Champagne Derrière les Murs**

The Moutard-Diligent company can trace its history back to the 17th century. It is now considered to be the most important traditional distillery in the Champagne area and produces some very individual spirits. In addition to its own brands, stripped pomace in 1,320 lb (600 kg) batches is distilled on commission for reputable champagne producers, followed by a minimum of three years' cask maturation. The marc, at 45% by volume alcohol, is significantly more intensive in its aromas than that which has only 40% by volume. The clear grapey notes, the fine wood spices, and striking style are convincing.

**Nusbaumer**
**Vieille Eau-de-Vie Marc de Muscat**

Since 1947 the traditional craft distillery in Steige in the Villé valley has undergone repeated modernization. However, batch distillation in pot stills (although state of the art) has retained its traditional character. By contrast with other Alsatian distillers, Nusbaumer did not become famous for the Marc de Gewürztraminer, but for Marc de Muscat. It is aged before bottling in oak barrels, and has muscat and vanilla spiced notes and a creamy, mellow structure.

**Louis Sipp**
**Eau-de-vie de Marc Riesling d'Alsace Égrappé**

The traditional company known for its wines is right in the middle of picturesque Ribeauvillé. For its Marc Egrappé made from Riesling pomace, Alsatian-born Étienne Sipp takes his raw material from the Kirchberg and Osterberg Grand-Cru vines. After pressing, the pomace is stored in airtight containers and double distilled during the winter in a traditional alembic. The marc is fragrant and floral, and has an impressively piquant acidic structure and long finish.

# German tresters

Unlike grappa, no international cult has been formed around alcohol distilled from grape skins and seeds in Germany. Major distilleries have been somewhat neglectful in their treatment of such spirits. Their production is almost exclusively in the hands of a select few specialists, wine growers, and fruit distillers. Nevertheless—or precisely for that reason—over recent years an impressive array of first rate tresterbrands that have no need to hide behind the grappas have found their way onto the market. They are biding their time—the German tresterbrands still await the recognition they deserve.

In Germany the large distilleries have not been interested in tresterbrand. Its production has been left to the wine growers themselves. The major distillers, since the 19th century, have concentrated on brandy, leaving its poor country relations well alone. This was quite all right for the wine producers on the Moselle, Rhine, Main, and Neckar, who initially processed the residues of wine making for their own consumption. The wine from the first pressing was sold, the second pressing of pomace mixed with water made tresterwein (pomace wine), and finally the distillate from the pomace remained on the wine growers' premises.

With a name like "Trester," or in southern Germany "Treber," this spirit did not give rise to any overambitious aspirations as regards quality. It is derived from the high German *trestir*, which roughly translated means dregs, and has word associations such as "turbid" and "dirty." Until well into the 20th century tresterbrand was an unpretentious rustic product. While German wines were already starting their world conquest by the end of the 19th century, nobody troubled themselves about trester. This meant that German wine growers and vintners for a long time were able to distill whatever was available, completely unchallenged by regulations. While on the Moselle it was mainly Riesling grapes that served as the basic ingredients for trester, vintners in the Markgräfler area used their Gutedel, and those in the Württemberg area the residues of Trollinger and Lemberger grapes. Right up to the second half of the 20th century, varieties were rarely mentioned on the label. Quality consciousness was a late development. Inspired by the successes of the Italian grappa distillers on the one hand and improvements in German wines on the other, however, the 1980s brought about a change in thinking. The first

vintage and specific variety tresters came onto the market, and some vintners began to regard distilling as a business in its own right rather than merely a source of extra income. Top producers in the 1990s began to sell tresterbrands that could rival the best grappas. Descriptions such as "Mosel grappa" are still only used verbally, however. They do not appear on labels as only pomace brandies from Italy and Italian-speaking regions are permitted to call themselves "grappa." Many producers like to use the French name "marc."

German tresters are mainly distilled in copper pot stills—single distilled in the more modern systems, and double in the old fashioned ones. By contrast with Italian grappa, there is no restriction on the residual moisture content of the pomace. The distinction between Italian-style pomace brandies and tresterbrand is therefore theoretically a fluid one. By contrast with industrially produced brandies, trester is rarely distilled on such a large scale as to make the use of column stills worthwhile. Nowadays most German tresters are sold only after a long maturation period. Some spend ten or more years in oak barrels. Only a few producers experiment with other kinds of wood such as acacia, cherry wood, or mulberry.

# Germany's best trester regions

Page 208: In the Palatinate, here at the Kirchenstück, near Forst and Deidesheim, many wine growers are proud of their trester tradition.

Page 209: Freshly fermented red-wine pomace—the stuff of which (a distiller's) dreams are made.

**Germany's trester regions**

Ahr
Mosel
Rheingau
Nahe
Rheinhessen
Pfalz
Franken
Baden
Württemberg
Saale-Unstrut

☐ Trester centers

In almost all the wine-growing regions of Germany vintners also distill their pomace, provided they have the right to do so. In particular in southern Germany, and especially in Baden, these "small distillery rights" are common. Small distillers, known as *Abfindungsbrenner*, are only authorized to produce a maximum of 80 gallons (300 liters) of alcohol per year as non-bonded distillers. When diluted to normal drinking strength however this still amounts to a considerable quantity of 1-pint (0.5 liter) or smaller bottles. For a wine-growing estate that only sells pomace schnapps as a sideline, this is usually completely sufficient. The law also permits the transfer of distilling rights if their holder does not use up his own quota, or uses less than 10% of it. Apart from these small operations pomace spirits are also distilled—although not to the same extent as wine and fruit brandies—in *Verschlussbrennereien*, licensed industrial operations, production of which is taxed and bonded by the customs authorities. In Germany pomace is distilled from aromatic grape varieties such as Gewürztraminer, Muscatel, Kerner, and Neuzüchtung Morio Muscat—out of the Burgundy varieties (white, gray, and late Burgundies)—and from Chardonnay. Riesling is traditional, especially along the Moselle. Experiments with Scheurebe, Sauvignon Blanc, and Siegerrebe are still the exception

## Baden

Many wine-growing estates produce their own tresterbrand. In the Ortenau and Kaiserstuhl districts the most interesting distillates are to be found. Pomace from late burgundy wine production are favorites. They are, after all, already fermented and can be distilled without wasting any time. Baden's most expensive tresterbrand comes from Lake Constance, where Heiner Renn produces his legendary Torkelwasser.

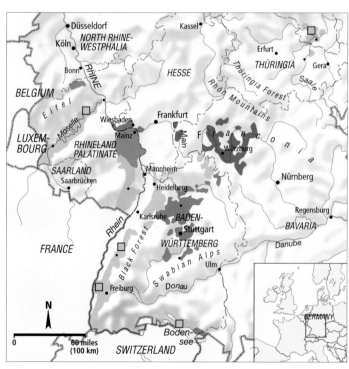

## Franconia

The Franconian trester tradition is not limited to spirits from late, gray, and white burgundies. Aromatic varieties or silvaners are processed into tresters too, the traditional rieslaners more rarely. Many wine growers distill pomace only if the vintage is suitable and stocks have sold out. Spirits distilled from Eiswein and Trockenbeerenauslese pomaces can also be found in small quantities.

## Mosel

Pomace from the Mosel area has long been almost exclusively distilled from Riesling and is often sold without having been barrel matured. It was not until recent times that high-quality cask matured spirits became established on the market. They sometimes originate in Riesling–Steillagen pomace from steep hillside vineyards and are matured for up to ten years in small casks. Certainly the most legendary Saar pomace distillates are produced in Austria by Hans Reisetbauer.

## Palatinate

Whereas many wine growers in the Palatinate prefer not to produce brandy, they do distill their pomace themselves. Just as wide ranging are the products between Alsenztal and the border with Alsatia. Outstanding are the Gewürztraminers, yielding some very vibrant, spicy pomaces, while those from Mittelhaardt often produce somewhat more elegantly fragrant spirits.

*Egon Müller's most outstanding wines come from the Wiltinger Scharzhofberg on the Saar. And from the best pomace comes an excellent tresterbrand in Upper Austria.*

*Opposite: Eiswein grapes too are given new life as pomace.*

# The finest hefebrand

Sometimes visitors get irritated. Vallendar is not only the name of a well-known distillery in the Eifel community of Kail. It is also the name of a small town just 30 miles (50 km) away. This can lead to confusion from time to time. Hubertus Vallendar merely smiles benignly—connoisseurs of high-class distillates almost always do seem to find their way to his showcase distillery experience, certainly the biggest attraction in the area. From wild raspberry through to banana or hazelnut spirits, dozens of subtle distillates are fragrantly waiting here to be discovered. Although the array of tresterbrands and hefebrands appears unprepossessing at first glance, they are Hubertus Vallendar's great passion in life. In particular heferschnaps, baby brother to tresterbrand, distilled from the lees remaining after the first decanting of the wine, has a long tradition in the Mosel area. Hubertus' father, who founded the distillery in 1967, used to experiment with hefebrand, and his son must have inherited a taste for the spirit early in life.

## Spontaneously fermented and distilled at low temperature

However, it was not until progress was made in distillation technology and wine production that the art of the hefebrand distiller could reach perfection. Huburtus Vallendar spent years making refinements to his distillery equipment in order to be able to limit the temperature, because the spirits become harsh and sharp if the temperature is too high. With the assistance of up-to-the-minute technology, Vallendar is now capable of completing the middle runnings at 181–183 °F (83 to 84 °C)—a value at which many other distillers are just beginning. The

Left: Lees are pumped into the pot still.

Right: In the combined distillation facility, the spirit is distilled in a single cycle.

aromatic components of the wine lees are transferred into the distillate with appropriate care.

Yet if the lees do not have the right provenance, all this effort would come to little. Hubertus Vallendar tried out several types of wine lees and long since ceased to use just any residues from wine preparation. The distiller now receives a supply of a mixture of wine and dead yeast cells from select producers of spontaneously fermenting wines. In particular, wine growers who allow their wines to remain on the lees until the summer or even longer can provide the distiller with aromatic, complex raw materials. In this way Vallendar can produce a citrus fruit tasting, creamy, and infinitely elegant top-quality hefebrand using 2003 riesling yeast from the Heymann-Löwenstein vineyard at Winningen by the Moselle. It has already been selected as the best European product of its kind and was awarded a legendary 96 out of 100 points at the World Spirit Awards.

The fact that the northern wine cultivations of Germany provide particularly good lees is easy to explain. Not only is acidity important for the taste of wines, but it also carries aromas into the distillation process. In the best cases it brings out in the taste the characteristics of individual vineyards, provided that the production process is not hurried. It can take quite a long time for a hefebrand to become mature enough to be diluted with spring water from prehistoric rocks to 45 or 40% by volume alcohol and then drunk. To contradict a popular misconception, spirits change not only when aged in wooden barrels, but also in stainless steel. Hubertus Vallendar has learnt that the aficionado may have to wait up to ten years before a distillate has reached the peak of perfect taste.

Left: Hubertus Vallendar checks the alcohol content.

Right: Fine yeast distillates are Vallendar's pet passion.

# Selected tresters

**Bosch Edelbrand**
**Tresterbrand vom Kerner**

Andreas Bosch is the third generation operator of the distillery in Lenningen in Swabia. He specializes in single variety fruit spirits and Swabian whisky. He obtains his pomace from the nearby wine cooperative in Neuffen in Württemberg. It is mashed on the day it is delivered and distilled immediately after fermentation. In character the spirit is surprisingly fine—you might say typically riesling—with slightly aromatic overtones and a very fruity resonance.

**Burgunderhof**
**Torkelwasser zweijährig**

Heiner Renn has become the trester specialist of Lake Constance and beyond. Although he still also distills Morello cherries, raspberries, and elderberries, it is the Torkelwasser, distilled from very moist Burgundy grape pomace, that steals the limelight here. The three variants mature for two, three, or six years in wooden barrels. The very best qualities mature in barriques. Even the two-year matured spirit has a striking fragrance of roasted nuts, dried fruit, and herbs—fiery, but soft as a plum.

**Destillerie Gutzler**
**Trester von Muskattrauben 1999**

Hardly any vintner in Germany can match the variety of trester and pomace distillates in Gerhard Gutzler's range. He has been distilling Gewürztraminer and Chardonnay grape pomace since 1991. Top-quality ingredients—moist pomace, with no added sugar—are an obvious formula for success. Gutzler has gained a reputation too for his 1999 Muscat tresters with their aromas of herbs and dates, as well as Riesling tresters with their scent of citrus. Part of the production is matured in mulberry wood barrels.

**Heinrich Männle**
**Weintresterbrand · Scheurebe Trauben Trester 1985**

The Ortenau vineyards are famous for red wines from late Burgundy grapes and white scheurebe wines. It is not surprising that Heinrich Männle and his daughter Sylvia also distill the pomace from these aromatic grapes. Their traditionally crafted 1985 scheurebe distillate has a smoky aroma reminiscent of cassis and ripe peaches. The spirit has a mature feel, having lost all its sharpness, and has a striking, almost silky structure.

**Holger Räch**
**Marc vom Gewürztraminer**

This small Palatinate distille has been making a name f itself since 1988 with Gewür traminer tresters and mar other spirits. It has won ma awards, among them the Worl Spirit Awards. Weinhefe and la Burgundy and Chardonna tresters (some in woode casks), and whole Gewür traminer grapes are als distilled. Holger Räch's Gewür traminer tresterbrand is ve typical of this grape variety lightly yeasty and reminisce of litchis, nectarines, and rose and clear as water.

**Johanninger**
**Marc**
**Sauvignon Blanc**

The three owners of this rath unusual wine factory own vine yards in Rheinhessen, in th Rheingau, and on the riv Nahe. In their tresterbrands the strive to preserve the fruity ch acteristics of the particular var ety of grape used. Silvaner an Chardonnay or the rare treste brands from Scheurebe Trock enbeerenauslese are distille in a small copper pot still an matured in glass or stainles steel. The Sauvignon Blanc is rarity, very typical of the grap variety with aromas of aspara gus and vanilla—fresh and livel

**Marder Fichtenhofbrennerei**
Weintrester Gewürztraminer

Edmund Marder has received multiple awards for his spirits—distilled using the most modern and delicate methods in a column still using a waterbath. Marder was three times in a row nominated most successful small distiller in the German Agricultural Society awards and won a gold award at Destillata 2007. His Gewürztraminer wine trester, the ingredients for which originate in the Palatinate district of Edesheim, has the clear, typical aromas of its variety: slightly earthy, very spicy to the taste, and with a distinctive presence.

**Peter Lauer**
Tresterbrand VXO

Young Florian Lauer from Ayl (in the Saar) has recently been assisting his father Peter with wine and tresterbrand production. V.X.O. is distilled in a very traditional way from riesling pomace from the best vineyards in the Saar. The spirit is then matured for eight years in used wooden barrels in a separate part of the cellar. The spirit, which has already received several awards for its category, has a distinct but very fine fruitiness with a nutty scent of dried fruits and plums. It is wonderfully delicate and highly complex.

**Rosenhut · Martin Fischer**
Tresterbrand vom fränkischen Spätburgunder

Joachim Fischer and his wife Elisabeth are members of the exclusive Rosenhut distillers' association. It imposes strict rules on its members' products. For example, the addition of sugar as a rounding element, in principle accepted in Germany, is taboo here. The late burgundy trester is distilled from their own pressing residues and aged in small barrels. It has an elegant trester aroma with slight woody tones. The woodiness is also perfectly integrated on the palate. A model Franconian trester.

**Theo Künstel**
Weintresterbrand
Im Holzfass gereift

In the middle of idyllic Waldulm is the small distillery run by the fourth generation Theo Künstel. As the Ortenau vineyards begin a very short distance away, the freshness of the pomace supplied to the distillery is guaranteed. The old distilling equipment, now on display in the garden, was replaced a long time ago by a modern installation. Double distilled tresterbrand is produced from several varieties of pomace, matures in wooden barrels, smells faintly of hazelnuts, and is spicy, dense, and has a superior resonance.

**Weingut Bercher**
1999er Burgunder Marc

The Bercher family can trace its wine-growing history back to 1457. The two brothers who now operate the estate have divided their work. Rainer Bercher is responsible for distillation, although he only distills late burgundy tresters every few years. After the 1996 came 1999, and, most recently, 2003. The 1999 currently available is double distilled and matured for between three and five years in oak barrels. The woody character is however muted. The spirit has a spicy taste and is slightly raisiny.

**Weingut Pawis**
Tresterbrand vom Edelacker Riesling

The small Saale-Unstrut cultivation area is not exactly known for its tresterbrands, but these can be of surprising quality. Weingut Pawis, one of the leading companies in the wine-growing area, distills its top spirit from very moist Riesling pomace from the noble Freyburger Edelacker vineyard. The Riesling tresterbrand is made from 2005 vintage grapes. It is as clear as water, and has the vintage-typical Riesling aromas of blossom, ripe fruit—including stone fruits and citrus—with a very delicate note of pomace.

# Tresters from Austria and Switzerland

It's not just the Italians that have developed a significant grappa tradition over the years. In Ticino pomace spirits are a part of daily life—even if this fact is studiously ignored across the Swiss–Italian border. In Lugano, Mendrisio, and Curio, vintners have been distilling the pomace of grapes from their own vineyards for centuries. Indigenous varieties such as Bonarda or Freisa were initially the main wine and grappa grapes. After the vine pest disaster, Merlot and what are known as American grapes were introduced. The latter are rarely vinified nowadays, but do play an essential role in grappa production. Ticino grappa has one further characteristic feature: it was (and still is) traditional to distill the pomace together with the lees remaining after the wine is racked off.

In particular in German-speaking Switzerland, trester production is inspired by Ticino tradition, whereas the western Swiss look rather to the practices of their French neighbors. In all three parts of the country, there are nowadays committed small and very

small producers, and also major distilleries such as Destillerie Humbel that make some noteworthy tresterbrands. Distillates from indigenous grape varieties such as Heida and Humagne Rouge are unique. Under an agreement with the European Union, Swiss tresterbrands can now call themselves grappa if they have been produced in Ticino or in the Italian-speaking valleys of Graubünden—i.e. in Val Mesolcina, Calancatal, Bergell, and Val Poschiavo, from grapes grown there. In German-speaking Switzerland they find ways to get around the prohibition on the use of the term "grappa" with the tongue-in-cheek "grappin." The traditional Swiss word "Träsch" is, however, well out of fashion.

Austria too, since the end of the 1980s, has been producing some increasingly exciting spirits. As has wine production in general, the production of pomace spirits has experienced an upturn in quality. Many wine growers distill their pomace brandies themselves and some have now become better known for their spirits than for their wines. Other producers allow the specialists to do their distilling for them. Alois Kracher, for instance, has had some success with spirits from grapes left partially to dry on the vine produced by Alois Gölles. Distiller Hans Reisetbauer seeks out the ingredients for his top-quality distillates both from among the vintners on the German Saar and in south Tyrol.

Austrian tresterbrands are distinctive for their clarity and variety of characteristics. Distillation techniques are almost always state of the art, and innovative filter systems—such as that, for instance, used by Styrian Franz Tinnauer—ensure that all remaining heads and tails are filtered out of the finished distillate.

# Selected tresters

### Alois Gölles
### Kracher Tresterbrand von Trockenbeeren

Many connoisseurs esteem Gölles as a pioneer of Austrian trester success. Top-quality double distilled spirits have been produced here since 1979. Gölles started a trend with the spirit from Trockenbeeren pomace supplied by the Kracher wine-growing estate in Burgenland (iodine, with a pinch of toasted sesame). Nowadays Sauvignon tresters from Tement or Veltliner tresters from F. X. Pichler are also used.

**Austria**

### Franz Tinnauer
### Traminer Tresterbrand

Vintner Franz Tinnauer in Gamlitz, Styria, has been specializing ever more intensively since 1990 in double distilled spirits. The tresterbränds from zweigelt and from sauvignon reserve are cask matured. The pomace from the classic series is clear and bottled at a fiery 44.5% by volume alcohol. It smells of dried blossoms and rose petals, with just a slight hint of bitterness in the resonance.

**Austria**

### Grafenwald
### Traubentrester Edelbrand

Gerd M. Jäger, Wolfgang Summer, and Bruno Ammann in Vorarlberg, Austria, have been distilling tiny amounts of every variety, but with infinite care. A raw spirit is succeeded by a fine spirit, often with an alcohol content of only 60–7% by volume. Sugar is not added under any circumstances. Maturing is partially in toasted stockinger barrels that are not used more often than twice.

**Austria**

### Jöbstl
### Tresterbrand vom Schilcher

The address of the distillery that has its own small vineyard attached speaks for itself. The name of the street in Wernersdorf/Wies in western Styria is Schilcherberg, and from the capricious, very acidic red Schilcher variety Waltraud Jöbstl distills grape and wine spirits and hefebrand as well as the pleasantly fine aromatic, fresh, zesty Schilcher tresterbrand. The wine character that remains distinctive in the distillate is notable.

**Austria**

### Reisetbauer
### 2006 Rosenberg Reserve Tresterbrand

Hans Reisetbauer was for a long time known for his fruit spirits. Then he began to scale the heights with quality tresterbrand. He has perfected the fine art of procuring the best ingredients available. German vintner Egon Müller supplies the Riesling pomace, Bernhard Ott from Wagram provides Grünen Veltiner from the high Rosenberg vineyards. The distillate is yeast, apricot, and apple scented, with a ripe, elegant, and complex character.

## Austria

### Weutz
### Arcana Rosso

The Styrian Arcana Rosso produced by Brigitte and Michael Weutz is double distilled from prefermented Merlot and Zweigelt pomace (the exact ratio is a trade secret) immediately after pressing. The select raw material comes in this case from vintner Hannes Harkamp. Weutz decided to mature his spirits in 15-gallon (56-liter) Limousin oak barrels. This process imparts to the spirit aromas of leather, yeast, and orange oil, and moreover remarkable length.

## Switzerland

### Cave Engloutie · Jürg Biber
### Humagne Rouge Marc et Lie

Jürg Biber processes in his distillery in the Swiss canton of Valais pomace (always with lees) from indigenous grape varieties such as Humagne Rouge and Heida. He experiments with the composition of the pomace and has even sieved the seeds from the grape skins, which gives a more mellow pomace brandy. The Johannisberg (Silvaner) has a grapey, discreetly bready character. The Humagne Rouge is considerably spicier.

## Switzerland

### Kunz-Keller
### Grappin Burgunder Marc und Lie

The eastern Swiss distiller of the year in 2007/8 distills in Maienfeld the prize winning grappin from his own blue Burgundy pomace. Traditionally the grape seeds and skins are distilled together with the wine lees. The grappin is clear, elegant, with just a hint of raisin, and full bodied. The Riesling x Sylvaner marc (Müller-Thurgau) and the blue Burgundy marc, matured for three years in oak barrels, have very distinctive tastes.

## Switzerland

### Sackmann
### Grappa Classico
### Roccolo alle Vigne

This little distillery in Curio in Ticino was taken over from the legendary Paul Schnell by Margrit and Rolf Sackmann. The couple now travel regularly from Truttikon in lower Zurich to Roccolo alle Vigne, where they press wine and distill Grappa Classico from American grapes. The clear spirit is considered to be one of the most famous and most prized pomace brandies in Ticino. It has a fine, neutral character and is strikingly fiery.

## Liechtenstein

### 2005er Marc
### Liechtensteiner Edelbrand

The Lichtenstein production of wine and grappa is as tiny as the principality itself. Hansjörg Goop fills just a few bottles per year, all of which are numbered. The 2005er marc was distilled from Pinot Gris and Chardonnay pomace and has no added sugar. It has a reticent, raisiny taste, with a slight hint of vanilla and dried apricot. It is surprisingly mellow and wonderfully full bodied.

# Spanish orujo

No *poteiro*, no orujo. No distiller, no pomace brandy, or to give it its correct name, no aguardiente de orujo. If the golden rule of Spanish pomace brandy production sounds at first like a truism, it still makes sense. It is not the equipment that is the most important thing, but the skill of those operating it. Particularly in the northwest Spanish region of Galicia, in the comparatively cool district between the Atlantic coast and the Portuguese border, there is a long tradition of distilling grape pomace. It is also to be found in the adjacent provinces, but more rarely in other parts of Spain. The fact that in Ribera del Duero too, top-quality orujo has recently been distilled from Tempranillo, Cabernet, and Merlot has less to do with tradition than a desire to experiment and improve quality. The same applies to marc from cava grapes that some Catalonian producers distill and market professionally, primarily from the classical cava grape varieties Xarel-Lo, Parellada, and Macabeo. The north–south divide in pomace brandy did not occur by chance. Just like in Italy or France, in Spain too the northern wine-growing areas offered better climatic conditions. The pomace did not spoil as quickly as in the hotter south. Another reason was that in a traditionally poor district such as Galicia, the vintners, more than anywhere else, were forced to exploit every available source of income.

## Poteiro and Pota

The most important tool of the *poteiros*, the distillers in Galicia, is, of course, the *pota*, the copper kettle into which the pomace is poured. More than anywhere else, distillation in Galicia is considered to be a craft, an almost magical activity, demanding an appropriate measure of creativity as well as much experience and expertise. The pomace, fermented in open buckets, and supplemented with a little wine, is carefully distilled, often over an open fire. One distillation cycle, the *porada*, traditionally takes at least six hours. Frequently the raw spirit is refined in a second cycle. The stuff that is eventually bottled, diluted with a little water to drinking strengths that are nevertheless quite strong, is the pride of many vintners in the country. At 37–50% by volume alcohol the rustic pomace brandies do generally seem somewhat crude. No matter how skillful the *poteiro*, you can generally expect some impurities, burnt flavors, or other imperfections in the taste of such distillates. Industrially produced orujos are often clearer and sound, but perhaps they lack that special quality, the individuality of the

A phalanx of Galician pomace brandies. They include some rustic, some somewhat neutral, and some real works of craftsmanship. Sometimes the bottle has to make up for what the spirit can't offer.

rustic spirit. No orujo is quite like any other to drink, and this too is attributable to the composition of the particular pomace from which it is made. Albariño, Loureira, Torrontés, and Treixadura are the favorite grapes for distilling, although at times rare indigenous red-wine varieties are also used. Orujo de Galicia at its best is awarded a quality seal (D.E.: Denominación Especifica) by the inspection authority. Water clear orujo and the rarer cask matured orujo envejecido are entitled to use the appellation.

Fresh, unstripped pomace ready for distilling. In Galicia, often very small *potas* are used for the purpose.

# Portuguese bagaceira

As is the case elsewhere with pomace brandies, in Portugal aguadente de bagaceira is mainly consumed in the country itself. By contrast, for instance, with port, the grape pomace spirit, also referred to as destilação do bagaço, has never achieved international significance. This is regrettable. The country's countless indigenous grape varieties are able to impart to Portugal's pomace brandy a highly unique taste and character. Bagaceira has a higher status in northern Portugal, although it is produced in other regions. Bagaceira do Minho and Bagaceira Vinho Verde are perhaps the most prestigious varieties. However, bagaceira also exists in the Rabatejo and in the Alentejo regions. In the better class bars of Lisbon and Oporto, bagaceira do Douro and bagaceira da Bairrada are also to be found. It is the custom to allow single or double distilled spirits to mature in oak barrels. The best (and so the most expensive) examples may be aged for 2 years or longer—15 years or even more is not unusual. The pomace brandy labeled *velha* in such cases is not necessarily more balanced or better than the clear variants, and may ultimately be too intensively permeated by the wood.

On the Douro, famous for its port wine and increasingly for great dry red wines, some good bagaceiras are also distilled.

## Caves Primavera

These cellars, about an hour's drive south from Porto in the Bairrada, were established in 1947 by brothers Vital and Lucénio de Almeida. They are renowned for their vibrant, long-lived red wines. The use of red wine pomace is discernable in their prestige pomace brandy Bagaceira Velha Balseirinha. It has a mellow golden hue, and distinct notes of plum and creme caramel. Mild and balanced in taste, it has a slightly peppery tone but a dominantly plummy finish.

## Cooperativa da Covilhã

This collective, which has almost 1,200 members, is located in the Beiras interior where the climate is quite harsh and both white and red wines have a good level of acidity. For this reason the pomace is highly suited to distillation and the spirits produced age very well. Evidence of this is furnished, for instance, by the Aguardente Bagaceira Velha Centum Cellars, barrel matured for 15 years. This amber colored spirit has an elegant aroma of plums and nuts, and a hint of tobacco. It has an echo of sweetness, but also a capricious, slightly dry woody note.

## Casal de Valle Pradinhos

Surrounded by unspoilt countryside, Rui Cunha, on a remote estate in the Minho region, makes highly characterful wines from traditional grape varieties Tinta Roriz and Touriga Naçional and from 30-year-old Cabernet Sauvignon vines. His Aguardente Bagaceira Velha (50% alcohol by volume) has a distinctive personality. This dark spirit has tones of vanilla, spice bread, and apples. It has a sweet fruitiness and would be even better had it been matured in better barrels.

## Vinhos Campelo

Joaquim Miranda Campelo began to make his own wine in 1923, and founded the wine company that exists today in 1951. Since then it has become one of the most important producers of vinho verde. Managed by the three Campelo brothers, it also sells Douro, Dao, and beiras wines, as well as four different bagaceiras. Its Morgadinha Aguardente Bagaceira Vinho Verde is clear as water, and has a crisp, sweetish pomace bouquet and a seductive apples and pears fruitiness. It has a fiery bite in keeping with its youth.

# Greece:
# tsipouro and tsikoudia

Distilling pomace brandy in Greece was always the prerogative of small vintners and wine growers. They sold the final product if they did not consume it themselves. The name of this spirit is directly derived from *tsipoura*, pomace, although it is commonly also called by other names. In Crete they call it "tsikoudia" or "raki" (not to be confused with the Turkish brandy) or "apostagma." The last named is generally used to refer, particularly if it is accompanied by the word *stafilis*, to a grape spirit—i.e. the distillate from whole, fermented grapes, including juice and fruit flesh, of which there is also a tradition in Greece.

Tsipouro production was characterized for centuries by old fashioned equipment and oral tradition. Between September and December, after the wine harvest, the vintners set to work, shoveling pomace into small, often hand beaten copper pot stills.

The distillate was quite often aromatized using aniseed before the second distillation cycle, to create a predecessor to the modern ouzo. It was the large producers, led by Tsantali a few decades ago, that took the initial steps toward making tsipouro into a quality product. Technology became more reliable, and the selection of available ingredients better. Nowadays just a few producers dominate the quality pomace brandy market, but tsipouro is still produced in a traditional manner, as at Tsantali, in hand beaten copper pot stills in a double distillation process. This takes place immediately after the grapes have been pressed and the pomace fermented. Long-term storage of the raw material is unusual, as is maturation of the distillate in wooden barrels. Tsipouro is generally stored in stainless steel, and bottled at the earliest opportunity.

In modern cellars in Drama, Costa Lazaridi keeps top-quality pomace for distilling some very respectable tsipouro.

# Selected tsipouros

**Kooperative von Ioannina**
**Tsipouro Epirotiko Zitsa**
Zitsa is the name of a municipality and of a designation of origin in the Epirus region of northwestern Greece. Like almost all tsipouros in the district, it too is distilled from grapes of the indigenous Debina white grape variety. They are fermented immediately after pressing and quickly distilled. A comparatively neutral scented, slightly floral distillate is concealed in the attractive bottle. It has a light and pleasant, fruity, sweetish character.

**Lazaridi**
**Tsipouro Idoniko**
Costa Lazaridi is considered to be one of the most innovative Greek producers of wine and pomace brandies, as well as grape spirits, the latter being distilled from single grape varieties such as Cabernet Sauvignon. Lazaridi pomace brandy is a mixture of various grape varieties. Double or triple distillation in ultramodern copper pot stills produces a remarkably fine spirit. Tsipouro has a clear, slightly fruity aroma, and it is mellow and pleasant to drink, with a sweet fruity finish.

**Lazaridi**
**Tsipouro Idoniko anisé**
Aromatized tsipouro is produced to the same criteria as the other distillates. Aniseed is added during the distillation process. By contrast with its non-aromatized cousin, this spirit should be enjoyed cold, preferably at 39–43 °F (4–6 °C). Its fine aniseed/licorice aroma then comes into its own. It also has a spicy taste and a surprisingly mellow character. Tsipouro Idoniko anisé deserves the recognition it has received at the International Wine and Spirit Competition.

**Tsantali**
**Tsipouro Alexander the Great**
Nowadays the company is considered to be one of Greece's major wine producers. Its history dates back to 1890. In addition to producing red and white wines, it has dedicated itself to making some very high-quality pomace brandies. The pomace for this tsipouro, with its 38% by volume alcohol content, comes from grapes from Mount Athos, such as the Asyrtiko and Roditis varieties. Aniseed is not used in its production. The spirit has a very clear and fruity bouquet. It has some light notes of pomace. It is pleasant, mellow, fruity, and mild on the palate.

**Tsantali**
**Makedoniko Tsipouro**
At 44% by volume alcohol, this tsipouro is rather fiery by northern Greek standards. But this Macedonian pomace brandy has another characteristic typical of its kind: its aniseed aroma. After the first distillation cycle aniseed is added to the raw spirit, then distilled with it into the final product. A faint hint of licorice is clearly detectable in the bouquet, but is pleasantly subtle. The distillate becomes slightly milky due to the essential oils once water is added—a reaction that is appreciated particularly in an aperitif.

# Pomace brandies worldwide

Nowadays pomace brandies are made almost everywhere that wine grows. But traditions vary and can be one way of dividing producing countries into two groups. Whereas some, over the centuries, have developed their own culture of rustic pomace spirits, others have taken modern grappa as their model. The first group includes pomace brandies such as can be found in Turkey, Russia, the Ukraine, and Georgia. In Luxembourg, Croatia, and Slovenia too, vintners have known for generations how to process pomace into alcoholic spirits. The synonyms are appropriately diverse. Hungary speaks of Törkölypálinka, in Bolivia people drink Singani, and Georgian distillers speak of Chacha.

The second group of pomace spirits is created across the oceans, and is an imitation of modern Italian grappa or top-quality German and Austrian spirits. They have been created wherever ambitious vintners, wine cellars, or specialist fruit distillers wanted to create a European-style spirit—for example in South Africa or in California. Even if some producers use the appellation "Grappa" unchallenged by law in their own countries as soon as they wish to market their products within the area of the European Union, their bottles must bear a different label. The French name "marc" is not a problem. It has become established even in English speaking countries, in particular to denote a particular quality.

Pinotage pomace makes a surprisingly fine spicy spirit.

# Selected pomace brandies

## Georgia

**Telavi Wine Cellar**
**Grape Chacha**
In 1997 the Wine Cellar, founded back in 1915, came under new management. Here pomace spirits are produced that reflect the whole range of indigenous grape varieties such as Saperavi and Rkatsiteli, without neglecting the international varieties Cabernet Sauvignon and Merlot. This pomace brandy is clear, floral, has a faint aroma of damp cellars, and comes across as somewhat oxidative.

## Israel

**Jonathan Tishbi**
**Alembic White Brandy**
The history of the Tishbi wine-growing estate can be traced back to the year 1882. Michael Chamiletzki, the grandfather of Jonathan Tishbi, was then working for Edmond de Rothschild, planting vines. Tishbi's White Brandy is distilled from residues of French Colombard grapes in an alembic that will soon be 100 years old. The pomace brandy is spicily sweet, and has a faintly raw but very individualistic character.

## Canada

**Okanangan Spirits**
**Gewürztraminer Marc**
Frank Deiter speaks with an unmistakable north German accent. No less German is the recipe for the pomace spirit from this small Canadian distillery. Here pomace is distilled from Pinot Gris, Riesling, Siegerrebe, and even from Auxerrois. The gewürztraminer is clearly fruity, with an aroma of litchis and tea roses. It's fresh and crisp on the palate.

## South Africa

**Wilderer**
**Edelbrand Pinotage**
German-born Helmut Wilderer has made a name for himself in South Africa as a maker of fruit spirits and Fynbos Kräuterschnaps. An ultramodern copper pot still is used for batch distillation, just once. The spirit leaves the installation with an alcohol content of 70–5% by volume before being reduced to drinking strength. The Pinotage pomace brandy that Wilderer produces, in addition to its Muscatel and Gewürztraminer pomace spirits, is an absolute rarity. Very spicy, herbal, slightly yeasty, and with its own wholly unique character.

## United States of America

**St. George Spirits**
**Marc of Zinfandel**
Jörg Rupf Carmyle, born in Alsace, Germany, became a specialist in fruit distillation in California in 1982. He distills in an ultramodern installation although only in small 26-gallon (100 kg) batches. The ingredients for Marc of Zinfandel come from Rosenblum Cellars. This mellow and very fruity spirit which smells of dried blueberries is produced in small quantities (around 400 cases per year).

# Ultimate pomace brandies: whole grape spirits

For a long time Italian distillers concentrated on grappa. Whole grape spirits were neglected to such an extent that *acquavite d'uve* for a time was even prohibited by law. For decades only wine or pomace with a restricted moisture content was permitted to be distilled. Then the Nonino family in Percoto in Friuli, on November 27, 1984, distilled the first official whole grape spirit. This meant that the Noninos, after harvesting, not only mashed the skins, seeds, and lees, but also used the entire stripped grape, including must and fruit flesh. They called their product Ùe and initially only made a couple of hundred bottles of it. As with the first single variety Nonino grappa a few years previously, once again it was the Picolit grape that served as guinea pig in the experiment.

Other producers such as Poli, Pojer & Sandri, and Marzadro soon followed suit and since then, *aquavite d'uve* has established itself as a spirit in its own right. Whole grape spirits are not just prestige gimmicks. They can possess a quite individual character, mellow and aromatic, without the sometimes raisiny, yeasty overtones of a pomace brandy. This has been recognized too by producers in Germany, Switzerland, and Austria. Nevertheless, only a tiny quantity of such specialties is made. Most of them are clear when they come onto the market—i.e. not cask matured.

Italy's first whole grape spirits were distilled by Nonino in these small stills in 1984.

**Italy**

### Nonino
### Üe Moscato Cru

...all started with a whole grape brandy from Picolit grapes. Later, the Noninos steadily expanded their range, and nowadays the precious Üe, presented in luxurious bottles, is also distilled from mixed white or red grapes. The variants from Fragolino or Traminer grapes and the dark amber coloured Riserva dei Cent'Anni, matured for 12 years in a barrique, have a particularly intensive taste. The Üe from Moscato grapes has an intensive fresh berry taste, and is very clear and brisk with a distinctly floral note and an almost exotic fruitiness, combined with a full body and length.

**Germany**

### Dirker · Traubenbrand von Morio-Muskat-Trauben

Franconian Arno Josef Dirker began with apple schnapps from his own orchards. Nowadays his range numbers around 50 distillates. The products vary from wild damson to hazelnut spirits. The distillery has now moved from Bavaria to Hesse. For the fine 2001 vintage Morio-Muskat grape spirit, the mash was fermented in small synthetic containers and was then distilled in copper stills. Variety as well as a typical mild Muscat aroma and a silky spiciness are the distinctive characteristics of this spirit.

**Germany**

### Hubert Gerhart
### Gewürztraminer-Traubenwasser

The small Jechtingen company has already won an array of medals for its spirits. In addition to tresterbrand, weinhefebrand, and fruit spirits, Hubert Gerhart distils grape spirits from Chardonnay and Muscatel grapes in his traditional copper pot still. The Gewürztraminer grape spirit matures in oak barrels and has an intriguing dark golden color and the aroma of ripe Traminer grapes.

**Germany**

### Weingut Göhring
### Siegerrebe · Weintraubenbrand

This wine-growing estate in Flörsheim-Dalsheim in Rheinhessen achieved uncommon fame with a quite common grape variety. The Siegerrebe is well known for wines that are only convincing where the must weight is extremely high. Yet there are no intrusive aromas in this double distilled spirit that has been the recipient of multiple awards—just pleasant notes of exotic fruits and mild spices.

**Switzerland**

### Humbel
### Muscat Bleu

This distillery in German-speaking Switzerland, founded in 1918, is considered to be a specialist in fruit and pomace spirits. Lorenz Humbel is even experimenting with sets containing one whole grape spirit, one pomace spirit, and one brandy of the same grape variety. Its Muscat Bleu, one of the varieties from the Muscatel family that is predominantly sold in Switzerland as a table wine, comes from grapes from his own little vineyard. The spirit smells of dried blueberries. It is sleek and straight with a piquant acidity.

# Savoring pomace brandies

Grappa for breakfast? A splash of marc with your coffee? Such delightful customs, widespread among the Italian and French rural populations just a few decades ago, are now a thing of the past. The custom of "killing the worm" in the morning, as the French would say, has disappeared together with the 60% volume, raw, burnt tasting rustic grappa of the old days. Nowadays pomace brandies are enjoyed as a stylish digestif—and unfortunately only rarely mixed.

A dégustatation of grappas or other pomace brandies has more in common with a wine tasting than many would believe. With a little experience the grape varieties used in a good, well-distilled grappa are often discernable in the taste. Connoisseurs can often even detect the origin of the barrel types used in maturing. For a more precise identification of the aromas, they often rub a couple of drops of grappa onto the palm of the hand to get a feel for the character of the spirit. Taste too, is, of course, very revealing. Acidity and bitter constituents betray a great

deal about the grape varieties or the work o the distiller, sharpness gives clues to filtra tion, maturation, and the type of distillatior process. A mouthful of milk is said to reneu tralize the palate between two spirits.

Anyone who does not taste grappa & co. pro fessionally but simply wants to enjoy them at their best needs only two things—the idea pomace brandy and the right glass. Repu table suppliers such as Schott-Zwiesel Spiegelau, and Riedel have not just one, bu several variants in their range. It is importan that the capacity of any glass is neither too large nor too small. In a glass that is too large the alcohol comes too intensively to the fore A glass that is too small prevents the aromas from unfolding properly. Glasses for aro matic spirits (gewürztraminer, moscato, and scheurebe) should be somewhat taller and like white wine glasses, first taper toward the top and then widen again. For barrel maturec grappas, glasses that are slightly more bul bous, opening into a straight cylinder at the top, have proved to be ideal. Traditiona

Left: Grappa from single grape varieties—here Arneis—is a taster's delight.

Middle: Romano Levi's grappa with chamomile flowers preserves an ancient tradition.

cylindrical schnapps glasses and tumblers, but also the very bulbous cognac balloons, are completely unsuitable for top-quality pomace brandies.

## Pleasantly warm

In any case, the temperature must be right. Below 46–50 °F (8–10 °C), no grappa can develop its aroma fully; and 57–61 °F (14–16 °C) is about right for high-grade, long cask matured marcs or tresters. Higher temperatures allow the alcohol to dominate and heavy odors to come to the fore. It should also be taken into account that the liquid, once in the glass, does quickly warm up.

If grappas and their cousins are to be used as bar mixers, the traditional cocktail rules should be observed, including those regarding temperature. The fact that pomace and whole grape spirits are hardly ever used as mixers is very regrettable and not to be explained by their quality. Countless short cocktails and long drinks would benefit from a subtle, barrel matured grappa in the place of brandy, and would taste all the more fine, elegant, and aromatic. Even classic cocktails such as the Side Car (perhaps with a not too strong barrel influenced Marc de Champagne) or an Alexander (with a decidedly spicy Moscato grappa from Berta) could be varied in this way, while aromatic, clear pomace or whole grape spirits such as Morio-Muskat from Dirker are best used in Sours. Pomace brandies are not to be underestimated as ingredients in fine cuisine. An ice parfait with a shot of Marc de Muscat, caramelized grappa grapes (with goose or duck liver or game terrines), and a riesling distillate in a sauce with breast of pheasant can have a wonderful effect on the taste of a meal. The only proviso is that the bottle should not have been standing open for months or years. Clear spirits quickly lose all fine aromatic components until only various oxidative odors remain.

Matured for years in oak barrels, this grappa from Berta is a versatile digestif.

# Fruit brandies

Today top-quality fruit brandy is produced in state-of-the-art distilling columns.

Opposite: Some types of brandy are made from fruit varieties grown solely for this purpose.

Page 232: Only fully ripe cherries produce a quality brandy.

# The soul of the fruit

Of all the spirits it is fruit brandy, or fruit schnapps, that conveys the purest taste of the fruit from which it is made. Certainly in the case of high-quality brandies, that is. A good distillate is not oversweet but is naturally fruity; it is not aggressive in the mouth, but flows gently down the throat. There is no irrevocable passing of the "good old days" to be mourned in the case of fruit brandy as the quality has never been as good and the range of products never as extensive as they are today, with high-quality raw materials and modern machinery producing distillates the like of which was unknown previously. Today's quality fruit brandy varieties extend to the bounds of what is possible—with the prices being no exception either.

On April 20, 2007 a group of enthusiasts met together with experts from the renowned Wädenswil research institute in Stetten, in the Swiss canton of Aargau, for the First Schnappsologist Congress. What sounds somewhat lighthearted was in fact a serious occasion. The subtitle "Controlled Spontaneous Fermentation," too, was less a provocative contradiction than an open-minded challenge to the participants to sound out the possibilities of a new fermentation technique.

Events such as these reflect current sentiment among the top distillers: they are eager to perfect their craft down to the finest detail, even if this means exploring unknown territory. There are, of course, still farmers using up left-over produce and these continue to make up the bulk of the farm-produced schnapps. In southern Germany alone 30,000 people are authorized to produce brandies and the situation is similar in Austria and Switzerland. Fruit brandy remains a part of national identity throughout the Balkans, where sensory quality often takes second place to alcohol content.

It was in the 1980s that the first rethinking took hold among distillers, especially in Austria. They were mostly young people who had taken over their parents' enterprises and were faced with the less than attractive prospect of spending the rest of their days producing fruit at cheap prices for bulk buyers. It was then that innovative new solutions became apparent. The first meaningful experiments took place in the washhouses of Vorarlberg and Styria. True miracles of taste were derived from fruit of outstanding quality in carefully pursued production processes. There was not yet a market for noble fruit brandy, but *digestifs* were just coming into fashion and many of the new fruit brandy varieties were thus able to capture their first niche market in the better restaurants. Instead of a basic fruit brandy distilled primarily for conserving fruit, there now appeared first-class Williams, apple, and damson brandy varieties, the aromatic clarity of which was and is unique. Once all of the difficulties of fermentation and distillation had been understood it became clear that small differences can have a big effect. A Gravenstein apple, distilled homogeneously, is able to retain its characteristic flavor just as an Elstar or a Cox Orange can, while the idiosyncratic Subirer pear with its small, hard fruit develops its very own flavor when distilled. Many top distillers today cultivate virtually extinct fruit varieties. Fruit, leaves, roots, and whatever is to be found on the wayside are what find their way into the mashing tub, be it mushrooms or geraniums from the window box. The circle of those keen on experimenting has since come to include distillers in the United States, South Africa, and Australia where fruit brandies and schnapps with a well-earned reputation are produced.

# The fruit brandy business

Fruit brandy is evidently a European development originally deriving from the Alemannic realm. It was in regions that did not enable wine production, at least not without considerable effort, but where the natural climate and soil conditions favored fruit farming, that the production of fruit brandy took hold—centuries later, and once fruit must, largely from apples, had long become established. This applied in particular to the northern side of the Alps and the Rhine Valley with the Vosges Mountains bordering it, and the Black Forest. If we ignore the period when distillates were significant only as remedies, the distilling of fruit only began to gain increasing popularity from the first half of the 16th century. It was an additional source of income for farmers (particularly if they did not own any forested land) who no longer had to despair at surpluses of fresh fruit on the market in good years as they were able to convert part of their perishable goods with very little effort into a product that was non-perishable and in demand. In bad years, on the other hand, when thunderstorms before the harvest had perhaps made the fruit unsalable, the windfall fruit could still be saved by mashing, fermentation, and distilling.

Over the course of time, and especially once agriculture had recovered from the devastating effects of the Thirty Years War, what was once a sideline developed into a lucrative source of income. A classic example is the Rench Valley in the Black Forest, where the coopers' guild attempted to secure a monopoly over distilling rights in the 18th century, an approach that threatened the survival of the farmers. The latter received unexpected support from the bishop of Strasbourg, Armand Gaston Maximilien de Rohan-Soubise, who was also the sovereign squire to whom a decree dating from 1726 granted the right to distill cherries and sell the brandy—albeit not without first committing them to the payment of taxes in return. Distilling also became a set feature of fruit utilization in other regions and countries while ultimately making the supply and/or drinking of fruit brandy an indispensable part of hospitality. This applies to Austria's Styria region, known as the fruit basket,

as well as to central and east European countries, and to the Balkans where plum brandy varieties in particular have established themselves as the national drink. There is evidence of their having been produced in Hungary since the 17th century.

Home distilling remains a part of everyday life to some extent in these countries today, while it has become a large-scale business in Germany, Austria, and Switzerland, depending on the quantity of (pure) distilled alcohol. In Germany, where 26 million bottles of fruit brandy are bought and therefore also drunk annually—making Germany the world's largest market for fruit brandy—the Spirits Monopoly Act distinguishes between sealed distillers, authorized sellers, and stock owners. The sealed distillers include commercial alcohol producers and small-scale farm distilleries producing up to 106 gallons (400 liters) of pure alcohol annually. Since in principle alcohol is subject to spirits tax, the treasury requires that those parts of the distillery where alcohol is produced be held under seal. Exceptions are granted by the customs authorities and the monopolies commission for authorized sellers who are permitted to produce a legally controlled amount of alcohol tax free using their own "simple distilling equipment." Authorized sellers without their own simple distilling equipment are the so-called stock owners: persons who have produced their alcohol-producing materials themselves. The amount of fruit brandy made in one year of operation may not exceed 13 gallons (50 liters) of pure alcohol. As already mentioned, distilling fruit brandy can be a large-scale business.

Of the 26 million bottles of fruit brandy consumed annually in Germany, about 60% is pit fruit brandy made from apples and/or pears (Williams pears are the most popular), quinces, and sorb fruit. This is followed by stone fruit brandy varieties such as cherry or damson brandy, yellow plum, sloe, or apricot, as well as elder brandy. Bringing up the rear are the berry brandy varieties or spirits made from raspberries, blackberries, red currants, blueberries, or cranberries, as well as from berries that are not in fact berries, such as rose hips, rowan berries, or medlars.

Farms, such as this one in Allgäu, that harvest their own raw materials for distilling, are officially known as stock owners.

# Before distilling the fruit

Distilling is a skilled trade with a three-year apprenticeship and anybody who has ever had anything to do with the distilling of fruit will know why. Fruit is delicate and perishable, unlike the robust barley used for whisky, the indestructible grain varieties (or other raw materials) used for vodka, or rum's tenacious molasses. And high-quality fruit brandy can only be made from high-quality raw materials. It is the sugar, acid, and water content of the fruit that determines whether it will produce a noble brandy, as well as its quantities of natural yeast, natural preservatives, and natural flavorings. Distillers increasingly opt for organically grown fruit with its unadulterated variety characteristics and lack of the pollutants that can lead to undesired results in the distillate.

## Flawless fruit mash?

The harvest is the next stage that determines the quality of the brandy as the fruit needs to be harvested in as unspoilt a condition as possible. Depending on the variety, the fruit is either picked by hand or shaken or knocked into nets spread out under the trees. Windfalls, which have already been exposed

to millions of microorganisms in the grass, increase the incalculable risk of spoiled fermentation in the mash.

Since all parts of the fruit obviously affect the flavor of the brandy, not always positively, the stalks and leaves are removed before mashing (they produce too much of a green note), while stone fruit is often completely pitted provided that no part of the stone is required for an almond nuance. If this is the case the mincing of the fruit must be done carefully to ensure that the stones do not crumble because they have substances on the inside that can be toxic (purist distillers even remove the core from pit fruit). It is clear that every fruit variety requires a different degree of mechanical manipulation in order to produce a mash with the ideal consistency. Some types of fruit, such as quinces for example, have such a firm cell structure that mechanical measures alone are not enough. The addition of enzymes that break down the pectin is recommended in such cases in order to liquefy the mash, together with the addition of water if necessary. Cavities where mold can develop are formed if the mash is too dry. Once the fruit has been

Left: The fruit is shaken from the tree using a stick and caught in nets.

Right: The leaves and stalks are then carefully removed and the fruit is sorted.

mashed the yeasts are able to come into ample contact with the sugar contained in the juice. Fermentation usually starts once the number of living yeast cells reaches at least 6,000/cubic inch (100,000/cm³) of mash.

## Bubbling away …

This is where the next problem comes in: only 3% of the large quantities of natural yeasts in the fruit peel that generate the fermentation are in fact desirable. The vast majority can produce the wrong nuances or render the spirit completely undrinkable. Hence the natural conditions in the mashing tub soon become an all or nothing gamble. In order to avoid fruit and time having been invested for nothing, the "good" yeasts are boosted with the addition of pure cultured yeast so that they gain the upper hand straight away. Spontaneous fermentation will set in if the right moment is missed, damaging the additional yeasts: the fermentation will be too strong, the related temperature increase too great, and a loss of flavor is the result. The living yeast cells need sufficient nourishment to be able to perform their task of converting the existing sugar into alcohol and carbon dioxide as efficiently as possible. Some fruit varieties, such as sloes or rose hips, do not always provide this nourishment, so the addition of mineral nutrients (nitrogen compounds) is then required—insofar as this is not prohibited, as it is in Germany.

Supplied with sugar, amino acids, and mineral nutrients in a healthy mash, the ideal fermentation temperature for the yeasts is 64–68 °F (18–20 °C). Undesired microorganisms such as acetic, lactic, and butyric acid bacteria also flourish under the same conditions. Fortunately, their acidic nature makes them more sensitive than the yeasts and they become inactive at a pH value of 3.3. If the fruit mash is not sour enough it needs to be further acidulated in order to prevent it spoiling. The mash containers are kept airtight for the same reason, in one direction at least: nothing is allowed to enter but it must be able to let things out. The fermentation of 660 lb (300 kg) of fruit mash can produce up to 2,380 gallons (9,000 liters) of carbon dioxide—up to 320 cubic feet (9 m³), which escapes through the sealing liquid in a specially constructed fermentation bung.

Left: The fruit is pitted in the next stage of the process.

Right: The fruit is now ready for mashing.

# Distilling starts

The ideal temperature should be kept as constant as possible during the fermentation process, which takes from ten days to several weeks, irrespective of the type of fruit. Modern stainless steel containers can therefore be temperature controlled as required. Distilling starts, again irrespective of the type of fruit, only once fermentation draws to an end or has already ended as the flavor reactions can otherwise interfere with the specific fruit aromas.

It takes a great deal of expertise before the mash is ready to go into the distilling tank and the last hurdle is checking that the fermentation is complete. The fact that no more gas is escaping only means that the yeast is no longer working. You cannot tell reliably from either the appearance or the taste of the mash whether fermentation has paused or come to an end. Commercial test methods are needed to ensure clarification and tables listing how much of which substances in which fruit mashes are to be expected following completion of fermentation are also helpful. Once fermentation has reached a satisfactory conclusion, you then have to be careful not to ruin a successful brandy in the distilling tank by heating the mash too quickly. The solid mash contents can catch and burn just as in a saucepan, resulting in fruit flavors being lost or superimposed with bitter, burnt nuances. Some fruit types, such as elder or morello cherries, can also froth to such an extent that the foam rises as far as the swan neck and/or the spirit tube intended for the liquid. Modern distilling tanks are therefore no longer subjected to direct heat but are heated using heating coils, preferably in a bain-marie. The temperature is continually measured at a number of points and a computer processes the data, controlling the distilling process at the optimal temperature.

The liquid that evaporates and condenses until the mash is heated to about 172 °F (78 °C) is considered to be unusable and is siphoned off as the first running. This is followed by the middle running—the focus of all of the distiller's efforts so far—and finally, once the alcohol and flavor content drop dramatically, the end running that is also siphoned off. Distillation takes place in a traditional distilling bubble in a single, largely curved, direction: the vapors rise in the heated tank, they exit via the swan neck where they are cooled and precipitate in

This state-of-the-art, computer-controlled distilling plant at Christoph Kössler's distillery in the Tyrol ensures that the distilling process produces the ideal flavor.

quid form into a second container. This so-called raw distillate is still unusable, however, and needs to be refined to a smooth distillate in a second process. Only then does the distiller separate the first, middle, and end running. Modern distilling columns, however, are constructed so that a circuit is created, thus producing a comparably smooth distillate in one process. Both systems have their advantages. A distilling column ensures a great deal of fresh primary aromas in the mash. The brandy aromas from a distilling bubble are reticent initially, but then develop their depth and sustainability. They linger longer in the mouth and even longer in the glass. With the effects of the air, an empty glass can give off even stronger aromas than a full one. Fruit brandy made in a distilling column on the other hand should not be stored for too long and should certainly not be left open.

# Tasting rituals

Connoisseurs all agree: the shape of the glass can release or suppress the aroma of its contents. What they cannot agree on, however, is the effect each shape has on the aroma. In the case of fruit brandy the verdict is made all the more difficult by the different properties of the processed fruit. Also fruit brandy is high proof and the alcohol rising up from the glass irritates the nose if the shape of the glass produces an unfavorable alcohol concentration. The fine fruit nuances, on the other hand, should be inhaled in as concentrated a form as possible. Wide goblets like the classic cognac snifter emphasize the alcohol at the expense of the fruit aromas. With some varieties of fruit brandy long flutes also tend to accumulate the alcohol rather than the aroma of the fruit.

Surprisingly, it is a relatively small goblet shaped rather like a closed tulip (No. 1) that is best suited as an all-round glass. Alternatively, the rim can extend outward slightly as with the Quinta Essentia glass (No. 2), devel-

oped by a group bearing the same name and comprising five of the best Austrian fruit brandy distillers. This shape transports the aromas of very different fruit brandies. Varieties that have matured in the barrel usually benefit from a somewhat larger goblet like a grappa glass (No. 3) or a snifter (No. 4).

Commercial suppliers willingly provide a wide selection for anyone looking for a glass for a specific brandy. Stone, pit, and berry fruit glasses are available on the market, while there are more goblet versions catering for pomace, herbal, and other brandy varieties. Even at professional tastings, however, such glasses seldom score points with the fruit varieties for which they are intended. Ultimately, it is the pit fruit glass that triumphs with the pomace brandy, and the whisk(e)y glass presents a Pear Williams brandy to its best advantage. You are better off relying on an all-round glass than on a whole range of glasses. What the glass must have, however, is a stem so that the goblet

Left: The World Spirits Glass WS 18.5 was designed by Austrian Wolfram Ortner, initiator of the World Spirits Festival.

Right: A typical calvados glass.

remains free of fingerprints and you do not mistakenly inhale perfume or body odors as well. The length of the stem is immaterial as long as it does not make the glass unwieldy. It goes without saying that embellishments and colors on such a glass are not desirable. Recommended materials include polished Pyrex, potash, and lead crystal. The last named is unsurpassed when it comes to clarity. An expensive glass is not necessarily better than an inexpensive one; it does not have to be hand blown glass either—even though this is very pleasant to the touch.

## Tasting delights

There are a few things to note once you have filled a well-tempered glass of your choice (preferably at a temperature a little cooler than a normal heated room) with brandy, particularly in contrast to a wine tasting. Fruit brandy should stand for a couple of minutes first as this often disperses any sharp nuances. Swiveling is avoided so as not to entice the strong alcohol out more. You slowly bring the glass to your nose and breathe in slowly. If the alcohol sticks in your nose, move the glass away again quickly. Any deficits will become apparent when you bring the glass closer a second time: solvent nuances indicate the presence of first running components and are a death sentence; rotten cabbage notes come from the end running and are at least as irritating as a pungent alcohol aroma. A good brandy has none of these, and all that enters the nose is the generous fruity nuances evoking all manner of associations from a flowering meadow through to grandma's preserving jars.

Fruit brandy is of course tasted in small sips, and how long you keep the distillate in contact with the tongue and mouth depends on the alcohol persistence. Even when strictly tasting, you should allow a little liquid to trickle down your throat, otherwise you will not be able to describe the aftertaste convincingly. It is advisable not to try different types of fruit brandy quickly after one another because the alcohol onslaught takes its toll on the mucus membranes. It is better to taste the same brandy a second time after a short interval. And do not forget to take a sniff of the freshly emptied glass.

Left:
1 All-round glass for fruit brandy
2 Quinta Essentia glass
3 Grappa glass
4 Snifter

Right: World Spirits glass (also see opposite left).

# Apples

The amount of apple distillate that has made its way down the throats of our hard-drinking forefathers over the centuries must amount to a veritable tide by now as apples were and are a set feature of rustic farmers' apple schnapps everywhere where this fruit is grown. In the German-speaking realm this type of schnapps is known as *Obstler*, and it owes its fame primarily to pears as well as plums, but ultimately to any kind of fruit that had to be disposed of. Apples are the most important fruit variety in the temperate climate regions and apple trees will grow in places unsuited to pear trees. They are undemanding; they can withstand the rain and cold of Normandy and northern Germany, Finland, Asturias, Michigan, and Oregon; they grow in the Caucasus—where they originate—and in China. There is evidence of the growing and storing of apples going back 5,000 years, and there are currently around 20,000 varieties worldwide (although the number is declining because many old varieties have been irretrievably lost). It is therefore no wonder that apples are right at the top of the list of distilled fruit. The forebears of all present-day (table) apples are the small, hard, crab apples (*Malus silvestris*) growing on thorny branches, and the bush-like Asian Paradise Apple (*Malus domestica* ssp. *occidentali-europaea* var. *paradisiacal*). This legacy has continually produced hybrids that are largely inedible when raw but have good fermenting and distilling properties. Hence two categories of apples have made their way into the mash tubs during the course of apple brandy history: at random, those that were no longer suitable for eating and, deliberately, those that were never suitable for consumption. Perhaps this explains the apple's solo career in the form of cider (apple wine)

Apples are often available in excess and many varieties are intended for distilling only.

distilled to apple brandy as calvados. *Obstler* and calvados have long been keeping a wide—even if not overlapping—public happy. Apples first earned gradual recognition as homogeneous noble brandy varieties, recognition that they had doubtlessly earned. Such apple brandy varieties, particularly those made from high-quality apples such as Gravensteiner, Cox Orange, or McIntosh, are delicately sophisticated, fruity taste experiences. Extracting the aromas of the individual varieties has been one of the most exciting chapters in the development of fruit brandies since the early part of the 1990s.

Many high-profile distillers in Germany, Austria, and Switzerland have taken up the challenge of reinstating the reputation of half-forgotten regional apple varieties. And apple varieties with a distinctive aroma and flavor typical of their variety prove to be an appreciated raw material, provided a few ground rules are adhered to. Farmers distinguish between picking ripe and tree-ripe apples. The distiller should select the latter

because they are able to develop an aroma that cannot be achieved through subsequent ripening. In addition, unripe or not quite ripe apples contain even more tannin and pectin, more acids, and less sugar. The tannins influence the taste of the brandy. The pectin, responsible for the cohesion of the cell tissue, hampers and extends the liquefying process for the mash (it can take up to ten days, increasing the risk of decay). A too viscous mash carries the risk that other, necessary mash additives will not disperse evenly within the mixture. It is also difficult or impossible to pump and burns more easily in the tank. Too little sugar and too much acid can cause fermentation to stop.

Today a noble, elegant apple brandy presents itself as light and clear, stored in a glass or stainless steel container. With its balance and longevity apple brandy also reacts exceptionally well to the characteristic influence of wooden barrels.

There are allegedly 2,000 different apple varieties in Normandy. They differ in color, shape, fragrance, flavor, and ripening time.

Page 246: Old varieties and old trees are cherished at Chateau de Hauteville in southern Normandy.

Page 247: This small alembic with open cooling coil was once in use at the Chateau du Breuil, which has become one of the most significant calvados producers.

# Apple concert: calvados

With its gentle hills and mellow valleys, Normandy has retained the charm of an old farming area. Streams wind through orchards with tall apple and pear trees, cows grazing underneath (their milk curdling into some of France's best-known cheeses: Camembert and Neufchâtel, Livarot, and Pont l'Evêque). The Normans have known how to treat apples and pears for centuries and the range of varieties grown here is legendary.

However, you need to be wary of simply biting into many of these fruit: they develop their unique charm only when they are ready for drinking, as cider and poiré, bitter or sweet, gently sparkling or bubbling vigorously, and ultimately reduced to their very essence as calvados. Once you know that some kinds of calvados are a combination of two, three, even four dozen different apple varieties—with Domfrontais even containing pears—then its wonderfully diverse bouquet and rounded flavor is no longer quite such a mystery.

Long before calvados was considered to be worthy of bearing the name of its home region, this apple brandy was helping the rural population to bear the cold and wet of Normandy. While cognac had risen to become the undisputed export hit, calvados remained the loyal farmers' schnapps, conquering nearby Paris at best—not the upmarket suburbs, but the working class areas. It was thanks not least to the circuitous route via the trenches of World War I that it became known throughout the whole of France. It was with the 1948 film version of Erich Maria Remarque's novel *Arc de Triomphe* in the Paris of the late 1930s, when Ingrid Bergmann and Charles Boyer as illegal refugees warmed themselves in a dreary bar with calvados instead of with cognac one evening, that this category made it as far as Hollywood. It became the custom in the working class bistros of Paris to follow a quick coffee with an equally short apple schnapps drunk from the small, thick rimmed and still warm cups: *café-calva*. Just the name of this proletarian pleasure is enough to provoke extreme unease among quality conscious distillers today. Yet anyone plucking up the courage to face the heinous challenge of drinking medium vintage calvados with a good, hot Arabica will discover that the combination does have some appeal. Some farms and distilleries that were already producing high-quality apple brandy around 1900 today have reserves that have matured over the decades. Calvados, even that aged for longer periods, has always had its clientele. Its real rise to fame, however, like that of cider too, began in the 1980s when the interest in authentic products grew worldwide.

On the coast of the Calvados *département*, in the fine hotels and in the Deauville casino, but also in Trouville and Honfleur, the barkeepers were among the first to create cocktails and long drinks using calvados, pommeau, and cider. Calvados, with its emphatically fruity aroma, now belongs to the basic supplies of any self-respecting bar. Calvados topped up with good cider is delicious, and if you like it a little sweeter, add a dash of pommeau as well. However, hors d'âge matured in the barrel for several years, or vintage calvados, deserves the same respect and the same tulip-shape glass as a fine, vintage cognac. You should take a moment and allow it to develop its aroma. Even if there is a hint of rust and spices from the wood maturation, or else fruit nuances that are owing to the use of port, sherry, cognac or rum barrels, in a good calvados—be it 2 or 40 years old—it is always the apples that set the tone.

# Real cider and a doubtful father

Normandy is proud of its apples. The 1920s—when the apple trees in the large province between Paris and the Channel numbered well over 20 million—may be over, but they continue to characterize the entire region, especially when in blossom. Although the actual calvados story started late, its foundation can be traced back to a long tradition: cider. Its origins will have been the fermented apple juice to which the Vikings readily and generously did justice. The Vikings were ravaging the coastal areas and Cotentin hinterland as early as the 9th century and ultimately established them-

selves there. Their leader Rollo negotiated a treaty with Charles the Simple, the king of Francia, in 911, making him the first duke of Normandy and its inhabitants Normans. There were already large numbers of apple and pear trees there, but Charlemagne ordered that still more be grown. The emperor without a capital issued a special decree in 812 ordering the cultivation of all the bases that he "visited" with his entire court during the course of his journeys in his extensive empire, together with the compilation of a plant list comprising 90 items. It detailed not just apple and other fruit trees

Calvados is distilled at the Domaine Coeur de Lion with its 17th-century manor (in the foreground) using traditionally produced cider.

in general, but even speaks of special apple varieties such as Gozmaringa, Geroldinga, Crevedella, and Spirauca.

The Norman apple mixture prior to the turn of the first millennium is unlikely to have tasted particularly good because beer and wine were obviously preferred. The term *sidre* was first recorded in Normandy in the 12th century. It is attributed to the words *shekar* or *shaker* originating from the Orient, which were general terms for fermented beverages. In Spain the latinized *sicera* refers to fermented apple juice. The Normans became familiar with *sicera* as a result of the trade relations that they maintained with the Basques as of the 12th century.

## A faithful apple friend

The Basque apple wine undoubtedly encouraged the Normans to improve the production and flavor of their own *sidre*. We are also told that a certain Guillaume d'Ursus, a Basque by origin, settled in Cotentin at the end of the 15th century, cultivating diverse apple varieties described as "aromatic" from his Spanish homeland on his Domaine de Lestres and from which he pressed an exceptionally good *sidre*. The journal of Gilles de Gouberville testifies to the significance of *sidre* as an everyday drink. In the surviving volume of his *Mises et Receptes*, which extend from 1549 to 1562, this royal functionary, responsible for watercourses and forestry, made careful note of everything that happened on his property, in particular his flourishing apple trees, of which he had more than 30 varieties.

For two years Gilles Picot, the lord of Gouberville, accommodated a young man from Tours named François on his property in Mesnil-au-Val. The latter was clearly interested in alchemy and built a distillery for his keeper in 1553, which he put together using specially constructed pots and ovens. What was distilled in it and with what degree of success is not disclosed; it is merely described as "the container for making eau-de-vie" when it had to be repaired by a brazier in 1554. Only at one point in his journal from 1561 does the writer mention a bottle

of eau-de-vie given to him by three visitors. Cider seemed to have been sufficient for his personal needs. The notes contain no reference at all to *eau-de-vie de cidre*, but the Normans at least view the meticulous functionary as the father of calvados.

Advertising sign for the Au Gars Normand restaurant in Honfleur, Normandy.

# *All of a sudden there was calvados*

It is obviously unclear exactly when the first cider vaporized in a distilling bubble. As already mentioned, the journals (1549–1562) of Gilles Picot, lord of Gouberville, are of no help in answering this question. All that has been passed down is the acknowledgment of the newly founded guild of *distillateurs d'eau-de-vie de cidre de Normandie* with a royal decree dated 1606. The often quoted treatise by the doctor Julien Le Paulmier, *De vino et Pomaceo* (1588), only details the effects of grape and apple wine on the human body (whereby Paulmier favors cider because its "warmth" matches the warmth of the human body, whereas wine is too "warm" and makes people ill), and makes no reference to distillates. Norman apple brandy has shown satisfactory progress, however, even without a certified "birth certificate." Apple growing, which was easily combined with dairy farming, continued to expand and remains a characteristic form of land use in Normandy today. However, a successful production concept always attracts the attention of the authorities and in the case of calvados the upper nobility were involved. The levy system introduced by Jean-Baptiste Colbert, Louis XIV's finance minister, in 1681 also applied to distillers and made their products expensive. As if that were not enough: a decree in 1713 permitted the free circulation of brandy only; other distillates could be transported and consequently consumed only in the region in which they were produced. It was only with the French Revolution that this restriction came to an end.

Left: Jean-Pierre Groult next to the photo of his great-grandfather Pierre, who won his first gold medal with his calvados in 1893.

Right: Mobile alembics remain in use in Normandy today.

## Explosive calvados

The new regime divided the whole of France into small *départements* that had to select a name for themselves. Part of Normandy became Calvados, named after a rocky reef off the coast at Asnelles.

Although the rustic apple brandy would now have been able to enter new markets unhindered, demand existed—with the exception of nearby Paris—in its home region only. It was the consequences of a catastrophe that provided a remedy: when phylloxera began to destroy entire vineyards in 1863 and wine and cognac production went into stark decline as of 1870, even non-Normans were forced to acquaint themselves with cider and calvados. Demand increased and the region made every effort to meet it. Farmers that did not own their own distilling equipment hired migrant distillers who moved from farm to farm with their apparatus, earning a good living in the process. Middlemen who bought up, assembled, and distributed calvados soon became established. The future looked promising when a second, more serious, catastrophe intervened in the calvados story.

With the outbreak of World War I the government enforced its increasing demand for more and more alcohol, which was needed for the production of explosives and as fuel. At the same time, the soldiers finally made whatever calvados was still available popular throughout France and beyond. Calvados as an export product was a child of war and benefited from World War II as well. As occupying forces, Hitler's troops requisitioned the entire distilled alcohol production with the exception of recognized appellations such as cognac and armagnac. The region of Pays d'Auge seized the opportunity and applied for the recognition of calvados as an *Appellation d'Origine Contrôlée*. This was granted in much haste in 1942 and the other production areas in Calvados were also accepted as controlled appellations. The Germans had been successfully outsmarted and the rest of the world was assured of the fine brandy with an individual character that calvados has since become.

The loft of the impressive Château du Breuil barrel storeroom was built by ship carpenters and based on the shape of a ship's hull.

# Apple school

Normandy currently has around 7 million apple trees whose fruit are intended for the mash tub and not for the table. They remain much smaller than table apples and it is estimated that there are close to 2,000 different varieties. Whether the cider is for drinking or distilling, it is always an accumulation of several varieties whose qualities complement each other. The appellation decree recommends 48 of these varieties, which are divided into four groups.

Sweet-sour: every second apple tree belongs to this category as these fruit form the basis of the cider with their distinct interaction between sweetness and tannins. The main varieties are Bedan, Benet Rouge, Bisquet, Noël des Champs, and Saint-Martin.

Bitter: they have an especially high tannin content and fortify the structure of the cider. The main varieties are Domaine, Fréquin Rouge, Mettais, and Moulin-à-Vent.

Sour: their high acid content gives the cider an extra freshness and storage life. The main varieties are Rambault and René Martin.

Sweet: they develop more sugar, are particularly aromatic, and increase the alcohol content. The main varieties are Germaine and Rouge Duret.

## Free standing or trellised

The traditional shape of the apple tree is that of the free-standing trees in the orchard, with between 28 and 73 trees per acre (70 and 180 trees per ha). The lowest branches are 6–8 feet (2–2.5 m) above the ground so that cows are able to graze comfortably beneath them. Wire mesh protects the trunks from the cows. Dairy farming and fruit growing go hand in hand in this two-tier form of land use characteristic of Normandy. The French state's decade-long support of apple growing for alcohol production came to an end in the 1950s when dairy farming took priority and uprooting bonuses were paid for apple trees.

When the interest in cider and calvados was revived some 30 years later, there was of course a lack of apples. Short apple trees were propagated as a modern growing method in order to close this gap as quickly

Left: This machine gathers the apples from the meadow like a mobile vacuum cleaner and places them in a bin.

Right: The apples are sprayed with water so that they are easier to mash.

s possible. This meant 162–260 or more trellised trees per acre (400–650 per ha) being planted, handled, and harvested mechanically. The trees reach their full production capacity in just seven years, while a free-standing tree needs at least 15 years. Furthermore, short trees yield 12 tons per acre (30 t/ha) and more, whereas no more than 8 tons per acre (20 t/ha) can be expected from free-standing trees. However, fast growth and higher yields often mean reduced quality. Wherever possible, reputable calvados distillers prefer to use apples from free-standing trees as these produce a more aromatic and complex distillate.

## Apple gathering and ripening

Apple varieties are distinguished not only in terms of the four flavors indicated above, but also according to ripening time. The summer varieties are disregarded in Normandy, where the focus is on the second (beginning of October), third (November), and fourth season (December and January) varieties. Jean-Pierre Vuilmet from Clos d'Orval waits until the apples are so ripe that they fall from the trees themselves because it is only then that they have developed their full sweetness. The harvest in his orchards therefore lasts through to November and the fruit is gathered at intervals of a few days. Many fruit farmers gather the apples twice only and then knock off the fruit still hanging on the trees by using a stick or shaking the trunk. The fruit then continues ripening for several weeks in high, well-ventilated wooden boxes. On the old farms in Normandy they are still spread out in the loft above the *cidrerie*. The ripened apples are then conveyed via a jet of water into a pool where they are washed, and then placed in a mill with a perpetual screw that grinds them into mush. The mush drops onto a conveyor belt press or a pneumatic press, or else it is pressed in traditional rack and cloth presses so that the juice, the basic ingredient for the cider, trickles off.

Left: Here the apples are ground and fall directly into the traditional rack and cloth press.

Right: A rack and cloth press in action. The pores of the fabric act as a filter and hold back all the coarse particles.

# Cider-making time

Of course, cider is not simply cider, for it is distinguished according to the apple combination that, for its part, is determined according to the type of cider. *Cidre à consommation* is bottled before the end of the apple juice fermentation with a proportion of residual sugar, starting the *prise de mousse* that gives the finished cider its characteristic sparkle due to the resultant carbonic acids. *Cidre à distiller*, on the other hand, has to be completely fermented before its distillation into calvados can begin.

Cider is often a combination of 30–40 different apple varieties (and pear varieties in as far as they are permitted). The fruit is milled and the juice usually remains with the solids for up to four hours before it is pressed. This period needs to be as long as possible in order for all of the natural yeasts and flavoring substances needed by the cider and later the calvados to dissolve out of the skins. It also needs to be kept as short as possible to avoid too much of the apple aroma being lost due to the oxidization of the fruit flesh. While the addition of pure cultured yeast during the second fermentation in the bottle is permitted for *cidre de consommation*, it is a legal requirement for *cidre à distiller* that it be fermented naturally only with its own yeasts derived from the apple skins. These yeasts make up just 3% of the unsolicited microorganisms that are provided by Mother Nature.

The separating of the solids, or the pressing, should not be too aggressive so that, ideally, no more than 170 gallons (650 liters) of juice are obtained from 1 ton/ne of apples; 210 gallons (800 liters) are however permitted.

The cider needs to ferment slowly in order to retain its fresh fruit aromas. In the past, before the advent of fermentation tanks with temperature controls, the fermentation of the tannin-rich, acidic apple juice took place at the required slow pace on its own due to what were usually low autumnal outside temperatures. Today the majority of producers are equipped with modern technology providing optimal control of the fermentation process as this is what determines the purity and intensity of the aromas. In Pays d'Auge a fermentation period of at least six weeks, and in Domfrontais eight, is

This modern alembic containing 660 gallons (2,500 liters) is heated with gas, both its shape and its materials—copper and brick—being based on old traditions. This enables precise control of the temperature.

prescribed. This produces a dry, full flavored cider with an alcohol content of 4.5–6%.

## Calvados throughout the year

It was once the custom on the farms to distill calvados only once the cider barrels needed to be emptied for the new harvest, i.e. in September. Most producers operate differently today. Père Magloire gets going every year by heating up the alembics for the fresh, young cider. Cellar master Michel Poulain took this idea from Cognac where the young wines produce very fine, floral, sweet alcohols. Other producers with their own alembics or distilling columns start in January and take their time over months. Farmers who have to wait for migrant distillers in order to be able to distill their small quantities are dependent on the latter's timing.

In the Pays d'Auge, where double distillation is prescribed, some producers do it differently. "We distill with significant time delays," explains Jean-Pierre Groult of Roger Groult. "In September we distill the previous year's cider to raw brandy with an alcohol content of about 30% vol. *Les petites eaux*, as we call them—elsewhere they talk of *brouillé*—enable us to empty and clean the tanks in time for the new harvest in the months of October and November. Once the work of producing the new juice is finished, we focus on the fine distilling of September's *petites eaux* in December, January, and February, which produces a calvados with a 70% vol. alcohol content. We work with small alembics as the wood furnaces that we prefer do not permit the even heating of large volumes. The concentration of alcohol is also more conclusive in small alembics." Apart from the terroir, it is this dedicated form of distillation that gives the brandy the best aging potential, upon which the prestige of the Pays d'Auge calvados is based. Calvados and Calvados Domfrontais, on the other hand, are largely distilled in a continual process. This process, more cost effective because it is less involved, produces a clean, fruity brandy that ripens comparatively quickly in oak barrels but that does not develop quite such complex aromas as a Pays d'Auge calvados.

The small, old alembic, which is heated with wood, requires a lot of experience and constant monitoring.

# Calvados cubed

The calvados-producing region extends over much of Normandy. It is divided into three different appellations, and the harvesting of the apples, the production of the cider, and the distillation thereof have to take place in the appropriate AOC region. The conditions also relate to the approved apple varieties, to maximum yields, to the pressing of the apples, and to the fermentation of the cider (and especially the fermentation period), as well as to the distilling process and the maturation time of the calvados in oak barrels. Of the 15,000 or so farmers harvesting cider apples and pears from registered orchards, only 445 produce calvados themselves today, while just 45 of those possess a supply of more than 13,200 gallons (50,000 liters) of pure alcohol, equal to about 3,300 gallons (12,500 liters) of calvados. There are 55 producers, retailers, or cooperatives tha process the harvest from the remaining farmers and sell around 6 million bottles of calvados, more than half of which are exported

## AOC Calvados Pays d'Auge

The oldest and most renowned AOC granted in 1942, bears the name of a historic landscape, most of which lies in the Calvados *département* and includes a number o municipalities in the adjoining Eure and Orne *départements*. The apple trees are grown on slopes with clay/lime and rather shallow soils. A minimum of 70% bitter or sweet sour and 10% sour varieties is prescribed The cider must be distilled in a dual process It has to pass an analytical and organoleptic

**The growing regions of the Calvados appellation**

- Regions assigned to AOC Calvados
- AOC Calvados
- AOC Calvados Domfrontais
- AOC Calvados Pays d'Auge

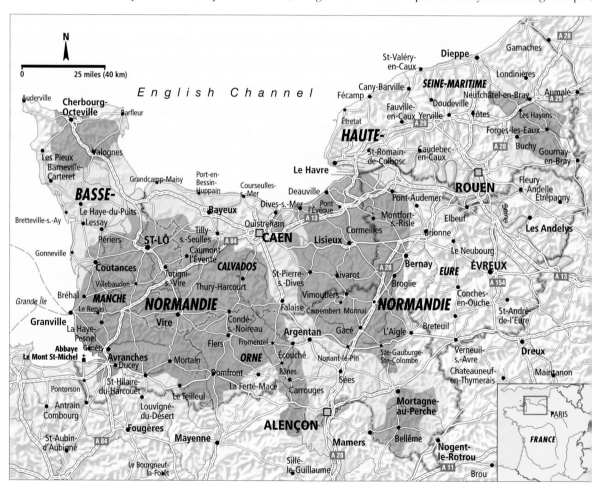

est and has to age in oak barrels for at least two years before it may be sold.

## AOC Calvados

The largest appellation, responsible for well over two thirds of production, was upgraded to an AOC in 1984. It extends over a large area of Lower Normandy. That means the Calvados, Orne, and Manche *départements*, also extending into Mayenne and Sarthe, and also applies to Pays de Bray in Seine-Maritime, the home of Neufchâtel cheese. Clay soils predominate here, with the exception of Cotentin and Bocage where slate and other rocks are dominant. Here, too, a minimum of 70% bitter or sweet-sour and 10% sour varieties has to be used. The distillation method is not prescribed but the large majority work with column distilleries. Analytical and organoleptic tests are also carried out here and the minimum age is two years.

## AOC Calvados Domfrontais

This appellation, first recognized in 1998, lies in the south of Normandy near the small town of Domfront. The 112 municipalities are located largely in Orne, although some are in Manche and Mayenne. It is thought that the Romans introduced pear trees to this region where the soils are comprised of granite and are more moist than those of the other two appellations, and they have been grown here ever since. Consequently, the region's inhabitants also produce poiré in addition to cider, and their especially fruity calvados always contains a specific proportion of pears. The appellation now requires that the orchards comprise at least 15% pear trees (25% as of the 16th year) and that the calvados contain a minimum of 30% pears. It is distilled in column tanks and has to mature in oak barrels for three years before being sold.

## Eau-de-vie de cidre

Cider that is distilled outside the Calvados appellations is labeled *Eau-de-vie de cidre*. This applies largely to the traditional apple growing areas of Brittany where the distillate is entitled to bear the endorsement *de Bretagne* and is recognized as an *Appellation d'Origine Réglementée* (AOR).

In Cornouaille *eau-de-vie de cidre de Bretagne* is referred to as *lambig*. As with calvados, the basic principles governing its production are set down in detail and regulated by law. Accordingly, only cider that is derived from at least 15% sour apple varieties is permitted. The density of the trees and their maximum yields are also stipulated. Both column tanks and dual distilling are permitted. Lambig may be offered for sale after three years of aging in barrels, but the better ones age for significantly longer, while rare varieties mature for up to 30 years.

If an apple brandy from the Calvados regions is not matured in oak barrels for the prescribed minimum period but is bottled young and light, it is labeled *Eau-de-vie de cidre de Normandie*.

# Of young pommeau and vintage calvados

Oak, be it new or reused, plays the key role in the maturation of calvados whereby the former sherry, port, cognac, or other barrels lend an additional complexity.

The young, colorless apple distillate with an alcohol content of around 70% vol. still has a long way to go and some of it never makes it as far as matured calvados, being destined for another honor, namely the prevention of fermentation in freshly pressed apple juice. This is how pommeau is produced, characterized by its full apple aroma, fruity sweetness, and pleasant acidity. Pommeau de Normandie was upgraded to an appellation in 1991, for which 30 apple varieties may be used, the selection of which determines th aroma. Storage in barrels for at least 1 months is prescribed. In 1997 Pommeau d Bretagne was made an AOC, and Pommea de Maine followed soon thereafter. The alc hol content is 17% vol. Pommeau is usuall drunk chilled as an aperitif but is also excep tionally well suited to dishes containin apples, especially apple desserts.

Younger apple brandy varieties that are nc blended with apple juice are initially left t rest in oak barrels. Only in this way do the become calvados. The prescribed matura tion period of two to three years really is th minimum because, as with cognac, the bes quality is achieved only after many mor years in oak barrels. However, apple brand is not able truly to rest in oak barrels. "W always start the maturation of young calva dos in new 106 gallon (400 liter) barrels i order to give it a bit of color and wood flavo right from the start," says Didier Bédu o Château du Breuil. "It is placed in large older barrels after six weeks at the latest otherwise the rust nuances will become to pronounced. The more often a barrel is used the longer the calvados can stay in it."

Of course, every producer has his own pro cedure, his own philosophy. Christia Drouin and his son Guillaume not only hav received recognition for their methods i which they dispense with new wood entirel using barrels from other provenances suc as port, sherry, banyuls, or cognac instead but have also provided important initiatives "For me the maturation comprises three dif ferent phenomena," explains Guillaume Drouin. "Firstly, there is the influence of th wood: it gives the calvados color, tannins and aromas and therefore structure and sub stance. The calvados then also comes int contact with the air on its surface and through the wood, causing oxidization. Thi changes not only the fruit aromas but als those introduced by the wood. A vanilla aroma, for example, derives from the oxidization in wooden barrels. Then there is also evaporation, referred to as the angel's share. Evaporation means concentration. If you want to produce a great calvados, one that is robust and complex, there is no way other than to allow part of it to evaporate; otherwise it will always resemble a young calvados." Almost all producers agree, calvados is at its best when it has 20 or more years to develop in the barrel.

Like all distillates, calvados starts out as a colorless brandy, taking on ever deeper color tones as the years go by.

## Labeling issues

A calvados must have been developed in oak barrels for at least two to three years.

### Vintages

For the vintage to appear on the label, the calvados has to derive from the stated year alone and from a single distillation. Important: the label should indicate the bottling date as calvados does not age in the bottle.

### Assemblage

The age appearing on the label refers to the assemblage's youngest brandy. It often contains much older ones as well.

### Conventional designations

Trois étoiles / Trois pommes (or similar)
    Two years of wooden barrel maturation
Vieux / Réserve
    At least three years of wooden barrel maturation
V.O. / Vieille réserve / V.S.O.P.
    At least four years of wooden barrel maturation
Extra / X.O. / Napoléon / Hors d'âge / Age Inconnu
    At least six years of wooden barrel maturation

### Calvados fermier

Such a calvados must have been produced on a single farm from the tree through to the bottle.

# Selected producers

### Eric Bordelet

The former sommelier at Arpège in Paris took over the family property Château de Hauteville in Charchigné in the so-called Normandie méridionale in 1992. Here he practices organic farming in his orchards that lie on granite and slate soils and in which some of the pear trees are 300 years old, producing top quality poirés and cidres. He produces single vintage—non-reduced—calvados, which captivates with its very intensive ripe apple and sweet cider aromas, is harmonious despite its strength, and has a mineral aftertaste.

### Château du Breuil

Château du Breuil is an architectural jewel from the 16th century, to which 40,000 visitors annually are testimony. It comprises 104 acres (42 ha) with 22,000 apple trees, the harvest being distilled in two large alembics and, since 1954, matured in the five floors of a former textile factory. Of particular appeal is the XO Réserve des Seigneurs, which matures for 20–25 years and features sweet, spicy nuances and a good complexity. Specialties: calvados with a 52.3% vol. alcohol content and double maturation with a six-year long finish in malt barrels.

### Roger Groult

"Anybody who wants to keep the term terroir may only source his apples locally," emphasizes Jean-Pierre Groult. His own property, Clos de la Hurvanière in Saint-Cyr-du-Ronceray, supplies half of his needs; the rest comes from direct neighbors. The cellar portrays the Groult family history—barrels have been added by each of the four generations—and tastings go back to the Réserve Ancestrale. Ever more diverse and sophisticated apple aromas always predominate with aging. Very good: Age d'Or.

### Christian Drouin

Christian Drouin has been producing calvados of the highest quality since 1980. Following very traditional cider production and distillation at the (extremely picturesque) Domaine Coeur de Lion, the maturation in used barrels characterizes the style. His son Guillaume, a qualified oenologist, contributes his wine-making expertise. Each vintage develops its own character, with honey and white blossom, sometimes nuts and cocoa, or fine wood and tobacco nuances, and always a common ripe apple, baked apple, or warm cider undertone.

## Clos d'Orval

In the Bocage region between Caën and Vire, Alain Aubrée and brother-in-law Jean-Paul Vuilmet run the family farm with a sense of tradition. Their cows graze in their 50 acre (20 ha) orchards where the 60 apple varieties are grown. They produce Jus de Pommeau, an excellent Cidre Brut, poiré, *pommeau, vinaigre de cidre*, and of course calvados as well, in a variety of vintages ranging up to those matured for 35 years. The hors d'âge, matured for over 10 years, has a pleasing, intensive baked apple aroma, good harmony, and stamina.

## Père Magloire

Cellar master Michel Poulain has been the force behind this leading calvados brand since 1974. He began by convincing farmers to keep their old apple trees. "Don't lose 15 years in one go," was his motto, for that is how long an apple tree needs to start yielding. He has been determining the house quality since 1991. Tasting is the focus of his work. His greatest successes include the Fine, the youngest calvados in the vintage hierarchy. The Pays d'Auge 20 ans d'âge displays a firm texture, sweet spices, and plenty of strength.

## Frédéric et Catherine Pacory

The Pacory family has been farming the 222 acre (90 ha) Ferme des Grimaux near Mantilly since 1939 with cows and chickens as well as growing 700 free-standing pear and 400 apple trees. With their modern presses they produce cidre fermier and poiré, Pommeau de Normandie, and its equivalent Grim' de Poire, as well as distilling Calvados Domfrontais with a high proportion of pears. The 20 ans therefore gives off candied pear and spice aromas and has a gentle balance of nut and rust nuances as well as elegant tannins as a finale.

## Philippe Daufresne

It was just for fun that he had pressed apples in the old press on his grandfather's farm near Ouilly-le-Vicomte and then fermented the juice, but his cider won a gold medal in Paris in 1970. He attributes its quality to the southern slopes with good clay soils and the free-standing trees, as well as to the very slow, cool fermentation that gives his Cidre Brut de Normandie a wonderfully fresh apple aroma. The clear, clean, fine fruity flavors are also to be found in the Calvados Pays d'Auge Hors d'âge.

# The AppleJack legacy

The Scotsman William Laird came to the United States in 1698 and settled in Monmouth County in New Jersey. He wanted to distill whisky as was the custom in his former homeland but soon realized that the requisite barley was lacking. Instead there were plenty of apples, so William made cider that he distilled into "AppleJack." Some of his competitors, not familiar with distilling, allowed the water in the cider to freeze in the cold winter temperatures, thus concentrating the alcohol. The brandy, also named AppleJack, is said to have caused the most awful hangovers.

The Lairds established an inn in Colts Neck in 1717, that also served as a staging post. When Robert Laird finally began keeping accounts in 1780 he recorded the price for a gallon (4 liters) of cider spirits, suggesting that the Lairds were still distilling cider. At that time apple brandy was a popular drink and was often consumed at breakfast, also being served by the future President Abra-ham Lincoln in his tavern in Illinois, where a half pint (0.25 liter) cost 12 cents in 1833. The distillery in Colts Neck went up in flames in 1849. After a breathing space of two years, the Lairds started again in Scobeyville, half a mile (about 1 km) away from Colts Neck, but this time in the fast lane: from then they distilled apple brandy on a larger scale, establishing a clientele in several states, particularly in the urban centers of Denver and Los Angeles.

## Concentration and respite

During Prohibition the family managed to market their apples as other apple products but was granted a license to produce alcohol for medicinal purposes prior to the lifting of the ban.

This meant that, immediately after the end of Prohibition, they were in a position to start supplying AppleJack again, which was still purely an apple brandy—and which was more than could be said for the produce of

Left: At Lairds in New Jersey the apples delivered are first crushed and then fermented into cider. Center: The residue provides valuable fodder and is distributed among the neighboring farms. Opposite bottom: The tried and tested distilling column is indestructible.

the former moonshiners. Since the Lairds, not without reason, feared damage to the reputation of their products if they were classed together with these lower quality products, they simply bought out their competitors' bootleg distilleries and today they own the only large distillery producing AppleJack in the USA.

When consumers turned away from aromatic, dark spirits in the 1970s, the Lairds followed the trend and created today's lighter AppleJack, comprising one third apple brandy and two thirds neutral alcohol. They responded to the demand for premium spirits with the 7½ Year Old barrel-aged Old Apple Brandy and the even more impressive 12 Year Old Rare Apple Brandy.

The family company now employs the ninth generation, and even though AppleJack now only makes up a small proportion of the production of the oldest distillery in the USA, it would be unthinkable for the Lairds to break with a tradition founded by their ancestor William in a time of need in 1698.

The apple aroma in Apple-Jack tends to be subtle, being more dominant in the apple brandies.

### Austria

**Weutz**
**Elstar Apfel**
Michael Weutz from Steiermark in Austria believes that far too often, apple brandy is undervalued, even now—not just because apples are regarded by consumers as all too common fruits, by comparison with raspberries or mirabelle plums. Distillers often underestimate the variations in vintage that can occur with apples. Michael Weutz mashes the fruit without stems and cores, to avoid green notes. This gives the final spirit very fresh, fruity flavors with vague hints of peel. The interplay can be savored at leisure in the long, persistent finish.

### Austria

**Tinnauer**
**Gravensteiner Apfel**
Franz Tinnauer is a trained wine grower. He still owns 20 acres (8 ha) of good sites in Steiermark, but he sells his grapes to wineries and cultivates other fruit instead. For some years now he has had to buy in extra supplies, otherwise he would not be able to satisfy the ever growing demand for his brandies. His reserve line concentrates deliberately on length on the palate; an exuberant bouquet is of secondary importance for him. Its fruitiness ensures that Gravensteiner is still pleasantly light in spite of its 50% vol. alcohol content. Tinnauer also lets the brandy rest for years to allow the alcohol and flavors to marry before bottling it.

### Switzerland

**Käser**
**Berner Rosen**
Berner Rosen is one of the many regional apple varieties rescued from obscurity by committed distillers like Ruedi Käser from Elfingen, Aargau. Keen on experimenting, this Swiss distiller with strong traditional links uses the variety to make a brandy with such an intensely fragrant apple bouquet that it really does remind you of roses or some other flower. This medium-weight spirit lingers on the palate in spite of its floral, fruity elegance.

### Germany

**Martin Fischer**
**Apfelbrand, im Holzfass gereift**
The Rosenhut distillers' cooperative named itself for the helmet shape of distiller's pots in Franconia. Its members, including Martin Fischer, are at pains to use native fruit varieties, refusing to add sugar or any other artificial ingredient to their products. Traditional meadow orchards are something of a hobby horse of Martin Fischer, so fruits from various old standard varieties come together in his apple brandy and age in small casks made from mulberry wood. This gives the spirit hints of pear, some vanilla and pine honey, and its deep color.

## Germany

**Marder · Gravensteiner Apfelbrand, im Holzfass gereift**

Brandies stored in casks are among the specialties of this Black Forest distiller. Even though Edmund Marder occasionally argues with his son Stefan about it (he has recently become the third generation to join the business), something exquisite always comes out of it. Gravensteiner Apfel has a pleasantly acidic, fruity taste, with cheeky notes of sour cherries and a hint of citrus fruit. The wood influence gives it stability.

## Spain

**L'Alquitara del Obispo Aguardente de Manzana**

Casería San Juan del Obispo is an estate not far from Oviedo, the capital of Asturias, belonging to the García Meana Menéndez-Fernández family. On their 50 acres (20 ha) of land, they cultivate 22 varieties of apple on 3,500 apple trees. The natural cider pressed from the fruit is distilled in pot stills heated by gas. This produces one of the country's most convincing fruit brandies, with clear, intense, and complex apple flavors—smooth, long, and remarkably harmonious on the palate.

## England

**Somerset Cider Brandy Company Alchemy Fifteen Years Old**

Burrow Hill in Somerset lies in the heart of one of the three English cultivation areas for cider apples. Julian Temperley, on whose farm they have fermented cider for over 150 years, acquired a full license to distill cider in 1989, the first to be issued in the history of English schnapps production. A hundred cider apple varieties grow on his 150 acres (60 ha) of land, 40 of which give substantial yields. Temperley's cider and cider brandy are the result of skillful mixtures of apples and are impressive, with their pure apple flavor that combines well with the fine woody notes. Alchemy has focused the spotlight firmly on Temperley's distillation art.

## Canada

**Michel Jodoin Calijo Apple Brandy**

With a great-grandfather who bought a fruit orchard with 100 apple trees at auction in 1901, it is no surprise that Michel Jodoin obtained the first license to produce cider in Quebec in 1988. At that time cider did not have any economic significance in Canada, though this has clearly changed. Michel Jodoin, who rose to become one of the biggest producers, opened the first apple microdistillery in Canada in 1999, where he distills his Calijo from cider. After aging for three years in small, new oak casks, this pleasantly sweet, appley brandy has intense flavors of vanilla and caramel.

# Pears

Anyone who has compared several Williams pear brandies at a tasting will know just how much they can vary. In the best-case scenario, the fruit predominates with delicate, smooth, subtly sweet flavors and is characteristically well rounded on the palate. As well as the full flavor of ripe pears, you can detect notes of aniseed, spice cake, licorice, tropical fruits, and white chocolate.

Yet all too often you are disappointed. "The fine fruit aromas are tricky," warns Hans Reisetbauer. "It only takes a tiny mistake in the fermentation process or distillation and you've had it." He knows exactly what he is talking about: since the mid 1990s, when ambitious distillers in Austria in particular were constantly raising the standards of fruit spirits, Reisetbauer has been producing a Williams brandy with flavors of unprecedented intensity.

Williams Bon Chrétien (known as Bartlett in North America) is the variety of pear introduced by the Englishman Richard Williams in the first part of the 19th century. It only develops its characteristic flavor after about 10 days' after-ripening; at a mash temperature of 63 °F (17 °C) it starts to lose its magic—if you can smell it, it is no use for the brandy. Cold fermentation is therefore required. The low acidic content of the fruit means that extra acid should be added to the mash as protection against bacteria, and the relatively low sugar content of Williams pear limits the amount of alcohol that can be produced. The delicate flavors of Williams can indicate distilling even if fermentation is weak. At the raw spirit stage the mash tends to build up a lot of froth, and the fine spirit reacts very sensitively to being heated too quickly. The relatively short aging period should take place at temperatures below 59 °F (15 °C), in the dark, and in full containers, as some of the classic Williams flavors do not tolerate warmth, light, or air. Williams is a diva, but as its temperamental nature is exceeded only by its quality—at least when handled correctly—and its fame, distillers take the risk.

Two pear experts
Left: Christoph Kössler from the Tyrol.
Right: Stephen R. McCarthy from the Clear Creek Distillery in Portland, Oregon, demonstrates how the pear gets into the bottle.

# Quinces

These fruits do not make life easy for the distiller either. After the harvest they have to after-ripen in order to strengthen the flavor. Before these very firm fruits are mashed, their furry bloom has to be removed as it contains an oil that can become rancid and even affect the final spirit. The fruit pulp is very dry, so water—or even better, quince juice—has to be added to the mash. Whether they are apple or pear quinces, the fruits are full of tannin and low in sugar—all factors preventing fermentation from taking place effectively. Even in ideal circumstances, only up to 1 gallon of spirit can be expected from 100 lb of fruit (3–4 liters per 100 kilos). Yet the intense fruit fragrances that rise from the glass, the fruity freshness on the palate, and the flavor that oscillates between apples, pears, and floral notes, are certainly worth all the effort.

Williams now has competition, however, for other pears among the 1,500 or so cultivars also provide a pretty comprehensive spectrum of flavors for making spirits, with notes that are both delicate and intensely fruity at the same time. Of the dessert pears, Dr. Guyot, Gute Luise, and Alexander Lucas are on sale as single variety brandies. The last two of these are characterized by a persistent note of nuts on the finish.

The juicy, flavor intensive must pear varieties are particularly popular in Austria, and also in German regions as well—the Pfalz and Swabia. They process well into a homogeneous mash, containing plenty of sugar and intense flavors that in purely chemical terms are often even higher than a Williams pear. The high tannin and sorbic acid content of some varieties can, however, cause a breakdown in fermentation. One of the best-known regional must pear varieties is Subirer from Vorarlberg. This was not always the case; it owes its renaissance in no small part to an Austrian distiller from Steyr, Alois Gölles. As he recalls, "The fruits that were barely edible raw were virtually ignored." At best they were used as a component in a mixed mash. "Few recognized the complexity of their flavors." Once they had been separately distilled as a single variety, the spirits won plenty of awards, with their fine fruit and distinctive notes ranging from green peel to chamomile and pine. Brandies made with Austrian dried pears are an unusual specialty in which the high sugar content of these fruits ensures an intensely sweet finish.

## Lantenhammer (D)
### Feiner Williamsbirnen Brand ungefiltert
"The art of doing nothing," is how they describe their company's philosophy at Lantenhammer. It has worked for nearly 80 years. High-quality brandies, stored until they have reached perfect harmony, come from this region in Schliersee, Upper Bavaria. Recently the firm's third-generation owner, Florian Stetter, has introduced his unfiltered Williams brandy. They have dispensed with filtration to keep all the flavors, making the brandy very concentrated and absolutely typical of the variety.

## Käser (CH)
### Williams Birnenbrand, unfiltriert
Nothing is safe, not even flowers in window boxes, when Swiss producer Ruedi Käser is about. The building where his tastings take place is called the "castle," and is suitably large; otherwise there would not be enough space for the extensive range on offer. This unfiltered Williams proves that Käser still knows his trade. While a few green notes are evident on the nose, in the mouth it is the crystal clarity of fruit that predominates.

## Metté (F)
### Eau-de-Vie de Poire Williams
There are plenty of French folk who believe that the Williams pear originated in a French monastery; an English teacher called Richard Williams happened to sell it, so his name has prevailed. And the best Williams brandies come from Alsace, of that they have no doubt. Jean-Paul Metté's distillery in Ribeauvillé produces a powerful Williams brandy with elegant, fruity sweetness that persists on the palate.

## Hämmerle (A)
### Subirer
The must pear variety Subirer had almost had its day when resourceful distillers rediscovered it. When freshly picked the fruits are seductively sweet, but are virtually inedible due to their grainy flesh. The brandy produced by Hämmerle in the westernmost corner of Austria is complex and bursting with fruity sweetness. Subirer is also characterized by a tangy note that makes it quite unusual.

## Freihof (A)
### Williamsbirne
Many have wondered how the pear gets into the bottle; and it is not quite that simple. As soon as the flower petals fall, and even before the little fruits reach the size of a cent, the bottle has to be attached onto it, bottom up so that it does not fill up with water. No matter how much care is taken, not many of the pears grow well enough in their glass casing for them to be filled later with fine Williams brandy and put on sale, as is done here in Hämmerle's parent company.

## Holzapfel (A)
### Williamsbirne 05
Wine was produced at Prandtauerhof, now owned by Karl Holzapfel, over 700 years ago. Today some of the best Austrian fruit brandies produced using the latest methods come from there. "Harvest the fruits at the peak of ripeness for eating" is his motto. Each fruit is hand picked, "then quickly cold mashed." The result is a pure tasting Williams brandy, in which the 45% vol. alcohol content strengthens the intensity of the fruit, while never becoming overdominant: smooth, fruity, and long.

## Pfau (A)
### Kärntner Mostbirne
Valentin Latschen, owner of the Pfau distillery in Kärnten, has been working with schnapps for over half his life. The 49-year-old was a founder member of the standards organization Quinta Essentia, and swears by the importance of high-quality fruits for distilling, as well as by must pears for his brandy. Not too fruity on the nose, it is defined by grassy, green aromas. In the mouth, however, it develops unimaginable sweetness: delicate and rounded, long and firm.

## Kössler (A)
### Edelbrand Birnen-Cuvée aus dem Akazienfass
Stanz is one of many little villages in the Tyrol, where over a third of households scattered over the mountains make their own fruit brandy. To do this Christoph Kössler uses one of the latest computer-controlled distilling systems. With his acacia casked pear cuvée, he shows the marriage of pear flavors and cask nuances. Rather difficult to define even at the nosing stage, rich fruity sweetness follows on the palate, blending perfectly with the unconventional wood note.

## Reisetbauer (A)
### Williams Brand
Hans Reisetbauer used to be called "Mr. Williams," and indeed his Williams brandy helped give him his breakthrough. He has planted 20,000 trees to date that are gradually providing the high-quality yield he had hoped for. The pear fruit is accompanied in his brandy by distinct notes of peel, adding complexity and full flavor. Suitable for storing.

## Tinnauer (A)
### Williams Brand
As a trained wine grower, Franz Tinnauer believes there are also good locations for fruit trees. For this reason the Williams trees stand on the exposed side of the Steinbach valley, right alongside his vines. If tasters judged his Williams as having too many green notes in the past, it is now distinctly sweet, even on the nose, with a hint of overripe fruit. On the palate the intensity persists, and the high concentration of fruit comes even more to the fore.

# "Obstler" and pomace

Rochelt's Williams, quince, and raspberry brandy from the Inntal valley

The type of fruit brandy known as Obstler is widely regarded as a rather unassuming schnapps, which is to some extent a byproduct of fruit growing. For centuries overripe fallen fruit has been made into a mash before the fruit rots completely, and then fermented and distilled. For a long time no one bothered about the quality of what was being used as leftovers. Blends from inferior distilling estates and spoiled must defined the market; they were inexpensive and therefore readily available. And up till now fruit farmers disposed of all the dessert fruit they could not sell by making plain spirits. Reinhard Wetter, a distiller from Lower Austria, and his colleagues were not happy to leave it at that, for if the whole is more than the sum of its parts, then there would have to be great Obstler as well, as long as the quality and technology were right. It turned out that combining different types of fruit, along the lines of the cuvée of a wine, produced greater harmony and complexity in the bottle.

Reinhard Wetter processes only hand-picked fruit from his own trees. Each fruit type is mashed separately, fermented, and distilled into a raw spirit. Only at the raw spirit stage are the fruit types mixed together and then refined by further distillation. The result is top-quality Obstler like his Wetter hexe made from apples, pears, and elderberries.

Apples and pears especially set the tone in Obstler, as their flavors complement each other well. Adding nuances with a third component is something that Günther Rochelt from the Tyrol has perfected. His Inntaler leaves us in no doubt about what a mixture of Williams pears, quinces, and raspberries can achieve. Rochelt's brandies represent the technical and financial upper limit of what can be done with fruit distillation at this time, so a bottle of his varietal brandies may cost up to 400 euros.

## Not fallen fruit, but traditional orchards

In the past the raw material for distillation came primarily from traditional orchards, a concept revived in the 1970s at a time when the tendency in Germany was exactly the opposite: commercial fruit growing with

A typical Black Forest landscape: Emersbach with traditional fruit fields and an orchard on the far slope.

dwarf varieties planted in symmetrical rows, if possible with 1,200 trees per acre (3,000 trees per ha).

Different fruit trees of varying ages, which grew high and with broad crowns at random across meadows, on which flowers bloomed and cattle grazed, were seen as an uneconomical, old-fashioned, and generally bad idea. It was not until later that it was understood that the value of this biotope lay not just in diversity of varieties for its own sake, but also in its effect on the quality of the fruits. The plants thrive so well there, and are less susceptible to diseases, that they do not need mineral fertilizers and pesticides—an idyllic scenario for environmentalists, organic farmers, and distillers. The number of traditional orchards is once more on the increase.

Farmers who sell the juice from the fruits retain the pomace, or marc. It contains about half of the weight of the fruit as well as a whole array of flavors, but (and Reinhard Wetter appreciates this especially) without all the pips and stalks you get with grape marc. These are the very components that are often responsible for the astringent, bitter flavors in brandies made from grape marc.

## Pear pomace

Reinhard Wetter was one of the first to distill his Williams pomace, with its bouquet bursting with the fruitiness of Williams pear and a tangy hint of green leaves. Earthy nuances add to the equation on the palate. Among other things, Jörg Geiger in Schlat (near Göppingen, Baden-Württemberg) has begun to use a variety of wine pear that has almost been forgotten. The production of sparkling wine from the Champagner Bratbirne variety was first mentioned in records back in 1760. The small, compact, yellow pears are sorted according to ripeness, washed, and then put in closed containers to after-ripen, for this is how they develop their luscious flavor. They are then ground and lightly pressed. The juice, which runs almost clear from the press, is made into sparkling pear wine using traditional methods. The leftover pomace with valuable fruit

## All about labels

The German terms "Obstler," "Obstbrand," and—prefixed by the name of the fruit—"-brand," "-wasser," or "-geist" on a label identify the contents of the bottle.

### (name of fruit)-brand

This term has now taken over as the generic name for fruit brandy, and denotes a spirit with an alcohol content of at least 37.5%. It may only be obtained using alcoholic fermentation and distillation of the fresh fruit or the fresh must from this fruit.

### (name of fruit)-wasser

The same requirements apply as for "-brand." In the case of some stone fruits, they tend to use "wasser" as a regional preference.

### Obstler, Obstbrand

A brandy made from two or more types or varieties of fruit that have been distilled together.

### (name of fruit)-geist

Whole, unfermented fruits, the sugar content of which is too low for alcoholic fermentation, are macerated in alcohol (ethyl alcohol of agricultural origin) and then distilled with this alcohol.

### (name of fruit) spirituose

The fruits are mashed in alcohol; added flavorings, even from fruits other than the ones being processed, are permitted.

pieces is still very moist, thanks to the gentle pressing; it is fermented immediately and then distilled without the solids. This retains all the pure pear flavors and gives it a convincing aroma, flavor, and finish.

Pomace made from the Champagner Bratbirne pear by Jörg Geiger.

Reinhard Wetter's Wetterhexe, a brandy made from apples, pears, and elderberry.

# Stone fruits

Alois Gölles had thought of everything: he had harvested only fully ripe fruit from his own trees, and fermented it according to all the rules of the game. He had looked over the shoulder of seasoned professionals, carefully distilling the mash and fine tuning the raw spirit through the distillation process. Finally he was able to bottle a pure, top-quality distillate. But when he released it onto the market in the early 1980s, full of expectation, it soon became clear what a mistake he had made: he did not use cherries! His plum brandy was faced with the prejudice that plums are inevitably associated with slivovitz, that simple, rustic schnapps from the eastern bloc.

Now this top distiller's wood aged Alte Zwetschge has long since become one of his classics. And in the intervening years other stone fruit varieties have taken their place alongside cherries, and are winning over, or back, the favor of a quality oriented clientele: greengages, mirabelles, sloe berries, wild plums, Austrian sour plums, apricots, and peaches. Cornel cherries that have till now

been handled as a stone fruit are actually nuts from a botanical point of view, though their nutty flavor is not so surprising any more.

## The almond question

The thing about all types of stone fruit is that they require a great deal of experience on the part of the distiller, as no pits should be broken open during the mashing process, if at all possible. They contain amygdalin, which is broken down into prussic acid (hydrogen cyanide), among other things, during processing. Apricots contain a particularly high level of it. Even unbroken pits give the brandy an unmistakable note ranging from almonds through to marzipan. Depending on how pronounced it is meant to be, the amount of pits left in the mash varies, and they can even be left in during distillation. At the end of the day it is a matter of taste, and is a way of differentiating these spirits as a distinct category.

Like no other fruit, ripe plums can give the distillate persistent depth. Their high sugar content means they produce high alcohol

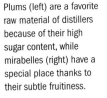

Plums (left) are a favorite raw material of distillers because of their high sugar content, while mirabelles (right) have a special place thanks to their subtle fruitiness.

alues. Their sweet flesh is rich in aromatic fruit notes.

The plum fragrance of the brandies is accompanied by marzipan, jasmine, nougat, and pear, and sometimes even hard cheese and roses. Sloes, native to the area stretching from north Africa across Europe to the Caucasus, are the ancestor of the plum. Their dark blue fruits—as big as cherries and with a comparable pit size —taste very tart and bitter when raw, but produce very distinctive brandies and spirits.

Apricots make impressive components in brandy with their intense fruit, though their reputation has unfortunately suffered as a result of cheaper mass produced products that unfortunately often have added flavoring. Good brandies are expressive but never heavy; instead they are subtly elegant. Wachau is famous for its high-quality apricot brandies, so it has protected designation of origin status. In Hungary and many other Balkan countries, barack palinka would seem to be an unchallenged feature of the national identity.

Cherry brandies and kirsch have a quite distinctive character from other stone fruits. When sweet and sour cherries without stalks and with few pits are mashed, the almond notes recede in favor of the primary flavor of the fruit; light, clear, and often bitter accents gain an upper hand. Varieties with a deep red flesh, like sour or morello cherries, can produce complex brandies that reveal nuances of bitter chocolate, cinnamon, and chamomile alongside those of the fruit. Specialists can even elicit flavors that are hard to extract from small fruited types like wild cherries.

Stone fruit brandies do well when given more time to reach the peak of maturity. Top Tyrol distiller Günther Rochelt allows them at least three years in large glass containers that are not completely filled to enable contact with the air; those are kept at different cellar temperatures depending on the type of fruit. Good brandies are even better after ten years. Thoughts then turned to cask aging, especially when they saw how the persistent fruity sweetness of some plum varieties reacted to the strong wood notes. So many a critic who absolutely rejected cask aging for many fruit brandies just a few years ago has now gone quiet, for more and more distillers are bringing a new deluxe class of fruit brandies onto the market using traditional cask aging.

Cherries (left) are classics in the distilleries of many regions, whereas peaches remain the preserve of leading experts, as their delicate flavors dissipate easily during distillation.

# Cherries

Using the modern equipment in his specialist distillery, Lorenz Humbel teases out the character from a range of cherry varieties.

Himmelrieder Herzkirsche and Bittere Brenzer, Ziesener Wilde and Werdersche Allerfrüheste, Schöne von Montreuil and Rheinfallkirsche—how to find the right cherry from 800 different varieties given in one Swiss database alone? For Lorenz Humbel, who took over his father's distillery in Stetten near Zurich, the question would more likely have been, which ones do you leave out? Using 126 varieties he has already found out that it is possible to "create a very distinctive profile." Small-fruited cherry varieties are sweeter and tastier than dessert cherries, sour cherries can have a higher sugar content than sweet cherries (it is just masked by the acidity), and early cherries are less expressive in a brandy than late cherries, just as dark cherries are more intense than pale ones.

Nowhere are cherry brandies as cultivated and celebrated as in Switzerland. There is hardly a region or large town that does not have its own version: Zuger Kirsch, Basler Kirsch, Berner Kirsch, and so on. So Swiss distillers reacted quite touchily in 1994 when permission was given to use foreign cherries as well in Swiss kirschwasser. Some of them formed a "Swiss kirsch" interest group, processing only home-grown cherries.

The Swiss fruit association compiled a list of requirements for distilling cherries in their "standards and regulations for cherries."

Accordingly, only fully ripe fruits can be used, without stalks, leaves, and twigs; bruised and damaged cherries only as long as they are not fermenting or spoiling; what are in fact rejects of dessert and preserve cherries are as inappropriate as fruits full of maggots.

## Small scale in the Black Forest

Black Forest kirschwasser may only be produced onsite from the fruit of the region without any added sugar. In spite of these measures to maintain quality, this cherry brandy has seen better times. Just after World War II it was the best-known version of this spirit in German-speaking countries as well as elsewhere. Yet in the decades that followed its halo slipped considerably. Against the background of 31,000 non-bonded distillers (Abfindungsbrenner) and 300,000 owners of raw materials (private individuals permitted to distill up to 13 gallons / 50 liters of pure alcohol per year) that together were processing some 200,000 tons of fruit across southern Germany, it is within the bounds of possibility that there was "too much mediocrity," as Edmund Marder admits. His sour cherry brandy is proof that this need not be the case. It combines lively fruit with an elegant hint of marzipan.

With cherry brandy the question of pits in the mash is more critical than with other stone fruits. Beside the light, acidic flavors of the fruit, the marzipan flavor of the pits asserts itself with particular clarity, and can easily become dominant. One exception is the rare wild cherry brandy. Here the fruit is captured harmoniously with hints of cocoa and coffee. "It is perfect with a good espresso," as Hubertus Vallendar recommends. Wild cherries, also known as bird cherries, thrive on tall trees in mixed forests that often bear no more than 45–65 lb (20–30 kg) of cherries. The fruits consist primarily of a large pit and not much flesh, and are extremely laborious to process.

For larger scale cultivation, increasing numbers of cherry varieties are catching on, which can be mechanically harvested using electrical shakers. Catching them in a net prevents them from getting damaged. They need to be modern cultivars, however, that can withstand the electrical vibrations to their delicate roots.

Left: Humbel's cherry brandies benefit from elaboration in large stoneware containers, or even in large barrels.

Right: Creativity and an extensive range go hand in hand.

# Selected cherry brandies

### Switzerland

**Etter**
**Zuger Kirsch 1996**
Internationally renowned, the Etter distillery displays modestly, though self-assuredly, on its label "100% pure fruit brandies from Switzerland." It is not just for their cherry version that they stress that the fruit "is grown in the vicinity of the distillery." Single origin fruit brandy from the Lauerzer mountain cherry variety of the region is only distilled in years of a good harvest. The brandies are bottled after at least 6–8 years in storage, the traditional way in 13-gallon (50-liter) demijohns. Etter has been distilling this varietal cherry brandy for over 50 years now. This means that the oldest kirsch still on the market is dated 1949.

### Switzerland

**Urs Hecht · Gunzwiler Destillate**
**Kirschbrand Lu Lauerzer**
Since Urs Hecht took over his father's old "for-hire" distillery (Lohnbrennerei) in 1984, his career has taken a sharp rise and he has won many awards. He has not forgotten the farmers, however, from whom his father before him bought fruit. While his fine brandies are aging at home, he travels around with his mobile still, distilling schnapps for his suppliers. "This way, I find out what matters to people," says Hecht, "for instance that small farmers are being hit hard by dumping prices." Hecht buys only high-quality material from Switzerland for his brandies, paying a decent price for it. This ensures the best basis for quality brandies like the Lu Lauerzer, which melts initially on the palate with buttery smooth fruit and finishes on ripe cherries.

### Switzerland

**Humbel**
**Cuvée Kirsch K126**
Lorenz Humbel is a man who is fond of precision. To find out about the production of cachaça, he even went on a cargo ship to Brazil. Back home his declared intention is to maintain the tradition of the Swiss cherry as a seal of quality. To this end, he examines every step of production for possible improvements—and he finds them. No other distiller experiments with so many different varieties, and none with such success. Altogether Humbel makes a few dozen different cherry brandies and every one of them is a gem. There is the dazzling morello cherry with crystal clear, ripe fruit that melts on the palate. The white wild cherry version, on the other hand, oscillates between marzipan, berry fruits, and a hint of vegetables, with a palette of flavors defined by its pits. Cuvée Kirsch is made up of 126 varieties, which combine with surprising harmony with the wood notes of this cask-aged brandy with its smooth, sweet fruit.

### Austria

**Mariell**
**Vogelkirsche vom Leithaberg**
There is a reluctance to recognize th[e] importance of geographical location fo[r] fruit brandies—the terroirs, with all the[ir] defining conditions from the soil to th[e] weather, that are valued so highly by win[e] drinkers. Wine producer Richard Mariell['s] fruit trees grow beside his vineyards i[n] the Leithaberg mountains in Burgenlan[d] province. The limestone and slate slope[s] store heat that they release again in th[e] evening. The European bird cherry variet[y] bears the best fruits on such calcareou[s] soils. This is also evident in the bird che[r]ries from the Leithaberg region. The[ir] intense cherry fruit is suffused with pow[-]erful yet elegant notes of the pit. Th[e] brandy is well rounded, sweet, and lon[g] on the palate, with a hint of vanilla.

## Germany

### ...arder
### ...auerkirsch

...Albbruck in the lower Alps, a stone's ...row from the Swiss border, Edmund ...arder has been making brandy all his ...e, always trying to use the best fruits and ...eadily improving each fruit variety. At ...ernational tastings his meticulous ...tention to detail has brought him enor-...ous success, and with fruits that are ...tually the Austrians' trump card—bird ...erries. So these brandies from the ...uthern Black Forest are now found even ...elegant hotels (like the Louis C. Jakob ...Hamburg and the Adlon in Berlin), in ...e Reichstag, and on Lufthansa air-...anes. The sour cherry is rather ...strained on the nose initially, and then ...nfolds it fruity, bitter almond flavors in the ...outh.

## Germany

### Ziegler
### Wildkirsch Nr. 1

Ziegler is a company that has been distilling fruit since 1865. The breakthrough came, however, when a group took over the family firm, improving both quality and marketing. The house's flagship since then has been its Wildkirsch No. 1, each bottle of which contains 3,000 ripe cherries, according to the company. With its distinctive carafe-shape bottle, Ziegler is now a familiar favorite in haute cuisine. This smooth brandy reveals a lively interplay between the flavors of sour cherries and their pits.

## Germany

### Vallendar
### Dollenseppler Kirschbrand

In 1998 Hubertus Vallendar built an ultramodern distillery in the village of Kail on the Eiffel mountains overlooking the Mosel river, not far from his home village of Pommern. There he just keeps on creating the most astonishing brandies. To get an idea of the quality of his spirits, it is best to start off with the classics, like this cherry brandy. For it he chose a sweet cherry variety characteristic of the Baden region—Dollenseppler cherries he sources from the Markgräferland. These brownish-red dark cherries develop plenty of sugar and flavor, which Vallendar captures in a pure, concentrated form.

## United States of America

### St. Georges Spirits
### Kirsch

Jörg Rupf opened his own distillery in California in 1980. Excited by the quality of the fruit, he began by distilling fruit brandies and then turned his attention to liqueurs, whisky, and vodka. To this day he still takes the trouble to buy in the fruits himself, as their quality determines that of his brandies. He gets the right type of sour cherry, the Montmorency variety, in Michigan. To bring out their flavor, he uses pinot yeast. "Tasters are often deceived by the delicate first impression of the kirsch," he says. "Beginning gently with almond, it ends in a spectacular, persistent cherry finale. I love the stunned silence that follows."

## France

### Distillerie Paul Devoille
### Eau de Cérises, Kirsch Grande Réserve

Fougerolles, in the north of the Haute-Saône *département*, is the gateway to Franche-Comté. Fruit trees were planted in this hilly region back in the Middle Ages, especially different soft fleshed, sweet cherry varieties. Ideal for distilling (as well as making preserves), they are responsible for this cherry brandy's special reputation. Today 40,000 cherry trees produce fruit here. Distillerie Paul Devoille, founded in 1859, has been in the Miscault family since 1985. It has a Grande Réserve, traditionally based on several varieties which are fermented and then double distilled: a powerfully expressive cherry flavor with a fine almond note.

# Plums and quetsches

It is certainly far from easy to tell the difference between plums and quetsches ("Zwetschgen" in German), especially as it is said in the Alpine region to be a vernacular rather than a botanical difference. Extensive hybridization also makes it even more confusing from the botanical perspective. The clue, or guideline literally, is perhaps to have a look at the seam on the skin: the oval-shape quetsches do not have any, unlike the rounded plums and the very round green-gages. With mirabelle plums, the size of cherries, it is just a matter of luck whether you find a seam. There are more indicators underneath the surface: the flesh of the quetsch is firm, sweet, and aromatic, and comes away easily from the pit, which is elongated, flat, and pointed at both ends. Plums on the other hand are reluctant to separate from their round, bulbous pits, as their flesh is not as firm. The adhesiveness of the pits can be significant for the distiller's choice of variety, for most plums and quetsches produce a similarly high level of alcohol.

## Rich in pits

When retained in the mash, and even the distillation, the pits make their presence felt with clear notes of almond and marzipan, giving the full bodied brandy an added striking component. If the pits are damaged when the fruit is crushed, then they are responsible for unpleasant, unwholesome notes of bitter almond that can spoil the distillate. Distillers looking for a pure fruit flavor remove all the pits from the raw material:

most find their own style somewhere in the middle. So what is usually a small proportion of pits makes its way into the mash and gives a smooth marzipan flavor to a brandy that is extremely fruity.

Other than plums and quetsches, a variety called Löhrpflaumen is good for distilling. This accidental hybrid originally came from Switzerland. The large, reddish-purple fruit have an intense flavor of cinnamon and almonds, but are also rather tart, which is also expressed forcefully in the spirit. Local types of quetsches, such as Bühler or Fellenberg types, are mainly of regional interest. Zibarte is a type of wild plum whose small yellowish green fruits with high tannin content are only used in fruit distillation. Black Forest zibarte is regarded as a premium specialty because of its low yield, partly caused by its low sugar content.

## Slivovitz

Being welcomed with a small glass of plum brandy is good manners in the Balkans. In Serbia alone 70% of harvested quetsches, some 424,000 tons, ends up as slivovitz. Many farmers still make their own schnapps and can look back on a long tradition of illicit distilling in the process. By far the most commonly used variety is Pocegaca (a cultivar of *Prunus domestica*, the common plum) that contains plenty of sugar, so alcohol fermentation is not usually a problem. However, during the mashing stage, not enough care is always taken to keep the pits intact. This explains the distinctive flavor of some brandies and also perhaps why evening

liberally quenched with slivovitz are so notorious for their aftereffects.

Fermentation is carried out at low temperatures to slow down the process. Once the mash has finally fermented, distillation takes place either immediately or it is left for a time, in which case this "Spätbrand" (late spirit) is regarded as the finer product. Part of the spirit is bottled soon after, while the rest is aged in casks. Oak casks, as well as barrels made from robinia and mulberry wood, are used, which occasionally gives the spirits a good finish. Exporting companies like Imperia, Stefan Nemenja, and Stara Sokolova age their slivovitz for up to 12 years. In spring 2007 the Czechs lost some of their proverbial saint-like patience. A formal error in an amendment to EU standards threatened to downgrade their high percentage fruit distillate, slivovice, to a nameless, alcoholic plum juice blend. It reached the stage of protests during which a total of 200 plum trees were planted and anointed with the offending spirit as "the plums of freedom." In September 2007 various Slavic states won EU-wide protection for their slivovitz, which they are allowed to prefix adjectivally with their names as a protected designation of origin. And the plum grove of freedom thrives on.

## A potential sharka attack?

Like all stone fruit, plums are under threat from the sharka (or plum pox) virus. Transmitted by aphids, it begins by leaving bright green spots on the leaves. The plums then develop little bumps, and the flesh hardens like rubber, making it inedible. Affected trees must be cleared, and the location can only be replanted in the second year at the earliest, and even then not with stone fruit. Urgent research is currently underway to find sharka-resistant varieties.

## Tuică

With a history said to date back to the 15th century, this schnapps is now so ubiquitous that in rural areas at least few meal begin without a small tuică, and at family celebrations they drink toasts with it instead of wine. This Romanian spirit with an alcohol content of 45% vol. is distilled from a regional plum variety that is grown exclusively for this purpose. A census in 2003 revealed the cultivation area as 136,000 acres (55,000 ha), and 75% of the harvest was used for tuică production. After 6–8 weeks' fermentation the mash is double distilled in copper pots over a wood or charcoal fire, and the distillate is then aged in oak casks for a period ranging between six months and ten years. The best-known growing regions are Buzau, Cimpulung, the Mures valley, and the mountains about Pitesti, where tuică is nicknamed "Ochii lui Dobrin"(Dobrin's eyes), after the 1970s footballer whose feel for the ball was matched only by his hard drinking. Tuică is a recognized product of protected origin within the EU. However the Romanians had to undertake to register the many private distilleries and comply with hygiene standards.

# Selected plum brandies

**Germany**

**Dirker**
**Feldzwetschgenwasser**

It all started with a glut of plums. There was such a bumper harvest from the traditional orchards in Franconia in 1986 that the farmers' own needs, as well as those of neighbors and friends, were more than met. Arno Dirker, a skilled carpenter, took the surplus to a friend, who distilled it. That was the beginning of a beautiful friendship—between Dirker and the pot still. His Feldzwetschgenwasser is characterized by a really pure fruit quality, a restrained cask note, and good length. Exactly how a plum brandy should be.

**Switzerland**

**Urs Hecht**
**Vielle Prune im Barrique**

Within a short time Urs Hecht from Lucerne has risen to become one of the hottest distillers, thanks to his meticulous work. As well as being intensely fruity, his spirits are skillfully balanced, in this instance between acidic fruit and new wood: lively, juicy, and syrupy on the palate.

**Austria**

**Alois Gölles**
**Alte Zwetschke, im Eichenfass gelagert**

Fruits ripen later when they have been subjected to warm days and cold nights; in return, they develop more flavor during the longer vegetation period. At least this applies to the domestic plums from traditional Steiermark orchards in this brandy. The spirit is aged for seven years in oak casks, giving it the rich brown color of cognac. Plenty of old, fine wood can be detected on the nose and palate, but it is never intrusive, while the ripe fruit is accentuated with a wonderfully lavish touch.

**Austria**

**Christoph Kössler**
**Zwetschkenbrand aus dem Eichenfass Reserve**

"The more often the raw material is distilled, the more quality is lost." This is Christoph Kössler's simple answer to the basic question of double or continuous distillation. In saying this, he has not made it easy for himself. The Tyrolean distiller has one of the latest computer-controlled systems in his distillery. His brandies reach a corresponding level of perfection. The 2003 oaked plum brandy is the embodiment of finesse, combining lively fruit with a little vanilla and peppermint.

**Austria**

**Tinnauer
Zwetschkenbrand
Reserve**

"The best spirits are created in the mind," as the Steyr distiller Franz Tinnauer once said to a journalist. And in fact he is seen as the thinker among Austrian distillers. Perhaps this is why his distillates are often bottled at a high spiritual level: his Zwetschkenbrand Reserve is distinguished by an alcohol content of 52.5% vol. It begins with fascinating intensity on the palate, and maintains it right through the long finish, with notes that oscillate between peppermint, frosting, and spicy wood. Exactly the right amount of alcohol.

**Austria**

**Weutz
Zwetschke**

In the old debate about double versus continuous distillation, Michael Weutz from Steiermark opted for the middle road. He had equipment custom built to suit his own ideas of what it should be, though he won't give out any information about it. Weutz pays meticulous attention to every last detail. Only top-quality fruit is harvested and the pits are removed by hand where necessary. The result speaks for itself. A lovely nuance of old wood, overlaid by some mint and herbs on the nose: plenty of fruit and dried fruit, sweet and long on the palate.

**Croatia**

**Badel
Stara Sljivovica**

Badel attaches great importance to the fact that this slivovitz is based on the Bistrica plum variety, grown near Zagreb, as well as the fact that it has been producing the Croatian national drink since 1862. The plum brandy is double distilled in the Zagreb distillery. Then Stara Sljivovica (stara means "old") is aged in casks made from Slavonic oak, which give it its clear amber color and a certain mildness. Well-chilled, slivovitz is used in Croatia as an aperitif, or to accompany or round off a meal. This versatility has made it into the brand leader there, as well as in Germany.

**Serbia**

**Bogdanovic
Stara Sokolova**

This old plum brandy was named for the falcon, which gave its name to its region of origin in the Mediterranean part of Serbia. There, on the Drina river, plums are the most important agricultural product. They are used in different ways, though the lion's share is destined for slivovitz. The Bogdanovic family, now into its seventh generation, has been distilling plums since 1830. It owes the quality of its consistently excellent spirit to the mixture of old and new plum varieties and the careful elaboration that gives the brandy its wonderfully smooth, harmonious profile.

**France**

**Etienne Brana
Eau-de-Vie de Prune Vieille**

Basque distiller Etienne Brana set up a distillery geared to produce the highest quality in Saint-Jean-Pied-de-Port in 1974, and planted pear trees for what has now become his famous Poire William. But his old plum brandy, made from the Prune d'Ente variety and greengages, is just as good. Selected fruits are fermented in stainless steel tanks and then double distilled in a charentais pot still. Martine Brana, who succeeded her father, ages a proportion of the eau-de-vie in oak casks, before blending it with fresh, fruity plum spirit. It has an intensely complex, pungently fruity aroma, and is very well balanced on the palate with an elegant spicy note and a persistent finish.

# Sloes and their spirit

Barely the size of a cherry, the blue-black fruits of the sloe, an ancestor of the cultivated plum, represent a challenge for the distiller. They taste sour, very tangy, astringent, and bitter. The fruits are at best only edible after the first frost, which destroys some of the tannins. Its scant flesh can only be removed from the pit with difficulty, making it harder to mash the fruit. The tannins and bitter constituents, levels of which are high even after the frost, impede fermentation. It is not impossible, as it can be helped along by adding enzymes, selected yeast, and warm water, but the alcohol yield will always be low, about half that of mirabelles. Many distillers therefore opt for maceration, in which the unfermented fruit is steeped in alcohol before being distilled.

Blackthorns, or sloes, grow wild in many areas, including the famous Champagne region. Seasonal pickers deliver the fruits to the distillery, where they have to macerate in wine spirit first of all.

In Distillerie Moutard in the Champagne region, they use wine spirit that has been distilled in house—they do, after all, specialize in marc de champagne—and leave the sloes to macerate for two years in it, allowing many of the fruit's flavors to transfer to the alcohol. It is then put into copper alembics that are heated very carefully; otherwise the sloe spirit develops unpleasant caramel notes. Moutard's Eau-de-vie de Prunelle de Champagne has a very intense flavor of almonds and marzipan. The sloe fruit is very pronounced on the palate, accompanied by sweet almonds and a delicate bitter note.

**Left (from top to bottom)**

Two basket sieves are fitted over each other inside the cylinder-shape alembics. The lower one is inserted empty.

The macerated fruits are only added when they are inside the alembic, so that no drop of the alcohol they have been soaked in is lost.

After the second basket sieve is put on top and filled, the fruits in it are evenly distributed. The alcohol is collected in the lower part of the alembic.

The lid is then put on the alembic and tightly screwed on.

**Right (from top to bottom)**

The characteristic onion-shape top is fixed to the middle of the lid. The swan's neck, or vapor pipe is attached to its opening at the top. The other end of this pipe is connected to the tank.

Stage one: the raw spirit. When the alembics are heated from below, the vaporizing alcohol rises through the macerated sloes, the vapor collects in the top, and then travels through the swan's neck to the tank, where it condenses.

After the raw spirit is produced, the sieves full of depleted fruit are lifted out of the alembic with a hoist. The equipment can then be properly cleaned.

The fruits have served their purpose and are removed, and if possible they are used as fertilizer for the fields.

# Apricots

One of the most remarkable manifestations of the apricot is found in Wachau, Austria, with its dry climate and clear changes in temperature between night and day, especially until the ripening period before the beginning of August. This led with justification to Wachau apricot brandy being given an EU protected designation of origin in 1996. At present some 100,000 apricot trees grow in the cultivation area. Most of these are dwarf trees of the Klosterneudorf variety, with an emphasis on generously measured planting density: after all, the fruits should get enough light, air, and sun. Again and again, distillers in particular are urged to process fruits grown in sunlight rather than shade, as only the former develop that particularly intense apricot flavor. So it is entirely fitting that, as early as 1600, the name of apricot was associated with the Latin term *apricus* (a sunny place) and taken to mean *in aprico coctus* (ripened in the sun), though this etymology is debatable.

If you want to harvest apricots fully sun ripened at the peak of their flavor, it is essential to know what you are doing; for, unlike stone fruits like pears and quinces, apricots do not after-ripen, especially the ones from Wachau. But if you get the plump orangey yellow fruits with the red blush into the mash tun at just the right time, then that perfect balance of high sugar content and acidic values—a result of the special climate conditions of Wachau—promises brandies with lusciously sweet flavors of ripe fruit and almonds (provided not too many of the large pits are broken during the mashing process). The yield of spirit from the mash is around 7%. Apricots are distilled in central and eastern Europe, from the Gallic abricotine to barack pálinka in Hungary and its other variations in the Balkans. At its best, apricot brandy is a warm spirit with profound sweetness and a persistent fruity appeal. Sometimes you also find playful flavors like aniseed, chocolate, or jasmine.

## Barack pálinka

Apricot brandies are highly valued east of lake Balaton, the political border between Austria and Hungary, as well, and in large areas of the Balkans.

At the time of the Ottoman empire, vast apricot groves had extended across the Hungarian plain since the mid 16th century. They were unable to withstand the vagaries of

To produce a convincing brandy, apricots have to reach the peak of ripeness on the tree.

Hungarian history, and were replanted in the early 19th century. To this day the area around the city of Kecskemét is famous for the quality of both its apricots and its barack pálinka.

It is said that the apricot schnapps (for this is what barack pálinka means) distilled there enjoyed the highest favor, after the duke of Windsor tasted it for the first time in an elegant Budapest bar in the 1930s. That said, barack pálinka has remained a down-to-earth drink. This fine brandy is often bottled at an alcohol content of 50% vol., and state certified as such on the label. High alcohol content is regarded as meaning higher in quality as well. Especially strong palinkás are approvingly called *kerítésszaggató* in Hungary. This means "fence ripper," an affectionate allusion to the effect that a few glasses can have on a person's balance.

As is the case just about everywhere in the Balkans, the házi pálinkák (domestic spirits) with the highest percentage of alcohol are often made at home. In Hungary private individuals are permitted to take their homemade mash to a distiller to make into a spirit of the desired strength. The expert's sure hand, however, ensures that the poisonous methyl alcohol and harmful fusel oils are properly separated off in the heads and tails. Viewed in this light, there is nothing wrong with a daily glass of apricot brandy.

From left to right: In Kecskemét they use modern distilling equipment. What is happening inside the column still can be observed through the bull's eye. In spite of computer-controlled technology, the practice of drawing and tasting samples has not been abandoned.

Hungary has a diverse range of barack pálinkas on the market.

# Unusual stone fruit brandies

**Christoph Kössler (A)**
**Edelbrand aus Vinschgauer Marillen**
Vinschgau apricots on Nördersberg near Schlanders in the Tyrol enjoy extraordinary growing conditions. With plenty of sun, cool nights, and a late harvest, the fruits form lots of acids that are full of flavor. The unassuming, pale green fruits of this individual variety are barely edible when fresh, and only play their olfactory trump cards in a processed state. Vinschgau residents know this, and make delicious preserves with them. Christoph Kössler knows it too. His brandy presents these apricots in all their complexity: fragrant, bursting with rich sweetness, and with a hint of menthol.

**Franz Tinnauer (A)**
**Weingartenpfirsich Brand**
It almost goes without saying that Franz Tinnauer, as a skilled wine grower, plants vineyard peaches near the sites where his vines grow. But distillation does not just happen by itself. The fine, complex flavors of peaches, which are so often found in wines like riesling, survive the distillation process with some difficulty. Very often the result is a tasteless brandy with a heavy marzipan flavor from the pits. Tinnauer has kept the bitter almond notes out completely, producing a smooth, fruity brandy in which the peach is quite evident in the finish.

**Karl Holzapfel (A)**
**Marille 05**
First, the apricot pits have to be removed. As Karl Holzapfel from Wachau is aware, "They intrude too much in the flavor." The fruit is then carefully mashed, and immediately cold fermented in a very slow process. After distillation it rests for two years in a demijohn—"This is better for concentrating the flavors." The apricot brandy is bottled at 45% ABV, "and ages a little more in the bottle." On the nose, it introduces a very elegant, playfully light array of fruit aromas, which continues seamlessly on the palate, amazingly intense and long.

**Georg Hiebl (A)**
**Schlehe Edelbrand**
Lots of pit, little flesh, hardly any water content, without which fermentation cannot begin; the sloe is a difficult fruit, but many distillers enjoy precisely this challenge, even if they later realize they were not up to it. In the must producing region of Lower Austria Georg Hiebl succeeds in breathing life into this wayward fruit. His fine sloe brandy exudes an intense flavor of pits, marzipan, pistachio, and plenty of almonds—full and delightful on the nose, complex and long on the palate, the finish revealing a touch of menthol and herb bitters.

### Guglhof (A)
**Marillen Brand**

Gugelhof, founded in 1641, is the oldest distillery in the Salzburg district. Anton Vogl describes himself as a traditionalist as well, as the business has been in his family for generations. This does not preclude, however, the use of modern distilling technology, such as fermentation in temperature-controlled stainless steel tanks. Vogl does, however, fully support the double distillation method as it gives the spirits a longer lifespan. The limited editions are bottled by hand at Gugelhof. The apricot brandy is full of juicy ripeness, with a touch of mint and pomace, robust on the palate, and with menthol in the finish.

### Franz Tinnauer (A)
**Kriecherl Brand**

Yellow mirabelle plums are called Kriecherl in Austria, but the same name is given to damsons, a type of wild blue plum. At Franz Tinnauer in Gamlitz, southern Steiermark, where they also produce excellent wines, you can taste this wild plum variety at its best. It has a subtle note of the pit, wrapped in plenty of fruit. On the palate, cherries, plums, cinnamon, and menthol unfold in a long finish.

### Jean-Paul Metté (F)
**Eau-de-Vie de Vieille Mirabelle**

The mirabelle plum has ideal growing conditions in eastern France, especially Lorraine. The region's fruits enjoy not only the protected designation of origin status, but also the esteem of the inhabitants of Lorraine, who celebrate the Fête de la Mirabelle each year in Metz. For over a century Metté has produced first-class brandies, now dozens of types, in the nearby town of Ribeauvillé. It was his mirabelle, however, that made distiller Jean-Paul Metté famous. Stone fruits are characterized by a restrained aroma. But on the palate the taste is powerful, with sweet fruit and a persistent finish.

### Martin Fischer (D)
**Mirabellenbrand, im Holzfass gereift**

In Wiesentheid, Franconia, Martin Fischer specializes in fruits from the region, and preferably the native varieties. He has a special preference for the modest mirabelle, even if it looks "from the outside like a small plum with pigmentation." His brandy, refined in wood casks, is proof of his enthusiasm. Its unusual aroma of finest marzipan and full milk chocolate aplenty conjures images of a well-appointed candy store. In the mouth, it exudes sweet, ripe fruit, accompanied by a modicum of chocolate, marzipan, and a hint of caramel.

# Fruit journeys

Styria, the southernmost of Austria's federal states, which borders on Slovenia, enjoys a pleasant Mediterranean climate as well as sufficient rainfall and good, fertile soils. The natural conditions are ideal for fruit growing (and wine growing), even though heavy snowfalls are frequent at the higher altitudes. While other fruit-growing regions in Europe find it more difficult to market their fruit varieties profitably, especially their apples, this is something in which the Styrians have been and remain accomplished. Styrian apples were known for their quality far and wide even during the era of the Austro-Hungarian monarchy, being very much sought after and a feature even at the court of the Russian czars. Today they carry a great deal of weight in the federal economy as they are the most important product in east, west, and southern Styria. These three regions supply 70% of all Austrian fruit, and nine out of ten apples on the domestic market—the latter being grown by 1,600 apple farmers on around 13,600 acres (5,500 ha). Fruit is grown on a total of 19,000 acres (7,800 ha) in Styria, wine growing now having reached about 8,000 acres (3,300 ha). Fruit trees and orchards therefore constitute a distinctive feature of the landscape, attracting undivided attention during the spring blossom season in particular. Styria has become a more or less mandatory travel destination, especially since the attractions of the fruit are not only optical. While the fresh fruit in season is clearly one factor, the opportunity to visit the many fruit farms welcoming guests is an even greater attraction. There you can quench your thirst with a glass of juice, must, or nectar; buy jams, chutneys, and dried fruit; and, last but not least

Styria is Austria's most important fruit-growing region as well as being the leading fruit brandy region.

taste the excellent quality fruit brandy varieties, of which there is now an astonishing range available.

## Distilled future

Distilling is an old tradition in fruit country as fertile as this. While, in the past, it largely presented an opportunity to be able to process the extra produce, the Styrian farmers have managed to elevate their schnapps to an entirely new level in terms of quality, turning them into successful niche products. They have succeeded in transforming their farms, deeply rooted in tradition and passed down through the generations, into modern, future oriented businesses where even the raw materials they produce themselves are processed innovatively. Of course, the varieties available were and remain first and foremost those characteristic of Styrian fruit growing. In addition to apples, with the well-known varieties such as Gravenstein, King of the Pippins, and Idared being distilled separately—as well as traditional varieties such as Maschansker—the distiller's attention was soon drawn to elderberries, the region's

second most important fruit variety, which is grown primarily for its coloring and requires a great deal of technical skill when it comes to distilling. In the order of their importance in terms of fruit growing the distillers convert pears, damsons, red currants, blackcurrants, peaches, strawberries, cherries, apricots, walnuts, and blackberries into clear fragrance and flavoring essences, as well as using wild fruit, especially the popular rowan berry, and more exotic raw materials.

The focus on ever more intense—but also more refined, clearer, and eccentric—aromas is a feature not only of the distillers in Styria, but also of their colleagues in all branches of the culinary and beverage industry. This has resulted in a movement that has transformed Styria into an indulgence region directing itself as Austria's culinary center at gourmets and quality-conscious customers throughout Europe, providing them with numerous opportunities to train and inspire their senses.

The flow of indulgence-seeking visitors begins as soon as the fruit blossom season begins in the spring.

The *klappotek* prevents the birds from simply gorging on the fruit.

# Berry fruit

Spirit made from berries is one of the most sought after and most expensive of the fruit brandy varieties. When fresh the small fruit have an intense flavor, but their distillation requires a great deal of skill and expertise. This begins with the harvesting—with the often rather evasive berries, it can sometimes be an unexpectedly long period of time before they make up a quantity worth distilling. If they are wild berries, they require even more work as they often have to be picked from inaccessible bushes, many of which bear thorns. At the top of the list are the wild varieties with significantly more concentrated aromas that have long since become rarities in central Europe. This makes the harvesting an expensive investment. Standing in front of the extensive range of "wild" products on the spirits shelf in the supermarket, you would be forgiven for thinking that that some of the names have more to do with the distributor's imagination than with the origin of the berries. Consumers whose sense of taste has possibly been manipulated by the artificial flavoring agents in fruit yogurt or jam to such an extent that they find fresh strawberries to be lacking the familiar strawberry taste easily succumb to the deceptive wealth of aromas.

## The fruit quantity lesson

With many berries such as blackberries and strawberries it is the quantity alone that makes the spirit expensive. "If you are lucky 100 liters of wild strawberry mash will produce 2 liters of brandy," explains Arno Dirker who distills a whole range of wild berry varieties (100 gallons produce 2 gallons). "Together with the production costs and tax that soon becomes unaffordable." What is almost more difficult is capturing the fine aromas. Even generous quantities of carefully processed fruit often produce no more than insipid schnapps. Other berries such as wild blueberries and elderberries have high pH values, meaning that they are not sour enough to prevent the undesired development of acetic, lactic, and butanoic acid bacteria. In expert hands, however, elderberries can produce a dense, spicy brandy. The

It is only since the 1990s that the new quality approach and modern technology have made it possible to distill berries such as red currants and blackberries into convincing fruit brandy varieties.

unwanted parts also have to be removed from the berries in what is a very time-consuming process, and the berries then finely ground. Fermentation can take four weeks, with the distilling producing no more than 2–3% of pure alcohol from the mash. Currants, especially white and blackcurrants, are much easier to process. The intense aroma in the skins is reflected in the brandy, as are the slightly astringent nuances from the foliage. White currants are an especially pleasant variety, being characteristically fruitier with elegant acids.

With high-quality berry brandy only being possible with plenty of experience and with modern technology, these varieties have come into existence since the 1990s. Raspberries are one exception, also having produced convincing results earlier when macerated in and distilled together with alcohol. This remains the most widespread method today. Approximately 13 lb (6 kg) of fruit produce a half gallon (2 liters) of 96% alcohol, very little of the alcohol content is lost during distilling, and when diluted to drinking strength there is correspondingly more raspberry essence. Raspberry liqueur, on the other hand, uses fermented fruit and a comparable quantity of alcohol requires 220 lb (100 kg) of raspberries. Applying the same method to wild blackberries or blueberries seemed futile up to a decade ago. Today berries in general provide a wide spectrum of intense, complex distillates, each with its own character.

Elderberries constitute a particular technical challenge for distillers and are distilled only seldom.

Producing top-quality brandy from berries such as raspberries or blackcurrants requires large quantities of the expensive fruit.

# Raspberries

The raw materials for fruit brandy can sometimes constitute a substantial financial burden, particularly in the case of raspberries. Even for a large-scale consumer such as a distiller, the sensitive fruit are often a major cost factor. Harvest quantities from wild raspberries—without doubt one of the highest quality raw materials for the distillate—are so small that the daily yield often has to be frozen first. The sensitive berries would otherwise spoil before enough of them had been gathered for the mash. Mold then develops if fermentation does not start quickly. In addition, the fruit have only a small amount of sugar that can ferment to produce alcohol. All of these are risk factors that make the product expensive.

Preserving the fruit in 96% alcohol is one way of saving money. The alcohol leaches out part of the rheosmin as well as another around 250 substances making up the raspberry aroma. When distilled, about 1½ lb of fruit is sufficient for 1 gallon of alcohol (3 kg for 1 liter). A raspberry liqueur, on the other

hand, requires more than 15 times as much. Quality-conscious distillers such as Günther Rochelt from the Tyrol in Austria crush up to 28 lb of fruit to distill just 1 gallon of raspberry liqueur (50 kg for 1 liter). Anybody who likes playing with numbers will be able to calculate what weight of raspberries was used to produce the next sip from the glass. Were it not for the fact that the majority of wild raspberries are harvested in eastern Europe the initial costs would in fact be totally unaffordable.

## Spirits or liqueur?

What with many other types of fruit ultimately amounts to a decision between first and second choice is not as clear cut with raspberries. The distilling ensures that the flavor nuances of the alcohol deriving from the fruity sugar end up well preserved in the bottle. They develop an unexpected depth and sustainability in the process. Wild raspberries can possess such a degree of transparency that you sometimes think you can feel the fruit's many tiny hairs on your tongue. When matured in the bottle many raspberry brandies improve to become even more harmonious. Some distillates continue to develop even once the bottle has been opened. The first aroma arising from a freshly poured glass, however, is sometimes reserved, if not insipid in fact. Even when the brandy "awakens" in the glass for a while there is often one thing lacking: fruity freshness. The magical, floral lightness of the raspberries that seems to dance on top of the liquid, on the other hand, seems to capture the spirit much better. Good spirits are present immediately and immerse the taste buds in fresh raspberry aromas that sometimes play out as dark fruit compote nuances as well as numbing overtones of hyacinth.

Framboise from St. George in California, USA.

Picking raspberries in Germany's Black Forest.

# Selected raspberry distillates

**Germany**

**Dirker**
**Waldhimbeergeist**
A 17th-century Irish sailor is the reason behind Arno Dirker's producing this fine wild raspberry brandy. If his forefather had not been "stranded" in Franconia and had not started a family there... Dirker knows the story in detail. With meticulous patience he manages to produce a distillate made from wild Romanian raspberries that retains the full raspberry fruit. Dense, sweet, with a touch of raspberry candy.

**Germany**

**Marder**
**Waldhimbeerbrand**
With reliable quality, Edmund Marder has worked his way up to be one of the top European distillers, now with the support of his son Stefan as well. The first of their joint efforts indicates that there are not going to be any major changes to the course taken so far. Full of fruit and dense on the palate, and ripe and creamy with a trace of candy and lemon that appear in the aftertaste.

**Switzerland**

**Käser**
**Waldhimbeerbrand**
"That won't amount to anything," claim some fruit distillers as soon as the talk turns to raspberry brandy. You need far too much fruit and they contain far too little sugar. Raspberry brandy really does need a professional. The Swiss fruit distiller Ruedi Käser produces this brandy by distilling 66 lb (30 kg) of fruit per bottle, extracting the pure fruit. The palate is stroked by the most gentle of aromas, incomparably fragrant, lively, and long.

**Austria**

**Kössler**
**Edelbrand Waldhimbeere**
The Austrian Christoph Kössler is one of the consistent winners in international competitions. Brandy from his range win prizes one after the other and he practically has a subscription to titles like "Distiller of the Year." Kössler runs one of the most modern distilling plants, using it to extract a very fine pit nuance from the wild raspberries as well as a very clear fruit style.

**France**

**Metté**
**Eau-de-Vie de Framboise Sauvage**
Until ten years ago, the word "Alsace" cropped up sooner or later in any discussion of top-quality fruit brandy. Ideal growing conditions, a long tradition, and the French awareness for preserving every culinary achievement were the prerequisites. With the endeavors of the young distillers in the neighboring countries to the west, however, there is now less talk of Alsace. Metté is one of the few remaining distilleries still flying the flag. Raspberries have always been a hallmark of the region. The distillate displays abundant fruit, pleasant body, and a touch of bitter sweet in the aftertaste, as well as length.

# The essence of indulgence

"Like a cartload of hay in the living room," says Ruedi Käser, amused at the somewhat bewildered faces of his guests who, like him, are holding a goblet in the hand. It seems impossible but the spirit gives off the intense fragrance of sun-dried grass. How did it get there? "Trial and error, elimination, and trial and error again," that is all the astonished audience gets out of him because of course Ruedi Käser does not allow anyone to look over his shoulder. Brandy varieties made from hay and lemon grass, asparagus, and rhubarb are the result of ongoing and persistent experimenting and their recipes remain a trade secret.

Ruedi Käser is one of a group of innovative distillers who have mastered a repertoire ranging from apples to damsons and who are no longer willing to settle for that alone. "Of course there is always room for improvement, but the incentive lies in finding something new."

## Crystal clear holidays

When someone like Georg Hiebl develops a passion for oranges while on holiday, the best fruit for classic fruit brandy varieties might be flourishing in the many orchards back home in Austria's fruit region, but he will nevertheless distill mandarins and mangos. And maracujas. And water melons. And dates. "Holiday in a glass," is what he calls it when every brandy variety gives off an exotic aroma. Armed with curiosity, enthusiasm, and old reference books on fruit growing, today these out-of-the ordinary distillers use their sound skills base to tackle limes, pine cones, and Jerusalem artichokes. And once they have figured out how to do it, it seems there is no stopping them. Dandelions per-

Chestnuts (left) and rose hips (right), the fruit of the wild rose, are among the unusual raw materials used for top-quality brandies.

haps? Or coriander? Ceps or perhaps holly ather? Anything goes, including poppy eeds, ginger, and rose hips.

And what on earth is an Oregon grape, Mr. Dirker? "*Mahonia aquifolium*—a type of barberry that produces pea-size, steel blue rosted berries with sweet-and-sour, dark red lesh." The German who (still) has a distillery in Hesse uses them to make a brandy full of earthy nuances, "a little like a good genian. I had tried it as a child and so I wanted o know what it tasted like as brandy." The listillers seem to prefer distilling according o their childhood memories: poppy seed ("because I used to love poppy seed bread") or Green Sauce. Arno Dirker prepares his crystal clear version of Hesse's national dish by distilling extracts of the seven prescribed fresh herbs for significantly longer than 12 hours, "and then it does taste just like real Green Sauce."

However, even if it is possible to distill plants about which hardly anyone knows more than the name, this does not mean that the end product is necessarily drinkable. Experiments with garlic are said to have produced such idiosyncratic results that the distillers are happy to change the subject quickly. Tenacity is therefore a basic requirement. With his first attempts at distilling hazelnuts Dirker was hardly able to detect the nuts at all. It worked much better with roasted nuts, but a great many nuts ended up in the trash before he had established the right degree of roasting. With the addition of vanilla and cocoa the end result was a spirit with elegant nougat nuances which is especially popular with his customers. No one has been able to imitate it to date.

Sour citrus fruit (left) and dried hazelnuts (right) present a particular challenge when it comes to distilling, but they can produce good results.

# Selected "exotic" brandy varieties

**Germany**

### Arno Dirker
### Haselnussgeist
Having once read in an old book that hazelnuts cannot be distilled, he decided to have a try himself, despite the "cannot be distilled." The author had not told any untruths, but Arno Dirker had a confectioner friend who gave him the key tip: roast the nuts. The addition of a little vanilla and cocoa, both thoroughly degreased, is what gave the Dirker hazelnut brandy, said to be the first of its kind, its fragrant hazelnut and milk chocolate bouquet. "You don't have to drink it," concedes Dirker himself: it goes very well with vanilla ice cream, in cakes, in an espresso. His regular customers drink it neat, however.

**Germany**

### Vallendar
### Bananenbrand-Ruanda
For his first attempt Hubertus Vallendar chose bananas from the Canary Islands, but then, his home region of Rhineland-Palatinate having entered into a partnership with Rwanda, using the delicious, small bananas from Rwanda became the obvious choice. The top-quality brandy produced from these bananas has complex aromas from the ripe, almost overripe fruit, and from the green skins. The ripe, almost baked fruit with its caramel sweetness predominates on the palate. The distillate was so well received in Rwanda that it has developed into an aid project with Vallendar assisting in the distillation of bananas locally.

**Germany**

### Vallendar
### Spargelgeist
With the still he constructed himself the distiller in Kail, high above the Moselle, is able to extract the aromas from all raw materials in overwhelming concentrations, this applying even to asparagus from Müden mountain in Germany. The glass gives off a wide variety of vegetable nuances ranging from earthy to cooking water, as well as green asparagus and leeks, more intense than in any cooked dish, with the asparagus providing a spicy flavor and plenty of aftertaste. An exceptional top-quality brandy.

**Austria**

### Georg Hiebl
### Kaffeegeist
When asked the question as to how he views his profession, the Austrian Georg Hiebl answers: "As a creative act aimed at perfect harmony." And he has no inhibitions in his pursuit of this ambitious goal. In addition to berries and stone fruit, he also distills corn, beer, and vegetables, as well as making a rum and a bourbon whiskey. He himself has still not found a category for the coffee brandy in his brochure, however. With its strong roast nuances the distillate is difficult to categorize but could produce its best results when used for cooking or for desserts.

**Austria**

### Georg Hiebl
### Rote Rüben Brand
"A crazy idea," is what Geor Hiebl called his distillery and h knows how to top anything tha the competition places in the stills in the way of fruit, veg etable, and grain varieties Envisaging beets as a brand variety is not really an obviou idea. However, in contrast to th many "exotic brandy varieties that you might taste out o curiosity but do not necessari want to drink again, beet brand is indeed pleasant. The earthy warm aroma of boiled beet rises from the bottle as soon a it is opened. The brandy is sur prisingly gentle on the palat and really is drinkable, with distinct aftertaste.

**Switzerland**

**Ruedi Käser**
**Thymiangeist**
It is possible! Thyme can be made into brandy, and a highly intense one at that. Käser, known for his extravagant brandy varieties, has proved it. This brandy brings the fragrance of a whole bunch of thyme into your nose. The leaves are perhaps a little dry, as if they had been picked a few days previously. On the palate, however, the essential oils from this Mediterranean herb suddenly become so dominant that you even feel their slightly numbing effect. "You don't have to drink this one either," says the distiller. The aromatic reserves are intended more for the kitchen: for a grilled steak, flambéed directly before serving, and for which the alcohol content of 55% vol. is ideal.

**Italy**

**Domenico Sciucchetti**
**Kastanie**
Domenico Sciucchetti smoke dried the chestnuts for this brandy very traditionally before Gian Andrea Scartazzini was then able to grind them in the Promontogno mill. That was in 2003 in Graubünden in the Swiss Alps, just a stone's throw from the Italian border. The results are also as authentic as this story would have you believe. The distillate gives off a smoky, chestnut flour aroma that is heavy, a little like a peaty Scottish whisky with medicinal nuances. On the palate, however, it is soft, again with these astounding smoky nuances, which are accompanied by a refined, subtle sweetness.

**France**

**Paul Devoille**
**Eau-de-Vie de Baies de Houx**
Holly, which flourishes as a bush or a tree in the forests of central Europe, is prized largely for its decorative, dark green leaves with their prickly edges and for its attractive small red fruit. They are considered to be poisonous but, when roasted, they used to be used as a coffee substitute. In Alsace, knowledge of the beneficial properties of *houx* has been retained together with the tradition of distilling it into brandy. This is done by leaving 220 lb (100 kg) of the fruit to macerate in 4 gallons (15 liters) of 96% alcohol. The fragrance and the flavor take you into the forest where you are surrounded by the spicy aromas of damp foliage and humus. Magical.

**France**

**Jean-Paul Metté**
**Spiritueux de Gingembre**
"You have to try this one," insists Philippe Traber. The head of the traditional distillery and godson of the legendary founder Jean-Paul Metté knows that he has to be firm. Who would want to have the floral, soapy aromas of ginger as an alcoholic beverage? You might give in out of politeness, but you remain skeptical. And then comes the surprise: the *Gingembre* has the unexpected aroma of the fruity part of the ginger root alone, as well as a fresh orange impression, paired with a touch of lemon grass. The floral side tends to dominate on the palate, but remains authentic and still fruity. An exotic that is guaranteed to get a reaction.

**Canada**

**Okanagan Spirits**
**Saskatoon**
The Native Canadians have long known the value of the Saskatoon berries, the small, blueblack fruit from this snowy mespilus variety (*Amelanchier alnifolia*), which in botanic terms are in fact not berries at all but a variety of pit fruit. Their high vitamin C content is balanced by an equally high sugar content so that they can be used in a similar way as cranberries. In 2004 the German Frank Deiter realized his dream of distilling the fruit from the region around Vernon. In addition to an apple brandy aged in barrels that happens to bear the name Canados, the results also include Saskatoon, which competently extracts the characteristics of this largely unknown fruit with its fruity-sweet and dry aromas, exhibiting a very subtle nuance of the pits.

# Gentians, rowan berries, etc.

Gentian is not everybody's cup of tea as the highly aromatic, bitter earthy distillate, although gentle on the stomach, is very idiosyncratic. Its aromas derive from oils, resins, alkaloids, bitters, and pectin. The brandy is made from the heavy roots—weighing up to 13 lb (6 kg)—of the protected yellow gentian (*Gentiana lutea*), a bush measuring up to 4½ feet (140 cm) in height, and has nothing at all to do with its blue namesake, as some labels might suggest. Without blossoms the yellow gentian is easily mistaken for white hellebore, one of the most dangerous of Europe's toxic plants, especially as they both grow in alpine meadows. However, although a fraction of an ounce (1 g) of dried hellebore root can be fatal, the same amount of gentian root is "only" enough to lend a slightly bitter taste to over 3 gallons (10 liters) of water. For the information of those complaining about the bitters in gentian brandy: the better part of it does not even make it into the distillate. Gentian production is a laborious process. "Even when the mash is very homogenous, fermentation takes two to three months because most of the sugar—up to 13% in fresh roots—is present as trisaccharide gentianose that first has to be broken down by the yeast's own enzymes into glucose and fructose in order to be able to ferment," explains Rudolf Walter. After distilling gentian needs at least another two years in order to be able to "round off" its edges. Rudolf Walter comes from Galtür in Austria, where there is evidence of gentian having been distilled as far back as around 1800. The quantities are now controlled in order to ensure the sustainable harvesting of the roots. Other producers obtain their gentian from Italy and eastern Europe. Only Bavarian mountain gentian brandy has to be made in the German federal state of Bavaria from Bavarian gentian roots, according to the EU regulations.

## Berries that are not berries

Long known in Alpine regions and highly prized today is brandy made from rowan berries (French *alisier*). In the autumn the wild variety bears podded fruit that is so bitter that the first frost is needed to alleviate the bitterness—an effect that can be imitated today in the deep freeze, albeit with the same minimal compromises in aroma. The harvest yields are low, and the fruit is very dry and low in sugar, but rich in the natural preservative sorbic acid. The mash needs to be diluted and the fermentation initiated by means of strong, pure culture yeasts (which then need sufficient nourishment). This is no deterrent for Alois Gölles because, like many of his colleagues, the Austrian from Styria sings the praises of this brandy with its unique bouquet and dense marzipan nuances, its idiosyncratic bitter aromas only developing into a complex brandy after a number of years. Nuances of bitter almond, licorice, nutmeg, bananas, and aniseed are then the reward.

The fruit of the wild service tree enjoys a similar reputation. The brandy with the dried pear aroma is one of the most expensive varieties because the fruit is so rarely available. However, it seems that it is the difficulties themselves that attract the distillers.

This also apples to medlars, an aggregate fruit that lost their significance as a dessert fruit way back at the end of the Middle Ages. Here, too, the low yields and long, difficult fermentation despite the high sugar content simply encourage the distillers.

Left and center:
The tall, yellow, gentian develops starchy roots that have been distilled to make a medicinal brandy in the Alpine regions for centuries.

Right:
The brandy made from the difficult rowan berries is now also considered a delicacy outside Austria.

**Germany**

**Bentenhammer**
**Holzfass Enzian**
Bentenhammer is proud of its company headquarters in the Bavarian Alps and it is therefore a must to have a gentian in the range. The roots of the yellow gentian, a plant that measures up to 4½ feet (140 cm) in height, are fermented and distilled according to the traditional method. Thereafter is where the small difference comes: the brandy is matured in wooden barrels. Once it is later diluted to drinking strength with spring water from the Bannwald spring at the foot of the Schliersee mountains the wooden nuances even dominate the earthy edges of the gentian flavor and give the brandy its gentle body.

**Austria**

**Hämmerle**
**Enzian ›Vom ganz Guten‹**
A bottle of "Really Good" is supplied with the harvest year, a bottle number, and a batch code—uncompromising quality control. The roots of this protected mountain bush are usually dried prior to processing and then distilled. Hämmerle, on the other hand, is proud of the fact that their mash is made from fresh roots only. It takes 27½ lb (12.5 kg) of them to distill one bottle of gentian. The tremendous amount of effort results in a highly concentrated brandy. The distillate with the earthy mushroomy aroma is surprisingly soft and round on the palate, with a hint of fruit and a subtle sweetness.

**Austria**

**Seyringer Schloss-Brände**
**Enzian**
The name comes from a former country estate dating from the era of the Austro-Hungarian monarchy. The name and the historic bottles are indicative of the old Viennese tradition behind the Seyringer Schloss-Brände. This brandy is also dominated by the gentian: the flavor is characterized by a rustic gentian nuance.

**Austria**

**Guglhof**
**Vogelbeer Brand Reserve**
Fruit has been distilled at Guglhof for generations and the almost 500-year-old building has now been modernized. The modern plant with which Anton Vogl distills brandy varieties such as this rowan berry brandy with its raisin, dark Bundt cake, and sweet berry aromas can be admired through the glass walls.

**Austria**

**Reisetbauer**
**Vogelbeer Brand**
Hans Reisetbauer travels as far as the Balkans if needs be. The Austrian distiller spares no effort when it comes to finding the best raw materials for his fruit brandies. The result is gems such as this rowan berry brandy, its bouquet alone being characterized by deep pit fruit nuances with a light, caramel sweetness. A wonderfully distinct flavor of berry fruit, often with a hint of marzipan, herbs, and nut chocolate, develops on the palate.

**Austria**

**Alois Gölles**
**Vogelbeere**
Only wild rowan berries from the mountain slopes of Styria are harvested for this brandy. "Wild rowan berries may have less sugar but they give the brandy more aroma," claims Alois Gölles from Styria. His bottles contain especially fine almond, marzipan, and bitter almond aromas but barely a trace of the astringent, dull tones that often dominate rowan berry brandy.

# Wood-matured and cigar brandies

Wood maturation—considered an indispensable career component for cognac and calvados—used to be considered an unsuitable means of maturing the majority of fruit brandy varieties. In contact with the wood the distillate acquires sweetness, density, and complexity, as well as typical barrel nuances that fruit are allegedly not able to cope with. However, this applies neither to apples and pears, nor to damsons and other stone fruit. Experiments with cherries are comparatively recent. Some of these brandy varieties have generous alcohol contents of 50% and more. This strength and intensity is valued by cigar smokers, amongst others, when seeking a spirit to harmonize with the intense aromas of their cigars. So-called cigar brandies each need to be "tried on" individually.

### Ruedi Käser (CH)
**Birnenbrand aus dem Kastanienfass**
The pear brandy is placed in the chestnut barrels with an alcohol content of 60% vol., 5–7% of which has evaporated after 16–20 months. It is then bottled, unfiltered, with this drinking strength. The fruity aroma of the ripe pears forms a pleasing combination with the fine wooden nuances.

### Urs Hecht (CH)
**Kirsch Teresa im Barrique**
As a native of Switzerland, Urs Hecht is not only a confirmed kirsch distiller, he is also a wine connoisseur and is therefore able to handle barrels and knows that the fruit should not be intimidated by the wood. In the Teresa, with a storage period of several years, the fine, bitter aromas of the pit, of sweet cherry, and a touch of oak wood mature combine into one, sometimes with the fruit, sometimes the marzipan, sometimes the toasty barrel nuances dominating.

### Lantenhammer (D)
**Quitten Brand aus dem Apfelholzfass**
The rare symbiosis between aged quinces and apple wood needs a sensitive expert such as Lantenhammer in Bavaria, Germany. The slightly bitter bouquet is immediately reminiscent of quinces. On the palate the abundant wooden influence alternates with the sour apple, cherry, pear, and lemon nuances, culminating in the bitter-sweet spices and subtle pit tone of the aftertaste.

### Guglhof (A)
**Alter Zwetschgenbrand**
The fruit for this brandy is harvested by hand from old damson trees in the Salzburg province. It takes ten years for the "old brandy" to mature in oak barrels before it is then bottled by hand. By then it is a combination of candy floss and damsons with a touch of cinnamon and raisons, as well as the exotic. The aftertaste is sweet, soft, round, and long.

### Edmund Marder (D)
**Zwetschgen Brand, im Eichenfass gereift**
Edmund Marder focuses on proximity: late ripening damson varieties from the Black Forest mountain villages of Unteralpfen, Birndorf, Birkingen, and Eschbach are matured in toasted barrels made from Swabian oak. The brandy gives off a sweet cinnamon aroma. A milder wooden nuance with a touch of vanilla on the palate, meltingly soft.

### Alois Gölles (A)
**XA Alter Apfel, 1989**
Alois Gölles was one of the first fruit distillers to adopt an uncompromising focus on quality, which is why he now has the oldest brandy varieties in store. There are only a couple of hundred bottles of the 1989 vintage. After so many years in oak barrels it still has the fresh fruit in the bouquet and this is retained on the palate, despite the sophisticated wooden nuances. A long aftertaste with touches of tobacco and leather in the empty glass.

### Alois Gölles (A)
**Alter Apfel aus dem Eichenfass**
As one of the pioneers Alois Gölles has been a consistent advocate of high-quality distillates, having one of the basic prerequisites outside the front door: Styria's volcanic soils that are ideal for fruit trees in particular. The Old Apple is distilled from regional varieties such as Maschansker and Starking before then being matured in oak barrels for seven years. It develops lively acids from the apple during this time, producing a soft, melting fruity aroma on the palate, underlined by typical barrel nuances.

### Arnold Dettling (CH)
**Kirsch, holzfassgereift**
The fruit for this barrel matured kirsch ripens on trees located on the slopes of the Rigi massif. The mountain cherries are small, dark in color, aromatic, and sugary sweet. Dettling carry out their own quality assurance: this brandy, for which only the best fruit are selected, spends a number of months in wooden barrels. During this time it acquires vanilla and butter nuances from the wood and these support the smooth fruit on the palate.

### Christoph Kössler (A)
**Apfelbrand aus dem Eichenfass**
Kössler's apple, pear, and damson schnapps have long since become known beyond the borders of Austria due to his mastery of the art of distilling temperatures. The man from the Tyrol is always on the lookout, however. This brandy is proof of his ability to keep apple brandy fresh and fruity in the barrel. Fruity, with green mint and a number of bitter nuances, a touch of pits, and plenty of sour apples: all of this competently accompanied by the finest wood.

# Whisk(e)y and bourbon

Starting with the mash, through to enjoying the drink, one thing is certain: without water there's no whisk(e)y.
Page 302: Strathisla has kept the atmosphere of times past.

# Smoke in abundance

Whisky. Whiskey. The word itself has a smoky ring to it. And it kindles associations. Images are evoked spontaneously: of distinctive pagoda towers, the landmark of distilleries in the Highlands; of Irish pubs in full swing; of the golden expanses of Kentucky and its racing horses. Anyone who appreciates whisk(e)y has a personal treasure trove of images and memories based on preference and travel experiences. For whisk(e)y—as the double way of spelling it suggests—is not a standard product. Quite the opposite, in fact. It is the multiplicity of different expressions that have won it its place in the world of spirits.

Irish and Scottish folk are fond of musing over the murky past, a time when their forefathers were being converted by plucky monks that brewed wonderful elixirs in stills they brought with them from faraway lands. Though the word "whisky" originally came from the term for "water of life," the only thing that present day whisk(e)y has in common with its ancestor is the alcohol content. The centuries of tradition certainly form a solid basis for its astonishing development, but in terms of taste, present-day versions have virtually nothing to do with their historical predecessors. For it was only in 1915 that an additional element was introduced to the production process in Scotland (officially, at least) that completely transformed the taste of whisky: the oak cask. There had, of course, been individual distillers in Scotland, Ireland, and the United States who stored their grain spirit in oak casks, thereby establishing that this maturation helped to improve the quality considerably. Widescale aging in casks in the main whisk(e)y regions is, however, a 20th-century development. Only then did the different whiskies develop the variety of aromas that make them so appealing, and acquire the mellowness that makes them so palatable.

What was originally drunk in the traditional whisk(e)y areas at first was a raw, high percent proof grain spirit, unless it was administered medicinally with added honey and herbs. Not until distillery owners and spirits merchants made a determined effort to tame its wild, fiery nature did it embark on its new course to global success. Achieving this was not just down to aging in casks, as blends (mixing lighter and stronger spirits together to make a harmonious whisky) also made a significant contribution. Although this is particularly typical of Scotland with its many malt and grain distilleries, it is equally applicable to Irish whiskey or American bourbon, even if distilleries there only use separate spirits, albeit different ones, and the term "blend" is not one they like to hear.

Thus whiskies were created that appealed to a wide audience, and still do: they are best drunk on the rocks, in long drinks, or in cocktails. They make up over 90% of the market and as a rule the best-known brands offer a good-quality product that is completely reliable. Today we would presumably be content with blended and vatted whisky, were it not for the fact that a section of consumers turned away from brown spirits in the 1970s, opting instead for clear spirits. The result was that Scottish distillers were left with a proportion of their unblended malts. This gave fascinated whisky aficionados the opportunity of rediscovering original whiskies. Glenfiddich had, admittedly, demonstrated back in 1963 just how appealing a single malt can be, but the real breakthrough came in the late 1980s. Since then the whole world has been enthusing about the rich diversity of malts. Not only that, the malt revolution awakened a completely new interest in whisk(e)y in general. Only then did people begin to discover the extraordinary richness of aromas and nuances that characterize top-class whiskies. Since then, producers of whisk(e)y and bourbon all over the world have been constantly coming up with new and fascinating spirits, and talented distillers in many countries of the whisk(e)y world have long been making a name for themselves.

# Uisge beatha from the whisky distillery

When Henry II conquered Ireland in the 12th century, his soldiers are said to have regaled themselves with the "water of life" they found there (Henry II, detail from an English book illustration of Peter Langtoft's Chronicle, ca. 1300).

For Irish and Scottish people whisk(e)y is part of their culture, lifestyle, and national identity. As each would readily claim whisk(e)y as their own, they excel themselves in inventing stories about it.

Exactly when the art of distillation reached the British Isles is unclear, but presumably Christian monks brought it with them even earlier than the 10th century. The first mention of *uisge beatha* (pronounced ish'ke-ba'ha', and often written as "usquebaugh") dates back to 1171, when Henry II asserted his claim to power in Ireland and his soldiers are said to have enjoyed this drink. The term means "water of life" in Gaelic, and the first part developed into the word "whisky."

There is evidence of distillation as an alchemic process in England in the 13th century, when Roger Bacon (1214–92), a Franciscan monk teaching in Oxford, alluded to it in his writings. The first recipe to mention the distillation of fermented grain was hidden by Geoffrey Chaucer in the prologue to his famous *Canterbury Tales*, where he refers to the distillation of alewort (beer wort made from malted grain). The first indisputable proof was an entry in the tax record in Scotland at the time, the Exchequer Rolls, in 1494: "Eight bolls of malt to Friar John Cor wherewith to make aqua vitae." A "boll" was an old measure consisting of six bushels each weighing 56 lb (25. kg), making it about 2,700 lb (1,220 kg) o grain! In September 1505, when the Scottish king James IV was staying in Inverness his treasurer noted two purchases of aqua vitae for the king, recorded as if they wer for medicinal purposes.

## Currency and cure

Distilling in Scotland and Ireland may hav been the initial preserve of monks, bu apothecaries soon followed suit, for aqua vitae was regarded as a cure-all. By this the meant not pure spirit, but a concoction o medicinal herbs, minerals, and honey. Onc the recipes for it appeared in books, pro duction began to spread across the Britis Isles. It was kicked off by *The Vertuose Bok of the Distyllacyon of all Maner of Waters o*

Left: in the 13th century Roger Bacon was versed in the art of distillation (statue of Roger Bacon in the Oxford University Museum of Natural History).

Right: in the 14th century Geoffrey Chaucer published the first recipe for grain distillation (engraving by Charles Knight, 1780).

the Herbes (1527), which was a translation of the *Liber de arte distillandi de simplicibus* (1505) by a doctor from Strasbourg called Hieronymus Brunschwig.

People distilled the sought-after water of life themselves using simple pot stills, enriching it with all sorts of ingredients to make it into herbal water. It was usually taken care of by the housewife, or the servants in the case of more genteel households. Farmers soon found that distilling allowed them to store surplus barley securely, preserving it to some extent, while the left-over mash was ideal as fodder for livestock. Their clear, unblended whisky also developed into a method of payment that the masters of estates readily accepted as rent.

## Forced to become legal

The first licenses for whiskey distillation such as the one granted to Sir Thomas Philipps in Country Antrim, Northern Ireland, in 1608 (the reason for the current Old Bushmills Distillery to celebrate its 400th anniversary in 2008) were the exception initially. They are evidence, however, of the authorities' keen interest in alcohol production, which in turn had implications for the quantities of alcohol already consumed. As long ago as 1644 the Scottish Parliament levied the first tax on strong spirit. Following the Act of Union in 1707, creating one United Kingdom of England and Scotland, the government increased duties on spirits,

which proved to be a lucrative source of income. As this measure was not met with wild enthusiasm by the rural population, illicit distilling and smuggling flourished noticeably. At the end of the 18th century in Ireland there were approaching 2,000 home-based distilleries that paid minimal taxes. The government thought about possible remedies for bringing whisk(e)y production into line, and in 1823 it passed the Excise Act. Only stills with a barrel capacity of more than 48 gallons (181.61 liters) were allowed, subject to an annual license fee of £10, and in addition there was a tax on each measure of pure alcohol distilled. At the same time, in Scotland as in Ireland, support was given to the establishment of new large distilleries and illicit distilling became a punishable offence, not just for the distiller but also for the owner of the land on which the stills were located. The only options were to give up or to distill whisky professionally.

Bowmore on Islay is one of Scotland's oldest officially licensed whisky distilleries.

# Religion, freedom, whisky

Robert Burns, poet and whisky drinker (grisaille painting ca. 1870, detail).

John Jameson in Dublin was the first to produce whiskey on an industrial scale, as illustrated by these pot stills.

In light of the taxes raised on the part of the government, every illicit distiller could liken himself to a freedom fighter. The Ferintosh Distillery on the Black Isle peninsula to the north of Inverness, on the other hand, found itself caught up in political turmoil. Its staunchly Presbyterian owner, Duncan Forbes of Culloden, had welcomed the overthrow in 1688 of James VII of Scotland and II of England (who granted Catholics more and more rights) by the Protestant William of Orange, his son-in-law. In doing so, however, he incurred the wrath of the Jacobites and it was not long before his distillery went up in flames. It turned out that this was the best thing that could have happened to him, for in compensation in 1690 the loyalist ex-distillery owner was awarded the privilege of being allowed to continue distilling on his estate without the deduction of any tax. Ferintosh, the first legal distillery in Scotland, became so famous that for some time the name became synonymous with whisky. When the privilege was finally revoked in

1785, Parliament compensated the owners to the tune of £20,000, whereupon the Forbes of Culloden shut down their distillery. "Thee, Ferintosh! O sadly lost! / Scotland lament frae coast to coast! / Now colic grips, an' barkin' hoast / May kill us a'; / For loyal Forbes's charter'd boast / Is ta'en awa!" With these words—full of dark foreboding and evoking an unhealthy future without the disinfectant properties of Ferintosh—the national bard Robert Burns (1759–96) bids farewell to his favorite whisky in the 21-verse epic "Scotch Drink." Burns, who immortalized his numerous love affairs in poems, loved to sit with friends in simple bars. "Freedom and whisky gang thegither," he mused in praise. After moving to Kilmarnock in 1784, Robert Burns had to make do with the whisky placed in front of him in Poosie Nansie's Tavern in Mauchline.

Frequented at that time by beggars, vagabonds, and loose women, the bar still exists to this day: it inspired the poet to write the cantata "The Jolly Beggars." Here in the

Lowlands they served rough whisky from the Kilbagie Distillery. Founded in 1700, the distillery was owned by the Stein family, who obtained its license in 1794. Just under 30 years later (see below) one of the sons, Robert Stein, was to make his mark.

Before that happened, however, attention was fixed firmly on the tighter excise laws of 1823. A few of the domestic and illicit distillers had managed the leap over to legality "voluntarily" before these came into force. In Dublin John Jameson founded his company in 1780, and John Power followed 11 years later. Thanks to the new support for large companies, both expanded their distilleries considerably and began to export their whiskey. With its lighter, less peaty character it became very popular in the British Empire and its close ally, even after independence, the United States.

## The grain whisky revolution

The distinctively smoky Scotch whisky could not keep pace and remained confined within its borders for the time being. In order to cut down the laborious double distillation method using traditional pot stills, around 1826 Robert Stein began to experiment in the Kilbagie Distillery with a continuous distillation process in patent stills, which would be faster and therefore more economical.

Aeneas Coffey, an Irish tax inspector and inventor, whose work had given him plenty of experience of pot stills, made significant improvements to this column still. Firstly he supplied his equipment—later named the Coffey still—to both Jameson and Powers, though the whiskey it produced was too bland for their taste. Coffey was more successful in Scotland. Using his technique large quantities of mostly unmalted barley could be processed into a purer distillate at low cost: it was the birth of grain whisky. With few exceptions it produces unconvincing results in its pure form, and is very rarely bottled singly; what it did make possible was the blend, which continues to make Scotch whisky the commercial success it is today.

Irish whiskey notched up considerable successes abroad in the second half of the 19th century, and was exported to the Commonwealth and the United States of America.

# Scotch floods the markets

A Scottish wine merchant in Edinburgh, Andrew Usher senior, is reputed to have been the first person in the 19th century to blend malt whiskies from different distilleries in order to offer his customers consistent quality. When the low-price, light grain whisky then came on the market, Andrew Usher junior set to work adding it to malts. By doing so he discovered that it mellowed the often powerful taste of pure malt. In 1860 he launched the Old Vatted Glenlivet, took over the distillery's production completely, and became the first to export blended whisky. Powerful malts blended with light grain whisky were in the air, as it were, and merchants like George Ballantine, James Chivas, John Dewar, Matthew Gloag, John Haig, William Sanderson, and John Walker also began to create reproducible blends of accessible character. At the same time the production of grain whisky also experienced breathtaking growth, especially after the six most important Lowland distilleries merged to form the Distillers Company Limited in 1877. Whisky had become an industrial product.

## The whisky question

From 1890 consumers were faced with a dazzling array of single malts, different blends, and young grain whiskies—all of which might well be offered by one single distillery—without any indication on the label of what was in the bottle. In Ireland the most famous distilleries took a clear position in favor of pure pot-still whiskey, but in Scotland there was resistance as some distillers continued to insist that only malts produced by the double distillation method could be described as genuine whiskies. Finally a legal action was brought in the London borough of Islington. Her Majesty's Government then decided to set up a commission that ruled in 1909 after widespread consultation with experts from both parties: the spirit made from mainly unmalted grain is

Bonded warehouses of Glenlivet, the home of the first blended Scotch.

also "whisky." This gave blends the official seal of approval.

## Irish whiskey in recession

Irish whiskey flourished in the 19th century, and was distributed throughout the British Empire and appreciated in North America as well. When continental Europe was hit by grape phylloxera and the flow of cognac and other brandies was in danger of trickling to a halt, the markets also dried up. Irish whiskey and blended Scotch, which was then gaining a foothold abroad, profited from this drought. Irish whiskey experienced its first setback when Prohibition came into force in the USA in 1920. At almost exactly the same time the establishment of the Irish Free State unleashed a trade war with England, resulting in Irish distilleries sustaining heavy losses in the British Empire. On top of all this the economically weak new government raised taxes. For most small distilleries this combination of circumstances spelled the end. Those that remained tried to keep their heads above water on the domestic front, but there was no energy left for forward planning.

So when Prohibition came to an end in 1933, there was a shortage of Irish whiskey while there was Scotch galore. It was the dawn of the golden age of blended Scotch whisky. From then on it conquered world markets and its curve of success rose unabated until the 1970s, when consumer tastes turned unexpectedly to clear spirits such as white rum and vodka, as well as to the colorful cocktails they went into. The whisky industry sank in a sea of oversupply— or rather, a whisky loch. Many distilleries were forced to close: the most devastating year was 1983, when 12 shut their doors for good.

However there was still a glimmer of hope: Glenfiddich Pure Single Malt, brought out by William Grant in 1963. What had then been the object more of derision than recognition would now prove itself to be the last chance for distilleries, which had been completely dependent on blends until that point. One after the other they moved over to bottling their own malts. And the market

Johnnie Walker "keeps walking," turning his back on visitors to the Cardhu Distillery, which provides the basis for his blend.

reacted, with curiosity to begin with and then with sustained enthusiasm that has lasted to this day, not just for Scotch whisky but for top-quality whiskies in general. This spawned a wide range of special bottlings, such as single cask or cask strength, but also an interest in other origins: bourbon from the USA, Canadian whisky, Japanese whisky (Japan is the fourth largest whisk(e)y nation), and a revived interest in Irish whiskey. Whiskies are made in many countries now, and artisan distillers are producing quality at the highest level. They represent a delightful contrast to the production style of the tightly organized, hierarchically structured whisk(e)y industry in the mother countries.

# Nosing and tasting

Anyone serious about getting to know whisky, whiskey, and bourbon stays well clear of ice, soda, cola, and other "bulking agents" with flavor. They will go for the traditional, tulip-shape glass also used in wine tasting. For whisk(e)y tasting, as celebrated by malt fans today, has borrowed its technique from the world of wine. In saying that, professional nosing—with tasting taking a secondary role, if it even happens at all— goes back a long way. It started out with whisky merchants like the Ushers, father and son, who created blended Scotch in the latter part of the 19th century. The main aim in doing so was to blend several powerful, heavy malt whiskies with light, neutral grain whisky in order to keep reproducing the blend they had created as consistently as possible. To do this, you need the right nose. It was essential to be able to distinguish the different malts from each other, in order to decide how they would work harmoniously together and with the grain whisky: a high art form reaching perfection purely through nasal expertise.

## A personal pleasure

As with wine, the nose of the whisk(e)y is actually far more complex than the taste, which is why the aroma is held in highest regard. If you want to follow the rules of the art to the letter, you will however examine the color first of all. A very light whisk(e)y has probably matured in bourbon casks while a darker one has probably done so in sherry casks. As the color tone of all blends and many malts is fine tuned with caramel however, the true value of this information is minimal. We are told more by the "legs," the pattern created on the inside of the glass after the whisk(e)y has been swirled about in it. If the legs are thin and run down

quickly, then it is a young spirit. An old malt has beautiful curves that linger for a long time. The same applies to whisk(e)y that has soaked up the wood finish of sherry or port, or is bottled at cask strength with a high percentage of alcohol. When it comes to nosing, exercise a degree of caution: it is best to hold your nose at a slight distance from the glass to begin with and pass it over it quickly. Then smell it more judiciously and at greater length. That is the first stage. The next involves adding a little still, soft, pure water to the whisk(e)y. How much? That's the crunch question. Some mix in a 1:1 ratio, but personally I prefer less water, at 1:4 or 1:3 at most. It is astonishing how so little water can open up the bouquet and release a whole series of other aromas. It is then advisable to leave the whisk(e)y to stand for a short while as the aromas change and develop within another quarter of an hour.

"Sniffing out" this complexity is one of the greatest pleasures for whisky lovers (and creates long lists of detected aromas). Not one of them would take even the smallest sip from the glass before fully savoring this nasal rush. Once in the mouth a further kaleidoscope of aromas unfolds, some of which announce the bouquet while others introduce fresh nuances and notes. This is accompanied by the "mouthfeel," the general impression in the mouth, which can be soft or harder, sweetish or drier, short or longer. The aromatic diversity is fascinating in the case of some whiskies, others are rather one dimensional, the fiery quality of some betrays their youth, and others still show their age in the gentle warmth. Adding a little water brings out the full enjoyment of some whiskies, while water seems instead to impair the flavor of others. Next time, try it straight.

Left: With an ordinary blend, the patterns formed on the inside of the glass are not clear: the "tears" run down close to each other.

Right: The "legs" of an 18-year-old whisk(e)y, on the other hand, form nicely separated curves.

# Grain and plenty of water

The traditional grain of Scotland is barley. It certainly loves deep soils, but it also grows on more barren ground. It was, and still is, cultivated as livestock fodder, but Scottish cuisine knows various ways of preparing it to bring out the best in barley, firstly as a basic foodstuff such as bannocks, bread baked on an open fire, or scotch broth, a nourishing soup which is often cooked with a piece of lamb in it. There are now dozens of recipes for more refined forms of cooking that like to adopt a more regional flair. But barley's greatest significance is associated with the production of whisky and beer.

Pure malt whisky, made from only malted barley, is the exception, however. The far commoner blended Scotch is based on a mixture of distilled malt mash and other spirit known as grain whisky. Corn may have been used mainly for this at first, but wheat replaced it as soon as it became cheaper. For there are no restrictions whatsoever in terms of the type of grain that can be used in grain whisky. The situation is quite different as far as its Irish neighbors are concerned. They too prefer barley, though they use both malted and unmalted grain, and like to add some wheat as well.

Corn and rye are predominant in North America. The Blue Grass region of Kentucky is one of the main growing areas for corn in the world. So it made sense to fill the mash tuns with corn, especially as it is rich in starch. A minimum of 51% corn is required for bourbon. Rye, which came to North America with European immigrants, is used both malted and unmalted, but mostly just as a minor addition. Straight rye, which must contain at least 51% rye, is the exception.

One of the reasons Speyside developed into the main region for malts is its excellent, thriving barley crop.

## The relationship between water and whisky quality

Whether and in what way water determines the quality of matured whisky is a subject that has been hotly and frequently debated. Most Scots ascribe the excellence of their malt not least to the softness of their water, but this does not prevent either Glenmorangie or Highland Park, for instance, producing outstanding malts, in spite of their use of hard water. On the other hand, the quality of bourbon is directly attributed to the chalky, hard water of Kentucky and Tennessee, which is also low in minerals. On Islay, where the water is obviously peaty, it has long since been seen as the main reason for the individual flavor of its malts. Now it is becoming increasingly evident that the influence on taste was thoroughly overestimated. This does not change the fact that without pure, unadulterated, and sufficient water there would be no whisky.

The soft, abundant water of the Campsie Fells supplies Glengoyne, the southernmost distillery in the Highlands.

## Without water, no whisky

A whisky distillery needs copious amounts of water, so it was only ever set up in a location with a plentiful supply. Previously, when every distiller still produced his own malt, water's first role was when the barley was soaked (known as "steeping"). Soft water is best for this, and many of the Scottish distilleries swear by this softness, which is especially assured when the water comes out of granite seams or when the water flows through peat. Water's next indispensable stage is when the mash is being made, and from then on the local water is a constituent part of the whisky. For most of the flavor is contained in it: the weak alcohol content is then concentrated in the distillation process, while the proportion of water decreases. Ice-cold water is essential for condensing the spirit, so much depends on having a low enough temperature. Some distilleries in Scotland close for a few weeks in summer because they do not have sufficient water and/or the water is too warm.

When the young whisky—the new make—condenses, water still makes up almost 30%. It is then promptly put into oak casks, but not before the alcohol content has been adjusted with water to what is normally the desired strength of 63–64% vol. When the whisky has reached the right age, it is (with rare exceptions) reduced to drinking strength. Only the few distilleries that bottle on site still do this with their own water. Each distillery strives to ensure its water supply, however, not just in relation to the quantity but also to its purity: wherever possible it has acquired the corresponding source or stream with all the surrounding land, which is cultivated according to ecological principles.

# Magic malt

Scottish whisky and barley are inextricably linked, for in all the distilleries in the Highlands and on the Islands, only malted barley is used for whisky, as stipulated by law. As barley often grows on more barren soils that are low in nitrogen, it develops proportionately more starch; this means it can give a higher alcohol content, which is seen as no bad thing by the Scots.

There are two different types, winter and summer barley. The former is sown in autumn and harvested the following summer. It is used primarily as an animal feed, but also for whisk(e)y, mainly in Ireland. Two-rowed summer barley is sown as early as possible in spring, that is in March or April at the latest. It needs only four months to ripen and is good for malting: over half of the barley harvested in Scotland is used to make whisky and some distilleries import additional barley from other countries.

Malt whisk(e)y must be produced exclusively from malted barley. But for nearly all whiskies, irrespective of where they are made in the world and whether mainly from corn or rye, malted barley plays an important role as it sets off the natural conversion of starches into sugars, which would otherwise have to be done by adding enzymes, as happens in Canada.

## A vital transformation

If grain is sown in spring, it begins to germinate with the help of moisture and heat from the sun. Inside the kernel, enzymes then develop that break the stored starch down into sugar. This sugar provides the diastatic power for sprouting, as well as for yeast in the fermentation process.

The sugar feeds the yeast, providing the force for propagation and leaving behind the desired alcohol and carbon dioxide as metabolic products. So in order to create the ideal conditions for yeast, it is essential to make the grain sprout. And as the grain is not supposed to use up the sugar required to make

Left: A mountain of fresh barley for malting.

Right: After steeping, the barley is spread out on large malting floors and must be turned regularly—a hard job.

he malt, growth must be halted by heating. : should not become too hot during this rocess; otherwise the enzymes will lose heir desired effectiveness. Barley is emi- ently suited to this stratagem as it contains large amount of starch, but rye, wheat, and ther types of grain are also suitable for use or malting.

n order to start the germination process arti- cially, the barley is soaked in water for two > five days until it is completely moist. It is hen spread out on the malting floor in a ayer about 12 inches (30 cm) thick. Once starts to sprout, the barley warms up and as to be turned over regularly to prevent too nuch heat from developing. The ideal sugar evel is reached after seven days at most, and he "green malt" is then dried out, or kilned, > halt the germination process.

'he landmarks of Scotland's distilleries, heir pagoda towers, are in fact just the chim- eys of the kiln ovens. The green malt is pread out on the kiln's drying floor. This is omposed mainly of tiles that have tiny holes n the top and larger ones on the underside, hrough which warm air rises. The oven is

also here, heated traditionally with peat that smokes the malt as it dries and gives it its characteristic flavor.

Very few distilleries still produce malt in this expensive, artisan way: these are Balvenie, Bowmore, Glendronach, Highland Park, Laphroaig, and Springbank.

Now malt is usually obtained from com- mercial maltings, where the barley is germi- nated and dried in drums. During the drying phase peat smoke is passed across the malt for a period of time determined according to the appropriate smoking needs of the par- ticular distillery.

Left: Grains of green malt.

Right: While the malt is spread out on the malting floor above, the kiln oven below provides hot air and varying degrees of smoke depending on how much peat is used.

# Of mash and beer

In the Highlands and Islands of Scotland each whisky distillery has its own special malt that is more or less peaty according to its tradition and profile. Apart from that the rest of the history of malt is basically the same. In countries like the USA they use not just barley malt but a mixture of different types of grain, and this mash bill has been elaborated by each bourbon distillery on an individual basis. The heat of the mash is determined by its composition, nearest to boiling point in the case of corn. Mashing begins with an extremely dangerous process for the distilleries—the grinding. If even a tiny spark ignites during this process, which can easily happen if a piece of metal falls into the malt, the mill will go up in flames. Powerful magnets now prevent this from happening as it used to be the main reason for a distillery burning down.

The malted barley is rough ground in the mill, after which the grist is agitated in the mash tun in hot water (the mash must not become hotter than 140 °F / 60 °C). This is mostly done in closed stainless steel tanks to keep the heat in: they are also fitted with mechanical stirrers. The enzymes are reactivated by the heat and moisture (one of which is sensitive to temperatures that are too high), and the starch is converted into sugar that dissolves into the water. The murky brown, sugary liquid produced is called "wort."

The mash tun can often be as deep as 10 feet (3 m) and has a perforated floor that has holes small enough to retain coarser particles while still large enough to allow the wort to flow freely into the wort's receiver, a holding tank underneath the tun. The *draff* remains in the tun—that is, the ground and soaked grain from which the carbohydrates have been extracted and which then makes excellent animal feed. (In the case of other corn spirits this separation only takes place during distillation, but the residue then still makes high-quality cattle fodder.)

Left: The malt bin is one of the most important items in the distillery.

Right: The mash is put into large tuns with hot water.

In Scotland the mashing process is completed in three passes, each lasting no longer than about 20 minutes, during which time the temperature is raised occasionally. The second pass releases the highest level of sugar extraction, while the third provides the rest of the remaining sugar, about 4%. This is used to start off the next mash.

## Wort and wash

The sweet wort collected in the receiver is cooled to 68–81 °F (20–27 °C), and then pumped into fermentation vats made from pine or larch wood, or now stainless steel, which are known as washbacks in Scotland. They vary greatly in size, so while older vats hold around 1,300 gallons (5,000) liters, modern fermentation tanks have a capacity of more than 13,000 gallons (50,000 liters), or even more than 21,000 gallons (80,000 liters) in North America. In any case, they are not filled completely, as enough space is left for froth buildup. Yeast is then added to the wort: most distilleries use commercial brewer's or distiller's yeast that is mixed to individual taste. The interest in customized yeast and its specific development is comparatively recent in Scotland, but in Kentucky some distilleries have taken an interest in obtaining and developing their own yeast strains for years. In the case of purely malt-based wort, the alcohol fermentation can be very volatile, producing strong surges and a lot of froth; they try to keep this in check with revolving switchers. Depending on the prevailing temperature (and the amount of phenols from the peat), fermentation is usually completed in 40–72 hours, with a longer period ensuring more aromas. The result is the wash, a beer around 8% alcohol by volume, commonly known as ale in Scotland.

Left: The ground grain is thoroughly stirred with water to release the sugar converted from the starch.

Right: Experts now are convinced that the wash ferments best in wooden vats.

# Malt distillation

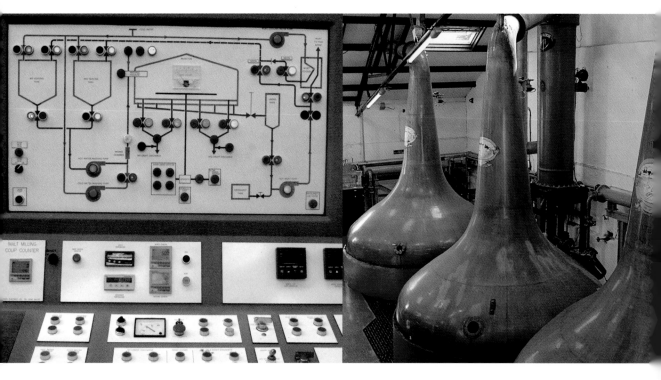

Left: Hi-tech has now arrived in the distilleries as well.

Right: The shape of the pot stills has a decisive influence on the new makes—the higher and narrower they are, the more refined the spirit.

By law, malt whisky must be distilled in pot stills in Scotland. These traditional copper stills help to create a part of the malt's identity, for every distillery uses quite distinctive shapes of pot still, from broad, flat ones to tall narrow ones with elegant necks. The higher the steam has to rise, the fewer of the heavy, volatile aromas manage to reach the condenser. This process makes it a lighter spirit, as otherwise overlaid floral notes would emerge.

The pot stills, formerly heated directly by charcoal and gas, now receive the heat they need from steam. Whisky could be distilled in one single pot still in two or three sequential passes, but in practice Scottish distilleries operate with pairs of pot stills: one (the wash still) is reserved for the wash, while the refined spirit is distilled in the spirit still. Often, though not always, the wash still is obviously bulkier. At first glance they can be distinguished from each other by the additional equipment on the spirit still: the spirit safe. This allows the stillman to intervene directly in the process.

## Low wine and new spirit

Malt distillation is traditionally carried out in two stages. The fermented, brownish colored yet clear beer, or wash, is poured into the first still, which can hold up to 8,000 gallons (30,000 liters), and then heated. The alcoholic vapors rise and pass through the pipe to the cooling coil, where they are condensed by cold running water. The low wine is collected, consisting mainly of water, but also 21–23% alcohol by volume at this stage. The residue from the pot still can be used for animal feed. Now the second (usually smaller) pot still is deployed, in which the low wines are distilled once more. In the process the clear spirit runs through the spirit safe, a glass box in which the stillman can observe the spirit. At the same time hydrometers indicate the specific gravity and therefore the alcohol content. Using a lever he can either direct the flow of the spirit back to the low wines or alternatively collect it in the spirit receiver.

At the beginning of the second distillation the foreshot, or head, runs off, but it contains

indesirable elements like aldehyde and ster as well. These foreshots are separated off by the stillman. He collects and separates off the spirit he judges to be pure (about 15 minutes into the run): this is the middle cut, spirit cut, or heart of the run.

Though this central cut usually starts with an alcohol content of around 74%, this level goes down steadily in the course of the distillation process, so that 3–5 hours later it has dropped to 62–65% vol. Next come the feints, or tails, which consist of the rougher alcohol and fusel oils that the stillman separates off and redirects into the pot still. So the alcohol content of the middle cut varies between 62 and 74%, which produces an average value of 70–72% vol. in the spirit receiver. Even if the separation of foreshot and feints can be achieved at a control desk in distilleries with the latest technology, what the stillman or master distiller decides and when is crucial for the quality of the future malt, tangibly influencing its character. The bigger the middle cut, the more of the heavy, aromatic components go into the spirit; the smaller it is, the lighter and more refined the end spirit. If the stillman allows too many feints through, there is a danger of the whisky developing unpleasant aromas, while if he is too restrictive with the middle cut then the whisky may later prove to be lacking in character. As a rule the middle cut makes up about three fifths of the total run. Reduced with spring water to give the ideal alcoholic strength of about 63%, the new spirit can then settle in the warehouse, its home for the years to come, and embark on what is now generally acknowledged to be the most important stage in its development.

Left: Pot stills are usually found in pairs: the wash and the spirit still.

Right: The fresh spirit flows through the spirit safe into tanks sealed by customs—the spirit receivers.

# Cask aging

When the new make is first put into a cask, it is crystal clear. The amber color and additional aromas that it will have acquired after years of maturation are directly related to the casks used and how long it has been kept in them. While Scottish, Irish, and most other whisky producers prefer used casks, it is a legal requirement for bourbon to be aged for at least two years in new, charred casks, most of which are made from American white oak (*Quercus albus*).

Bourbons are often bottled after four years' cask aging as they have absorbed sufficient aromas from the new wood by then. These used casks are a godsend for other whisky producers. The taste profile of whisky is inextricably linked with maturation in oak casks, irrespective of their origin. This was not always the case. Even until 1915 most whisk(e)y was consumed "fresh" as a raw grain whisk(e)y. The first record of malt aged in casks occurs in the *Diary of a Highland Lady*, in which Elizabeth Grant remembers her father sending "pure Glenlivet whisky" to Edinburgh in 1822 for King George IV. This was her favorite cask, "in which whisky had been in the wood, then in uncorked bottles, for a long time, as mild as milk and with a real taste of contraband." Such whiskies, however, remained the exception.

Opposite: Selected casks in which malts have aged over many years.

Warehouse men record on the first barrel of a row which and how many malts are maturing in them.

## Legally enforced rest

Nowadays Scotch whisky must mature for at least three years in casks, a requirement we owe to David Lloyd George (1863–1945). The British prime minister would have gladly banned every form of alcoholic beverage, but realized that such a measure would hardly make him popular with the general public. So he took up the suggestion of his colleague, James Stevenson, the director of Johnny Walker: the sale of young spirit (which caused the most social damage) was banned and the minimum maturation period for whisky was laid down in the Immature Spirits Act of 1915.

Whisky producers had already accumulated initial experience of dealing with casks, but now it became exciting as there was much to discover about it. They were able to discern a distinct change in the whisky after just three years in the young casks used for the first fill, which had previously contained bourbon or sherry. What was lost in terms of harshness it gained in complexity: through the exchange with the aromas and flavors present in the wood, through the chemical reaction of the charred wood on the inside of the barrel, and as a result of the slow but steady oxidization through the wood pores and bunghole.

Once the distilleries had become aware of the effect of maturation, they began to experiment with longer aging periods and learned how to judge the wide range of factors affecting the process: the choice of casks (bourbon, sherry, or other types) and whether they were first fill or older ones; they found out about the importance of the atmosphere in the warehouse, whether it was dry or moist, cool or warm; and whether the ground was made of stone or stomped earth. They came to understand that there could be no universal rules. In one distillery the most expressive malt can be a 10-year-old, while in another it might be the one aged for 25 years—it is all a matter of taste.

# A Scottish whisky journey

Whisky blazes a fiery red trail into and through Scotland. Every distillery has its own individual style—an amalgam of its situation, the shape of its pot stills, and last but not least the connection of the site with its environment. You have to experience this aura first hand, ideally while tasting some of the malts distilled there. Only then do you appreciate how everything is interconnected, how the character of the whisky is sustained and shaped by the individual landscape. And before you know it, you are captivated by the fascination of malts.

If you talk to the people who work in a distillery, you find out a great deal about the particular malt in terms of its typical characteristics and influences. That can amount to quite a lot of information, all apparently with one single aim—to give each malt its own distinctive profile so that no two malts taste the same. It means that a varying palette of aromas is created inside the pot stills, depending on their shape, and the young malt spirit will be transformed by its particular maturation period and according to the type of cask.

The topic of water always comes up, and often the source or stream beside a distillery is a lovely spot well worth a look; besides, the best way to find out about the different distillery sites is to walk about them. Then you might come across the granite that is in evidence in many places and characterizes the wildly rugged Highland landscape. You can often detect the different microclimates as well, if a river like the Spey is flowing nearby or the sea is lapping against the foundation walls of the warehouses. They talk about dry and moist warehouses, and how the malts age quite differently in them: in the former, more volume is lost and in the latter, more alcohol.

For anyone with particular favorites among the malts, nothing is more interesting than to pay a visit to the distilleries that produce them. They will often come across special bottlings, of which there are only a small number; they can be purchased on site, whereas they are difficult to obtain elsewhere. Often distilleries not only offer a dram of their most recent whisky, but also have informative tastings led by experts.

Take the opportunity of following the fiery red whisky trail and at the same time discover the different regions of Scotland. This way you will get to know the Lowlands by visiting Glenkinchie, on the edge of the Lammermuir hills to the south of Edinburgh. Then forge ahead to the beautiful scenery of the Grampian mountains, aiming for Dalwhinnie, the highest lying distillery in Scotland and set in spectacular surroundings. On then to Speyside, the stronghold of malts.

To the north of Inverness, Glenmorangie near Tain awaits, and then a good bit further up the coast, as the land flattens out, Wick and the Pulteney Distillery await you, renowned for the salty finish of its malts. From Scrabster near Thurso take the ferry across to the Orkney Islands, well worth seeing not just for Highland Park, but also for the Skara Brae prehistoric settlement with its stone furniture.

Starting out along Loch Ness a lovely route leads from Inverness to Oban, where the distillery is located right in the harbor town. Here you can pick up one of the infrequent ferries to Islay, finally reaching the heaven for heavily peated malts.

# Lowlands, Highlands, and Islands

Page 324: Lagavulin on Islay is a mecca for those who love heavily peated malts.

Page 325: Bed and breakfast accommodation add to the charm of a whisky tour.

Scotland's whisky regions are roughly split into the Lowlands, Highlands, and Islands. The first of these begins at the English border, and stretches as far as an imaginary line between Greenock, on the river Clyde near Glasgow, and Dundee. The landscape of the Lowlands also has its charms, with rolling hills, vast forests, walled fields and meadows, and numerous crystal clear streams and rivers. There were dozens of distilleries here in the mid-19th century using pot stills, but the main thing was that they had to compete with the grain distilleries producing cheap grain spirit in large amounts. Only three distilleries have survived to the present day, producing malts with very little peatiness, or none at all, which are lighter in character, with subtle aromas, and often triple distilled. They mostly have a dry and by no means disagreeable finish.

The next whisky region is the Highlands, stretching north from the Lowlands as far as Orkney, covering the rest of Scotland apart from Islay and Campbeltown. This area is usually split into four sections—Eastern,

The road leading to Glenmorangie House near Tain, north of Inverness.

Central & Southern, Western, and Northern Highlands—as well as a special section of its own for the many distilleries of Speyside. And the Islands? It is tempting to group the islands of Orkney, Skye, Mull, Islay, Jura, and Arran together, on the assumption that their seaside location and often large quantities of peat would link them. It is not quite so simple, however, and this is why the islands on the west coast are normally associated with the Western Highlands region, while all malt lovers would agree that Islay (pronounced "ei-la") with its eight working distilleries deserves to be looked at and valued in its own right. The Kintyre peninsula with Campbeltown at its center has also maintained its special status, even if there are only three distilleries still operational there, the last of which is not due to release its first malt until 2014.

**Whisky regions of Scotland**

- Highlands
- Lowlands
- Campbeltown
- Islay

**Important distilleries in the subregions**

- Northern Highlands
- Western Highlands
- Eastern Highlands
- Central & Southern Highlands
- Lowlands
- Campbeltown
- Islay
- Speyside region

# The blends

If "Scotch" has become the global concept for Scottish whisky, then it is really as much down to the blends as to the 90 or so distilleries in Scotland still marketing their own single malt. We also have to thank the thriving whisky industry, which provides a living for thousands of people. Nowadays the blends make up over 90% of the total Scottish whisky output.

When the introduction of column-still distillation brought a more economical and blander tasting whisky onto the market, increasing numbers of merchants decided to follow the example set by Andrew Usher in 1853 with his Old Vatted Glenlivet and create their own blended Scotch. These men included Haig, Bell, Dewar, Walker, Sanderson, and Buchanan. It was all about mixing the light grain whisky with powerful, expressive malts—this is what is meant by "blending"—in order to obtain a pleasant, easy-drinking whisky. They then had to learn the art of being able to repeat the blend again

and again, so that the greatest possible consistency was obtained.

For this a very experienced nose is required. You have to be able to distinguish the various malts from each other, and then work out how to combine them in such a way that they act in harmony with each other and with the grain whiskies. Anyone fortunate enough to follow a master blender into the laboratory can experience a crash course in "nosing." Dozens, if not hundreds, of samples from the distilleries of the Lowlands, Highlands, and Islands are lined up there in small bottles on shelves. In the twinkling of an eye the master can cover the whole range: from light to floral, fruity ones; and from spicy to the big, powerful peaty ones. Only the nose is used for this process as tasting would very quickly numb the sensory organs. Experts rely solely on nosing.

## Moderate mixing

Only a tenth of the malts distilled and aged in the many distilleries of Scotland come onto the market as single malts. The rest goes to the well-known brands, each of which uses 15–50 different malts and 3–4 grain whiskies to make a blend, and often they have several blends in their range.

Every blend has its own profile that relies primarily on a small number of specific grain and malt whiskies, forming the basis of the blend in terms of origin and age. In addition other (rather interchangeable) malts are used which are grouped by type—according to whether they are fruity, sweet, smoky, etc. For a blend is not based on a precise recipe in which every ingredient is added in exactly the same amount each time: the master blender knows how to work with the palette of his whiskies in order that he can create an identical overall picture every time, even if he cannot always use exactly the same splashes of color.

Blends are true works of art that usually hark back to the first brushstroke of their creators but have subsequently been modified. Even

Strathisla is the true home of the famous Chivas Regal as it provides the basis for its blend.

the direct heirs who brought international acclaim frequently perfected the recipe. Later external circumstances were the reason for adaptations—if a distillery that had been the main supplier closed down, for instance. In some cases the blend was deliberately given a relaunch to bring it up to date, a measure that would be repeated every few years in future.

The way in which grain and malt whiskies are combined with each other depends on the tradition of the particular whisky house. The proportion of malt can be just 10% or over half, even though grain whisky usually predominates in terms of volume. As a rule the malts and the grain whiskies are assembled separately, and only combined when they "get to know each other" for a further few months in oak casks.

The higher the percentage of malt and the older the whisky, the higher the quality—though the label must always state the youngest component. The most recent blends often do not give the age, though this is no reflection on their quality. Luxury blends, on the other hand, clearly indicate their old age on the label with pride; these are usually really excellent and extremely complex whiskies.

The greatest challenge for all blended Scotch whiskies is forward planning for sales. The various young distillates—new spirits, new makes, or baby whiskies—must be warehoused now and be capable of convincing the market in five, ten, or fifteen years, which ties up a lot of capital and is a risky venture.

Chivas Regal and Ballantine's, displayed in front of the Strathisla still house, along with some of the malts that go into their blends.

# Selected Scotch blends

**Ballantine's**
**17 Years Old**

In 1827 George Ballantine took the bold step of leaving his parents' farm and opened a general store in Edinburgh. He established another larger company that specialized in wine and spirits in Glasgow in 1865. Under his son George it was granted a Royal Warrant in 1903. Its most successful brand to date, Ballantine's Finest, was launched in 1910. The family sold the business in 1920. Owned since 1937 by the Canadian company Hiram Walker, Ballantine's went on to become the leading whisky in Europe. By 1930 the premium 17 Years Old brand had appeared: its assertive blend of complex aromas of peat, smoke, and baked fruit, and its full, sweetly spiced flavor make it extremely palatable. Ballantine's is now part of the Pernod Ricard group.

**Black Bottle**

This unusual blend has now found a fitting home with Bunnahabhain on Islay. The whisky with the black label and a bottle shaped like a pot still brings together all seven Islay malts. It was created in 1879 by tea merchant Gordon Graham and his brother, initially mostly for personal consumption, until the blend won more and more fans, especially in Scotland. Uniquely for a blend, smoky, peaty notes predominate, especially when a little water is added, but this is overlaid by a sweet quality that keeps the drier grain component in check. It has also captured the salty air of the island.

**Buchanan's**
**Aged 18 Years**
**Special Reserve**

James Buchanan (1849–1935), later Baron Woolavington, is one of the major figures in the history of whisky. When this whisky firm representative was sent to London in 1879, he soon realized that it was easier to sell whisky in bottles than in casks, and just five years later he set up his own business. He sold his own "Buchanan's Blend" in black bottles with a white label, but when he noticed that people were simply asking for "the black and white whisky" he changed the labeling and created one of the most successful whisky brands ever. This 18-year-old Reserve is extremely smooth and complex, with hints of dried fruit, nuts, vanilla, and subtle smokiness.

**Chivas Brothers**
**Royal Salute**
**Hundred Cask Selection**

Brothers James and John Chivas ran a specialist shop in Aberdeen and were granted a Royal Warrant in 1843 when Queen Victoria acquired Balmoral Castle. From early on their smooth blends earned them a dazzling reputation. Their big break, in the export market in particular, came when they bottled their Chivas Regal 12 Year Old for the first time in 1909. Strathisla in Keith became the base for Chivas after the company was taken over by Seagram in 1949. Royal Salute was brought out to mark the coronation of Queen Elizabeth II in 1953. Although reoriented, the blend remained faithful to its original style—rich, sweet, and complex with a dense, velvety texture in which old malts set the tone.

**Cutty Sark**
**Scots Whisky**
**Aged 12 Years**

On March 20, 1923, Francis Berry and Hugh Rudd (partners of Berry Bros. & Rudd, wine merchants founded in 1698 in St James's Street, London) sat down together and talked about the time being right for a lighter whisky in both taste and color, for the market was defined at that time by dark and heavy blended Scotch. They decided to create a naturally light blend made from elegant Speyside malts. For their emblem they chose the *Cutty Sark*, a clipper used in the tea trade that was launched in Dumbarton in 1869 and was reputed to be the fastest ship of its day. The Aged 12 Years also demonstrates a light, fresh touch, with a subtle sherry note and appealing spiciness.

**ewar's**
**ecial Reserve**
**ed 12 Years**

rmer's son John Dewar set up
s own business on Perth's
gh Street in 1846, thus cre-
ng the foundation for a whisky
mpany made internationally
mous by his sons, John
exander and Thomas Robert.
vas the work of Tommy Dewar
particular, whose trips up
vertising campaigns paved
e way for their White Label
unch in 1899: it is still the
stselling Scotch in the USA
day. The Dewars, both of whom
re knighted for their services
whisky, founded the distillery
r their blend in Aberfeldy back
1896. The Special Reserve
nounces its malty character
d is well rounded, with a
easant spiciness tinged with
oke and honey.

### William Grant's
### Cask Selection
### 12 Years Old

With the opening of Glenfiddich
in 1886 William Grant laid the
foundation for the company that
is still run by his heirs. When
Scotch whisky experienced its
first major crisis in the late 19th
century, he saw his opportunity
and expanded into wholesale.
He then created a blend that
was introduced in Canada by
his son John. Today the grain
whiskies of the Girvan Distillery,
built in 1963 by the family, form
the basis for the blends and in
particular the amazingly successful Grant's Family Reserve,
which includes Glenfiddich and
Balvenie malts. For the new
Cask Selection range they make
use of special wood finishing in
bourbon casks, which gives the
whisky a stronger emphasis of
wood and smoke, though it is
still a perfectly balanced,
supremely elegant whisky.

### The Famous Grouse

The Scottish grouse on the label
made the blend so well known,
in the Perth area initially, that it
earned the additional epithet
"famous." It still bears the name
today, quite rightly as the blend
created in 1897 by Matthew
Gloag is the Scots' own favorite.
This rise to fame only happened
after the company was taken
over in 1970 by Highland Distilleries. Now it is part of the
Edrington Group, who ear-
marked the famous Glenturret
Distillery as its new home,
although its malts are not in fact
used in "Grouse," as the Scots
call it. It is pleasantly rich and
fruity, with a touch of smoke,
sweet spiciness, and creamy
toffee.

### J & B Rare

Giacomo Justerini came to
London in 1749 to woo a
famous opera singer (successfully, as it turned out). There he
set up in business as a spirits
merchant, and when Alfred
Brooks took over the company
in 1831 he added his name to
it as well. The breakthrough
came with J&B Rare, which was
launched just after the end of
Prohibition in the USA. Its light,
mellow style took it to second
place worldwide. This popularity is down to its successful
blend, at the heart of which are
four Speyside malts led by
Knockando. In all a total of 36
malts and 6 grain whiskies
come together to create this
fresh, smooth blend with notes
of grass, citrus, subtle spice,
and nuts.

### Johnnie Walker
### Premier
### Rare Old Scotch Whisky

The most famous whisky in the
world started with John Walker,
who opened a store in Kilmarnock in 1820 when he was
just 15 years old. In it he also
sold whiskies, preferably the
powerful Islay ones. His grandson Alexander Walker brought
out the Red Label and Black
Label blends as brand names in
1909, and even then they were
sold in the square bottle. The
same year saw the introduction
of the "striding man" emblem,
the dandy in the red riding frock
coat. With its sweet-flavored,
spicy-smoky aroma, Red Label
is still as convincing today as is
the more intensely complex
Black Label. The Premier is a
luxury blend in which long aged
malts ensure plenty of body,
wood notes, and nutty toffee
aromas.

# Highland whiskies

The Highlands have some of the most spectacular and the most sparsely populated scenery in Europe. As might be expected, they are mountainous in contrast to the Lowlands. Ben Nevis, their highest peak and the highest in Britain, towers 4,406 feet (1,343 m) into the sky, and there are also another 300 mountains of 2,950 feet (900 m) or more. Their parallel mountain ranges alternate with picturesque glens and ravines, and are traversed by numerous rivers and lochs.

The Southern Highlands are defined by the varied landscape of the Grampians, with the Tay and Spey rivers flowing on either side down to the North Sea. From Inverness on the Moray Firth the Great Glen runs southwest to Fort William with its series of lochs (including the famous Loch Ness) and draws a dividing line to the North West Highlands with their rugged mountains and the Hebrides lying off the coast.

While the influence of England took hold in the Lowlands at an early stage, Highlanders preserved their language and customs far longer, including the taste for whiskies with a distinctive character. This heritage has not just been maintained. In spite of substantial concentration in the whisky industry, it is nurtured even more than ever, thanks to the global interest in single malt whiskies.

## Single malt is back

In the past Highland folk only drank whisky made at home or in illicit stills. The arrival of blends turned Scotch whisky into an international spirit. The single malt has picked up the old tradition and developed it further—only whisky from one single distillery can bear this name, and it must be made exclusively from malted barley. Numerous other distilleries, especially in the 1980s, followed the pioneering example set by Glenfiddich in 1963. Of all the Scottish distilleries, which number over 120, some 30 are located in the Highlands and just under 60 in Speyside. Their number varies, for sometimes they are mothballed for a time and then reopened, depending on the market situation. Since 2000 five new distilleries have been established, though no single malt from them are on the shelves yet.

Single malts are often sold according to specific age categories (10, 12, 15, 18, and 2 years) though these grades are mixed from casks of different ages and sometimes even

of different origin in order to maintain consistency in the aromatic profile. As with blended Scotch the age on the label always refers to the youngest malt in the mixture, but as all the components come from a single distillery it is not called "blended." By contrast there are "vatted malts," though these tend to be somewhat rare; usually described on the label as "pure malt," they are made by blending malts from different distilleries.

The ultimate in malt uniqueness is the "single cask," in which case the contents of one individual barrel are bottled and labeled. To a greater or lesser degree they are distinctly different from other bottlings, and set the heart of every whisky collector racing.

At about 1,150 feet (350 m) above sea level, Dalwhinnie is the highest distillery in Scotland.

# Speyside

Speyside is regarded as the heart of malt production in Scotland. The area, through which the river Spey flows, lies between Inverness and Aberdeen. To the south it extends into the Cairngorms National Park, while in the north it is bordered by the coast between the rivers Findhorn and Deveron.

Almost half of all working distilleries are located here. The oldest and prettiest distillery on Speyside is Strathisla, which was founded back in 1786 and retains much of its original style. It was said of Dufftown, the self-styled Malt Whisky Capital of the World, that "Rome was built on seven hills, Dufftown stands on seven stills." Included in this cluster are Dufftown, Kininvie, and Pittyvaich, as well as Glenfiddich, Balvenie, Glendullan, and Mortlach. Convalmore and Parkmore are closed. Other important whisky villages are Rothes, with five distilleries, and Keith, which has four.

Before Speyside became famous Glenlivet was already a household name. George Smith was the first to obtain an official license in 1823 for his distillery situated in the river glen of the same name. As an illicit distiller he was already well known for his whiskies and Glenlivet earned him such a good reputation that other local distilleries—including Glenfarclas, Aberlour, Macallan, and the further flung Longmorn—also added Glenlivet to their name. As far back as the 19th century this led to the Smiths being granted the legal right to use the name "The Glenlivet" for their malt. The glen of the Livet is also home to malts from the Braeval Distillery (which has since closed down) and the busy Tamnavulin.

Speyside offered distillers a number of advantages, including an ample supply of barley, especially in the Elgin area, an abundance of good water, and plenty of peat. It is

The river Spey is a vital lifeline flowing through Speyside, where the largest concentration of distilleries in the world can be found.

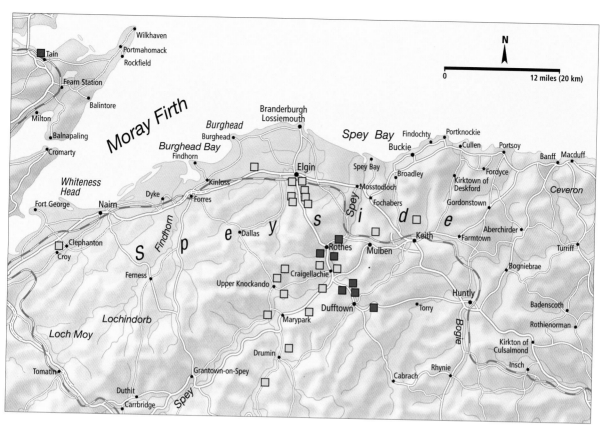

often said that Speyside has its own distinctive style of whisky, which is characterized as elegant, well balanced, and round, with plenty of finesse. The distilleries in this area certainly hold back on the peat level, but it is equally true that every company in Speyside has developed its own house style, which is defined, however, more by factors such as the shape of the pot stills and the type of casks used than by the natural conditions of their shared environment.

**Major distilleries in Speyside**

| | |
|---|---|
| ☐ | Speyside |
| ■ | Dufftown |
| ■ | Rothes |
| ■ | Northern Highlands region |

## The malt whisky trail

To convey the sense of Speyside, seven distilleries and a cooperage made a special joint effort to welcome tourists. They flagged up the attractions of exploring the region as a whole, and of discovering how there can be such a wide variety of distilleries and malts. Most of the other distilleries are of course open to visitors as well, so Speyside may also be explored on an individual basis.
www.maltwhiskytrail.com

Visitors are given a warm welcome by most distilleries.

# Selected producers

## Aberlour

The distillery owes its name to the site of its foundation in 1826—at the confluence of the Lour with the river Spey. It was one of the first distilleries to offer single malt, after it was taken over by Pernod Ricard in 1974. Sherry casks are preferred for aging as they ensure a certain sweetness and dried fruit aromas. A'bunadh, bottled at cask strength, is a lovely whisky, with aromas of Christmas cake, raisins, candied peel, honey, and smoke.

## Glenfiddich

Clan Grant, one of the last independent Scottish whisky families, can trace its roots back to the 14th century. The part of the family history associated with whisky is rather more recent however: after 20 years with Mortlach William Grant founded his own distillery, Glenfiddich, in 1886. The first single malt emerged from it in 1963, and in spite of its lack of distinction it is still the most popular. On the other hand the Aged 18 Years Ancient Reserve is convincing—its fresh, fruity nose is followed by a magnificently smooth and elegant finish.

## Glenrothes

The distillery on the outskirts of Rothes began its operations on December 28, 1879. Its malts soon met with the approval of master blenders and became a standard component of The Famous Grouse and later Cutty Sark. Glenrothes gained an excellent reputation among experts for its vintage malts. With its Select Reserve it created a vatted malt that reflects the house style beautifully; its intense peach aroma tinged with citrus and vanilla, its roasted nutty notes, and its creamy texture.

## Glenlivet

In the early 19th century there were almost 200 illicit distillers in the glen of the Livet. In 1823 George Smith was first to register his distillery legally. It operates with four each of wash stills and pot stills with long necks; these produce lighter malt when used in conjunction with lightly peated malt. Nàdura 16 Year Old Cask Strength is a delightful exception: unfiltered with a very creamy texture, lots of vanilla, dark chocolate, sweetly exotic spices, and delicate roasted notes, it packs a punch.

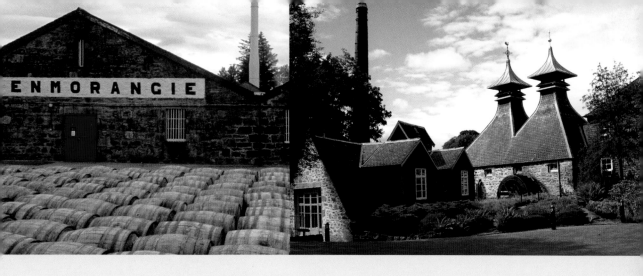

## Glenmorangie

Two things stand out in this distillery founded in 1843: its eight pot stills with unusually long necks and the low, old warehouses beside the sea. This is where the Scots' favorite malt is made, for Glenmorangie (with the accent on the second syllable), or to be more precise the 10 year-old Original, boasts wonderfully intense aromas of flowers, citrus fruits, and a distant whiff of smoke. It is subtly sweet on the palate, smooth, fruity with a hint of vanilla, and ends on a very rounded finish.

## Macallan

Malt has been officially distilled beside the 300-year-old Easter Elchies House overlooking the river Spey since 1824. Its fame became established in 1892, initially as a component of blends such as The Famous Grouse, then thanks to the full, supple style of the single malts produced in oloroso sherry casks. The 21 astonishingly small pot stills are remarkable and, what is more, the heart of the spirit or spirit cut, is restricted to 16% of the run. The wonderfully rich 18 Years Old Fine Oak is outstanding.

## Strathisla

The charm of its natural stone buildings, pagodas, and water wheel make this without doubt the most beautiful distillery in Scotland. Its four squat pot stills produce a full-bodied malt that forms the basis of Chivas Regal and is only sold as a single malt in very small quantities. Even the 12 Year Old announces its robustness, bursting with aromas of citrus fruits, baked fruit, malt, and cocoa. It is full and long on the palate, with notes of herbs, dried apricots, nuts, and honey.

## Glenfarclas

In the Grant family since 1865, this distillery operates the six biggest pot stills on Speyside. Oloroso sherry casks are preferred for maturation: 52,000 casks age in their warehouses, the oldest of which contain malt made in 1952. This inspired John Grant in 2007 to bring out the Family Casks range, one cask of malt from 43 vintages. The 105 Cask Strength is also famous, a younger malt with distinctive sherry, malt, and honeyed notes, with a persistent finish.

# Selected Highland malts

**The Balvenie**
**Single Barrel · Aged 15 Years**

The Balvenie is not just a neighbor to Glenfiddich geographically; it is part of the family, so to speak. It was William Grant himself who set up the Balvenie Distillery with his sons in 1892 in the old farmhouse of the nearby castle—this was six years after he had founded his own first distillery. It has one of the last working traditional malting floors in Scotland, as well as large, bulbous pot stills. Although the external conditions are identical, and the same malt master works in both locations, the malts of the two distilleries are quite different. Experts tend to prefer Balvenie malts, such as its 15-year-old, a single malt drawn from a single bourbon cask: its intensely complex array of aromas is impressive, revealing an infusion of malt, oaky notes, and honey.

**Cardhu**
**Aged 12 Years**

John and Helen Cummings began to distil small quantities of malt in 1811 on Cardow Farm in Mannoch Hill. Helen is said to have been in charge of the pot still. Her daughter Elizabeth took over in 1872, moved the distillery to its present location in 1885, and tripled production. The main customer for this renowned malt became the Johnnie Walker brand, and the Cardhu heir, John Fleetwood Cummings, was later offered a place in the company's senior management. The disadvantage of this arrangement is that far too small a proportion was bottled as Single Malt Aged 12 Years. It is a light, smooth, and sweet representative of Speyside, with subtle notes of apple and vanilla.

**Cragganmore**
**12 Years Old**

Part of Speyside, the distillery was set up in 1869 by an industry expert. Its founder, John Smith, had previously worked for Macallan, Glenfarclas, and even Glenlivet. He knew his trade so well that all the master blenders scrambled to get his spirits. Malt from Elgin with very low phenol content is now used. The complexity of its 12-year-old flagship malt presumably stems from the strange T-shape attachment through which the rising vapors of the two flat spirit stills must pass in order to condense. Its floral nose has a hint of grass and smoke, and it has a smooth, light and slightly sweetish flavor, with subtle notes of malt and honey.

**Dalmore**
**Aged 12 Years**

Built in 1839 on the banks of the Cromarty Firth by Alexander Matheson, the distillery experienced an upturn from 1867 under the Mackenzie family, whose clan symbol is a royal stag. It has enjoyed excellent relations with the trading company founded in 1882, Whyte & Mackay, which took over Dalmore in 1960. Since 1870 a feature of the house style of Dalmore has been to store the malt in oloroso sherry casks. The proportion of these used in the Aged 12 Years was only recently increased, making its already characteristic full-bodied quality and nutty sweetness even more pronounced. Its typical features are an aroma of bitter orange marmalade, and a spicily sweet, long finish.

**Dalwhinnie**
**15 Years Old**

At an altitude of 1,150 feet (350 m) in the Grampians, Dalwhinnie holds the record as the highest Scottish distillery. It stands at an ancient rendezvous point where drovers came with their herds from the north and west to rest, and presumably enjoyed the warmth of a dram from early times on. With a plentiful supply of good water and situated on the crossroads to the south, a distillery was first set up here in 1898. It was taken over in 1926 by the Distiller's Company Ltd., and its malt was mainly used for Black & White blends. Nosing reveals a lovely aroma of peat and heather honey, very smooth on the palate with notes of orange, subtle spice, wax, and honey.

### Glenfarclas
### 50 Years Old

This expensive bottle commemorates the bicentenary of the birth of John Grant, who acquired the distillery in Ballindalloch, founded in 1836, at the age of 60. A total of 110 bottles of this rarity were produced, selected by his direct descendant George Grant. It was distilled in 1955 and exactly 50 years to the day later it was bottled: a wonderful old malt with a very complex bouquet of sherry, nuts, and spices, overlaid by a full-bodied flavor of toffee and wood. Within this selection it is an example of the huge range of bottlings on offer to malt fans today, from younger single cask editions to vintage malts and treasures such as this one, aged for decades.

### Glengoyne
### Aged 21 Years

Easily reached from Glasgow and close to Loch Lomond, this distillery, officially opened in 1833, marks the border between the Lowlands and Highlands, though it comes into the latter category. This small company, which developed from a farm, has two spirit stills with a capacity of just 925 gallons (3,500 liters). It has always been able to sell its output easily to the whisky firms of the nearby city, and in 1876 it was acquired by the Lang brothers for their company. In the 1960s it went over to the Edrington Group, but later transferred to the Scottish company Macleod Distillers in 2003. As well as the smooth, light 10 Years Old, particular pride is taken in the Aged 21 Years, which clearly announces the influence of the sherry casks: with honey notes, dried fruit, and sweet spice.

### Glenmorangie
### The Quinta Ruban
### Port Cask Extra Matured

The distillery of the "Sixteen Men of Tain" on the Dornoch Firth, which is famous for its very delicate 10-year-old malt, is regarded as the stronghold of wood finishing. Its director, Bill Lumsden, has experimented more than anyone else with the effects of different casks on the taste of malts. His great classic, the Port Wood Finish, has recently been reissued under a different name and style. Its expression is captured unadulterated, without chill filtration, in the new bottle. The nose is very complex: an infusion of butterscotch, cocoa, orange peel, and a hint of sandalwood. It proves to be pleasantly smooth, full, and sweet on the palate, with aromas of cherry preserve, dark chocolate, mint, nuts, and a touch of wood.

### Loch Lomond
### 21 Years

This distillery is the only one in Scotland to produce both malt and grain whisky. It is located near to the famous loch, though not right beside it, so it only just qualifies as part of the Highlands whisky region. It was not established until 1965, and 20 years later it was acquired by Alexander Bulloch for the purpose of supplying his chain of stores with whisky. Bottling was also taken care of by its own Glen Catrine Bonded Warehouses Company, which is now one of the biggest bottling companies in Scotland (Glen Scotia in Campbeltown is also part of the group). A peculiar feature of the distillery is the four pot stills with rectifying heads, in addition to the two traditional pot stills, which allow the distillery to make eight completely different malts, ranging from very peaty to extra light. Very lightly peated malt was used for the 21 Years and it has kept an intense aroma of barley, combined with notes of raisins, oranges, ginger, and creamy toffee. On the palate it presents as pleasantly dry with rancio notes of nuts and almonds, macerated raisins, and a subtly sweet taste of grain.

### Old Pulteney
### 12 Years

Pulteney, the northernmost distillery on the mainland, is in Wick, which used to be famous as a herring port. Named after a politician who campaigned tirelessly on behalf of fishermen in the early 19th century, it was founded in 1826 by James Henderson and equipped with just two pot stills. Its own bottling only appeared after the takeover by Inver House. Although this single malt is aged exclusively in old bourbon casks, it is regarded as the "manzanilla of the north," thanks to the salty aromas contributed by the North Sea. Added notes of malt, grain, and pit fruits are succeeded by a lovely sweetness, subtle oak, and the tang of the sea.

# The whisky islands

The Isle of Jura (literally meaning deer island) is dominated by the bare conical mountains known as the "Paps."

With the exception of Islay the Scottish islands do not constitute one uniform whisky region. They are all different in terms of their natural environment, and therefore their malts. Highland Park on Orkney is still the northernmost distillery in Scotland (operating legally since 1798), even if Blackwood on the Shetland Isles is planning one further north. Yet Highland Park will remain unique, with its malting floors and two kilns from which peat smoke emanates, and the incomparable style of its malt. Scapa, the second distillery on the main island, lies right beside the sea, always seems rather somber, and is now producing individual 12 and 14 Years Old single malts that are very promising.

While you have to take a boat (or a plane) to Orkney, the Isle of Skye can be reached by a much maligned but functional bridge from the mainland. The largest island of the Inner Hebrides has a ruggedly romantic coastline and is dominated to the south by the Black Cuilins, the highest peak of which is 3,061 feet (933 m). Not far from Loch Haport on its west side is Talisker, the only distillery on the island and widely known for its distinctive, smoky peppery malt.

With its brightly colored house facades, Tobermory harbor is the most beautiful in the Hebrides.

You also have to take a ferry to reach the Isle of Mull, and for whisky aficionados this is best done from Oban. You arrive at Tobermory harbor, which is the most beautiful in the Hebrides with its colorful facades. The only distillery is also located there, offering a dram to both friends and foes of peat. Like Highland Park it has been licensed to distil since 1798, though initially for beer rather than whisky.

To reach the Isle of Jura, you have to sail first to Islay and then from Port Askaig—it is only a few minutes on the ferry. Jura's landscape is defined by the three Paps—stark, conical mountains 2,526 feet (770 m) high—and supports a population of over 5,000 deer, while the human contingent has fallen to 160. Craighouse in the southeast is home to the only distillery. Its lodge is an irresistible attraction for whisky fans. The Isle of Arran, where master blender Harold Currie opened his own distillery in 1995, is also one of the whisky islands: it has already gained a very good reputation.

# Selected island whiskies

**Highland Park**
**Aged 18 Years**
The distillery on the outskirts of Kirkwall, the capital of the Orkney Islands, has been in operation since 1798 and has earned itself an excellent reputation for its single malts. Underlying this success are quite specific natural conditions such as hard water and a particularly cool climate, as well as a conscious effort to preserve traditions, coupled with a realistic openness to innovation. One fifth of the barley used is germinated in house on malting floors and kiln dried using very aromatic peat that they have dug themselves from the local moor; this means it has 20 times more phenols than malt bought in from the mainland. Sherry casks made from either American or Spanish oak are preferred for aging. The typical aromas are of heather, subtle peat smoke, sweet spice, orange marmalade, and honey: the Aged 12 Years is exceptionally smooth, while the Aged 18 Years is bigger, sweeter, spicier, and smokier.

**Talisker**
**Aged 10 Years**
When the MacAskill brothers founded Talisker on the Isle of Skye in 1830, they chose the location on the banks of Loch Harport on economic grounds. Everything had to be transported by sea (and it turned out that the most suitable in terms of logistics was also the most scenic spot). They were dependent on low tides for unloading the cargoes until Thomas MacKenzie, the manager and major shareholder, built a landing stage and trolley system to transport the casks from the warehouses. Following a fire in the still house in 1960 the five pot stills were faithfully rebuilt. They produce a very striking malt, helped along by the heavily peated malt they use. The nose is therefore characterized by an intensely peaty aroma, alongside the pungency of spices and sea air. With an alcohol content of just below 46% vol., the Aged 10 Years explodes on the palate, then evokes more smoke, salt, and a characteristically peppery note.

**Tobermory**
**Aged 10 Years**
Tobermory, the main town on the Isle of Mull with its pretty, brightly colored houses, gave its name to the distillery. In 1798 it was called Ledaig after the bay in which it is located: it was initially a brewery, which then began distilling whisky in 1823. In the next 170 years of its existence it experienced only sporadic phases of success. The comeback began after they were bought over by the firm Burn Stewart in 1993. Now two different ranges of malt are produced there, one from peated malt under the Ledaig label, and Tobermory from unpeated malt. The Aged 10 Years is very convincing: a fresh aroma of citrus fruit, mint, and a tang of the sea, developing into an extremely smooth palate with just a hint of smoke and salt.

**Isle of Jura**
**Superstition**
The island is reached by ferry from Islay. The distillery is located in the only village, Craighouse. It was set up in 1810, though it had to be rebuilt in 1876 and was mothballed during World War I. It remained out of commission for half a century. When distillation began again in 1963, it was decided that unpeated malt should be used, unlike the practice of its neighbors on Islay. It is mainly a light, clean spirit that is produced in unusually tall, slim stills—it retains its fruitiness over many years, But there are also peaty exceptions, such as Superstition, the liquid expression of the islanders' beliefs. It combines honey and spices with a smooth creaminess, the tang of the sea, and a trace of salt.

# A test of courage with peat

It is fairly safe to assume that you will only meet tried and tested whisky fans on the ferry from Kennacraig to the two ports of the southernmost Hebridean island, Port Askaig and Port Ellen. For Islay (pronounced "eye-la") is a special kind of mecca. The island, which is recognized as a separate whisky region, is famous—or notorious—for its malt style with an extremely high peat smoke content, as represented by Ardbeg, Laphroaig, and Lagavulin.

In its heyday in the 19th century there were 21 distilleries on the island, and from around 1760—when Killarow Distillery, now long gone, was firing up its pot still— to the present day there have been a total of 26 or 27 companies, the youngest of which, Kilchoman, was only established in 2005. Today eight distilleries operate on the island and this will rise to nine in 2009 when Port Charlotte begins to produce whisky again. The spectrum of aromas in Islay malts certainly requires a bit of getting used to, as it contains not just peat and smoke, but also tar, iodine, salt, the tang of the sea, medicine, car tires, and even docks and fish oil, both in the nose and on the palate. And that's not all: added to the notes of kiln-dried peat smoke and salty tangy proximity to the sea, you find the sweet and spicy aromas of cask aging, which give the big peaty malts the rich smoothness of velvet. You also come across aromas of orange and lemon peel, fruit compote, baked fruit, rum-macerated fruit, roasted nuts, licorice, dark chocolate, cocoa, and coffee, and many more.

## Firmly rooted in the sea

Landing in Port Ellen it is not far to the three superstars of the south coast, the first of which is Laphroaig. Its official founding date is uncertain but it is presumed to be around 1820. Before that time the islands were firmly in the hands of illicit distillers for many years. Farms malted their home-grown barley, the kilns were fired with peat they had dug themselves, and after fermentation and distillation the spirit was smuggled onto the

Ardbeg, which almost foundered, celebrates its revival with its exceptionally smoky, complex malt.

mainland. As the buildings indicate, Laphroaig was a farm too, and even now it makes some of its own malt in house. At its neighbor and rival, Lagavulin, which means "the hollow where the mill is," you can visit the ruins of Dunivaig Castle, the seat of the Lords of the Isles, who ruled over the Hebrides from this base in the Middle Ages. Peter Mackie, one of the innovative whisky barons, learnt the craft of distilling in Lagavulin and inherited the distillery in 1889; he made its malt into a component of the successful brand White Horse.

The easternmost distillery of the peat trio is Ardbeg. Farmer John McDougall acquired the island's second license for it in 1815 (the first went to Bowmore). It remained under family ownership until 1973. Highly esteemed for its extremely peaty malt (only small amounts were needed to give profile to a blend), the high quality became its downfall. Demand was too low and from 1981 Ardbeg was only sporadically in operation, or not at all, until it was taken over in 1997 by Glenmorangie, which lead to a comeback.

The oldest distillery shares its name with the main town, Bowmore, where it is also located.

Founded in 1779, the distillery has its roots—at times literally— in Loch Indaal. Here they keep up tradition, malting a proportion of the barley themselves. They also donate the excess warmth from the still house to heat the local swimming pool in a former warehouse.

On the opposite side of the loch, Bruichladdich—valued on Islay for its light malt—has been experiencing an upturn since 2001. Bruichladdich have rolled out this success by rebuilding a distillery in the neighboring village of Port Charlotte in 2007. Nearby Kilchoman Distillery on Rockside Farm, which also processes its own home-grown barley, was opened in 2005, the first new distillery on the island for 124 years.

In the northeast on the Sound of Islay, Caol Ila (established 1846) and Bunnahabhain (1881) are working distilleries. The first of these began mainly producing for blends but is now becoming known for its appealing malts, which are still typical of Islay. The second distillery abandoned its peaty character at some point, and now produces a light malt, though its origins are betrayed by the salty note.

Laphroaig divides the whisky community into two camps: those who adore the "medicinal" malt, and those who run a mile from it.

# The taste of the moor

Islay malt owes its unique reputation to peat. Its most famous distilleries use malt that has dried for several hours over peat smoke, the distinctive aroma of which is passed on, first to the barley, and then to the whisky. Peat found its way into the production process simply by being there, not as a consciously chosen flavoring.

Heat is needed over a lengthy period in order to halt the artificially induced germination of the barley. This must be done after the grains have formed the enzyme needed to turn the starch into sugars—that is to say when the barley has turned into malt, which is then easier to process in a dried form.

To generate heat they had recourse to local fuels. These could be wood and charcoal, but in many places, on the islands especially, it was peat. Peat is formed when plants—primarily peat moss (sphagnum), heather, and grasses—die off in marshes or other wetlands. They sink into the soil but do not decompose because their acid content is too high and there is not enough oxygen, so they accumulate and compress together. In this way around 3 feet (1 m) of peat "grows" in 1,000 years.

Before cutting the peat irrigation ditches are dug out and the top layer of marsh and turf is removed. Plant roots can still be discerned in the white peat underneath, and it is not until the next layer that the sought-after brown peat with high fuel value is found. It is cut into peat sods and piled into pyramids to allow the waterlogged peat to drain and dry out. Peat cutting on Islay begins in April. With enough wind and not too much rain, the peat will have dried out in time by the end of the summer.

## Providing the smoke for the whisky

Large areas of Scotland are covered in a layer of peat, which has been used as a fuel there since time immemorial. In many places they even heated the pot stills with peat until they could afford charcoal.

The effect of peat on the taste of whisky only found true expression when malt was kiln dried over peat smoke. This is because the grains absorb phenols from the peat as they dry, and a large proportion of these phenols survive the distillation and make it into the final whisky.

With the boom in blended Scotch after World War II whisky production underwent a rationalization process, with the result that malt was made by more industrialized processes and peat smoking was seen as uneconomical. Instead, the desired peat notes were added at the blending stage.

This ensured the fame of the Islay malts—malt continued to be kiln dried in the traditional way there. On an island of which a quarter is made up of peat, they don't skimp on its smoke. A twentieth part of Islay malt is often sufficient to put the peat into a blend. Today, now that most malt is made in large maltings like the one in Port Ellen on Islay, they know how to peat the barley exactly the way the customer wants it. Since it has been possible to measure the peat content, they

also know how long the peat smoke has to last to produce a particular measurement: this is given as ppm (phenol parts per million of malt). Ardbeg traditionally used the most phenol-rich malt with a good 56 ppm, followed by Laphroaig and Lagavulin with 35–40 ppm and Caol Ila with 30–35 ppm. These are classed as very peaty malts. Bowmore leads the middle group with 20 ppm, while a lighter malt like Glenmorangie just about manages 1 ppm as even unpeated malt contains this amount of phenol.

At most 60% of these remain in the whisky, and are gradually broken down with age. Bruichladdich, wanting to set its own personal peat record, managed to reach a whopping 167 ppm with its Octomore II—The Beast. In reality, then, the distinctively smoky peatiness of a malt is not—and never has been—dependent on the location of the distillery, but rather on the phenol content of the malt used, and on tradition, of course, which on Islay is peaty.

Today the pagoda-style chimneys are often just decorative, but originally the smoke was drawn up through them from the kiln ovens.

Opposite: In order to cut peat, drainage ditches have to be created first of all, and then the natural fuel can be dug out with a spade and left to dry in the open air.

# Islay malts

The Islay malts demonstrate the potential of the single malt. Each one has its own individual character. Lagavulin is Islay's most famous international ambassador, and its Aged 16 Years is a colossus. It boldly announces the smoky peat and iodine smell of the bay where it is made, but these are sustained by the sweet aromas of sherry casks, as well as dried fruit and spices—powerful, dry, and vigorous.

Ardbeg has dedicated a bottling, Uigeadail (meaning "mystical place") to the distillery's own water source. In contrast to the 10 Years Old—which captures the essence of its habitat with aromas of smoke, peat, tar, heather, and sea air—Uigeadail has a seductive bouquet of fruit cake, cocoa, spicy smoke, and leather which then become full, sweet, and oily on the palate.

Laphroiag 10 Years Old exudes the strong aroma of peat and peat fires, mixed together with the penetrating smell experienced when you stand near the most westerly distillery on Islay's Atlantic-facing south coast:

blend of sea tang, iodine, fish and salt, wrapped in sweet malt.

Moving on: to the west Bruichladdich (the distillery suggests pronouncing it "Brookladdie") 17 Years Old is proof of a subtler approach, even if they are now building up a new line there using extremely peaty malts. A wonderfully smooth, elegant, round, and delicately spiced whisky.

The 12 Years Old from Bunnahabhain (pronounced "Boo-na-há-ven") is also on the light end of the spectrum, starting with a fresh zing, followed by notes of smoke, salt, citrus, ginger, and toffee, and ending on a smooth, malty finish.

Its neighbor Caol Ila (pronounced "Col eela") just down the Sound to the south demonstrates the connection to the sea in its 12 Years Old: aromas of sea tang and soap give way to an oily flavor, with a hint of sweet smoke and caramel.

While all of the Islay styles are harmoniously married in Bowmore's legendary 17 Years Old, its Legend is more representative of an entry level or aperitif malt, very fresh and appealing, with an emphasis on smoke.

The Isle of Jura 16 Years Old beckons from the neighboring island, with notes of oranges, honey, and toffee, mellow and out of this world …

A selection of all the malts from Islay and Jura, against Port Ellen bay.

# Campbeltown

Opposite: Looking up Loch Fyne from Inverary, at the end of which lies the adjoining Kintyre peninsula.

Campbeltown, on the eastern end of the narrow Kintyre peninsula—the tip of which is only 9 miles (15 km) from the northern Antrim coast—held itself up as the whisky capital of the world in the 19th century and is still recognized today as a whisky region in its own right. In fact it is said that between 1880 and 1920 there were 34 distilleries in this small town. Its sheltered harbor made it easy to transport the whisky by boat, whether to the whisky companies of nearby Glasgow or else to the USA. What had initially proved to be an advantage was reversed when Prohibition was introduced. Demand collapsed and many distilleries were forced to close down. Only two survived: Springbank and Glen Scotia.

Springbank has been run by the Mitchell family since 1828, in just the same way as it was then, which has carved a special niche for the brand in the whisky world. All the

Springbank's malts are rare treasures, cherished by whisky lovers.

stages of whisky production are carried out in house in the original buildings, from malting through to bottling. For the descendant it would be unthinkable to color their malt with caramel or use chill filtration, so they are all bottled with an alcohol content of at least 46% vol. The malt may be only lightly peated for Springbank, but for Longrow they indulge in robust peating. On the other hand there is no smokiness at all in the triple distilled Hazelburn (a nod to nearby Ireland). With Springbank you can often enjoy the finish in rum, port, or sherry casks, and the distillery offers a fantastic collection of malts aged for a long time, often decades, bringing out the particularly round, complex style of the region with the characteristic salty note of the sea.

In 2004 the family renovated the old Glengyle Distillery in the town center, reactivating it with the expressed aim of issuing

ts first malt in 2012, which will be known as Kilkerran.

Glen Scotia, founded in 1832, is the other surviving distillery in Campbeltown, though it was only sporadically in production, or mothballed completely, in the last century. Yet they still manage to produce very convincing malts, with only one wash and one spirit still. It now seems to be on an upward trajectory, the proof of which is its very good, complex, and delicately spiced 14 Years Old.

## Single grain has its day

Fortunately there is no law forbidding Scottish distilleries from making whisky from corn or wheat, aging this product without blending, and then bottling it as it stands. What used to be seen as sacrilege is now finding favor with more and more fans. These single grain whiskies are closer in style to bourbons or Canadian ryes, and after 20, 30, or more years especially, they are astonishing—extremely smooth with a lovely vanilla flavor.

## Lowlands malts

During the 19th century the Lowlands too had many malt distilleries and developed a light, appealing style of whisky. They could not, however, compete with the large distilleries that were producing grain whisky. Only three have survived to this day: Glenkinchie near Edinburgh, Auchentoshan on the river Clyde on the outskirts of Glasgow, and Bladnoch in the southwest near Dumfries. The Lowlands malt style is characterized by the use of unpeated malt as a rule, and triple distillation. This produces lighter, distinctly fruitier whiskies, with elegant notes of fresh herbs, grass, and citrus fruits, and they age surprisingly well. Highly recommended typical examples are Auchentoshan Aged 12 years and Bladnoch 10 Years Old.

# The wood finish

It has been well known since the 19th century that storing whisky in casks previously used for other spirits can improve it. Yet cask maturation only became standard practice in 1915, after the minimum age regulation was introduced. As sherry was not only a popular drink at that time, but was also transported to Britain in casks, the warehouses were left with empty butts in abundance. Hence the first generation of modern whiskies was aged in sherry casks.

After World War II this would all change. The Spanish then started to bottle their wines themselves, so sherry casks became both expensive and rare. Luckily there was a convenient alternative: bourbon casks. By law Americans are only allowed to use new casks for their whisky, and once only. As a result they were left with a large surplus of used casks. The Scots changed over with clear conscience to the far more favorabl bourbon barrels, especially as new cask were incompatible with their malt anyway So nine out of ten Scotch whisky casks now come from the USA.

When the independent bottler Gordon & MacPhail boasted of refining Speysid malts, first in port wine and then brand casks, it was not long before Balveni brought out its Doublewood in 1992. But n one tested this method as thoroughly as Bi Lumsden at Glenmorangie. In the mean time many other distilleries and companie have changed over, thus providing a far wide range of products.

To begin with the malts undergo their basi aging in bourbon casks made from America white oak. The finishing then takes place the aim of which is to increase their com plexity: this can last between six months an two years, or even for five years in excep tional cases. The most common, and satis fying, method is a finish in sherry or por casks, but nowadays you also find casks use that previously contained madeira, malaga marsala, cognac, calvados, and sometime rum, as well as wine casks from famous cul tivation regions or the great chateaux. Often this is spectacularly successful.

Many malts now get their finishing touch by aging in special casks, which adds considerably to their complexity.

## Owners and bottlers

The structure of Scottish distilleries is in state of flux. Now only a few are still unde family ownership, such as Springbank o Glenfarclas. By contrast many family firm have been taken over by large-scale compa nies. Diageo in particular has excelled exclusively owning the Johnnie Walker, J&B Bell's, Buchanan's, Black & White, Dimple and Haig brands, as well as distilleries like Caol Ila, Cardhu, Clynelish, Cragganmore Dalwhinnie, Glen Elgin, Glen Ord, Glen kinchie, Knockando, Lagavulin, Oban Royal Lochnager, and Talisker. Perno Ricard is a similar big player, with Chiva Regal, Ballantine's, Clan Campbell, Lon

## Scotch whisky: what's in a label?

Scotch whisky must be made in a Scottish distillery from water and malted barley, or be distilled from another grain, in which the alcohol content following the last distillation must not exceed 94.8% vol. It must age for a minimum of three years in oak casks and contain no added ingredients other than water and caramel. It must be bottled at an alcohol strength of 40% vol.

Basically there are two types of Scotch: single and blended. "Single" means that the whisky comes from a single distillery. "Blended" means that it has been blended together from spirits from more than one distillery.

**Single malt whisky:** whisky from 100% malted barley from a single distillery.

**Single grain whisky:** whisky from one or several types of grain from a single distillery.

**Vatted, pure, or blended malt whisky:** whisky made from several malts from two or more distilleries.

**Blended grain whisky:** whisky from one or more grain types, from two or more distilleries.

**Blended Scotch whisky:** mixture of single malts and grain whiskies, mostly from different distilleries.

**Other designations:**
**Cask strength:** unreduced malt, which normally has an alcohol content of 50-60% vol.

**Single cask:** malt from a single cask (but this may be reduced).

John, and the single malts The Glenlivet, Aberlour, Glendronach, Longmorn, Strathisla, Scapa, and Tormore; the Edrington Group, whose international distributor is MaxXium Worldwide, can claim The Famous Grouse, Cutty Sark, The Macallan, Highland Park, The Glenrothes, Glenturret, and Tamdhu. The family firm of William Grant & Sons has a share in some of these brands and with the Glenfiddich, Balvenie, and Girvan distilleries it is the third largest whisky producer in Scotland.

Since time immemorial malt distilleries have sold proportions of their output by the cask, initially to independent bottlers and later to the blended Scotch brands. This put independent bottlers at the forefront of the malt revolution, and to this day they are still a dynamic force as they frequently offer single cask bottlings from the distilleries, which can differentiate themselves clearly from the owner's bottlings. Some big names in this respect are Gordon & MacPhail, David Laing, Murray McDavid, Cadenhead, The Bottlers, Signatory, and even the Scotch Malt Whisky Society, to name but a few. Recently others have decided to take the position of supplying, to some extent, only certain countries.

Glenmorangie is one of the pioneers of wood finish, and one of its highlights is its 1988 malt, which completed its maturation in madeira casks.

Mysterious graffiti on a whisky cask.

# The Irish whiskey revival

Considered the whiskey par excellence during the 19th century, "pure pot still" from Ireland had to be more or less reinvented after World War II. Irish whiskey is now typically smooth and light, with floral notes and a hint of citrus fruit that give way to vanilla, dried fruit, and nuts, producing an especially well-balanced flavor. This profile has guaranteed it a place alongside Scotch and Bourbon. It is still a rather modest place, but Irish whiskey has once more become a household name.

Irish whiskey was in a precarious situation at the end of World War II, with the six surviving distilleries producing little or none at all. Light came at the end of the tunnel in the form of an invention by Joe Sheridan. Joe was a barkeeper in Foynes near Shannon, where the "flying boats" (seaplanes like the Boeing 314 Clipper) refueled on their transatlantic flights. He wanted to give passengers a bit of Dutch courage, but as tea with whiskey did not seem to soothe the nerves of the Americans he added a decent shot of whiskey to hot, sweetened coffee and then topped it with a spoonful of semiwhipped cream. His Irish coffee caught on. When travel writer Stanton Delaplane of the San Francisco *Chronicle* tasted it on a stopover, he was so excited about it that in 1952 he introduced the recipe to his local bar, the Buena Vista Cafe on Fisherman's Wharf. Irish coffee became a hit there: as many as 2,000 glasses a day were poured and 2,000 crates of whiskey were sold to San Francisco every year. For many years this represented the only export of any real significance.

Meanwhile in the Republic of Ireland three of the surviving distilleries—Jameson, John Power & Son, and Cork Distilleries—became embroiled in relentless competition. As John Clement Ryan, a descendent of John Power and urbane ambassador for Irish whiskey, recalls, 'My father was then the managing director of John Power & Son, which had already taken over Tullamore Dew a few years earlier. At that point he had very hush-hush talks with Jameson and Cork Distilleries, and in 1966 they finally announced the founding of the Irish Distillers Group. The hatchet was buried, but decades of competition made cooperation difficult. The aim of the agreement was to establish a place again for Irish whiskey on the world market." In a skillful move the Irish Distillers Group acquired the Old Bushmills Distillery in Northern Ireland (which also owned the Coleraine Distillery)

in 1972, thus securing the monopoly on Irish whiskey for itself with the five most important brands.

Jameson was by far the leading brand internationally, while Power's was the most popular in Ireland. Paddy was very well known in the Irish Republic, as was Bushmills in Northern Ireland— and the latter also commanded an extensive export portfolio. Tullamore was strong in Germany, Austria, Denmark, and France.

To optimize profit with six different distilleries did not seem to make economic sense, especially as two of them were cramped together in the center of Dublin and there were three in and around Cork. The group reached a revolutionary decision when it opted to close down all the operations apart from Bushmills and set up a new, state-of-the-art distillery in Midleton, which opened in 1975. There they could distill both grain and pot-still whiskies, and make all the types of whiskey they needed. Yet the group still seemed too small to be able to win back the old market. So in 1988 Irish Distillers became part of the Pernod Ricard group. Irish whiskey has now become a new dynamic force, making it all the more exciting for whiskey fans.

# Illicit water of life

Page 352: The largest pot still in Ireland enjoys its retirement in the Jameson Heritage Centre in Midleton.

Page 353: Power's is the most popular whiskey on the Emerald Isle.

Leaving aside for a moment all the romantic accounts of its origin, the first mention of *uisge beatha* in a document in Ireland was in a notice about a death. The "Annals of Loch Cé" tell of a certain Richard Mac Raghnaill, who in 1405 lay down to rest after excessive indulgence in uisce beatha, whereupon "it was a water of death for him." What doomed him in his sleep was likely to have been brandy, as no written evidence for grain spirits has yet been handed down from this time. We can only surmise that in the remains of pot stills dating back to the end of the 14th century, some grain was distilled. The contexts of these discoveries make it clear that, even at that time, distillation was taking place outside monasteries.

Consumption of alcohol increased apace in Ireland as well, and when Parliament under Henry VIII granted the aristocracy and affluent citizens the right to distill without a license, this regulation represented a rather unsuccessful attempt at dealing with alcohol abuse. Distilling eau-de-vie, which by that time was mainly based on grain, was widespread in the country: it was "a beverage, that brought no benefit whatsoever when drunk on a daily basis …, and it uses up much yeast, grain, and other things in the process as well." From then on it would be permitted only for those who had obtained a license, while illegal distillation would be prosecuted. What looked quite good on paper had no chance of succeeding in 16th-century Ireland as the population just ignored it.

## The tax code: "Run like the devil from the excise man"

The Tudors and then the Stuarts who ruled over Ireland helped to fill their coffers there by selling so-called patents that gave their owners the right to pursue a trade as a monopoly in a specific region. As far as whiskey is concerned, the first patents were issued in 1608. One of these was to Sir Thomas Phillips in Bushmills, County Antrim, from which it can be assumed that he was operating his distillery as a business. The present day distillery regards this as its foundation date, irrespective of its own official registration 176 years later.

Before long the lucrative system of patents was serving the interests of civil servants more than the state, so it was abolished in 1644 in favor of tax laws. On the occasion of

Left: Henry VIII tried in vain to ban Irish people from distilling (portrait of Henry VIII by Hans Holbein the Younger, 1497-1543).

Right: Charles II bestowed a spirit tax on his Irish subjects (portrait from the workshop of Adriaen Hannemann, 1603-71).

The Old Bushmills Distillery in Northern Ireland boasts a 400-year-old history.

the coronation of Charles II in 1661, Ireland received the special Christmas present of the duty on spirits. That divided the country into two unequal halves: the few legal distillers who paid excise duties, and the majority of the population who did not. The populace had recourse to distilling for more than one reason: surplus barley could be preserved to protect it from pests, and in the process produce high-quality animal feed; and, on top of this, landlords accepted alcohol in lieu of rent. The golden age of *poitín* (known in English as potcheen or poteen) or "moonshine" began, and it made its way into many Irish folksongs.

In spite of a stream of new regulations and the pretty rough pursuit of illicit distillers by excise men, the government proved incapable of bringing alcohol production and consumption under control for the next 150 years. This eventually was to happen in quite a different way.

## The Rare Old Mountain Dew
**(first published in 1916)**

At the foot of the hill there's a neat little still
Where the smoke curls up to the sky.
By the whiff of the smell you can plainly tell
There's poitín boys nearby.
For it fills the air, with a perfume rare
That betwixt both me and you.
And as on we roll, we'll drink a bowl
Or a bucketfull of mountain dew.

## The Hills of Connemara

Gather up the pots and the old tin cans
The mash, the corn, the barley and the bran.
Run like the devil from the excise man.
Keep the smoke from rising, Barney.
Keep your eyes well peeled today
The excise men are on their way
Searching for the mountain tay
In the hills of Connemara.

# Rise and fall

At the end of the 18th century, when almost 2,000 stills were operational in Ireland, forward-looking businessmen like John Jameson and John Power realized that the Industrial Revolution would bring considerable change, affecting sales of whiskey. They invested in its production in spite of the tax on pot stills at the time. They were vindicated when the law was changed across Great Britain as a whole in 1823. Output was taxed from then on and bigger companies were the beneficiaries. Illicit distillers seized the opportunity and became fully legal, while the small, unregistered distilleries in the countryside found themselves under increasing pressure.

The six top-selling distilleries among Irish whiskey producers were owned by John Jameson, John Power, George Roe, William Jameson (all in Dublin), Andrew Watt (Derry), and the Murphy brothers in Midleton. The largest of their pot stills had a capacity of 392,300 gallons (148,500 liters) and was located at Midleton. They changed over to a triple distillation process that produced rich, smooth whiskies known as "pure pot still." They were well received on export markets and demand rose in the United Kingdom. At the same time life in Ireland was becoming harder and harder. British commentators warned that the country was on the brink of famine: population numbers were rising rapidly, three quarters of workers were unemployed, living conditions were horrendous, and the standard of living was extremely low. Alcohol abuse was the order of the day.

One man led a campaign against this, the Capuchin friar Father Mathew, who founded the Total Abstinence Society in 1838. He traveled tirelessly across the country, challenging people irrespective of their social class to take "The Pledge"—and thereby promise never to drink alcohol again. In the next six years around three million Irish people took the vow, more than half of the adult population. But catastrophe could not be avoided.

Left: Malting floors at Jameson in Dublin.

Right: Filling the casks with "new make."

The Great Irish Famine struck the country from 1845 to 1848, during which time a million people, an eighth of the population, starved to death, a million and a half emigrated, and many more left their homeland in the years following. In 1841 the country had a population of 8 million and 60 years later it had dropped to scarcely more than half of that.

## The decline

During the disastrous famine the distilleries had to curtail production, but as soon as it was over Irish whiskey experienced an unprecedented boom as grape phylloxera eliminated its strongest rival, cognac, for years to come. Irish pure pot still triumphed in North America in particular, but also in England, where Scotch whisky still had not managed to break through, and the rest of the Empire. In Ireland then more than 160 distilleries were working at full throttle. But then Irish whiskey production suffered several serious blows. American markets were closed by Prohibition, and almost immediately after that England's trade boycott against the newly independent Irish Republic blocked off the United Kingdom markets. On top of all this duties on spirits rose drastically at home. One distillery after the other collapsed. While the Scots tried their utmost to circumvent Prohibition, the Irish accepted it as an act of God. When it was repealed in 1933 Scotch had created a marvelous starting basis, while the few Irish distilleries still surviving lacked both product and capital. In the USA in particular blended Scotch also expanded sales during World War II, helped along by Churchill's patronage, though Irish whiskey was limited by export restrictions.

When the war was over only four distilleries remained in the Republic of Ireland: Jameson and John Power & Son in Dublin, Cork Distilleries in Midleton, and Tullamore Distillery in Offaly, which had already been mothballed—it finally closed down in 1953. In Northern Ireland Bushmills, Coleraine, and the Upper Comber Distillery had survived, but the last of the three ceased production in 1953 as well. Only a couple of beleaguered veterans remained of what was once a booming industry.

Left: Bottles being carefully packaged.

Right: Shipping crates of whiskey in Dublin harbor.

# *A dream comes true*

The former Jameson Distillery in Dublin has been turned into an attractive visitor's center.

Only three distilleries have survived in Ireland: Midleton, Cooley, and Bushmills.

The distillery founded by John Jameson in Bow Street outside the city walls in 1780 is now in the center of Dublin. Skillfully converted into a visitor's center, it provides a way into the history and taste of Irish whiskey. No actual distillation takes place here, nor in the Jameson Experience, which used to be the Jameson Heritage Centre in Midleton. The distillery, brought into operation by the Murphy brothers in 1825, has now been restored as a visitor attraction, featuring the world's largest wash still, a water wheel, and an impressive stationary steam engine. At one time 500 people worked there.

Not many whiskey fans know that one of the biggest, most up-to-date, and efficient whisk(e)y distilleries in the world is located behind the old distillery site, along with huge warehouses. When it was rebuilt in 1975 the Irish were a match for all their global rivals in terms of technology, confidently looking to the future for their whiskey. In Midleton they reinvented the well-known

brands and the styles associated with them, working along with the old master distillers whose successors are held in the highest esteem for the outstanding palette of whiskies they are producing.

However it was not just the Irish that bemoaned the fact that Irish whiskey had become a monopoly enterprise. The small-scale Old Bushmills Distillery at the other end of the island was included in this, and it continued to cultivate its own style although the bulk of Irish whiskey, with which it shared the name, came from Midleton. When the French group Pernod Ricard took over Irish Distillers in 1988, new export opportunities were certainly opened up, but whiskey lovers were worried that the diversity might become even more restricted.

## Cooley is pretty cool

At the same time there was a glimmer of hope on the horizon, though (almost) no one knew about it yet. As far back as 1987 an internationally successful Irish entrepreneur, Dr John Teeling, took a notion to buy the state-owned potato alcohol plant that was for sale on the Cooley peninsula. He acquired it, along with its ten column stills, for a token sum with the intention of distilling whiskey there.

He attracted support from a number of quarters: a friend from his student days, Willie McCarter, who owned shares in the former Watt Distillery in Derry; Lee Mallagahan, the former owner of the famous Locke's Distillery; and the entrepreneur Paul Power. Together they founded Cooley, though lack of capital almost made them founder in the beginning. They were nearly bought out by their big rival, purely with the mischievous aim of taking the ambitious distillery out of circulation.

They have now established themselves as a small, but effective and inspirational, counterforce, thanks to their smart vision— they would distill malt in Ireland, make only double distilled pot still whiskey, and breathe new life into the old whiskey brands. However, it is not the old names that are winning over whiskey fans, but the quality, which is growing year by year as its stock ages. Cooley even created the first peated malt in Ireland with its Connemara Single Malt.

Competition is indeed reviving the industry, for the range at Jameson has expanded significantly in the interim, not least by adding excellent pure pot still whiskies like Green Spot or Jameson 15 Years Old to the traditional Redbreast. Blends that combine grain and pot-still whiskey are also achieving top quality, like the Jameson 12 Years Old.

It is likely to become even more vibrant in years to come as a third force has emerged. Bushmills changed camp and is now owned by Diageo, who have invested heavily and more than tripled production. The established blends such as the excellent Black Bush with its sherry cask profile still have a loyal following, of course, but the "1608," produced without chill filtration and with an alcohol content of 46% vol., has been brought out to celebrate the 400th centenary. They are still going strong today…

The old pot still in front of the Jameson Experience in Midleton.

Locke's old Kilbeggan Distillery is now used by Cooley as a visitor's center and for aging their whiskey.

# Making whiskey the Irish way

Everything was straightforward when Irish Distillers had the monopoly as their philosophy reigned supreme. Then Cooley came along, however, and did all the things they were not doing, which were also seen as being not typically Irish. The fact remains that Irish Distillers maintained and developed certain traditions which differentiate their whiskies from other types, especially Scotch, and for this they deserve credit.

The difference begins with the barley. In Midleton they use both malted and unmalted barley. While malted barley gives the spirit a full, distinctive flavor, master distillers Barry Crocket and David Quinn prefer a mixture of roughly equal parts, producing "a cleaner, smoother, and rounder taste, verging on sweetness." They now add some wheat as well, but under no circumstances do they use barley that has been kiln dried over a peat fire for smoky notes are banned in Midleton.

Within four hours the necessary enzymes have broken down the starch in the unmalted barley into sugars in the mash tun. The warm, sweet liquid is then pumped into the wash backs, the temperature is lowered, and in about 80 hours it has fermented into a cloudy, strong beer with an alcohol content by volume of about 9.5%.

## A very versatile site

Though built back in 1975 the distillery in Midleton is still the only one in the world where pot stills and column stills stand side by side and can be used together in various combinations. It is specially set up for triple distillation, and to distill all sorts of whiskies in one single site. It has four pot stills: two of these are wash stills, the third is dedicated to the second distillation run, and the fourth to the third run. Alongside these are seven column stills. All whiskies are triple distilled, but where, when, and how this is done determines the subsequent taste profile. So a lighter grain whiskey is passed once through a pot still, and twice through a column. If it were put through the column first, then through the pot still, and finally through the column again, it would produce a slightly more robust result.

Triple distillation was introduced by the big distilleries around 1820, while many of the smaller companies left it at two passes. Although all the big brands brought together under Irish Distillers were distilled three

Left: Mashed barley being thoroughly stirred.

Right: These two pot stills are used only for distilling the wash.

mes, they kept their individual characteristics. The megadistillery in Midleton was set up only on the understanding that it would be capable of delivering all of these whiskey styles.

With the expertise brought on board by the master distillers from the old distilleries, they did in fact manage to coax the old style out of the new plant. The different shapes of pot stills helped in this respect, but the temperature of the run is also important as this determines which ingredients in the vapor are transferred through the neck, or "lyne arm," and which are left behind.

As in Scotland whiskey in Ireland must age for three years in oak casks by law, and the wood also has a similarly important influence on the taste of the final product. Around seven out of ten casks in Midleton have previously contained bourbon and are made from American white oak, though sherry casks are also used very selectively. They have had them made in Andalusia for many years, "soaking" in oloroso in three bodegas for two years, before the new make is entrusted to them. Casks used for marsala, malaga, madeira, and port are used now as well, in order to develop greater diversity in the whiskies. This is less to do with wood finishing, as is currently trendy. As master distiller David Quinn explains: "We don't want

to lose the elegant aroma and taste of our triple distilled whiskies. Using casks with overpowering aromas can all too quickly compromise the balance that they have taken such pains to create in the still house."

The art of Midleton's master distillers is revealed in the quite different character of their whiskies.

Left: New make is distilled here, in a pot still (in foreground), and a column still (behind it).

Right: The prosaic spirit safe allows master distillers to identify the strength of the spirit at a glance.

# Irish whiskey tasting

From 1975 to 1992 all the Irish whiskies made by Irish Distillers came from Midleton, where the best-known brands are still distilled and aged today, including the global market leader, Jameson. Even its standard version is convincing, with its subtle note of barley and vanilla, beginning smoothly with a hint of sherry and then ending on a pleasantly sharp finish. If the aromas of dried fruit, nuts, and spices are more pronounced in the Jameson 1780 12 Years Old, the reason lies in the sherry cask aging, which is enhanced still further in the 18 Years Old, giving it greater intensity, sweet fruitiness, and a very long finish.

While in Scotland a blend is made up of many different grain and malt whiskies from various distilleries, the great feat of the three Irish distilleries lies in the fact that they produce all the necessary components themselves. Their mastery of this art is proved not least by the Redbreast 12 Years, a pure pot

The spectrum of Irish whiskies in all its splendor ranges from the light Tullamore Dew to the powerful Redbreast.

still that is big and powerful, yet velvety an seductively sweet at the same time. Hewitt reveals itself to be an exciting mixture c fruity, malty notes and a full-bodied flavo The favorite whiskey of the Irish, Joh Power's Gold Label, shows the clear influ ence of the pot still, combined with plent of fruit and spice, and a hint of crunchy ba ley. Tullamore Dew, distilled in Midleto but marketed by Cantrell & Cochrane, is light, pleasant Irish whiskey, well balance with a subtle toffee note.

If there are almost 100 different Iris whiskies on the market, we owe this not leas to the Cooley Distillery, which has revived whole series of old brands and labels. Coo ley uses both grain whiskey and double dis tilled malt. You won't find malted barley i the mash bills, and no whiskey is triple dis tilled. Blends like the appealing Wild Gees are in the range, but the strong point is th single malts. First of all John Teeling brough

...ut The Tyrconnell, the new edition of a
...hiskey by Andrew A. Watt, named after a
...acehorse. With an aroma of orange, white
...hocolate, and grain, it is smooth on the
...alate, with notes of malt, spices, and oak
...Aged 10 Years is now available as well).
...hanahans announces a fresher character,
...ith a distinct aroma of barley, and vanilla
...nd citrus notes.

...he sherry cask finish of Magilligan may
...ave made it a talking point, but with Con-
...emara Cooley has produced a masterpiece.
...t is the first Irish whiskey to be distilled
...sing heavily peated malt. The special cask
...trength edition, like the 12 Years Old, is
...xtremely complex, weaving together smoke,
...weet spice, roasted aromas, and malt.
...ushmills—officially called The Old Bush-
...ills Distillery—has always occupied a spe-
...ial place, not just because of its location in
...County Antrim and its history. For over 100
...ears malt whiskey has been triple distilled
...here. It now comes in a range of vintages but
...lso in numerous single cask bottlings, some
...f which are real gems. The malt is also partly

responsible for the outstanding quality of
the blends. It makes up four fifths of the
famous Black Bush, which ages into a deliciously smooth whiskey with aromas of
sweet dried fruits, nuts, and toffee, thanks
to the extensive use of sherry wood.

The Old Bushmills Dis-
tillery maintains its special position with a range
of single malts and the
excellent Black Bush.

The dynamic approach of
Cooley contributes a great
deal to the present diversity of Irish whiskey— and
they are still going strong
today ... not least with
Connemara, the island's
first peated malt.

# Bourbon and Tennessee whiskey

Jim Beam and Jack Daniel's are familiar sights in bars across the world, but the journey of American whiskey was not a smooth one. For too long it was tainted by the dubious atmosphere of the saloon, where bartenders slid bottles vigorously along to the end of the counter so that gunslingers could throw it back by the tumblerfull. The image of bourbon has now been radically transformed. The four big brands offer special bottlings alongside the popular versions. Aficionados value "small batch" or "single barrel editions" that reveal bourbon in all its individual diversity and are responsible for spawning a new generation of American whiskies.

Bourbon and Tennessee whiskey experienced their golden age in the early 19th century, when they reached New Orleans and the big cities of the east coast. Fifty years later the Midwest opened up, and grain spirit became the tough guys' drink of choice in Arkansas, Missouri, Texas, and Oklahoma. But the abstinence movement, which was fueled by religion and culminated in Prohibition in 1920, almost killed off American whiskey, while at the same time leading to a steep rise in alcohol abuse and criminality.

After Prohibition Americans had almost lost their taste for their own spirits. Originally whiskey had been distilled from rye in Pennsylvania and Maryland, producing a strong, dry, and pungent spirit. Blended Scotch, which flooded the USA as soon as Prohibition was over, offered an especially subtle and light alternative. Bourbon and Tennessee whiskeys did in fact start to win back ground in the 1950s, and a very small number of them managed to access international markets. When bourbon was officially recognized as a distinctive product of the United States by the US Congress for the first time in 1964, however, it was just when clear spirits and long drinks were in fashion. From what were once thousands of distilleries, a total of only 11 still remain. And Bourbon County, once extensive, has now shrunk to a small area of Kentucky where bourbon has not been distilled for a very long time. Today it is made in Kentucky in Frankfort, Lawrenceburg, Clermont, Bardstown, Louisville, Loretto, and Versailles; and in Tennessee it is produced in Lynchburg and Tullahoma.

The renewed interest in special quality products has now ensured a far richer range of whiskies. The impetus for this has come not least from those who worked, and are still working, in the few distilleries still operational and the adjoining rackhouses. This led Booker Noe, Jim Beam's grandson, to bring out the unreduced, unfiltered small batch Booker's Bourbon at around 63% alcohol by volume (ABV) in 1988, thus unleashing a revolution.

From then on connoisseurs of bourbon realized that they had to be more discerning. They may have been persuaded previously that bourbon matures faster in new casks and has reached its peak after four years, but their demand then began to support the efforts of non-mainstream distillers, who were creating whiskies that were twice, three, or even five times as old, and far outclassed the four-year-olds. Till then they had catered for the average consumer, serving smooth whiskies reduced to an ABV of 40% which were, however, distinctly lacking in character. Now the master distillers were given *carte blanche* in the warehouses, and were allowed to fill the casks as they thought best. So the big distilleries now offer a fascinating palette of American whiskeys, as do a few maverick distillers on the west coast.

# Rebels and bans

Jack Daniel, who worked in the whiskey business from the age of 14, founded his own distillery just six years later in 1866, and became a legend.

Page 364: A touch of Wild West myth at George Dickel in Tennessee.

Page 365: All casks must be labeled in detail.

It is no secret that the art of whiskey distilling in the United States can be traced back to Scottish and Irish immigrants. After the 1745 Jacobite Rebellion in Scotland, the notorious Highland Clearances took place, as a result of which thousands of peasant farmers were driven from their leaseholdings and force to emigrate. Mass emigration also took place in Ireland. The destination of choice for those emigrating, many of whom were skilled in the art of distillation, was the east coast of North America. Though barley was not a thriving crop there, rye made up for it—especially in Pennsylvania and Maryland. So the first American whiskey was almost certainly a rye. The earliest recorded distillery, Michter's, was founded in Schaeferstown in 1753 and continued to operate until 1988.

The immigrants traveled further west across the Allegheny mountains, where they were promised land on condition that they raise crops on it. Bourbon County (now part of Virginia and Kentucky) was founded there in 1785, and was named for the French royal house that had supported America's fight for independence. Corn grew in abundance on the vast plains, presenting a downright invitation to distill it. As whiskey sold well, many farmers made it their main source of income. They labeled their casks "Old Bourbon" and shipped them over the Ohio and Mississippi rivers to New Orleans. There folk enjoyed the taste of the unusual whiskey with its sweet, full flavor, and soon it became known as "bourbon."

## Rolling with the punches

After the wars of independence against England, the young nation was in urgent need of cash to secure its infrastructure, maintain its army, and pay its debts. The only way to fill the empty coffers was with taxes, so the first president of the United States, George Washington (who was himself a whiskey distiller—his distillery in Mount Vernon has been restored), decided to tax spirits in 1791. This did not go down well with settlers, who did not appreciate handing over the meager profits from their grain harvests, and they not only threatened, but actually tarred and feathered, the tax collectors. In 1794 they united and engaged in open revolt, which became known as the Whiskey Rebellion. A

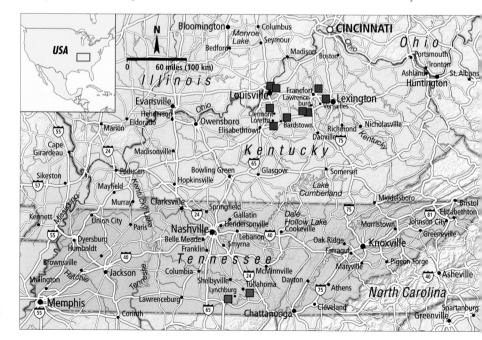

■ In Kentucky just nine distilleries are still operational today.
■ In Tennessee only two are companies left.

a result Washington mobilized around 13,000 soldiers, advancing even into Pennsylvania against the farmers, who had to back down in the face of such a massive demonstration of state power.

The taxes did not stop farmers and the first commercial distillers like Evan Williams and Jacob Beam from continuing to make whiskey. In the first half of the 19th century there were over 3,500 pot stills in Pennsylvania, around 2,000 in Kentucky, and in Tennessee alcohol production rose above the 7,900,000-gallon (3 million-liter) level. Inventors like Elijah Craig and James Crow made technical improvements, and when they found out about column distillation bourbon distillers were happy to change over to the new process.

The rise in production saw a growth not only in the social problems caused by alcohol abuse, but also in the abstinence movement. By 1855 12 states were already "dry" and in 1920 Prohibition finally came into force across the whole country. Only a few producers had the courage to start over in 1933, and Jim Beam was the first. As if he had just been waiting at the age of 70 to be able to carry on the family tradition, he set up the new distillery in Clermont in 1934. Heaven Hill in Bardstown opened the following year. In the decades that followed a few companies managed to establish a name for themselves internationally. Alongside Jim Beam there were Wild Turkey, Four Roses, and Jack Daniel's. It took until 1964, however, for the US Congress to recognize bourbon as a "distinctive product of the United States," defining and protecting it by law.

This measure was not enough to save ailing distilleries. One after the other closed down: Weston, Missouri, in 1985; Virginia Gentleman, Virginia, in 1987; and Michter's Distillery, Pennsylvania, in 1988. Seagram's Distillery, Indiana, now produces mainly gin and vodka. It left only nine bourbon distilleries in Kentucky, and two in Tennessee. Yet these are now delivering bourbon of an almost unprecedented quality.

Left: Life in Lynchburg has always been rural, then and now.

Right: Casks on their way to a towering rackhouse in the Jack Daniel's distillery.

# Sour mash and beer stills

Water, spent beer or backset, and meal are used to make the mash.

Left: A fermentation vat in which distiller's beer is produced.

Right: Most distillation is done in columns, known as beer stills.

Opposite: Freshly distilled "white dog" is transferred to spirit receivers.

Corn—the most important crop in the United States—also has the starring role in American whiskey. If the whiskey has been made with at least 51% corn, then it can call itself bourbon; the proportion of corn is usually 70% or more. It is mixed together with small grains—rye, or less frequently, wheat, and 5–15% malted barley, which is needed to convert the starch into sugar. Of course every distillery swears by its own mash bill(s), as the grain recipe is called.

Corn is not as easy to mash as the smaller grains as it has to be cooked after grinding in order to release the starch. It is then cooled to about 140 °F (60 °C) and the crushed rye and malt are added. The water, needed in large quantities for mashing, is hard in Kentucky and Tennessee, and the layers of limestone act as ideal filters.

In both states they use the sour mash process. This involves using the sugarless, liquid leftovers from the first distillation in the beer still, while the solid parts serve as animal feed. This thin stillage, backset, or spent beer, is added to the mash by the master distiller according to his own experience, and this can be done before, during, or after the fermentation process. It constitutes at least one fifth of the volume and works in two ways: it prevents the growth of harmful bacteria by creating a proper pH balance, and helps to maintain consistency in the distiller's beer.

Unlike their Scottish counterparts, distillers in Kentucky and Tennessee put special emphasis on the yeasts, carefully cultivating their own traditional strains.

They often use different yeasts for different bourbons, for according to them the aromas

re mainly formed by the yeasts. They also
allow longer fermentation periods of 72–96
or more hours, more than is usually the case
with whisky.

## Doublers and thumpers

With the exception of Woodford Reserve,
bourbon is distilled in beer stills—that is in
continuous columns. These columns vary
greatly in size, reaching a height of 16–66
feet (5–20 m) and with a diameter of 28–59
inches (70–150 cm). They produce low wine
with an alcohol content of 45–60% vol.,
which is then usually transferred to the "doubler" for a second distillation; this is a type
of pot still, from which the low wine condenses at around 65% ABV. Sometimes the
alcohol-containing vapors are led directly
into the "thumper," which takes on the same
function as the doubler, producing the fresh
spirit also known as white dog. In Tennessee—and this gives the whiskey produced there its unique style—the spirit is
filtered through sugar maple charcoal before
being stored in casks; this is officially known
as the Lincoln County process.

## American Whiskey

In 1964 the US Congress declared that
**Bourbon**
- must be produced in the United States;
- must be made from a grain mixture containing at least 51% corn;
- may not be distilled with an alcohol content exceeding 80% vol.;
- must be 100% natural (only water can be added);
- must be aged in new, charred casks made from American white oak.

**Straight Bourbon** meets these requirements and has been aged for at least two years; if matured less than four years, the age must be indicated on the label.

**Rye Whiskey** must meet the same requirements, and be made from at least 51% rye.

**Wheat Whiskey** also has to meet the same requirements and be made from at least 51% wheat.

**Corn Whiskey** must be distilled from a minimum of 80% corn.

**American Light Whiskey** is a blend of light grain whiskies that have been distilled at a minimum alcohol content of 80% vol.

**Blended Whiskey** must contain at least 20% whiskey, blended with neutral, 95% grain spirit.

**Tennessee Whiskey** is actually a bourbon, the only differences being that it is filtered in sugar maple charcoal before aging, and may only be produced in that state.

# Highs and lows of aging

Every whiskey distillery needs warehouses, and in Kentucky and Tennessee these are called rackhouses. Often they are fascinating wooden buildings, not particularly good to look at, which are 10 or 12 stories high, with wooden mountings from floor to ceiling filled with oak casks. A traditional rackhouse is a huge shed exposed to the elements that protects the precious barrels from rain and snow.

Bourbon must be aged in new, 48-gallon (180-liter) casks made from American oak and freshly charred—brand new, in other words. Coopers still apply heat to bend the staves, but the toasting level (graded from I to IV) depends on how long they are fired for. The top layer of the wood chars, while below the heat causes caramelization of the sugars contained in the wood, thus forming the vital flavors for the bourbon.

When the new whiskey in the new cask is put in the warehouse, an exchange takes place between them which is influenced by temperature and humidity. These vary according to which level the cask is on, th[e] most dynamic effect occurring at the to[p] where it is warmest. So each cask develop[s] in a different way. To put together his bou[r]bon, the master distiller selects casks fro[m] every level of a range of warehouses. Whe[n] he needs a single barrel bottling, howeve[r] he chooses the casks which have reached well-balanced maturity, and these are no[r]mally stored on the middle levels.

Whiskey certainly acquires more distin[ct] aromas, and faster, in new casks, but it ha[s] by no means reached its peak after fou[r] years. Top-quality whiskeys—which are le[ft] for seven, eight, or more years—prove ju[st] how much even bourbon can benefit from [a] long aging process. Unlike other whiskie[s] in which the shade is usually adjusted b[y] adding caramel, the color of bourbon i[s] always the natural result of the years it ha[s] spent aging in wooden casks.

View of a rackhouse with its wooden mounted casks.

Steve McCarthy with his surprising Oregon Single Malt.

# The American Dream

Steve McCarthy is a textbook example of how an American lives his dream. He comes from a family that has been fruit farming in Oregon for 100 years, and together with his brothers he cultivates 620 acres (250 ha) of apple and pear trees near to the Columbia river. But he was never completely satisfied with the way they were marketing their fruit. His penchant for "good old Europe" then took over—he had come to know it in his schooldays and he later visited on business when he worked for a company selling hunting equipment. He then attended a trade fair in Nuremberg in the 1980s and became acquainted with fruit spirits, which were especially interesting for him, given his family background.

"My wife and I traveled up from Lisbon to Alsace, then on to Germany, and everywhere we tasted fruit schnapps and found out about the equipment needed to produce it. At that time you didn't have eaux-de-vie in the States, and you couldn't just 'google' it," he quips. He was determined to give it a try and distill an eau-de-vie made from pears. Back in America he heard about a German by the name of Jörg Rupf who had just opened the St. George Spirits Distillery in Oakland, near San Francisco, and was the first to start distilling fruit spirits. Steve hired the German pioneer to teach him the fundamentals, and then he founded the Clear Creek Distillery and began to work out the finer points painstakingly for himself. Since then Steve McCarthy has assembled more than just an extraordinary palette of eaux-de-vies. He also produces grappas, brandies, and—most recently—liqueurs. The whiskey was added on in the 1990s, after his experiences on a trip to Ireland. But Steve McCarthy wanted to make a peated malt. So he ordered the raw materials in Scotland, and commissioned the Widmer brothers to make the wash for him in their brewery in Portland; "all" he needed to do was to distill it in his Holstein pot stills, and then mature the spirit in casks made of Oregon oak for three years. The result is a complex, well-balanced malt with notes of peat and smoked fish, sweet fruit, and appealing wood notes—a milestone in the history of American whiskey.

The Anchor Distillery in San Francisco has contributed another such milestone by creating their Old Potrero Single Malt Straight Rye Whiskey, made from malted rye.

# Selected American whiskies

### Booker's
### Small Batch Aged 7 Years
Booker Noe, Jim Beam's grandson who died in 2004 aged 75, worked for decades as a master distiller and was an ambassador for bourbon *par excellence*. For his small batch he took pleasure in bottling a whiskey unfiltered at cask strength, as was standard in the 19th century. This means that the exact strength (which is around 63% ABV) differs from one bottling to the next, as do the age and the character to a certain extent. On the other hand, what does remain constant is the extraordinary intensity and complexity of the aroma, as well as the impressive power and length on the palate. Monumental.

### Elijah Craig
### 12 Years Old
The Shapiro family, which owns the Heaven Hill Distillery in Bardstown (founded in 1935), offer their bourbons under many different names, but they dedicated the best to the great bourbon personalities like Evan Williams and Elijah Craig. Craig was a lay preacher who distilled whiskey himself and is sometimes cited as the inventor of bourbon—though not necessarily by Heaven Hill and its master distillers, Parker and Craig Beam, who are indirectly related to the founder of the leading bourbon brand. The distillery has done pioneering work with long-aged bourbons, thus demonstrating the benefits of aging. This is impressively underlined by their 12 Years Old, which has developed a very complex and appealing aroma with notes of orange, pear, vanilla, pepper, and smoke. This is followed by sweet fruit and spice, elegant toasted notes, and a persistent dry finish that is long on the palate.

### Elmer T. Lee
### Single Barrel
Buffalo Trace is the Frankfort distillery that produces this bourbon, named for the former master distiller. The company dates back to around 1860, when it was founded by Benjamin Harrison Blanton. His son, Albert B. Blanton, took over as director in 1897 and, with George T. Stagg as a partner, the company became famous as the Ancient Age Distillery. Today it offers a range of brands including Old Charter, George T. Stagg, Blanton's Single Barrel, Eagle Rare, and W. L. Weller. It is a lovely bourbon, with sweet roasted corn notes, bursting with toffee aroma and a distinct hint of oak.

### Four Roses
### Single Barrel
Few distilleries have such an imposing home as Four Roses in Lawrenceburg in the heart of Kentucky. Built in 1910, it looks like a Spanish mission station. Originally an Irish immigrant called Joe Peyton began to distill his famous Old Joe on this site in 1818. At the end of the 19th century he was succeeded by Paul Jones, who created the Four Roses brand, which became an international name after the company was taken over by Seagram in 1943. To make it, a number of bourbons with different mash bills were produced, as well as a blend of different yeasts. The single barrel bottling, symptomatic of the recent trend, is a revelation, with clear notes of rye and malt, plenty of fruity sweetness, and roasted notes.

### Jack Daniel's
### Silver Select Single Barrel
Jack Daniel's has become synonymous with American whisk per se, and is always characterized by a sweet, smoky, charre note. An additional stage in fi ishing is responsible for th and distinguishes Tennesse whiskey from bourbon: filtrati through a layer of up to 10 fe (3 m) thick of sugar maple cha coal before the young whiskey put into casks. The founder, Ja Daniel, was already distilling the age of 14, and from 186 he was able to do this in his ow distillery, in the Hollow at Ca Spring near Lynchburg. Th pure deluxe whiskey come from individual, specially age casks that give it more colo richness, and complexity, as w as dryness.

## Jim Beam
### Straight Rye Whiskey

The first whiskey in the USA was distilled from rye as the Scottish and Irish settlers found hardly any barley. The mash bill of this outstanding classic is made from well over 51% rye, with some corn and malted barley. At a time when rye whiskeys are now rare, it is heartening that one internationally best-known brand of bourbon is maintaining this tradition. Rye whiskey is characterized by its intensity, in this case with hints of lemon peel and rancio. Plenty of citrus fruit and mint are revealed on the palate, but also a powerful rye note that is balanced by sweet fruit and coconut.

## Knob Creek
### Small Batch Aged 9 Years

Knob Creek, bottled at 100 proof (50% ABV) is part of a small batch range by Jim Beam that also includes Basil Hayden 8 Years Old 40% vol., Baker's 7 Years Old and Booker's 7 Years Old. It is a good example of the diversity that bourbons can offer. The company can be traced back to Jakob Boehm, a German who came to Kentucky around 1785 and later founded the Old Tub Distillery there. His direct descendant James "Jim" Beam directed the company's fortunes from 1892 until it was mothballed in 1919: he started it up again however in 1933 at the age of 70. Knob Creek is the name of the stream where Abraham Lincoln spent many of his childhood years. This is a honeyed bourbon bursting with fruit, with a deliciously well-balanced and spicy taste and a distinct note of vanilla.

## Maker's Mark

Every bottle that comes from this beautiful old distillery in Loretto is sealed with the wax stamp of its maker, an individual style that also applies to the contents. Here wheat is added to the corn and malt to give smoothness to the bourbon. The air-dried casks are also seen as an important factor, as they produce a full-bodied bourbon with a sweet and spicy complexity, honey aromas, followed by butterscotch, nuts, honey, and spice—distinctly nippy on the palate. The Samuels family is behind Maker's Mark (even though it no longer owns the company) and it can trace its whisky-making tradition back to 1780—the spelling "whisky" goes back to the company's Scottish origins.

## Wild Turkey
### Aged 12 Years

Austin, Nichols & Company was a wholesale grocer founded in New York in 1855. After Prohibition was lifted, its president, Thomas McCarthy, decided to trade in wine and spirits also, so he commissioned existing distilleries to produce bourbon and rye whiskey. The company did not expand this division until 1970, when it acquired the Old Moore Distillery in Lawrenceburg owned by the Ripy brothers in order to distill its Wild Turkey brand there. Master distiller Jimmy Russell is responsible for the high quality of their whiskeys and has worked in the distillery since back in 1954. The ripe fruit of peaches and oranges is most prominent in the Aged 12 Years, followed by the sweetness of corn, plenty of nuts and vanilla, and a hint of licorice.

## Woodford Reserve

This bourbon is unusual for at least two reasons: it is the only one that is distilled three times in pot stills, and it comes from the oldest working distillery in Kentucky. After it was mothballed in 1971 it had to be completely restored, a task undertaken by Brown-Forman. The distillery reopened in 1996. The pioneer Elijah Pepper distilled on this site as early as 1812, and it was here that his colleague James Crow perfected the sour mash process around 20 years later. In 1878 the distillery was taken over by Labrot & Graham. Woodford Reserve is a dark shade, with a nose revealing notes of toffee, vanilla and smoke, followed by sweet spice, nuts, honey, and a pleasantly dry hint of oak cask on the palate.

# Canadian whisky

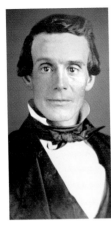

Hiram Walker, a grain merchant and whisky distiller, was also a visionary who founded a town.

The distillery employed hundreds of people, not least in the in-house cooperage.

Surplus grain was distilled by Scottish and Irish immigrants in the 17th century in Canada too, and naturally they chose the grain varieties that were available. At first this was rye, giving rise to the mistaken belief that has persisted until now that Canadian whisky is mainly made from rye. The existence of grain as a raw material in Canada paved the way for it to be turned into a lucrative liquid form, especially for millers. The pioneers were William Gooderham and James Wort, who initially built a mill in present day Ontario in 1832 and started distilling there five years later. It was to become the biggest distillery in the country, merging a good hundred years later with Hiram Walker & Sons. Walker himself, a grain merchant born in Massachusetts in 1816, opened the Windsor Distillery and Flouring Mill facing Detroit on the Canadian side, and it grew to become Walkerville, a town in its own right. He equipped the distillery with a column still and began to make a very light, smooth whisky that he marketed in bottles (unlike his competitors) and called "Club." He sold it primarily in the United States, where it became the successful brand it is today, Canadian Club.

Hiram Walker & Sons was later outstripped by Seagram, a company founded by Joseph Emm Seagram. He started out as a bookkeeper in a malt mill in 1864, became a partner five years later, and then took it over in 1883. That same year he launched his first whisky, a mixture of several spirits that produced the first Canadian blended whisky. With the launch of Seagram's V.O. (Very Own) in 1911, he created one of the most successful Canadian whiskies. After Joseph Seagram's death Samuel Bronfman took over the company in 1928 and merged it with the Distillers Corporation Limited, which his family had founded back in 1924.

During Prohibition in America Canadian distilleries worked at full throttle, producing mostly light whiskies. These were smuggled across the border, where they became well established. When Bronfman saw the end of

There was cause for celebration at the end of the 1920s in Walkerville when the dynamic Harry Hatch took over the distillery, radically improving the sales figures.

the alcohol ban in sight, he built up surplus stocks. In this way he was in an ideal position in 1933 to satisfy soaring demand in the neighboring country. His rival, Hiram Walker, had made similar preparations. Sales and profits in both companies rocketed, and they had the foresight to reinvest their surpluses in expansion by taking over whisky brands and distilleries, especially in Scotland. Seagram proved especially successful in this regard, and by the end of the 1950s it had grown to be the largest spirit company in the world. In 2001 it was divided up between Diageo and Pernod Ricard.

## A more liberal approach

The sale of alcohol may be strictly controlled and, above all, highly taxed in Canada, but in terms of production the distilleries have decidedly more freedom than their competitors in the USA, Scotland, and Ireland. The usual grain types are used as raw material—rye, wheat, barley, and corn—which on the one hand are distilled in column stills to produce a base spirit of up to 95% vol., making it practically neutral alcohol. On the other hand the companies distill a range of the different components they need for their blends. For this, they distill various grains in a range of mixtures, as well as individually:

this can be the Irish way, with unmalted and malted barley; with just malted barley, as is done in Scotland; or bourbon style, with a high proportion of corn. Column stills are mostly used, but pot stills are also brought into service for small batches.

By law a minimum age of three years is prescribed, though Canadian producers are not restricted in terms of the casks they use. These are mainly preused bourbon barrels, but can also be new casks or ones that have previously held sherry. And the most special feature is that they can add up to 9.09% of "non-Canadian whiskies," involving the addition of flavorings which are by no means just other types of whisk(e)y, but can also be sweet or fruit wines, or other spirits.

# Less is not more after all

At the end of World War II Canadian whisky experienced an upturn similar to the one that followed the end of Prohibition, thanks to its US sales. At the same time a market restructuring took place in Canada. The large companies like Hiram Walker & Sons and Seagram mothballed more and more of their old distilleries and concentrated production on one single up-to-date site that had been rationalized. Smaller companies could not keep pace, and fell by the wayside. As far as marketing was concerned, they decided to continue investing in the big, well-established brands like Canadian Club, Crown Royal, Seagram's V.O., and Canadian Mist, rather than assembling a comprehensive palette of differentiated qualities. But when the market began to move in another direction, the Canadians missed their chance. Although a few classic brands like Alberta, Century Reserve, Gibson's Finest, Gooderham & Worts, Potter's, Schenley, and Wiser's brought a degree of variety to the product range, it is insignificant in comparison to bourbons and Irish whiskeys, let alone Scotch.

The tide finally seems to be turning. Glenora, a distillery founded in Nova Scotia in 1990 with a heavy Scottish influence, was in the vanguard of this change: as it proudly declares, it is "the only single malt distillery in North America." After a lot of initial problems not only has Glenora developed into a charming tourist attraction, but its malt is getting better and better.

Another breath of fresh air on the Canadian whisky scene is the wine maker John Hall. In 1992 he took over the distillery in Grimsby, Ontario, that had been founded two decades earlier by the Swiss master distiller Otto Rieder, and renamed it Kittling Ridge. Ten years later he brought out his first Forty Creek, a conscious reference to the first Canadian whiskies. To make it, he distills corn, rye, and barley separately in two small pot stills, and then ages them individually in specially selected casks in order to bring out the character of each grain spirit. In the case of whisky, however, it needs time to reach the desired quality. Enough years have now passed and Forty Creek whiskies are proof that John Hall's painstaking craftsmanship is paying off. What is more, they are providing the fresh inspiration that Canadian whisky desperately needs.

Wine maker John Hall has brought fresh inspiration to Canadian whisky.

# Selected Canadian whiskies

### The Crown Royal Distilling Company
### Crown Royal

The most successful Canadian whisky of the former Seagram empire has now added its name to the only distillery to survive. Founded in 1968, it is situated in Gimli, Manitoba, on the western shore of Lake Winnipeg. There 1.25 million casks are maturing in 46 warehouses, with 1,000 casks per day destined for Crown Royal. Sam Bronfman, who took over Seagram in the early 1930s, created this premium whisky to celebrate the visit by King George VI and Queen Elizabeth in 1939. Until recently it certainly warranted the deluxe rating, and was seen as the epitome of the Canadian style: sweet, appealing, very full bodied and spicy, thanks to the addition of rye. It now has a sweeter, blander style, so you have to go for the more expensive Special Reserve, Crown Royal XR, or Cask No 16 to find the regal taste.

### Hiram Walker & Sons
### Canadian Club

This whisky is an institution, for Canadian whisky owes its success in no small part to it. Shortly after Hiram Walker built his distillery on the Detroit river in 1858, he began to bottle his whisky and sell it on the other side of the river in America, as Walker's Club Whisky. His competitors there managed to push through the regulation making him indicate the origin of his whisky, and the brand Canadian Club was born. Walker started to use column stills early on, and the rye that gives the aroma to the blend has been distilled separately for a long time. A subtle whisky with a hint of fresh fruit, smoke, and vanilla, very smooth, with a faintly spicy rye note: it is very good for mixing.

### Kittling Ridge Distillery
### Forty Creek
### Barrel Select

In alluding to the name of a settlement that was founded around 1750 (beside the waterfall that operated the distillery's malt mill), this whisky positions itself within the production tradition of the early farmers who pioneered Canadian whisky. Distilled in small batches in two pot stills, the spirit derives its complexity from several sources: the fruity-spicy rye spirit that ages in very lightly toasted casks, the nutty barley spirit from casks with a medium level of toasting, and the rich, sweet corn spirit from very heavily charred casks. The final touch is given to the blend in sherry casks, which give it plenty of sweet fruitiness and a distinctive character, with aromas of honey, nuts, spices, and roasted notes.

### McGuinness
### Old Canada

The long-established whisky firm of L. J. McGuinness & Co. from Toronto went the way of many of its competitors. It was taken over by Corby Distilleries in 1988 as part of the concentration in the Canadian whisky industry. The majority shares in Corby itself had belonged to Hiram Walker & Sons since 1935, when the director was the legendary Harry Hatch. Thus Old Canada is now made in the distillery in Windsor, Ontario, where it is column distilled and blended with more flavorsome grain spirits. It is available as six- to eight-years-old editions. Quite dark in color, it has the characteristically mild style of Canadian whiskies, being very smooth and sweet with notes of caramel.

### Schenley
### OFC
### Original Fine Canadian

This great classic comes from the only whisky distillery in Canada where French is spoken, for Schenley Distillery is situated in Valleyfield in Quebec. It was built in 1945 on an industrial site on an island in the Saint Lawrence River. Its famous OFC—only convincing in its original 8-year-old Canadian version—was created in 1955. It is a blend strongly characterized by pungent rye whisky that is distilled in a pot still. A light golden color, it has a lovely sweet bouquet which reveals an interplay of corn and vanilla notes. The palate is exquisitely balanced, full bodied, and sweetly spicy, with an elegant note of honey and a deliciously dry finish.

# Japan: the rise of whisky in the east

If Japan is one of the most important whisky-producing nations in the world today, then it is because of two men, Shinjiro Torii and Masataka Taketsuru. As a young man Torii worked for an uncle who produced and sold various alcoholic beverages, presumably including whisky, which became known in Japan from around 1870. Torii foresaw the future in whisky, for once he had started his own wholesale business he brought out his first Finest Liqueur Old Scotch Whisky in 1919: according to the label, it was bottled by "Torys Distillery," four years before he actually opened his own Yamazaki distillery.

Whiskies are distilled in copper pot stills in Yamazaki, near Kyoto.

Taketsuru, the offspring of an esteemed sake brewing family, came to whisky by a quite different route. He attended the Technical University in Osaka, where he was recruited by the owner of the spirit merchant Settsu Shuzo and entrusted with the production of various types of alcohol. He apparently proved himself; the company sent him to Scotland in 1918, where he picked up all the production techniques for making whisky. He attended chemistry courses at the University of Glasgow, and in the spring of 1919 he gained his first practical experiences for five days in the very accommodating Long-morn Distillery.

This gave him a more profound insight into a distillery that made grain whisky, and then a chemistry professor arranged for him to go to the Hazelburn Distillery in Campbel-town. For five months Taketsuru conscientiously noted down every detail relating to whisky production and then compiled a comprehensive report for his company in Osaka. When he returned home in 1920 with his Scottish bride, he was the most experienced whisky expert in Japan, commanding a wealth of knowledge that would shape his whole life.

## The first whisky distilleries

In 1923 Torii built Japan's first whisky distillery, in Yamazaki, not far from Kyoto, in a spot famed for the excellent quality of its water. He hired Taketsuru as his manager, who worked for the next ten years for this company (still called Kotobukiya then) which produced the first commercial whiskies in Japan. The opening gambit came with Suntory Shirofuda in 1929. Heavily influenced from the outset by the Scottish role model, Japanese whiskies remained blends for a long time, with each distillery using only its own spirits (rather than buying them in from their domestic counterparts), though they did import Scottish malts as ingredients.

Taketsuru went on to found his own whisky company in 1934, as well as the Yoichi distillery in Hokkaido, which reminded him of Scotland. When war broke out he began to meet the needs of the army with just one pot still, along with his competitors. After the war he continued his operations, now as Nikka Whisky Distilling. While he produced a powerful and complex peated malt in direct fired pot stills in Yoichi, he founded the Miyagikyo distillery in 1969, which was responsible for light, smooth malt.

Torii's son Saji followed in his father's footsteps. He renamed the company Suntory in 1963, and ten years later he built his second whisky distillery, in Hakushu, which was the largest in the world. He freed himself from the constraints of Japanese blends, creating a variety of different malt whiskies. So Suntory is now home to Yamazaki, the first Japanese single malt, as well as the top-quality blend Hibiki.

Japanese whisky has moved on from strength to strength since then. The distilleries offer a wide spectrum of styles—from the light, floral spirits, to those with a distinctive sherry cask influence, and heavily peated, smoky ones. At the same time the two giants, Suntory and Nikka, are outdoing each other with premium quality products, whether long aged or single barrel bottlings. Since 2001, when a Yoichi malt was selected by an expert panel as the best in the world, international interest in the whisky art of Japan has been growing, and so it should.

A photo of the kilns from the early days of the Yamazaki distillery.

Four whiskies from Suntory, including the elegant, extremely complex blend Hibiki and the wonderful Yamazaki Single Malt Aged 18 Years.

# Whisky worldwide

Whisky has long since ceased to be the sole province of the Irish, Scots, Americans, and Canadians. Today there are whisky producers in many countries, divided into two groups. The older of these takes its inspiration from the successes of blended Scotch for producing and selling whisky in its own country, in the hope of sharing in the profit of the original. A few who have approached it with a seriously professional attitude have managed to bring out products that are extremely convincing, bringing some of them a considerable degree of success. The younger group is made up of committed distillers, who in many cases have already produced very high-quality spirits with other raw materials, and looked to the outstanding malts for inspiration to create their own versions of whisky. Not all have been immediate hits, but some show great originality and top quality.

## Whisky in India

India occupies a special place as a large-scale producer, already established with brandy, gin, and vodka. The country's annual consumption of whisky alone is calculated at 150 million gallons (570 million liters). Introduced during British colonial rule, whisky has risen to become the most popular spirit drunk by Indians today. High import duties protect the market for Indian products, 90% of which are based on molasses and therefore not allowed to be sold as whisky in Europe.

The leading brand in India is Bagpiper from United Breweries, which has an annual turnover of over 10 million crates. The group also sells 16 other big whisky brands, including McDowell No. 1, sales of which now exceed 6 million crates. Their flagship brand is McDowell's Single Malt Whisky, distilled in Goa, which is based on local malted barley and is aged for three years in oak casks. Amrut distilleries are their competitors in terms of malt: they distill their Amrut Single Malt Whisky from barley grown at the foot of the Himalayas which is then allowed to age in Bangalore at an altitude of 3,300 feet (1,000 m) under tropical conditions with very high humidity.

The small pot still of Ruedi Käser's Whisky Castle in the Swiss canton of Aargau.

# Whiskies from other countries

## Germany

### Slyrs

**Bavarian Single Malt Whisky**
This whisky comes from Schliersee in the heart of the Bavarian mountains, and is created by master distiller Florian Stetter following an inspirational trip to Scotland in 1994. He also has the right qualifications for this project, for as director of the Lantenhammer distillery he is not only versed in the production of fine spirits, but has also completed training as a brewer. Since 1999 he has been distilling Slyrs (pronounced "shloors"), which is based on malted barley that has been smoked over beech wood. It is then aged for three years in new 60-gallon (225-liter) casks made from American white oak and finally bottled under a vintage label. Slightly nippy, and heavily influenced by the new oak wood, it has floral notes and is clearly too young, but shows definite potential.

## France

### Distillerie Guillon

**Whisky 46 % vol, Single Malt de la Montagne de Reims**
Oenologist Thierry Guillon set up his whisky distillery in Champagne in 1997, where he found a suitable plot with an excellent spring on the edge of a wood. He sources barley from the region and smokes part of the malt over oak or beech chips instead of peat. After double distillation the whisky is aged in oak casks, for which Guillon partly uses new barrels and partly ones that have previously contained Sauternes, Meursault, or Maury wines. It is very complex with sweet spiciness, herbs, malt and a subtle smoky note; it has plums, as well as cherries, tobacco, cocoa, and just a hint of smoke on the palate—full of character.

## Austria

### Weutz

**Flamberger Hot Stone**
Michael and Brigitte Weutz have made a name for themselves in southern Styria with their fine fruit spirits. In their village of St. Nikolai im Sausal there was also the Löscher microbrewery. What could be more obvious than for them to cooperate? Michael Löscher supplies the wash that Michael Weutz then distills. This has produced half a dozen single malts to date, such as Black Peat (peat smoked), White Smoke (beech smoked), and Golden Wheat (made from wheat). Recommended as a good whisky to accompany a cigar, Hot Stone has the aromas of smoke, malt, vanilla, and fruits, with a subtly bitter taste of fresh fruit, sweet spice, and elegant wood notes.

## Switzerland

### Humbel Distillery

**Ourbeer Single Malt Whisky**
**Aged 36 Months**
The Humbel family has been distilling in Stetten since 1918. The grandfather began with cherry spirits, the father added different types of fruit, and the son—Lorenz—uses organic fruit and likes to distill unusual ingredients. His malt is a joint venture with the Basel brewery Unser Bier. In the context of a whisky seminar once a year it delivers barley wort without hops to Humbel, where it is distilled according to the craft; it is then committed to three years' cask aging, the last six months of which are in tokay casks. This produces a fruity whisky, with aromas of orange and apricot; it is smooth tasting and distinctly sweet, with a subtle smoky note, and a hint of cocoa and orange peel.

## Switzerland

### Whisky Castle

**Single Malt Whisky**
**Smoke Barley**
At Käsers Schloss (in Fricktal in the Swiss canton of Aargau) master distiller Ruedi Käser had a long track record of distilling more than just fruit by the time he opened his new distillery, Whisky Castle, in 2005. He housed his own maltings there, as well as a Scottish pot still with a capacity of 160 gallons (600 liters), making it the smallest whisky distillery in the world, according to him. In it he distills oats, spelt, barley, rye, wheat, and corn, aging the whisky for at least three years in casks that are used for single cask bottlings. His Smoke Barley spends precisely 1,160 days in a sherry cask, revealing itself to be very complex, with plenty of fermented corn, smoke, malt candy, and menthol, followed by a full-bodied palate of roasted, smoky notes, sweet vanilla, and a dense texture.

# Collecting and enjoying

Every whisk(e)y has its own individual character and, of course, quality. There are now thousands of different bottlings, and no end seems to be in sight. This is exciting news for the whisky aficionado and collector, but how does someone who likes a drink of whisky go about trying different brands?

To engage seriously with the subject matter, you need a solid point of departure—and there is no substitute for first hand experience. This does not have to involve an expensive outlay as many whiskies are available in the form of miniatures. In this way you can dip into different regions and countries, starting by choosing a malt each from the Lowlands, the Highlands, Speyside, and Islay and comparing them with one of the well-known blended Scotches. If you want to move beyond Scotland, then try samples from Ireland, Kentucky, Tennessee, and Canada. This will act as a good basis from which to start. The next lesson can deal with the age of the whiskies and can span the range of blends and five- or six-year-old malts, or even up to 8, 10, 12, 15, 18, 21, and more years.

Whisk(e)y in miniature bottles provides a broad picture of the many diverse styles.

Another exciting aspect is the much sought-after wood finishes, from sherry, port, madeira, marsala, malaga, and even rum or other dry wines. If you have a preference, perhaps for the Speyside malts, you will be faced with a wide subject there, with over 40 working distilleries. If you prefer the peaty malts of Islay, you may want to gain an insight into the different styles of the distilleries there. If you like Kentucky, then tackle the best-known bourbons from its nine distilleries, while Irish whiskey fans can start by testing themselves with the most famous brands. And if you get the chance, you should supplement your latest passion with onsite experiences. Collectors will find real treasure troves in the specialty stores that are now found in many countries. You will find not only the popular bottlings but also special, rare ones, and maybe even the proprietor's own bottling from selected single casks.

## The rules of the game?

Distilleries are normally reticent about dictating to their customers how whiskies should be drunk. However it is wise to make certain distinctions. The quality of a long-aged malt or bourbon can be enjoyed properly only if you choose a tulip-shape glass for tasting, serve it at room temperature (64–68 °F/18–20 °C), and add pure spring water according to taste. Some bourbon distilleries have even bottled their own water for this purpose. Old whiskies, then, should never be stored in the refrigerator or served on the rocks, which would kill the taste.

In pubs and bars, and frequently at home as well, whisk(e)y often has a different status: blended Scotch or popular qualities of different origin are usually drunk in tumblers, with water or ice cubes depending on taste, as a long drink, or in a cocktail. With soda it becomes a highball. The Manhattan is famous, causing quite a stir in New York when it appeared in 1890: it was the first to unite rye whiskey with sweet vermouth, though this is now uncommon. There is now an abundance of variations with different whiskies, often with shots of angostura bitters and dry vermouth. Many classic cocktails now have a variation that includes whisk(e)y, whether it is a Collins, a Cooler, a Sling, or a Smash. Whisk(e)y Sour is a very well-known mixture of whisk(e)y, lemon juice, and sugar. The Old Fashioned is a specialty from Kentucky, so bourbon should be used in this cocktail, along with just a little sugar, angostura, and a slice of lemon. And for cold days eggnogs or Irish coffee are highly recommended.

In pubs and bars, whisk(e)y is often served in a tumbler.

# Grain

# spirits

Top-quality grain spirits are often distilled in ultra-modern column stills.

Opposite: Cereal fields, in particular in northern and eastern Europe, supply the distilleries with their raw materials.

Page 384: Barley is the star among grains giving the best-quality spirits.

# Bread or brandy

Anyone who wishes to make alcohol out of grain rather than fruit has always had to face somewhat greater difficulties, and not just from a moral standpoint. Diverting "our daily bread" for other uses was only possible in peaceful times when harvests were plentiful. Distillation posed technical difficulties too as, unlike fruit sugar, the starch in corn cannot be fermented as such. It must first be broken down into sugar, which requires greater expertise and is a more laborious process. But that has never stopped anyone who has neither grapes nor other fruits to distill. And that is why, wherever grains grow in abundance, there are also corn spirits.

Many corn spirits have, over the years, become inextricably linked in people's minds with their countries of origin. Even someone who has never drunk a glass in their life will automatically associate korn with Germany, vodka with Russia and Poland, genever with Holland, gin with England, and aquavit with Denmark and Norway. All the grain spirits listed above have one trait in common: when they are distilled in a traditional manner, they are very neutral in taste, which opens up a great many possibilities. When combined with aromatic additives, they take on a national identity such as that given by the juniper in genever and gin, or the caraway in aquavit. Left pure and unadulterated, as korn and vodka are in their original state, they go with many dishes and just as many occasions, which has never been in dispute in the home of vodka. The neutrality of grain spirits means, of course, that natural factors such as water quality and the aromas imparted by the cask have a particularly strong influence. This has long been exploited in one large group of their most famous representatives, the whiskies.

Where once the roles were very clearly defined, over recent decades the composition of grain spirits has started to change. The initiative here came from vodka—now the world's most popular spirit—and, first and foremost, Swedish absolut. Although even before it made its appearance on the American market toward the end of the 1970s some brands had managed to carve out market shares for themselves (the prevalent belief being that vodka in cocktails really only affected the alcohol content), absolut became the first real star in the premium vodka segment. The fact that it became chic to drink a particular brand was not least due to a brilliant marketing strategy and a new bottle design.

In the early 1990s international vodka brands such as Moskovskaya and Stolichnaya added prestige variants to their normal products. For the past ten years or so, vodkas have been available that can only be described as ultra-premium. Starting from the assumption that nothing is as luxurious as the purest of the pure, experts have developed sophisticated concepts for making their distillates ever more mellow, ever clearer, and ever more elegant. Only water from a glacier or from a well 330 feet (100 m) deep will do to dilute the six or seven times distilled noble spirit to drinking strength. Activated carbon must be used for filtration at precisely 32 °F (0 °C) or, even better, silver or diamonds. Bottling must be at least into crystal.

Quality is evaluated to the limits of the imagination, although experts say that it has not been possible to improve on the manufacturing methods for years. The example set by vodka is now being imitated by the aromatic grain spirits. Constant refinements in quality portend yet greater things to come.

# Swine and swill

Cereal cultivation, bread, and beer can look back together over a very long common history. Whether it all began 7,000 years ago in Mesopotamia or even earlier is, at least for now, lost in the mists of time. Even more obscure is the early history of cereals used for distilling rather than brewing. Although the basic skills needed to ferment grain had been gained in beer brewing, distilling beer quickly proved unprofitable for the nascent grain distilling industry. From its agricultural beginnings toward the end of the 15th century, for a long time distillation only paid off if its waste was used too. The watery mush (swill or slops) from which the alcohol was removed in grain distillation proved to be an excellent concentrated food for fattening pigs that, in the early days of industrial grain distillation, begged the question of which was the byproduct, the alcohol or the animal food. Writings from the time decrying excessive alcohol consumption furnish evidence of the pleasurable being combined with the functional. Since the middle of the 16th century alcohol has been produced in large quantities from grain, wherever grapes do not grow but grain is in abundance and where there is sufficient water and wood—that is in northern Europe and Asia. Production grew, as did the interest of the authorities. One of the first German brandy taxes was enforced in 1507 in the free Reich city of Nordhausen in Thuringia, Germany. The first clear documentary evidence of grain distilling is dated 1545 and is its prohibition, in no other town than Nordhausen itself. Since then the history of grain distillation has been rich in both prohibition and promise.

In northern and eastern Europe, the home of the most famous grain spirits, some towns and cities established themselves as distillery centers. Some have now lost that reputation, while in others the industry is flourishing better than ever before.

- ■ Grain spirits
- ■ Vodka
- ■ Genever
- □ Gin
- ■ Aquavit

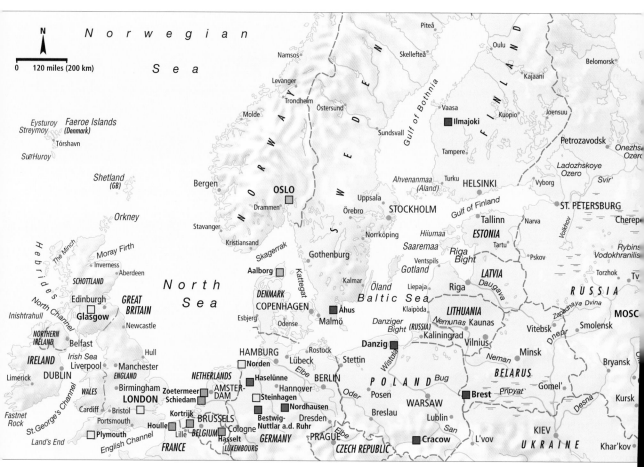

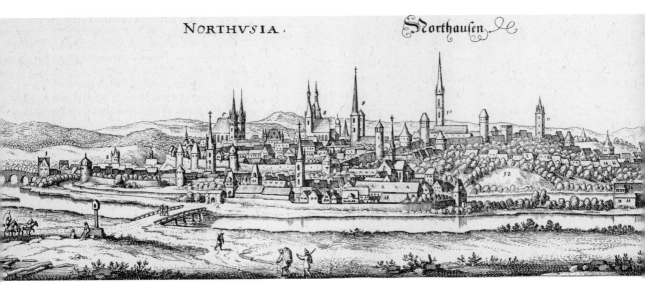

NORTHVSIA. Northausen

## Unfettered spirits

One Polish document dated 1544 bears witness to the large-scale production of a clear grain spirit. In 1550 what was almost definitely the first consignment of genever was supplied (in Leyden). It would be some time before the juniper spirit would make the voyage across the English Channel, but the British Isles could wait. After all, they had been consoling themselves with whisky for quite a while there already. When the Thirty Years War broke out in 1618 and times became more troubled, two things happened, among many others: rulers needed soldiers and soldiers needed alcohol. The former had a direct effect on the taxation of spirits and the latter—for instance in Nordhausen—produced rare fruits such as the order that each distillery and brewery should cater for 30 soldiers. As, for many reasons, the undisturbed cultivation of cereal fields is not conducive to war, the balance of this fragile interdependence became increasingly precarious.

After the Thirty Years War rulers and authorities continued to require one thing above all else: money. The Great Elector Frederick William accomplished a stroke of genius in the Brandenburg Recess of 1653 in this context. Paragraph 20 states: "We want to encourage the cities to distill brandy for their own sustenance … which the rural areas must not claim exclusively for themselves."

In the face of a limited number of officials, tax control was very much more efficient in the cities than in the country, once the preserve of korn distilling. A second example shows the intimate relationship between alcohol and wealth. In Russia the brewing of vodka was initially the privilege of the landowning nobility. This changed under the rule of Peter the Great (1672–1725), who is said to have taught himself distilling and had developed his knowledge of the art further during his visit to The Netherlands in 1698. With the help of state-licensed manufacturers and vendors, he turned vodka into a bubbling source of finance for his fleet, but then decided to liberalize production once again and to tax it instead. Moscow became the Russian stronghold of vodka production. In Poland it was Danzig, Lemberg, Cracow, and Posen (where 500 breweries were counted as early as in 1580) that grew into the most important centers of production—and grew rich at the same time.

Top: Nordhausen in Thuringia, depicted here in an engraving from the Upper Saxony volume of the *Topographia Germaniae* by Matthäus Merian published in 1650. In the 16th century the town grew into a center of the distilling industry.

Bottom: Peter the Great in a painting by Jean-Henri Benner.

# Grains for distilling

In principle, any grain can be distilled into alcohol. The best however are varieties with high starch content as more starch means more fermentable sugar after pretreatment, which ultimately results in a higher alcohol content, said to give greater mellowness. As nowadays the starch source has become more interchangeable, the very essence of a vodka's quality being thought to lie in its neutral taste arising from repeated distillation, the starch source can be selected in good conscience according to profitability. This has not always been the case everywhere. The German *Brennerei-Zeitung*, a distillers' publication, dated January 1,1886, reacted defensively to one korn distiller having been accused of adulteration due to the fusel oil content in his spirits. "The spirit only acquires its special grain taste from the grain fusel oil. If you were to take away the grain fusel oil completely, the spirit would no longer be a grain spirit and a distiller refining so much that the fusel oil disappears altogether would no longer find a single customer for his grain brandy."

Wheat (left), the most demanding but most widespread cereal crop, was often used for distilling because it was cheap. Rye (right) is considered in Russia to be the best vodka base.

## Wheat

Wheat is the basis of most grain spirits as it is the world's most cultivated cereal crop. Until now, it has been high yielding and cheap to produce, even though it is among the grain types that require the most heat and water.

Common or bread wheat (*Triticum aestivum*) is best suited to distillation. Some varieties however do have a high protein content, which increases frothing. The alcohol yield is 40–5 gallons of pure alcohol per 100 lb (34–8 liters per 100 kg) of raw material—these values are based on complete saccharification of the starch and include the total alcohol from the first, middle, and final fractions: the head, heart, and tails. Gin and genever, aquavit, and German korn are most often produced from wheat. Many of the Scandinavian vodkas too are wheat based.

## Rye

Rye is the hardiest cereal variety. It will withstand drought and semistarvation. Many Russians continue to consider rye to be the best grain for the distillation of real vodka, even if they have been drinking something quite different for a long time now. The alcohol yield is 39–44 gallons per 100 lb (33–7 liters per 100 kg). Rye has a high proportion of its own amylase enzymes that break down the starch in sugar so that the yeast is able to work.

## Barley

Barley is seldom used "raw," but grain-based alcoholic drinks that contain no barley are rare.

## Malt

It is mainly barley that is malted and malt, or its constituents, is essential in the fermentation of starchy base materials. The starch stored in the kernel is the seed's store room. So that it can derive nourishment from it (and that which can be processed by the seed can also be used by yeast in the fermentation of the mash) it must be broken down into sugar, the task of enzymes that are released as soon as germination starts. Cereal grains are softened for about two days in water before ideal germination conditions are created for them under controlled temperature and a constant flow of air. After 4–5 days the sprouted radicles are approximately as long as the grain and the acrospires immediately before they break through. This green malt is now exposed to increasing temperature to protect it, and kiln dried to stop the germination process (new plants are not what is required here), without destroying the enzymes required to break down the starch—these being susceptible to excessive heat. In its basic characteristics, preparation of kiln dried (cured) malt is the same regardless of whether it is to be used for brewing or distillation. Many differences in the finished malt (essential for beer) are the result of the degree and source of heat during kiln drying. By contrast with distillery malt, brewery malt is made from particularly high starch cultivations of grain: more starch means more sugar and results in higher alcohol content. As well as barley, rye, wheat, and spelt are also malted.

## Other sources of starch

In addition to rye, wheat, and barley, EU directives on the production of grain spirits also permit oats and buckwheat. The Sasse brewery in Münsterland in Germany has rediscovered the properties of emmer wheat, one of the oldest cultivated wheat varieties. Since distillers have been experimenting with arable crops, distillates can also be enjoyed from "old" grains such as spelt, millet, amaranth, and kamut.

Depending on the climate, in some regions and in some countries maize and potatoes are also distilled. The potato distilleries in particular have at times presented serious competition for grain distilleries (in Germany) and have indeed prevailed as far as vodka is concerned.

Rice is not used as a starch source in alcoholic drinks in Europe and America, but is intensively used in Asia—for instance in sake, often misleadingly described as "rice wine," but actually a type of beer. However, rice spirits too have a long tradition. In Thailand a whisky is produced from rice. Arrack, and in particular Batavia arrack, can be produced from it. One Vietnamese spirit is ruou. Soju is a Korean version. It is popular in Japan as shochu. All three are usually, but not necessarily, made from distilled rice.

Emmer, one of the oldest cultivated varieties of wheat.

Barley (left) is only rarely used "straight from the ear." It is usually first left to germinate. As a sweet malt (right), it is highly useful in grain mixtures in converting starch into sugar.

# One more korn

Korn was to Germany as gin was to England and vodka to Russia. Yet times change and korn is struggling to imitate the success of vodka and gin in achieving a more refined image for a simple common folk's drink. Its rustic, working-class background is hardly its strongest selling point, and qualities such as "hard," "rough," "raw," and "down to earth" are probably best left unmentioned. As a traditional drink korn holds its head above water, but a flash of marketing inspiration would do it no harm at all.

In the days of the economic miracle, korn was the most commonly ordered spirit in German pubs. And the second went down just as easily as the first. Heinz Erhardt, a German comedian, wit, and poet in the 1960s, sang about its immoderate consumption. "Immer wenn ich traurig bin, trink ich einen Korn. Wenn ich dann noch traurig bin, trink ich noch 'n Korn … Und wenn ich dann noch traurig bin, fang ich an von vorn." (Whenever I am feeling sad, I drink a glass of korn. When I find that I'm still sad, I drink another korn … and when I find I'm just as sad, I start all over again.) Lines such as these made their mark.

Modern Germany loves Horst Schlämmer but it isn't going to sit about drinking Doornkaat or Bommerlunder for his sake, just because dead fellows sing about them. It isn't the first crisis that the national spirit has had to overcome. Up to the beginning of the 19th century life was steady for the korn distillers, korn drinkers, and imposers of taxes—they all knew what to expect. The areas of Westphalia and Lower Saxony, owing to the high yielding grain cultivation, had become centers of korn distilling. Distillers such as Schwarze in Oelde can trace their corporate history back to the beginning of the 17th century. The Thirty Years War—no matter how severe its consequences while it was raging (1618–48)—had few permanent effects on the distillation of korn. As soon as the fields could once more be cultivated, it did not take much longer than a few crop cycles before everything was almost back to normal again. Around 150 years later, a certain distinguished businessman, a Mr. Neuenhahn, since 1778 owner of a Nordhausen brewery, described his profits as follows in *Das Ganze der Branntweinbrennerei* (About brandy distilling): "with a daily processed quantity of 12 bushels of rye grain [around 105 gallons / 400 kg] one pot still will give an annual yield of 274 barrels [each containing 54 gallons / 206 liters] of grain spirit as well as feed for fattening 250 pigs (at a profit of 3 taler). A bushel of rye costs around 26 groschen, a liter [about 2 pints] of korn will make about 33 pfennigs." If a taler is worth 30 groschen or 360 pfennigs, this would give a pretax income of less than 100% (especially as expenses for wood, barrels, and workers have not been taken into account here).

In the year 1820 a decision was made that would make life extremely difficult for the korn distillers in Germany. Prussia introduced the mash room tax on the processing of farinaceous substances which, in principle, would remain in force until 1909. Whereas previously duties were calculated on the basis of the quantity of raw materials or capacity of the still, now the volume of the mash tun was the decisive factor. At the time of this change there was a total of around 22,000 korn distilleries in Prussia. Fifty years later the number of distillers had changed little, but only a sixth of them were distilling grain. The majority of them had shifted toward potato distilling, not least because potatoes have a much more viscous mash than grain and a full mash tun taxed at the same rate yields more distillate. Laborers and farmers continued to drink clear spirits as before, with (in)decent regularity, but in very few cases was this korn. The revenue from the brandy tax was gratifying, but the korn distilling industry was on the brink of ruin. It did however cling to existence and, when the brandy taxation law was updated in 1909, it was no longer at a disadvantage and was able to boast quality, once a purity order came into force stating that korn should only call itself korn if it actually contains grain. No sooner was this order signed and sealed than it began to create problems of its own, however, when grain was prevented from being used for korn. It was not until 1954 that the prohibition on distilling bread cereals was officially lifted. The korn distilleries were reduced to just a few centers, but the industry had survived.

# In vats and kettles

Page 392: At the Sasse distillery an ample sample of the matured korn is drawn off from the vat using an outsize pipette.

Left: Organic grain is now often used for the best korn.

Right: Mash tuns like this one in the Fabry Museum at the historical korn distillery in Hilden, with special suspended cooling coil to keep the temperature right for the yeast, are no longer in use.

"To start with, a big kettle, holding about four or five bucketsful / is placed full of water over a fire / to heat up well / but not boil; then a half metze [former dry measure approximately equivalent to 10 gallons / 40 liters] of malt is placed in a large vat or barrel / hot water is poured over it / and it is stirred (as in beer brewing) thoroughly / after this, half a metze of crushed wheat or barley is added to the malt in the vat / it is all stirred together thoroughly / so that no lumps remain; then, the water left in the large kettle / which should be about two bucketsful / is boiled well / and should be poured onto the grain and malt in the vat / covered well / allowed to stand thus for three or four hours, after which it is opened up / and cooled down with one or more tubs of cold water / it is stirred once again well and if anything has baked hard together, this should be rubbed loose using the fingers / and fresh yeast or / ferment added / as for beer or wine … / and it is then left for three or four days / until it has settled again / and is finely covered." This is how Wolff Helmhard von Hohberg,

in 1701 in his book *Georgica curiosa aucta. Oder: Adelichen Land- und Feld-Lebens. Auf alle in Teutschland übliche Land- und Hauswirtschafften* (The rural and agricultural life of a nobleman. On all agricultural and domestic practices common in Germany), began his description of the production "of brandy / distilled from grain." In principle, mashing and fermentation in the mash kettles of today, equipped with agitator, cooling coils, and temperature gauges, has changed little. Malt and grain are crushed, nowadays as finely as possible, and everything is thoroughly mixed with water, avoiding the formation of clumps because the processes in the mash kettle operate best only on contact with all the ingredients. In those early days people knew the importance of getting the temperatures right, even if they were not yet able to explain why. The enzymes in the malt—one for liquefying the starch (and for agglutination) and the other for the conversion of starch into sugar—require relatively high, but not the same, temperatures (and pH values) for optimum

efficiency. Whereas the alpha amylase only becomes fully effective at 158 °F (70 °C), the beta amylase is damaged at temperatures as low as 140 °F (60 °C). The mash temperature therefore must be below this, even if this makes liquefaction of the starch take longer. As soon as the starch has been converted into sugar, which can be easily checked using a color reaction iodine test, the mash must be cooled to around 77 °F (22 °C) as otherwise it would be too hot for the yeast that is to be added. Mashing and starch conversion lasts for about 90 minutes, after which it is poured into the fermentation vat. Fermentation takes a further 3–5 days. The fermented mash is distilled with the solids (by contrast with whisky, for which it is filtered off in advance). Factory distillation takes place in sealed distillation equipment, mainly (continuous) column stills, in which 40 or more bubble trays may be used. The more bubble trays, the purer the distillate. The objective is a refined spirit with 85% alcohol content by volume. Private distilleries such as Rüdiger Sasse in Schöppingen in Münsterland distill their grain, which is often organically cultivated, in the traditional manner using pot stills, swan neck lid, or spirit tube and condenser and have to process raw spirit and refined spirit in separate stages.

## Korn, kornbrand, and doppelkorn

The distilled spirit is diluted to drinking strength using water. This water must, above all, be soft water. Any hardness from calcium or magnesium will cloud an alcohol solution. The alcohol content also determines the label on the bottle: korn has at least 32% alcohol by volume; kornbrand, doppelkorn, and edelkorn are at least 38% volume. "Korn" and "kornbrand" as names are authorized in countries where the official language is German, provided that the distillate is exclusively produced from full-grain wheat, rye, barley, oats, or buckwheat in which the proportion of malted grain is a maximum of 25%.

Cask maturating of grain spirits is still rare. Rüdiger Sasse is one of the few companies that have been experimenting with this for decades, using cognac, bourbon, and more recently muscatel barrels.

Left: Only rarely are grain spirits double distilled in pot stills.

Right: Maturing in oak casks is unusual, although some excellent results can be achieved.

# Selected korn

**Berentzen**
**Edelkorn vom alten Fass**
Berentzen had resigned itself to the fact that there were no longer any customers that wanted a good grain spirit from the barrel. They faced up to the consequences and stopped production. Hardly had the korn been taken off the market than there came a tide of demand for it—sufficient demand to revive this traditional wheat-based korn. Indeed, the distillate, "gilded" in oak barrels, has quite a following. In 2001 a specialty was re-created at Germany's largest korn distillery and is now mainly supplied to regional restaurants. An unlikely tale, with a happy ending.

**Doornkaat**
**Feine Kornspezialität**
Jan ten Doornkaat Koolman knew what he was doing when he distilled his korn three times. In 1806 he came out top of a series of competitors in the east Frisian town of Norden. Doornkaat still holds second place in the hit parade of German doppelkorns, although the square-bottled spirit has not been the product of family enterprise for quite a long time now, its competitor Berentzen having come to Doornkaat's rescue. However, a publicity boost not exactly celebrated at Berentzen came from an unexpected source. Comedian Hape Kerkeling has made Doornkaat the favorite tipple of his brilliant character Horst Schlämmer. Doornkaat no doubt has gained in popularity on account of this, but sales figures have not as yet begun to show a marked profit as a result.

**Fürst Bismarck**
**Original**
No, this grain spirit is not just named in honor of the former German head of state. The distillery actually belonged to the Iron Chancellor and has enjoyed widespread success across many regions. The product owed its good fortunes not only to its name. Rye, wheat, and barley malt were its raw materials. A harmonization phase after distillation and soft water create a crisp, smooth spirit with a hint of sweetness in its taste.

**Hullmann's**
**Alter Korn**
Its family tree dates back to the year 1469 when Hanneken Hullemann, steward of the abbey at Rastede, bought his daughter's freedom from serfdom. The family established themselves in the Oldenburg region as hardworking and successful farmers. In 1807 they founded a distillery with the profits from which they increased their land holding to more than 740 acres (300 hectares). Even if the family fortunes were fleeting, the mature 36% volume korn lives on thanks to the H. Heydt private distillery in Haselünne. It is now matured in Limousin oak barrels that give the spirit its mellowness and the fine notes of vanilla, without losing any of its grain-spirit taste.

**Nordhäuser**
**Eiskorn**
Perhaps Nordhäuser is the father of all korn spirits. It does come from the greatest and oldest korn-distilling city in Germany. Over its 500-year company history Nordhäuser has seen a few things: the Thirty Years War, Napoleonic occupation, the National Socialists, and a period as a state-owned enterprise. Real Nordhäuser, as always, is only distilled from rye and malt, which give it plenty of body. The korn is diluted to drinking strength with ice-age spring water that is reputed to be of extraordinary purity, originating in 300-foot (100-meter) deep wells in Mecklenburg-Vorpommern.

**Sasse**
**Münsterländer Lagerkorn**

As was the case with many distilleries, the production facilities at Sasse were demolished after 1945 and their stocks destroyed. When production resumed the new product was needed too quickly to enable the young distillate to be matured for long. "So at some point we forgot the art," admits Rüdiger Sasse. But the company has long since made up for this deficiency. Since the beginning of the 1980s the Münster distillers have concentrated on producing matured korn (lagerkorn). Spirits with a high cost of sales using twice as much grain as those produced in industrial distilleries form the basic stock, matured in macerated cognac barrels.

**Sasse**
**T. S. Privat**

Without question, T.S. Privat has reached the pinnacle of what can be achieved by artisanal methods. For at least 20 years, and sometimes far longer, the spirits for this cuvée are matured in wooden casks once used to hold sherry or bourbon. The result is a spirit that combines the sweet tannin aromas from young casks with the oxidative aspects of the old into one perfect distillate. T.S. is mild and complex, abounding in tones of sherry, caramel, and vanilla.

**Schneider**
**Ganz Alter Schneider**

Solid quality gives this spirit its presence, even without sensational marketing. Alter Schneider has not bent to the demands of the cheap retail sector price war. This grain spirit with 38% alcohol by volume is aged for at least two years in old sherry barrels, giving it an amber tone, mellowness, and a complex woody aroma. The H. & F. Schneider company had been distilling its grain spirits in Bestwig-Nuttlar in Sauerland for more than 130 years, so intensively that apparently they had given no thought to a successor. The company has now been taken over by Schwarze & Schlichte and production goes on as before.

**Schwarze**
**Weizen Frühstückskorn**

The name comes from the time when strong spirits were a routine part of daily sustenance. Farm workers who needed a second breakfast during their hard labor were often given korn that was as mellow as possible. Since 1927 the name has been protected as a trademark. The black Frühstückskorn has a markedly grainy bouquet and is clear on the palate, but it cannot be denied that a farm laborer's life in those days was not an easy one.

**Strothmann**
**Weizenkorn**

Strothmann korn is available in nearly every north German supermarket. The market leader in the 32% by volume alcohol korn segment presents itself as a typical wheat-based korn in somewhat inconspicuous packaging. Technically flawless, it is matured in wood for a short enough time not to affect the neutral aroma. It is a mainstay in German pubs and the most popular choice for consumers looking for a cheap mixer ingredient. But none of this guarantees sales, as the Berentzen group found out when it took over the brand in 1996 and then watched as shares slumped. They more than recovered a long time ago now, and Strohmann has stubbornly held onto its position as top dog.

# Clear as vodka

Unfortunately the origin of this most international of national drinks is anything but clear. The Poles point us to a reference to vodka in official records from San-domierz dated 1405, while the Russians appealed to the European Court of Justice for clarification and felt themselves vindicated. The chronology of events is controversial because the original ingredients and purpose of the spirit whose name is a diminutive of the word "water" remain obscure, even in the documentary evidence that does exist. In such circumstances it may take on enormous importance that vodka was used as an aftershave lotion or as a mouthwash.

Like other distillates, vodka was not intended to be drunk for pleasure in its early days. In the first printed Polish herbal, published in 1534 in Cracow, the author Stefan Falimirz recommends to his masculine readers a "vodka" laced with chamomile as an aftershave rub to soothe irritated skin. It burns but smells pleasant. After a bath it does no harm to extend external use to the entire body. The herbalist names more than 70 further uses for vodka, together with ingredients that can be combined with it. However, it is not vodka for external use that is our main focus here. If the spirit was known in Russia (and not only there) since the beginning of the 16th century at the very latest—as vodka, a diminutive of water (*voda* in Russian and *woda* in Polish)—this encapsulates very neatly the change in attitude of the "patients" to their one-time medicine. What could be more routine and harmless than a little water? The name took root and proved, through the centuries, to be an inspiration in many respects. It bore no reference whatsoever to the content. Actually, it might be made from anything at all that came to hand which could be distilled into alcohol (by contrast with korn, the very name of which restricts the list of possible ingredients immediately). For vodka, if rye was in surplus supply rye would be distilled, if not some other grain would be used, or potatoes or even molasses. As long as it was not the taste of the raw ingredients but the alcohol, becoming ever stronger through repeated distillation, that was the main concern the distillers had plenty of scope. Using the knowledge described in his dissertation of 1865, "The combination of alcohol and water," Russian chemist Dimitri Mendelev was able to improve the quality of vodka still further. The list of his scientific achievements ranges from the design of the periodic table of elements through

to the invention of the *stopka*, the traditional Russian vodka glass.

Yet it matters little what vessel vodka is consumed from as long as it is indeed consumed. And consumed it has been, in vast quantities, for centuries. Alcohol has been recognized and used everywhere as the ideal taxable commodity, but in Russia it has influenced politics more than in practically any other country. Fleets, wars, and police forces have been financed by it. Whoever had control over vodka and whoever had the proceeds of its taxation in their pockets had the power to do anything but one thing: limit vodka consumption. Anyone who has tried this over the past hundred years has been doomed to failure, whether it be Czar Nicholas II, Leon Trotski, or Mikhail Gorbachov. Vodka has undeniably been the most important source of income for czars of every kind. Since the 18th century it has represented a third of state income. Vodka dependency is universal.

# Cottage industry

Page 398: It isn't just the Russian gourmets who appreciate vodka, caviar, and blinis as an hors d'oeuvre.

Page 393: A freshly labeled bottle is checked at the Kostroma vodka factory.

Top: To produce *samogon*, home-distilled vodka, plenty of water and yeast is needed and, of course, plenty of the basic ingredient—which may be grain, potatoes, or molasses.

Middle: Nobody knows exactly how much samogon is created annually in private kitchens. A distillery can be improvised with a couple of tubs and buckets and a few lengths of hose.

Bottom: The match is a good test of alcohol content as the samogon will burn only if the spirit is at least 50% alcohol by volume.

Making vodka is in principle not much more difficult than making soup. First you stir crushed ungerminated and germinated grain in hot but not boiling water, allow it to infuse, pour in enough cold water to make it cool enough for the yeast, mix everything together well, and allow it to ferment. This eventually produces a light alcoholic brew that is slowly heated while stirring, but must not be allowed to boil. Once you have found a way of catching the evaporating liquid and drawing it off into another vessel, the most difficult part is done. The final stage—heating the (condensed) liquid, collecting, and drawing off the vapor—can be repeated as often as you like. With some practice the vodka will become stronger and purer each time. Many Russians, over the generations, have built up amazing skills in this art, using just their own kitchen stoves. Home-made *samogon* is a part of daily life in Russia and there are as many recipes covering both basic material and any flavorings to be added later as there are *samogontschik* (home distillers). The professional producers have, of course, optimized their technical processes as far as possible. When they consider the distillation process to be complete—by the end of the 17th century four distillation cycles were considered necessary—they subject the distillate to various further filtering processes using activated carbon, paper, protein, and freezing, each one using their own recipe and their own equipment: for instance the base material of the activated carbon. Another important factor is the water used to dilute this almost clinically pure product to drinking strength. Opinions differ greatly as to whether mineral-rich or low-mineral water is best suited, and which pH value is most beneficial. Every major distillery has its own spring or, if not, its own glacier, from which it derives its water. Occasional vodka-drinkers might be forgiven for thinking that its producers take the same care to eliminate any hint of distinctiveness as distillers of fruit-based spirits devote to bringing out in e schnapps glass specific flavors from a rticular variety of apple. Vodka aficiona-s however speak of character when refer-ng to the taste of a vodka. Actually, these aits are distinctive more for the sensation ey arouse in the mouth than because of ing experiences of taste, and they differ cording to the base ingredients.

ecently some northern European manu-cturing countries such as Poland, Swe-n, and the Baltic states have attempted to ve official restrictions imposed on the nge of base materials in the spirits referred as vodka, to allow just grain and potatoes. he attempt failed. Since December 2007 has been decreed that distillates made om grapes or molasses can continue to be arketed as vodka. Vodka from raw materi-s other than the traditional ones will enceforth bear the words "distilled from…" d the name of the base material used.

he name "vodka" is completely unrelated the country of origin. Gorbatschow comes om Berlin and Eristoff comes from Italy. slanov is produced in Ghent in Belgium, d Smirnoff has been produced in New rk for a long time now. How it arrived there quite a tale of adventure. Piotr Smirnov unded his distillery in Moscow in 1860. 1886 he was appointed supplier to the urt and, by the turn of the century, his fac-ry had a capacity of 3.5 million cases per ar. Incidentally, around the turn of the illennium approximately 80% of Russian en were drinking on average 29 gallons 10 liters) of vodka every year. Piotr's son adimir took over the distillery in 1910, nortly before the October Revolution, at ne end of which the factory was national-ed and its owners sentenced to death. He ed via Constantinople to Paris, where in 925 he established a new but unsuccess-l distillery. A former supplier traveled to merica in 1934 with just a license to pro-ace "Smirnoff" in his luggage—but that as all it took!

## Aromatic vodkas

Fruit or spices are generally used to produce aromatic vodkas. These are added to the purified distillate or to the finished vodka to add flavor. Some of them might sound like a western party gimmick but they are commonly enjoyed on the rivers Volga and Don where aromatic vodkas are appreciated in certain circles. The bitter Jubileynaja (Birthday Vodka) and Pertsowka (Pepper Vodka) are two examples. In the Ukraine there is amber-flavored vodka, in Poland buffalo grass and honey (Krupnik), and even Scandinavians traditionally serve the flavored vodka *kryddat brännvin* on midsummer night. There are said to be at least 40 versions—which makes Russians smile as they know that there are many more. The range covers aniseed (An Isovaya) and sesame (Staraja Skaska), bread (Artelnaja Chlebnaja) and hemp (Cannabiskaja), vanilla (Stoli Vanil) and horseradish (Jat s Chrenom), and cranberry (Mjakow Kljukwa) through to Parliament Mandarin, also familiar west of the Volga.

# Selected classic vodkas

**Russia**

### Green Mark Traditional
If in the 1950s a vodka was presented to the state authorities for approval, it would receive the coveted "Green Mark" only if its quality was designated as outstanding. Launched in 2001, Green Mark—produced at the Moscow Topaz Distillery—rose to top vodka on the Russian market in just a few years, and delights the Russian palate and soul with its traditional wheat and rye aromas. Its distinctive features are the raw materials of wheat and rye, flavored with cedar nut aromas and filtered through activated carbon and silver. On the palate it is pleasantly mellow and slightly nutty.

**Russia**

### Ruskij Standart Imperia
In 1998 entrepreneur Tariko Roustam established the Standart brand which is anything but standard. In Russia it is one of the most expensive, but also one of the most popular. Winter wheat from the Russian Steppes, glacier water from Lake Ladoga in the north, and octuple distillation using silver and crystal quartz filters are the factors that make this vodka not only crystal clear but silky smooth.

**Russia**

### Moskovskaya Cristall
For Russians, Russian vodka has some decidedly unbeatable advantages: indigenous rye creating a slightly sweet taste and soft water from springs and woodland rivers in the region around Moscow. After distillation the crystal is filtered through wood carbon and quartz sand. While standard Moskovskaya is bottled in Latvia, its nobler brother actually comes from Moscow and sells very well internationally, despite the bottles containing one eighth of a gallon (0.5 liter), unfamiliar in many markets.

**Russia**

### Kauffman Private Collection
The Private Collection Vintage vodka is expensive. But what you get is both a slightly sugared grain spirit and the world's only vintage vodka. The company assures us that the current vintage is almost sold out, so customers will have to wait for the new vintage. Why have a vintage vodka? Because wheat is not of the same quality every year, is our answer. This is news to the average consumer. Nevertheless, Kauffman is limited to 25,000 jaunty Saint-Gobain acrylic bottles. Anyone who can get one will enjoy a mellow spirit with flavors of toast and a hint of peppermint.

**Russia**

### Kalashnikov
Water from Lake Ladoga, northeast of St. Petersburg, dilutes Kalashnikov to 41% by volume alcohol. This "military strength" was introduced to the Red Army to enable the military to distinguish approved vodka from adulterated or cheap vodka. The officers needed only to measure the alcohol content in quality controls. Kalashnikov has a clear, distinctive scent of threshed grain with a slight note of eucalyptus in the finish.

**Russia**

### Stolichnaja Elit
Before the collapse of communism, standard Stolichnaja was the vodka most popularly consumed in Russia and in the world. For its noble brother E the winter wheat was distille much more slowly. Only th finest proportion, known as L vodka, is processed furthe After traditional filtering throug birch carbon and quartz sar the distillate is chilled sever times to 0 °F (−18 °C), freezin all impurities to the sides of th barrel.

**Poland**

### Chopin

Potatoes are not considered everywhere to be the ideal raw material for vodka. The Polmos Siedlce company from Poland manufacture the spirit from the mash of cooked Stobrava potatoes. It is distilled four times, then filtered several times. This gives it just a trace of the earthiness that characterizes other potato spirits. It has a mellow taste with a medium body and a hint of apple.

**Poland**

### Wyborowa Exquisite

Since vodka has been a popular drink, the manufacturers have been vying with one another with their marketing ploys—the more offbeat, the better. Wyborowa has chosen a bottle designed by star architect Frank Gehry. Despite its modern appearance, the Poles are proud of the superb quality of traditional workmanship in the glass. The grain for this pure rye vodka comes from a unique area of cultivation in the northwest of the country where the soils are especially fertile. Triple distilled, triple filtered, triple purified—it results in a distillate that has an impressive bouquet with a spicy note of rye and a creamy texture on the palate.

**Sweden**

### Absolut

The vodka that sparked the vodka revolution in the 1980s boasts the world's longest ever uninterrupted advertising campaign. In 1879 entrepreneur Lars Olsson in Åhus in southwestern Sweden distilled a pure spirit for the first time using a new kind of distillery. His Absolut Renat Brännvin (absolutely pure spirit) was registered as a trademark. The bottle in which Absolut was first launched onto the market in 1979 was modeled on an apothecary's bottle and still has a contemporary look. The bottle has been painted by artists such as Andy Warhol, Keith Haring, and Damien Hirst. Absolut is now the third biggest spirits brand in the world. The Swedes have also successfully launched a series of flavored vodkas.

**Sweden**

### Svedka

Svedka wants to be the universe's no. 1 vodka. A high hope indeed, and one that depends on there being no shortage of wheat supplies. For now, Svedka vodka is the fastest-growing Swedish vodka brand in the world. About 3 lb (1.5 kg) of grain is distilled for 40 hours for one bottle. To live up to its forward-looking image it is, of course, five times distilled in a modern column.

**Norway**

### VikingFjord

The raw materials for VikingFjord are specially selected potatoes from the region around Lake Mjosu. Their starch is more difficult to release than that of grains. They are selected and cooked, then mashed for three days. The most popular Norwegian premium vodka has to be distilled six times through the still until the distillate is pure enough. As the finishing touch only pure Josteldalsbreen glacier water can be used to dilute it to drinking strength.

**Italy**

### Eristoff

Eristoff vodka originally came from Georgia, where it was first distilled in 1806 by Prince Ivan Eristoff. Triple distillation and wood carbon filtering are techniques that were being developed at the time in Russia. The October Revolution drove the nobleman to Italy and he continued to produce his vodka in Milan. The last member of his family died in 1991. The distillery is now owned by Martini & Rossi. The vodka with the howling wolf on the label has a gentle aroma of unripened apples, a slightly creamy texture, and a hint of licorice in the mouth.

# Vodkas from other countries

**France**

### Cîroc

For some it was a stylish premium vodka with a novel sales pitch, for others it was an object of hate. When in 2003 Diageo distilled his noble vodka from grapes, tradition-conscious manufacturers were outraged. To their minds vodka should only be distilled from arable crops or molasses. The argument raged on up to EU level. The product has a seductive ring: two different sorts of grape are each distilled four times, then blended and once again distilled in an armagnac pot still.

**France**

### Jean-Marc XO

A vodka with a local complexion: in the *département* of Cognac Jean-Marc Daucourt processed four select varieties of wheat (Ysengrain, Orvantis, Azteque, and Chargeur) in order to eliminate any trace of bitterness from his vodka. He distills nine times in traditional copper alembics. There then follows microoxidation and filtering through special Limoges oak carbon. The result is silky smooth with a hint of citrus.

**France**

### Idôl Vodka

Idôl is made from small, hand selected Pinot-Noir and Chardonnay grapes. The spirit is distilled no fewer than seven times and filtered five times to achieve optimum purity. Like the grapes, the water comes from one of France's best wine-growing regions, Burgundy—or more accurately the Côte d'Or. A vodka for wine lovers.

**France**

### Alpha Noble

After being distilled six times and given one further cycle in a traditional pot still, then double filtered and cooled to a precise 32 °F (0 °C), this vodka can claim to have undergone the "alpha ennobling method." The distillery in Fougerolles only produces small batches that are diluted to drinking strength with spring water from the Vosges.

**France**

### Grey Goose

"I told [the waiter] I wanted a Grey Goose on the rocks a fuckin' hour ago! Chop, chop!" Not every media mention is worth its weight in gold, but when it comes in a TV series like *Sex and the City*, it's another matter. Grey Goose is the epitome of the "scene" premium vodka. It has no need to boast about its origins in the Cognac wheat from which the French also bake their famous pastries, the pure spring water it contains, or the fact that it is filtered through Champagne limestone.

**Austria**

### Oval

"An unashamedly intelligent vodka" is Oval's promise. Open-mindedness doesn't do any harm anyway. In a process patented by Russian professor Valery Sorokin, pure wheat alcohol and water are molecularly restructured in such a way that the water molecules envelop the alcohol. Proton-containing substances are also intended to neutralize all undesirable contents. *Na sdorowje*.

## Austria

### Pfau Bramburus

In the making of one eighth of a gallon (0.5 liter) of spirit 55 of the newest potatoes are used. This is the proud claim of distillery owner Valentin Latschen. Old varieties of potato yield a spirit that has an earthy aroma of bread and freshly peeled potatoes. Right through to the long finish, you can taste a vodka that has a well-rounded body and is much more mellow than the modern equivalents.

## Germany

### Puschkin

Even if it is named after Russia's national poet, Puschkin is a German vodka and is actually Germany's second biggest vodka brand. For some time now the mother company Berentzen has been using an ice filtration process in production in which all undesirable constituents are crystallized out.

## Switzerland

### Xellent

There is one thing that you are bound to find in a Swiss noble vodka, and that is pure Swiss glacier water. It is obtained around 10,000 feet (more than 3,000 m) above sea level while Swiss rye fortunately grows at somewhat lower altitudes: between 1,600 and 2,600 feet (500–800 m). The fermented rye mash is carefully distilled in traditional small copper stills, which gives Xellent a distinct density.

## Scotland

### Blackwood

The Shetland Islands, in the northernmost tip of Scotland, are not too far from the Norwegian coast. Here for a long time the only visitor was the odd Viking. But it is here that a wheat-based vodka is three times distilled, then filtered first through wood carbon from Nordic birch, then through ice. Its water comes from an island stream, of course. The label on the bottle becomes a bluish color as soon as Premium Nordic Vodka is placed in the fridge and reaches the right temperature.

## Netherlands

### Ursus Classic

The Dutch have used an old Icelandic recipe for this premium vodka. Pure wheat (although this is little cultivated in Iceland) is the base material for the mash, which, after five times distillation, produces an unusually smooth drink.

## United States of America

### Smirnoff Penka

Penka is distilled many times using the pot-still method and the best rye. After each cycle the master distiller checks the distillate for impurities. Any remaining impurities are then removed by repeated filtering. Very clear and almost creamy.

# Genever career

Although its career has been well documented, the circumstances of its birth, or more precisely who the father was, remain a mystery. The invention of genever in the middle of the 16th century is popularly linked with one name. But this is where the flaw in the story lies. Without this name it is as plausible as the legends surrounding many other spirits: a doctor or apothecary (often indissociable from one another) looking for a cure—in this case, for kidney disease. For the purpose he macerated juniper berries—prized for their beneficial effect on kidney function—in alcohol, little suspecting what a force he would set in motion.

Anyone who wanders through the small town of Schiedam in The Netherlands will, at almost every step, encounter evidence of an affluent past. The town boasts 225 memorials that only a well-heeled community could have afforded. They are also proud there of the six tallest windmills in the world. Stretching in a line along the Nieuwe Waterweg down almost as far as the Rhine delta, they seem to be just waiting to have their sails turned by the wind, eager to start work once more, grinding malt and grain for Holland's most important alcoholic drink. By the end of the 19th century, around 400 distilleries were in operation in Schiedam. Nowadays fewer than a handful remain, among them Nolet (Ketel 1) and De Kuyper. For a long time now no genever has been transported in freight barges across the Schie, but the tank loads rolling out of the distilleries each day bring quite enough money into the town's coffers. In The Netherlands Schiedam is synonymous with good genever. The city on the river owes its life to the spirit. Who knows if it would have survived without the alcohol production that established it here at the beginning of the 17th century? After all, the harbor had silted up repeatedly before then, and faced overwhelming competition from Rotterdam and Amsterdam. Perhaps a certain Dirk Bokel made an unpromising choice around 1250 when he erected his castle and built a dam right here. But with genever came fame.

The spirit owes its lasting success to its medicinal properties, as many of its devotees will tell you. It is said to have been invented by Franz de le Boe, also known as Franciscus Sylvius, a famous physician and professor at the University of Leyden. He wrote various scientific treatises and was one of the first doctors in Holland to recognize the existence of the human circulatory system. The furrow between the parietal and temporal lobes in the cerebral cortex, the *fissura Sylvii*, is named for him. No alcoholic drink could wish for an inventor with better credentials. His only defect was that he was born too late, in 1614 (which would have pushed genever out of the race and put gin first). It is therefore not possible for him to have been concocting cures in 1550. Even Bols admits that at the end of the 16th century (its distillery and liqueur factory was not established until 1575) its genever was being produced on the basis of recipes already existing. One Sylvius de Bouve, pharmacist, chemist, and alchemist as well as professor at Leyden, that might well have been pickling juniper berries at the time in question is cited …

Anyway, genever gained a following and drew, in the composition of its aromatic ingredients—juniper berries were not the only additive—on the abundance of exotic herbs and spices brought back from all over the world by Dutch merchants sailing practically past Schiedam's city gates. In its turn the finished product became part of the trade network, itself branching out in all directions across the globe. Many leading spirits manufacturers can trace their origins back to the 17th or even the 16th century, among them Lucas Bols and Petrus de Kuyper (1695). With the raw ingredients available, each one was able to develop its own style.

Even before the popular juniper spirit set sail for foreign shores with the ships of the British navy, it was finding its way into its neighbor countries. Korn genever on the German side of the Frisian Islands was in high demand, and brands such as Schinkenhäger even after World War II were staple drinks in any working-man's pub in the Ruhr district. The Belgians and Flemings too love their genever or genièvre, which has an equally long tradition.

# Genever and genièvre

Hasselt, where the Genever Museum now brings to life the history of grain spirits, would become the center of genever production in Belgium. In 1601 the reigning monarchs of Flanders, Archduke Albert of Austria and his wife the Infanta Isabella of Spain, gave the town its first real boost when they prohibited the sale of spirits distilled from grain, fruit, and vegetables in the southern Netherlands. Grain should—in those stricken times of war, hunger, failed harvests, and incipient alcohol abuse—be baked into bread rather than being distilled.

Hasselt remained unaffected by the ban, as it was at that time part of the prince-bishopric of Liège. However, the town's distilleries experienced a real boom between 1675 and 1681 under Dutch occupation, when the distilleries supplied the occupiers with schnapps that they spiced up with all kinds of aromatic substances as required. Ever since then the Hasselt distillers remained loyal to the heavily aromatic style. The arch-

duke's prohibition was lifted in the Austrian Netherlands formed in 1714. The aim was to promote agriculture and prevent land from lying fallow, as was normal in the three-field system of crop rotation. Livestock were fed over winter on the swill created during grain distilling, and the resultant dung was used in the spring as fertilizer. For this reason most farms equipped themselves with a pot still so as to be able to distill their own grain.

## Belgian rustic liquor

After the establishment of the kingdom of Belgium in 1830 there followed a period of increased economic prosperity, not least in its Flemish part. Sweeping industrialization did not bypass the distilleries. They improved production using steam generators and modernized their processes with the column still invented by Jean-Baptiste Cellier-Blumenthal. Not only was continuous distillation now possible, but also the use

of field crops such as sugar beet, maize, and potatoes that were harder to process. Cheap genever found a ready market among the new working class and was soon the cause of serious social problems. To counter this evil the distilling landowners, who could not in any case compete with the alcohol industrialists, were stripped of their tax concessions—which put an effective end to rural genever production. When the Germans invaded Belgium during World War I, they requisitioned the copper stills as raw materials valuable to the war effort, melting them down to make shell cases. The industry recovered with difficulty from the removal of its basic tools of production. At the same time the Vandervelde law, passed in 1919, prohibited public bars and taxed the sale of alcohol so severely that genever became unaffordable to workers. Even when the economy turned round once more, genever never recovered from its ill repute as the poor man's schnapps, while sales of other spirits rose. It was not until the 1980s that Belgium began to take a new interest in genever. As in the other countries in Europe, in Belgium regional specialties started to gain a following. It was repackaged emphasizing the fruit content, and found a new clientele, among women too.

## Liquid cultural history

All of a sudden, genever was available in the better pubs and shops, although there were few top-quality Belgian grain spirits. Genever tourist trails were marked out and in 1987 the Genever Museum was set up in a former distillery. With attached living quarters, distillery, stables, and barn, the facilities provide an insight into the production of grain genever in the 19th century. Once a year the distillery comes to life for ten weeks and produces genever just like in the "good old days."

Before the invention of bottling plants children were employed to fill the genever bottles and young men to cork them.

# Juniperus appears

Juniper is the defining spice in the genever mix.

Opposite: With the introduction of the column still a new day dawned for genever.

Bottom: For ten weeks every year, the distillery at the Hasselt museum springs back into life. The old malt mill starts to grind grain (left) and the tall, slim columns (right) are heated up once more.

A very strange natural phenomenon earned the juniper berry its botanical name juniperus (derived from *junior pario*, the junior appears). The young, green berries appear while bunches of black fruits are still hanging in their second year. Another derivation theory, by contrast, speaks of *juveni paros* meaning giving birth (too) early, and is a reference to the abortive effect once attributed to a few juniperus varieties that are poisonous in all parts. If the origin of the name is not clear, the names derived from it are: the word genever, then gin, came from "juniperus." Jeneverbes (*Juniperus communis*) is an essential ingredient of genever, even if other herbs such as mugwort, caraway, amber, aniseed, and coriander may come into play to varying extents.

## Genever stages

A mixture of rye and/or wheat (since 1878 also maize) and malted barley in equal proportions is stirred into water at the *branderij*, fermented with yeast, then distilled three times in copper stills. The alcohol content is increased first in the *ruwnat* (about 15% by volume), then in the *enkelnat* (about 25% by volume) and finally in the *bestnat* or *moutwijn* to more than 45% by volume. Moutwijn is very malty and cannot hide its fusel oil content.

This "semi-finished product" was and still is processed further in various ways. In the *distilleerderij* juniper berries, a mixture of other herbs and spices without juniper berries, or all aromatic ingredients together are macerated and then finely distilled. After separation of heads and tails, aromatic spirits with an alcohol content of around 70% by volume (*gestookte moutwijn*) are obtained. They may be blended with one another and diluted to drinking strength as desired. These have been produced using the traditional (Schiedam) process and so are known as Oude Genever. They may have up to 3 oz per gallon (20 g/liter) of added sugar and must contain at least 15% moutwijn. An old gold hue may come from barrel maturation or from caramel.

Pure grain spirit with at least 51% moutwijn may be labeled Korenwijn. It has a minimum alcohol content of 38% by volume and is supplemented with up to 1½ oz per gallon (10 g/liter) sugar. After barrel maturation it becomes a quite respectable aperitif if not exactly a bestseller. Oude Genever and Korenwijn together only represent 1.1% of Dutch spirits consumed.

With the introduction of continuous column stills in the 19th century, it became more economical to distill the initial moutwijn with an alcohol content of up to 92% by volume. Using just four "building blocks"—pure moutwijn, moutwijn with aromatic substances, moutwijn with juniper, and almost neutral strong alcohol—some highly diverse genever taste profiles can be formulated before being diluted to drinking strength. If grain and malt alone are processed, they are now distinctively labeled as *graanjenever*. In quality-conscious distilleries aromatic substances are also distilled with the alcohol, instead of being added at the end.

## The younger and lighter, the better

A light, *jonge* genever style with no malty or grainy character reigned supreme during World War II because grain for moutwijn production was rationed or even excluded. In the course of the price war in the 1970s, when only the most neutral tasting products stood a chance, rougher edged genever made from the "oude" recipe for a time almost disappeared from the market. Jonge genever currently makes up 24% of spirits consumed in Holland and so takes first place. It is supplemented with a maximum of 1½ oz per gallon (10 g/liter) sugar and can now once more contain up to 15% moutwijn.

# Selected juniper-flavored spirits

**Netherlands**
**Bokma**
**Oude Friesche Genever**
Bokma is one of the best-known genever brands. Around 1890 the striking square bottles were already standing row upon row on the shelves of spirits merchants and pubs. The company is now a fifth-generation family enterprise. Oude Friesche Genever is one of Bokma's most popular products. The company is very proud of its closely guarded secret recipe. The soul of this genever is the moutwijn, to which Bokma add an aromatic blend of herbs including angelica, juniper berries, licorice, star anise, cloves, dill, and more besides.

**Netherlands**

**De Kuyper · Jenever**
Apparently rated more critically in its own country, De Kuyper is the genever market leader in Germany. Its image is by no means outdated, which is more than can be said of most clear schnapps drinks there. Keeping a wary eye on market trends and a good nose for the right degree of modernity in its image have brought success to this Dutch brand. Not least, the aromatic variants Bessen Genever have enjoyed popularity for several years now, ensuring some gratifying sales figures. De Kuyper has grown into the world's no. 1 liqueur producer, for which it was appointed Royal Distiller by Queen Beatrix.

**Netherlands**

**Nolet · Ketel 1 Graanjenever**
Although the Nolet family was distilling its first spirits in 1691, the Dutch company is less well known for its homespun genever than for its vodkas, which have almost cult status. But "Kettle 1" is still the godfather of the brand. In true artisan tradition an 866 gallon (3,277 liter) container is heated by a coal fire to create a remarkably mild rye spirit. The company refuses to reveal the actual recipe. According to its managers it is one of the most closely guarded secrets in Schiedam, genever capital of The Netherlands.

**Netherlands**

**Zuidam · Rogge Genever**
Triple distillation—a time-consuming, laborious process compared with column distillation—is part of Patrick and Fred Zuidam's production philosophy, as are their hand worked copper stills heated over a coal fire. The master distiller separates off the heads and tails in each of the three cycles. Rye as a basic ingredient guarantees a certain body and a highly individual character. More than 150 herbs are used in Zuidam's stills, if not in each still. But a select mixture is evident in the mellow rye spirit's taste.

**Netherlands**

**Zuidam · Zeer Oude Genever**
The Zuidam brothers must have been driven by curiosity when they were inspired to launch this *zeer oude Genever* (very old genever). In the shadow of other major grain spirits such as old Scotch whiskies the juniper spirit was generally drunk young and very quickly. But why should that be the case? The ingredients: a high proportion of moutwijn and three years of absolute seclusion in small French oak barrels. "Single barrel" means that the genever content of each barrel matures undisturbed, undergoes no filtering process, and is not blended at the end. The result is a complex spirit that exudes subtle herby aromas to complement its mature tone.

**France**

**Persyn · Houlle · Genièvre de France**

Since 1812 this family distillery has been producing its genièvre exclusively from grain from the northern Pas de Calais. Rye with malted barley and a little oats are mixed, ground, and mashed with hot water. A little later yeast is added and when, three days later, the mash has reached approximately 3% by volume alcohol, it can be distilled. This is also done in a traditional way, three times, in *alambics à feu nu*, stills heated up over an open fire. After distillation the genièvre is aged in wooden barrels. After a few years' maturation eaux de vie of various ages are blended to combine the vitality of the young with the charm of the old into a top-quality mellow, aromatic drink.

**Germany**

**Heydt · Schinkenhäger**

Its real name is Kruke, but for hardened Schinkenhäger fans this stoneware vessel will always remain the *Betonbuddel* (the concrete bottle). In any case it is a historic example of the successful combination of heritage (Steinhagen, Westphalia) and brand image (homespun). The stoneware vessel was registered as a trademark with a high recognition value. The pun on the word *Schinken* (which means bacon) expressed in the still-life depicted on the label is no doubt intended to establish the grain spirit as an excellent accompaniment to meals. Over the years the company has confidently pushed this image. Its 1960s advertising slogan was *Drink the one with the Schinken!* Even today, Schinkenhäger is the leading Steinhäger brand in Germany.

**Germany**

**Heydt · Urkönig · Steinhäger with black juniper berries**

Although not much evidence remains in Steinhagen in Westphalia of the former distilling tradition and the few surviving producers have long since been taken over by outside concerns, real Steinhäger has to be produced in its original home. The EU sees to this. The König company bottled its last Steinhäger "distilled according to the ancient recipe of Henrich Christoph König" under its own management in the 1960s. Nowadays the brand is owned by Heydt. For Urkönig the spices are distilled into the raw alcohol. In parallel the master distiller creates a pure grain distillate. Both are distilled once more and diluted with water from the company's own spring, to drinking strength. This German version of genever uses only juniper as the conifer thrives on the southern slopes of the Teutoburg forest that provided Steinhäger with a protected origin label very early in its history.

**Germany**

**Heydt · Wacholder**

The private grain distillery H. Heydt belongs to an ancient landowning family of aristocratic descent from Haselünne. In this town in Lower Saxony the distillers are the major employers. Heydt has been one of them since 1860, when agriculture went hand in hand with distilling. But over the years this medium-size family concern purchased a small collection of brands that, incidentally, included Schinkenhäger. The Emslanders like to emphasize the homespun nature of the product as their core asset, although the berries for this Wacholder are brought in from Tuscany.

**Germany**

**Original Schlichte**

In 1766 H. W. Schlichte was the first grain distillery in Steinhagen, which would then become a mecca for juniper spirits, with more than 20 distillers. Around 1900 Schlichte became the official supplier to the German armed forces and even today Original Schlichte is shipped "to all five continents," as they proudly claim. The earthenware bottle is not practical for such travels but it is a trademark, as is the pure juniper aroma that once earned Steinhäger the commendation of being "highly digestible."

# Timid gin

From 1580 British and Dutch soldiers were fighting the same battles in the Dutch/Spanish War. What could be more natural than to encourage them with the same genever in their cups? The ranks were convinced by this boost to morale that they would drink first after, then also before, they saw action. In officers' circles the effect was referred to disparagingly as "Dutch courage."

When Protestant Wilhelm of Orange acceded to the British throne in 1689, one of his first official acts was to impose high taxes on the distillation of brandy and to prescribe genever—or gin as his new subjects dubbed it—under law. In this way he stepped up trade for his fellow countrymen while driving their Catholic competitors out of the field, together with their cognac. The British did not object.

Over the next 20 years gin consumption rose to around 22,700,000 gallons (86 million liters). The government liberalized production and soon an estimated 25% of households were making and selling gin, the common ingredients of which included turpentine—which gave it a resinous piney taste but was highly dangerous to health. At the height of the gin craze six times as much gin was being produced as beer. In the more than 7,500 London gin shops it was predominantly the poor that consumed the cheap spirit which quite often came from one of the 1,500 illegal distilleries. As a consequence social dissipation was rife among the lower classes and the death rate rose drastically among the rapidly growing population. The reaction to an emergency tax increase on gin pushed through in 1736 led to riots and even more illegal distilling. In his etching *Gin Lane* (1751), copper engraver William Hogarth caricatured the scenario. With the burgeoning affluence of a new middle class as a result of the Industrial Revolution, the situation in the second half of the 18th century relaxed appreciably. The old gin shops were now simply too sordid, as was gin itself.

It was not until the Roaring Twenties that gin became a socially acceptable drink. On the eastern side of the Atlantic it was mixed into cocktails and on the western side into politics too. Gin could be very cheaply produced and could be consumed very quickly thereafter. Mixed in a tub with juniper oil and other intensively flavored herbs, not-so-pure bathtub gin circumvented Prohibition across the board. After World War II gin became a social high climber and fashion drink. No American star would have passed up the opportunity to declare it their favorite tipple for maximum media impact. But nothing lasts forever and the aromatic, slightly sweet pizzazz that made gin cocktails so appealing was overtaken by the attractions of neutrality. By the 1980s vodka was the drink of choice in fashionable circles. It was clear that gin would not lie down and die. Large distilleries and small specialty distillers have discovered the grain spirit with a taste of juniper for themselves, devoting all their considerable skills and talents to creating a sensation of aromatic perfection.

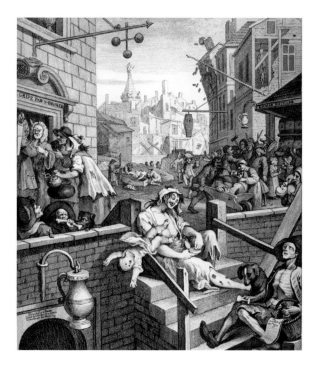

# Gin secrets

Page 414: Sean Harrison, master distiller of Plymouth Gin, checks the clarity of his product.

Page 415: In his etching *Gin Lane* (1751), William Hogarth caricatured the excesses of gin consumption.

Common gin ingredients (left to right)
Top: Juniper, coriander, angelica, almonds, and cassia.
Bottom: Malaguetta pepper, violet root, cubeb pepper, licorice, and lemon zest.

Gin owes its taste not to the basic grain. Maturation in barrels has little to do with it either. Gin takes its life from spices, and in particular juniper. Nevertheless, gins differ widely depending on the recipe used.

Old Tom is a gin in the slightly sweet style of the 18th century. Gin historians like to refer to it as the missing link between original Dutch genever and the English style. Old Tom style gins—the most famous brands include Booth's, Gilbey's, and Boord's—have become a rarity. All the more reason for distillers to revive their interest in them.

Somewhat drier but solid is Plymouth Gin, which likes to portray itself as mellowest of the world's gins. Aromatic herbs and fewer bitter flavors with soft water to round off distinguish the Plymouth style. Blow its own trumpet as it might, the spirit from the old naval port is actually very full bodied, roundly sweet, without any hint of sharpness.

Unsweetened but often aromatic gins are characteristic of the British production and bear the label "London dry." As well as junipers, there dominate here often lemon and orange zest, together with aniseed, cinnamon, coriander, violet root, licorice, and angelica. No matter how the aromatic herbs may differ in intensity, the spirit always remains free of sugary sweetness. London dry gins are now the most widespread. A brand such as Gordon's is produced under license to the original recipe as far away as Oceania. The USA is one of the former colonies too. American dry gins, or soft gins as the local juniper spirits are known, have a lower alcohol content and less body.

## Aroma down to a fine art

By contrast with many other alcohol producers, gin producers generally avoid distilling their base spirit themselves, preferring to be supplied with neutral 96% by volume alcohol. However, all brand producers stress their preference for grain as being a finer, more aromatic base and refuse alcohol from other raw ingredients, in particular molasses.

Therefore the gin distilleries concentrate from the start on the fine art of aromatization. Each brand has its own recipe in which various natural aromatic substances appear in varying combinations. More often than not house methods are maintained—usually out of tradition.

In England, the stronghold of gin distillation, this second cycle takes place in copper pot stills. Normally pure alcohol and water are placed in the pot still. Its quality will have an effect on the final product that is not to be underestimated. Then the aromatic mixture is poured straight into the liquid and distilled. Other distilleries have moved towards suspending their aromatic substances in a heat-resistant net or basket in the still—there are models designed with an appropriate device—so that the rising alcohol vapor is drawn through them and takes on the volatile aromatic substances. Some traditional producers are proud of the fact that the mixture of various plants and plant parts is macerated for some time in alcohol first, so that the aromatic molecules are more thoroughly absorbed.

## The ultimate recipe

The recipe would appear to be more important than the method of extraction, and each distiller swears by his own. The obligatory juniper is accompanied by a series of intensive spices such as coriander, ginger and nutmeg, lemon and orange zest, and also ingredients such as malaguetta pepper and violet root. The strong violet perfume of this variety of iris was considered in the Middle Ages to be an emetic and may be responsible for the apparent soapy taste that its decriers never tire of discerning in gin. A total of around 120 different plant substances may be used in the production of gin. Neutral grain spirit is referred to as compound gin (by contrast with distilled gin)—to which the aroma of juniper berries, for example in the form of juniper oil, was added. It may not be sold as gin in Germany and other countries. With their low sugar content the dry gins are ideal in cocktails with sweet components, such as gin and tonic. Perhaps this is yet another reason for the triumphant advance of gin round the world in the luggage of soldiers of the British Empire.

The master distiller at Bombay Sapphire weighs ingredients with precision (left) and will then extract their aromas in the pot stills (right) through distillation.

# Selected classic gins

### England

**Bombay Sapphire**
Launched in the middle of the 1980s as the intellectual product of a marketing agency, Bombay Sapphire quickly established itself. The transparent blue bottle proved to be an eye-catcher and an immediate reminder of the popularity of gin in India. Occasional events such as the Bombay Sapphire Designer Glass Competition and the Bombay Sapphire Prize are intended to reinforce the image. The recipe for the three times distilled spirit has ten different ingredients: cassia, malaguetta pepper, and Indonesian cubeb pepper are just a few. Water from the Welsh lake Vyrnwy is used to dilute the spirit. The result is a complex and less juniper-influenced aroma.

### England

**Beefeater Crown Jewel**
The Yeomen Warders, guardians of the Tower of London, embellish the label of the famous Beefeater Gin. They may be responsible for looking after the crown jewels, but the nobler variant of the gin, Crown Jewel, is guarded only by a tinted designer bottle. In it is a triple distilled gin with an unexpectedly well-rounded body. In addition to junipers, there are notes of pepper and candied fruits.

### England

**Cadenhead's Old Raj**
The William Cadenhead company is known for seeking out disused barrels in Scottish whisky distilleries which it then purchases. There are few left of such venerable companies from the 19th century. When such a company makes a gin, it will certainly not be commonplace. This one is fragrant, aromatic, and mellow on the palate. The most unusual feature is not revealed until the end. Old Raj is spiced with saffron, which is detectable not only in the bright yellow coloration, but also in a distinctive finish.

### England

**Blackwood's Vintage Dry Gin**
Being the inventor of Bailey's Irish Cream, Blackwood boss Tom Jago has already made quite a stir in the spirits business. There are only as many bottles of his Vintage Gin produced annually as there are inhabitants of the Shetland Islands. Wild water mint is harvested by the banks of their lochs, as are angelica and sea pinks that bloom in the short island summer. Coriander is cultivated in special tubular greenhouses, and the juniper comes from Umbria. Highly aromatic.

### England

**Gordon's London Dry Gin**
Gordon's is one of the best-known gin brands and has two faces. Only in England is the bottle green. In the rest of the world it is as clear as water. The gin was distilled for the first time in 1769 by a Scotsman named Alexander Gordon in the Southwark district of London. Since then the recipe has remained unchanged, we are assured, but by comparison with the early days the alcohol content and intensity of taste have been reduced. The triple distilled gin is "by appointment to Her Majesty the Queen" and has featured in music, art, and film. Its appearance in the John Houston film *The African Queen* (1951) is considered to be an early example of product placement—dozens of Gordon's bottles were poured into the river with the empty bottles bobbing like a string of pearls on the surface of the water.

### England

**Hendrick's**
If you wish to put distance between yourself and the crowd, you should go the extra mile. Just like Hendrick's. The venerable spirit that had a rather fusty image just a few years ago is now five times distilled ("for purity and smoothness," as we are assured with incomparable understatement) and with 11 select aromatic substances added, including rose leaves and cucumbers, putting true British style in the bottle. Barrel maturation at the factory in Ayrshire in Scotland finishes off the process. After freshening up its image recently with new packaging, Hendrick's is on its way to becoming a cult drink.

### England

#### Miller's

Beautiful Angela does one of the most important jobs at Miller, we are eagerly told. The distillers, at least, are so keen on their gin that they even give their pot still a girl's name. The signature "London Dry Gin" is not quite accurate in the case of Miller's. The young gin, with its 92% by volume alcohol, sets out on its travels to Iceland from the Black Country, among the old coal pits where England's Industrial Revolution began. In Iceland it is diluted to drinking strength with what is said to be the purest water there is before being shipped back to London. At exactly which stage in the production process the gin takes on its distinctively complex taste is a secret. In any case, tones of grapefruit, violet, and cucumber can be detected.

### England

#### Plymouth Gin

Anyone who counted Churchill, Roosevelt, and Mr. Hitchcock among their clients can be certain to have made a name for themselves in the Anglo-Saxon world. Anyone who once supplied standard rations to the Royal Navy has a right to brag about it. Plymouth gin can boast both these claims. It stands for an entire stylistic genre of gins with multilayered aromas, but in particular great mellowness. Hitherto, Plymouth was distilled in an early 15th-century monastery. Its slight sweetness carries a whole bouquet of herbal aromas from juniper through to lemon and from lilac through to damp earth.

### England

#### Tanqueray

The high alcohol content of 47.3% by volume is justified by Tanqueray on the label with the note "Export Strength." In its many foreign markets hardly anyone is aware that the bottle is modeled on the shape of a London fire hydrant. Tanqueray is a very tactile spirit. The juniper berries are hand picked in September in Tuscany. The coriander comes from the Crimea and the angelica root from Saxony. The gin is very popular in the USA, Canada, Japan, and Spain. Sleek, dry Tanqueray is the ideal partner in cocktails. Anyone who likes their Martini extra dry should try Tanqueray.

### England

#### Whitley Neill

A premium gin must be inspired. Whitley Neill London Dry Gin draws its inspiration from African aromas, from Cape gooseberry, and the baobab tree—also known as the tree of life. Together with juniper, lemon and orange zest, coriander, angelica, and cassia are the aromatic substances added to the alcohol a few hours before distillation. The result is an extraordinarily fruity gin in which the juniper berries are accompanied by candied fruits and floral tones.

### United States of America

#### Seagram's Gin

The history of the leading American gin begins in 1857 and stretches almost without interruption through to the present day. Only the Prohibition enforced a break. The distillery In Lawrenceburg, Indiana, was reopened in 1939 and Extra Dry was born again. In its aroma—in addition to junipers—cardamom, coriander, cassia, orange zest, and angelica play a major part. In the first distillation neutral alcohol is extracted from American grain, and the plants are then distilled with it in a vacuum at a low temperature for a second time, which gently removes their aromatic essences. Maturation in old whiskey barrels is one of its unusual features, imparting a distinct mellowness and a pale coloration to the gin.

### France

#### Saffron Gin

Since 1874 Gabriel Boudier has been producing Burgundy liquor Crème de Cassis de Dijon. Trendy drinks are not really what you might expect from a venerable firm that has kept its label unchanged since time immemorial. Saffron Gin is not a scene drink, but a painstakingly produced artisan product. It is only created in small batches in traditional pot stills. It is based on a recipe from colonial times to which saffron was used to give a little color and an elegantly spicy character.

# Blessing the empire

Gin owes its world fame to the British, or more precisely the British navy. They drank the juniper spirit whether stationed in Australia or in India. Not even the officers' mess was safe from gin, which earned the grain spirit its respectable reputation wherever it found a new home—be that even in the remotest corner of the world.

The spirit's world conquest did not stop short of a tiny Balearic island such as Menorca. During British rule over that island in the 18th century gin became so firmly entrenched in the island's culture that Menorquines see it even today as a part of their cultural identity—and have the same attitude towards drinking it. When the distillery was built in the 18th century, column distillation had not yet been invented. Ginebra de Mahón is made in pot stills. As grain in the warm Mediterranean island was harder to come by than grapes, it is mainly based on alcohol made from wine. The mat-

uration phase in white oak barrels is reminiscent of wine-making tradition too.

The other ingredients were easily procured. On the island the coniferous juniper grows at an altitude of 2,600–3,300 feet (800–1,000 m), and the berries are considered to be extra juicy. Aromatic ingredients such as angelica, cinnamon, caraway, orange zest, and coriander were added to satisfy the tastes of British soldiers.

Menorcan gin is dry with a clear note of juniper, but is also herby and spicy. It is still double distilled over a wood fire, and no additives or extracts are allowed. Since 1997 Ginebra de Mahón has been protected as a designation of origin. Even on the Spanish mainland its distinctive aroma is appreciated—the Spaniards are the nation with the world's highest gin consumption per capita.

Just as in the days of the British Empire, gin is distilled in these old pot stills on Menorca and matured in oak barrels.

# Unusual gins

### Germany

**Noordkorn**
A distiller of choice fruits that has won international competitions and success in the best restaurants with his distillates is on a continual search for ever more exotic ingredients for his spirits. Hubertus Vallendar has set himself another challenge, setting standards with a juniper spirit in the tradition of a German korn. Vallendar's homage to the former Frisian korn metropolis of Norden has a convincing fragrance of juniper and sauna herbs, with tangy citrus fruits such as oranges and kumquats.

### Austria

**Blue Gin**
Whatever would make an Austrian want to produce gin? Hans Reisetbauer has no time for such questions. The successful fruit distiller is on a constant lookout for new ingredients for his distillery to experiment with. The fact that he is a master distiller of juniper spirits is obvious here. The effort involved is enormous. The ingredients originate in ten countries, including Egypt, Vietnam, and China. The spirit exudes a fine juniper and lemon fragrance, and is mellow and elegant on the palate. Once it's all sold out, we'll just have to wait patiently for next year.

### Spain

**Gin Xoriguer**
Intensive herbal tones, and in particular a strong aroma of juniper, are the characteristic features of this Ginebra de Mahón, together with a woody note. It is based on a wine brandy, as is the tradition on Menorca. Xoriguer is a family-run business and we are assured that it will never be otherwise. Only true heirs know the secret recipe and only they, behind closed doors and with their own hands, are permitted to place the aromatic mixture into the stills. Gin has a long tradition on Menorca, and Xoriguer is one of the few major operations whose products are available on the mainland.

### Switzerland

**Humbel Gin**
In the rural Swiss canton of Aargau, Lorenz Humbel worked very hard to become one of the best fruit distillers in his country. In the process he discovered that there are more than 800 varieties of cherry growing in his homeland. He is also interested in other fruit besides. He works on the principle that everything has to be pure. That is why only distillate from organic grains can go to make up his gin. The herbs are allowed to infuse for some weeks before they are distilled. The result is a particularly delicate, clear, mellow juniper spirit.

### France

**Citadelle**
This gin is said to have originated in 1771 in a distillery in Dunkirk, once a major spice port. The recipe calls for 19 different plants and spices, more than for any other gin, it is said. Apart from juniper, licorice, cardamom, nutmeg, star anise, cinnamon, and many others are required. The basic ingredient is French wheat, fermented with spring water and distilled three times. The aromatic ingredients are allowed to macerate in this spirit before they are distilled into gin. The bouquet has dominant notes of juniper and citrus fruits and the taste is complex, round, and elegant.

### Netherlands

**Van Gogh**
The Dutch should really call their gin genever, but never mind! The list of ingredients reads like a herbalist's catalogue: juniper berries from Italy, coriander from Morocco, Indonesian cubeb pepper, licorice, malaguetta pepper, almonds, angelica, and violet root. Van Gogh tastes like a bouquet of fine herbal aromas, a mellow, low-alcohol gin that is long and complex on the palate.

# A pure question of taste

People can be divided quite clearly by their reaction to caraway: either you like aquavit or you don't drink it at all. There doesn't seem to be any gray area of indecision—the caraway is always too distinctive for that. Probably for that very reason aquavit has not achieved worldwide distribution like vodka or white rum which, with their light, reticent style, took the foreign markets by storm. But aquavit has a loyal following that cannot be defined in strictly geographical terms. Its "district" stretches from Norway through to Lower Saxony and from Iceland to where the Finns once met the Iron Curtain.

On April 13, 1531, a certain Mr. Eske Bille, residing at Bergenshus Castle, Denmark, sent the last archbishop of Norway, Olav Engelbretsson, a quite special bottle. The "Aqua Vite" it contained was a cure "for all kinds of suffering that a man might have, outward or inward," the noble donor effused in his accompanying letter, thus leaving us with the oldest known documentary evidence of aquavit. What mixture of herbs made the distillate so universally effective, and whether caraway was in it, remain unclear, just like the state of health of the addressee after receiving it.

Whatever befell him, if it was misfortune there is no reason to believe that this had anything to do with the bottle. The recipient seemed happy and he obviously saw no reason to prevent aquavit from blazing onward with its trail of success, and its beneficial effects on health remained undiminished. So throughout centuries to come, ground grain was mashed, fermented, enriched with local herbs and spices, and double distilled. Dill and juniper might appear in the recipe, but the Danes liked their aquavit to taste of caraway.

It would be an outsider who brought change to the well-established distillery scene. In 1846 Isidor Henius, a brandy distiller from Thorn in West Prussia, came to live in Aalborg where the aquavit, produced by about a hundred small artisan distillers, already enjoyed a fine reputation. Henius set up his distillery on the south bank of the Limfjord and fitted it out with one of the new column stills. And that was how the industrialization of spirits production in Aalborg quietly took root. The aquavit, of which Henius with his column still was able to produce a great deal more in a very short space of time, was convincing in its greater purity and more distinctive caraway aroma.

Over the decades to come Henius would put most of the small distillers out of business. In 1881 his company was taken over and renamed Danske Spritfabrikker. The company, which cultivated its own caraway on 49 acres (20 hectares) of land, in 1923 took over the Danish spirit and aquavit monopoly. Even today, under Swedish ownership as it now is, it is the only spirits producer in Denmark. Aalborg is the undisputed capital of aquavit. A total of 15 varieties have been created here, including Dild, Jule, and Jubilee Aquavit.

Denmark's Scandinavian neighbors were inspired by aquavit and developed their own recipes so that each country now claims its own style. In Norway the finished spirit is often matured in barrels, which suits it very well. In Germany in the early 1920s aquavit was so successful that Aalborg took the offensive when exports became unprofitable due to high customs duties and restrictions. In 1924 it made Berlin its production site, followed by Buxtehude. As the designation "Aalborg" was not permitted to appear in the name, the producers called their drink, which was distilled in accordance with the original recipe, Malteserkreuz after their imported logo, the Maltese Cross. The bottles with the white cross have been a fixed part of spirits culture in northern Germany ever since. Even today every second aquavit ordered in restaurants is a Malteser—popularly accompanied by the advertising catchphrase: *Man gönnt sich ja sonst nichts* (Nothing else will do).

# All about aquavit

Page 422: True to style, aquavit is served in a deep-frozen special cup.

Today aquavit is based on 96% by volume alcohol of rural origin, which means that it can only be distilled from arable crops. The first aquavits were distilled from grain. But when in the 18th century potatoes became naturalized in Scandinavia, it proved that the starch-rich tuber could bring in a considerably higher alcohol yield than grain. Many distillers then decided against grain. In the taste of the finished aquavit, the raw ingredient is not an important factor since the use of such a high alcohol content is stipulated, and most aromatic substances are eliminated, together with any impurities, during the distillation process. The spice mix distilled in a second cycle with the alcohol and water therefore takes on an even greater significance. The caraway taste is vital and must be clearly distinguishable in an aquavit, according to one EU ordinance. Dill, fennel, cinnamon, coriander, and other ingredients can only be added with appro-

Nowadays the oak casks of Line Aquavit are stowed in containers for their sea voyage around the world.

priate restraint. Ether oils are not permitted, but natural and nature identical aromatic substances are tolerated as long as the majority of the aroma comes, as stipulated, from the distillation of caraway and/or dill seeds. A resting period for the distillate after the second cycle, taking between a few weeks and several months, permits a small part of the contents to form ester compounds. This chemical process ensures that the taste of the still young aquavit becomes more rounded and harmonious. If the aquavit is to be barrel matured, old 132-gallon (500-liter) sherry casks are generally used, the wine and wood tones of which will combine with the herbal aromas of the aquavit into a complex ensemble. The noblest qualities spend ten years or more in the cask and so take on a pleasant, warm color. Aquavits that are too light, however, may be colored with caramel instead.

## Caraway loses its way

What does barrel maturation have to do with an undeliverable cargo? Nothing—unless that cargo consists of sherry barrels full of aquavit and the port of destination is abroad, for example Australia. It was highly annoying when a batch of barrels that could not be sold on the other side of the globe were unexpectedly still cluttering up the cargo hold. But the story has a happy ending. After crossing the equator twice, it returned to its home port where an angry captain noticed the amazing change in the furthest-traveled aquavit in the world.

Line Aquavit is no ordinary caraway spirit. After the lucky unlucky delivery, the company decided to subscribe to this positive effect, so to speak, and since then has routinely sent its aquavit barrels on a journey round the world.

Skeptics who doubt this onboard harmonization might like to present to producer Arcus the results of an experiment with aquavit barrels that simulates the conditions of the long sea voyage on land. Continuous fluctuations in temperature and atmospheric humidity, sometimes with extreme values, combine with continuous movement of the aquavit. The result is convincing, but far from the quality of a real Line Aquavit, says Arcus.

So up to now every drop of Line Aquavit voyages for 19 weeks by sea—to Australia and back once. In the current market the company states that at any one time more than a thousand barrels of aquavit are voyaging across the world's oceans in order to give its taste profile a positive travel experience. And the traveling itinerary is documented on the back of every label.

Back from the long sea voyage, the ennobled aquavit is bottled at Arcus' modern plant in Oslo.

The passport of a Line Aquavit bottle.

# Just the right temperature

Presumably it is less a question of spirit than character. The dynamic, quick decision makers like their aquavit cold, preferably ice cold and out of a shot glass or a Y-shape goblet. The thin glass, often pre-iced in the deep freezer, does not take away much of the coldness of the liquid. If you pick it up by the stem the aquavit will remain even icier. Calm, reflective types perhaps only occasionally drink an aquavit, but will also enjoy malt whisky, Armagnac, or rum. They savor their drinks and so will drink their aquavit from a snifter or similar small balloon glass from which they are able to appreciate the aromas that the spirit exudes at room temperature. This will probably be a long barrel matured quality. To speak of the right or wrong way to drink aquavit would be to do both types a disservice. The epicure will linger, immersing themselves in the more complex aromatic polish that the sherry cask has exuded into a strongly spiced aquavit. The aromas of herbs have become significantly more subtle over the years, producing mellowness and reticence. The sherry and wood notes give body. What an impressive harmony of different aromas.

## Drinking data

Traditionally, in Denmark and Scandinavia aquavit is a social drink. In Norway it is served on National Day, May 17. In Sweden it is served at the evening meal on midsummer night, accompanied by a drinking song or two. Aquavit goes down well with hors d'oeuvres such as herring, crab, and smoked fish. A fish, after all, as they say, has to swim. The dill in many aquavits is a further encouragement here.

Danes drink aquavit at Christmas and actually on any other occasion that presents itself. Shots are often downed in one. The drinker brings the glass to the lips, pauses, looks each person in turn in the eye, and gestures a toast to each. After the obligatory "Skøl," most empty their glasses in one swallow before once more making eye contact, as if in approbation. Often a Karlsborg or Tuborg will follow this aromatic attack on the palate. The beer will be enjoyed by those who don't like the taste of caraway to linger too long. It neutralizes the palate, or prepares it for the next shot of aquavit.

Aquavit has won itself a firm place as an accompaniment to meals. According to Scandinavian tradition, it should be drunk with crab, fish pie, or any smoked fish.

# Selected aquavits

### Denmark

**Aalborg · Jubilæums Aquavit**
The Aalborg producers were appointed "suppliers to the royal court" with their aquavits. No alcoholic drink can aim much higher. Since there has been aquavit, the Nordic city of Aalborg has been its uncontested capital. Jubilæums Aquavit was launched in 1946 on the company's 100th anniversary and since then has been one of the most-exported aquavits. Notes of coriander, aniseed, and lemon can be discerned on the palate. Another reason for "Jubi's" export success is the interplay of caraway and dill.

### Norway

**Line Aquavit**
Its competitors would love to have a sales pitch like that of Line Aquavit. Before it is bottled, each drop travels on board ship to Australia and back. On the long voyage it is stored in old sherry casks and takes on their aromas, intended to render the drink more mellow and milder. Its inventor Jørgen B. Lysholm was a merchant himself and in the middle of the 19th century shipped various cargoes including codfish to South America. But the Line quickly became his company's most successful brand and brings in healthy profits even today. For this reason the company insists on the importance of crossing the equator twice. Line Aquavit stands head and shoulders above most other aquavits in both character and expression.

### Germany

**Malteser Aquavit**
The Aalborg company only wanted to circumvent excessive import taxes when they began in 1924 to produce Malteser Aquavit in Berlin. This spur-of-the-moment creation proved a long-term success. In the 1970s a second factory had to be set up in Buxtehude. Perhaps it is the pleasantly delicate interplay of caraway and plenty of dill that appeals to Germans so much at 0 °F (–18 °C). The Malteser, unlike many comparable spirits, has never really fallen out of fashion. Plenty of consumers cannot resist the view of that slender, iced Malteser glass.

### Germany

**Bommerlunder**
To avoid having to wash up, a French horseman who could not pay his bill gave the innkeeper the recipe for an alcoholic drink. Peter Schwennesen accepted and became rich. The legend is entrenched in the history of the village of Bommerlund near Flensburg. Bommerlunder in any case has sold millions. A down-to-earth, aromatic, somewhat rustic spirit with 38% by volume alcohol that became a bestseller, perhaps when the old folk of Düsseldorf used to recommend it with a bacon sandwich back in the 1980s. In addition to caraway, other spices find their way into the distillation. According to the producers, the result is best enjoyed cold. Ice-cold Bommi. Mmmm.

### Germany

**Helbing · Hamburgs Kümmel**
This aquavit, created in 1836 by Johann Peter Hinrich Helbing, is Hamburg's oldest spirit, and Hamburg is a town that really does not lack breweries and distilleries. Around 1900 more than 400 workers were employed by the Helbingsche Dampf-Kornbrennerei und Presshefefabrik AG and even roads were named after the meritorious producers. The distillate contains the "finest caraway seeds" and "purest grain alcohol," and the present owners, the Matthiesen family, continue to follow the recipe—secret, of course—unchanged for more than 170 years.

### Germany

**Gilka · Kaiser-Kümmel**
"Der Kurze von Berlin" is an early example of snappy brand image creation. When the 38% spirit from a Berlin distillery founded in 1836 made it somehow onto the table of the German emperor, the name "Gilka Kaiser-Kümmel" was immediately invented. (It means the emperor's caraway.) The company has retained its nose for metropolitan marketing. On the label a penguin with spiked helmet and monocle is a humorous reminder of the Hohenzollern dynasty. Publicity campaigns too have involved gifts of pieces of the Berlin Wall. Kaiser-Kümmel is double distilled and slightly sweetened, just how they like it in Berlin.

# Clarity from the Far East

Gun powder, paper, porcelain—the Chinese have often been several steps ahead of the Europeans and they are said to have been drinking wine made from rice or fruit as far back as 9,000 years ago. Spirits have been popular in China for centuries and there is hardly an emperor or military leader who was not renowned for his capacity for alcohol. While distilling apparatus is still claimed to have been an Arab–European invention, there are Chinese records of distillates dating from the Yuan dynasty in the early 14th century. Consumption has risen continuously ever since then and is today six times greater than that of rice wine.

On display in the Shanghai Museum is bronze distilling apparatus dating from the Han dynasty at around the time of the birth of Christ. It remains unclear whether it was also used to distill alcohol, but what is certain is that alcohol has been distilled in China since the start of the 17th century, using the apparatus and skills acquired from the Dutch. The distillers adopted the fermentation techniques used in the production of rice wine. The microbiological activity making up the fermentation process was researched after the founding of the People's Republic of China, so that temperature controls and maturation in individual barrels have today enabled the improvement of the distillation results. The spirits' basic ingredients are bran, grain fermented in a variety of different ways, and of course rice. Their alcohol content is at least 30, mostly between 55 and 60, and occasionally as high as 80 vol. percent.

Most spirits are distilled once with little filtering. They are therefore often very harsh on the European palate—such as the millet schnapps Kao Liang, for example. Rose petals are among the typical flavorings used in Mei Kuei Lu Chiew, the back of the bottles displaying the image of a rose as a quality feature. Luzhou is also one of the most popular spirits; made primarily from Chinese millet, wheat, barley, and rice, it has a fragrant bouquet. The ingredients are added partly fermented and partly unfermented and are distilled together. Fen, which is initially fermented in ceramic containers half submerged in the ground, is a more neutral spirit that is sweet and soft on the palate, the best of them having an aromatic aftertaste.

Maotai holds the unofficial title of high-proof national drink. It is distilled from millet and another grain component, with water from mountain streams. Its flavoring is reminiscent of rice and sometimes sugar icing. The premium spirits age for years in buried clay containers that are opened for special occasions, such as weddings. An alcoholic beverage bearing the name Maotai can be traced back 2,000 years and, although its origins lie deep in the country's feudal past, it became the favorite drink of generations of Chinese communists and a feature at Chinese state banquets.

Such illustrious guests as Margaret Thatcher and Kim Il Sung drank toasts with Kweichow Maotai. The spirit containing the water of the Chishui river in the southwestern province of Guizhou is considered to be one of the best, and the founder of the nation, Zhou Enlai, toasted the founding of the People's Republic with it in 1949, personally forbidding any industrial establishment within a 60-mile (100 km) radius.

When more and more, at times illegal, distilleries established themselves there at the start of the century as a result of the continual rise in Maotai demand in the upand-coming economic nation, even the otherwise indifferent official news agency Xinhua reported with great concern that the "production basis was under threat."

# Shochu is everything

Page 428: Far Eastern clear spirits are enjoyed neat or mixed, ice cold, or warmed, with shochu also being savored with salted plums or in cocktails.

Page 429: First choice among Chinese heads of states is Maotai (1st and 2nd. from left); Fen Chiew (3rd), made from millet, and Chu Yeh Ching Chiew (4th), made from bamboo, are regional products.

Good spirits also need an attractive external appearance. This applies to the Japanese Iichiko, the standard shochu (2nd from right), and to the upmarket versions aged in barrels. Calligraphy and ink drawings emphasize the complex production methods.

Neat or on ice? That is not the only decision required of a shochu drinker. The Japanese willingly mix their favorite spirit with water—hot or cold—as well as with sake, jasmine tea, or Campari. Considered to be modern in Japan, shochu, which has been distilled since the 16th century, has overtaken sake, seen as old fashioned in the country of its origin— hundreds of shochu brands being available in well-stocked Japanese spirits retailers—as well as making a name for itself in western metropolises such as New York and London. Here its much acclaimed health benefits are of particular interest.

With shochu having had to battle with serious image problems not all that long ago, it has been successful in dispelling its negative associations as a lower class drink. Today the old man's drink *oyaji* holds particular appeal for urban women. Since the turn of the century, the consumption of shochu in Japan has outstripped that of sake. The enzyme urokinase contained in shochu is alleged to have a variety of beneficial effects on health and has also contributed to the success of the low calorie shochu in the USA. The 120-year-old Japanese Shigechiyo Izumi announced in *The Guinness Book of Records* that he drank shochu daily.

Shochu is made by initially fermenting a variety of grains with *koji* mold (*Aspergillus oryzae*). Koji, its different varieties influencing the flavor of the end product, is also used in the fermentation of rice to make sake as well as soya. Of course it is primarily the processed basis ingredients that are responsible for the flavor of the distillate. Barley produces clear, lean spirits that are also aged in barrels. Sweet potatoes contribute light, earthy, peaty aromas, the best examples of which are reminiscent of almonds (the

dramatic rise in shochu demand has resulted in shortages in the supply of sweet potatoes). Spirits made from rice, on the other hand, are characterized by a sweet depth. Japanese legislation also allows raw materials such as sesame, chestnuts, carrots, or perilla and/or sesame leaves—an unusual labiate that contains the sweet, mint-like perilla aldehyde. Today shochu is usually distilled in a single run in copper stills and then reduced to an alcohol content of about 25% vol. Contents with 40% vol and more are as rare as twice distilled shochus, which have a more neutral flavor and are therefore less popular. Awamori, distilled only on Okinawa from ground Thai long-grain rice, is considered to be the best shochu. The black koji, responsible for the fermentation, is also found only on the southern islands. Large quantities of citric acid are produced during the fermentation process, which is why the mash remains stable even in the humid, tropical climate. Good awamoris are stored in underground clay vessels for several years. The famous shochu reserves, some of which were up to 300 years old, were destroyed in their entirety during the battle of Okinawa in 1945.

The Korean national drink, soju, is related to shochu and has been distilled since the Mongolian wars of around 1300. The better varieties being made from rice, wheat, barley, or sweet potatoes, soju can also be based solely on flavored, neutral alcohol and may not contain more than 35% vol. alcohol. Largely unknown outside the country's borders, it is nevertheless able to hold its own with the big names in the business in terms of quantity. The worldwide statistics for 2006 put Jinro Soju in first place ahead of international brands such as Smirnoff and Bacardi. Overall the 49 million South Koreans consume a phenomenal three billion bottles of soju annually.

Earthenware bottles are an indication not of rustic but of especially valuable contents. Chinese spirits such as the millet schnapps Kao Liang Chiew and Mei Kuei Lu Chiew (4th and 5th from the left) are flavored with rose petal extracts.

# Rum, cachaça, and tequila

Sugar cane comes in different varieties.

Right: The Fonds Préville distillery near Macouba on Martinique, home of Rhum J.M.

Page 432: Vast sugar cane fields provide the raw materials for the Caribbean and South American rum.

# Caribbean cheer

Mojitos, daiquiris, caipirinhas, and margaritas are some of the cocktails most frequently enjoyed in fashionable bars everywhere today. Their world conquest, which started at the beginning of the 20th century, has accelerated over recent decades, not least due to the growing popularity of their countries of origin—Cuba, Brazil, Mexico, and the West Indies—as tourist destinations. The hot rhythms of salsa, samba, tango, and bossa nova have invaded bars and discotheques, awakening a thirst for cocktails with a shot of rum, cachaça, or tequila.

The Spanish and Portuguese brought sugar cane to Central and South America, where it flourished and soon provided a commodity in great demand in Europe and the USA: sugar. It was not until the beginning of the 19th century that the discovery of beet sugar emancipated the European politicians from their dependence on colonial sugar, and the cane-sugar market began to suffer. The plantation owners intensified their stake in what was previously a secondary source of income, but had been registering growth for some centuries already: rum.

When sugar is boiled, a sweet, viscous byproduct is created that quickly decomposes in the tropical climate. This is molasses. Fermented and distilled, it became the potent alcoholic intoxicant that helped make the colonial day bearable. Rum has come a long way since then. Changes in ownership of the Caribbean islands from the 17th century onward opened up markets for rum in England, Holland, France, Denmark, and the USA. From there the new drink spread unstoppably. It gained adherents on the Central and South American mainland too. In Mexico rum was probably distilled before tequila. Guatemala, Nicaragua, Venezuela, and Guyana also followed suit.

In Brazil, in addition to rum production from fermented molasses, rum was also produced from the sugar-cane juice itself. The resulting *aguardente de cana* was known as cachaça and, mixed with lime juice and sugar, would become caipirinha, the national drink. On the French islands of Martinique, Guadeloupe, and Haiti, sugar-cane wine, also known as rum, was distilled and enjoyed in particular in the form of ti punch.

Wherever sugar cane grows—whether in India, Nepal, the Philippines, or the Canary Islands, in Australia or China—sooner or later rum has been distilled. Yet not until the raw rotgut was tamed into a clear, mellow, light alcoholic beverage, excellent for mixing, did it become popular beyond bounds. Over recent years there has been a growing interest in finer versions of the spirit, aged for lengthy periods in casks, complex and full of character, and with an intensive taste.

In Mexico rum was pushed into second place by tequila, distilled from agaves. The Mexican national drink too has enjoyed international success and has followed a similar course. In addition to brands that contain a considerable proportion of white rum, high-quality 100% pure agave liquors are gaining an increasing following. Quality takes priority over quantity.

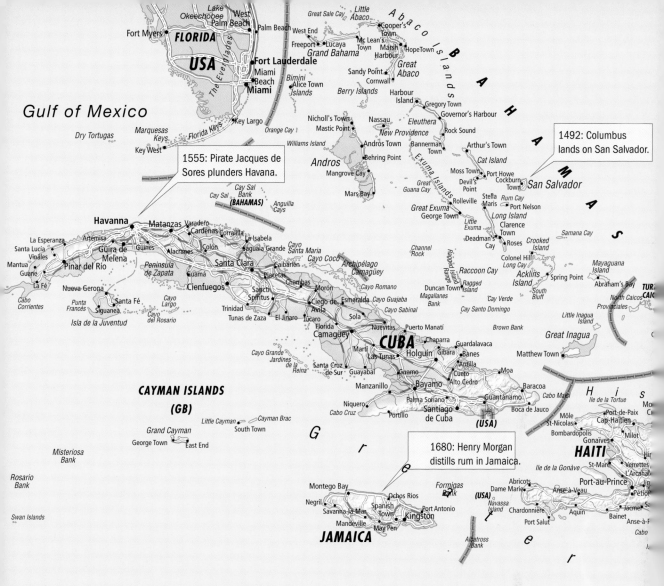

The map contains the following labels and callout boxes:

**Callout boxes:**
- 1555: Pirate Jacques de Sores plunders Havana.
- 1492: Columbus lands on San Salvador.
- 1680: Henry Morgan distills rum in Jamaica.

**Major regions:** USA, FLORIDA, Gulf of Mexico, BAHAMAS, CUBA, HAITI, JAMAICA, CAYMAN ISLANDS (GB), Andros, Great Abaco, Little Abaco, Grand Bahama, Eleuthera, Long Island, Acklins Island, Crooked Island, Great Inagua, Mayaguana Island

# Caribbean adventure

| | |
|---|---|
| 1492 | Christopher Columbus discovers the Antilles. He lands on San Salvador. |
| 1493 | Columbus introduces sugar cane. |
| 1536 | Pedro Campo discovers Barbados. |
| 1555 | Jacques de Sores sacks Havana. |
| 1572 | Francis Drake attacks two harbors in Panama. |
| 1586 | Francis Drake attacks Cartagena. |
| 1625 | British occupy Barbados. |
| 1628 | Dutch land in Tobago after a raid on a Spanish cargo of silver. |
| 1634 | Dutch take over Curaçao. |
| 1636 | French take over Martinique and Guadeloupe. |
| 1642 | Peter Stuyvesant becomes governor of Curaçao and neighboring islands. |
| 1655 | Sailors of the Royal Navy are allowed a daily ration of a UK pint (47 cl) of rum. |
| 1670 | Henry Morgan invades Cuba. |
| 1671 | Danes occupy St. Thomas. |
| 1674 | Henry Morgan is pardoned, and made a nobleman and lieutenant governor of Jamaica, where he distills rum from 1680. |
| 1694 | Père Labat, father of quality rum, arrives in Martinique. |
| 1703 | Foundation of the Mount Gay distillery in Barbados. |
| 1718 | British governor on the Bahamas combats the pirates; death of Blackbeard the pirate. |
| 1733 | British crown taxes molasses imports in New England. |
| 1739 | Admiral Edward Vernon conquers Puerto Bello. |
| 1740 | Vernon orders rum ration in the Royal Navy to be mixed with water. |
| 1767 | First rum exported from St. Thomas to Flensburg. |
| 1797 | British take over Trinidad. |
| 1850 | Rum ration in the Royal Navy is reduced to an eighth of a UK pint (6 cl) per day. |
| 1862 | Bacardi establishes a distillery in Santiago de Cuba. |
| 1865 | Slavery is abolished in the USA. |
| 1880 | Cuba abolishes slavery. |
| 1888 | Brazil is the last country in Latin America to abolish slavery. |
| 1899 | Spanish relinquish control of Cuba. |
| 1902 | Eruption of Mount Pelée on Martinique; 26,000 people are killed. |
| 1929 | Ernest Hemingway visits Havana for the first time. |
| 1934 | Bacardi establishes a distillery on Puerto Rico. |
| 1944 | Captain Morgan brand of rum is launched in Jamaica. |
| 1959 | Fidel Castro becomes head of state in Cuba. |
| 1993 | Pernod Ricard and a Cuban state company market the Havana Club brand of rum. |

**N**

0    60 miles (100 km)

*Atlantic*

*Ocean*

1934: Bacardi sets up a distillery on Puerto Rico.

1767: First exports of rum from St. Thomas to Flensburg.

BRITISH VIRGIN ISLANDS (GB)

Anegada

Sombrero

ANGUILLA (GB)

Virgin Gorda

Anguilla

St-Martin (F)

Charlotte Amalie

Tortola

Sint Maarten

St-Barthélemy

DUTCH ANTILLES (NL)

Barbuda

St. Thomas

St. John

Saba

St. Kitts

ANTIGUA & BARBUDA

San Juan

Virgin Passage

Sint Eustatius

Basseterre

Arecibo

Fajardo

St. Croix

Nevis

St. John's

Antigua

Aguadilla

Bayamón

Redonda

Mayagüez

Utuado

Caguas

Isla de Vieque

ST. KITTS & NEVIS

San Germán

Ponce

VIRGIN ISLANDS (USA)

MONTSERRAT (GB)

Guadeloupe Passage

Grande Terre

La Désirade

Cabo Rojo

PUERTO RICO (USA)

Isla Mona

DOMINICAN REPUBLIC

Santo Domingo

Cabarete

Santiago de los Cabelleros

Samaná

La Vega

Sabana de la Mar

Cotuí

Miches

El Seibo

Higüey

Villa Altagracia

La Romana

Punta Cana

San Pedro de Macorís

Boca de Yuma

Basse Terre

Basse-Terre

GUADELOUPE (F)

Pointe-à-Pitre

Marie-Galante

Les Saintes

*Lesser*

Dominica Passage

Portsmouth

Roseau

DOMINICA

Martinique Passage

Ste-Marie

*Antilles*

Fort-de-France

MARTINIQUE (F)

St. Lucia Channel

Castries

*Caribbean*

ST. LUCIA

Vieux Fort

BARBADOS

1703: Establishment of Mt. Gay distillery on Barbados.

Speightstown

Bridgetown

*Sea*

St. Vincent Channel

Kingstown

Georgetown

St. Vincent

ST. VINCENT & THE GRENADINES

Bequia

Mustique

Mayreau

Canouan

Union Island

Petit St. Vincent

Carriacou

Petite Martinique

GRENADA

St. George's

1642: Stuyvesant becomes governor of Curaçao.

*Lesser*

Aruba

DUTCH ANTILLES (NL)

Noordpunt

Bonaire

*Antilles*

Oranjestad

Curaçao

Islas los Roques

Isla Blanquilla

Tobago

Charlotteville

La Macolla

Willemstad

Kralendijk

Isla Orchilla

Los Testigos

Scarborough

Peninsula de Paraguana

Adicora

Punta Manzanillo

Punto Fijo

Urumaco

Coro

Mirimire

Dabajuro

R. Pedregal

S. Luis Hueque

Churuguara

R. Hueque

Golfo Triste

Tucacas

Catia la Mar

Cabo Codero

Isla de Tortuga

La Asunción

Isla Margarita

Porlamar

Carúpano

San Juan de los Galdonas

Güiria

TRINIDAD & TOBAGO

Port of Spain

Sangre Grande

*Trinidad*

Cumaná

Rio Claro

San Fernando

Boca de la Serpiente

Bonasse

Peninsule de Araya

Golfo de Paria

Casanay

Caripito

San Felipe

R. Tocuyo

Puerto Cabello

Guarenas

Puerto La Cruz

Barcelona

Maturía

Carora

CARACAS

Maracay

Sta. Teresa del Tuy

Barquisimeto

Valencia

San Juan

Cua

Altagarcia de Orituco

VENEZUELA

Yaritagua

Tinaco

rk Island

n Town

ands

Passage

# The kill-devil and the pirates

Christopher Columbus (1451-1506), the discoverer of America, on his first landing at Guanahani on October 12, 1492; copperplate engraving by Theodor de Bry (1528-98), from H. Bergoni, *Historien, America pars quarta*, Frankfurt am Main, 1594.

Columbus' landing in 1492 on the island of San Salvador in the Antilles heralded an age in which sugar and rum would take on considerable importance in the region—it was Columbus that prepared the way for sugar-cane cultivation in the West Indies. By the 16th century it had been discovered on the sugar-cane plantations that strong liquor could be distilled from molasses, a byproduct of the processing of sugar cane. This rough and raw alcoholic beverage was initially only given to slaves and foremen, as a consolation for their backbreaking labor, while the wealthy colonial overlords preferred imports of European spirits.

Among the first people to be aware of the market for high-quality rum were the Dutch, who were strengthening their hold in northern Brazil under Governor Johann Moritz from 1636 and attempting to bring the country under their control. Experienced brandy producers and traders, they knew what profit they could make from the sugar-cane liquor. When in 1654 they were ousted by the Portuguese and sought refuge in other colonies of the Caribbean, they took with them their knowledge of the craft of the distillery.

In its original, rustic form, rum was soon decried as a kill-devil or *guildive*. In the Creole language it was named *rumbullion*, meaning a stew of boiled sugar-cane stems, as well as being a corruption of the English word "rebellion"—literally a great tumult—a reference to the intoxicating effects of the drink. The true origin of the word "rum" remains unexplained, but by about 1660 it had come into use all over the West Indies, whatever the nationality of the colonial overlords.

## Rum and mutiny

In 1494 the Spaniards had secured South and Latin America in the treaty of Tordesilla—with the exception of Portuguese Brazil. The exploitation of the silver mines in Peru and Mexico earned the Spanish crown enormous profits, but sailing ships piled high with bullion soon aroused the avarice of pirates. From 1560 great convoys were therefore organized that, escorted by warships, embarked on the return journey to Europe together. They gathered in the Lesser Antilles, steered through the Yucatan canal between Mexico and Cuba, then set a course past the Bahamas for Seville and later to Cadiz. Pirates and freebooters were undaunted by the convoys. Quite the reverse. The dominant position of Catholic Spain in Latin America and the West Indies could not go unchallenged by the Protestant realms of England and The Netherlands, and even France found it intolerable. As in the 16th and 17th centuries none of these countries had sufficient ships with which to oppose the Spaniards, they devised a mischievous and expedient solution. They

gave sea captains carte blanche to keep any booty they might seize, provided that they inflicted sufficient damage on their Spanish opponents in doing so. Businessmen and noblemen, anticipating prodigious wealth, financed the freebooters. One of the most feared was Francis Drake, whose first attack on Spanish posts and harbors took place in 1572 in Panama.

At the time sailors were treated little better than slaves. They were subjected to iron discipline and brutal punishments while shipowners and merchants often raked in incredible riches. The only consolation below decks was rum, which was, since the 17th century, an entitlement that was particularly welcome as everything else on board was consumed with extreme caution. Perhaps rum gave the sailors courage. The heyday of piracy was in the decades between 1640 and 1680. In the Caribbean, far from the reigning powers, several crews succumbed to the temptation of ridding themselves of the yoke of servitude in order to plunder and line their own pockets. The pirates were surprisingly often democratically organized, electing their own leaders who had to behave in an exemplary manner during engagement and afterward were expected to distribute the booty fairly.

Henry Morgan, born in 1635 in Wales, achieved nobility and notoriety. He was a reckless freebooter and pirate. From the governor of Jamaica he received his first official commission in 1668 to reconnoiter Cuba.

He took it upon himself to sack the ports of Puerto Principe in Cuba and Puerto Bello in Panama, both the governor and the English crown being completely unaware of his ruthless escapades. As commander of the Jamaican fleet in 1670 he captured Cuba, set sail for Panama, took the capital by storm, and seized £100,000 sterling. In 1672 he fell into disfavor and was taken prisoner and brought to England, where King Charles II knighted him two years later and sent him back to Jamaica as lieutenant governor. He is said to have begun to distill rum there in 1680, eight years before his death. Captain Morgan Rum, now produced in Puerto Rico, was named in his honor in 1944.

Robert Louis Stevenson is said to have based his novel *Treasure Island*, first published in 1883, on the story of Edward Teach, who from around 1700 plied his brutal trade from Nassau under the name of Blackbeard. Before each raid he is said to have stuck slowburning hemp cord into his beard so that it glowed and smoked. The sight filled many merchants with such fear that they surrendered immediately. When Blackbeard was intercepted off the coast of Virginia in 1718, he toasted his enemy with rum before engaging battle. He suffered 5 shot wounds and 20 cuts of the saber before he died.

Blackbeard the pirate, whose real name was Edward Teach, killed on December 3, 1718; copperplate engraving by B. Cole from Daniel Defoe, *A General History of the Robberies and Murders of the most Notorious Pirates*, 1725.

A carousing Sir Henry Morgan, pirate chief and acting governor of Jamaica (ca. 1635-88); steel plate engraving after a drawing by Alexandre Debelle (1805-97), from: P. Christian, *Histoire des Pirates*, Paris, 1846-52.

Fifteen men on a dead man's chest
Yo ho ho and a bottle of rum
Drink and the devil had done for the rest
Yo ho ho and a bottle of rum.

Robert Louis Stevenson claimed that the idea for his adventure novel *Treasure Island* came to him after reading Charles Kingsley's *At Last: A Christmas in the West Indies* (1871), in which a pirates' island in the Caribbean named Dead Man's Chest is mentioned.

# Slave trade and independence

Harvesting sugar cane on Cuba. French colored wood engraving from the second half of the 19th century.

No other spirit is associated with as much cruelty as rum. The European craving for sweet things, excited further by the new drinks of chocolate, coffee, and tea, made sugar exporting a gold mine in the 18th century. The sugar-cane plantations in the West Indies flourished, not least due to cheap labor provided by slaves. After the discovery of the New World, the Europeans established their ill-famed transatlantic trade triangle, with new profits awaiting them at every transshipment stage. In the case of rum the process was as follows. Rum and, in particular, molasses were shipped from the Caribbean to New England, where they were distilled. Then, laden with barrels of rum, the ships sailed on to west Africa, where the spirit was sold at a high price and slaves were taken on board as a replacement cargo. They then set sail back to the Caribbean to sell the surviving slaves to plantation owners. Millions of Africans lost their home, died

a pitiful death, or scraped an inhuman existence until the keeping of slaves was finally abolished in the 19th century. Nowadays the progeny of slaves form the majority of the population of the West Indies.

## Rum in politics

In the British colonies of the American east coast rum was not only a highly prized drink. There were restrictions on the shipments to France of rum from the French islands of Martinique and Guadeloupe to ensure that it could not compete with wine and cognac, and New England was a godsend as the new market for molasses, either direct or via Dutch intermediaries. The distilleries there produced copious quantities of rum with the natives "drowning" in the glut, so the links in the slave trade chain in which the New Englanders took the lead meshed perfectly together.

This trade with archenemy France was a thorn in the flesh of the British crown. As early as 1733 the British government tried to sabotage it with customs duties. When this did not have the required effect, it intensified controls and taxes in 1763 with the Sugar Act, arousing protest in the east American colonies. Even before Boston and tea, it was rum that first stirred American longing for independence.

Doling out the daily rum ration on British naval cruiser HMS *Endymion* in 1905.

## Death and grog

Ships' crews in the 17th century were allowed daily rum rations. The sailors of the Royal Navy, from 1655, received their tot twice a day, half a UK pint of rum (about 0.5 liters). The ship's paymaster, the purser, doled out a dark, heavy rum that became known as "Pusser's." It replaced the daily UK gallon (4.5 liters) of beer that spoilt too quickly in the Caribbean heat. Up to 1740 the rum was distributed neat and drunk neat. Then Admiral Edward Vernon, who had the previous year won a sensational victory in Puerto Bello near Panama, ordered that the rum should henceforth only be distributed mixed with water. He was convinced that the same quantity of spirit consumed diluted would lead to less drunkenness. He also ordered that those who were good workers should receive extra lemon juice and sugar, which would make it more palatable for them. Because Vernon, in poor weather, always used to wear a wrap of *grogram*, a kind of coarse fabric, his crew called him "Old Grog." Accordingly, the mixture he ordered came to be known disparagingly as "grog." Grog was therefore originally cold and consisted of Pusser's Rum, water, lemon juice, and sugar. For more than 300 years, until 1970, the daily rum ration was customary in the Royal Navy, even though, from the 1850s onward, it was reduced to 1/8 of a pint (6 cl) per day.

Sugar-cane processing in Cuba. Lithograph by Justos Cantera from: *Vistas de los principales ingenios de Cuba*, 1857.

# The rise of Carta Blanca

The 19th century threw sugar cultivation and rum production into a state of drastic crisis. In 1806 Napoleon I imposed the Continental Blockade against England, obstructing colonial goods, including sugar supplies, from the West Indies. But an alternative was already available. In 1747 Andreas Sigismund Marggraf had discovered the high sugar content of beet, from which his student Franz Carl Achard cultivated the sugar beet. The first beet-sugar factory was established in 1801 in Silesia. It was not long before beet sugar became a serious competitor to cane sugar. Strict quotas were enforced on Caribbean sugar producers, which meant economic catastrophe for the Antilles. Many sugar-cane plantations, together with the distilleries, were ruined. In parallel, in the 19th century rum became a social drink. In the United States it did have a fierce adversary in bourbon, but in Europe it was considered to be chic to drink a cold or hot rum punch. In particular British, Dutch, and Danish traders—who often operated their own distilleries on the islands—were selling rum, which they matured, refined, colored, or blended themselves. Lamb, Old Holborn, and Pusser's were well known in England. Pott der Gute and Der alte Hansen came from what was then Danish Flensburg. In France Negrita was a favorite tipple.

Soon it was not only merchants and seamen who realized that rum improved in wooden barrels, and learned to make the most of this phenomenon. On the islands too, a distinction began to be made between freshly distilled spirit and mature rum colored with caramel. On Martinique the French champion of the abolition of slavery and politician

In the 19th century steam engines were used to make crushing the sugar cane easier. A view inside the Dillon distillery, Fort-de-France.

Victor Schoelcher in 1842 described the first type of spirit as tafia, and only the second variety as rum.

With the abolition of slavery between 1833 and 1888 a new era dawned in the West Indies, in which the great plantations disappeared. As for sugar processing and rum, steam engines and distilleries brought about a revolution in the 1860s. The sugar crisis meant that rum gained in economic value and, by the end of the 19th century, had superseded sugar as a prime export on many islands.

On Martinique, Guadeloupe, and Marie-Galante, small planters struggled through the crisis as best they could, beginning to ferment the sugar-cane juice itself and to distill it themselves. *Rhum agricole* was born. For decades it was not traded, but drunk exclusively by the resident population. Only recently has its special quality gained the recognition it deserves.

From the 1870s Europe was afflicted by the vine pest that destroyed almost all grapevines. The consequence was not only less wine, but also less alcohol, a dearth that the rum distilleries were all too eager to help fill. Hardly had the resistant vines begun to produce a normal harvest than World War I broke out, with many soldiers trying to muster courage by drinking rum. After the war rum too underwent an economic crisis and, when radical restructuring measures came into force during World War II, hundreds of small distilleries were forced to close down.

## A change in style

Before all this another change in style had taken place. Catalonian wine merchant Don Facundo Bacardi Massó attempted to improve the rum production process in Cuba further, until he succeeded—primarily with the help of a Coffey column still and charcoal filtration—in turning the heavy, crude distillate into a clear, light, more mellow spirit. This *ron superior*, due to its white label, was known as Carta Blanca and soon found imitators in Spain and the Spanish colonies.

In the wake of the Cuban war of independence against the Spanish colonial power in 1898, war broke out between the USA and Spain. While they were stationed on the islands, American soldiers developed a taste for light Cuban rum, in particular mixed with cola, lemon, and ice. They toasted one another with the battle cry "Cuba libre!" (Spanish for "free Cuba!"), giving the most popular long drink in the world its name.

When at the end of 1920 prohibition came into force in the USA, smuggling from Cuba flourished, on ships that went down in history as the Rum Row Fleet. Rum became the basis for many new, innocent-looking cocktail recipes. After Prohibition was lifted in 1933, cocktails and long drinks could be enjoyed freely. Light-colored rum grew in international popularity as a mixer, while darker spirits often had a harder time of it. Daiquiri, Mojito, and the cachaça-based caipirinha have preserved their popularity to this day. More recently there has been increasing interest in aromatically appealing, more complex, and darker qualities. Flavored with aromatic spices, mature, golden rums are experiencing a promising growth rate. At the same time there has been an increase in the number of aficionados who appreciate that mature and vintage rums are among the most complex and refined spirits in the world. The rough firewater drunk by slaves and pirates has come a long way!

The old Bacardi distillery in Santiago de Cuba

Don Facundo Bacardi Jr. refined the mild, white rum developed by his father.

# Havana

If you only have an hour in Havana, you should spend it at the Malécon! Both a promenade and a sea defense, the 4 mile (7 km) coast road curves like a bow along Havana Bay, around the old city centre and Vedado. It is an informal meeting place for anyone and everyone, young and old, singles and couples. Here you can stretch your legs and revive your spirits, fish and swim, chat, or make and listen to music. Here everyone feels they belong. In the evening this is the most wonderful place in the city to watch the sun go down. Just a few steps away is the heart of Havana Viega, amidst a mixture of old fortifications and churches, palaces and mansions, wide squares, "avenidas," and narrow alleyways, where luxury meets poverty, and glittering renewal meets abject decay.

Even if many splendid buildings from colonial times have now been transformed into cultural centers, Havana is anything but a museum. In hidden alleyways the pulse of life throbs on, just as we always imagine it doing: everywhere can be heard Latin American and Caribbean rhythms and in the evening the groups retreat into clubs and bars, playing well into the night.

## Dangerous abundance

In the final year of the 19th century the Cubans succeeded in ridding themselves of their Spanish colonial overlords, albeit with the help of the Americans who exerted influence for the next 60 years over both politics and the economy in Cuba. When, from 1929, Prohibition in the USA by no means had the desired effect, Havana became a favorite tourist destination where alcohol was not the only vice that could be freely indulged in. From the 1930s luxury hotels and flashy casinos began to define the cityscape. At the same time, behind the scenes, the Mafia was infecting the leading political clique, making Havana a stronghold of glamor, games of chance, drugs, and prostitution. The city retained this dubious reputation even after World War II, exerting a fatal attraction on the rich, the beautiful,

The Malécon is the most popular meeting place in Cuba's capital.

nd the unscrupulous. Outside the seemingly never-ending party, the local population became poorer and poorer. Corruption and social abuses were rampant. In 1959, after some initial failed attempts, a young former law student and his guerilla forces not only succeeded in ousting the dictator Batista, Fidel Castro also swept away his moribund system. An attempted coup by the USA in 1961 failed. The trading embargo that it then imposed on Cuba exists even to this day.

## Papa's Daiquiri

Ernest Hemingway came to Havana for the first time in 1929 and was immediately fascinated by the city. When he returned to Cuba to catch swordfish three years later, Havana captivated him for good. He took lodgings in room 511 of the elegant hotel Ambos Mundos, from where he enjoyed a marvelous view past the cathedral to the sea. For years he returned to the hotel and this room again and again, finishing his novel *For Whom the Bell Tolls* there.

From his lodgings in the liveliest alley in the whole of the old city, Calle Obispo, it was not far for Hemingway to walk to his two favorite bars. He liked his rum in two different ways. In La Bodeguita del Medio on the Empedrado, which has lost some of its charm over the years, he would order a Mojito. If he felt like a daiquiri, he just strolled up the Obispo to the Floridita where this drink was a spe-

cialty at the time. When he tried the cocktail of white rum, lime juice, sugar syrup, and crushed ice there for the first time, he is reported to have said that it was "not bad," but that he would prefer it without the sugar and with twice the rum. Cantinero Constante is said to have granted him his wish and served him with the words "There it is, papa!"—and Papa's Daiquiri was born. With a splash of grapefruit juice rounded off with a shot of maraschino, it is served even today as the Hemingway Special in the Floridita bar, which is still as charming as ever.

Hot rhythms seem to accompany the Cubans day and night.

Ernest Hemingway drank in the Floridita, the birthplace of the daiquiri.

# Raw sugar cane

Without this tropical grass, there would be no rum. Nowadays, it is the high-yielding *Saccharum officinarum*, true sugar cane, and the hardier wild varieties *Saccharum robustum* and *Saccharum spontaneum* that combine all the best properties of the original plants. When sugar cane matures, a soft sap forms inside the rigid stems in which the plant can store an unusually large amount of the sugar created during photosynthesis.

The original home of the sugar cane is tropical New Guinea, from where it spread via the Philippines as far as India and China. From India it reached Persia, where, as early as AD 600, a process was developed for purifying the concentrated raw sap of many undesirable substances—to refine the sugar and press it into conical shapes: the first sugar loaves, which were commonplace for a long time. From the 7th century onward, with the spread of Islam, sugar cane became known in the Near East, in north Africa, and in Spain. Sugar was carried by the Crusaders in the 12th century to the courts of central and northern Europe. In 1493 Columbus took sugar cane to the Antilles, as sugar was one of the most sought-after commodities of the time. Just a decade later the first slaves were being sold to the rapidly expanding plantations in the West Indies. Sugar soon replaced gold, which had so often been sought in vain.

Sugar cane is propagated from cuttings, which led, over the centuries, to a weakening of the genotype, even when new plants were introduced from Java and Tahiti in the 19th century. At the beginning of the 20th century cultivations were established on the islands of varieties which were intended to be as well adapted as possible to the prevailing natural conditions of soil and climate. Since then various research institutes—that in Barbados has a particularly high reputation—have supplied clones selected from individual islands. The new hybrids give rich yields, high sucrose content, and also resistance to disease and pests, as well as good sap extractability.

Nine months after planting, the sugar-cane crop is ready for harvesting.

## Commercial crop par excellence

Sugar cane is cultivated in tropical regions throughout the world. Depending on variety and conditions of growth, the yield may be around 45 tons per acre (100 tonnes per hectare) a year. The average sugar yield from this is 10%—that is worldwide about 120 million tons (110 million tonnes) of sugar per year (corresponding to 74% of total sugar production). When 10 tons of sugar are produced from 100 tons of cane, 5 tons of molasses are created, which contain almost 50% of the sugar present in the stems. The majority of production residue, the *bagasse*, consists almost completely of cellulose. It is heated in the sugar factories and processed to create paper, cardboard, or fiber board and, increasingly, ethanol (biofuel). This energy concept from sustainable raw materials (oil palms as well as sugar cane) is in the process of transforming expanding areas of rainforest into tracts of land for cultivation, and converting ever more foodstuffs into combustible fuel to produce power.

## High-strength grass

Cuttings 12–20 inches (30–50 cm) long are laid flat in furrows. After about four months they have put out roots and shoots and formed several stems. A mature plant bears a stand of 5–20 stems which may be 8–16 feet (2.5–5 m) high and ½–2 inches (1.5–6 cm) thick, depending on the variety. The stems are divided into 4–6 inch (10–15 cm) long internodes, from which alternate leaves sprout that may be up to 3 feet (1 meter) long, in a similar way to maize plants. Being a tropical plant the sugar cane requires sufficient heat (the annual average temperature must not fall below 64 °F (18 °C)) and high rainfall. As the plants mature the lower leaves dry and fall off. The lower part of the stem, covered by a thin layer of wax, becomes bald and smooth. Some varieties form high, feathery, silvery shimmering stands of blooms. This perennial grass provides good harvests for five to eight years, after which the sugar content declines and it has to be replaced.

## Machete versus machine

The vegetative cycle of the sugar cane is 12 months. Nine months after the stems are planted, the cane is usually mature and the cane-sugar content has reached a maximum level. In the West Indies harvesting takes place between January and July. The daily harvest is determined by the capacity of the processing factories as the cut stems must not be stored longer than 24 hours. In the tropical heat microorganisms will drastically reduce the sugar content.

Traditionally the cane is cut short just above ground using a machete. The upper part of the stem with the green leaves is topped and left in the field as mulch. These methods are used in particular in small operations or on steep ground. Some farmers even today set fire to the fields before the harvest in order to drive away snakes and insects and to remove the unpleasantly sharp-edged leaves. This also makes the stems lighter.

For larger fields a mechanical cane loader loads the cut sugar cane onto waiting trailers. On fields in flat areas the harvest can be carried out entirely by machines that cut off the top part of the stems with the green leaves, and immediately chop the rest into 8–12-inch (20–30 cm) pieces, while blowing away the dry leaves.

Sugar cane is cut by hand—often once the dry leaves have been burnt off—or harvested by machine.

# Rum from molasses

Molasses, the viscous residue from sugar production, is fermented with water and yeast.

Rum has remained a byproduct of sugar production, even if it has well exceeded domestic sugar in economic importance on the French Antilles and many other islands.

To obtain sugar the sugar cane is first cut into pieces, shredded, and milled in order to extract its juice. This cloudy liquid undergoes several purification processes and is then heated with liquid lime in order to eliminate the non-sugar substances. After filtering these can be used as fertilizer. The thin juice is concentrated by boiling in pans until the sugar begins to crystallize due to supersaturation of the solution. This process is accelerated by the addition of sugar crystals. It ends when the magma consists of half crystals and half syrup. The sugar crystals are removed from the syrup by water and steam in centrifuges. This raw sugar is light in color but not white as yet, and will be refined at least one more time. The dark, viscous syrup remaining after the final crystallization is known as molasses.

## Rapidly fermenting residues

The molasses contains almost 50% of the original sugar content of the plant. Before fermentation it is diluted with water. The foam (skimmings) removed during boiling of the sugar-cane juice and the acidic yeast residues (dunder) are also added to the final distillation. In addition more yeast—cultivated from the establishment's own or commercially available yeast strains—is stirred in. All these additives, together with the fermentation itself, affect the aroma of the mature rum. For light varieties of rum a short, rapid fermentation lasting two to three days is sufficient. If, as in Jamaica, a richer, heavier distillation is desired, the fermentation period is extended by a week or more using temperature control. Efforts are made, in subsequent distillation, to preserve the more complex aromas created in this way in the rum. The liquor obtained from molasses, the mash, contains no more than 5–9% alcohol.

## Distilling progress

The molasses fermented into mash was originally distilled twice in pot stills imported from Europe—in sheds to one side of the sugar refineries. The two separate distillation processes resulted in a high alcohol content exceeding 80% by volume. To avoid a second distillation, in the Caribbean too people soon began not to allow the vapor rising from the first distillation to condense immediately but to use it to reheat the raw liquor from the previous distillation process. This meant that distillation could take place twice in a single cycle. A second vessel was added and only the vapor rising from this was allowed to condense. Such a distillation system was known as a retort. It might have up to three additional stills. In each of them, aroma and alcohol become more concentrated. In this way highly alcoholic, intensive Jamaican rum is distilled forming the basis for a *Rum-Verschnitt* (rum blend) in Germany, Holland, and Austria, or domestic rum. The column-shape apparatus now used particularly by the larger producers,

developed in Ireland and Scotland at the end of the 1820s, can be thought of as stills in a vertical arrangement. The mash is heated in them in a continuous uninterrupted process, in which liquids with various boiling points vaporize, condense, and can then be drawn off as required. The most modern equipment consists of several interlinked distillation columns, enabling the master distiller to collect distillates of various strengths and different aromatic constituents. He is then able to compose blends that differ significantly in style.

Top left: Rum is now predominantly distilled in modern column-shape systems in continuous operation, as here at Bacardi in the Bermudas.

Top right: Old copper pot stills for double discontinuous distillation at Mount Gay on Barbados.

# Rum from sugar-cane juice

On some islands in the Antilles the sugar sales crisis in the 19th century resulted in rum no longer being produced from molasses, the byproduct of sugar manufacture, but from top-quality sugar-cane juice itself. This meant that rum had become the main product.

It wheezes and puffs, hisses, clacks, clatters, and chuffs—today as always: the old steam engine on Martinique, where each of the seven still-active distilleries depends on a similar monstrosity, is still used to power shredders and mills that divest the tough sugar cane of its fibers and break it down. As a rule these consist of three wheels in series that crush the stems. Stream water flows in to allow the sugar to be extracted better. This juice, known as *vesou*, is filtered and pumped into open tanks, combined with yeast, and stocked in vats.

In 24 to 72 hours it ferments and becomes *vin de canne*, the 3.5–6% by volume alcohol sugar-cane wine that can be distilled. The steam furnace is filled with bagasse, the crushed sugar-cane fibers. This not only supplies the steam engine with power, but also heats the distillation columns and drives a turbine for electricity. Perfect recycling. And should there be any bagasse left over, it can be used as cattle fodder or processed to make paper or cardboard.

## Exciting columns

On the French islands of Martinique, Guadeloupe, and Marie-Galante, pot stills or alembics were often abandoned in favor of distillery apparatus consisting not of two columns like the Coffey or patent stills, but having only one column. Nevertheless, they operate continuously and so save both time and money.

When "rhumiers" speak of the advantages of their columns, they tend to get excited. First of all they will point out that each column—

Steam engines drive shredders and mills that crush the tough sugar cane.

and each still—is a unique, handcrafted piece of equipment. That is why each produces rum with a quite distinctive character that influences its quality to a considerable extent. Whereas, for reasons of cost, there is now a trend toward merging originally separate distilleries into large groups, the individual character of the traditional brands has largely been preserved by the transfer of their distillation apparatus and its continued use.

The copper distillation apparatus typical of the Antilles consists of a tall column divided into 15 to 20 levels. The sugar-cane wine is preheated in the *chauffe-vin* to 150–67 °F (65–75 °C) and fed up through the column at this temperature. On the way from top to bottom it passes through the various levels, being sprayed through a metal bell on each level. At the bottom vapor is introduced into the column. This rises up stage by stage. Where wine and vapor encounter one another, a violent, continuous bubbling takes place that can be observed through circular inspection windows also used for cleaning purposes. Gradually the vapor becomes laden with volatile components—alcohol, ester, aldehyde. Thus enriched, it makes its way up to the top of the column, from where it is fed through the swan neck and the chauffe-vin which it heats, and into the condenser. Here it cools and liquefies, and is collected as clear rum with an alcohol content of 65–75% by volume. The non-alcoholic residues, the slops, can now be drawn off from the bottom of the column. From 1 ton of sugar cane, the juice of which is fermented directly into wine, the distillery obtains around 24 gallons of strong white rum with an alcohol content of 55% by volume (1 tonne of sugar cane produces about 100 liters); and 2,640 gallons of sugar-cane wine will yield about 193 gallons of rum (10,000 liters of wine yields about 730 liters of rum).

The juice ferments into weak sugar-cane wine that is distilled in columns (continuous distillation plants) into rum.

# Growing old in the tropics

The condensate from the distillation process is by no means drinkable yet. Depending on the process used, this rum contains 65–90% alcohol by volume. If it is to be sold quickly as white rum, it is usually decanted into stainless steel tanks for a period of three months, where it is regularly agitated in order to aerate it. Contact with oxygen makes the bitter volatile constituents vaporize, mellowing what was initially a very aggressive liquor. Only rarely is rum bottled at its original strength as overproof. It is most often reduced with distilled water to a drinkable strength which, for the international brands, is between 37.5 and 43% alcohol by volume, but for the rums of the French islands is 50, 55, or even 62% by volume.

Some brands in the Cuban tradition mature for up to three years in old oak barrels, giving them a light, mellow, balanced character without becoming too dark in color. Before bottling, this rum is charcoal filtered to remove any coloring substances. The word *añejo* on the label refers to the fact that this is matured rum. In general for "blanco" especially light, aromatic distillates are used, while the *maestro ronero* (master rum maker) selects stronger spirits for lengthier maturing.

A tried and trusted method of aging rum is in used bourbon barrels. It has not been until recent years that new oak barrels, or barrels that have contained other whisky, cognac, or wine, have been used. Maturing in wood intensifies the color of the rum, giving it first a light gold tone, then amber or mahogany tones that some cellarers will assist by adding caramel.

One peculiarity of the maturing of rum in the West Indies consists in the effects of the hot tropical climate. Anyone entering a warehouse full of barrels will be overwhelmed by the intensive odor. The proportion of distillate evaporating at high temperatures is considered to be 7–8% per year. An increasing number of producers have started to air condition their halls in order to reduce the "angels' share," yet even when such measures are taken, it still remains above the level of moderate or cooler climate zones. In the heat the alcohol draws tannins and aromas from the wood much more rapidly. This is why new barrels are rarely used, and only ever with extreme caution, as they can quickly give the rum an unpleasant and bitter flavor.

With accelerated aging, rum can be classified as mature after just three years. It will then, depending on whether new or older barrels were used, have a more or less intensely spicy or roasted note. However, to be able to develop multilayered aromas blending notes of tropical fruits, spices, cocoa, and tobacco, rum requires a significantly longer maturation period. It will reach the next stage after 6 to 8 years, while the most outstanding rums are left to mature for longer than 10, 15, or 20 years.

The art of the *maestro ronero* consists in recomposing the best-known blends of his company at each stage of maturity in order to preserve their style and quality. Each has his own recipe, often handed down from his predecessors. Apprenticeship often lasts ten years. For a blend rums of various ages are always combined, and the age stated on the label is that of the newest ingredient.

In Cuba a special aging method has been developed, consisting of two separate processes. In order to obtain the base for

Bottom left: The skill of the "maestro ronero" is a decisive factor in the style of the rum.

Bottom right: The oldest surviving vintage rum at the St. James distillery was made in 1885.

future blends, freshly distilled aguardiente is subjected to aging for several years so that the blend master achieves the desired character of the "madre" by blending and selecting, and by periods spent in older or newer casks. If he wants to produce a particular blend for his company, he mixes a precise quantity of the madre with fresh distillate into *ron fresco* that he once more matures, and develops further by mixing again until the aroma and flavor profile of the blend required is created.

If white rums, depending on their origin, display fine differences in aroma and character, the profile is considerably more distinctive among older rums. The location of the distillery is of subordinate importance in this. Far more significant are local traditions and, even more, house style and the signature of the blend master. Rum, therefore, can offer an extraordinarily diverse range of expression.

Vintage rums are a relatively new development, even though there are some old bottles that date back to 1885. In the past distilleries rarely set aside vintage spirits with the intention of bottling them separately. They were intended rather for blends. It was not until the 1980s that some producers began deliberately to store and mature vintages, so that now a range from various countries and islands can reveal a surprising difference in production year to year.

Top left: Large oak barrels are also used for a shorter aging period.

Top right: Rum is usually aged in small bourbon barrels.

# Best of rum—Caribbean highlights

## Bahamas

**Bacardi Ron 8 Años – Reserva Superior**
Under Fidel Castro's communist regime the Bacardi distillery in Santiago de Cuba was nationalized. By that time the company had already established distilleries on other islands, for example on Puerto Rico, known for light and dry rum. In 1965 Bacardi moved its headquarters to New Providence on the Bahamas, where it set up one of the most modern distilleries in the world—one that is always state of the art. In the five-story distillery tower stand five columns with an annual capacity of over 7 million gallons (27,000,000 liters) of distillate. The company has seven warehouses where it ages the rum. Each contains 44,000 barrels. The mature rum is transported by the company's own fleet in tanks to the various bottling plants operated by the company throughout the world. The eight-year-old Reserva Superior is a mellow, balanced rum with a discreet hint of vanilla, Cuban style.

## Cuba

**Havana Club Añejo 7 Años**
The Cuban government was committed to rum and created a high-efficiency distillery in Santa Cruz del Norte in the province of Havana. It revived the Havana Club brand that dated back to 1878 and entered into a joint venture in 1993 with Pernod Ricard in which the French group undertook international marketing operations. Havana Club—although, as a Cuban product, prohibited on the leading US market—has risen to become the third largest rum brand in the world. The quality of its rums and the craftsmanship of its blend masters are expressed in its flagship, 7 Años, a very mellow, full-bodied, versatile rum with sweet spices.

Also:
Arecha; Caney; Legendario; Liberación; Mulata de Cuba; Santa Cruz; Varadero

## Jamaica

**Appleton Estate Extra 12 Años**
Jamaica was famous for dark, heavy, highly flavored rums, of which many were bottled in England as Navy Rum. Others were used in Germany, Holland, and Austria as *Verschnitt* (blends). Despite adaptation to a lighter style, even today there are still some wonderfully mature, spicy, full-bodied rums such as Extra, aged for more than 12 years by the oldest rum producer on the island, the Appleton estate founded in 1825.

Also:
Captain Morgan; Coruba; Alfred Lamb's; Lemon Hart;
Myers's; Sangster's;
Southard's; Wray & Nephew

## Haiti

**Barbancourt Réserve Especial 8**
When Dupré Barbancourt from Charente founded the distillery in 1862, he brought double distillation with him from his homeland. The family firm has remained true to this process to this day. Sugar cane from 1,500-acre (600 ha) plantations—a fifth of which are owned by the company, the rest being owned by 200 farmers—supply the annual requirement. As in Martinique, vesou is obtained straight from the sugar cane, then distilled twice and finally matured exclusively in French oak barrels—an exception in the West Indies. This top-quality liquor has a fascinating aroma of candied peel, rancio, and smoke, and is velvety and full-bodied, with a strong note of fruit and cinnamon that lingers on the palate.

Also:
Marie Colas; Nazon; Tesserot

## Dominican Republic

**Brugal Siglo de Oro**
In the Dominican Republic—as in neighboring Haiti—sugar still represents one of the most important national products. However, rum is valued more highly in the republic. Since the mid 1970s older qualities have been deliberately developed, and the very intensive, heavy but mellow Siglo de Oro from Brugal, a rum-producing company established about 120 years ago by a Spaniard, is a top-quality product.

Also:
Barceló; Bermúdez; Caribe Azul;
Cubaney; Matusalem

## Puerto Rico

Bacardi; Captain Morgan;
Don Q; Palo Viejo;
Ron del Barrilito; Ronrico

## Virgin Islands of the USA

### Cruzan Estate Single Barrel

As early as in 1760 sugar-cane plantations were being established on the
island of St. Croix, from which this distillery developed. Its rums are based on
molasses diluted with rainwater and fermented with the company's own yeast
cultures at a controlled temperature. Distillation takes place in a modern five-column system. The best quality is matured
for up to 12 years in American oak, then
blended, and undergoes an additional
finish in barrels that are individually filled.
The result is a light-colored, mellow, balanced rum with a discreet fruity, toffee
aroma.

Also:
Conch

## British Virgin Islands

### Pusser's British Navy Rum

For more than 300 years Pusser's was
issued daily to the crew on the ships of
the Royal Navy. It was a special blend of
five West Indian rums. After this custom
was abandoned in 1970, entrepreneur
and round-the-world yachtsman Charles
Tobias took over rights and recipe in
1979. He made Tortola the headquarters
of Pusser's and revived the strong, complex blend that basically originates in
wooden pot stills.

Also:
Calwood

## Anguilla
Pyrat

## Antigua and Barbuda
Cavalier; English Harbour

## Guadeloupe

### Damoiseau Vieux 8 Ans d'Age

On Guadeloupe sugar-cane juice is fermented and the wine distilled, which
results in a particularly aromatic eau de
vie. The Domaine Bellevue de Moule,
founded at the end of the 19th century,
was taken over with its distillery in 1942
by the Damoiseau family. The cuvée,
matured for more than eight years in
cognac barrels, perfectly expresses the
style of the islands, with its markedly
sweet fruity, spicy notes, balance, and
finesse.

Also:
Bourdon; Domaine de Séverin;
Longueteau; Montebello;
on Marie-Galante: Bielle; Père Labat

## Martinique

Rum brands: see chapter entitled "Old
rums from Martinique";
Bally; Clement; Depaz; Dillon;
Habitation St. Etienne; La Favorite;
La Mauny; Negrita; Neisson; Old Nick;
Rhum J.M; Trois Rivière; St. James.

## Barbados

### Mount Gay Eclipse

At Mount Gay on Barbados rum is said to
have been distilled as early as 1663. The
very fruity, mellow, often light, smoky
island rums, some of which are distilled
in pot stills, have an excellent reputation.
Mount Gay produces a large proportion
of these. Even Eclipse that has been
matured barely more than two years is
very convincing. The best quality is the
Extra Old.

Also:
Cockspur; Doorly's; E.S.A: Field;
Foursquare; Kaniche; Malibu Rum;
R. L. Seale

## Trinidad and Tobago

### Angostura 1824 Limited Reserve

Trinidad is known as the home of Angostura Bitters. However, the company,
founded in the 1820s by German doctor
Johann Siegert, has developed into one
of the largest rum producers in the world.
It has one of the most modern distillery
plants. Formerly predominantly active in
the bulk sector, it now emphasizes the
marketing of premium rums under its own
name as well as under the name of local
rum legend Joseph Bento Fernandes—
such as the 12-year-matured, very intensive, full-bodied, mellow 1824 with
aromas of candied orange and papaya,
currants, honey, cinnamon, and tobacco.

Also:
Fernandes Vat 19; Forres Park; Kairi;
Old Oak

## Guatemala

### Ron Zacapa Centenario 23 Años

Industrias Licoreras de Guatemala, the leading spirits group in the country, formed in 1944 from the merger of four distilleries, supplies high-quality rums. Their history dates back to Spanish doctor and chemist Alejandro Burdaleta who distilled rum from sugar-cane syrup, maturing it using the solera system. Ron Zacapa was launched in 1976 on the occasion of the centenary celebrations of the city of Zacapa. The 23 Años, voted best premium rum in the world five times in a row in the Caribbean Weeks' Rum Festival competition, is matured first in bourbon casks before receiving its final polish for the last years, first in sherry, then in Málaga barrels. This explains its pleasant mellowness and the aromas of roast nuts, cocoa, toffee, and coffee.

Also:
Botran; Malteco

## Mexico

In Mexico rum or *aguardiente de caña* plays an important role even if it is seldom bottled neat, but is usually used for blending with simpler tequilas.

Also:
Cabeza; Porfidio Sugar Cane; Xtabentun D'Aristi

## Nicaragua

### Flor de Caña Centenario 18 Años

The rum from Chichigalpa dates back to a sugar-cane plantation founded in 1890. Here it was decided in 1937 to concentrate on rum. The first exports to neighboring countries were made in 1959, but it was not until 1994 that the brand was marketed internationally. After 12 years Centenario is full bodied, with aromas of butter, baked apple, cocoa, and toffee. Also available are 15- and 18-year-old bottles.

Also:
Cerro Negro; Concepcion; King Managua; Masaya; Mombacho; Momotombo; Ron Plata; San Cristobal; Zapatera

## Panama

### Malecon Reserva Imperial 21 Años

After the separation of Panama from Colombia in 1903, José Varelo Bianco, a young Spanish immigrant, founded the republic's first new sugar factory in Pese. It was his sons, Manuel, Plinio, and Julio, who began to produce rum in 1936, when Varela Hermanos launched the brand name Abuela. The company Caribbean Spirits, which produces Malecon, has distinguished itself in particular with the long-matured rums in its Imperial range, for example the very mellow, delicately spicy, 21-year-old rums that have clear roasted and apricot aromas. Over recent years rum has been increasing in importance as an export item for Panama.

Also:
Cortez; La Cruz Anejo; Portobelo; Panama Jack

## Colombia

### Hemingway 7 Años

Santana Liquors procure young sugarcane distillate from the Caribbean, which they then mature for seven years in bourbon barrels into their top Hemingway brand, a mild, balanced rum with a pleasantly discreet hint of vanilla. The Relicardo brand is also bottled by them.

Also:
Caldos; Juan de la Cruz; Medellin; Trapiche; Tres Equinas

## Venezuela

### Pampero Aniversario

Venezuela too has made matured rums its specialty and has even written into its laws that rum must age for at least two years. The Pampero distillery, established in 1938 in Caracas, launched Aniversario to celebrate its 25th anniversary in 1963, matured for 12 years in bourbon barrels. Since then, it has become established as one of the most popular premium rums. It has a pleasant taste, with hints of vanilla and roast, candied citrus fruits and honey, a full body, roundness, and harmony.

Also:
Aruka; Cacique: Carupano; Diplomático; El Descubrimiento; El Muco; Libertador; Ocumare; Santa Teresa

**Peru**

**Cartavio Aniversario 12 Años**
The national drink of Peru, as in Chile, is pisco. However, in the valleys of the Andes sugar cane is also cultivated, from the molasses of which high-quality rum is distilled at Destilerias Unidas Peruano. The company, modernized in 2005 on its 75th anniversary, reports increasing export success. Its jubilee bottling is aged according to the solera system for at least 12 years in barrels of Slovenian oak. Very mild and well rounded, this dark rum has a pleasant spicy, nutty, dried fruit, cocoa, coffee aroma, with a very discreet hint of tobacco.

**Brazil**

**Muraro**
Brazil is a world leader in sugar-cane cultivation. From some of it cachaça—which may be the most frequently drunk spirit in the world—is distilled. Otherwise, *aguardente de cana*, of which there are dozens of brands, is bottled rather than rum. In addition to Ypiócas, Muraro from Flores da Cuhna has become famous with its Bird's Rum. The ceramic bottle is decorated with a toucan, the company logo, referring to Brazil's rich birdlife. The dark rum is distilled from molasses and matured for a long time in oak in order to obtain its special, mild, sweet character. Some international companies such as Ron Montilla use the abundance of Brazilian sugar cane for their own rums.

**Guyana**

**El Dorado 21 Years Old**
Guyana is the home of Demerara rum, and currently its only distillery stands on the eastern bank of the river of the same name. The former colony is known for its strong British-style export rum, shipped in tanks, and for the spicy rums preferred in the country itself, but nowadays also exported. Demerara Distillers have the only surviving timber Coffey column in the world, as well as an additional wooden pot still, producing particularly rich, heavy rums that are aged in 50,000 bourbon barrels. Under their own brand El Dorado, high-quality, dark old rums are also sold, such as the excellent 15 Years Old and the 21 Years Old that adds extra silkiness to the intensive spicy sweet aromas and distinct roasted notes.

Also:
Courantin; Lemon Hart; Royal; Sea Wynde; Wood's Old Navy Rum

**Surinam**

**Borgoe 82 Gold**
This pleasant rum with a clear toffee aroma was launched on the market for the hundredth anniversary of the Marienburg Estate now owned by Surinam Alcoholic Beverages, of which Angostura is a member. The company has its own distillery in which rum is distilled in a three-column system, and finally matured in oak barrels. The eight-year matured, comparatively light-colored Black Cat Reserve is also interesting.

Also:
Black Cat; Borgoe; Mariënburg

**French Guyana**

Coeur de Chauffe; La Cayennaise; La Belle Cabresse

**Ecuador**

Azuaya; Estelar; Ron Royale; San Miguel; Zhumir

**Bolivia**

Kayana

# Old rums from Martinique

Martinique seems very French. It has a high standard of living, a lack of commitment, lots of officials and just as much unemployment, daily traffic chaos in the capital Fort-de-France, and an A.O.C.—an Appellation d'Origine Contrôlée. Otherwise reserved for wine and cheese varieties, but also cognac, armagnac, and calvados, it has finally been granted—the one and only rum appellation in the world. After 20 years' stubborn determination, the rum producers of the Antilles islands succeeded in obtaining it in 1996.

The fields that should be planted with sugar cane were stipulated, as was the variety and how it was to be cultivated. The permitted maximum yield is 108 tons per acre (120 tonnes per hectare). Then the sugar cane has to be cold pressed and the vesou fermented in open fermentation tanks into *vin de canne*, sugar-cane wine, which must have a minimum alcohol content of 3.5% by volume and a pH value of 4.7. Distillation can only take place in officially approved columns, and the rum collected must have a minimum alcohol content of 65% by volume and a maximum of 75% by volume.

If it is to be labeled *Rhum blanc*, it can be brought onto the market after only three months. If it is matured in large barrels, *élevé sous bois*, it must spend a minimum of 12 months there, during which time it takes on a light golden color. *Rhum vieux* may appear on the label if the distillate is aged for at least three years in barrels containing less than 170 gallons (650 liters). Usually small

A selection of the best rums of the island, matured for a long time in oak barrels

oak barrels of about 53 gallons (200 liters) volume are used, and the favorites are those that once held bourbon. Designations such as "très vieux," "hors d'âge," and X.O., or vintage details, are evidence of longer aging. Before a rum is awarded an A.O.C. label, it must pass an organoleptic test.

Typical aromas of Rhum blanc are: floral notes such as sugar cane, orange blossom, honey; fruity aromas such as citrus fruits, bananas, pineapple, and other exotic fruits; vegetable aromas such as herbal tea, dried leaves; spicy notes such as pepper; aniseed; and balsamic aromas such as tea tree and eucalyptus.

The following aromas are considered characteristic of Rhum vieux: roasted notes such as coffee, mocha, cocoa, chocolate, cigars; spices and aromas such as vanilla, cinnamon, muscat nuts; fruity notes such as jam, fruit sauce, dried figs, dates, baked plums, fruits in alcohol; and balsamic aromas of tea tree and eucalyptus.

The rum manufactured from sugar-cane juice is labeled *Rhum agricole*, while rum from the French Antilles produced from molasses is known as *Rhum industriel*. The bottles illustrated above are some of the best Appellation d'Origine Contrôlée Martinique rums available and can make a stay on the island an unforgettable experience.

# Rum from further afield

Rum is bottled and distributed in many countries of the world. It would be impossible, even within the scope of this book, to mention every brand and company. The following selection from the range of rum producers in various countries shows clearly that rum has for a long time been a universal spirit. Of late, darker, spicy rums have gained an increasing following, and the finest, long matured in oak barrels, are very highly regarded.

## Spain

### Arehucas 12 Años
On the subtropical islands off the west coast of Africa occupied in 1479 by the Spaniards, sugar cane began to be cultivated from 1489. Nowadays, plantations remain only on Gran Canaria to the north of Las Palmas and in Arucas. Destilerías Arehucas are famous for their rum, which gains significantly in balance with age without losing any of its rich taste.

Also:
Amazona Ron Dulce, Artemi, Guajro Ron Miel Canario

## Mauritius

### Green Island
The first sugar factories opened here in the 18th century when the French ruled the islands. Even today sugar is one of the main products of Mauritius, which has been independent since 1968. However, an increasing quantity of sugar cane is being used to produce ethanol. The island's best-known rum brands are produced by International Distillers Ltd. These are Green Island, White Diamond, Power's No. 1, and Flamboyant. There are some new initiatives on the restored Domaines Les Pailles and at Saint-Aubin, which distilled the island's first Rhum agricole in 2003.

## Nepal

### Khukri
In Nepal the leading brand is Khukri produced in Kathmandu, where cool weather and spring water offer very favorable conditions for maturing and reduction. The Nepal Distillery, which began in 1960 with an old-fashioned pot still, is now equipped with a powerful three-column distillation plant in which it rectifies the liquor. The rum is then matured for at least eight months in wooden barrels.
The khukri, a curved knife, replicated in the shape of the bottle, is the pride of the Nepalese.

## Réunion

### Isautier 5 Ans
The first distillery on Réunion was opened in 1815. Some 30 years later the Isautier brothers established the first large-scale distillery. By this time, there were 40 distilleries, which together produced around 530,000 gallons (2 million liters) of rum. The fact that the island's rum should only be produced from molasses—*Rhum de sucrerie*—or from sugar-cane juice—*Rhum agricole*—was stipulated in 1921. While Isautier at that time was selling bottled rum and punch, the smaller distilleries openly set themselves apart from them, founding in 1972 the Charrette brand that did its own bottling and marketing. Nowadays the following brands exist on Réunion: Isautier, Chatel, Charrette, Rivière du Mât, and Savanna. The majority of the production consists of young, fruity Rhum blanc, but when matured it gains significantly in balance and length, without forfeiting any of its fruitiness.

## Madagascar

### Dzama 10 Years
There is a rum tradition, too, on the island off the east coast of Africa. Sugar cane cultivated in the tropical plains of the coast of Madagascar facing the Indian Ocean, sugar is produced and rum distilled. At Dzamandar, after a maturation period of ten or more years in French oak barrels, an excellent rum is produced with delightful roasted and nutty aromas and a spicy mellow quality.

### India

#### Old Monk Rum

In the western world we like to concentrate on a few well-known brands and overlook the fact that other continents nurture their own traditions and have their own market leaders. The Indian rum Old Monk is now one of the world's most popular rums. India is the second largest sugar producer and, as a market, has an extremely promising future.

The brand dates back to Englishman Edward Dyer, who began to brew Lion, India's first beer, in the 1820s in the Himalayas, not far from Shimla. Shortly afterward he established a distillery. The rapidly expanding company came under Indian management after independence, and today, as Mohan Meakins Ltd., produces—among other things—India's favorite whisky, Solan. Its seven-year-old, very mild rum with fine, sweet spicy aromas, has a very fierce competitor in its own country in McDowell's Celebration Rum, produced by United Breweries.

### Philippines

Tanduay, the dominant Philippine rum brand, dates back to the family firm of Elizaides, which began with the Manila Steamship Company in 1854 and owned the first distillery just a few years later. The family invested in sugar-cane plantations in Panay and West Negros, the harvests from which they transported by their steamships to the distillery in Manila where they distilled rum and other spirits. When in 1988 the Lucio Tan group purchased Tanduay, there followed modernization and expansion of the distillery, which multiplied its capacity almost five times. Nowadays Tanduay obtains distillate from molasses that have been aged in oak barrels for two years or longer, mixes it with sugar, aromatic ingredients, and demineralized water, and then bottles it. Tanduay—which can be obtained in the Philippines at bargain prices—is after Bacardi the most frequently consumed rum in the world.

### Tahiti
French Polynesia

#### Noa Noa

Rum is being produced on small islands such as Tahiti in the Pacific Ocean, relatively close to the original home of sugar cane. The spicy Noa Noa, named after Paul Gauguin's book (1897), a journal of his life on Tahiti, has been produced by Marc Jones Tahitian Import Export since the 1980s. Jones enjoyed initial success exporting vanilla from Tahiti. The company soon expanded its range to other natural products from the island, and then moved on to produce rum, coconut, chocolate, beer, and juice.

### Fiji

South Pacific Distillers, founded in 1980, have made a name for themselves with their Bounty brand. They have also repeatedly won international awards for their rum. As early as in 1890 the Colonial Sugar Refinery, which would later produce Inner Circle Rum, established a distillery at Nausori.

### Australia

#### Bundaberg Black

Rum has a special place in Australia's history. Its trade was the monopoly of British officers, and rum became a form of currency at the end of the 18th century in New South Wales. When William Bligh wanted to abolish this officers' privilege, the Rum Rebellion broke out in 1808 and Bligh found himself back in prison. Nevertheless, it was not until 1884 in Beenleigh, south of Brisbane, that the first rum distillery was established after its owners had for some years made do with a floating distillery installed on a ship named the *Walrus*. Purchased in 2004 by Inner Circle Rum revived by Stuart Gilbert, Beenleigh with its pot stills is the oldest working Australian distillery.

Number one among Australian spirits is Bundaberg Rum. In the small coastal town of the same name north of Brisbane, four sugar millers joined together in 1888 to distill molasses. From 1942 the company also marketed ready-to-drink mixtures that since 2001 have also been dispensed from the barrel in Australia. From 2004 the Bundaberg Distilling Company expanded its capacities considerably. Initially the wash is distilled in columns and then the low wines are distilled a second time in pot stills. Then maturation takes place in 200 wooden tanks, each containing about 20,000 gallons (75,000 liters), for at least two years. Bundaberg Black, matured for eight years, is the company's best product.

Also:
Inner Circle, Beenleigh, Stubbs

# Flensburg and rum

German rum has its own history, which begins in Denmark—or more precisely in Flensburg. This city in the north of Schleswig-Holstein from the 15th century until 1864 was part of the kingdom of Denmark, and was its second most important port after Copenhagen. The *Neptunus*, which sailed to the Danish West Indies in 1755, heralded in the city's golden age. It was to bring back one of the most sought-after commodities at the time: cane sugar, to be refined in Flensburg.

The West Indian trade—Denmark owned the islands of St. Croix, St. John, and St. Thomas, now the US Virgin Islands—gave the city a significant boost. Its merchant fleet

Advertisement for the Hermann G. Dethleffsen company

tripled in number. The harbor was widened. New warehouses and workshops were built. The population grew. Flensburg became one of the most important transshipment points from which goods imported from the Caribbean and the Mediterranean were shipped to the neighboring Balkan states and to Norway.

In addition to coffee, cocoa, tobacco, rice, indigo, cotton, and precious woods, the Flensburg merchants were also increasingly interested in rum. The first barrels of high-proof molasses-based liquor—which, by contrast with many other goods, actually improved over the course of the months at sea—were imported in 1767. At that time Flensburg was a stronghold of alcohol distilleries and exported 3.8 million gallons (1 million liters) of high-proof alcohol, predominantly to Norway. If the harvest was poor, or if there was some other crisis, however, distilling was prohibited. In such cases, the distillers could now resort to rum. So, with all the specialist knowledge at their disposal, they began to mature and reduce pure imported rum, and to transform it into a drinkable spirit.

Distillers such as O.C. Balle (founded in 1717), Hermann G. Dethleffsen (1738), and Thomas Nissen (1748) began to trade in rum. Hans Christian Henningsen (later Sonnberg), who himself had sailed to the Caribbean, was the first to specialize in rum, in 1781. In 1848 Captain Hans Hinrich Pott joined the highly promising rum trade, and wine merchant Hans Hansen followed suit 20 years later. Over the course of almost 100 years, during which Flensburg ships transported pure rum from the West Indian islands under the Daneborg, the Danish flag, the merchants learned to refine it and to market it to profit. Then, when in 1867 the duchies of Schleswig and Holstein were annexed by Prussia, a new era in rum production began, that of the rum blend known as *Rum-Verschnitt*.

## Rum-Verschnitt

The merchants survived the change of flag relatively unscathed. It is true that they had to seek a new rum source. This was to be—as was soon apparent—Jamaica where, under English government, particularly heavy qualities were produced. The Flensburg people deliberately selected aromatic liquors with high ester content which soon became known as German flavored rum and which were shipped at an alcohol content of 75–80% by volume.

Now subject to German regulations, the rum producers were confronted with a monopoly law that demanded that alcohol imports should be taxed according to weight. It was obvious that rum should not only be reduced but should be blended with other, neutral alcohol distilled in Flensburg. Due to the predominant aromatic intensity of the original rum from Jamaica, only small quantities of it were necessary to give the Verschnitt or blend a distinctive profile.

In the 1920s Rum-Verschnitt became a famous and highly sought-after spirit and various brands such as Hansen, Pott, Balle, Nissen, Asmussen, Andresen, Sonnberg, J.C. Schmidt, and others gained in importance. After World War II around 30 companies resumed production. However in the 1960s the first takeovers occurred, and in 1974 the Grün and Dethleffsen families joined together and the famous brands of Hansen, Balle, and five others came to be produced by one company.

Taken over by the Berentzen distilleries in 1998, the company now exclusively concentrates on the Hansen brands with their successful Hansen-Präsident—named after Hindenburg. Der Gute Pott, Der Milde Balle, Boddel 40, Asmussen, and various smaller brands continue to supply the German market. In Flensburg only the family firm of A.H. Johannsen (founded in 1878) has survived.

In the courtyard of a famous Flensburg rum company at the beginning of the 20th century when the city still had around 30 producers.

## Rum qualities in Germany

Original rum is imported as white or matured rum from the country of origin and has to be bottled at its original strength of 72–4% vol. alcohol. The term "original" appears only on this label, together with the region of origin—for example "Original Jamaica rum."

*Echter Rum* (authentic rum) is an original rum that has been reduced in Germany to a drinking strength of at least 37.5% by vol. alcohol, but usually contains 40–54% by vol. alcohol. The word *Echter* (authentic) can appear only on this label, together with the region of origin—in the case of blends with a collective label such as Echter Westindien-Rum (Authentic West Indian Rum).

Within the European Union Rum-Verschnitt can be produced only in Germany. It consists of a mixture of original rum, neutral alcohol, water, and caramel coloring in which rum must form at least 5% of the total alcohol content.

## Original Stroh

Austria's most famous spirit is based on several varieties of overseas rum blended and refined with essences and aromatic substances. The company began with Sebastien Stroh in 1832. In 1997 the Klagenfurt-based company merged with Stock in Linz, where its headquarters now are. Stroh is exported into 30 different countries. Austrian Original Stroh, formerly Inländer Rum (obtainable in strengths 80, 60, 40% by vol. alcohol), is a spirit produced in the country that is predominantly used to flavor cakes and baked items, in Rumtopf, and also as a mixer drink; 80% Stroh is particularly suitable for use in burnt punch.

# Mojito and planter's punch

The Creole people have preserved their predilection for rum. On all the islands it is the favorite drink of the native population and a significant percentage of production is consumed in the country of origin, although tourists now are eager to help too. As early as the 18th century, when slavery was still recent history, the first bars were set up. For example, in 1763 a dozen existed on Martinique in Fort Royal, now known as Fort-de-France, whereas in the capital city of the time Saint-Pierre, there were 40.

Rum is no longer a source of comfort for those having to do hard manual labor, but a lifestyle drink. On the Antilles it is hardly ever drunk neat. It is served in the form of punch. The only thing that this punch has in common with the hot beverage served in northern countries, however, is the rum. Punch is thought to have been derived from a Sanskrit word—Indians too were used as cheap labor on the sugar-cane plantations—and refers to the five main ingredients.

Cuba's Mojito too is a traditional punch. It is possible that its name derives from a diminutive of *mojo*, a blend of spices stirred into lime juice. The ingredient that gives Mojito its quite special aroma is *hierbabuena* (the good spice, *Mentha nemorosa*), a Cuban variety of mint that is milder and sweeter than traditional peppermint and is a stock Cuban traditional herbal remedy.

## Ti punch and fine rums

On the Lesser Antilles, which include the islands of Guadeloupe and Martinique, people clink glasses of ti punch. This is a variant with a shot of molasses, and a dash of lime in addition to the rum. Usually, it is the clear, fruity, young rum that is used here, but indeed many Creoles now prefer three-year-matured, golden or amber colored rum, just as on the other islands often three- to five-year-old rums are used in the punch.

Not only does every island have its own special regional recipe for punch, each family cultivates its own formula and, what is more, has its own preferred brand of rum. If you visit a traditional bar and name your brand, the waiter is likely to bring over an entire bottle. As on the Antilles delicious fruits grow in abundance, it is an obvious thing to mix their juices with rum to make planter's punch. Only in hotels and elegant bars is it served with a pretty little garnish. Usually it is pushed across the counter in a large beaker. The quality of the rum and the freshly squeezed juices make all the difference.

# Cachaça

Cachaça is often made by smaller producers who harvest the sugar cane by hand, as is the case here in Vale Uruguai.

Neat or as caipirinha with lime, sugar, and ice—cachaça is, without contest, Brazil's national drink. Around 30,000 producers supply the market, including some major industrial firms, but the almost 5,000 brands on the market predominantly originate in small and sometimes tiny distilleries. More than 340 million gallons (1.3 billion liters) per year are produced, making cachaça the third major spirit in the world in terms of quantity, after vodka and soju. Only 1% of it, a paltry 3.4 million gallons (13 million liters), is exported. The Brazilians drink their cachaça themselves. Their folk drink has a long tradition, even if it has been fashionable only since the 1990s.

Cachaça—pronounced cashassa—is a distillate from sugar-cane juice and Brazil is the world's foremost sugar-cane producer. As in the islands of the Caribbean, the sweet grass was brought to the country by the colonial overlords. Around the middle of the 16th century, sugar-cane cultivation and the slave trade had become established on the coastal plains. Even then how quickly sugar-cane juice ferments must have been known. The first spirits were distilled back at the beginning of the 17th century when rough alcohol was dispensed to African slaves as a

motivation for their forced labor on the plantations and in the mines. Soon, the infamous trade triangle encompassed Brazil too, with "aguardente de cana" being used as currency for new slaves and the distilleries expanding alongside the sugar-cane plantations.

The spirit very quickly gained in popularity among the Brazilian population too. Portugal which recognized in cachaça a serious competitor for its own wine and Bagaçeira, a Portuguese wine spirit, tried in vain to repress its production. "Finally Portugal decided to levy a tax on production," says cachaça expert Marlene Elvira Seitz. "The extra income helped finance, for instance, the recovery in 1756 of earthquake-ravaged Lisbon. In the Brazilian war of independence from Portuguese rule toward the end of the 18th century, in which taxes were a major issue, duties on cachaça were an important factor. Soon it was a sign of patriotism to drink cachaça and to drink wine was to show your loyalty to Portugal. Cachaça became a symbol for the Brazilian independence movement." After the abolition of slavery that started in Brazil in 1888, cachaça remained the drink of ordinary people.

# Green sugar-cane juice

The most extensive sugar-cane plantations were in northeastern and central Brazil. Even today there are some plantations the size of which is difficult to imagine. The famous family-owned brand Ypióca, for instance, operates cultivations the size of Belgium. From the captaincy of São Vincente (now São Paulo) and the province of Pernambuco, cachaça production spread throughout the country, with a second stronghold in Minas Gerais, north of Rio de Janeiro. Nowadays the state of São Paulo is the major producer, followed at some distance by Pernambuco, Ceará, Minas Gerais, and Paraiba.

By contrast with the majority of rums, cachaça is based not on molasses but on freshly pressed and immediately fermented sugar-cane juice. Depending on the region, harvesting is between May and November, when the green sugar cane is cut short just above the ground and the leaves are removed as they contain no sugar.

In recent years several projects have been launched in Brazil to encourage organic culture of sugar cane. Cooperatives are taking part in these, enabling the associated small farmers to retain the fertility of their fields while obtaining a better income. Harvesting manually, they dispense with the normal burning of the fields to protect soil and wildlife. They compost the cut residues or leave them on the field as mulch.

Usually the distilleries are close to the fields and the harvested sugar cane can be processed the very same day. For traditionally produced Cachaça Artesanal the sugar cane must first be washed. Then it is fed into the mill, where it is chopped and crushed before the *garapa*, the juice, is pressed out with, in Brazil too, a little water being added to improve sugar extraction.

The filtered garapa is placed in fermentation tanks. While some small producers rely on natural yeast, cultivated yeast is generally used as well as natural additives that promote its development. Traditional maize flour—*fubá*—is the most usual, but other sorts of grain are also being used now, in particular rice starch. Sometimes freshly pressed lemon juice is used to improve the pH value. However, larger operations use chemical acidifiers. Each operation has its own special fermentation recipe that gives additional aromas to the "vinho" that is completely fermented in one or a maximum of three days.

First the sugar cane is crushed, diluted with a little water, and pressed. The juice is fermented and can then be distilled.

# Of alembics and exotic woods

Terra Vermelha is an outstanding example of an organic distillery.

Even at this stage, the qualities of the sugarcane wine (it is called simply *vinho*) can differ widely. It is approximately 8% by volume alcohol and forms the basis of all cachaças. Finally, distillation and further processing ensure a very wide range of different qualities. Larger distilleries are equipped with fast, cost-efficient continuous distillation plants (column distillation) and supply the majority of cachaça, dominating the domestic as well as the export market.

Smaller operations, focusing on delivering higher quality, use *alambiques*, traditional, often wood-fired stills that distill in batches. It is an art in itself to keep the constant temperature essential in perfect distillation. The distillery master naturally, in the production of cachaça as for other spirits, separates the first fraction or heads (*caheca*) and the last fraction or tails (*cauda*) and uses only the middle or heart (*coracão*) of the distillate. In the case of many simple traditionally made cachaças these are often unreduced or only slightly reduced raw spirits. They are then distilled a second time for the better qualities. Where the sugar cane is of high quality, in particular when it originates in an organic cultivation, this is not necessary. High-proof Cachaça Artesanal is distilled in multistage *alambiques*. In the quality-focused opera-

tions, heads and tails are not distilled again but processed further to make biofuel (ethanol), in the production of which Brazil is the world leader. However, ever more rain forests are being felled, and small farms expropriated, for the purpose.

The water-clear distillate that runs from the condenser is usually rough, raw, and barely drinkable. While clearer spirits do continue to come on the market, the better qualities undergo a maturing phase in wooden barrels. To be labeled as barrel matured—*envelhecida em barril*—cachaça has to be aged for at least a year in a cask. The special quality provided by maturing may be attributed to the exotic varieties of wood used (see box on this page) that can give the spirit a high level of quite unique complexity, together with the increasing mellowness and balance that come with age.

The water-clear, freshly distilled cachaça drains from the condenser.

## Coarse and fine differences

In Brazil people speak not only of cachaça. It is also known as *aguardente*, which is both the general Portuguese term for an alcoholic spirit and, in Brazil, also a synonym for sugarcane spirit, although of an inferior variety. Both terms are legally authorized and regulated. Cachaça must be of 38–48% by vol. alcohol and *aguardente* may be up to 54%. The popular word for the spirit, *pinga*, literally means a drop, and usually refers to cheap aguardente. As cachaça is based on fresh sugar cane, its aromas—reminiscent of blossom, exotic fruits, and honey—also give it its distinctive profile. The better the distillation, the finer its expression. One ton/tonne of sugar cane gives approximately 26 gallons (100 liters) of distillate at 40% by vol. alcohol. One acre yields on average about 185 tons (1 hectare, 75 tonnes). Cachaças from the famous regions of Pernambuco and Minas have a very good reputation. Golden, amber, or golden brown cachaça is matured in wood and now has cult status. Particularly fine are the clear cachaças matured in wood that does not give off its color, such as Jequitibá rosa. These are often expensive rarities that are seldom sold abroad and are enjoyed neat.

## Exotic woods

The types of wood used to make barrels for cachaça maturation, and their influence:

· Balsamo (*Myroxylon balsamum*, Tolubalsam): a yellowish gold color, strong influence on taste
· Ipê Amarelo (*Tabebuia serratifolia*, Trumpet tree): orangey tone, mild taste
· Vinhático (*Platymenia reticulata*, yellowwood): yellow coloration, creates a typical cachaça taste
· Imburana (*Amburana cearensis*): reduces acidity and alcohol content; the taste becomes more mellow and well rounded
· Jequitibá rosa (*Cariniana legalis*): purifies the cachaça, which retains its flavor and does not change color; the cachaça becomes milder; the finest wood for maturation
· Carvalho (oak): classic barrique maturation with golden tone, spicy and roasted aromas

Marlene Elvira Seitz

# Caipirinha and fine cachaças

Caipirinha is the agent that helped cachaça to international stardom. This refreshing short drink was only able to achieve such widespread fame when its second essential ingredient, lime, became a permanent occupant of fruit and vegetable displays the world over. This unobtrusive and hard to pinpoint event took place sometime in the 1990s, and since then cachaça has claimed its place in every bar and discotheque, even if it is merely as a component of caipirinha and, for that very reason, only in the most basic qualities. A Brazilian saying goes like this: *quanto pior a cachaça, melhor a caipirinha*—the poorer the cachaça, the better the caipirinha. Anyone who has ever tried a caipirinha made with a very good cachaça will doubt the wisdom of proverbs. It may be that the origin of the saying should be sought in the origin of the drink. Its name derives from the word *caipira*, meaning a hillbilly, softened with the diminutive suffix *inha*. Up to now, cachaça has predominantly been made in small rural factories, this usually crude raw spirit being sold mainly in the local area. Brazilians swear by these individualistic cachaça suppliers and point out that the rougher brands make a tastier mixture. A really convincing caipirinha is always based on a good, perfectly distilled cachaça with a clear, crisp, intensive aroma, in which the sugar cane from which it was made can be detected. In Brazil caipirinha is never served with brown sugar as is customary in Europe, but only white, fine-grained cane sugar. It is enjoyed rather sweet. The best limes for the purpose are small and thin skinned and should be unsprayed. They are cut into slices, only lightly squeezed, and their juice is stirred in with the sugar. Whereas crushed ice is used in other countries, which makes the caipirinha lighter, in Brazil ice cubes are preferred, allowing more space for the cachaça. Batidas too are based on cachaça, and are mixed with fruits, fruit juice or milk, sugar, and ice.

## Caipirinha

2 bsp cane sugar
1 organic lime, sliced
2 oz. (6 cl) cachaça
Crushed ice or
ice cubes
1 pinch cinnamon
(optional)

Place the cane sugar in a beaker. Add the slices of lime and crush them lightly with a pestle. Mix the juice into the sugar and then add the Cachaça, stirring well until all of the sugar is dissolved. Top up with crushed ice or ice cubes and stir. Sprinkle with a pinch of cinnamon if desired, or use lime peel.

# Selected cachaças

Outside Brazil, different cachaça brands and qualities have hitherto been of little importance. Bars tended to stock the cheapest cachaça possible for making caipirinha. Gradually a change is taking place, not least due to committed importers. At the same time Brazil is also showing interest in expanding its exports. The range is growing in Europe and in America, and with it an awareness of the considerable differences existing among cachaças. In addition to the market leaders, intended only for mixing, Pirassunga (available on the export market as Cachaça 51), Pitú, and Velho Barreiro—as well as a phalanx of more basic competing qualities—better quality products are also beginning to find their way abroad. Some examples are Sagatiba, Rochinha, Beluza Pura, Fabulosa, Fazenda Mãe de Ouro, and Lebion.

### Iguaçu
A collective organic project in Capanema in southern Brazil, not far from the famous Iguaçu waterfalls. Agronomist César Colussi produces the cachaça by double distillation, which lends the fine distillate very intensive aromas of exotic fruits, making it excellent for caipirinha. It also tastes good neat.

### Terra Vermelha
The Engenho Terra Vermelha, just 124 acres (50 ha) in area, with its sugar-cane plantations, is in the center of an area of red soil in the southern state of Paraná best known for its coffee and soya plantations, and operates on an organic basis. Its fine cachaça is best enjoyed neat. It is matured for six to seven months in casks made from Jequitibá rosa wood, which gives it a highly balanced quality without robbing it of the precious sugar-cane aroma.

### Colônia Nova
An association of small sugar-cane farmers in the Vale do Rio Uruguai in the southern state of Rio Grande do Sul, near the border with Argentina, focusing on organic cultivation and traditional cachaça production methods. Its brand Tropical Brazils has a clear quality, with a distinct sugar-cane taste for mixing, and as well there is a version that has been matured for four years in oak barrels and is spicy and smoky.

### Ypióca
A family firm founded in 1846 with sugar-cane plantations the size of Belgium. Even the standard versions, Crystal and Oro, designed for mixing, are aged for 12 months in balsa or other exotic wood barrels. The 150, launched for the company's 150th anniversary, is matured for six years in wood and is best enjoyed neat.

### Nêga Fulô
The Fazenda Soledade distillery, founded in 1827 in the state of Rio, uses a fractional distillation method for its cachaça, maturing it for three years in oak barrels, which gives it its mellow, well-rounded taste. Although the recommendation is to enjoy it neat, it also makes a convincing caipirinha.

### Cachaça 51
Founded around 1900 by the German Müller family, this brand produced in the city of Pirassununga in the state of São Paulo has crept into first place in Brazil. With its annual sales of around 250 million, it is also among the leading spirits in the world for caipirinha.

### Cachaça do Box 32
The name refers to a famous bar in the southern Brazilian state of Santa Caterina, Box 32, opened in 1984 in the market hall of the city of Fiorianópolis. Since 1990 they have been producing their own cachaça by traditional methods. It is distilled twice in copper pot stills and then matured for two years in oak barrels, which gives it its golden color, mellowness, and discreet vanilla aroma.

# Tequila and mezcal

For more than 8,000 years the versatile agave has been cultivated in Central America. This fruit's sweet flesh can be eaten and its fibers are woven into fabrics and carpets, braided into cords and threads, and processed into paper. The leaves have been used to cover roofs, its thorns have been used as sewing needles. Agaves have been used as medicinal plants. Their fermented juice, *pulque*, played an important role in the Aztec religion as an intoxicating and sacrificial drink. After an initiation into the art of distilling by the Spanish conquistadors, agaves were made into mezcal, and later tequila. Since then, both have become established as Mexican national drinks. They have become part of the cultural heritage of Mexico.

The Olmecs, around 3,000 years ago, are said to have drunk the juice of the agave. This juice is obtained by scratching the core or, more poetically, the heart of the plant. As the liquid begins to ferment quickly, it can be assumed that they were also already familiar with the milky pulque. According to Aztec legend, agaves owe their existence, shape, bluish color, and heavenward growth to fallen stars. But the pulque itself was considered to have been heaven sent. It is said that lightning struck an agave and set its heart on fire. A wonderful nectar remained, which the astounded native people acknowledged as a gift from the gods. Therefore they drank it with reverence, celebrated its taste, and considered themselves to be transported into a state that brought them nearer to their gods. It is almost certain that the priests, warriors, and wise men largely reserved the pulque for themselves, as too much intoxication for everyone is not good. Ordinary people were only permitted to enter an intoxicated state of rapture at the end of the calendar year, at the time when dead ancestors were honored.

Not long after the conquest of Mexico by Hernando Cortés in 1521, the Spaniards brought the first pot stills to the country. Initial attempts to distill the low alcohol, 5–7% by vol. pulque and obtain a stronger spirit failed. The milky agave brew was simply unsuitable. The reason for this, as was later discovered, is the long-chain molecular structure of the starch. It was not until the agave hearts were cooked over wood fires before the juice was extracted and fermented that the desired result was achieved and the liquid could be distilled. This produced a spirit with a characteristic smoky aroma referred to in its name: *mescal* in the local Nahuátl language is the word for agave heart.

The production of "vino mescal" quickly became widespread throughout Mexico, but was particularly concentrated in the west, in an area known as Jalisco that the Spaniards, who conquered it in 1530, renamed Nueva Galicia, valuing it highly due to its rich silver mines. Nowadays the region bears its old name once again, but it owes its significance to the Spaniards. When Don Pedro Sanches de Tagle, Marqués of Altamira, cultivated agaves in 1600 on his Hacienda de Cuisillos in Nueva Galicia, purely to distill them, he could have had no idea just what he was starting. Governor Nuno de Guzmán had a better idea when he levied the first tax on mezcal wine in 1608. Not long afterward distillation was officially approved in order to be able to control its production better and tax it more efficiently.

With the growing popularity of mezcal, the considerable tax revenue increased too. Nevertheless, the distillation of spirits in Mexico was a thorn in the flesh of the Spanish crown, which believed that it could make more money in the colonies with the sale of Spanish wines and spirits, and so prohibited the production of mezcal in 1785. However, the Spanish government had miscalculated and in 1792 the new King Ferdinand IV had to reauthorize distilling. Three years later he signed a license granted to José-Maria Guadaloupe Cuervo from Tequila to distill mezcal. And that was how the modern story of mezcal and tequila began.

# The home of tequila

Page 472: Agaves are the
secret behind both Tequila
and Mescal.

Tequila is Mexico's hallmark. Like all Mexican products, it is subject to NORMA, a control system that issues a number to every single bottle. This N.O.M. (Norma Oficial Mexicana) enables each bottle of tequila to be traced back to its producer. The law has set out precise rules on the production of tequila, stipulating where and how it should be made.

Its main production area, which has been declared Denominación de Origen, is the state of Jalisco on the Pacific side of Mexico. There are also 56 other communities in the neighboring states of Guanajuato, Nayarit, and Michoacán. Tamaulipas on the Gulf of Mexico is another. However, there are only two distilleries in Guanajuato and one in Tamaulipas, while the other 117 operations are concentrated in Jalisco. All other agave spirits are referred to as mezcal, which also has a Denominación de Origen and is mainly distilled in the area round the city of Oaxaca, even if its production is officially authorized for the states of Guerrero, Durango, San Luis Potosi, and Zacatecas. Jalisco is one of Mexico's most fascinating states, and has a flourishing and broadranging economy producing industrial, artisanal, special artistic, and craft and agricultural commodities. Moreover, Jalisco has a wonderfully varied landscape, and tourism is a continually growing source of income. From the impressive, in part still unspoilt Pacific coast, the land rises to the Sierra Madre. Jalisco's Spanish-founded capital, Guadalajara, with its 1.7 million inhabitants, the second-largest city in Mexico, used to be the most important market for tequila and itself has two distilleries. The city lies in a valley at an altitude of approximately 5,600 feet (1,700 m). It is surrounded by mountains, and to the east and north by a

2,600-foot (800 m) high mountain plateau that has developed into the most important agave cultivation area.

## Agaves as far as the eye can see

The small city of Tequila is 50 miles (80 km) to the northwest. It lies at the foot of the extinct volcano Cerro de Tequila, the cone of which towers about 4,000 feet (1,200 m) above it, in the middle of the gentle hilly landscape with narrow valleys that mostly contain agave plantations. In 2006 UNESCO declared the agave area, together with historic tequila production works between Tequila and the Rio Grande, a world cultural heritage site. Both have shaped the landscape since the 16th century and are an essential part of Mexico's national identity. This was the organization's reason for its decision.

The 6,000 fields on which the blue agave *Agave tequilana* F.A.C. Weber required for tequila is cultivated add up to a total of over 106,000 acres (43,000 ha), on which 150 million agaves thrive at altitudes between 2,300 and 9,500 feet (700–2,900 m) above sea level. It is not rare for individual fields to stretch over an area of 490 acres (200 ha).

In 1944 the Mexican government decreed that only agave distillate from the state of Jalisco could be designated tequila. The first official guidelines on its production followed three years later. In 1977 the authorities raised the status of tequila to a recognized designation of origin, but it was not until 1994 that the Consejo Regulador del Tequila that strictly monitors its production was formed. The brand has also received international protection since then, correcting a past omission. This was necessary as, out of the annual production of 52 million gallons (195 million liters), nowadays more than four fifths are exported. The USA is the main client, but tequila is exported to around 100 other countries. The increase in demand has driven prices up, so that ironically many Mexicans can no longer afford tequila—even though the spirit distilled from the fermented juice of the agave is a part of the Mexican way of life.

Only a certain blue agave variety is authorized for use in tequila and is cultivated on extensive tracts of land.

# Blue agaves and drunken heroes

Don José Antonio de Cuervo received from the Spanish king in 1758 a tract of land in the region of Jalisco. That was the beginning of tequila's rise to success.

When José Maria Guadaloupe Cuervo, son of José Antonio, opened the first distillery in the small town of Tequila in 1795, he soon found that he had imitators. Yet for the *tabernos*, as the distillers were known, these were uncertain times. Not only during the Mexican struggle for independence that began in 1810 and rumbled on for 11 years, but also during the decades afterward, the political situation remained unstable. Troops and bands generally supplied their requirements for mezcal by confiscating it. Although independence in 1821 saw demand for home-produced spirits rise, as there were hardly any imports, it was not until Porfirio Diaz came to power that a period of economic upswing began in 1876 that would also benefit the distilleries.

Hardly any distilleries from the foundation period survived. One of these was Taberna La Cruz founded in 1805, purchased in 1873 by Cenobio Sauza, which survives even today as La Perseverancia. In those days mezcal was distilled even in Tequila, out of

various sorts of agave. Each distillery experimented and selected its favorites. It is said to have been Sauza who, at the end of the 19th century, finally concentrated on the blue agave (*maguey azul*), which was classified in 1902 by French military physician and botanist Frédéric Albert Constantin Weber, and was later named after him. Gradually other tabernos followed Sauza's example. Many ceased to produce aguardiente from sugar cane and moved over to the promising Weber agave whose fermented juice was double distilled. It was not long before their products distinguished themselves significantly from the mezcals of other regions. Even in Mexico City the spirits from Tequila soon became legendary.

## National symbol

Cuervo claimed right from the beginning to be the greatest producer, a position that he has been able to defend to date. In the 1880s alone, he supplied 10,000 barrels of "vino mescal" per year to Guadalajara. By 1910 the

Mexican revolutionary leader Pancho Villa (1878–1923) on horseback; photograph, January 1, 1911.

number of tabernas in Jalisco had grown to almost 90. The introduction of bottling from 1906 made a decisive contribution to their success. The Mexican revolution once more threw the country into a phase of political and economic uncertainty, and most distillers had to cease operation. Yet the spirit from the blue agave owes its legendary reputation precisely to those troubled times. It inspired and sustained the heroes of the revolution. Between 1930 and 1960 Mexican movies glorified hard heroes, and tequila features significantly as a rule in at least one scene of brotherhood and comradeship in each, and this proved to be excellent promotion for the spirit.

After the economic crisis of 1929 tequila profited, as did Cuban rum, from the Prohibition in the neighboring United States. Demand rose sharply in the 1930s, which entailed a supply bottleneck in blue agaves. If tequila was originally distilled 100% from blue agaves, the state—in this emergency situation—permitted a stretching of the quality of sugar required for the alcohol content to include other plants. The mixto was born and, although it was less authentic and of poorer quality, it developed surprisingly quickly into an export hit and its production began in earnest.

When, during the course of World War II, imports of spirits from Europe into the USA became scarce, tequila was able to gain a stronger foothold there. At the end of the 1940s the margarita cocktail conquered the United States, starting with California, and in a very short time achieved such popularity that the export of tequila, or rather of mixto, rose considerably.

A decade later it was the example of the beatnik generation of Jack Kerouac and William S. Burroughs that cranked up tequila consumption. In 1968 the Olympic Games helped Mexico in general and tequila in particular to hitherto unprecedented fame. Tequila became a youth culture drink, enjoyed with salt and lemon or two-handedly with Sangrita, but always downed in one. It was not until the boom in the tourist trade of the 1980s, in particular from the USA, that high-quality brands with 100% agave opened up a new interest in tequila as a premium spirit.

Tequila is usually drunk from small shot glasses and is often downed in one.

# Tequila's successes and setbacks

The city of Tequila is a delightful tourist destination, not just for those who appreciate the spirit of the agave.

Tequila has become a bustling small city of 20,000 inhabitants, but in some parts it has retained its friendly village atmosphere, regardless of the world fame brought to it by its fiery spirit. It is now trying to attract tourists. The Tequila Express already travels in every weekend from Guadalajara, and the Tequila Trail guides foreign visitors to the appropriate locations. The Mexicans are convinced that tequila, its birthplace, and its culture have to be experienced if you wish to understand the Mexican soul.

Tequila has emerged as a major economic factor. Over the past 25 years the number of *fábricas*, as the modern tequila distilleries are known, has tripled to around 100 operations. Yet tequila's recent success story has not been without its setbacks and imponderables. Part of this stems from the length of time, 8–12 years, it takes for an agave plant to mature. Production of the raw materials therefore can respond only clumsily to the supply and demand of tequila. For the farm-

ers it was often safer to plant maize or beans, especially as tequila producers were able to dictate prices for a time. In 1996 angry farmers erected barricades in front of tequila factories to protest against the companies lowering the price of agave hearts from 1,000 pesos per ton/tonne (approx. 70 euros at the end of the 1980s) to 600 pesos. Only when a guaranteed price increase of 30% was granted were the farmers satisfied. Three years later the price had climbed to 3,500 and by 2001 to 5,000 pesos, and nowadays it is calculated by much smaller units. It has reached the equivalent of up to 1,400 euros per ton/tonne.

## Controls and crises

Such price increases had serious consequences. The best-known entry brands of 100% blue agave tequila came under pressure. Their producers did not want to pass the costs on to the consumer. They therefore decided to add sugar from other plants to their tequilas, transforming them into mixtos. This aroused the protest of a group of small, quality oriented tequila producers who pleaded openly for a tightening up of the rules governing production and for obligatory bottling in Mexico. Their spokesman Don Jesus Lopez Roman, owner of the San Matías distillery founded in 1884, was killed in 1997 in a gangland-style shooting in front of his distillery.

In the same year the control board decreed internationally that a mixto had to contain at least 51% blue agave and in the following year introduced stringent controls that resulted in the temporary closure of some distilleries and a prohibition on the sale of 67 bottled brands. Since then the Consejo Regulador del Tequila has made enormous efforts to control even tequila exported in tanks and bottled outside Mexico, and so to ensure that it corresponds to the stipula-

tions governing the country's first Denominación de Origen.

Shortly before the turn of the millennium, agave farmers found themselves facing a new problem. Weakened by propagation from cuttings, the *Agave tequilana* F.A.C. Weber became susceptible to diseases such as T.M.A. (*Tristeza y Muerte de Agave*—wilting and death of the agave) caused by a fungus. This has reached catastrophic proportions and now approximately 40% of all blue agaves in Mexico have fallen victim to it. Affected plants die within a few months. The steeply climbing prices for *piñas*, the agave hearts, are a consequence of this acute threat facing 50,000 farming families. While they are demanding a large-scale state project for the restoration of the plantations, the large tequila companies— some of which are already struggling against shortages of supply—are exerting pressure on the government to reduce the obligatory proportion of blue agaves in mixto. Many small tequila producers see this as a loss of identity that they are not prepared to accept. Despite these grave problems, tequila is experiencing a boom. While the major mixto brands are gaining ground internationally, demand for premium and super premium tequilas is also flourishing. The range of 100% agave tequilas that have to be bottled in Mexico, by contrast with the mixto varieties, is greater than ever and is selling at constantly rising prices. About half of the overall production goes to the USA, but Europeans too are showing an increasing interest in tequila. Bottling into extravagant, often hand-blown bottles is also kindling the market. In 2006 Tequila Ley.925 brought out its six-year matured Pasión Azteca in a limited edition of 33 bottles. Some of them were made from pure platinum. They can be personally delivered at a price of US$225,000. The company is now planning a $1 million bottle. There is certainly no other spirit for which there is such a great divergence between production costs and end price.

The tequila phenomenon is characterized by ever poorer basic qualities on the one hand, ever more expensive, luxury bottlings on the other hand, and around 1,000 different brands on the market.

Bottom left: World record bottle of Pasión Azteca.

Bottom right: It is hoped that agave disease can be combated with resistant new cultivations.

# Agave abundance

Agaves grow in the wild in South and Central America. They are not cacti but succulents, classified with the lily and amaryllis families before they were given their own genus, *Agavaceae*, which includes more than 400 types. The value of the agave has been known in Mexico for at least 8,000 years. Here, where the plant is called "maguey," "mescal," or "agave," there are around 140 different varieties of which nowadays only the slender, greenish blue *Agave tequilana* F.A.C. Weber is permitted for use to produce tequila. Mezcal may be made from other types of agave, or their juice is fermented and sold as pulque.

Agaves will grow to an age of 8–15 years old. The lance-like thorny leaves reach a length of between 5 and 6 feet (1.5–1.8 m). Their diameter can exceed 10 feet (3 m). It is not until almost the end of their life that they develop a tall inflorescence and fruit, the *quiote*, after which they die off.

Agaves reproduce less by seed, as these appear far too rarely, than from shoots growing from the axils of dead leaves. The young plants developing in this way are separated out in the rainy season between the months of June and October.

## Harvest

The harvester, the *jimador*, checks to see whether the plants are beginning to put forth blooms. If so he will cut off the flower at once. This makes the agave heart swell even more. When the leaves have rust colored spots near their center and it looks as if the plant has shriveled, it is at its optimum ripeness. It is time for the harvest. The plant is now 8–12 years old and it is destroyed by harvesting. Long-term planning is all the more important in order to ensure continuous yields.

The jimador takes up his *coa*, a special, round, razor-sharp ax with a long handle. First he separates the agave from its roots by pushing aside the plant with one foot, then wielding the coa. With precision blows he chops off the long, fleshy, sharp leaves until

On harvesting, the agaves are first separated from their roots, then the *jimador* removes the leaves with a sharp axe, the *coa*.

all that is left is the *piña*, the heart of the agave, which at first glance looks like an outsize pineapple—*piña* is the Spanish word for pineapple or fir cone. An experienced *jimador* takes about four minutes to harvest an agave and to trim it ready for transport.

## Processing

In lower lying valleys, piñas may weigh around 77–165 lb (35–75 kg). On the high plateau around the city of Tequila they may weigh as much as 110–200 lb (50–90 kg). They are transported by lorry to the distillery, where they are first halved or quartered and then loaded into vast ovens or pressure cookers known as autoclaves.

Slow cooking of the agave at approximately 140 °F (60 °C) is necessary so that the starch contained in their fibers can be converted to sugar. In the stone ovens that are steam heated this process takes 36–48 hours, depending on the size of the hearts, resulting in a flow of sweet liquid from the agave flesh which is drained off. Finally the agaves are allowed to cool for 24 hours.

If the agaves are cooked in autoclaves, the fermentation time can be reduced by half or by three quarters. This process does have a negative effect on the quality of the subsequent distillate, at least according to traditionalists.

The cooked, now dark brown agaves are shredded and crushed. Heavy millstones used to serve this purpose, but nowadays machines are used similar to those for sugar cane. As with sugar cane, water is added at this stage, to facilitate sugar extraction. In this way, *aguamiel* or honey water is obtained, together with the pressed fibers. At one time the honey water—the sweet liquid from the cooking process—and fibers were fermented and distilled together, which was one of the reasons why this was such a lengthy process. However, the distilleries, with a very few exceptions, have now started to separate the juice from the fibers and to carry out fermentation with a comparatively clear juice that is easy to pump.

The agave hearts are known as *piñas*. They are baked in large ovens in order to break down their starches into sugar.

# 100% tequila and mixto

The fábricas swear by tequila consisting of 100% blue agave, fermented with natural yeast existing in the vats that have been used over the years, from which however they have often cultivated their own strains. Depending on the variety of yeast and temperature, fermentation can last from 5 to 12 days and has a significant impact on the aromas of the *mosto* or must and the subsequent tequila. Soil, altitude, climate, location, and also the degree of maturity and time of harvesting—as well as the cooking method—are other factors affecting the character of the aroma.

As soon as the agave must is fully fermented, it is filtered and pumped into the pot still. Distillation is in two cycles: first the *ordinario*, which is between 20 and 30% alcohol by vol., condenses. It is distilled the second time into tequila. As with all fractional distillation processes, the distiller separates off the heads and tails (*cabeza* and *cola*), and only collects the heart (*corazon*). Traditionally tequila is distilled with an alcohol content of 55% by vol.—i.e. the heart is rather great, which gives the distillate more bite and aroma—but also means that it contains more fusel oil. Modern producers distill at a higher degree, often as much as three times as high, in order to achieve greater mellowness (and more neutrality) and finally to reduce the distillate to a drinkable strength. The American market in particular prefers more mellow qualities. On average 15 lb (7 kg) of agave hearts are required for 2 pints (1 liter) of tequila.

Maturation has considerable influence on the fragrance and flavor of the tequila. Many aficionados swear by the young, white, unmatured qualities because these have the purest agave aromas. After a few months in a small barrel made from American, or more rarely French, oak the tequila will take on roasted and spicy notes that become ever more dominant as the maturation period lengthens. However, at the same time it gains in mellowness and elegance. Only rarely is maturation extended to more than three years.

## A mixto history

Mixto was born when demand for tequila exceeded supplies of agaves. In the 1970s the Mexican government permitted sugar from other plants to be added to tequila, up to 49%. Since then methods of production and marketing have varied. In the case of mixto, costs are kept as low as possible, which has resulted in some changes in the production process. The most cost-effective production method is as follows:

The piñas are fast cooked in large autoclaves and the aguamiel is extracted after cooling. It is pumped into fermentation tanks and 49% other sugars dissolved in water are added. The best of these are industrial sugar and maize syrup, but most frequently granulated cane sugar is used. The entire mixture is thinned down until the sugar concentration is 6–10%, which makes the work easier for the yeast.

For the fermentation commercial yeast is used and nitrocompound accelerators are added that ensure rapid development of the yeast bacteria, which then succeed in reducing the fermentation period to 24 hours or less. The must obtained in this way is then continuously distilled in modern column distilleries and bottled as quickly as possible. Very little remains of what made up the original quality of a tequila; however, this process does save well over half the production costs of the traditional agave spirit.

Many companies bottle simple, cheap, mixed tequila, as well as high-quality tequilas made from 100% agave. Some only produce cheap mixtos, others only expensive, pure agave spirits.

Opposite: top to bottom: When the must, the alcohol content of which is being checked here, is thoroughly fermented, it is distilled in pot stills. The maturing of an añejo must take place in small, oak barrels. Such expensive qualities are often labeled by hand.

# Tequila qualities and categories

**Officially, there are two qualities of tequila:**
The better and original quality is exclusively distilled from blue agaves, clearly indicated on the label: 100% agave.

The more common quality, mixto in the jargon of the trade—a term that never appears on the label—must be distilled from at least 51% blue agaves and may contain a maximum of 49% other sugars. The most widely distributed international tequila brands are mixtos. This can be deduced from the fact that unmatured mixto is exported in tanks, bottled abroad, and can be reduced to drinking strength, while all other varieties of tequila have to be bottled in the country of origin.

After maturation and processing, there are five different tequila categories, monitored by the control board:

**Plata, Blanco, White or Silver**
Clear, unmatured, uncolored tequila reduced after distillation to drinking strength and bottled quickly.

**Joven, Abocado, Oro or Gold**
Unmatured, usually colored and flavored with caramel and/or other additives, not to be confused with matured tequila.

**Reposado or Rested**
Matured for at least 2, and a maximum of 12, months in large or small barrels made from American or French oak, with a pale golden tone, mellow character, and a fine agave taste.

**Añejo or Aged**
Matured for at least a year in oak barrels with a maximum capacity of 160 gallons (600 liters)—usually former bourbon or, more rarely, cognac barrels—this is somewhat deeper gold in tone, with a more balanced, more mellow character, complex aromas with vanilla, and spicy notes.

**Extra Añejo or Ultra-Aged**
The newest category, matured for at least three years in oak barrels with a maximum capacity of 160 gallons (600 liters), appropriately dark, complex and long, previously often marketed as reserva.

Both 100% agave spirits and mixtos are available as blanco, reposado, and añejo, but only mixtos are available as oro. A reposado mixto generally has a significantly higher proportion of blue agave than 51%, whereas añejos are practically exclusively spirits made from 100% blue agave. The alcohol content of tequilas reduced with distilled water must be between 38 and 55% vol. alcohol but generally does not exceed 40%.

# Selected tequilas

This list can represent only a small selection of the 100 or so distilleries, approximately 800 individual brands, and around 200 brands bottled outside Mexico. Due to the increasing worldwide demand for premium and ultra-premium qualities, some companies exclusively offer 100% agave brands in expensive designer bottles. The distillates themselves are from long-established fábricas, while there are often variations between suppliers.

## El Conquistador

### El Conquistador Añejo

This very spicy, 18-month matured añejo with slightly sweet finale is produced by El Viejito in Atontonilco el Alto. The family firm that has been in existence since 1937 expanded considerably under Antonio Nuñez from 1973, in particular in the export market. It supplies a series of brands such as El Viejito, Hussong's, Distinct, Don Quijote; and Sierra, the leading brand on the German market. The family's greatest triumphs are the 100% agave tequilas Aguila and El Conquistador.

## Casa Herradura

### Herradura Selección Suprema

Feliciano Romo established his distillery in 1870 in the Amatitan Valley at the foot of the Tequila volcano, at Hacienda San José del Refugio, which is now a museum. Herradura, which has more than 11,000 acres (4,500 ha) of its own and a further 8,700 acres (3,500 ha) leased with a total of 25 million blue agaves, made a name for itself with 100% agave tequilas appreciated by Bing Crosby and bandleader Phil Harris back in the 1950s. The third largest producer nevertheless felt itself forced to convert its second brand, El Jimador, a leader in Mexico, to mixto. Up to now pure agave tequilas have remained under the company's own name. In 1995 Herradura launched its five-year-old oak-matured, highly complex, and elegant Selección Suprema, the first super premium tequila, which prepared the way for current luxury bottles.

## Casa Noble

### Casa Noble Blanco

Distilled by La Cofradia, this brand deserves an entry of its own. It offers only 100% agave tequilas in which selected 10-year-old plants are used, the hearts of which are cooked for 38 hours in stone ovens. Fermentation is without additives, and is followed by triple distillation. Crystal is an extraordinarily mellow tequila with clear, intensive agave aromas and is considered to be one of the best in the blanco category. Just as outstanding are the reposado, aged for 12 months in French oak barrels, and the añejo, aged for five years, both bottled in expensive, colorful porcelain decanters.

## Cabo Wabo

This brand, awarded the highest accolades, was created by rock musician Sammy Haggar for his Cabo Wabo Cantina in Cabo San Lucas. To do this, he joined forces with the Rivera family, a small tequila producer that had been distilling since 1937. In 2007 the Campari Group took over the majority shares. A very mild and crisp 100% agave spirit.

## Jose Cuervo

### 1800 Reserva Antigua Añejo

José Maria Guadaloupe Cuervo, in 1795 was the first to receive a license to distill his agave spirit. In 1812 he founded the visitor-friendly Fábrica La Rojeña where even today some of Cuervo's tequila is produced, although the majority comes from the company's second factory in Guadalajara. Fábrica Agavera Camichines is also owned by the number one mixto producer (every third bottle of tequila comes from Cuervo). It has now converted to 100% agave tequilas. Here Gran Centenario and the extremely complex, spicy, and well-balanced 1800 are produced, on the label of which the name Cuervo no longer appears.

## La Cofradia

### La Cofradia Reposado

The modern distillery, founded in 1992 in Tequila—whose owners, the Hernandez Cousins, can look back over 50 years of family tradition—has established itself as a supplier of convincing distillates marketed under various brands such as Amate, Los Dorados, and Cava de Villano. The 100% Reposado has a pleasant aroma of cooked agaves and good presence on the palate. See also Casa Noble.

### Milagro

#### Leyendra de Milagro Añejo

Milagro is a tequila company that not only knows what it wants, but also knows where to get it. In just a few years it has built up an impressive reputation with 100% agave distillates, with its three-times-distilled blanco, its reposado, and the Leyendra de Milagro Añejo Barrel Select, rested for 18 months in American oak and with very convincing mellowness and finely spiced and ripe fruity notes. The spirits are distilled in Tepatitian by Industrializadora de Agave San Isidro.

### Porfidio

#### Porfidio Plato

This extravagant brand was created by Austrian Martin Grassi, who was just 30 years old at the time. He moved to Mexico in 1990 and for a certain time began to rent distilleries and, with his own team, began to distill tequila—so to speak, following his own instinct—as a pure agave spirit. He thought up the facetious name of Ponciano Porfidio; bottled his exquisite distillates into the now famous highly symbolic cactus bottles; and gained respect, recognition, and some animosity with the quality, appearance, and high prices of his products. Since then, Grassi has founded the Destilería Ponciano Porfidio y Hijos in Puerto Vallata that combines state-of-the-art technology with the highest standards (here too he also distills an excellent rum). Award-winning, highly complex, fruity, and spicy, Porfidio Single Barrel has a distinctive agave aroma and intensive honey overtones.

### Sauza

#### Hornitos Reposado

Don Cenobia Sauza purchased an old mezcal distillery in 1873 in Tequila that he renamed La Perseverancia. It is now a modern production facility where agave hearts are cooked in just eight hours and then fermented in large stainless-steel tanks. The second-largest tequila producer distills in 1,060 gallon (4,000 liter) plants. In addition to the dominant mixtos, the company makes Hornitos, a popular, typical 100% agave reposado with a distinctive aroma of agaves. Tres Generaciónes Añejo 100% Agave is its best product, and is matured for three years. The Rancho El Indio plantation with its attractive bar is well worth a visit.

### Tequila 1921

#### 1921 Blanco

Finding a horde of treasures in the Hacienda La Colorado—including some sensational, decade-old tequilas—inspired Swiss-born Beat Aerne and a group of tequila aficionados to set up a traditional tequila factory in the state of Guanajuato using methods and equipment handed down through generations. Even the bottle they use is a replica. The distinctive properties of the agave are the main feature of the three qualities of 100% blue agave tequilas made by the Corporación Licorera in Léon. In the reposado and the reserva especial matured for 8–12 months in barrels this is associated with fine roast and spicy notes.

### Tequila Esperantó

#### Esperantó Blanco

This subsidiary of the Pastrana Group founded in 2002 in Coyoacán, the famous district of Mexico City, obtains its outstanding 100% agave tequilas from various distilleries, but in particular from the Destiladora Azteca in Tequila. The fábrica, known as El Uano, has been operated by the Orendain family since 1900 (restored between 1976 and 1978). The name of their own famous brand, Arette, is derived from the horse of the same name whose rider won a gold medal for jumping in the 1948 Olympic Games in London.

### Sierra

#### Milenario Extra Anejo

Destilerías Sierra Unidas, in the center of Guadalajara, export their tequila to 90 countries and are the leading producer in Europe. Double distillation takes place in modern copper stills. After their Antiguo, they are now marketing Milenario, a super-premium brand from selected agave fields, matured for four years in bourbon barrels. It has a convincingly complex aroma of sweet agaves and fine wood spices, and is mild and spicy to the taste with hints of chocolate and tobacco.

# Untamed mezcal

Like Scorpion, this very smoky mezcal from the Caballeros company comes with intensive citrus, earthy, and salty aromas.

Mezcal and tequila can look back over a common history—at any rate, to the time when the distilleries in Tequila insisted on the exclusive use of Weber's blue agave, making a name for themselves with it. Mezcal has remained closer to simple folk, as in almost every village and small town in its district it was and often still is produced in a timeless, traditional way that gives it its distinctive character. Since mezcal achieved Denominación de Origen status in 2005, 18 types of agave in Mexico, collectively referred to as *maguey*, may be used to make the spirit. The most widespread is espadin, and the best known is wild tobalá that produces an excellent mezcal. Its main territory is the state of Oaxaca, with 50 distilleries concentrated in Santiago Matatlán del Mezcal. These produce almost 60% of the total mezcal requirement.

## Trusted souls

A decisive factor in the aroma of mezcal is the cooking of the piñas in the *palenque*, a conical pit in the ground, 8 feet (2.5 m) deep that generally has a diameter of 11 feet 6 inches (3.5 m). In it are heated stones on which the agave hearts are layered. They are then covered with agave leaves, palm mats, and earth. They are cooked in this manner for three to five days and take on the aromas of smoke and earth. They are then left to cool for a week, covered with palm mats, during which time fermentation has already started. After this, the hearts are placed in a stone mill, where they are crushed by a millstone driven by a horse or donkey, in just the same way as tequila was generally formerly made. The pulp is mixed with a little water and fermented in large vats. After fermentation is complete, the contents are poured into the fermentation kettles made from either copper or ceramic, which rarely have a capacity exceeding 26 gallons (100 liters). On top of them is placed a copper swan neck, the *sombrero*, and they are then heated on a wood fire. The first distillation process lasts approximately 24 hours and produces clear "punta." The palenquero distills it again to obtain mezcal.

A mezcal produced in this highly traditional, artisan way has preserved its soul and has its own individual, smoky, earthy character, which clearly distinguishes it from tequila. Just as clearly is it distinguished from the increasing production of commercial mezcal which—just like tequila—is now being produced using modern ovens, fermentation tanks, and distilleries in which no more than 51% of the sugar required for the alcohol content has to originate in agaves. The legally stipulated maturity grades for mezcal—blanco, reposado, and añejo—are similar to those for tequila.

## The infamous worm

At the beginning of the 1950s mezcal bottles that contained a red or golden worm attracted much attention. This was a marketing gag by Jacobo Lozano Páez, who operated a drinks company in Mexico City. The worm is a skipper caterpillar that either eats its way through the heart of the agave—the much prized *gusano rojo*—or nourishes itself on the leaves (*gusano de oro*). Both caterpillars are considered to be particular delicacies and are sold at Zapotec markets. They do not have any special aphrodisiac or psychedelic effects, but have been a tried and trusted sales aid for cheap mezcal—however, never for tequila—just as effective as an attached sachet of Gusano salt. While top quality mezcals never contain a captive caterpillar, some bottles of the best brands of Scorpion have been embellished with this non-nutritious additive.

# Selected mezcals

## Del Maguey

The company founded by American artist Ron Cooper in Oaxaca focuses entirely on mezcals produced in certain villages by families following an artisan tradition dating back more than 400 years. It began in 1995 with the villages of Chicicapa and San Luis del Rio. Nowadays, it offers seven highly distinctive Single Village mezcals, obviously 100% agave. They are all only available in small quantities. However, the greatest of rarities are Tobola, obtained from a small, broadleaved wild agave, and Pechuga (chicken breast), a third distillation in which not only does the double-distilled mezcal have mountain apples and plums added to it, but the palenquero also hangs a skinned chicken breast in the still to ensure that the fruity notes do not dominate. Liquid cultural heritage.

## Caballeros Inc.

### Mezcal Añejo 5 Years

Roberta French and her son Douglas began to establish a textile firm in Oaxaca in 1985. Ten years later they started to export small quantities of select, traditionally produced spirits under the brand name of Scorpion, becoming pioneers of high-quality mezcal. Particularly the seven- and five-year oak barrel-matured Super Premium qualities have been very highly distinguished in competitions held by the American Beverage Testing Institute. Caballeros Inc. also sells other mezcal brands, including Mystique, Toba-lá, La Reliquia, and Embajador.

## Sociedad de Productores del Sur

Don Luis Mezcal, with its 12-month oak-matured, slightly smoky, fruity, and creamy añejo, is a member of this active association, which covers a good 300 villages from the area around San Luis Amatián. As for the Armados brand, the agaves come from organic cultivations and are fermented without additives. The Sociedad has opened the elegant Plaza del Mezcal in the center of Oaxaca, with a small museum and well-stocked shop.

## Hacienda de Chihuahua

Sotol is a specialty originating in the Chihuahua desert in northern Mexico. Here the wild *Agavacea dasylirion* flourishes, for centuries cultivated by native tribes. This variety of agave takes 15 years to mature. Only then can the hearts be cooked for three days in ceramic ovens. The French-trained oenologist José Daumas Gil de Partearroyo ferments the must, using champagne yeast, and distills twice—for the añejo three times. For maturation he uses French oak casks. The six-month aged, pleasant, and mild Sotol Reposado Wild Agave has a beautiful, strong, spicy aroma of agaves, with a discreet note of roast.

# How to drink tequila

Slightly dampen the back of the hand, sprinkle some sea salt on it, lick off the salt, bite into a piece of lime, then swallow the tequila, or vice versa. This is how tequila, as a shot in pubs and discos, became a cult drink, but strict rituals are generally only practiced in certain friendly cliques. Some also like oranges and cinnamon, and drop into the glass a coffee bean that they then crunch up to finish. A typical routine is a two-handed one, with a tequila in one hand and a Sangrita, a sharp Mexican juice cocktail, in the other. Tequila aficionados, the largest communities of which are in the USA and Mexico itself, are repelled by such drinking customs. They sip their 100% agave spirits—whether it be platos, reposados, or añejos—out of sherry glasses or cognac balloons, reveling in the multilayered aromas.

## A whole realm of aromas

The generally water-clear Plato has a predominant aroma of fruit, primarily agave, and then citrus, pear, apricots, banana; also pepper and paprika and sometimes sour cream, wet stones, and earth. It tastes above all of agaves and tropical fruits, of wild blossom honey, vanilla, and cinnamon, often of black pepper and sea salt, sometimes also of green herbs and peppermint. Whilst simple qualities may burn the back of the throat, the better ones are warm and mild.

A reposado generally glints with a light golden color. The nose often detects aromas of baked agaves, dried yellow fruits and baked apples, honey and roasted nuts, caramel, vanilla, cinnamon, carnations and pepper, more rarely also cheese, or sweat. The aromas of ripe agaves, dried or grilled tropical fruits and roast nuts often fill the mouth, followed by sweet spices, honey and roasted paprika, pepper, sea salt, but also leather, soil, sour cream, or smoky wood notes. It often has a very spicy, dry aftertaste, very intensive on the palate.

In the case of amber or copper-colored añejo, long maturation in oak barrels comes to the fore with distinctive roasted aromas reminiscent of nuts, chocolate, mocha, or toffee, which may be combined with notes of grilled pineapple or yellow dried fruits, but also ripened cheese, leather, or olive oil. In the mouth, aromas of sweet spices and honey, ripe, cooked and grilled tropical fruits, cooked agaves, roasted nuts, and other distinctively roasted and woody notes dominate. The taste is often very mellow, oily, full bodied, and lingering. Good tequila always (also) tastes of agaves.

Mezcals have similar aromas, but are somewhat smokier and earthier, sometimes more floral or mineral, and occasionally also possess more idiosyncratic aromas reminiscent of paraffin and ashes, arising from the highly traditional methods of production.

Tequila owes its international popularity not least to two cocktails, Margarita and Tequila Sunrise, for which mixtos are generally used.

Tequila travels well. With a little salt and lemon juice, it is often drunk in bars. Brown tequila also goes well with orange and cinnamon. Simple qualities in particular benefit from good modifiers, perhaps a few coffee beans in the glass or a swallow of sharp Sangrita with it. There is only one way to drink matured, 100% agave tequilas: from a crystal goblet that releases all the aromas to their best advantage.

# Absinthe, pastis, and aniseed

- · The feeling on the tip of the tongue
- · The green fairy's spell
- · Ritual and renaissance
- · Cult-like activities
- · Premier pastis
- · Aniseed, fennel, licorice
- · Raki: grapes with aniseed
- · Ouzo in independent Greece
- · Raki and ouzo with pleasure
- · Aniseed from Chinchón
- · Super sweet aniseed

**ANISETTA**

**MELETTI**

Advertising poster from the Italian liqueur company Meletti in Ascoli Piceno (detail).

Opposite: The Lemercier Frères distillery yard in Fougerolles from where eaux-de-vie and absinthe are dispatched.

Page 490: Even the new generation absinthe is sweetened according to the familiar ritual.

# The feeling on the tip of the tongue

Anyone who has been to Turkey or Greece on vacation is familiar with the fascinating array of appetizers called *meze* or *mezédes*, as well as the raki or ouzo that follow these tempting culinary offerings. Those visiting France will be able to observe guests in any bistro at midday or in the early evening celebrating their pastis, which they dilute according to personal taste and with ritual earnest. In Italy, on the other hand, there is little chance of escaping a sambuca or anisetta after a meal. Aniseed is simply everywhere.

The distinctive aroma that characterizes not only aniseed but also the sloe liqueur Pacharán is also highly prized in Spain, while the Portuguese enjoy their own version. In Bulgaria fans of the "biting" seeds order Mastika liqueur. Aniseed wafts around the Mediterranean like an aromatic breeze—the seeds are used primarily to flavor drinks, playing only a secondary role as food flavoring. Combined with cold, fresh water, aniseed drinks are thirst quenching, low in alcohol in comparison to other spirits, and easily digestible.

*Pimpinella anisum* seeds were a set feature of Greek pharmaceutics as early as the 6th century BC. They combat flatulence, relieve pain, and help with asthma. In 5th-century Indian and Chinese medicine they were administered to new mothers as a milk stimulant. In traditional medicine aphrodisiacs are then only a small step away. Your reasons for drinking aniseed schnapps are up to you…

This annual plant with its cluster of flowers originates from the eastern Mediterranean, having since spread to Asia and Europe. However, it is there where the plants receive enough light, warmth, and sufficiently fertile soils for the seeds to ripen fully, making their cultivation worthwhile—that is in the south of the Italian marches or in the area around Chinchón, south of Madrid. The quality of this region's aniseed liqueurs is based on the local cultivation.

In other regions aniseed proved to be a costly raw material, which is why spirits manufacturers preferred Chinese star aniseed, which found buyers in Europe from the 16th century as soon as it became available in larger quantities. Although not related to aniseed, it contains the sought-after flavoring anethol which, to our taste, is what makes aniseed aniseed.

However, it is not only about aniseed: think of the elixirs that were produced in medieval monasteries where the blossoms, fruit, bark, and roots of other plants were also added. Every recipe is, of course, the closely guarded secret of every manufacturer.

Wormwood, *Artemisia absinthium*, was often included in the ingredients, and the ratio was reversed in the French Jura so that alcohol, water, and sugar were added to the absinthe and the flavor was refined with aniseed and all kinds of other condiments. What had started out as a remedy became something of a calamity in France in particular toward the *fin de siècle* as absinthe drinking became fashionable and the most persistent of absinthe drinkers became ill, this being attributed to a neurotoxin contained in wormwood. It took Prohibition (and war) to bring a necessary end to the abuse of absinthe.

However, the French were unwilling to dispense with the popular aniseed flavor, which is why pastis became the national drink in the 1950s with record-breaking speed, leaving all of the traditional schnapps varieties in its wake. A "defused" absinthe has been available since the end of the 1990s and has established a small band of faithful followers.

# The green fairy's spell

People used to meet for an absinthe at the "green hour" in the late afternoon and prior to a rich evening meal in the large boulevard cafés. The "people" were the French bourgeoisie, who took pride in displaying their well-being during the second half of the 19th century. Drinking absinthe was considered chic and was a relatively costly indulgence. It was drunk diluted with water, making it milky green in color: large sections of the middle class—male and female—paid homage to the "green fairy," among them poets such as Baudelaire and Apollinaire, Verlaine, and Rimbaud, not to mention numerous others. Absinthe was already well established at that time but was rescued from anonymity as a household remedy by the French doctor

Degas painted the absinthe-drinking couple Ellen Andrée and Marcellin Desboutin in a Paris café in 1876. (Edgar Degas, *In a café* or *Absinthe*, 1876, oil on canvas, Musée d'Orsay, Paris)

Pierre Ordinaire (1741–1821) in Val-de-Travers in the Swiss canton of Neuenburg, who administered his own *élixir d'absinthe* to his patients. What (or who) inspired his recipe is a matter for speculation, only coming to light again in the kitchens of the Henriod sisters in Couvet after Ordinaire's death. These unmarried ladies used to produce a *liqueur d'absinthe* that they sold with modest success. It appealed to the residents of the Jura not only for medicinal reasons. Major Daniel-Henri Dubied was hoping for even greater commercial success when he acquired the recipe in 1798, set up a distillery in the small town, and began selling his *Extrait d'absinthe*.

His son-in-law Henri-Louis Pernod very successfully took charge of sales in the French Jura. When Napoleon III imposed drastic increases in the customs duties for spirits, Pernod decided to open an absinthe factory in France in 1805, albeit on the other side of the border in Pontarlier. Production began with an output of 4 gallons (16 liters) per day, reaching a daily production of 5,300 gallons (20,000 liters) 100 years later.

Pernod profited from the Algerian crisis of 1830 because the morale—and the stomachs—of the soldiers stationed there was in dire need of a tonic. Once the officers returned home after 1860 demand in France increased, initially in the upper classes. The social barriers had, however, fallen by the last quarter of the 19th century: liberty, equality, drunkenness.

The excessive and chronic enjoyment of absinthe caused hallucinations and led to both physical and psychiatric impairment. This was attributed to a neurotoxin contained in wormwood. However, many of the symptoms were also due to poor-quality alcohol. What made the situation all the more nebulous was the fact that too much alcohol prevented the absorption of thujone, while nicotine increased the effect of thujone.

Business flourished. Pernod was the leading company in Pontarlier but there were now

The famous poster artist Leonetto Cappiello designed this advertisement for a company in Lunel wanting to benefit from the success of the original Pernod with their signboard.

also a further 21 distilleries. The heavily taxed absinthe was a very welcome source of income for the French state with more than 58 million gallons (220 million liters) being consumed annually. Doctors' warnings were therefore inopportune and while reactions in Belgium and the USA were more prompt, the sale of absinthe in France was only forbidden at the outbreak of World War I, prohibition being imposed in 1915.

# Ritual and renaissance

Opposite top: The captured green fairy is of course set free for the *Fête de l'Absinthe*.

Opposite bottom: High-quality Val-de-Travers absinthe is diluted with cold water only and enjoyed without sugar.

Left: *Grande* wormwood grows exceptionally well in Val-de-Travers.

Right: This imposing drying shed in Boveresse was built in 1893.

Absinth—*Artemisia absinthium* or *grande* wormwood—is an ancient medicinal plant with a variety of uses in traditional medicine, particularly for stomach and digestive complaints. With wine often being added to it even as a household remedy, this tincture formed the basis for vermouth in Turin at the end of the 18th century. The plant's properties have long been known in the Alps and in the Jura in particular, so that the doctor Pierre Ordinaire was not the first to use wormwood. The geographic origin of the *élixier d'absinthe* is more certain than the question of who invented it: it originates from Val-de-Travers in Switzerland.

The success of absinthe as a *fin de siècle* drink was due not least to its unusual flavor. People were already familiar with vermouth and the first quinquinas, but absinthe with its aniseed flavor was something entirely new. Then there was also the fact that it was not drunk alone but in company in the cafés. Its enjoyment also required a special ritual, increasing its appeal even further.

Absinthe, a very high-proof and bitter herbal spirit, had to be diluted with water and sweetened with sugar in order to make it at all enjoyable. The cafés provided water containers, *fontaines*, on the tables for this purpose and these had small taps so that several guests could make use of them at the same time. A special flat spoon with holes was laid across the goblet-shape glasses to add one or two sugar cubes to each glass. The water was slowly poured into the glass over the sugar, which "opalized" the absinthe because

the essential oil anethol contained therein—although soluble in alcohol—is barely soluble in water. The tiny drops of oil in the alcohol are enclosed in water. This coat of water blocks the light and the previously clear drink becomes cloudy. The green fairy's animations were prized not only by writers and men of letters, but also by artists such as Van Gogh, Gauguin, and Toulouse-Lautrec. The ban that was ultimately imposed on absinthe reinforced its secretive flair and the infamous lure of the Bohemian lifestyle. It escaped being banned in Spain and Portugal, while in Val-de-Travers, where absinthe originates, the ban was simply ignored. A number of moonshiners kept the tradition alive there in hiding, secretly distilling *La Bleue* in the smallest of quantities that were available to insiders only. Once it became apparent in 2004 that absinthe would again be permitted in Switzerland—and without the imposition of significant restrictions apart from the thujone content—its supporters, both active and passive, joined forces. They demanded a recognized appellation in order to provide official protection for the position of Val-de-Travers as the home of absinthe. Since an A.O.C. would have entailed too many conditions, they settled for an I.G.P., an *Indication Géographique Protégée*. It is hoped that this will provide a boost for the valley and beyond—also for the Jura—and that absinthe will become a Swiss specialty distributed internationally.

Val-de-Travers saw the liberalization of absinthe production in EU countries as the prelude to a renaissance for its revered *Bleue* and as a cause for celebration. The *Fête de l'Absinthe* has been taking place in mid-June in Boveresse since 1998 and has developed into a veritable institution during which the green fairy, locked up for a year, is unashamedly set free and homage is paid to her opaque qualities.

# Cult-like activities

Legendary intoxicating, hallucinogenic, and erotic effects—they all kept the interest in absinthe alive, all the more so while it was largely unobtainable. That changed when, at the beginning of the 1990s, Hill's Liqueurs began marketing a bilious green-colored absinthe made in the Czech Republic with 70% vol. alcohol content. It was at around the same time that absinthe appeared in Francis Ford Coppola's *Bram Stoker's Dracula* (1992). Shortly thereafter rock star Marilyn Manson did demonstrative justice to absinthe, as did Johnny Depp even more effectively as Inspector Frederick Abberline in *From Hell* (2001) in the hunt for Jack the Ripper.

The changes made to the EU aroma regulations in 1991 had already set a limit for the amount of thujone permitted in bitter spirits, but it was only with the relaxing of production regulations in 1998 that the path was cleared for production and distribution. One thing remains forbidden: in France the green fairy is not allowed to be called absinthe as such, it has to hide behind designations such as *extrait (de plantes) d'absinthe* or *à base des plantes d'absinthe*.

While a variety of spirits companies tried to launch hastily produced absinthe brands, the real interest lay in the former strongholds of Val-de-Travers, Pontarlier, and Fougerolles.

A single commercial distillery had survived in Switzerland's Jura valley, run by Yves Kübler whose forefathers used to operate one of the largest absinthe distilleries in Switzerland. In 1992 Kübler brought the herb distillate La Rincette onto the market; it did not contain wormwood but was very similar in taste to absinthe.

Left: *Grande* wormwood is harvested by hand using a sickle.

Right: The plants are hung to dry in drying sheds or in attics.

Following liberalization throughout Europe the Swiss federal government then also gave in and granted Kübler permission to distill absinthe, subject to specific conditions, in October 2001. In Pontarlier, just 16 miles (25 km) away, Pierre Guy also revived the family tradition and started distilling the first absinthe in 2001. Old stills in the French Jura have since been reactivated or else old absinthe recipes have been revived by traditional distilleries. The second important date in absinthe's recent history is March 1, 2005, which is when production was legalized again in Switzerland. A number of illegal stills subsequently ceased their underground activities and are now official distillers. The Val-de-Travers association today numbers nine distilleries, including one cooperative.

Conditions in the Jura are ideal on both the Swiss and the French sides as *grande* wormwood and a multitude of other herbs flourish particularly well there. There has since been a conversion to cultivating these raw materials using organic methods. The plants are harvested when their essential oil content is at its highest—usually prior to their blooming in full—and are then dried. For the production process, wormwood and other herbs are first macerated in high-proof alcohol. The flavored alcohol is then drawn off and for all high-quality absinthes it is distilled again, while the commercial brands make do with the maceration. The result is a crystal clear "white" absinthe, while plants containing chlorophyll are used for the "green" version. The less it is reduced, the more aromatic it is. It then needs to be diluted and can also be sweetened, although this is not essential. The old absinthe ritual is undergoing a sudden revival and the green fairy is back. We just have to hope that she will be treated a little more courteously this time round.

Left: Distilling used to take place in secret in small distilling cauldrons such as this one (and that above) belonging to Claude-Alain Bugnon.

Right: La Clandestine has expanded following official registration but the distilling remains a true craft.

# Selected absinthes

France

### Doubs Mystique Carte d'Or
### Aux Extraits de Plantes
### d'Absinthe 65%

The company Oxygénée Ltd., based in England, is the name behind this new age absinthe and is one of the leading absinthe specialists with The Virtual Absinthe Museum on the internet and with sales of old, rare absinthes. The company acquired two historic Egrot stills, one with 240-gallon (900-liters) capacity and the other holding 53 gallons (200 liters), and distills in Pontarlier. Its secret is the multitude of plants used, all of which are indigenous to the Pontarlier area. The youngest Doubs Mystique distillates age for six months, the older ones for more than a year. With an attractive yellow-green color and a bouquet very much characterized by wormwood, its flavor has a surprising, biting freshness before it mellows out.

France

### François Guy
### Plantes d'Absinthe 45%

Founded in 1890, this distillery was part of the golden age of absinthe in Pontarlier and its Pontarlier-Anis, launched in 1921, was the only aperitif based on distilled green aniseed. In April 2001 the distillery planted 55,000 wormwood plants in the same fields near Pontarlier that have been used for time immemorial. They were harvested in September, dried for the whole of October, and then distilled. The in-house recipe used to prepare absinthe in 1914 is still adhered to precisely, with due attention being paid to the ratio of wormwood to aniseed, and the old stills also being used. The special wormwood aroma is unmistakable but blends pleasantly with the aniseed.

France

### Libertine
### Spiritueux aux Plantes
### d'Absinthe 55%

Next to Pontarlier, Fougerolles was the second absinthe capital and it was here that the Paul Devoille distillery was founded in 1859, producing kirsch and absinthe. René de Miscault took over the distillery in 1985 because he wanted to pursue the earlier tradition together with his son Hugues. They created the Absinthe Libertine based on a recipe dating from 1894 that Miscault keeps in his Musée des Eaux de Vie de Lapoutroie. They also planted wormwood on the Fougerolles heights. Every single plant ingredient—and these include green aniseed, star aniseed, fennel, coriander, melissa, licorice, and hyssop in addition to wormwood—is distilled separately, and this is noticeable in the very refined absinthe. It is also available with 72% vol. alcohol.

France

### Lemercier
### Absinthe Amer 72%

The Lemercier company in Fougerolles dates back to a farming family that started out distilling kirsch only. To boost sales Desle Nicolas Lemercier began bartering with Burgundian wine makers, distributing their wines in the Franche-Comté. His successors Constant and Isidor Lemercier built a new distillery at the railway station in 1881 that contained a special absinthe distillery, their main product at the time. The family concern managed to defy crises and wars with their production of eaux-de-vie, liqueurs, vinegar, and their barrel-making business, so that after 1998 they were able to take up their own tradition in the production of a very convincing absinthe, available with 45% vol. alcohol as well as in two especially intense versions with 72% vol.

France

### Pernod
### Aux Extraits de Plantes
### d'Absinthe 68%

Henri-Louis Pernod was the pioneer of factory-scale absinthe production when he started out in Pontarlier in 1805. During its boom years the distillery achieved a production rate of more than 6,600 gallons (25,000 liters) daily. The absinthe ban put an end to that and the company went downhill rapidly. It was only after 1951 that Pernod 45 was able to emulate the achievements of the past. In 2001 the company benefited from the new wave of interest, the original recipe allegedly having served as inspiration. However, apart from the typical absinthe alcohol content and the lack of sugar, the result is more reminiscent of the company's own pastis as the aniseed aroma dominates, the wormwood providing only subtle bitterness on the palate.

## France

**Roquette 1797**
**Aux Extraits de Plantes d'Absinthe 75 %**

David Nathan-Maister from Oxygénée and Peter Schaf have joined forces in order to revive old absinthe recipes under the Archive Spirits brand. These are produced in the Emile Pernot distillery in Pontarlier using two old stills. This first attempt from the year in question—named after Dr. Pierre Ordinaire's horse —also uses local, more unusual herbs in addition to wormwood, fennel, and aniseed. They give this absinthe a green color that turns cloudy when mixed with water. The aroma is pleasantly complex and spicy, while the wormwood gives the flavor a refined touch of bitterness over and above the other herbs and the touch of lemon.

## Germany

**Eichelberger**
**Absinth 70 verte 70 %**

Lili and Rudi Wild run a specialty distillery and apiary in Taxöldern, in the midst of the Upper Palatinate lake district of Germany. High-quality fruit schnapps varieties are produced in the small, modern distillery at the lowest possible temperatures and in deliberately slow cycles. Inspired by the www.absinth-guide.de forum, this absinthe was created in 2005 using only macerated and then distilled natural herbs, and immediately became one of the best wormwood distillates. It is conspicuous for its attractive green color, which then slowly takes on a distinct opaqueness. The bouquet is dominated by complex herbal nuances, while the classic wormwood and fennel aromas develop on the tongue with an appealingly fresh touch of lemon.

## Switzerland

**La Clandestine**
**Absinthe du Val-de-Travers 53 %**

This absinthe originates from the new Artemisia distillery authorized in 2005 as the first in Switzerland's Val-de-Travers since the absinthe ban of 1910. Its owner, Claude-Alain Bugnon, started out distilling illegally in 2000 but now distills according to the recipe that gave the moonshiner Charlotte Vaucher her best *Bleue* in 1935. Bugnon continues to use this recipe today, only using plants from the valley and heating his small still directly. With its fresh, intense wormwood, aniseed, wild flower, and herb aroma—as well as its wonderful roundness and length—La Clandestine is one of the best absinthes there is and is enjoyed without sugar.

## Switzerland

**Kübler**
**Absinthe Véritable Fée Verte 53 %**

Kübler was number two in Switzerland during the golden age of absinthe when the Swiss cross was a symbol of quality everywhere. Yves Kübler therefore dreamed early on of continuing his family's tradition. With the takeover of the Blackmint distillery, the only commercial distillery in Val-de-Travers, and with his La Rincette—a pastis very similar to absinthe— in 1990, Yves Kübler was well on the way to making his dream come true. He was the first to distill absinthe in Switzerland again following the liberalization in 1998. His Fée Verte is Kübler's best distillate to date, crystal clear, with an intense aniseed aroma, unmistakably soft on the tongue, and with a wonderfully fresh character.

## Czech Republic

**Cami**
**Absinthe Toulouse-Lautrec 68 %**

The Czech Republic produces a variety of absinthes that perhaps contributed to the renaissance of this spirit but that have not yet been able to measure up to their French and Swiss competitors. The Cami distillery has outdone itself with this absinthe, dedicated to the famous painter and passionate admirer of the green fairy. Developed together with the shipper www.absinth-oase.de, this absinthe is characterized by the restriction of the natural ingredients (with the exception of the color) to partly fresh herbs and green aniseed. There are a total of 14 flavorings that are distilled in small batches. Diluted with water it has a very appealing opaqueness. The wormwood aroma is subtle while aniseed and herb aromas predominate, as does its own spiciness.

# Premier pastis

In the 1920s more and more customers in the bistros and cafés of Marseilles were surreptitiously ordering "tiger milk." Every landlord in the capital of Provence kept his own mixture under the counter—known as *pastis* in the local Provençal dialect—comprising alcohol, aniseed, a little licorice, and a variety of other herbs and spices as well as a little sugar, as a replacement for absinthe. The French missed their green fairy after the ban of 1915 and the inhabitants of Provence, who were as resourceful as they were obstreperous, did not simply given in without putting up some resistance. Although the liqueur manufacturers had convinced the legislators of the harmlessness of aniseed so that an aniseed liqueur was permitted in 1922, the related conditions requiring a maximum of 40% vol. alcohol content and at least 22 oz of sugar per gallon (150 g per liter) produced a very sweet liqueur but no new absinthe—much to the dismay of the manufacturer and the consumer, because it was not everywhere in France that landlords were as

accommodating of their customers as those in Marseilles. There the pastis had a different flavor in every bar and some were better than others.

There was a young man paying particular attention to these differences at that time: as deliveryman for his father's wine business Paul Ricard visited the bars and bistros on a regular basis, using these visits as an advertising opportunity for his own table wine. He had designed the label himself—with vines, olive trees, and sunshine symbolizing his homeland Provence—as he had wanted to become a painter but his father would hear nothing of it. He was therefore constantly in search of the commercial success that would have given him financial independence to do what he wanted to do. Up until that time he had worked in his father's wine business, had acquired bookkeeping skills, and was racking his brains to find what could bring him closer to his goal. *Vin ordinaire* was certainly not the answer. Perhaps pastis? The bistro customers seemed to be crazy about it.

Paul Ricard would have liked to have become an artist and dedicated every free minute to his hobby: in addition to paintings he also produced posters, using his pastime to the benefit of his company.

## Provençal self-improvement

He set about developing his own version of pastis, spending his evenings composing new variations. "I developed the habit of taking a sample with me on my rounds the day after my distilling, macerating, and filtering," he recounted in his autobiography *La passion de créer*. "Encouraged by the comments of my tasters and inspired by their wishes, I continued to refine the mixture so as to then continue my survey in another bar the next day." A number of months passed in this fashion before he was happy with the outcome.

There was in fact still just one obstacle: the ban. When it was lifted in 1932, when Paul was aged 23, he began producing Ricard in the yard of his parents' home in the Saint-Marthe suburb of Marseilles. He set about selling with a great deal of verve and managed to achieve a turnover of 66,000 gallons (250,000 liters) in his first year.

The aniseed aperitif with the 45% vol. alcohol content ideal for the absorption of anethol was allowed to be produced from 1938 and Paul Ricard set about conquering the Paris bistros. He launched his *vrai Pastis de Marseille* with its significant Mediterranean character, personified by the singer Darcelys, a mischievous Provence inhabitant with an open shirt and brash charm. By contrast, the advertising symbol of the competitor Pernod, now also producing a pastis, seemed to embody the less positive drinking habits of the absinthe era, which provided the 1940 Vichy government with a welcome pretext for what was already an inevitable ban on alcohol.

Even during the time when the advertising of alcoholic drinks was forbidden during the initial years after the war, the name Ricard was to be seen as sponsor at all major events, stealing a substantial lead on all pastis competitors. Its labels after 1951 were surreptitiously reminiscent of those forbidden precursors.

Paul Ricard knew that his outstanding success was due not only to his own efforts but also to those of his employees. He distributed company shares among them for the first time back in 1938 and he was always one step ahead of the statutory requirements with his social services provision. On top of that he built houses and holiday homes for his employees. On the side he created the Castillet international racetrack and founded a marine biology institute on the island of Embriêz, amongst other things. Today, under the management of his son Patrick Ricard, Pernod-Ricard has grown to become the world's second largest spirits group.

With esthetically appealing advertising and clever marketing Ricard was streaks ahead of the competition right from the start.

# Aniseed, fennel, licorice

Aniseed had characterized the flavor of the absinthe distributed by Pernod and other distilleries and it was in this way that the residents of northern France were confronted with its characteristic flavor for the first time. The seeds of this flowering plant, which had been a popular flavoring in Provence since time immemorial, clearly appealed to them. Fennel, which was also popular and which contained the same essential oil, also grew wild there. Provence was therefore destined to produce the successor to absinthe.

However, as already demonstrated by the example of the Marseilles bistro landlords, each of whom prepared their own version, with pastis in Provence the focus was more on the result than on the processing. A typical *pastis de Marseille* was a mixture of neutral alcohol, water, sugar, and aromas. The latter were added as distillates and macerations—that is as infusions.

The most important component is the anethol, an essential oil present in green aniseed. *Pimpinella anisum* is a difficult plant to cultivate, needing plenty of light as well as a certain amount of humidity, and it does not ripen reliably under unsuitable climatic conditions.

Consequently, the seeds are expensive and not always available in sufficient quantities.

What aniseed is allowed to contain:

1 Mint
2 Birch leaves
3 Verbena
4 Quassia wood
5 Licorice
6 Saffron strands
7 Cassia leaves
8 Chamomile
9 Poppy seeds
10 Thyme
11 Coriander
12 Cardamom
13 Cinnamon
14 Star aniseed
15 Fennel
16 Summer savory
17 Turmeric
18 Aniseed

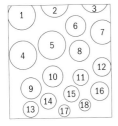

Help was forthcoming from southern China, from the Guangxi region where star aniseed (*Illicium verum*) grows. It is a type of magnolia with leaves similar to bay leaves. The tree, which grows up to 66 feet (20 m) in height, needs 25 years to reach maturity and bears an average of 100 lb (45 kg) of the characteristic, usually eight-point, fruit twice a year. Although it is not related to green aniseed it contains anethol (which is extracted before it leaves China). French fennel or tarragon is used to provide additional anethol.

The second important pastis ingredient is licorice (*Glycyrrhiza glabra*), a perennial bush indigenous to the Mediterranean and west Asia. It is the dried roots that are crushed and softened, and used to obtain the licorice-flavored juice that gives pastis its yellow color.

The recipe can comprise up to 72 further ingredients, including herbs and spices such as thyme, rosemary, sage, melissa, mint, coriander, chamomile, cloves, and cinnamon.

## Use

Pastis production always follows the same principle. The dried plants and flavorings are placed in an alcohol–water mixture whereby the alcohol content—amounting to 30–96% vol.—must be matched to the respective ingredients. Sometimes this maceration takes no longer than 24–72 hours, but is usually two to eight weeks long. The liquid is then drawn off and the plants are pressed in order to obtain all of the extract. The major brands work solely on the basis of maceration.

The handcrafted distilleries take it a step further, however. Since the plants contain further aromas these are distilled after pressing. Some of the macerations are then also refined and concentrated by distilling, although this is not necessary for all of them (such as licorice, for example).

The most demanding phase is the blending of the macerations and distillates with the anethol and sugar to produce the essence. This is responsible for the aroma and flavor of the pastis and is usually brought up to a

strength of 45% vol. with water and alcohol. Filtering then ensures that the pastis flows clearly into the glass.

With pastis only having been produced by large companies who have consistently rationalized their production, small distilleries have been producing handcrafted pastis since the end of the 1980s, providing an appealing range of different styles depending on which herbs and flavorings dominate the recipe. Usually bottled unfiltered, uncolored, and sometimes unsweetened, they provide considerably more finesse. There is one thing that all pastis have in common, however: they are drunk diluted. Connoisseurs add only ice-cold water, never ice cubes that cause the anethol to separate.

Henri Bardouin in Fourcalquier was one of the pioneers of the new, handcrafted pastis.

# Selected pastis

### Casanis
### Pastis de Marseille
Half Corsican, half Provençal, this pastis was being produced on Corsica as far back as 1925. After the distillery was destroyed in 1942, its owner Emmanuel Casabianca started out again in 1951 near Marseilles with the new brand name. However, he retained his proven recipe and macerated licorice, but distilled green aniseed and star aniseed together for the blend. This is what gives the Casanis its aromatic finesse, whereby as a *pastis de Marseille* it also contains the prescribed 2 g anethol per liter instead of the usual 1.5 g. Still the Corsicans' favorite pastis, it has flourished as an *apéritif du Terroir*—owned by the Burgundian Boisset family since 2000, to whom the renowned Pastis Duval also belongs.

### Distilleries et Domaines de Provence
### Pastis HB Henri Bardouin
The residents of Fourcalquier, Haute Provence, have been collecting medicinal herbs in the Montagne de Lure for centuries and these were also being distilled as far back as the Middle Ages. This is a tradition that has produced druggists and apothecaries, pharmacists, and distillers. The distillery was founded in 1898 and has been working with wine and alcohol, maceration, and distillation ever since in order to extract all of the aromas and active agents from the plants. A somewhat different, handcrafted pastis has been created in memory of the former owner, Henri Bardouin, who was a passionate collector of herbs and mushrooms, its complex aromas being produced by 65 plants and flavorings including melegueta pepper and nutmeg, as well as a little gentian.

### Ferme des Homs
### Pastis des Homs
Pierre-Yves de Boissieu and Maria Möller Kräuter grow organic herbs such as thyme, rosemary, oregano, and fennel on the *Ferme des Homs* in the northeast of the sparse Larzac plateau near Millau, or else they gather herbs and wild fruit in the Parc Naturel Régional des Grands Causses. They dry the plants and use them to flavor their *Vinaigres de Vin Vieux* or flavored salts, as well as their handcrafted pastis. They add a total of 15 different herbs and wild plants to the aromatic aniseed and licorice base, but do not add coloring agents. Their pastis therefore retains its pale color and develops an intense herb aroma.

### Jean Boyer
### Pastis Eméraude
Jean Boyer, who died in 1992, was a cleric who founded a community in the region in 1957 that runs two restaurants as a means of livelihood. Boyer began to import the best Scottish whisky after a customer had complained about the whisky served there, resulting in the company Auxil—today Le Palais des Alcools are specialists in top-class spirits. It was therefore only a matter of time before he began to produce something himself, and the four Jean Boyer pastis were the result. These require selected plants to be macerated in alcohol for up to 96 hours. The resulting *teinture* matures for several months until the aromas harmonize with one another. The popular Pastis Eméraude appeals with its diversity, length, delicate bitterness, and substantial herb aromas.

## Jules Girard
### Pastis de Provence

In 1924 Jules Girard founded a small *atelier* for producing pastis, liqueurs, and eaux-de-vie in Jonquières, his home town at the foot of Mont Ventoux, between Orange and Avignon. He made use of recipes deriving from local tradition in Provence, a region that has always been known for its wealth of culinary and medicinal herbs. These local herbs were supplemented with spices from Asia and the Far East such as vanilla, coriander, cinnamon, cardamom, and of course star aniseed. Vincent Méry, head of the distillery, macerates them for weeks before pressing them, distilling some of them further, and then selecting the very best to blend into a pastis that is in a class of its own with its golden color, its sweet and spicy aroma, and its subtle hint of bitterness.

## Lemercier
### La Bleue

This pastis takes its name from absinthe, known in Switzerland as *une bleue* (a blue). The distillery in Fougerolles was already experimenting with a pastis recipe back in the 1920s, one that was dominated by star aniseed, wormwood, fennel, and other flavorings. Once they were happy with the results they secured *La Bleue* as a trademark in 1939. Based on their substantial experience in the production of absinthe, they also decided on a combination of maceration and distillation for the pastis in which the intensity and resilience of the aromas are unmistakable. This comparatively sweet pastis is dominated by the aniseed flavor, together with nuances of fennel and other herbs.

## Ricard
### Pastis de Marseille

The market leader when it comes to pastis is still based in Marseilles where Paul Ricard started out in 1932—albeit his son Patrick has turned it into a multinational company that he runs from Paris. The *crème de Ricard*, however, is produced in Bessan in Languedoc, and is the aromatic essence that gives the Ricard its special touch. The company monitors the recipe ingredients right from the cultivation stage, be it star aniseed from China, licorice from Syria, or herbs from Provence. The resulting essence is then sent to the company's own bottling plants where it is used to flavor the base comprising alcohol, sugar, and water. Ricard then comes onto the market after three weeks of blending.

## Pernod
### Pernod

The largest absinthe brand launched Pernod 45 in 1938 in order to reinvent itself with pastis. It struggled initially to free itself of the stuffy and preponderant past, but that changed in 1951 when the sale of aniseed aperitifs was again given the green light by legislators, and Pernod brought out its spinoff, Pastis 51, with outstanding success. Pernod was able to regain significant market share, enjoying on the export market what it was denied at home, namely first place. The merger with its archrival in 1975 created the basis for what is today the world's second largest spirits concern.

# Raki: grapes with aniseed

It was allegedly Greek wine makers in Asia Minor that first produced raki from grape pomace in the 15th century. Raki was drunk throughout the Ottoman Empire around 1700. It was so popular that a separate treasury was set up in 1792 for the taxation of alcoholic beverages. Religious bans have never been able to pose a serious threat to raki production as many local authorities simply turned a blind eye to it. Raki became the most important alcoholic beverage in Turkey and the country came to monopolize its production after being proclaimed a republic in 1923. A copious Turkish evening meal without raki is unthinkable. Raki consumption in Turkey currently amounts to around 15,850,000 gallons (60 million liters) annually—more than all other alcoholic drinks together.

The Tekel (*monopoly* in Turkish) company has been producing all alcoholic beverages since 1931. Sugar-beet molasses has been used in its production since 1947; it used to impart a certain bitterness to Yeni Rakı (New Raki).

## Raisins and figs

Present day raki is largely based on grapes—mainly raisins—or, particularly in southern Turkey, dried figs. The fruit is ground and mashed together with water at a ratio of 1:4. Once fermentation starts at 82–90 °F (28–32 °C), batches of cooled mash are added to keep a constant temperature. The usual rise in temperature during the fermentation process would otherwise endanger the yeast cultures.

The so-called *suma*, with an alcohol content of 93.4–94% vol., is produced using column distillation. It is diluted to an alcohol content of 45% vol. and contains 15 oz per gallon (100 g per liter) aniseed— or else fennel seeds, softened in water. The entire mixture is then distilled slowly a second time in a copper still with a capacity of up to 1,320 gallons (5,000 liters). It is during this process

Left: *Suma* is produced in distillation columns in this modern distillery in Izmir.

Right: The copper stills are used for the second cycle with the aniseed.

hat the middle runnings, with an alcohol content of 75–84% vol., are drawn off.

The freshly distilled raki matures for a while in wooden barrels or in stainless steel tanks before reaching a strength of 43–50% vol. Up to 1 oz of sugar per gallon (4–6 g per liter) is added and this is followed by a further aging period of up to three months.

As with most quality products, raki has its myths. The *dip rakısı*, the residue that remains in the tank after production, is said to be especially aromatic. It does not come onto the market and there are very few people who have ever tasted it because the producers present it to special customers and prominent public personalities as a gift, which is why it is referred to as *özel rakı* (exclusive raki).

The monopoly era finally came to an end on February 27, 2004, initiating considerable movement on the raki market. A number of new brands have emerged, some of which provide a high-quality grape raki as well as some of the first varietal rakis.

## Arak, not arrak

A distilled, unsweetened aniseed schnapps based on grape brandy and known as arak is drunk in the region extending from Turkey to Jordan. It is diluted with ice-cold water (turning it milky white) and is usually served with a variety of appetizers. It can also be mixed with tea or fruit juice. There are a number of theories about the origin of the name: one option is the Iranian town of Arak as well as Iraq itself; another is the Razaki grape.

Arak is not to be confused with arrak, a spirit that is widespread well beyond the eastern and southern Asian region and does not constitute a uniform category. The first arrak reached Europe in 1596 and came from Java. Arrak is similar to rum but is more neutral and often has a high alcohol content. Rice as well as molasses and palm syrup form the basis for the alcohol.

Left: The aniseed distillate is fed into stainless steel tanks.

Right: The clarity of the raki is reviewed under a microscope in a laboratory.

# Selected rakis

**Elda**
**Enfes Rakı Fresh Grapes (Yas üzüm)**
Izmir, home of the parent company Elda, is a trade and cultural center dating back to antiquity. The top-quality grape-growing areas are situated in the hinterland on the Turkish Aegean Sea. Enfes—Turkish for delicious—is produced from grapes and not from raisins. It is somewhat lighter and more rounded in comparison to the standard products. The rest of the recipe is otherwise identical. Despite their intense aniseed aroma, which sometimes covers up the character of the alcohol base, rakis made from fresh grapes are currently especially popular in Turkey. Yas üzüm is bottled in limited editions in order to emphasize its exclusivity.

**Elda**
**Enfes Rakı**
The Elda group of companies built Turkey's most modern raki distillery in Tekeli near Izmir while the state restructuring was still going on. The region is known for the quality of its grapes and raisins. A high-quality raki has been produced here since the end of the monopoly and bears the well-known brand name Efes in Turkey, although in Germany it is labeled as Enfes for statutory reasons. The aniseed comes from the area around the upmarket holiday region of Çesme, also known for the quality of its water. This twice-distilled schnapps is characterized by an especially high proportion of aniseed.

**Mey**
**Altınbas Rakı**
Altınbas is one of the most renowned rakis in Turkey and, like Yeni, is produced by the Mey company. In contrast to brands such as Yeni, which is distilled at several of the five distillery locations, the Altınbas always comes from Istanbul. Even without the modern trimmings it is considered to be very pleasant to drink, and rightly so. Despite the high proportion of aniseed and a relatively high alcohol content at 50% vol., its bouquet is very pleasantly subtle. It has been produced using double distillation since 1967.

**Mey**
**Club Raki · Kulüp rakısı**
Similar to Altınbas Raki, which is also produced by the house of Mey, Club Raki (Turkish kulüp rakısı) is somewhat milder. The dominant aniseed is accompanied by mint nuances, producing a harmonious schnapps either neat or diluted with water and giving it a softness despite its 50% vol. alcohol content. Club is the oldest of the Mey brands and has been produced in Istanbul since 1932, the recipe remaining unchanged since then. Kulüp rakısı has retained its very traditional nature despite the fact that the American investment company Texas Pacific Group has long held a majority shareholding in the parent company Mey.

**Mey**

**Tekirdag Rakısı Gold Serie**

Unlike the majority of its competitors, the Gold Series Tekirdag is brown in color, emphasizing the fact that it is matured in *barriques*. The brand's flagship is milder and oilier than the rest of the fleet.

In addition to the fresh grapes, this raki is characterized by its high proportion of essential aniseed oils. This schnapps in its distinctive bottle and with its intensive aroma is considered to be an upmarket gift for friends. The distillery producing this famous brand is located in the town of Tekirdag, close to the local prison. It is alleged that the aniseed aroma can be smelt in the penitentiary, making the conditions all the more difficult for the inmates.

**Mey**

**Yeni Rakı**

Yeni positions itself as the world's most renowned raki and is produced by Mey, the successor company to the Tekel monopoly. The producer emphasizes its lifestyle character with a modern bottle design, distinguishing Yeni from many of its competitors. According to the company the precise recipe and the distilling process are a "century-old secret" that is "closely guarded." The basis for the double distillation is a mixture of raisins and grapes. The schnapps is stored in oak barrels for several months to round it off. The high proportion of aniseed intensifies the aniseed-licorice aroma that is considered to be Yeni's hallmark.

**Nevsehir Distillery**

**Mest Rakı**

Mest is one of the first rakis to be distilled on a varietal basis. Only grapes from the white Sultaniye variety—popular in Europe as a table grape—are used. The grapes come from the historic Denizli province with its early Christian and ancient Greek artifacts, as well as the famous calcified terraces that are a UNESCO World Heritage Site. Wine has been produced in this west Anatolian region for centuries. It has a mild climate, albeit with temperature fluctuations from –18 to 113 °F (–10 to 45 °C), resulting in an especially soft raki.

**Sarper**

**Beylerbeyi Rakı**

Having first appeared in summer 2007, Beylerbeyi is one of the youngest brands on the flourishing Turkish raki market. The parent company Sarper, which produces this raki in the Izmir and Manisa region, a center for the raisin trade, has made substantial investments with the new production plant allegedly having cost 18 million dollars, also making it one of the most modern in Europe. Beylerbeyi Rakı is one of the few rakis on the market that is distilled three times, giving it a certain mildness. Sarper is also proud of the fact that it is easy to digest.

# Ouzo in independent Greece

Together with feta cheese, ouzo is the most well known of Greek specialties. However, it does not have a particularly extensive tradition, neither in the Peloponnese nor in other regions, which is in complete contrast to the millennia-old wine tradition and even to the distillation of *tsipouro* from grape pomace that has been practiced for a century. It is assumed that it was Greeks in Asia Minor who flavored grape pomace with aniseed.

The large-scale production of aniseed schnapps under the name ouzo only began with the independence of Greece in 1830, but the origin of the Greek word *ouzo* remains unclear. A popular theory is that the designation goes back to the labeling of freight coffers with *uso di Marsiglia* (for use in Marseilles). Etymologically it could derive from the Turkish word *üzüm* meaning a concoction from grapes.

The Asia Minor Catastrophe saw a rapid increase in ouzo sales—this was the defeat of Greece at the hands of Mustafa Kemal's army in 1922, leading to the expulsion of more than 1.5 million Greeks from Turkey (and 360,000 Turks from Greece), including many wine makers who were also familiar with aniseed schnapps. The island of Lesbos, known for its particularly intense aniseed, became a center of ouzo production and is considered to be the home of the best ouzo in Greece today.

Pure alcohol of agricultural origin is used as the main ingredient for ouzo, although the type of agricultural origin is not stipulated. The alcohol is diluted with water and placed in stills. A mixture of aniseed and other herbs is then added, their composition determining the flavor and quality of the ouzo. Many smaller producers pay special attention to the quality and the processing of the aniseed. Some of them still complete steps such as *drimonisma*, the separating of the seeds entirely by hand.

Star aniseed, fennel seeds, coriander, cardamom, nutmeg, cinnamon, ginger, angel

Left: The most important ouzo flavorings are (from below center clockwise) cardamom, aniseed, coriander, lime blossom, fennel, angelica, and star aniseed in the center.

Right: Ouzo is also available in very small bottles, the miniature size in this case being a feature of the brand.

## Mastika

The pine bush mastika, *Pistacia lentiscus*, has been used for centuries because it contains a resin suited to many uses, such as for setting the varnish for violins as well as for stabilizing oil paints. Originating from the island of Chios, it has an intense aroma and is distilled together with aniseed and other flavorings used in ouzo. Mastika, with an alcohol content of up to 80% and produced largely from figs or plums, is diluted to drinking strength. Versions with an alcohol content of significantly more than 40% vol. are available in Bulgaria and Macedonia, which also have a mastika tradition. Some of these are sweetened with up to 2 lb of sugar per gallon (180 g per liter) and have a liqueur character. Mastix is usually drunk chilled and with water, like raki and ouzo.

ica, chamomile, and mastika are used in addition to aniseed or aniseed oil. A single still typically contains 22–66 lb (10–30 kg) of flavorings.

Traditional copper stills with a maximum capacity of 260 gallons (1,000 liters) are prescribed for the distillation of aniseed and herb extracts, meaning that the larger producers need whole rows of stills in order to be able to produce the required quantities. The *kefáli* (first runnings) and *urá* (last runnings) are drawn off during the first distillation and the *kardiá* (middle runnings) are separated. Some producers distill the middle runnings a third time, sometimes with additional flavorings. This produces the *adoloto*, the ouzo essence, which is left to mature in tanks for a while.

The best producers add nothing more than pure water and sugar to the *adoloto*, although 20% is prescribed for the end product and the addition of neutral alcohol is also permitted. The final drinking strength has to have a minimum alcohol content of 37.5% vol. Ouzo is recognized in the EU as a protected origin beverage. It may only be produced in Greece and in the Greek section of the island of Cyprus, and may not contain more than 7½ oz sugar per gallon (50 g per liter). The generous sweetening and the relatively low alcohol content make ouzo sweet and soft. In Greece it is often drunk with water, resulting in the familiar cloudy appearance. With the revival of the cocktail culture many producers recommend ouzo as an ingredient for mixed drinks, mixtures with tomato or orange juice having their appeal. Ouzo is popularly served in *ouzeries* together with *meze* (appetizers).

Sampling is one of the ongoing quality controls to which ouzo is subjected.

# Selected ouzos

### Barbayannis
### Aphrodite

Anyone who names his ouzo after the Greek goddess of love and beauty must be very sure of his product. And that is indeed the case: the company maintains that its hallmark provides the "perfect flavor" combined with the "impression of classic beauty and timeless elegance." High demands indeed, but they match the quality of Aphrodite. Distilled three times, this ouzo flows full of strong, sweet aromas. Its 48% vol. alcohol content exceeds that of many of its competitors and produces a pleasant warmth on the palate—and not only there. The complex aniseed aroma that it then develops is especially impressive.

### Barbayannis
### Ouzo

Lesbos is said to have been fertile and sunny when Efstathios J. Barbayannis arrived there in 1860, according to the company history. He reached the harbor town of Plomari by ship from Odessa in Russia, where he had been able to gather a great deal of distilling experience. Barbayannis founded his own distillery and used the wealth of aromatic herbs from the region for his ouzo. Barbayannis is today owned by the fifth generation of the family and the ouzo production remains unchanged, without the addition of neutral alcohol. The company maintains that the water comes from the mountains near Plomari and contains salts and minerals.

### Giokarinis
### Giokarinis Ouzo

The fact that a widow is responsible for this ouzo is vaguely reminiscent of champagne. It comes from the island of Samos, however. Eleni Giokarinis launched this schnapps in 1910 and it soon became known as the "widow's ouzo." Giokarinis is very mild with a pleasant licorice flavor. The only ingredients revealed by the producer are aniseed, fennel, cardamom, and the seeds of the mastix tree. The ouzo is carefully distilled in handmade copper stills, with any unwanted aromas being diligently removed. The middle runnings are then distilled for a second time. Giokarinis Ouzo is now produced by the third generation and remains unchanged.

### Kaloylannis
### Ouzo 12

The Kaloyiannis distillery has been producing this ouzo comprising nine different herbs since 1880, granting it a sophisticated ripening process in barrels. Until the 1920s the family used to run a tavern in Constantinople where the schnapps was served directly from the wooden barrels. Over the course of time the customers came to want to be served from the twelfth barrel—so the legend has it—because they were convinced that this was the barrel containing the best ouzo. The company had to move its base to Greece in 1925 but the name Ouzo 12 remained. Fact or fiction? Either way, Ouzo 12 is today one of the best-known ouzos in the world.

### Katsarou
### Ouzo Tirnavos

The antique town of Tirnavos in Thessaly made a name for itself with silkworms and grapes. Nikos Katsarou was given a still as part of a dowry in 1850, and ouzo has since become a further hallmark of the town. Katsarou experimented for a long while with the distillation of herbal extracts, and in 1856 the state finally permitted the family to produce *Apostagma os uso Tyrnaboy* (as distilled in Tirnavos), which was soon to become the Greeks' national drink. Katsarou today refers to its Tirnavou as the "oldest ouzo in the world," claiming the label "World's Finest Ouzo" at the same time. Proof thereof is difficult to come upon, even though the recipe remains unchanged.

### Pilavas
### Ouzo Nektar

The Pilavas family produced their first ouzo in 1940. More so than brandy and liqueur, it has remained the company's main product up to the present day, the company now being in the hands of the third generation. The parent company likes to describe the recipe as comprising "first class raw materials." Ouzo distillers closely guard the nature and quantity of their ingredients, as if they were state secrets. According to Nikolas Pilavas' traditional recipe, the double distillation in a modern distilling plant is followed by a three-month resting period. A very mild ouzo is the end result. Irrespective of the long-standing tradition, Pilavas is available in 37 different forms of packaging.

### Plomari
### Ouzo of Plomari

This is the most widely drunk ouzo in Greece. Plomari, on the island of Lesbos, is considered to be one of the best sources of ouzo because the aniseed bushes flourish particularly well there. Plomari considers them to be the best in the world. The Greek market leader has been produced since 1894 with its creator, Isidoros Arvanitis, having managed to distill a truly harmonious mixture in his still. The recipe's herb mixture also includes mastix resin. However, as with so many producers, the precise recipe remains confidential and unchanged. The company management maintains that even the old still in which Arvanitis composed his elegant mixture is still in use. For certain, however, it is not the only still, otherwise Plomari would not be able to cater for the international market.

### Sans Rival
### Ouzo Sans Rival

The majority of ouzo manufacturers promote the fact that their ouzo has long been prepared according to a secret, unchanged recipe, a fact that they willingly prove on the basis of dates that extend back to the 19th century. Sans Rival, however, really is one of the oldest ouzos. It is distilled twice, and it has an aromatic fullness and a pleasant, mild taste. Its special touch comes from a herbal mixture and a little mastix resin, making it more complex than some other ouzos that focus primarily on aniseed flavors. Sans Rival comprises a pure, flavored schnapps without added neutral alcohol.

### Tsantali
### Tsantali Ouzo

Georgios Tsantali is now the third generation in charge of the brand's destiny, a fact of which the Tsantali company is proud. The ouzo has been produced according to the old family recipe ever since the company was founded in 1890: aniseed, fennel, cloves, cinnamon, coriander, and a range of other ingredients are macerated in a mixture of water and pure alcohol for 24 hours. The outfit itself appears a little overprocessed by comparison. Modernized and with an antique backdrop adapted to the current image, the bottle shaped like an antique column is also popular in the domestic market. Tsantali claims to operate the largest ouzo distillery in the world. The product comprises 100% schnapps distilled with flavorings.

### Tsilili
### Ouzo

Kostas Tsililis has been endeavoring to produce only the best quality ever since founding his wine estate in 1989. He has gathered together the ideal grape varieties for his wines and brandies near Raxa in Thessaly. He selects aniseed from Euboea in order to give his quality ouzo the desired aroma. He always buys from the same farmers to be able to ensure a consistent style. Together with the alcohol, the flavorings are distilled twice in small copper stills. The Tsilili version of the national drink is popularly equated with the Greek way of life has an especially strong aniseed aroma as well as a touch of cinnamon.

# Raki and ouzo with pleasure

Turks and Greeks alike value the diversity of their aniseed schnapps, which is not only suited to every occasion but is also healthy. Such is the opinion of raki and ouzo fans at least. They therefore appear on the table as aperitifs, meal accompaniments, digestifs, or simply for in between. They embody the best of everyday culture, both on the Peloponnese and in the Bosporus. Relaxed gatherings with aniseed schnapps and delicious appetizers are a regular feature, although they can also develop into raucous revelry. Raki and ouzo have to be enjoyed slowly; you need to take your time. That begins with the serving. In a restaurant the waiter brings a cylindrical glass measuring just under a half pint (around 0.2 liters) and fills it about a third or half full with crystal clear schnapps. In better restaurants the guests indicate the quantity they require. The majority of cafés or *ouzeries* serve it by the glass, or in half and/or whole bottles. The order is based on the size and the mood of the party. Cold water is added—mineral water is permitted—as well as ice cubes that are usually added by the guests themselves. The order is fixed. If ice is added to neat raki this can result in crystals formed by the aniseed. This freezing out compromises the quality of the schnapps and its flavor is impaired. The combination of water and spirits, however, produces an opal-colored cloudy effect that spreads throughout the glass.

Some connoisseurs prefer to enjoy the distinctive aniseed flavor neat, but then they require a glass of cold water on the side. Alternatively, raki with *ayran*, the salty yogurt drink, and—particularly with a *kebab*—*salgam*, a fermented, salty juice made from turnips and carrots, is added.

## Small sips

Like raki, ouzo is always drunk slowly and in sips so that the intense aniseed flavor can be

Turkish fishermen in Antalya harbor enjoy a morning snack and a glass of raki.

properly appreciated. Despite what is sometimes a high alcohol content of up to 50% vol., this means that the aniseed schnapps can be enjoyed for a long while without any side effects. This applies even on hot days. Anyone finding the alcohol a bit much can dilute it with more water, which has a double benefit: even at larger raki gatherings glasses are only refilled once the last person's glass is empty.

With their proportion of aniseed, raki and ouzo are considered to be remedies for a variety of complaints and are also especially easy to digest. This is indeed a good thing because the first of the tasty appetizers appears as soon as it has been served. Cold and warm appetizers, known as *meze* or *mezédes*, for which both countries are renowned, often get the party going.

Typical appetizers include sheep's milk cheese and honeydew melon. Salted almonds, tomatoes, cucumbers, salad leaves, sardines, and chickpeas can also put in an appearance on the table. Small cooked appetizers are also popular, such as red lentil balls, calamari, and other types of seafood, stuffed brinjals, and grilled vegetables with the yogurt sauce *cacık*. The glasses are often retained for the second course, particularly if it contains fish. However, *köfte*, *shish kebab*, and other grilled meats also go very well with ouzo and raki, as do even the sweet baked desserts. In fact, the characteristic flavors of Turkish cuisine such as dill, mint, parsley, garlic, caraway, and lemon always go well with aniseed.

If a normal evening meal requires all the aniseed's strength, this is even more the case with a *rakı sofrası*. At these raki gatherings the host takes pride in constantly bringing new appetizers to the table while the guests chat for hours on end, sipping their raki.

Ouzo is an essential feature of the Easter celebrations in Krasi on the island of Crete.

# Aniseed from Chinchón

Aniseed develops an especially intense flavor under the Spanish sun. It is therefore produced throughout Spain, but the most famous comes from Chinchón, south of the city of Madrid.

A contract dating from 1777 is the oldest written mention of the aniseed schnapps from Chinchón, even though it must already have been well established by then. The contract relates to an order from the Spanish royal court for no fewer than 26,400 gallons (100,000 liters) per year. The large-scale cultivation of aniseed in central Spain began at this time, the focus being on quality. In the 19th century Queen María Cristina appointed the Chinchón distillers as her

court purveyors. The aniseed from this little town south of Madrid was awarded gold medals at the world exhibitions in Chicago in 1893 and in Paris in 1900.

The cultivation of aniseed is relatively labor intensive but the town remains true to its tradition. Even today the Anís de Chinchón contains nothing more than what is on the label, although flavorings with a similar taste are available at a significantly lower cost. Wine is used to form the basis for the distil-

late but the more cost-effective grain alcohol produced by column distillation has brought about changes even here. Only a few wine-based aniseed schnapps have survived. As with French or Greek aniseed schnapps, Chinchón is today also based on neutral alcohol. Together with macerated aniseed, this mixture is then distilled again in copper stills. The alcohol content of the end product fluctuates between 35% vol. for Chinchón dulce to over 70% vol. for Chinchón seco especial. The EU certificate of origin guarantees that only aniseed schnapps from the municipal district of the same name southeast of Madrid may call itself Chinchón.

Aniseed schnapps is produced throughout Spain, however. In addition to *Pimpinella anisum*, star aniseed, fennel, or other plants which develop similar aromas are commonly used. A variety of processes is permitted, such as the repeated addition of seeds or other parts of plants with aniseed-like flavors. The only condition is that the aniseed flavor predominates. However, the most well-known aniseed spirits such as Chinchón stick to aniseed and are involved in the cultivation of the plants in their district—such as the Destilerías de Rute with the aniseed museum and the Anís seco from Cazalla de la Sierra in the province of Seville. Well-known aniseed brands include Miura, Castellana, Tunel, Machaquito, and Anis del Mono, which last belongs to the Osborne company.

Aniseed spirits have formed part of the Spanish drinking culture for centuries and gender-specific drinking rituals have developed as a result. Men usually order aniseed mixed with brandy as *sol y sombra* with coffee and cigars. Elderly ladies sip sweetened aniseed at their coffee parties, valuing both its digestive and its antiaging properties. The latter is a property that does not seem to work for aniseed itself. Many specialist distilleries have had to close and in Chinchón only the Sociedad Alcoholera has survived, having been taken under the wing of the sherry giant Gonzalez Byass.

Chinchón is the capital of Spanish aniseed production. Religious plays are performed on the town plaza (in the background).

# Super sweet aniseed

With sufficient sugar, aniseed changes from a medicine to pure indulgence, a fact that the liqueur manufacturers—after the monks—soon realized. The first recipe for an aniseed liqueur came from a West Indian sailor. Marie Brizard, daughter of a barrel maker and wine producer in Bordeaux, nursed the ailing sailor back to health. As a gesture of thanks he left her with the recipe for a cordial based on aniseed and 11 other flavorings. In 1755, at the age of 41, she decided to produce and sell the liqueur. Countless flavorings, and more especially raw sugar—which is essential for the production of liqueurs—were imported via Bordeaux harbor in those days. And so the charitable lady's company became just one of more than three dozen small distilleries producing sweet alcoholic beverages in the harbor town.

The Italians joined in much later—at least officially. The entrepreneur Luigi Manzi (1809–73), who established thermal baths in Casamicciola and the first electricity plant, is considered to be the inventor of sambuca, for which he used Chinese star aniseed and which is produced and bott[led] in Civitavecchia. This is where the succe[ss] of sambuca, which the law requires to [be] crystal clear, was launched. It went on [to] inspire liqueur manufacturers through t[he] whole of Italy.

Sambuca Manzi is still available today bu[t] did not remain the only Italian anise[ed] liqueur. For example, Silvio Meletti creat[ed] his anisetta in Ascoli Piceno in the southe[rn] marches in 1870 because he wanted to p[ro]vide a competitor for the expensi[ve] imported products. His advantage lay in t[he] quality of the aniseed harvested from t[he] clay soils of his home province. In 1904 t[he] company was able to afford a new distille[ry] near the railway station. Mistrà is the nam[e] of another version in the marches, and Sa[s]solino comes from Emilia-Romagna.

Anisette, Anisetta, Mistrà, Sambuca, a[nd] their close relatives from other countries a[re] usually drunk neat, the glass often decorat[ed] with three coffee beans, sometimes serv[ed] on ice or else with a dash of water. It can a[lso] be set alight, with the flames extinguish[ed] before drinking it warm.

Left: The charitable Marie Brizard displayed a great deal of business sense with her Anisette.

Right: In the 1950s all of the bottles from Meletti in Ascoli Piceno were wrapped in tissue paper.

# Selected aniseed liqueurs

### Destilerías de Cazalla
### Miura Anis Dulce

Cazalla de la Sierra, a good 50 miles (80 km) north of Seville, is located in the middle of a national park in the heavily wooded Sierra Norte. Wine making and the art of distilling developed in the 16th century in the region around the small town with its impressive architecture. Two hundred years later the residents were focused primarily on *aguardientes* and there were around 40 distilleries in the 19th century. Aniseed developed into one of their specialties. A number of the small distilleries joined forces after 1945 as the Destilerías de Cazalla, which has belonged to Caballero since 1995. An essence is distilled from aniseed in old *alambiques* and is then blended to produce this intense liqueur.

### Marie Brizard
### Anisette

Marie Brizard, daughter of a barrel maker from Bordeaux, was given the recipe in 1755 by a West Indian sailor whom she had found desperately ill on the street and had nursed back to health. The recipe has been handed down over the generations, being carefully modernized as required. This clear liqueur is based on green aniseed from the Mediterranean region. The recipe also includes ten other plants, fruit, and flavorings. This liqueur comprising only natural ingredients with an alcohol content of 25% vol. is enjoyed neat on ice. Anisette has also become very popular as an ingredient in numerous cocktails. It is flavored with lemon juice to produce Anisette Limón.

### Molinari
### Sambuca extra

Sambuca from the house of Molinari is one of the most well-known brands. It is produced on the basis of star aniseed, neutral alcohol made from wheat, and sugar, as well as a little ash. All of the other ingredients are kept secret. Like all sambucas it is enjoyed neat or *con la mosca* with three coffee beans—often also set alight. It is also drunk with ice or chilled to a temperature of 32 °F (0 °C), mixed with grapefruit juice, and of course as *espresso corretto*. Sambuca Molinari al Caffè constitutes a special version. Enriched with diverse coffee varieties and other ingredients, it has a very appealing combination of flavors. It is drunk neat at a temperature of 46 °F (8 °C).

### Silvio Meletti
### Anisetta

Meletti's Anisetta is an institution. Initially produced by the founder's mother for her own shop in Ascoli Piceno, it became a liqueur brand in 1870. The company founder designed his still heated in a *bain marie* himself in order to achieve as aromatic a distillate as possible, using locally grown, high-quality aniseed. Today the family company still follows the process as handed down, according to which an aniseed essence, the *aniciato*, is distilled first of all. Other flavorings are also distilled in order to compose the Anisetta, which rests in large steel tanks before bottling and is characterized by its refined, pure, sweet aniseed aroma.

### Wenneker
### Anisette

This clear aniseed liqueur comes from Wenneker, one of the largest liqueur manufacturers in The Netherlands. Its aroma is based on aniseed, it has a sweet flavor, and it displays plenty of fresh licorice nuances. With its soft, rounded flavor it is ideal for enjoying neat but is also suitable as an ingredient in numerous mixed drinks. Wenneker Anisette has an alcohol content of 25% vol. This liqueur is just one example from the extensive range offering a variety of basic liqueurs. All of the products are produced without added chemicals and contain only natural flavoring and coloring agents.

# Vermouth and wine-based aperitifs

Numerous aromatic ingredients give vermouth its special character: these spices, flowers, seeds, and barks, for instance, are the mark of Noilly Prat.

Opposite: In Turin bars, an aperitif is obligatory.

Page 522: Vermouth companies were among the pioneers of advertising, commissioning posters from the best-known lithographers, such as this work for Martini in 1918 by Marcello Dudovich (1878–1962).

# That certain aroma

Whether it is a glass of champagne, a dry white wine, a malt, or a predinner cocktail, the aperitif has been a popular habit in Europe and beyond for a long time. Yet the outright winners are vermouth and other wine-based aperitifs, those Mediterranean invaders that vanquished preprandial tedium and ensured the smooth passage of food to the stomach. Who, then, can claim to have invented the aperitif? There is no shortage of contenders: the French and Italians each think it is their right, Spaniards view this with skepticism, and as far as the Greeks are concerned, it must surely have been them.

In Turin they have no doubt at all that their city, and nowhere else, has been the aperitif capital from over a century ago through to the present day. For its inhabitants an aperitif is such an integral part of a meal that when the glass is set down, it is now automatically accompanied by a plate of something to eat, which is included in the price. Bars tout for their customers' favor with tasty nibbles. Some even present window displays of the extra side dishes that visitors can expect. Of course, even in Turin bars what is meant by "aperitif" has now acquired a more liberal interpretation, but vermouth—either with or without a shot of bitters—has held its ground, even though it has long since been known as Americano and is available as a ready mixed drink in bottles.

With a glass of vermouth in your hand, it is easy to imagine yourself transported back around a hundred years to the time when the great Italian brands had a high public profile thanks to their outstanding advertising campaigns, which are now well established as documents of the *Zeitgeist*. Their French competitors, who were targeting the same corner of the market with similar products, matched them in this respect, and poster art surpassed itself. This was the heyday of what were known as wine-based aperitifs, such as Byrrh, Dubonnet, and Saint-Raphaël, among others. The comforting time-filler before the meal was meant to be rich, sweet, and aromatic. Nowadays tastes have changed, and many of the oldest suppliers were unable to keep up, the result being that only the big names survived, with only a few exceptions. These too, however, have long since been incorporated into global companies, losing their halo of glory to the bigger picture: in fact, they are now often a subsidized part of the enterprise.

They should not be forgotten though, not just because of the tradition behind them but because of the quality of their preparation and the often surprising complexity of their taste. Astonishing skill underlies the harmonization of aromas and taste, created by fusing the base wine with dozens of natural ingredients such as flowers, leaves, fruits, seeds, roots, and barks.

At least vermouth brands—with their distinctive aromatic profile—have managed to carve out a permanent niche for themselves in bars across the world: no bar can afford to be without martini. And this does not mean the best-known international brand of vermouth, but the classic cocktail that originally consisted of one part dry vermouth and four parts gin. There are also dozens of other recipes that use dry and sweet versions of vermouth (and, less often, wine-based aperitifs) including cocktails like the Americano, Negroni, American Beauty, Claridge, Devil's, Duchesse, Miami Beach, Queen's, Shamrock, and Tipperary.

# A wormwood solution

"The name of the star is 'Wormwood'. A third of the waters turned bitter... ." In Revelation 8:11, the third angel sounds his trumpet and a star falls down from the sky onto a third of the rivers and springs. Even outside the biblical context, the "drop of wormwood" has a proverbial status. Common wormwood (*Artemisia absinthium*) has been valued for centuries as a medicinal herb, due not least to its notorious bitter constituents. Illness was believed to indicate an imbalance in the four body fluids (humors), so recovery was dependent on restoring the balance. If a deficiency of yellow bile was responsible for the disorder, then the restorative medicine had to be bitter. Hippocrates, who developed this theory in the 4–5th century BC, is reputed to have personally macerated wormwood in sweet wine together with oregano. The result was a stimulating tonic that aided the digestion, and its formula could dispense with any ingredient but wormwood. It flourished at any rate in the centuries that followed, and became the standard medicine used in the art of healing throughout Europe: it was known and valued as *vinum absinthiatum* or Hippocratic wine.

Over the centuries wormwood has had a wide range of applications, from treating worm infestation and plague wounds, to inducing labor and suppressing sexual urges in the clergy, so it is hardly surprising that the tonic has never been completely forgotten. In Italy during the 16th century the term *vermut* or *vermouth* became part of the vernacular. Yet for clear evidence of wormwood wine, we have to wait until 1773 when Cosimo Villifranchi mentions it in his treatise on Tuscan wines, *Oenologia toscana*.

## A healthy indulgence

Turin developed (along with Florence and Venice initially) into the center for wormwood wine production. From the end of the 15th century, it had been the official residence of the dukes of Savoy, who stayed loyal to their main city when they also became

kings of Sardinia around 1720. Aromatized wines had featured in the large provinces of Sardinia and in Piedmont and Savoy since olden times, and both viticulture and herb collecting had already been practiced there for many years. Thus Turin had all the necessary prerequisites for it to rise to become the stronghold of vermouth.

Right in the center of Turin, on what is now the Piazza Castello (on the corner of Via Viotti) opposite the Royal Palace, a gentleman called Marendazzo opened an elegant bar that was a combination of a spirits merchant's and a coffee house (it was destroyed in 1943). His assistant and eventual successor, Antonio Benedetto Carpano, created a new drink called *vermuth* in 1786, though wormwood was only one of its many ingredients. Carpano was the first to incorporate local recipes to make an aromatized wine with a sophisticated taste, one that had a beneficial effect and also appealed to the ladies. Soon Carpano was indulging the elegant circles of Turin society with his "luxury wine," as it was described by the national encyclopedia, entitled *Enciclopedia Italiana Treccani*.

It was only when his nephew inherited his estate that the brand name was registered and a company was founded. Guiseppe Bernardino Carpano made his uncle's vermouth famous and turned the bar into a meeting place for politicians and artists. The people in Turin loved the vermouth and ambiance so much that Carpano opened round the clock.

At that time sweet vermouth was seldom drunk straight up. Whether you opted for sweet or dry was a matter of personal taste. The most popular additives were vanilla and bitters. One morning in 1870 a group of stockbrokers and speculators met up in Carpano's for an aperitif. There was a fierce debate about the prices of some securities that had gone up by one and a half points. Caught up in the argument, one of them ordered his favorite vermouth and bitters mixture with the words *punt e mes*, Piedmontese for "one and a half"—one part vermouth and a half part bitters. The mixture and its name became so well established that Carpano decided to produce and bottle it as Punt e Mes, now the most successful aperitif of the brand.

Vermouth has survived as an aperitif, along with the traditional bars and cafes in the old town of Turin.

Opposite top: This illustration from the Latin edition of an Arabic doctrine on health, *The Medical House-book of the Cerruti family* (1390), depicts a physician picking wormwood.

Opposite bottom: The Carpano laboratory: the factory in Turin was turned into the Eataly food and wine center, with a vermouth museum.

# Brands emerge

In Turin patissiers and wine distillers were held in high esteem. Like other craft sectors, they were organized in guilds that bound masters and apprentices to an agreed set of rules. The Cinzano brothers are named in the minutes of a meeting dating back to 1757. A license enabled them to sell their products in their home town of Pecetto and in Turin. As they were expert liquor manufacturers and shrewd merchants, it was not long before the Cinzanos had created their own vermouth, especially as they had experience in dealing with aromatized wines.

Francesco Cinzano, one of Turin's most distinguished citizens, advised the Sardinian government on behalf of brandy manufacturers in 1816, and held public office over the next 20 years. He had been producing his own vermouth for years, which he sold in his shop in Dora Grossa (now Via Garibaldi). In 1862 his son traveled to London to exhibit the Cinzano products at the International Exhibition. He met with con-siderable success there, bringing home two gold medals.

## Vermouth heralds profits

The successes of the Carpanos and Cinzanos caught on. All the liquor producers in the city and many a wine grower from Piedmont made their own versions of the luxury wine. Among them was the son of a wine grower, Carlo Gancia, who established his company in Canelli in 1850. Following a visit to Reims in France, he produced the first Italian sparkling wine in 1865, setting the asti spumante tide of popularity in motion. In 1920 he introduced his famous white vermouth and a blend of red vermouth and bitters called Americano. The list of vermouth producers in Turin at this time is a long one, starting with Anselmo, Arlorio, Ballar, Bianchi & Cie, Calissano, Chazalettes and Cora. But liquor manufacturers elsewhere in Italy also caught a whiff of the business potential: Bosca, Cyrano, Gambarotta

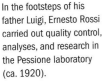

In the footsteps of his father Luigi, Ernesto Rossi carried out quality control, analyses, and research in the Pessione laboratory (ca. 1920).

Pio Cesare, Ramazotti, Riccadonna, Soldi, and Venici were just some of the new brands, many of which have long since sunk into oblivion. The most successful vermouth brand has been in existence since 1863, when Alessandro Martini and Teofilo Sola took over a drinks company and brought on board their liquor expert, Luigi Rossi, as a third partner. By the next year, on Rossi's advice, manufacture had been moved to Pessione, a good 12 miles (20 km) southeast of Turin and located on the Turin–Asti–Genoa rail link. This meant that the export routes opened up to the same extent as the Monferrato wine-growing region. To the present day the main center of the company is still located in the impressive estate house that the partners acquired there.

The company, renamed Martini & Rossi after the death of Sola, went on from strength to strength, not least thanks to the involvement of the four Rossi sons. By the end of the 19th century they had made Martini & Rossi vermouth one of the greatest Italian exports and had opened branches in Buenos Aires (1884), Geneva (1886), and Barcelona (1893). The eldest son, Teofilo Rossi, held important political offices, from the mayor of Turin to the Italian minister of industry and commerce; he also created the global communications and sales policy of the company. As mayor he organized the 1911 International Exhibition in Turin, which brought long-term advantages to the city. In 1911 King Victor Emmanuel III elevated the Rossis to an earldom for their services to society and politics. During World War II the company suffered losses in many countries, but the four cousins that headed the company from 1930 to 1970 managed to inject new life into it after the end of the war. The company made an important decision in 1977 when they grouped all of the international branches under one umbrella organization, the General Beverage Corporation, which merged with Bacardi in 1993 to become the Bacardi–Martini group. Martini is still one of the best-known Italian brands to this day.

The importance attached to advertising can be seen from this picture of the Martini & Rossi storeroom (ca. 1920).

# Advertising and marketing

of a new medium and put it to the service of profit making: and that was advertising. Lithography, the printing technique perfected in the 19th century, enabled artists to design and duplicate colorful posters. They became a mainstay of advertising, bringing the products under their brand name to a wide public. The best-known exponents at that time were Jules Chéret, Marcello Dudovich, and Leonetto Cappiello, and though many others were also involved, poster art was initially concentrated in Paris and the north of Italy. Carpano, Cinzano, Gancia, and other vermouth brands made use of the new medium, but it was the Rossi brothers who were the first to recognize the value of advertising and marketing, making the most extensive use of both. They soon promoted the image and profile of their brand not only with posters, but also through the sponsorship of concerts (which included Maria Callas), and movie and sporting events.

Effective sponsorship: Jeanne Moreau, Monica Vitti, Maria Pia Luzi, and Marcello Mastroianni with the director Michelangelo Antonini at the premiere of the film *La Notte* (1960).

Right: D. Lubatti created this poster using the tempera technique in 1936.

Opposite: Leonetto Cappiello (1875–1942), the most sought-after poster artist of the day, designed this poster in 1910.

Clutching an aperitif glass, the consumer approached the end of the 19th century and moved into a new age: the era of the brand name, and in this case that of the branded drink. Many of these drinks had been produced for decades, but it was only now—for various factors had to come into play to enable this to happen—that they became brand names with market share, firstly in their own region and then beyond its borders. Industrial development formed the basis for this, along with the expansion of the transport infrastructure, particularly in terms of railways and shipping. The exchange of goods increased, and in the cities there was a growth in the areas for workers and wage earners, from which a new middle class emerged. People's lifestyles and needs changed, and in turn the demand for a greater variety of products grew and needed to be satisfied.

In this mood of limitless possibilities, many of the established drinks managed to adapt to a new, industrial scale, especially those that were quick to recognize the importance

# The vermouth "apothecary"

*Acorus calamus* – sweet flag
Root: aromatic; pleasantly scented; bitter constituents; stimulant. Southeast Asia.

*Angelica archangelica* – garden angelica
Seeds: similar to licorice, aromatic; good for the stomach, stimulant. Central Europe.

*Artemisia absinthium* – wormwood
Leaves and flowers: strong, distinctive smell; stimulates appetite. Central Europe

*Chamaemelum nobile* – Roman chamomile
Flowers: intensely fruity aroma; good for stomach and cramps. Central Europe.

*Cinchona officinalis* – quinine bark
Bark: distinctly bitter; stimulates appetite, aids digestion. South America.

*Cinnamomum zeylanicum* – cinnamon
Bark: intense, sweet and spicy aroma an taste. Sri Lanka.

*Croton eluteria* – cascarilla
Bark: slightly bitter, mild stimulant, aids digestion. Central America, Caribbean.

*Dipteryx odorata* – tonka bean
Seeds: intense, sweet, nutty smell; used to treat neuralgia. Guyana.

*Elettaria cardamomum* – cardamom
Seeds: strong, pleasantly sweet smell a taste. South India.

*Glycyrrhiza glabra* – licorice
Root: distinctive sweetness, similar to aniseed; settles the stomach. China.

*Hypericum perforatum* – St John's wort
Flowers: red dye; fragrant; mild antidepressant, used for neuralgia. Central Europe.

*Illicium verum* – star anise
Pod fruit: intense, characteristically sweet aroma; stimulant. China.

*Iris germanica* 'Florentina' – orris root
Rhizome: fragrant, with distinctive aroma of violets; calming. Italy.

*Lavandula angustifolia* – lavender
Flowers: very aromatic, fragrant, and spicy; good for heart and circulation. S. Europe.

*Origanum dictamnus* – dittany of Crete
Flowers and leaves: pleasantly spicy, slightly bitter smell; stimulant. S. Europe.

*Pterocarpus santalinus* – red sandalwood
Rasped wood: produces red dye; pleasant, subtle smell. Southeast Asia.

*Rosa gallica* – Gallic rose
Flowers: strong scent of roses; astringent; wound healing. Central Europe.

*Syzygium aromaticum* – cloves
Buds: spicy, sweet, slightly peppery; stimulates appetite. Madagascar.

# The vermouth "kitchen"

Vermouth is a wine with aromatic herbal ingredients added, known collectively as "botanicals." Sugar is also added, and sometimes a little grape juice and alcohol. And that's all. This may sound rather unimpressive today, but there is a fascinating story behind the development of the recipes, at a time when they had to establish which herbs—how much and in which form—worked best together and in harmony with the base wine.

The first stage in the production process involves extracting the botanicals. They play the crucial role in vermouth, as their blending defines the smell and taste profile. Each brand has its own recipe, which is, of course, jealously guarded.

In a company like Martini & Rossi, with branches in many different countries, it is vital that the aromatic blend is identical everywhere. For this reason it is prepared centrally in Switzerland.

Legal considerations have to be taken into account as well as house recipes, so at least one type of artemesia has to be used, for instance, in order to ensure the typical vermouth flavor. Sometimes botanical extracts are produced by macerating them for a period of time in alcohol and water, and sometimes they are distilled in alcohol and water. Depending on the size of the stills, up to 530 lb (240 kg) of dried botanicals are needed for one distillation. Here too, every manufacturer has their own unique recipe:

The real secret to vermouth lies in its unique blend of botanicals, which Martini & Rossi distill in house in a large still in Pessione.

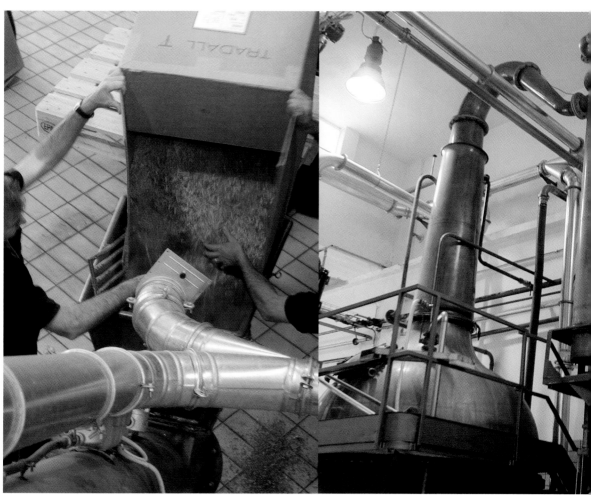

anyone who values quality brews their own "natural flavorings."

## A bitter-sweet balance

As stipulated by law, vermouth must contain at least 75% wine. White wine is used primarily as the base, though in the case of vermouth rosé a little red wine is added for color. Today neutral, non-oxidized wines made from Trebbiano grapes from the Emilia-Romagna region, for instance, or white wines from Puglia or Sicily, are used. For each brand the wines from different origins are blended together to give a base wine with a consistently identical taste.

Other ingredients are then added to this main consituent of vermouth: firstly sugar, as a rule, either in the form of mistelle (grape juice and alcohol) or pure white sugar. Sweetness is particularly important for the overall balance as it takes the edge off the bitter constituents.

The botanicals distillate is added (sometimes with more spices, herbs, and flavorings) and then alcohol to bring the alcoholic strength of the wine up to the desired level of 15–16%. Occasionally a little water is required to fine tune the mixture. Caramel is the only ingredient allowed to add color to red vermouth, which is actually amber colored in daylight. It also gives rosso vermouth a particular flavor.

The mixture is often left for another few weeks to "rest," so that the ingredients integrate completely before being stabilized through refrigeration, and are then filtered and bottled.

The slow distillation process produces the aromatic essence, which is then blended with wine, alcohol, and sugar in large vats before being bottled as vermouth.

# Dry French vermouth

As far back as 1896 Thomas Stuart mentions in his manual *Stuart's Fancy Drinks and How to Mix Them* a forerunner of the famous martini cocktail, made from a dash of orange bitters, two parts Plymouth gin, and one part French vermouth. He was talking about Noilly Prat, whose sales figures rose in the United States with the popularity of this drink, and trebled in the first decade of the 20th century to 75,000 crates per year. Dry French vermouth has remained the classic ingredient of a martini to this day, even though the Italian brands have long since caught up. Noilly Prat comes from Marseillan, a small port on the Etang de Thau, an inland lake on the French Mediterrannean coast between Sète and Agde. To this day it is still produced there over a two-year period using the original process.

The basic recipe for the first French vermouth was developed by a liquor manufacturer and wine merchant from Lyons, Joseph Noilly, in 1813. He obtained most of the ingredients from Marseilles, where Claudius Prat began to work for him in 1837. His son, Louis Noilly, decided to relocate the company to Marseilles in 1843, and from 1850 he matured the base wines for the vermouth in Marseillan. Prat, who was now his son-in-law, joined the company in 1855 and the brand was born.

## White wine in a sea of red

Marseillan was ideally suited to vermouth production, as it lies in the wine-growing region for the Picpoul white grape variety. It is situated close to the important wine-producing villages of Pinet and Pomérols, which represent one of the rare white wine regions within Languedoc, otherwise dominated by red wine. The second white wine used by Noilly Prat also grows on the doorstep, as it were: that is Clairette grapes from Languedoc. In the early days producers themselves took the wine distillate they had made to the winery owners, fortified the selected wines on site to stabilize them, and then fetched them after a year's maturation for further processing. Now this all takes place in their own cellar halls, where the wines—separated according to variety and fortified to an alcohol content of 16%—mature for eight months in large oak vats containing up to 10,600 gallons (40,000) liters. The pale, fruity wine is then transferred into aged 160-gallon (600-liter) casks, or demi-muids, and stored in the enclosed, open-air courtyard of the winery. There, it sweats under the Mediterranean sun or shivers when the cold northwest wind blows down from the Cévennes mountains in winter. The changes in temperature and contact with the air cause the wine to oxidize. Pouring it after about a year reveals it to be a gleaming, golden color; with an aroma of fresh nuts and toasted wood, reminiscent of dry sherry, it is a reminder of just how much the final Noilly Prat owes to wine. It is quite different from its Italian cousins with their bland vino. Monsieur Noilly was afraid of losing the secret of this successful aperitif, and so he kept the different stages of production in separate places. The wine was only matured in Marseillan, and it stayed that way for 123 years.

Noilly Prat owes its quality to a great extent to its wines, which are left to mature in 160-gallon (600-liter) madeira casks in the open air.

It was not until 1973, when the family business was sold because there were no heirs, that all the production processes moved to Marseillan—with the exception of bottling. After the glorious transformation in the casks in the open air, the wines, mistelle made from muscat wine, and house-distilled fruit essences of raspberry and lemon are all mixed together and put into 530-gallon (2,000-liter) casks. To each of these is added 44 lb (20 kg) of a blend made up of dried plants, chamomile flowers, coriander, teasel, Egyptian cornflower, bitter orange, quinine,

orris root, nutmeg, and a dozen other ingredients. The botanicals are left to macerate for three weeks, and have to be stirred daily with a scythe-shape stick. The vermouth is then filtered and rests for another six weeks before being stabilized by refrigeration. It has now acquired its complex bouquet and the distinctive taste that has made it so famous. And it even improves in the bottle, if it is given enough time… .

Louis Noilly found good local wines and the perfect storage conditions for his dry vermouth in the little port of Marseillan on the Etang de Thau.

# Chambéry cousins

CELLO

**VERMOUT**
LE PLUS APPRÉCIÉ

**CHAMBÉRY · DOLIN**
INVENTEUR DU VERMOUT DE CHAMBÉRY

Chambéry vermouth acquired distinguished fans on Lac du Bourget and its famous spa, Aix-les-Bains.

When you consider that Turin (in Piedmont), where vermouth rose to become a fashionable drink in the early 19th century, had been the capital of Savoy-Piedmont since 1563 and had not been seen as a foreign country for centuries by Chambéry inhabitants (in Savoy)—which became the main area for "French-style" vermouth production—vermouth begins to take on a political dimension. Whether French troops marched into Savoy and occupied the northern part of the duchy, or whether the Vienna Congress restored the old balance of power, the people on both sides of the Alps tried not to let it affect the way they conducted their affairs with each other.

The flourishing capital in Piedmont was a permanent destination for aspiring businessmen from the duchy of Savoy. Thus Joseph Chavasse, a young liquor manufacturer who had founded his own distillery in his home town of Echelles at the tender age of 25, would often have set off for Turin to sell his *crème royale* or *élixir d'amour*. No doubt he became acquainted with Carpano's new luxury wine on these visits and decided to create his own vermouth. In combining his ingredients, he had recourse to regional produce—perhaps following traditional local recipes for the cureall wormwood wine. He processed a large amount of healing plants and herbs from the Alpine region, macerating them for several months in the local white wines, which were dry, fruity, slightly tart, and fortified.

When he finally brought his Chambéry-style vermouth onto the market in 1821, Joseph Chavasse founded a tradition that spawned

many successors and won the *Appellation d'Origine Contrôlée* status for Chambéry vermouth in 1932—making it the only vermouth with a guarantee of origin.

## The Queen's blessing

Chambéry prospered under Piedmont administration. The grand boulevard, lined with tasteful shops, was extended in 1830. That same year Joseph Chavasse realized his dream. He became a burgher of the town and set up a new distillery in the Reclus quarter. It was inspected annually for the "good management of the premises and the high quality of the raw materials," for the ducal town put great emphasis on impeccable business practices. His son-in-law, Louis Ferdinand Dolin, concentrated all his energies on the vermouth business, which took his name and brought him awards at the international exhibitions in Philadelphia and Paris. But above all, it was Queen Victoria who helped him to sell his aperitif.

The Queen came to Aix-les-Bains on Lac du Bourget for the first time in 1852. Later—after the eventual annexation of Savoy by France in 1860 and her reappearance in society after the death of her husband—she visited the spa more frequently, making it a magnet to many of her compatriots. This brought considerable benefit, not only to the town, but also to Chambéry vermouth. Even to this day, it is better known in England than in the regions of France. In its heyday there were a dozen vermouth producers in Chambéry, including Marke Boissière, which is now made by Dolin. Since 2000 Routin vermouth has experienced a well-deserved renaissance, for it is once again being made according to the original recipe that its founder created in 1883 and is based on 35 different botanicals.

A vermouth dispenser from the time when English high society took the cure in the Savoy Alps.

Dolin makes the herbal essences for the vermouth bottled in Chambéry in these small stills.

# Selected vermouths

### Italy

#### Carpano Antica Formula

The Rolls-Royce of vermouths—Antonio Benedetto Carpano's first recipe (secret, of course) from 1786, containing 50 different herbs and spices, is presented in its original bottle design. After the success of Punt e Mes, Carpano brought out Rosso, Bianco, and then dry versions that were more in line with the market. Fratelli Branca, which took over the old company in 1982, went back to the roots, bringing out the original Carpano for aficionados. Surprisingly uncharacteristic of vermouth, it has the wonderful spiciness of gingerbread and lingers persistently on the palate.

### Italy

#### Punt e Mes

In Turin vermouth was served in mixes according to personal taste, with vanilla or bitters, for instance. One day in 1870 a few stockbrokers met in Carpano's for an aperitif. They had a heated debate about share prices, which had risen one and a half points. Caught up in the argument, one of them ordered his favorite vermouth with the words *punt e mes*, Piedmontese for one and a half, meaning one part vermouth and a half part bitters. As he was not the only one to drink his vermouth this way, Carpano decided to bottle the mixture and call it Punt e Mes. It is still the most popular aperitif of the brand today.

### Italy

#### Cinzano Bianco

Although Cinzano is available as rosso, extra dry, and most recently limeto (with extracts of lime) and orancio (with orange and vanilla), the breakthrough for the famous vermouth house came with its sweet bianco, with its characteristic aroma of cinnamon and cloves and persistent dry, bitter note. The Cinzano brothers were the second liquor company to bring out vermouth after Carpano, and became court-appointed purveyors. Like their competitors, they quickly recognized the importance of advertising, which helped their vermouth to become internationally famous. It is now part of the Campari group.

### Italy

#### Gancia Dry

The Gancia family launched their sweet, intensely fragrant, white vermouth in 1921, and it became their most successful product in this range. Its secret lies in Muscat wines from the Monferrato and other Piedmont wine regions, providing the wonderful aromas for the base wines. The flavor is then elaborated further with plant extracts. Carlos Gancia, the founder of the family business, began his career in 1850 with vermouth, though the family's core business has always been sparkling wines. The house has however remained loyal to vermouth production to the present day, and now has a very impressive dry in the range.

### Italy

#### Gancia Americano

In Turin and Milan it was the custom to pep up vermouth with a shot of bitters—this is regarded as the first Italian cocktail, generally attributed to Gaspare Campari. The mixture only really became famous during Prohibition when it was known as an Americano, because of the pleasure American tourists were said to have obtained from it. Subsequently many producers went on to offer a premixed drink in bottles. Gancia's Americano combines the characteristically pungent, bitter-sweet aroma with a low alcohol content of 14.5% vol., making it an excellent base for long drinks.

## Italy

### Martini Rosso

The different types of Martini & Rosso vermouth have become known internationally simply as "martini," in particular the rosso. No vermouth is actually red as such, but is colored amber using caramel. With its perfect balance between sweetness and acidity, and its intensely fruity, spicy aroma and taste, this vermouth has made widespread use of advertising and sponsorship to maintain its top position among wine-based aperitifs, unaffected by changes in fashion and by a wide margin. Martini Rosso has proved its value as a pungent, aromatic flavoring for many cocktails. In 1993 Martini & Rossi merged with Bacardi.

## France

### Noilly Prat

This dry vermouth from the south of France is something of an outsider. It has won a place for itself in just about every bar as the classic component of the martini cocktail. Compared to the extra dry of other houses, it comes out in front in terms of taste, thanks to the two grape varieties in the recipe (bursting with flavor) and the forced aging of the wines that results in a slight madierization. It even has a place in the kitchen—Noilly Prat is ideally suited for deglazing and for sauces. The traditional production method and high quality have been maintained since it became part of the Bacardi–Martini group.

## France

### Dolin

Chambéry vermouth proves itself to be one of the most refined examples of wine-based aperitifs, which is immediately evident in its clear, pale green, shimmering color. Its bouquet boldly unfolds the aromas of herbs, roots, and wormwood, more Alpine than Mediterranean in character, and with an unmistakeable dryness. The taste is also defined by herbs, yet it preserves an appealing lightness, irrespective of its characteristically persistent bitter note. It is very good as an aperitif with ice, straight up, or even with a dash of fruit liqueur. Dolin's Chambéryzette, a sweet, fruity aperitif created in 1904, combines its vermouth with strawberry liqueur.

## France

### Routin

Philibert Routin's company, founded in 1883, produced its first well-known product in the form of vermouth based on his own recipe. René Clochet extended the existing range to include syrups, liqueurs, and wines when the company was taken over in 1938. Over the years the vermouth recipe became more and more "commercial," with the result that the aperitif lost some of its special character. This all changed in 2000, when Georges Clochet went back to the original recipe with its 35 different herbs and botanicals. Vermouth Routin has regained its complex aroma and flavor since then, as well as its former success.

## USA

### Vya Extra Dry & Vya Sweet

The United States owes its great vermouth tradition to its Italian immigrants. Important brands are Gallo, Gambarelli & Davitto, Tribuno, and Lejon. Vermouth is drunk in cocktails, however, rather than straight up. Andrew Quady, a Central Valley vintner well known for sweet wines, created an excellent aperitif with a fresh bouquet and slightly bitter note: it was based on dry Colombard and Orange Muscat wines, as well as lime blossom, alfalfa, elecampane, and rose petals. Vya Sweet is made from Orange Muscat and Tinta Roriz sweet wine. The botanicals used to infuse flavor include gentian, blessed thistle, nutmeg, galangal, cloves, and the rind of bitter Seville oranges.

# Vermouth in combinations

Vermouth straight up fails to impress in the long run, as was evident back in Carpano's bar, where it was mostly drunk with a dash of bitters. With the enduring success of the martini cocktail, which bears no relation to the famous brand of vermouth, the doors of bars across the world opened to vermouth and bartenders were inspired. Even the basic recipe of four parts gin to one part dry vermouth was a variation of an earlier version pepped up with orange bitters. In *Modern American Drinks* in 1885, George J. Kappeler records a version made from one part sweet red vermouth, one part gin, and a dash of orange bitters. Charly, the bartender in the Raquet Club in New York in 1910, also took

sweet instead of dry vermouth, mixed it wi two parts gin and garnished it with a st each of lemon and orange peel—and t Old Army Martini was born. Someone ga nished the classic version with an oli which is said to have inspired President Ro sevelt to create the Dirty Martini, which h a dash of olive juice. Dry vermouth was th mixed into dozens of cocktails. In the bar Claridge's hotel in London, they use tv parts dry vermouth, two parts gin, one pa triple sec, and one part apricot brandy make the Claridge cocktail. Gin and ve mouth is truly a never-ending story.
For a Washington cocktail, take two parts d vermouth to one part brandy, and two dash

In the house bar of the impressive Martini headquarters in Pessione, they know how to make dozens of cocktails, starting with the classic martini.

each of Angostura bitters and sugar syrup. Or how about a Miami Beach? You need equal measures of scotch, vermouth, and freshly squeezed grapefruit juice. Then there is a Black Devil, with four parts rum, one part dry vermouth, and one black olive.

## Dry, sweet, and bitter

The bitters that have been mentioned, of which Campari is the best-known brand, seduced Milan and Turin folk early on to produce a range of mixtures, such as the Americano (consisting of just vermouth and bitters) and Negroni (with an added part gin) which caused quite a furor. Often though, not just dry but also sweet vermouth is brought into play. An example is the Cooperstown cocktail, for which one part each of dry and sweet vermouth are mixed in a shaker with two parts gin, and then poured into a cocktail glass with a sprig of mint. Gin is also a player in the Bloodhound cocktail, for which two parts gin are shaken together with one part each of dry and sweet vermouth and one part strawberry liqueur, then decorated with two fresh strawberries in a glass. In a Queens cocktail, the mixture consists of one part each of gin, dry vermouth, sweet vermouth, and pineapple juice. If you are not in the mood for gin, try the match of

one part each of scotch and of sweet and dry vermouth, stirred with two dashes angostura bitters, and garnished with some lemon peel. Sometimes sweet vermouth is enough on its own—Rosso or Bianco for taste and visual effect—as in a Metropolitan, where it is mixed in a shaker along with an equal measure of brandy, a half teaspoon sugar syrup, and a dash of angostura. If you prefer rum, make a Little Princess by stirring one part each of white rum and Bianco vermouth with ice, then pouring it into a chilled cocktail glass. The home of Italian vermouth is also the region for asti spumante, so many vermouth producers also make sparkling wine—for some, like Gancia, it is even the main part of the business. What would be more natural than to put both in a glass together? In this case Martini is banking on being the ladies' choice: for a vivacious Sylvia, put one part vodka, two parts Martini Dry, and two parts Martini Rosé in a cocktail glass and top it up with five parts asti. The seductive Lady Laura is made with four parts Martini Dry, one part peach vodka, and five parts asti, poured into an ice-filled Old Fashioned glass and then garnished with a slice of peach and a cherry.

The genesis of the vermouth bottle: Martini from 1865 to the present day.

TONIQUE
HYGIÉNIQUE
"BYRRH"
A BASE DE VINS GÉNÉREUX & QUINQUI

# Sweet and fruity aperitifs

Martini may be familiar to young frequenters of bars, but many have never heard the names Dubonnet or Saint-Raphaël, and have no idea what a wine-based aperitif tastes like. Of course the wine-based aperitif family has never been as successful internationally as whisk(e)y or vodka, but in the history of spirits they too had their good times, when millions of drinks in which they featured were drunk with judicious pleasure, year in and year out. They have kept their charm and quality and, like the non-aromatized liqueur wines, they are in the process of once again arousing interest as drinks with their own particular character and often with their own distinctly regional roots.

There is no denying the fact that wine-based aperitifs have seen far better times. This is certainly true of many of the vermouth types, and it applies even more to their French cousins, Dubonnet, Saint-Raphaël, and Byrrh. The family of wine-based aperitifs is basically divided into two groups. Vermouth consists mainly of fermented wine that is then aromatized. The so-called wine-based aperitifs, on the other hand, nearly all use mistelle as the base—that is, grape juice in which fermentation has been prevented by the addition of a sufficient quantity of alcohol. This fortified grape juice is then aromatized in the classic varieties, but in a few of the more modern ones it is sold as pure mistelle, which has tax advantages. This special kind of wine-based aperitif is very similar to liqueur wines, such as Pineau des Charentes, where cognac is added to the grape juice, and Floc de Gascogne, where armagnac takes on this role (liqueur wines are introduced at the end of this chapter).

Unlike vermouth, branded versions of which are made in nearly every Mediterranean and wine-producing country, actual wine-based aperitifs have in principle remained a purely French undertaking. Like so many other spirits, they began their career as an elixir. They were chosen as the means of administering a fever-reducing medicine—quinine or cinchona bark, named after the Countess of Cinchón, the wife of the Spanish viceroy of Peru, who was apparently cured by the bark. The drinks rose to become brand names at the end of the 19th and beginning of the 20th centuries. One of the technical prerequisites was the laying of railway lines, which linked the production regions in the south of France with potential customers in the industrial north and the capital. As with vermouth, advertising was the second factor, especially the new poster art. With all the

brand names that have survived to the present day, it is certainly no coincidence that their managements realized at an early stage that the success of the business was inextricably linked to the level of awareness of the product. This is precisely where advertising comes into play. Simon Violet, owner of the company Byrrh in the northern Catalan town of Thuir, was just such a visionary who knew how to make consumers aware of his wine-based aperitif by using advertising and business acumen. As a result, Byrrh rose to become the market leader between the world wars, when absinthe was banned in France.

A new period began in the 1950s, when consumer attitudes began to change. The internationally fashionable drink was scotch. In Paris it was pastis, the safe reincarnation of absinthe, though that too was squeezed out by whisky, at least as far as the taste of the male population was concerned. At the same time aperitif wines—with Dubonnet leading the way—managed to gain a foothold abroad.

And today? Now it is all about nostalgia and tourism. With the largest vat in the world, Byrrh in Thuir near Perpignan has become a popular tourist attraction. And more and more fans of sweet drinks are taking an interest in Pineau des Charentes and Floc de Gascogne, which may still be for the initiated but continue to represent a good additional source of income for many producers. Anyone fond of sweet, fruity drinks will get their full money's worth with liqueur wines.

# Bitter and healthy

In the 19th century quinine bark was seen as a miracle cure for malaria and as an all-round remedy and tonic in general. It was administered as a prophylactic to soldiers in the French colonial army, though it met with opposition on the part of the recipients as quinine bark has an extremely bitter taste. Liquor manufacturer Joseph Dubonnet, the proud owner of a store in the Paris Opera quarter since 1846, began to think of a remedy. In his cellar he mixed together a slightly bitter, but quite pleasant, drink made from mistelle and herbs, and enhanced with quinine bark. It was not just soldiers who liked his elixir. Parisians in increasing numbers enjoyed it as an aperitif, christening it simply Quinquina Dubonnet. This was how Dubonnet became the forerunner of a fashion for wine- or grape juice-based aperitifs containing quinine bark, which also highlighted their digestive properties.

Even before Dubonnet, around 1830, a doctor in Lyons called Juppet had developed a tonic containing quinine. As he was in danger of losing his sight, he begged the archangel Raphael for help, vowing to dedicate his tonic to him if he did. Considerable help was forthcoming, for Saint-Raphaël flourished as a wine-based aperitif from 1897 on, with its headquarters in Paris. As did Byrrh.

## Successful material

The Violets were itinerant drapers in Roussillon before they opened a store selling material and dry goods in Thuir, not far from Perpignan. To begin with they produced their stimulating drink based on wine and quinine bark (a monk is said to have revealed the recipe to them) for their own use alone. As the wine trade had become a very lucrative business in the second half of the 19th century, however, they began to market their tonic on a commercial basis. When the growing success of their quinine-based tonic unleashed increasingly vehement protests by apothecaries against unfair competition, Simon and Pallade Violet went on the offensive in 1873. They registered the brand name Byrrh—it was said to have got its name from

A worker in the Congo gathers quinine bark on a cloth.

## Quinine bark—the magic ingredient

The fever-reducing effects of the bark of the cinchona tree, native to the Peruvian Andes, were already known to the Incas: they called it Quina-Quina, meaning bark of bark. With its botanical name, *Cinchona officinalis*, Carl von Linné immortalized the wife of the Spanish viceroy of Peru, who was said to have been cured of fever attacks by a Jesuit using quinine bark—a nice story, but no more than that. The viceroy's diaries, preserved completely intact, make no mention of any illness. Nonetheless the Jesuits distributed the medicine across Europe in the 17th century in the form of a powder (known as Jesuits' or Cardinal's bark). In France its benefits became well known under Louis XIV. Today the tropical tree is cultivated in Ecuador and Guatemala, as well as in Java, Sri Lanka, India, South Vietnam, Malaysia, the Congo, and other parts of Africa. The dried bark of trees which are at least six years old is used. Quinine bark is used to treat, among other things, neuralgia, bronchitis, flu, fever, malaria, gout, and stomach and gall bladder problems, and is seen as an invigorating remedy, even for virility. The chemical form of its active agent, quinine, was identified in 1820 by two Frenchmen, Joseph Bienaimé Caventou and Pierre Joseph Pelletier. Quinine is still a constituent of many medicines to the present day.

the purely random order of letters on bales of cloth—as a consumer product and founded a factory.

Fifteen years later the brothers literally reached a parting of the ways. Their Byrrh was so successful that they had no choice but to build another factory. Pallade refused, and Simon Violet took over as sole proprietor, acquiring a site of 17 acres (7 hectares) in 1892, where he set up the huge winery in Thuir that is still operational today. His son Lambert's expertise made Byrrh a well-established name in France. A natural in public relations, he recognized the signs of the times and concentrated on advertising. Long before others thought of it, he allowed Byrrh to be used for sponsorship, supporting village festivals, competitions for fishing, playing boules, rugby games of course, and many other sporting events. Byrrh was ubiquitous, and became the top-selling aperitif in France between the wars.

# Fermentation is stopped

Left: Botanicals for the classic aperitif are weighed as they were 100 years ago in the Byrrh winery near Perpignan.

Right: Byrrh is aromatized mainly with quinine bark, dried orange peel, and coffee and cocoa beans.

Byrrh is best drunk straight up, without ice, but slightly chilled.

With their delicious aroma, grapes are among the most popular dessert fruits. If grapes are used instead to make wine—and with few exceptions this involves special varieties with smaller berries and thicker skins—the fruity aromas often dissipate during fermentation or at least undergo a considerable process of change. Back at the end of the 13th century the doctor, academic and Templar knight Arnaldus von Villanova

discovered on the Templar estate, Mas Deu near Perpignan that the fermentation o alcohol can be inhibited by adding a certain amount of brandy to the must. Furthe experiments to establish the required amount soon led to the realization that mus fermentation can be halted completely if a least 15% vol. of alcohol, or even slightly more, is added to it.

This process of stopping the fermentation o the must is known as *mutage* in French, and is the basis for producing liqueur wines. The result is that the enticing aromas of the freshly pressed grape juice are retained, as well as all the natural grape sugar content For clean, natural fruit aromas the grapes must be picked carefully by hand. On no account should they be allowed to burst, as they might then begin to ferment before the *mutage* takes place, thus impairing the aroma. (It is now possible to achieve perfect results even with mechanical pickers.)

For red versions of wine-based aperitifs unlike the vermouth recipes, they use red grape varieties that are immediately de-stemmed to stop the must from absorbing

any "green" tannins from the stalks and stems. Neutral 96% alcohol is then added. Depending on the quality and style of the particular brand, the mashed red grapes are left to macerate in their skins for up to a month, bringing out the best colors, aromas, and fine tannins. They are then pressed. For aperitifs based on white wines, the pressing takes place immediately and the alcohol is added to the must.

The second stage of the production process involves maturing the mistelle, the grape juice fortified with alcohol, in order to get rid of the initial taste of raw spirit. The main Byrrh winery in Thuir is most impressive. At one time, 70 oak vats (each with a capacity of 53,000 gallons / 200,000 liters) and two huge casks (one holding 111,000 gallons / 420,500 liters and the other —the largest wooden cask in the world—264,000 gallons / 1,000,200 liters) were all dedicated exclusively to this aperitif. Today Dubonnet, Ambassadeur, Cinzano under license, and others are matured here, but the capacity is still too big.

## Perfect percolation

As in vermouth, botanicals like quinine bark are essential components of this aperitif. For this reason great importance is attached to a direct exchange between the mistelle and the botanicals. In the case of Byrrh and the French (aromatized) aperitif Dubonnet, this process works according to the same principle as a coffee machine, and is called percolation. The plant matter, most of which is dried, is put into boilers, beneath which there are containers with mistelle. They are steeped under pressure for five to six hours and then rested for the same length of time in order to reconstitute before the process begins again. After a week the plants have yielded all their aromatic substances to the mistelle. This extract is mixed with the base wine that has aged in casks. After several processes of filtration and stabilization, the aperitif is ready to be bottled.

Left: The largest wooden vat in the world holds 264,000 gallons (1 million liters) and is a popular tourist attraction in Roussillon.

Right: When Byrrh was still the most consumed aperitif in France, tankers ran regularly across the track lines custom built in the factory.

# Aperitif, latitude southwest

The aperitif from Bordeaux, Lillet, naturally owes the special place it has occupied since the 1950s to its well-rounded aromatic qualities, but it is also thanks to the New York wine merchant Michel Dreyfus. The importer of Château Pétrus and Mateus Rosé discovered the taste in 1946 and brought Lillet to the United States. While wine-based aperitifs did not catch on in other markets, they caused a sensation in America, and in the 1980s four fifths of Lillet production traveled across the Atlantic. To survive, a wine-based aperitif needs a bit of luck as well: after all, the Kina Lillet created in 1895 by liquor manufacturers Paul and Raymond Lillet only extolled the virtues of quinine when the Bordeaux wine merchant Bruno Borie took it on board in 1985. Borie modernized the plant and brought the product up-to-date so that in 1986 Lillet entered a new dynamic phase following an oenological makeover.

Lillet is a blend of wines and liqueurs. First, wines from the Gironde are selected, some of which are vinified in house. The first blending and elaboration then takes place. The ingredients used for aromatization include the peel of sweet oranges from the south of Spain, bitter oranges from Haiti, and green oranges from Morocco and Tunisia, and of course quinine bark from Peru. The botanicals are cold brewed in alcohol and macerated for four to six months, and then the infusion is strained and pressed. Next, the wines and liqueurs are thoroughly mixed together in the blending process. Lillet is then matured for six to fourteen months in oak casks and vats before younger and older vintages are blended together to produce added compexity.

Left: The Lillet museum in Podensac near Bordeaux with its old distilling equipment.

Right: This poster was designed by the illustrator G. Dola—the client's name is wrongly spelled.

# Selected aperitifs

### White Lillet

The classic aperitif from Bordeaux is a lovely golden yellow color and has an intense bouquet (the red version was not developed until 1962). Though it reveals floral notes and honey, the aromas of candied oranges and limes are more pronounced, as is the fresh hint of mint. Distinctly fruity and sweet, it is generous and long on the palate, redolent of the sweet wines of the Gironde. Since 1999 it has marketed itself as the "French heavyweight in cocktails" and Lillet has organized the Feast of the Senses in Chelsea, New York, which brings together art, cooking, and Lillet.

### Byrrh Rare Assemblage

Mistelle that has matured for many years is selected for this special edition of Byrrh. Normally Carignan and Grenache Noir grape varieties are used, which provide the structure, richness, and aromas of small red fruits. They are aromatized the traditional way with a total of 18 different plants, especially cinchona bark, cinnamon, bitter colombo root, dried orange peel, and cocoa and coffee beans. The bouquet may be dominated by candied cherries and other berries, but its harmonious, rich flavor is characterized by elegant notes of vanilla, cinnamon, chocolate, and coffee.

### Dubonnet

Quinine bark is, of course, one of the ingredients of this classic drink, and it was responsible for its success, as Dubonnet made the bitter medicine for soldiers palatable. Originally it was based on mistelle made from ripe, red grapes: these now come from Roussillon, where Dubonnet is produced by Cusenier in the Byrrh winery. Dubonnet is lighter and fruitier than Byrrh. It became popular with the slogan "Dubo, Dubon, Dubonnet" and is used in cocktails by aficionados.

### Saint-Raphaël

There are white and red versions of this aperitif, which was made in 1830 with quinine bark by a doctor named Juppet from Lyons. The advertising posters are famous, depicting one red and one white waiter rushing across the Paris skies against a blue cloud background. They are each balancing a bottle of Quinquina in front of them, one red and one white. Saint-Raphaël is a classic wine-based aperitif (although its base is fortified must, not wine) with the typical botanicals of quinine bark, bitter orange, and cocoa beans. It is well rounded, and has a regular clientele in Quebec.

### Ambassadeur

Ambassadeur, devised in 1936 by Pierre Pourchet in Marseilles, is one of the best-known wine-based aperitifs. Like Byrrh and Dubonnet, it is produced in Thuir by Cusenier and based on mistelle, which matures for a minimum of two years in casks. It owes its very fruity aroma to orange peel, which comes from sweet oranges and bitter oranges from Curaçao. Vanilla also plays a significant role in its taste profile.

### RinQuinQuin

In the Rhône valley, *RinQuinQuin* is the term for the local cartagene or ratafia liqueur, while in Provence it means the favorite aperitif, which is often brewed at home, mainly based on white wine rather than must. Dry white wine from Lubéron is used to make RinQuinQuin, and aromatized with peaches and peach tree leaves. These are macerated separately in alcohol for six to twelve months, and then the liquid is strained off and added direct to the wine with sugar, while the solids are distilled and then added as peach spirit.

# The wine distiller's honor

It has had a bad name for centuries; for no sooner had the craft of wine distilling been established than the first misfortunes became known. At any rate, in the brandy strongholds of Charente and Gascogne these "glitches" are said to have happened in the late 16th century. In the Cognac region they have an even more precise date for it—when Henry IV came to the throne in 1589. The blame is always attributed to the carelessness of a wine maker or distiller, because all the stories do in fact concur: by accident he is said to have poured freshly pressed grape must into a cask of brandy. Angry about his mistake, he then rolled the cask into a far corner of his cellar and forgot all about it. A few years later the wine grower's silly mistake had instead miraculously transformed into a sweet and fruity, robust drink.

The first Pineau des Charentes is said to have been made during the reign of Henry IV. It is certainly a drink fit for kings.

Why should not a wine grower or wine distiller have in fact deliberately mixed together grape must and grape spirit? After all, in those days the latter was harsh, strong, and not exactly fit for drinking straight up.

## A personal liquor treat

Wine growers and distillers must have experimented much earlier with wine and grape spirit, as shown by the history of fortified wines, which are closely related. What is certain is that growers in many wine-producing regions where distillation also took place—in France, Spain, Portugal, Italy, and Greece, for instance—blended must and brandy to make a wonderfully sweet and fruity drink, which they served on special occasions and at celebrations, initially for their personal enjoyment and that of their family. Some liked to create a more elegant taste by adding herbs, leaves of fruit trees, and spices, while others stuck to the unmodified blend. Such customs were preserved in many areas, but only a few regions created a product that went on sale and was appreciated on a wider scale. All of the vermouth varieties and wine-based aperitifs that became fashionable from the mid 19th century and accessible to an ever wider group of customers have their origins in simple, home-made mistelle, exactly like fortified wines—whether sherry, malaga, port, marsala, or mavrodaphne.

Nowadays it is only in France that areas have emerged where the blend of must and grape spirit, mistelle, acquired its own individual profile. In this respect the Jura region certainly has one of the oldest traditions, though the oldest recorded recipe goes back to must that is concentrated by boiling. Producers finally agreed in 1976 on the production of pure mistelle, which was given the status of *Appellation d'Origine Contrôlée* Macvin in 1991, though terms like "maquevin" and "marc-vin" are no longer used. For a long time the happy marriage between must and marc (or pomace brandy) has been well known, even in the Champagne region: there, as in

Burgundy in particular, it is called ratafia. Ratafia—the term used in Spain and Italy for liqueur made from herbs, fruit, or nuts—has its origins in the Latin *rata fiat conventio*, indicating the conclusion of an agreement. It was the custom to make a toast with liqueur wine, thus "ratifying" the deal.

Wherever liqueur wine was produced from must and grape spirit, locally grown grape varieties were used. In the Jura region there were five standard grapes: the three reds, Poulsard, Trousseau, and Pinot Noir; and the two whites, Chardonnay and Savagnin. In the Champagne region mainly Pinot Noir and Chardonnay are grown, producing red or rosé, and white liqueur wines respectively. Liqueur wines are also popular as an aperitif in Languedoc, although they are only sold commercially by a few estates and merchants. They are known as *cartagene* there, and thanks to the wide range of grape varieties used in production, the aromas are all quite different from each other. They are often served in Languedoc as an accompaniment to the blue-veined cheese Roquefort.

The best-known liqueur wines however still come, as always, from the traditional areas, Cognac and Armagnac.

The recipe for Vin de Liqueur, a forerunner of mistelle, is attributed to the nuns of Château-Chalon in the French Jura.

The house of Moutard Diligent in Buxeuil produces not only a most excellent champagne, but also the typical ratafia.

# The Cognac connection

The grape varieties Sauvignon Blanc (left) and Cabernet Franc (right) give Pineau des Charentes its special fruity elegance.

Pineau des Charentes is said to have been produced for the past 400 years, though it was only in 1945 that it obtained the official status of *Appellation d'Origine Contrôlée*, allowing it to be sold by the glass. Now over 16 million bottles are sold each year, of which around 10 million are Pineau Blanc and 6 million Rosé. It is a growing trend.

The pineau region is identical to that of cognac, as practically all of its grape must has to originate from the same vineyards as cognac, with which it is blended. For pineau, which to a certain extent is a sideline of cognac, the grapes have to yield an alcohol content of at least 10% vol.—that is, 22 oz grape sugar per gallon (170 g per liter) of must, while in the case of cognac 8% vol. is sufficient. So wine growers and legislators set high demands on the grapes destined for pineau: for good pineau they have to be ripe and absolutely perfect, as their primary aroma is very important. This means that there are significant fluctuations in amounts from one harvest to the next, all the more so as any addition of preserved, concentrated, or chaptalized (with added sugar) must is strictly forbidden.

In both Grande and Petite Champagne crus, the grapes are reserved for distillation, so pineau has developed primarily in the less exclusive Cognac regions, Fins Bois and Borderies and especially Bons Bois and Bois Ordinaires. Originally, only grapes also allowed for cognac were used: Ugni Blanc was by far the most predominant, even though Folle Blanche and Colombard were used occasionally. Others such as Montils, Meslier, Saint-François, Jurançon Blanc, and Merlot Blanc existed on paper as lesser varieties, while in practice they are scarcely found now, either for cognac or pineau. The estates outside the two top crus however often have a broader spectrum of varieties, as they mainly produce not only cognac but also *vin ordinaire*, and rely on direct marketing. In this way Pineau des Charentes came to have access to a charming range of grape varieties, which also includes Sémillon and Sauvignon Blanc, as well as Merlot Noir, Cabernet Sauvignon, and Cabernet Franc. This enabled the production of a red version, Pineau Rosé.

## A rigorous procedure

As soon as the grapes are brought to the cellar, they are pressed gently, and young cognac is immediately added to the grape juice. The cognac, which must be a minimum age of one year and have an alcohol content of at least 60% vol., ensures that the must does not begin to ferment, a reliable way of preserving the fresh grape aromas.

At this stage the sweet must has not really coalesced with the cognac, and the alcohol in particular seems overpowering. For this reason, pineau (with 16–20 oz sugar per gallon / 125–140 g per liter) needs a brief maturation period, which is set at eight months for the very fruity rosé, usually much sweeter, and at twelve for the more restrained and usually drier white. In both cases the time is calculated from 1 April after the harvest. If the producer wants to bottle it, his pineau is tasted by a commission which has to pass it before it can be put on the market. As far as the alcohol content is concerned, wine growers have a certain

amount of latitude. It ranges from a sweet and fruity 16% vol. to 22% vol., at which level the pineau is much drier and reveals a much greater intensity.

A small amount of the output is left to age in oak casks, Pineau Vieux for at least five years, and Pineau Extra or Très Vieux for at least ten. They too have to be approved by a tasting before their age status is recognized. A young Pineau Blanc des Charentes makes its entrance in a robe of antique gold or amber, always bearing an intense bouquet—a melody of floral notes (such as lime blossom), dominated by aromas of quince paste, candied citrus fruits and melon, dried figs and honey, as well as dried fruits, almonds, and nuts. Its pleasant flavor is light and harmonious, with strong notes of honey, candied and dried fruit, and spices. It becomes more intense with age, until the classic rancio revered by connoisseurs begins to emerge. A Très Vieux Pineau is a subtle expression of the balmy Charente region.

Red Bordeaux varieties of grape are used to make Pineau Rosé, with its beautiful copper to reddish brown color, produced through aging in casks. The grapes give it the pungent berry aromas of blackcurrants or blackberries, combined with sweet spices, lovely toasted notes, and honey. Its distinctly fruity taste lingers long on the palate. A 5–10-year-old Pineau Rosé reveals notes of dried fruit, cocoa, and roasted nuts. The perfect type of glass for Pineau des Charentes is a small, tulip-shape wine glass that encapsulates the concentration of aromas. The wine is best served at a drinking temperature of 46–50 °F (8–10 °C), which tempers the sweetness slightly, while emphasizing the fruit.

A glass of Pineau Blanc, with just some of its characteristic aromatic ingredients.

# Packing a punch with velvet gloves

Needless to say, wine growers in Gascony were not lining up to mix grape juice with armagnac: whether it was by accident or design is unimportant as it is the result that mattered. By 1954 they wanted no longer to keep it just for themselves, but to be able to sell it commercially. Wine growers had coined the term *Lou Floc de nouste* (our local bouquet of flowers), but the flowers refused to flourish in official circles. The sought-after recognition did not come until 1976, once Floc de Gascogne was in full bloom. Today, around 200 wine growers and 6 cooperatives produce about 1.3 million bottles per year, in roughly equal quantities of white and rosé. The Gers *département* is responsible for the lion's share of four fifths, while the rest comes from the Landes and Lot-et-Garonne. Floc is in fact produced in the Armagnac region, however the parcels of land designated for it have to be registered each year before the harvest begins in a laborious process.

For white floc mainly Colombard, Ugni Blanc, and Gros Manseng grapes are used, although Folle Blanche, Baroque, Petit Manseng, Mauzac, Sémillon, and Sauvignon are also permitted. For rosé the two Cabernet varieties and Merlot set the tone, though Tannat, Fer Servadou, and Malbec are good for adding extra body.

The yield in the vineyard must not exceed 6,500 gallons per acre (60,000 liters per hectare), and the grapes have to indicate at least 22 oz grape sugar per gallon (170 g per liter). The armagnac, which is added after the grapes have been gently pressed, has a minimum age of one year and an alcohol content of at least 52% vol. The mixture is left to rest and blend until the following spring or beyond, when the floc is filtered and bottled. Only then does a commission carry out an analysis and tasting to determine whether it meets the standards of the appellation, granting it the recognition needed for commercial sale. In the poultry paradise of southwest France, it is, of course, served as an accompaniment to foie gras.

# Selected liqueur wines

**Château de Beaulon**
**Pineau des Charentes**
**Collection Privée**
**20 year old**

Both pineau and cognac are made at this chateau near the Gironde. The proximity to Bordeaux ensures that not only the classic grape varieties needed for cognac are grown on the 220-acre (90-hectare) vineyards of the estate, it also has the five main varieties of the Bordeaux region—Sémillon, Sauvignon, Cabernet Sauvignon, Cabernet Franc, and Merlot. This outstanding antique gold pineau, which has matured in casks for 20 years, combines Sémillon-based must with the Sauvignon of cognac. The intense complexity of its bouquet reveals candied fruits, nuts, and rancio, while its exquisite sweetness and delicate acidity ensure a sublime and persistent finish on the palate.

**Château de Salles**
**Floc de Gascogne**

The vineyards of this old family estate in the village of Salle d'Armagnac lie mainly in the famous, pale red, sandy soils of Bas Armagnac. Its brandies age wonderfully, especially in the centuries-old chai of the chateau, which is worth a visit. Benoît Hébert harvests the grapes for his floc from a south-facing slope as they ripen better there and develop a higher sugar content. He has grown the two Cabernet varieties and Merlot for the rosé. As soon as the grapes are pressed, he adds young armagnac, preserving the intense aromas of blackcurrants and red cherries. It is best served young as an aperitif, or with fresh strawberries sprinkled with sugar.

**Domaine Baud**
**Macvin**

Brothers Jean-Michel and Alain Baud run the 42-acre (17-hectare) estate together in the heart of the Jura region in the village of Le Vernois. It has been in the family since at least the 18th century, and the Bauds have extended the cultivation area in the past 20 years in Château-Chalon and Etoile. Renowned for their excellent *vin jaune*, they offer the whole range of different Jura wines, from *crémant* to dry white, red and rich, sweet straw wines—not forgetting the Macvin, all the more so because the brothers also distill marc and other eaux-de-vie: intensely fruity and sweet, the marc is well integrated, and the Macvin is delicious either as an aperitif or with desserts.

**René Geoffroy**
**Ratafia**

Wine growers since the early 17th century in Cumières in the Marne valley, the Geoffroy family has a profound connection to their vineyards and the land, as well as to the traditions of the Champagne region, including ratafia. In the amber version the freshly pressed must made from Pinot Noir announces it character upfront: it has both richness and the acidity born of the climate, which is also responsible for the scent of preserved wild cherries in this liqueur wine, and its well-balanced sweetness and fruitiness. The Geoffroys recommend drinking it with tiramisu and red berries, crème brulée, or chocolate desserts and wild cherries.

**Château Ricardelle**
**Cartagène**

La Clape, the former island facing Narbonne, is a wild Mediterranean landscape filled with scented scrubland. The 100 acres (40 hectares) of Château Ricardelle extending across the southwest tip are reserved for Appellation-class red wines that are marked with the pungent notes of the soil. For the cartagène they use only gently pressed Grenache Noir grapes that have been picked by hand. The free-run must is then strained off, filtered, and fortified immediately with high percentage grape spirit to give an alcohol content of 16% vol. and prevent fermentation. After a minimum of three years' barrel aging, it is a real treat, with aromas of candied orange peel and apricots, and a delightfully sweet, persistent palate.

# Liqueurs

**FERNET-BRANCA**
*digerire e vivere*

As the epitome of health, red beets stan[d] for Fernet Branca's beneficial effect.

Opposite: Fruits and plants steeped in alcohol release their aromas during mac[c]eration.

Page 558: Numerous aromatics are pre-cisely weighed out to produce Benedicti[ne]

# Sugar makes all the difference

Eggs and cream, litchis and kumquats, coffee and cocoa, china bark and herbs, cherries and berries—all those, and much more, can be turned into delicious drinks by expert hands. Tasting them is a pleasurable experience that induces a sense of well-being. The appeal of this mixture of sugar, water, alcohol, and flavorings lies both in the astonishing balance of a wealth of ingredients, and in the concentration on one main ingredient in the purest possible form in terms of taste. Rich in colors, flavors, aromas, and textures, liqueurs seduce several of our senses at the same time.

In the world of spirits liqueurs are something extra special. Their colors alone give an immediate hint of what is to come, confirmed by the first sip. From curative herbal elixirs to enticing creations made from exotic fruits, liqueurs conjure up dreams, making them far more than just a combination of color, smell, taste, and mouthfeel.

At the same time these magical potions have been treated very unimaginatively by the powers that be: according to European Union spirit regulations, all an alcoholic drink made for human consumption needs in order to call itself a "liqueur" is a minimum sugar content of 15 oz per gallon (100 grams per liter)—less in exceptional cases—and an alcohol content by volume of at least 15%. This prosaic approach to the phenomenon of liqueurs seems astonishing at first glance. Since when has it been possible to sum up one of life's mysteries in a few meager paragraphs?

It is no surprise that liqueurs are so popular, for in the current profusion of choice there will be one to suit everybody. The palette ranges from rich, dry herbal cordials to fresh, fruity specialties and velvety, sweet temptations made with cream and honey. It is hard to imagine there were times when most folk had to do without these indulgences. Sugar was expensive and it took so much of it to produce liqueurs that they became delicacies beyond the reach of the average citizen (this also explains why many of the old recipes use the natural sweetness of honey). In the good old days those without means would only get the chance to sip the mysterious concoctions if they were sick, for monks skilled in the art of healing would mix liqueurs as medicine.

At the beginning of the 19th century sugar from the colonies and from domestic fields became cheaper, so liqueurs have long since changed from status symbols to public property. There is a liqueur for every occasion: the elegant bitter liqueur as an aperitif, the robust herbal cordial as a digestif, the sweet fruit creme liqueur with coffee, and the seductive cream-based liqueur in any of the intervening moments...

Liqueurs also open up endless possibilities for mixing creative drinks and are great for sweetening and flavoring desserts, or even savory dishes. No home bar should therefore be without a basic selection of liqueurs.

Many of the sweet spirits have successfully shed their frumpy image and transformed themselves into the partygoer's new best friend. And of course there is a constant stream of new, trendy products hitting the market that rapidly become the must-have accessory of a fun loving clientele.

So a foray into the realm of liqueurs will become an unforeseen journey around the world. No matter what direction you take, you are bound to strike gold.

# Of monks and mixtures

The liqueur was born, not of pleasure seeking, but of a desire to aid recovery. The first to produce aromatic elixirs from secret herbal mixtures in the Middle Ages would certainly have been monks, who knew not only how to grow medicinal herbs in the gardens of their monasteries, but also how to preserve their healing powers in alcohol. They were not afraid to apply their knowledge of healing in a palliative way in cases where the few doctors were nowhere to be seen. In order to make the herbal medicine (which was often extremely bitter) more palatable to their grateful patients, it was heavily sweetened, and this suited the taste of those recuperating. This means that the Middle Ages may be seen as the first heyday of the art of liqueur-making, even if this was completely unintentional, as far as we know. At the same time, to the south of the Alps they were also mixing *liquidi* from high-quality herbs and alcohol—that is to say, liquids with beneficial effects. One such brew, a rose-based liqueur, proved so popular that the name "rosolio" became the general term for Italian liqueurs.

Liqueurs have been made in the Leyre monastery on the Spanish side of the Pyrenees since the Middle Ages.

Their pleasant taste was the real reason that elixirs based on herbs and alcohol— known as "liquore"—became popular spirits in aristocratic circles. For her marriage to the French king Henri II in 1532, Catherine de Medici's retinue included a whole troop of specialists in liqueur production, so that she would not have to live without this treat from her native country.

So we owe it not least to Catherine de Medici that a rich culture of liqueur-making flourished from an early stage in France as well. Here too it developed first behind monastery walls. The Carthusian and Benedictine orders in particular distinguished themselves in this respect: Benedictine and Chartreuse are still famous liqueurs today, and date back to that era.

## A popular source of comfort

As a result of the exorbitant price of sugar the consumption of liqueurs for pleasure was initially the preserve of the affluent classes. When sugar then became more affordable during the colonial period, and was subsequently replaced by beet sugar, a plethora of popular liqueurs quickly developed. After the French Revolution a whole nation discovered the comfortingly sweet liqueurs and soon every town had at least one *liquoriste*. Some of the truly great figures in the trade included, among many others, Edouard Cointreau, Louis-Alexandre Marnier, and Gaëtan Picon, who pioneered bitter spirits.

Other countries also ensure that there are no gaps on the world map of liqueurs. The caraway liqueur Allasch comes from Latvia; then there is Slovenia with its nut liqueur Orehovec and its herbal bitters Pelinkovec; in Lithuania they love Trauktine, a classic bitter liqueur; Jarcebinka, a rowanberry liqueur from the Czech Republic, has a lovely dry and fruity flavor; the Polish honey liqueur Krupnik, on the other hand, is indulgently sweet. Other Polish specialties include Nalewka, a rich and fruity liqueur, and Kontuczowka, which is aniseed based. The Netherlands can look back on a unique liqueur tradition. Here too monks created

the first versions of liqueurs. The actual birth of Dutch liqueur took place in Amsterdam in 1575. Lucas Bols distilled his first liqueurs in a woodshed. At that time, Amsterdam was the international center of the spice trade. Lucas Bols made liqueurs with caraway, aniseed, and sweet or bitter oranges, which he shipped in from the Caribbean island of Curaçao, then part of the Dutch Antilles. One hundred and twenty years after Bols, Johannes de Kuyper built his first distillery in Rotterdam. While Bols was sold off in 1816 and is now privately owned by a Dutch company, De Kuyper remained under family ownership, now in the eleventh generation. The most famous Dutch liqueurs are without doubt advocaat and apricot brandy.

"Anyone with cares also has liqueur." In his famous illustrated story "Pious Helene" (1872) Wilhelm Busch uses this motto to portray the fruitless battle of his troubled heroine.

# Shrouded in mystery

Detractors maintain that liqueurs are down to the failures of early distillers: the art of distillation has occasionally produced such unpleasant results that their taste had to be mercifully concealed behind all sorts of juices, herbs, and honey. Whether you believe this or not, it cannot be denied that liqueurs exist by virtue of the smells, flavor, and colors of their ingredients like no other spirits. Is it not the deep, flavorsome, fruity quality of a cherry brandy; the warm, round nutty aromas of Nocino; or the smooth, full-bodied roasted notes of coffee liqueur that we cherish? And who could forgo the deep cherry red, golden orange, or saffron yellow colors, or the appetizing creamy shades of a cream liqueur? We allow ourselves to be mesmerized without considering the craft that allows the essence of all the fruits, herbs, and spices to be captured in bottles. Mind you, it is an art form, and not magic—though people were not always quite so sure of this. Liqueur production and alchemy once went hand in hand. Only a few initiates were entrusted with the arcane, secret recipes, and this is still partly the case even these days.

## The magic solution

In order to get the aroma, flavor, and color into the liqueur, it has to be extracted from where nature stores them. One option is maceration, also known as "cold soaking." For this the raw ingredients (mostly herbs and spices—in other words the botanicals—or fruits, are soaked in a mixture of alcohol and water. The liquid penetrates the cells and flushes out the desired substances, provided that they are soluble in alcohol or water. Essential oils, for instance, which are practically insoluble in water, are soluble in alcohol as well as being distillable thanks to their volatility. The bitter constituents vital for some liqueurs are, on the other hand, more readily soluble in water than alcohol, and this is why care is taken to macerate gentian root, say, in a lower percentage of alcohol containing more water. (In the event

Left: The correct degree of ripeness is important for the cherry harvest.

Right: To preserve their flavors blackcurrants are flash frozen as soon as they are picked.

that the bitters are not appreciated, distillation is a possible option as the bitter constituents are not volatile, and will not transfer to the condensate.)

The individual behavior of each of the aromatics, flavorings, and colorings in solution therefore determines the concentration of alcohol: as a rule of thumb fresh raw ingredients (with a higher proportion of water) are macerated in high percentage alcohol, while dried raw materials are best steeped in distillates with an alcohol content of 40–60% as the water content absorbs the water-soluble substances.

The period of maceration is also determined by the soluble behavior, as well as the alcohol concentration. Floral substances and the more valuable ingredients in general are more quickly soluble. Fresh herbs and citrus peel release their entire aroma after just a few hours, and even the bitter constituents are extracted after a longer period of maceration. Some botanicals remain for weeks in alcohol, and others are macerated several times.

So there can be no single recipe for the perfect maceration. Every ingredient must be treated individually, even before soaking: some must not be chopped too coarsely, some not too finely. Some are even adversely affected by being heated during the milling process, and therefore have to be chilled while this is happening. And so on.

## Comforting warmth?

Substances not sensitive to heat can be more easily extracted through exposure to heat, in what is known as infusion, or hot extraction. This can be likened to making tea. The containers used for this are double walled in order to keep the outside surrounded by hot fluid, usually at a temperature of 104–140 °F (40–60 °C). One special process involves infusion with simultaneous distillation, in which the distillate obtained flows back repeatedly over the botanicals: special equipment is available for this. The duration and temperature are vital for the quality of the extract, and are often regulated automatically nowadays. The liquid drawn from the hot extraction is called an infusion.

When concentrated flavors are required, distillation plays an important part in liqueur-making as well. The porthole (left) allows you to see the "red-hot action."

# Percolating and evaporating

In the Zuidam distillery in The Netherlands they know not only how to distill genever and malt, but also how to create liqueurs.

A more effective form of maceration is percolation, in which the raw materials do not steep placidly in liquid, but gradually release their aromas, flavors, and coloring through a slow steady flow. In special equipment called percolators, alcohol at mainly 40–60% vol. constantly trickles down over the dried ingredients that have, however, been premoistened with some alcohol. In the course of this process the cells fill up with liquid and a continuous interchange takes place. Finally water is diffused in order to rinse the remaining alcohol out of the cells. This method is akin to the way filter coffee is made, only in liqueur percolation it takes place at room temperature. While the alcohol remaining in the base materials is often extracted through pressing and distilling in the case of maceration and infusion, this is unnecessary when percolation is used.

## Distilling thoroughly

Other base materials for liqueurs are extracted by distillation, which releases the volatile herbal and botanical substances contained in the hot alcohol and water vapors, and they are then condensed again by cooling. Instead of being suspended in the steam, the herbs can be steeped directly in the alcohol. Corn and fermented fruits can also be distilled to produce liqueurs. Not only can the botanicals themselves be distilled, but

also the products which have previously been left after maceration, infusion, and percolation. This can produce especially pure aromas. For even greater purity sometimes distillation takes place several times. One special technique involves a combination of infusion and distillation. In this case the distillate extracted runs back into the pot still for final distillation.

The important thing when distilling is to look out for the good middle parts of the run, for at the beginning and the end the distillation draws a lot of undesirable aromas out of the ingredients, which on no account should reach the liqueur. As they still contain pretty good substances for taste and smell, the heads and the tails are often purified and then redistilled. Equipment for herb distillation generally looks very much like traditional pot stills.

## A delicious composition

As well as extracts and distillates—the exact production method of which is kept strictly secret—other base materials are available to the liqueur manufacturer. Fruit juices and their concentrates are often used as constituents. If the recipes involve cream then emulsion liqueurs are the end result. Then there is alcohol. Neutral 96% alcohol acts as the flavor carrier for the other ingredients, while other liqueurs use the flavors of more elegant spirits like cognac or whisky.

Finally, no liqueur can do without an appropriate portion of sugar. Some types are also sweetened with honey, and frequently cask aging refines and captures the aroma. And there is always a little secret ingredient, a few spices perhaps, a special flavoring that makes this particular liqueur so incomparable…

The composition of the different flavorings and other ingredients gives every liqueur its distinctiveness, as seen here in a monastery high in the Navarre mountains.

# Nicely related

### Herb- and spice-based liqueurs

These have existed since the early days of the liqueur-making art. Back in the Middle Ages monks experimented with medicinal herbs to make up all sorts of health-promoting drinks. Often they tasted good to more than just sick people, and from modest beginnings outstanding specialties developed, some of which became world famous. Many plants, both native and exotic, find a use in herb- and spice-based liqueurs, and if a little saffron with its subtle taste is added it also turns into an appealing color.

### Bitter liqueurs

These liqueurs all have one ingredient in common: china bark, an ancient remedy for stomach ailments and fever, even malaria—so bitter liqueurs also began their career as medicine. With their shockingly contradictory taste, these liqueurs became the cult drink of upwardly mobile industrial societies in the 19th century—and not least the source of inspiration for advertising campaigns with artistic aspirations, which even now still focus on the relaxed Mediterranean image of bitter liqueurs.

### Fruit-juice liqueurs

If golden yellow apricot juice, fiery red cherry juice, the deep violet juice of blackcurrants, or other juices and concentrates are used, then these are fruit-juice liqueurs. They are wonderfully sweet—so much so that they often come into the category of "creme," which must contain the highest sugar content of all liqueurs. The Netherlands in particular developed an extensive palette of fruit-juice liqueurs; no fruit can be too exotic to be poured into a long-stemmed liqueur glass.

### Fruit-essence liqueurs

These encapsulate the essence of the fruit. They are made not with plain fruit juice, but with expertly created fruit extracts. Citrus fruits—or to be more precise, their peels, which are mostly dried and then leached out in different ways—usually form the basis of these liqueurs. The bitter herbal extracts are partly refined even further by distillation, or the distillates are obtained directly from the peels. The substances produced are mixed with alcohol, water, sugar, and subtle spices.

## Fruit brandies

In this case the fruits reveal their true spirit. A distillate of the relevant fruit type is always added to fruit brandies, in addition to the neutral alcohol that forms the backbone of most liqueurs. Typical representatives of this category are apricot brandy and cherry brandy. The inclusion of "brandy" in the name of these liqueurs often causes confusion as the wine-based spirit called brandy is absent: the term indicates the distillate of the type of fruit used.

## Emulsion liqueurs

You have already succumbed to the creamy, sweet taste and the silky-smooth mouthfeel by the time you savor the knowledge that opposites like cream and eggs make an enduring combination with alcohol. These liqueurs are often among the bestsellers. Their range includes some very big names, and some have almost become the national drink—you need think only of the egg liqueur, advocaat, or the famous Irish whisky cream liqueur, which is regarded as economically important on the Emerald Isle.

## Coffee and cocoa liqueurs

These are enjoyed not just by aficionados of liqueurs; coffee and chocolate lovers also get their money's worth, and these liqueurs play skillfully with the possibilities of the ingredients. Depending on the ingredients, emulsion liqueurs made with cream are also in this group, as well as those with fine spirits, meaning that strictly speaking they should be assigned to the spirit-based liqueur category. And as both ingredients often occur together anyway, we should not be too rigid with the designation, but simply enjoy them.

## Spirit-based liqueurs

The delicate aroma of fine spirits defines the taste profile of these liqueurs. The warm intensity of good cognac, the gnarled elegance of old whisky—these are ingredients with a powerful character that are the mark of unmistakable liqueurs. It is no surprise, therefore, that some world-famous products come from the family of spirit-based liqueurs. A second branch—the fruit-spirit liqueurs—grows more quietly. The distilleries, where exquisite delicacies are made from the distillates of regional fruits, are often small and long established.

# Herbal liqueurs: hidden health

Herbal liqueurs made in monasteries and abbeys are certainly among the most ambivalent phenomena in the world of spirits. Exotic spices grown in places that few people could barely imagine were supplemented by native herbs, quite a few of which had a dubious reputation in an age obsessed with witches. And in the days of infamous murders by poison, the relationship of the sick person toward the healer would certainly have been characterized by gratitude, but perhaps not been completely free from mistrust. Secret recipes of reclusive monastery denizens—without doubt, a shiver from the Middle Ages still makes itself felt today.

As we know from the tension filled *The Name of the Rose* (an apothecary in a monastery features there), both remedy and poison have a role to play. Monks who knew about plants recorded their knowledge in documents, but also made sure that not everyone had access to them. With the decline of monasteries in the early 19th century, much of this will have been lost: the desire for secrecy is not a good breeding ground for backup copies. If some of the ancient liqueurs are still being produced today, the tradition was carried on unbroken at best, or their recipes have been preserved and rediscovered. Once you have the recipes you still have to understand them. Frequently they present conundrums galore: plant names cannot be correlated and quantities are baffling. What is more, they have to be adjusted to present day production techniques. If the temptation to simplify the elaborate and therefore expensive production method for purely commercial reasons is resisted, this essential modernization passes off easily—that is, without any loss of quality.

The number of herbs and spices used in the production of liqueurs is huge. Everything has its place, from aniseed to cinnamon, irrespective of how rare and expensive it may be. Some ingredients are only deployed in narrowly defined regions, and are partly responsible for the wealth of unusual regional variations. Some have slipped into oblivion, like Krambambuli, the specialty from Gdansk, but many continue to make their mark on the culinary profile of their homeland today. Thus lavender liqueur is valued in Provence, as is the dark red cherry liqueur Nalewka in Poland. Liqueurs like Mentuccia, a peppermint cordial from Abruzzia, are typically Italian. Herbal liqueurs from Majorca and Ibiza add to the holiday mood, and Spain as a whole has a range of creations that enrich this category. Many liqueurs are now well known beyond their own borders, so that you do not have to go on trips to find them; your search will be successful right on your own doorstep. Similarly, many of the monastery liqueurs have exchanged the contemplative silence behind monastic walls for the hurly burly of the world—and it certainly agrees with them.

The possible uses for this liqueur group are extraordinarily varied. Firstly, each one can be enjoyed neat. After a meal especially, it is good to take a sip of these drinks that are as tasty as they are beneficial. In recent times, comparatively in relation to their often long history, many of these liqueurs have been discovered to be delightful additions to cocktails and long drinks. Their special charms reside however in the mysterious effect that was attributed to their ingredients—and still is today.

# Chartreuse

Page 570: The Benedictine palace in Normandy owes its existence to the liqueur recipe of a Benedictine monk.

Page 571: The Venetian monk Bernardo Vincelli (left) developed the recipe for Benedictine in the abbey of Fécamp.

The Chartreuse monastery in the French Alps, the spiritual home of a liqueur legend.

The history of the Grande Chartreuse monastery started with Saint Bruno, who was born around 1030 in Cologne and later taught at the cathedral school in Reims. As he was more driven by the search for the eternal than earthly success, he set off to see his friend in Grenoble, Saint Hugo, in 1084. An inhospitable place had appeared to Hugo in a dream, and it was there that they, along with just a few monks, built a chapel and wooden cells. These buildings were destroyed by an avalanche in 1132, but the new monastery that was subsequently set up nearby went on to become the headquarters of the order. It too was not spared disasters, and the impressive building today dates back to the 17th century.

The history of the liqueur began in 1605, over 500 years after the order was founded. A certain Marschall d'Estrées (King Henri IV's marshal of artillery) gave the monks in the Carthusian monastery near Paris a recipe for an herbal elixir by an unknown author. Apparently no one in the mother house of the order understood the nature of the treasure they had been given, as the monks were at that time concerned with iron mining in the mountains.

It took until 1737 for the manuscript to arouse the curiosity of Brother Jérôme Maubec, who served as the apothecary in the monastery. He then used it to put the recipe into practice. Since then, the *Elixier Végétal de la Grande-Chartreuse*, a curative medicine with an alcohol content of 71% vol., has been produced. Brother Jérôme's successor, Brother Antoine, perfected the production process, and in 1764 he developed a tasty and health-promoting liqueur from it which had an alcohol content of 55% vol.—the famous Green Chartreuse. The manuscript's odyssey did not end there however. During the French Revolution the monks had to leave their monastery.

They managed to save the manuscript, but the monk who was charged with preserving it did not believe that his order would revive, and handed the manuscript over to Liotard, an apothecary from Grenoble. Like all medical formulae at that time, this recipe had to be submitted to the Ministry of the Interior for approval, but it was refused. After the death of the apothecary it was given back to the monastery.

In 1838 Brother Bruno Jacquet used the original elixir as the basis for producing another liqueur which was sweeter, smoother, and contained 40% alcohol by volume. He used plants to give it a yellow color and it became especially popular with the ladies. By 1869 the elixir and green and yellow chartreuse were all being made in the monastery, but production was subsequently moved to a distillery in the more remote Fourvoirie.

When the Carthusian monks were forced to leave France in 1903, the three brothers who held the secret recipe settled in Tarragona in Spain and founded a new distillery there. Their fortunes in France only began to improve again after the mother house of the order was returned to the monks in 1940. The commercial company called Chartreuse Diffusion in Voiron became the location for production in 1970, and so it remains today. The monks oversee the production of both the elixirs and liqueurs, and the income is used to finance the monastery.

Then and now, the monks have maintained a vow of silence about the exact production process. Only this much is known: around 130 different plants and herbs are macerated in selected alcohol and distilled several times. The liqueurs are stored in oak casks for over eight years until they reach full maturity in the world's largest liqueur cellar, and then they are bottled under the label "V.E.P" (Vieillissement Exceptionnellement Prolongé, meaning "extra-long aging"). The liqueurs are consumed as a digestif, straight with ice, or as a long drink with juices or tonic, in a totally worldly fashion. Three brothers continue to guard the recipe, which has long since represented a valuable company asset.

# A passion for art and liqueurs

In 1510 Bernardo Vincelli, a Benedictine monk in the abbey of Fécamp in Normandy, succeeded in creating a particularly tasty concoction as a result of his experiments: this was the original Benedictine recipe. When the monks were driven from the abbey in the 18th century, the recipe was lost in the turmoil of the French Revolution. The wine merchant Alexandre Le Grand discovered it again in 1863 in the books of the former abbey, which his family had saved from destruction.

This advertising poster is a good illustration of the elegant world of the urbane liqueur consumer.

He refined the recipe to make a liqueur, named it Benedictine in homage to the order of the founding monk, and gave it the epithet "D.O.M."—Deo Optimo Maximo (to the greatest and best God)—as an indication of its monastic origins.

As a passionate art collector and patron, Le Grand built a magnificent castle for his two great loves, art and the liqueur Benedictine: the Benedictine palace, which, like the abbey itself, is located in Fécamp in Normandy. Next to the production site for Benedictine Dom liqueur, still partly produced there today, it houses the exhibition rooms for Le Grand's extensive collection of 15th- and 16th-century art. There was enough space left for a temporary exhibition gallery for contemporary artists, including Miró, Picasso, and Andy Warhol.

The house passion for the visual arts was reciprocated by artists: painters like Paul Gauguin, Rousseau, Carl Larsson, and Wesley Webber incorporated Benedictine, which was popular in affluent society, into their pictures. The company's founder was able to attract renowned poster artists to design his advertising material: Benedictine posters by the art nouveau masters Alfons Maria Mucha, Lucien Lopes Silva, and "Sem" (George Goursat) are classics of poster art. Today, the varied exhibitions make the Benedictine palace a worthwhile tourist attraction, confirmed not least by the 155,000 visitors it receives each year.

## The secret of the palace

Coriander from Morocco, tea and cinnamon from Sri Lanka, thyme from Provence, vanilla from Madagascar—a total of 27 different herbs and oriental spices form the basis of the secret recipe for Benedictine. They give the world famous liqueur its honey-sweet, full-bodied taste, which also has a spicy hint of vanilla. The monastery

liqueur has been produced since 1863 according to the original recipe.

The proportions of the carefully selected herbs and spices must be exactly right. The precise composition of ingredients is known to only a few initiates. The complete production process is protracted and carefully monitored. In order to release the aromas of the individual herbs and spices fully, the ingredients have to be processed in various ways, including maceration, which means steeping in a mixture of alcohol and water. In addition, a range of distillation processes is involved, for which the Benedictine palace houses a massive hall full of pot stills. The distillates and macerates then mature for three months in oak casks. After this they are combined and stored once again for eight months. Benedictine finally gets its characteristic consistency from the addition of water, cognac, syrup, honey, and caramel, after which the liqueur completes a further three month aging period.

Benedictine is drunk neat with ice, and is used for mixing, for example with champagne, or orange or grapefruit juice. B & B has now become a well-established, real

classic cocktail; it is a mixture of equal parts Benedictine and cognac. Benedictine is also indispensable as an ingredient of the legendary Singapore Sling, which originated in the Raffles Hotel in Singapore.

The old distillation hall in the Benedictine palace in Fécamp.

The ingredients must be weighed out exactly.

# Four hundred years of drinkable gold

The clear glass bottle, which was not introduced until 1996, shows the beautifully floating gold leaf. Until then brown glass was meant to shield the medicinal properties from the light.

Opposite: Becherovka acquires the final touch in this cellar.

The history of Danziger Goldwasser can be traced back to 1606, when Ambrosius Vermöllen, the owner of a liqueur factory founded in Danzig (now Gdansk) in 1598, developed the recipe for this unique liqueur and began selling it as a medicine. These were dark times, when medical care was poor—as you might imagine—and many sick people set their hopes on the new potion. After all, even the famous doctor Paracelsus (1494–1541) had attributed healing powers to gold.

Even with all the herbal strength of the contents, a little extra magic would not go amiss, so a pentagram was displayed on the label of the dark brown, square-side bottle with its wax-sealed top; this was the well-known symbol used to ward off evil, also worn as an amulet throughout Europe and often hung up in inns to represent health and well-being. The aristocracy soon discovered the new drink for themselves (for it must be a most unsatisfying feeling to have all one's gold on the outside) and helped to spread it beyond the Danzig city limits. Many a regal ruler was also firmly convinced that it was their right above all others'.

Goldwasser signaled the beginning of Danzig's history as a European center in the craft of distillation. This specialty was initially called "The Salmon" when the factory moved to a new quarter in 1704, for in place of a house number it featured a salmon hewn in stone. For over 300 years Danzig was to remain the home of the liqueur. When the city was cut off after the treaty of Versailles, another factory was set up—in Berlin in 1922—which became the sole production site after World War II. Today "Der Lachs" Original Danziger Goldwasser is produced in Nörten-Hardenberg.

Even before tasting it, the floating little gold flakes underline the special nature of this spice-based liqueur. The pungent, spicy

Genuine gold leaf is the attractive feature in Danziger Goldwasser. Healing properties were attributed to the precious metal in times past.

liqueur is made from 13 different aromatics, including aniseed, apricot kernel, cardamom, coriander, lavender, mace, cloves, bitter orange peel, juniper berries, lemon peel, and cinnamon. The ingredients are macerated in a mixture of alcohol and water and then distilled. Other ingredients are then added to the distillate, such as kirsch (cherry spirit), rosewater, and invert sugar, thus bringing it to a drinking strength of 40% alcohol by volume. It is then filtered, and the little flecks of gold (worth around 23 cents per 1 pint / 0.5 liter bottle) are added using a special metering device. They have no taste and their curative powers are illusory, but they look pretty. The flavors are best appreciated at 39 °F (4 °C), or else the modern way, on ice, or with champagne.

## English bitter in Beton

This golden yellow liqueur with notes of caramel, cinnamon, and cloves was invented by a British doctor, Frobrig, who stayed in Carlsbad in 1805 as the personal physician to Count Plettenberg-Mietingen. In his spare time he assembled curative mixtures made from herbs, oils, and alcohol in the laboratory of Josef Becher, the apothecary to whom he eventually entrusted his recipe. Becher refined it and in 1807 he put it on the market as Carlsbader English Bitter. When Czechoslovakia was founded after World War I the liqueur was renamed Becherovka. To produce it cloth sacks made from natural fibers are filled with a special mixture of 20 herbs and spices, known to only two people, and then soaked for a week in alcohol. The extract obtained from it is cut with water, sweetened with sugar, and then aged for two months in oak casks. The most famous mix using Becherovka, called Beton (German, meaning concrete), is combined with tonic water: it was created to mark the World Fair in 1967.

# Selected herbal liqueurs

### Belgium

#### Elixir d'Anvers

The Flemish doctor François-Xavier de Beukelaer had been experimenting for years by the time he finalized his recipe for Elixir d'Anvers, one of the most famous Belgian spirits. Soon valued for its health-promoting properties, the liqueur is still produced according to the original recipe today. It involves 32 different plants and herbs, which are first macerated and then distilled. The distillate is cut with neutral alcohol, water, and sugar. The liqueur owes its pleasantly smooth taste to aging in oak casks. The whole production process lasts some five months. The F.X. de Beukelaer distillery is one of the oldest and most renowned in Belgium, and is of course a Royal Warrant holder.

### Germany

#### Echter Leipziger Allasch

This specialty of Leipzig, named for the Latvian estate of Allasch not far from Riga, was introduced for the first time by Baltic merchants at the Leipzig Trade Fair in 1830. In 1917 the October Revolution halted production for the time being. But by 1923 Wilhelm Horn had founded a brandy and liqueur factory in Leipzig, and he adopted the specialty; it owes its well-balanced flavor to a high percentage of caraway spirit and plenty of sugar. Today the long-established company is based in the tavern brewery Bayerischer Bahnhof in Leipzig, where the local beer specialty Gose is also brewed. It is customary in Leipzig to drink Allasch alongside Gose, and if they are mixed together they make an "Umbrella."

### Germany

#### Borgmann Kräuterlikör

This premium German herbal liqueur has a history going back over a century. It is filtered and bottled using traditional artisan methods in the court-appointed pharmacy in Braunschweig, Lower Saxony. The recipe and production process have always been passed down by word of mouth. The taste of this semibitter liqueur is rounded off by curative plants and spices such as cinchona, galangal, cloves, and cinnamon. Borgmann was initially intended only for family and friends, but the liqueur went into larger scale production in 2006. The distinctive aluminum bottle is designed by international artists and appears in limited editions.

### Germany

#### Ettaler Klosterliqueur

Back in the Middle Ages a brother and apothecary at the Benedictine abbey of Ettal developed the recipes that formed the basis for this characteristically green monastery liqueur with an alcohol content of 42% vol. that is still produced today. Over 40 different herbs are needed to make it. Oak cask aging rounds off the fine, scented aroma. The Ettaler liqueur is also available in a yellow version, which owes its vibrant color to saffron. Its strength is only 40% ABV, and its floral bouquet is a good match for the lovely honey notes that enfold the many herbs. Other specialties of this Bavarian monastery are a liqueur made from hops, and the Ammergauer hay liqueur with herbs from sheltered, hand-mown mountain pastures.

**Italy**

## Galliano

This Italian herbal liqueur is made from over 30 herbs, flowers, roots, and berries—some of which are native to the Alps, and some to the tropics. The subtly sweet taste is permeated with a hint of aniseed and herbs, and has an underlying note of vanilla. The intense golden yellow color of the liqueur, with a faint tinge of soft green, is seen to best advantage in the elegant, slim bottle. Created in 1896 by Arturo Vaccari, a wine distiller from Livorno in Tuscany, Galliano was originally intended only for the domestic market, but travelers took it to every corner of the globe. A cocktail containing Galliano that has become famous is the Harvey Wallbanger, with vodka and orange juice.

**Italy**

## Liquore Strega

Strega, the witch, is wicked. In Benevento (a papal enclave between Rome and Naples and a place where witches met, according to legend) Guiseppe Alberti developed the herbal liqueur in 1860, and had the ingenious idea of selling it as a love potion. Still owned by the Alberti family today, Strega is made from some 70 different herbs and spices, including cinnamon, orris root, juniper, peppermint, and wild mint. The ingredients are macerated and then distilled. Saffron gives it its golden yellow color and its special aroma. Finally Strega is aged in oak casks. Strega, a significant prop in the movie *The Godfather*, is mainly served as a digestif, neat, and is also popular on ice, as well as in cocktails and long drinks.

**Spain**

## Hierbas Ibicencas

You find this liqueur, made from native plants and herbs, in every restaurant and bar on Ibiza. In the past every family used to make its own recipe, by simply putting a bunch of herbs into a bottle of alcohol. Over a century ago the Marí Mayans family began to study this recipe and the effects of the different herbs. The outcome is Hierbas Ibicencas. Its characteristic aroma comes from a blend of the leaves, fruits, and seeds of 18 plants that are reputed to be especially good for the digestion. A high-quality extract is obtained from each plant, and all of the extracts are finally amalgamated in special proportions. Adjusted to 30% ABV drinking strength, the liqueur is at its best drunk neat or with ice.

**Spain**

## Licor 43

A soft hint of vanilla defines the aroma of Licor 43, with a subtle but firm expression. Other components are Spanish citrus and other fruits, extracts and essences, Mediterranean herbs, and spices. The Romans are said to have found out about the mysterious liqueur as a strengthening tonic used by their warlike opponents when they subjugated what is now Cartagena in 206 BC and promptly banned the "magic potion"—in vain, for it was not long before the whole Roman Empire was imbibing the refreshment, Liquor Mirabilis. In the 20th century a young visionary entrepreneur from Cartagena took over its production. Licor 43 is usually served neat over ice. It is good mixed, and the latest fad of the young crowd is to combine it with milk.

# Bitter liqueurs: love the frisson

The special charm of bitter liqueurs lies in the astonishing, almost contradictory, combination of bitter and sweet flavors. It comes as no surprise that they are served on all sorts of occasions. The palette of these versatile spirits ranges from the elegant aperitif to the hearty digestif, and for precisely this reason they have produced more classics than any other liqueur category. Bartenders love the bitter-sweet, incomparable flair that they give to cocktails and long drinks. Campari Soda is just one of the drinks to become internationally famous, and of course the legendary angostura bitters add the final touch to countless recipes.

The secret behind the pleasurable hint of bitters lies mainly in two ingredients, cinchona and bitter orange peel, which are found in most bitter liqueurs. Often, extracts or distillates of gentian root are also used. The ingredients and their production method are therefore similar to those of herbal liqueurs. Even all the secretive palaver is comparable, if somewhat irritating, though it has aroused curiosity and, with it, continued interest in the products. What is more, the Italian and French provenance of most classics in this category is associated with a relaxed *laissez-faire* and *dolce far niente* approach. These bitter liqueurs cover a wide range, then: from sweet, bitter almond liqueur amaretto, to sambuca with its cool, aniseed flavor (see "Absinthe, Pastis, and Aniseed" chapter); and from the elegant, bitter aperitifs to the dry, bitter *amaro* that is predominantly enjoyed as a digestif. In Italy you find plenty of bitter liqueurs, and France too has a rich culture of bitter aperitifs to offer. Robust stomach bitters, often available in miniatures, come from Germany.

The particular lifestyle that the many bitter liqueurs, especially elegant aperitifs, seemed to exude is no accident. It was certainly the contradictory flavor that fitted so well in a society in upheaval, marked out by looming industrialization, but that was not the only reason. At the turn of the 19th century the art of advertising was being discovered, and very soon its power of manipulation was recognized. Notable artists became involved in the design of pithy company logos and evocative art nouveau posters. Brand names suddenly became more important and, in today's parlance, that is why completely new product worlds were constructed around them.

The pioneer of bitters was Gaëtan Picon, born in 1809 in Provence, who learned the craft of schnapps distillation in Toulon, Marseilles, and Aix-en-Provence. He arrived in Constantine in 1837 along with the French army, which was in the process of conquering Algeria. Picon and his comrades found it difficult to cope with the forced marches under the blazing sun. Fever and foul water made their greatest torment—thirst—even worse. Picon realized that this was his main enemy, and from then on he fought thirst instead of the indigenous population. That same year he set up his first distillery in a little market town that would later become Philippeville. Picon had developed a liqueur with an alcohol content of 30% vol., containing cinchona and gentian root— which were known for their antifebrile properties, as well as being good for the digestion. Distillate of sweet orange peel ensured the pleasant taste. As would be expected, the first enthusiastic customers were the colonial soldiers, and Amer Picon accompanied them on their journey home across the Mediterranean. In 1872 Gaëtan Picon returned home and settled in Marseilles. By the time of his death ten years later, three factories were producing Amer Picon. Picon was the favorite aperitif of the French even during the period between the wars. Then it went the way of many of the prewar brands, however, as the more rounded style did not fit into the 1950s. Now only one factory has survived; it makes Picon Bière, a beer accompaniment to which the northern French and Belgians are rather partial. Italian bitters have managed to adapt best to the changing times, especially Campari— the success of which has proved that the elegantly bitter taste can still be very modern.

# Success in carmine red

Milan, mid 19th century: liqueur manufacturer Gaspare Campari opens an elegant cafe, the Camparino, in the posh Galleria Vittorio Emanuele II (built in 1867) in the shopping mall beside the cathedral. To mark the occasion he presents the guests with something new—a vibrant red, unique dry aperitif that meets with instant approval. The only thing they do not like much is the cumbersome name "Bitter all'uso di Hollanda," so it is soon changed to simply Campari Bitter.

His son Guido built the first small factory in 1892—which was soon too small, thanks to the efforts of his older brother Davide, just as the second, larger factory soon was too. So they took the audacious next step and built a new plant in 1903, in Sesto San Giovanni on the outskirts of Milan; its innovative design anticipated all their needs up until 1948.

If the father's invention achieved worldwide recognition, it was in no small part owing to the passionate but unrequited love of Davide for the opera singer Lina Cavalieri. Wherever he followed his goddess he forged trade links, which later prepared the ground for exporting Campari. He built up the first markets in Argentina and Switzerland, then France, Russia, and America, rapidly raising his father's brand to world class status.

Today Campari is part of the basic stock of every good bar. Bartenders love its versatility, serving it on ice, mixed the classic way with orange juice as an Americano or Negroni, or else composing modern drinks such as Camparinha, Campari Red Bull, or Maracuja.

## Pure extraction

Gaspare Campari worked on polishing the recipe for the red bitters from 1862 until 1867. The aperitif is still produced according to the original recipe to this day, based on an alcoholic extract of 86 bitter and aromatic herbs, fruits, and spices. The exact recipe is, of course, a secret, but some of the

## In light of the design

As early as 1932 Davide Campari decided to bottle the popular long drink Campari Soda, ready mixed. This made the single portion drink, with its moderate alcohol content of 10% vol., the first of its kind in the world. Fortunato Depero, one of the most famous futurist artists of his day, was entrusted with the design of the small 3–4 fl oz (0.1 liter) bottles; he had already brought a new, futurist-inspired dynamism to the advertising language of Campari. Seventy-five years later the little tapered bottle has risen, practically unchanged, to the status of design icon in Italian culture. It inspired numerous works of art, including Raffaele Celentanos's *Campari Light*, and the bottles themselves became ranked in Italy in the list of "1,000 timeless design objects."

Page 580: Bitters are based on a wide range of aromatics, which are mostly processed in dried form.

Opposite top: Its color was definitely a factor in Campari's amazing success.

Opposite bottom: Like other liqueur brands at that time, Campari proved innovative in every sector, including logistics.

The Camparino cafe in Galleria Vittorio Emanuele II was the nucleus of Campari.

ingredients are known, including cinchona, bitter herbs, rhubarb, pomegranate, ginseng, citrus oil, and orange peel. One of the main ingredients is the bark of cascarilla trees which grow in the Bahamas. The mixture is put into hot, distilled water and neutral alcohol is added. As it rests for several days, a high percentage, aromatic, and slightly bitter macerate is produced. This extract is filtered in a complicated process until clear liquid remains, which has previously been colored using natural carmine dye made from cochineal insects. The concentrate is brought to drinking strength by adding water and a sugar solution. It has an alcohol content of 25% vol.

At one point Campari supported 20 sites in Italy alone, but in 2005 production was concentrated in the state-of-the-art factory in Novi Ligure. The bitters are also made in a subsidiary in both Brazil and France. Campari is drunk in 190 countries and is one of the most famous brand names in the world.

# Gentian: bitter by nature

After yellow gentian became subject to ever stricter regulation, even Bavarian producers resorted to blue Hungarian gentian. As long as it is harvested in Bavaria, however, the protected designation of origin applies to the spirit.

Left: The "root diggers" coax out the 3-foot (1-meter) long gentian roots with special hoes.

Right: The mashed roots are distilled in traditional copper pot stills. Part of the spirit is used to refine liqueurs.

Gentian roots contain extremely strong bitter constituents that can only be processed as an extract as they are soluble and not volatile, and so hardly appear in the distillate at all. So for the really bitter liqueurs that have to contain at least 12 oz of sugar per gallon (80 g per liter), small quantities of the gentian root macerate are processed along with flowers and parts of the leaves.

Gentian, which is a protected plant in Germany, has flowers in all sorts of colors. Yellow gentian (*Gentiana lutea*), red gentian (*Gentiana purpurea*), spotted gentian (*Gentiana punctata*), and the most common variety, Hungarian gentian (*Gentiana pannonica*) can all be used in distillation.

Unlike the small, blue, stemless gentian known to most walkers, this particular variety involves tall-growing shrubs with a strong root to match. Since yellow gentian is now scarce, Hungarian gentian is being increasingly used as a substitute for it in gentian distillation.

Gentian liqueurs evolved naturally in areas where the rare plants grow. They are now found in regions of the French Massif Central (where the shrubs thrive in the rich volcanic soils) and in the Alps.

In Berchtesgaden in Bavaria the gentian distillery Grassl produces the most famous German spirits based on gentian. As well as the clear, high percentage spirit, they also offer a gentian-based herbal liqueur. Original documents show that the Grassl family of innkeepers acquired distillation rights as early as around 1600. Gentian distilling was a laborious business. The distiller spent the fall in the mountains, firstly harvesting the 110–220 lb (50–100 kg) of roots a day they needed at that time, and then in October distilling in huts at 3,300 feet (1,000 meters) or higher. With the first snows the casks of gentian were brought down to the valley.

# Selected gentian liqueurs

**Germany**

### Grassl
### Enzian Kräuter

This liqueur from the Bavarian gentian distillery Grassl is a painstaking combination of many different tried and tested Alpine herbs. Extracts are obtained from them, using recipes that have been handed down, and these are then refined with gentian distillates that have been stored for many years. Flowers and leaf parts of the rare, high-growing gentian varieties are also used in the process. This very smooth liqueur is distinguished by its characteristically unique taste, full bodied and aromatic. It has an alcohol content of 35% vol. Other traditional herbal liqueurs are also available. The most famous product is however Gebirgs Enzian, a cask aged spirit that flaunts the flamboyant, earthy flavor of gentian root to best advantage.

**France**

### Avèze
### Gentiane Fraiche

A merchant, Emile Refouvelet, created this gentian liqueur in Riom-lès-Montagnes in 1929 under the name Auvergne Gentiane, and the spirit's rich, spicy quality made it an instant success. From 1962 the liqueur was sold under the name Avèze. It is made only with gentian roots from the regional national park of the Auvergne volcanoes, an origin that can be indicated on the label; it is also an acknowledgment of *savoir-faire* and concern for protecting the environment. Roots around 45 years of age are freshly processed and then macerated for nine months in alcohol. Two liqueurs are then produced from the macerate: the one at 15% ABV is smooth and fruity, while the 20% vol. version is more robust and slightly bitter.

**France**

### Salers
### Gentiane d'Auvergne

Distillerie de Salers in the Auvergne prepares its gentian according to a recipe dating back to 1885, making it the oldest brand of gentian in the Massif Central. The roots of yellow gentian, which thrives in the volcanic soils of the region, form the base. Only after about 20 years' growth are they gently dug out of the ground, and the roots are finely chopped and macerated for several months in alcohol. Next, the macerate is distilled carefully in alembics along with aromatic plants. The distillation guarantees a complex aroma, but also gets rid of allergenic substances. The spirit then ages for a time in casks made of Limousin oak, before being supplemented with water, neutral alcohol, and sugar, and then filtered.

**France**

### Suze
### Liqueur

This golden yellow gentian liqueur has been produced since 1889. Half of its aromatic base consists of mashed gentian roots which are not dug out of the ground in the Jura mountains and the Auvergne until they are some ten years old. Their taste is rounded off with aromatic plants, and then distillation gives the mixture a subtle flavor. As well as gentian, the aroma and taste reveal notes of citrus, apricots, vanilla, caramel, and earthy, smoky notes. It is served cold as a long drink, as a cocktail, or neat with ice, ideally as an aperitif. The popularity of Suze is enhanced by the designer bottles that are created at Christmas time by famous fashion designers like Jean-Charles de Castelbajac and Sonia Rykiel.

# The world gripped by eagle's claws

Opposite: Fernet Branca rounds off for a full year in 550 of these imposing tuns.

Left: A historic Branca writing desk in the company's own museum.

Right: In spite of traditional tendencies, the quality at Fernet Branca is constantly checked using the latest methods.

If you tilt a glass of Fernet Branca, you can clearly see the bitters' yellow rim: saffron, the king of its ingredients, as they say in house. It takes almost 40 aromatics to make the recipe, still unchanged to this day. These include aloe, juniper, musk milfoil, columbo root, Chinese rhubarb, and coffee. Only natural flavorings are used, which are extracted by either maceration or cold soaking, depending on the properties of the raw material. Once all the ingredients are properly mixed, the bitters are put into large tuns made of Slovenian oak in the extensive cellars of the company headquarters in the center of Milan: 550 of these huge casks are dedicated to the bitters, where they are kept quietly for about a year. All of the production stages are now controlled by the latest technology, but the time consuming procedure has remained unchanged.

If you are acquainted with the laborious production process, you will find it hardly surprising that Fernet Branca turns out to be a very complex and digestible liqueur. At the same time the first sip can prove a bit of a shock. This may be why a young clientele has specifically introduced new ways of drinking it, enjoying Fernet as a shot, a cocktail, a long drink with ginger ale (as in California), and with cola. Brancamenta, the version with peppermint, is a popular choice for this. But in Italy they adore Fernet in coffee, as *cafè coretto e la morte* (espresso with death).

## "Renew but conserve"

Fernet Branca is said to be the most famous bitter in the world. With its international presence and modern appearance, it might be reasonable to assume that it comes from a modern factory, like so many of the big brands. But Fernet Branca is still produced in the extensive complex of buildings that Fratelli Branca built in Via Resegone in Milan in 1911, and that is right in the heart of the now expanded metropolis. "Renew but conserve" is the motto of the family

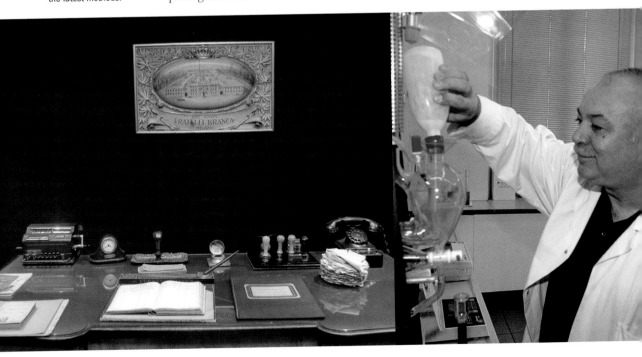

whose fifth generation now runs the company. The founder, Bernadino Branca, a well-to-do citizen, knew about herbs and had his own laboratory at home, where he perfected a recipe that came from a Swedish doctor called Fernet. He used family members as guinea pigs for his attempts. When a cholera epidemic broke out in 1836, he made his elixir available as a remedy. It went on general sale in 1845, but it was only turned into a commercial product by his sons, Giuseppe, Luigi, and Stefano.

At the end of the 19th century Milan saw an unprecedented economic boom and showcased its industry in an international exhibition organized by Stefano Branca, along with Giovanni Pirelli. At the turn of the century Fernet Branca opened up its first foreign markets and was particularly successful in South America, as it still is today. The only other factory in the world producing the bitters is in Argentina.

When Stefano died prematurely in 1891, his widow Maria Scala assumed control of the company. Her prudent management led Fernet Branca on to further successes, from 1893 under the symbol of the eagle soaring above the world. The Maria Branca Scala research center is named for her; it is an institution of worldwide importance in researching medicinal plants and is responsible for developing Fernet Branca's current quality control system. The next chapter in the company's history then began with her son Dino, as it was he who made Fernet internationally famous.

# Bitters in striking poster art

The Parisian agency Maga designed the alligator, visibly content thanks to a belly full of Fernet.

Left and right: Marcello Dudovich was one of the big-name poster artists, famous for his ironic exaggeration.

Center: In the early 19th century Leonetto Cappiello was the most sought-after poster artist, and was commissioned by just about every big brand at that time.

Many commercial goods, including spirits, benefited from the new lithographic techniques at the beginning of the 20th century, once the value in it for advertising was recognized. The bitter liqueurs were no exception. Barba di Rame (copper beard), as Davide Campari was known to his friends, had as much of a flair for it as Maria Branca Scala—the posters for both companies made history.

To begin with newspaper ads showed Fernet Branca as a cureall, not least for menstrual problems, and depicted women with a glass in their hand. Calendar boards distributed to vendors—the collection in the Branca museum is well worth a look—may have had exotic themes, but they were still very conventional in terms of style, in the manner of the company logo of the eagle designed by the Italian illustrator Leopoldo Metlicovitz. Maria Scala, on the other hand, attracted sought-after artists and agencies to create advertising posters: Maga in Paris, for instance, produced the euphoric alligator as

the symbol of good digestion, and the renowned Leonetto Cappiello designed the caricature "The King of Bitters," advertising Fernet as both aperitif and digestif.

Campari hired Marcello Dudovich on many occasions. Born in Trieste in 1878, the poster artist also worked as an illustrator for the Munich-based satirical journal *Simplizissimus* until the outbreak of World War I. His ironic touch is evident even in the advertising posters, and perhaps this is the secret of their impact. The scenes devised by Dudovich were all just slightly exaggerated. The kissing couple, bathed in Campari red, seem to be teetering with passion, and the stylish, rather scantily clad Charleston beauty at the art deco bar is being chatted up by a man wrapped in a cloak and wearing a top hat. There was no place for false modesty—Fernet Branca was advertised in 1922 simply as Italy's top product.

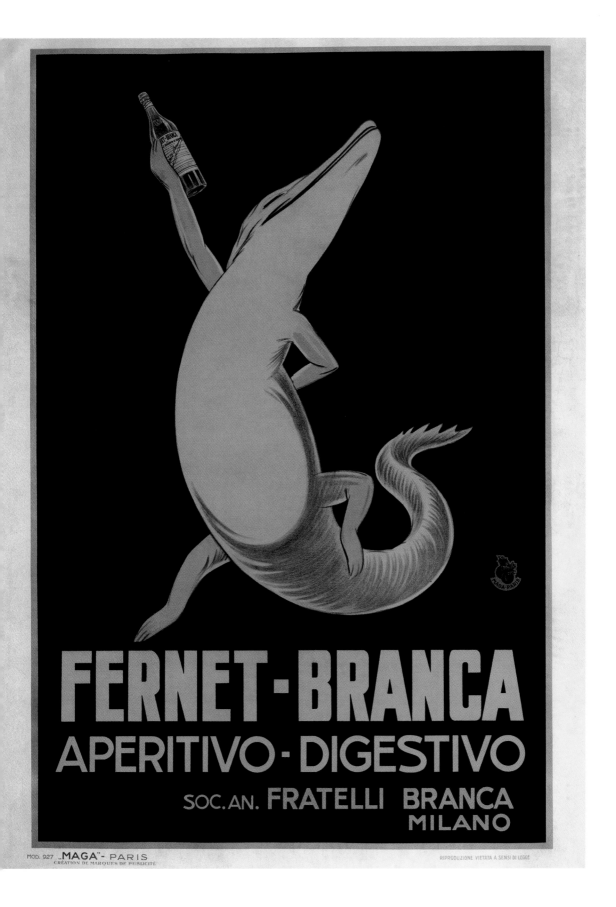

# Bitters without angostura

The history of Angostura Bitters began in Venezuela, where the German doctor Johann Gottlieb Benjamin Siegert served the South American liberator Simon Bolivar during the wars of independence against the Spanish. Bolivar posted his army doctor as head of the field hospital in the Venezuelan town of Angostura (now Cuidad Bolivar). To alleviate the tropical diseases the soldiers were suffering from, Dr. Siegert searched for an antifebrile tonic. For four years he carried out research on tropical herbs, before being able to produce the curative Amargo Aromatico (aromatic bitters). The ingredients list includes angelica, cinchona, gentian, galangal, ginger, red sandalwood, and cinnamon, as well as cardamom, nutmeg, mace, cloves, bitter orange peel, and tonka beans. What is missing is angostura bark, which is part of the outer bark of a tree native to the Orinoco; the indigenous people were familiar with its antifebrile properties. The macerate is dark reddish-brown and very bitter.

Why Dr. Siegert's Angostura gets by without angostura is unexplained, though this was immaterial to his fever-sick patients, whose numbers gradually went down. Word spread about the success, and the proximity of the trading port, Angostura, made such a radical difference to its export that the doctor exchanged his white coat for the overalls of a bitter liqueur manufacturer. Only then did he name his product for the town in which it originated. In 1875, when the political situation became more uncertain, the doctor emigrated to Trinidad with his sons and his company.

Their top seller soon became less important as a domestic remedy, but became a flavor enhancer instead. Not unknown in cookies, fruit salads, soups, sauces, and desserts, Angostura Bitters is most at home in the bar, where it forms part of the basic equipment. Many recipes testify to its versatility, but it is best known as a cleverly added dash to cocktails like the Mojito or the Manhattan.

The Trinidad firm later added other products to the world famous Angostura Bitters, including its flagship rum in 1919.

# Two Unicums

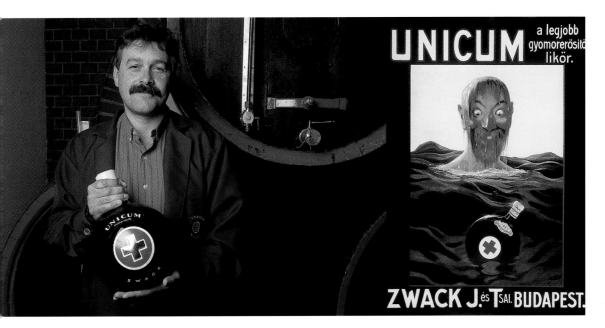

It was no less a figure than the court physician to the Habsburg emperor Joseph II, József Zwack, who created a bitter herbal liqueur for medicinal purposes at the request of his monarch. The emperor is said to have shouted *Das ist ein Unicum* (This is a specialty!) upon tasting the extraordinary herbal mixture in 1790. Thus began the success story of this famous Hungarian liqueur, which has lasted for over 200 years; it is mainly drunk as a digestif, but has now also become popular as a long drink with ice, and in mixed drinks.

Over 40 hand-picked herbs from all corners of the globe go to make this brand of stomach bitters. In order to extract the active ingredients and flavors, some of them are macerated for 30 days, while the other plants are distilled. In this way they can achieve exactly the right mixture ratio to create the striking flavor of Unicum, which has an alcohol content of 42%. To give a fully rounded taste, the bitter is aged for at least six months in oak casks.

Fifty years after this bitter was invented, the heirs of the court physician founded their own liqueur factory in Pest. Unicum has been distilled there since 1840 according to the original recipe, apart from a break of 40 years. For when the company was nationalized after World War II, the Zwacks fled to Italy, clutching the recipe. They started up production there again as soon as possible, while in Budapest they began to make a poor imitation of the original. After liberation from communist rule the fourth generation of the family took a chance and bought their old company back from the state, thus restoring order to this part of the world.

Unicum is an apt epithet for its full bodied, pleasantly bitter taste, its golden brown color that reflects vibrantly in the light, and its oily consistency. On tasting, sweetness is the first sensation, and then the multiplicity of herbal flavors unfolds as it lingers on the palate, with an accompanying hint of oranges. A persistent, sweet, yet bitter herbal taste lingers for several minutes in the mouth after consumption. The aroma strikes the right balance between sweet and bitter. We are told that the recipe for the liqueur in the round bottle with the distinctive St Stephen's cross is apparently stored in four separate parts, in four different banks, on four different continents.

A large-size bottle of Unicum, available locally in Budapest. The poster designed by an unknown artist now has cult status.

# The inexorable rise of the stag

Opposite: Jägermeister celebrated hunting folklore in the past.

Jägermeister is now a cult drink, especially in the USA.

Hubertus, the eldest son of Bertrand, duke of Aquitaine, was obsessed with hunting. One Good Friday he chased a mighty stag with his hunting companions, but when he launched his spear at it, it was deflected by the antlers, between which a cross then appeared. Thereupon Hubertus renounced hunting and later became bishop of Liège. All of this would have nothing to do with alcohol, were it not for Curt Mast, who developed Jägermeister in 1934 and was passionate about hunting. No one was very surprised, then, to see a stag's head with a shining cross stamped on the label, reminding us of the Hubertus tale and the patron saint of hunters.

Fifty-six herbs, flowers, roots, and fruits from countries all over the world are used to produce the base for Jägermeister, including cinnamon bark from Sri Lanka, bitter orange peel from Australia, red sandalwood from the East Indies, and ginger from South East Asia. The materials are weighed out in accordance with the secret recipe, then ground to different degrees and grouped together. They macerate for about a week in large containers in an alcohol and water mixture of 70% vol., which extracts only part of the ingredients. For this reason the procedure is repeated several times over a period of five weeks.

The extracts obtained through maceration are mixed to make the Jägermeister base, which is then filtered and stored for a year in oak casks. Alcohol, sugar solution, caramel, and softened water are added to the base, bringing the drinking strength to 35% vol. Jägermeister, the classic German herbal liqueur, was transformed from being unadventurous schnapps for the digestion to a cult drink for the young generation, especially the over 21s in America. This was achieved in no small part by clever advertising strategies—targeting gastro pubs with the bubbly Jägerettes, for instance, a PR team of young women who set the Jägermeister trail blazing. And the New York advertising themes photographed by Jan Michael since the late 1970s have given impetus to sales of the herbal spirit, which is now consumed in 80 countries. Finally, the Tap Machines ensured a sustained rise in turnover: these allow Jägermeister to be served ice cold as if from the freezer compartment, without losing sight of the bottles. They are simply placed top down over the cooling machine, putting them right in the spotlight.

## Remedies for the stomach

### Boonekamp

At the end of the 18th century an apothecary called Kamp from Leidschendam in The Netherlands developed this bitter herbal drink. He perfected it for commercial sale in 1805, though it did not become a brand name. For this reason Boonekamp, which is at the higher end of liqueur strength with an alcohol content of 40% vol., can be advertised by different producers, all of whom use their own herb mixture. Common to all varieties, including Kaiserkrone, is the distinctly bitter note—after all, this herbal specialty was originally intended as a medicinal remedy.

### Kuemmerling

After spending more than 15 years refining his invention, Hugo Kümmerling produced this successful recipe for herbal liqueur in Deesbach, Thuringia, in 1938. Production was moved from Thuringia to Coburg, Franconia, in 1949. Today the 35% vol. liqueur is manufactured in Bodenheim, Rhineland-Palatinate, in one of the most up-to-date production sites in Europe—around 1 million of the classic little tapered bottles (holding 7 fl oz / 0.02 liters) run off the production line each day. It is characterized by its smooth bittersweet taste. A fruity version, Kuemmerling Orange, was added to the range in 2004.

### Underberg

The miniature wrapped in straw paper is the signature feature of Underberg. Its beneficial effects on the digestion are based on herbs from 43 countries: these are finely chopped just before the production process begins. The herbal bitters were launched in 1851 by Hubert Underberg-Albrecht after many years of development work. Even today, the recipe is known only to three family members, who see to the selection and mixing of the herbs. The active substances and aromatics are gently released from the ingredients and the young Underberg is aged for another few months in wood casks, after the alcohol content has been adjusted to 44% vol. with fresh spring water. Underberg is now enjoyed in over 100 countries all over the world.

# Selected bitter liqueurs

**Denmark**

### Gammel Dansk Bitter Dram

The "Old Danish bitter drink" (the literal translation of the name) is the Danish national drink, alongside aquavit. Traditionally, in Denmark it can be served at breakfast, certainly at lunchtime, with coffee, in the evening, or any time in between. Gammel Dansk, produced near Aalborg, took many years to develop. The base is made up of neutral alcohol and 29 ingredients such as herbs, spices, and fruits from just about every continent—for instance star anise, cinnamon, cinchona, wormwood, Chinese rhubarb, and rowan berries. A total of 650 tons of spices are processed annually. From starting maceration to bottling, the final bitter takes five months.

**Italy**

### Cynar

This subtle amaro was developed over 50 years ago in Termoli, a town in central Italy. The first bottle was sold over the counter in a drugstore. Its dry taste is characterized by the flavor of artichokes. Using cold infusion, 13 herbs and artichoke extract are slowly mixed together with alcohol. Then water, sugar, and alcohol are added to bring it to the required alcohol strength of 16.5% vol. Caramel gives it the amber color. Cynar is the only bitter liqueur based on artichokes. The name Cynar comes from cynarin, the healthy, bitter constituent in the artichoke. Cynar is enjoyed neat on ice, or with a slice of orange and a dash of soda water.

**Italy**

### Amaro Montenegro

With its introduction in Italy in 1896, this specialty became a real classic of the amaro genre. These typical bitters represent part of the Italian way of life, punctuating mealtimes, before, during and after. Amaro Montenegro is made from over 40 herbs, which give this light liqueur (at only 23% vol.) its distinctive, fine herb, and fruity note. It is very good as an aperitif or digestif. It can be enjoyed neat, on ice, with a slice of lemon, or as a long drink. The liqueur is named for Princess Helena of Montenegro, who married the Italian Crown Prince (later King Vittorio Emanuele III) in the year the bitter was launched.

**Italy**

### Aperol

Brothers Luigi and Silvio Barbieri first brought out this aperitif to mark an exhibition in Padua. It was the latest creation of the company set up by their father in 1891, which produced a whole range of liqueurs. Since then, this classic has been produced exactly according to the original recipe. Its orangey red color comes from a mixture of rhubarb, cinchona, gentian, bitter oranges, herbs, and alcohol. Its bitter-fruity flavor goes exceptionally well with freshly squeezed juices and soda. Italy is the home of the "sprizz," a mixture of Aperol, prosecco, and a shot of soda water, adored by young Italians and now popular in other countries as a new trendy alcoholic drink.

## Italy

### Averna

The Averna family in Caltanissetta, Sicily, has been making this herbal liqueur since 1868. A monk from the San Spirito monastery is said to have given the recipe to the family, and it has remained unchanged to the present day. More than 60 different herbs, roots, and fruit peels are used, traditionally involving a lot of manual work, as it still does today. By the late 19th century the herbal liqueur had won countless international awards and medals, and it is now regarded as a classic in the gastronomic trade. Long drinks with Averna are fashionable. An especially tasty way to drink Averna is with ice cubes containing Mediterranean herbs such as rosemary, thyme, oregano, lavender, or basil.

## Italy

### Ramazzotti

Ausano Ramazzotti developed this Italian amaro in 1815, the year of the Congress of Vienna. Ramazzotti had a store and laboratory near to the Milan Arena at that time, where he made his liqueur from 33 different herbs and roots. The herbal liqueur is still produced according to his original recipe to this day. In 1848 Ausano Ramazzotti opened a bar near La Scala in Milan, where his amaro was served. This medium bitter is traditionally drunk neat, on ice, with lemon or with lemon soda. As well as the Amaro version, there is also Ramazzotti Menta with fresh mint, which is served neat with an ice cube, but is also excellent with hot chocolate. In Italy Menta is a particular favorite in the Veneto region.

## Spain

### Palo

This traditional aperitif, one of the specialties typical of Majorca and Ibiza, exploits the health-promoting properties of cinchona. It is said to have originated in the 16th century on Majorca as a medicine against rampant malaria; alcohol was added later to help preserve it. The recipe contains extracts of cinchona and gentian root, and caramelized sugar gives it its slightly viscous consistency and dark color. The taste is characterized by caramel notes, and some types also reveal a hint of licorice. This particular *palo* from the Juan Marí Mayan distillery on Ibiza is drunk by aficionados with a little lemon juice and a few drops of gin.

## Spain

### Túnel de Mallorca

The brand name, which refers to Majorca's railway tunnel, was developed in 1898, when Antonio Nadal Muntaner began to produce the island's liqueur specialties using artisan methods. The most successful of these is this pleasant semibitter liqueur, which is said to be based on a medieval monk's recipe. It is characterized by the typical flavors of the island, such as lemon verbena, coriander, mint, marjoram, chamomile, fennel, rosemary, juniper, orange blossom, and aniseed. It comes in a sweet version (22% vol.) for drinking neat, or a *seco* (40% vol.) with a dry herbal taste used for mixing. Mezcladas, the classic version with 30% ABV, is a mixture of the other two, and is used in long drinks.

# Summer in a glass: fruit liqueurs

The ability to capture the aroma of fresh fruits and re-create it authentically in liqueurs is an art form that deserves to be taken very seriously, and should not be underestimated. Guidance was given in the old recipes of early healers, who had already used herbs and spices to show how to catch the essence, the true heart, of the ingredients. Through time resourceful minds developed the most diverse ways of preserving the flavors of just about every fruit imaginable in bottles, so that they were both tasty and invigorating. On miserable, gray winter days these bottles have the capacity to conjure up pleasant memories of summer harvests.

Fruit liqueurs now offer a wealth of variety that is unmatched by any other liqueur category. Producers play around skillfully with an amazing range of constituents. Some use only fresh juices, others the extracts of fruits soaked in alcohol. Sometimes these extracts are then distilled to filter out only the finest, purest flavors. Those creating fruit liqueurs also have other ingredients at their fingertips, such as spices, different types of sugar, and of course the base alcohol—which can include fruit spirits as well as neutral alcohol.

So it is no surprise that each fruit liqueur accentuates its individuality. And the palette ranges from the simple home-made version—fruit soaked in alcohol and sugar in a bottle, still made by many families—to the intricate creation made from fruit extracts obtained through painstaking processes, mysterious spices, and carefully balanced mixtures of alcohol. For the penultimate resting period these elaborately produced works of art are often put into a fine oak cask.

Producers are reluctant to allow a peek into the process—after all, these complex recipes often contain the knowledge gleaned from generations of experience. Without giving away any company secrets, we can hold onto the idea that most fruit liqueurs can be assigned to one of three main categories.

The first of these groups is fruit juice liqueurs, which get their fruity flavor from fresh juices. Many producers also use a concentrate, and you have to be an expert to taste the difference really. Typical representatives of this category are cherry liqueurs, or the famous crème de cassis (blackcurrant liqueur from Dijon) that is enjoyed in Kir. With their marked sweetness, fruit juice liqueurs often fall into the category of "cremes" or creme liqueurs, which are defined according to EU spirits regulations as having a minimum sugar content of 37 oz per gallon (250 g per liter). Even this high level is exceeded by a further 23 oz per gallon (150 g per liter) in the case of crème de cassis.

While fruit juice liqueurs flaunt the vibrant colors of their fruits, fruit zest liqueurs generally appear clear, or at most slightly tinted. In these products the extracts obtained through maceration, infusion, or percolation are added. Often it is the peels of oranges or other citrus fruits that give their bittersweet flavor to this type of liqueur. One of the best-loved classics among the fruit zest liqueurs is curaçao, with its deep blue color. A centuries-old Dutch invention, it is now produced by many different companies.

Fruit brandies are liqueurs with their own quite distinctive charms. As well as neutral alcohol, they contain real fruit spirits which strongly emphasize the flavor of the fruit in question. The best known are apricot brandy and cherry brandy. Though not in the same league, the Spanish specialty *pacharán* is a traditional liqueur from Navarre that is made from sloes soaked in anise spirit and does not fit into any category.

Normally fruit liqueurs are served neat and chilled, or with juice, seltzer, or sodas as a long drink. In the past they were mixed only with champagne and dry white wine, but their qualities when combined with other spirits have been appreciated for a long time—they certainly add delightful fruity notes to cocktails. Incidentally, fruit juice liqueurs have a sensitive reaction to oxygen, so lengthy storage is not appropriate. But of course it does not necessarily have to come to that…

# Plucky cherries

Page 596: Distillers like to use ripe elderberries as the base for spirits and liqueurs.

Opposite top: Fruit grower Leo Weisrock is pleased with the quality of his cherries.

Opposite bottom: Eckes Edelkirsch banks on pure fruit flavors.

The Rhine plain on the right bank of the river between Worms and Mainz is the largest cherry-growing area in Germany.

Eckes Edelkirsch has practically been an institution in Germany for generations. Developed back in 1931, it became an indispensable item of its "economic miracle" during the 1950s. The memorable slogan "Only kisses taste better" has been used to advertise this cherry liqueur since 1969.

Plenty of competitors naturally try to take a share of the market away from the biggest selling German cherry liqueur, even though they only use cherry concentrate. So in 2005 Eckes went on the offensive and developed a new process that uses only fresh sour cherries. Compared to their sweet counterparts, sour cherries have appreciably more flavor, juice, acidity, and color. The secret of Eckes lies in the cherry varieties, the names of which are kept secret. It is a traditional variety with a distinctive flavor and deep red color, as well as a new cultivar, that rounds off the taste so amazingly.

They also decided to use native cherries from the Rhine-Hesse region, the largest German wine-growing area that is also Europe's second largest in terms of cherry cultivation. Here, within sight of the Rhine, the fertile loess soils provide the optimum conditions for healthy growth of the magnificent red, plump fruits.

More than anything else, the quality of the liqueur depends on the fruit being at the peak of ripeness. For this, the experience and sure touch of the fruit grower are needed. The right moment has come as soon as the cherries drop from their stems of their own accord, and speed is of the essence.

Modern technology has been introduced even to fruit orchards these days. Harvesting is done with a mechanical shaker, the arm of which grips the trunk of the tree and shakes it for three seconds. This brings down about 30 lb (15 kg) of fruit onto broad catching frames, as also happens during olive picking. The freshly harvested fruits are weighed in

the facility, carefully pressed until the skin of the fruit is broken, and covered in alcohol that has been distilled several times in the in-house distillery located in Nordhausen, Thuringia. The cherries are macerated in alcohol for four weeks or more in chilled mixing containers over 66 feet (20 m) high, during which time the mash is stirred occasionally by powerful rotors. In this way the flavors and colors are extracted.

## Testing the cherries

The production manager checks the progress of the extraction every week. Admittedly measuring equipment shows him the sugar content and the acidity level, but what really matters is the tasting. He will have tasted the mash up to 50 times by the time he gets the desired cherry flavor exactly right, with its fiery, sour note. The alcoholic juice is then drained off, the fruit flesh, pits, and skins are separated off, and the fruit left in the tank is gently squeezed in hydraulic presses. After further filtration only a deep red alcoholic cherry extract is left, the base for the liqueur. These finished extracts have a pleasantly acidic taste, slightly smoky and spicy, or like marzipan, depending on the cherry variety.

The final stage then takes place in Nordhausen, where the Edelkirsch liqueur is put together. For this the extracts of both cherry varieties are blended together, like a cuvee in the case of wine, and more than 10% sugar is added. According to the well-guarded house recipe, other ingredients are added to help round off the taste. Finally, the prepared mixture, with an alcohol content of just 20% vol., rests for up to a week to allow the flavors to marry. In mid October, some 50 days after the cherry harvest, the first bottles of the new product arrive on the shelves for sale.

The famous liqueur used to be drunk neat. Now it is enjoyed just as much with ice or as a mixed drink, for instance stirred with champagne or bitter lemon to make an interesting refreshment.

# Berries and the Occupation

Crème de cassis, a liqueur made from black-currants, would presumably be virtually unknown today were it not for the cathedral canon Félix Kir. Born in 1878, this priest was a well-known opponent of Nazism and helped thousands of prisoners-of-war to escape. He was already over 60 years of age when he was elected mayor of Dijon. As the local liqueur factories were fighting for survival after the war, he developed an effective advertising strategy to help them: every official visitor to the capital of Burgundy was offered *blanc-cassis*, a dry white Aligoté wine with a good shot of crème de cassis.

During the four-year Occupation, when cafes (once the second sitting rooms of the French) were languishing because sitting together and talking presented a risk, many a famous aperitif, including *blanc-cassis*, faded into obscurity. Mayor Kir's successful attempts to revive it earned him the honor, very rare in France, of having the drink named for him. At one time two merchants had brought *blanc-cassis* to Dijon. After getting a taste of it in Neuilly, they began producing crème de cassis in their home town in 1841. However, hardly anyone was growing the tangy fruits. Crème de cassis did become successful, however, and by 1914 there were 80 liqueur houses. More and more wine growers' wives planted blackcurrant bushes on the edge of the vineyards to boost their income with the sought-after fruit. Crème de Cassis de Dijon now enjoys the protected designation of origin status. It is only produced in Dijon, with fresh fruit from France.

Blackcurrants are still grown in Burgundy, and also in parts of the Loire and Rhône valleys, and farmers have specialized in cultivating them for a long time now. The shrubs need several weeks of subzero temperatures in winter, which triggers the profusion of buds. The flavor of the ripe berries is only at

Left: The defrosted black-currants are separated from their stems and lightly crushed.

Right: At Gabriel Boudier they are then put into these rotation tanks for maceration.

its peak for one day, so rapid machine harvesting is absolutely essential.

## Flash frozen cassis

The latest, and most efficient, method of preserving all the flavors, the high vitamin C content, and the deep violet color is to flash freeze the berries at –22 °F (–30 °C). In this way the fruits can then be processed as required. This involves warming them up to a temperature of 23 °F (–5 °C) and spraying them with alcohol, which makes diffusion—and thus the release of flavors and color in the subsequent maceration—easier.

The fruits macerate for up to five weeks in rotation tanks in a mixture of alcohol and water. Artisan producers even soak them for as much as three months in wine spirit. Then the first juice, which is reserved for the top qualities, is drained off; it is then pressed and sugar is finally added.

Fruit liqueurs described as "creme" are made exclusively using maceration, not pressing. To make the acidity in the berries work harmoniously in the liqueur, it must be perfectly balanced with sugar and alcohol. At an alcohol level of 20% vol. the liqueur has absorbed the best part of the fruit, and at 78 oz per gallon (520 g per liter), the sugar content is at just the right level. So in this case the volume percentages are an indicator of quality, for a creme with 16% vol. contains only half as many fruit extracts, but only 9 oz (60 g) less sugar.

Crème de cassis used to be available free in cafes, to add flavor to drinks, for no one in France drinks it neat. However not only does it go with wine, champagne, vermouth, and mineral water; cakes and ice cream taste even better with it as well. Even dishes with duck or pork benefit from the tangy liqueur.

Left: The berry extract is stirred in mixing tanks with sugar and water.

Right: The high color intensity of crème de cassis is a sign of its quality.

# Selected fruit liqueurs I

**Denmark**

### Heering
### Cherry Liqueur

What must be the oldest brand of cherry liqueur in the world comes from Denmark. The liqueur was first sold in 1818 in the merchant's store opened by Peter Heering, who had been given the recipe by his teacher. It is made from Stevns cherries, a deep red variety that grows on the island of Sjælland (Zealand), near the town of Dalby. The liqueur's characteristic almond note derives from the fact that the cherries are pressed along with their pits. This mash is soaked in alcohol and refined with a secret blend of spices. When maceration is complete, the liqueur is aged for a further three years in oak casks. It is drunk as an aperitif, a digestif, or in between, at room temperature or slightly chilled, on crushed ice or on the rocks—and in long drinks or cocktails.

**Denmark**

### V&S Danmark
### Kirsberry

This light cherry liqueur is another well-known Danish specialty. It is made from fresh cherries according to an old family recipe dating back to 1891. It comes from Sjælland, where cherry trees grow in large orchards under optimum growing conditions. Carl Theodor Jespersen, a wine merchant, was the inspiration behind Kirsberry. This liqueur is characterized by its distinctly fruity flavor and its low alcohol content of just 15% vol. Its special note comes from a distillate made from the fruit. Kirsberry tastes best chilled, whether neat, with lemon juice and ice, or in long drinks with cola or bitter lemon on ice. This liqueur also adds an elegant touch to desserts.

**Germany**

### Semper idem
### Xuxu

This trendy strawberry drink from the house of Semper idem Underberg is extremely fresh and fruity. The alcoholic beverage, which is made with high-quality vodka, is distinguished by its very high proportion of fruit pulp (66%) and the absence of added sweetening in the form of crystalline sugar. Since its introduction onto the market, the alcohol content has been raised from 10 to 15% vol. and lime is now used to round it off instead of lemon, giving this strawberry-colored drink its particularly zesty taste. No preservatives are used to make it. Xuxu is drunk neat and ice cold, and is also an excellent ingredient for a whole range of mixed drinks.

**Germany**

### Thienelt
### Echte Kroatzbeere

This fruit juice liqueur is made from blackberries, known locally as "Kroatzbeere." However this has now come to mean the dry, fruity liqueur that is sold by various producers. A classic version by Thienelt has been produced for around 100 years. Wild forest blackberries provide the aromatic juice for this specialty, as well as the ruby-red color of the fruits.
Thienelt's Echte Kroatzbeere is mostly drunk neat and chilled, or with ice. It makes a lovely aperitif when sparkling wine, prosecco, or champagne is added to it. The bottle, always wrapped in clear film, is the trademark of this classic liqueur.

**France**

### Gabriel Boudier
### Crème de Cassis de Dijon

Crème de Cassis de Dijon from the house of Gabriel Boudier, founded in 1874, is one of the best-known blackcurrant liqueurs. The incomparably well-balanced blend of berries, alcohol, and sugar, and its deep violet color, make this liqueur a real classic. Gabriel Boudier's Crème de Cassis de Dijon is still sold to this day in the original bottle with its label design dating back to 1874. In a conscious bow to tradition, it is enjoyed as blanc-cassis or kir with dry white wine. Boudier recommends one fifth crème de cassis to four fifths bourgogne. The company also produces creme liqueurs in the classic flavors of strawberry, wild raspberry, and peach.

# Fruit juice liqueurs

### France

**Joseph Cartron · Crème de Pêche de Vigne de Bourgogne**
The long-established distillery of Joseph Cartron in Nuits-Saint-Georges in Burgundy has been in existence since 1882. This creme is made from peaches, which wine growers used to plant between the vines but now grow alongside them. The little fruits are fully ripe and ready for picking in September. Their light flesh, marbled in soft pink, gives this liqueur its golden yellow color. To make the liqueur, these fruits are macerated for 10 to 12 weeks in neutral alcohol, and then the macerate is filtered and sweetened with crystalline sugar. At 18% vol. the alcohol content of this liqueur is very moderate indeed. Its pleasant, fruity flavor reveals the unmistakable taste of peach. It makes a very refreshing drink mixed with champagne or *crémant*.

### France

**L'Héritier-Guyot Crème de Framboise**
This Dijon liqueur firm developed out of the inn run by Louis L'Héritier and his wife, Claudine Guyot, from Meursault, who married in 1855. Their liqueurs had soon gained an excellent reputation and by 1883 their heirs were able to build the first large distillery. The company grew in importance by taking over several competitors, the oldest of which had been founded in 1845. Today it is the market leader for crème de cassis, but also has a diverse portfolio of other liqueurs—including their raspberry-based one, crème de framboise: produced from fresh fruit macerated in alcohol, its clear, intense flavor of raspberries is convincing.

### Italy

**Toschi Fragoli**
This Italian liqueur from Emilia Romagna represents something really special, which is immediately evident from its striking appearance. Not only that, the wild strawberries floating in the liqueur are an experience in themselves. It is served at room temperature or slightly chilled, but without ice. Drunk neat this liqueur is a rounded digestif, and with prosecco or sparkling wine it becomes a lovely aperitif. Toschi Fragoli enriches a whole range of cocktails and is good poured over fruit salad or ice cream. Toschi also has a version called Mirtilli, which has floating blueberries. Both liqueurs won the Gold Medal in an international spirits competition in 2004 as the most innovative spirits of the year.

### Austria

**Bailoni Wachauer Goldmarillenlikör**
This Austrian apricot liqueur trades under the protected designation "Wachauer Goldmarillenlikör," which means that it must be produced exclusively in the Wachau region of the Danube in Lower Austria. The family firm of Bailoni has been distilling in its ancestral home in Krems-Stein on the banks of the Danube since 1872. In the 1930s Bailoni specialized in the production of Wachauer Goldmarillenlikör. The spirit is made from the juice of ripe, freshly picked apricots. The color and flavor come from the juice alone. Fine apricot spirits give the liqueur an elegant note. The precise production process of this powerful liqueur with an alcohol content of 30% vol. is kept secret.

### Spain

**Olatz Pacharán**
This traditional Spanish liqueur from Navarre gets its characteristic flavor from sloes. Originally this national liqueur of Navarre could only be found on farms, where the fruit was usually soaked in anise spirit by grandmothers, who used cinnamon sticks or coffee beans to refine the taste. Today it is also produced in factories, and various brands are on the market. Adequate supplies of wild sloes have long since ceased to meet demand; since 1992 there have been special blackthorn plantations in Navarre for pacharán production. The liqueur has an alcohol content of 25–30% vol. It goes extremely well with orange or pineapple juice, topped up with a dash of sherry.

# Famous liqueur houses

### Monin

Liqueurs have been produced in the French family firm in Bourges in the Loire valley since 1912. The great classics are part of their range: peach liqueur, green mint liqueur, and blue curaçao, as well as their strawberry, cherry, and other versions. Their portfolio also includes a crème de cassis de Dijon. Monin now offers bar professionals a unique product line. Many types of fruit liqueur in user friendly bottles are there to meet every need. The house is equally well known for its syrups.

### Choya

In 1924 this Japanese company, based in Osaka, started up a wine-growing business. It has been famous since 1959 for its *umeshu*, the traditional Japanese liqueur made from the ume fruit, which is often described as a plum, but is more akin to an apricot. This Japanese product has a rich history, and is made by soaking ume fruits in alcohol; it has been part of the gastronomic culture for centuries. Low in alcohol, it is great for all sorts of mixed drinks, even with beer or in hot tea.

### Marie Brizard

In 1755 Marie Brizard, a cooper's daughter, was given the recipe for an aniseed liqueur by a sailor whom she had cured. That same year she founded a liqueur factory with her nephew. As well as its legendary anisette, Marie Brizard produces a wide range of liqueurs much loved by professionals, including such classics as cherry brandy, peach, amaretto, triple sec, curaçao, Madagascar vanilla, and a coconut liqueur. All of their liqueurs are macerated and distilled using traditional methods.

### Wenneker

This well-established Dutch brand was launched in 1693 by the founder of the company, Hendrick Steemann, in Schiedam. Joannes Wenneker took over the company in 1812, but as he had no heirs it went over to the Van der Tuijn family in 1903. The company headquarters moved from Schiedam to Rosendaal (between Rotterdam and Antwerp) in 1967. Tailored to professional needs, the range includes an amazing number of different liqueur types, from amaretto to kiwi, maraschino, vanilla, and watermelon.

## Bols

This Dutch company claims to be the oldest distillery brand in the world. In 1575 the Bols family founded its distillery in Amsterdam. Lucas Bols (born 1652) developed the original wooden shed into a prospering enterprise of international stature. The distillery remained under family ownership until 1816, and is now once again an independent Dutch company. In addition to the comprehensive selection of liqueurs, the company, which has representatives in 110 countries, also produces jenever/genever, gin, and vodka.

## De Kuyper

This liqueur house in Schiedam/Rotterdam was founded in 1695, and is regarded as a world leader among liqueur producers. The company has been in the family for eleven generations, and was appointed Royal Distillers in 1995. De Kuyper's extensive range is distributed in over 90 countries, and the whole production process takes place in Schiedam/Rotterdam. With its specialty liqueurs De Kuyper covers the whole spectrum of popular flavors, even including a rhubarb liqueur.

## Luxardo

The company was founded in 1821 in Zadar, a town on the Dalmatian coast. Now part of Croatia, at that time it was the capital of the kingdom of Dalmatia under Austrian sovereignty, which became annexed to Italy after World War I. The factory and most of the family were destroyed during World War II. Giorgio Luxardo survived and built up the company to new heights in Torreglia near Padua. As well as maraschino, it produces sambuca, amaretto, limoncello, triple sec, mint liqueur, espresso liqueur, and other classics.

## Toschi

The mild climate and fertile soils of the Po delta make Emilia Romagna one of the best fruit-growing regions in Italy. In 1945 brothers Giancarlo and Lanfranco Toschi had the idea of producing liqueurs from local fruits. Not long after Distilleria Toschi was built in Vignola, between Bologna and Modena. Its products now enjoy worldwide acclaim. The portfolio contains classics: from limoncello, sambuca, maraschino, and amaretto to nocello and liqueurs with floating fruit.

# Heavenly fruits from the south

Whether it is Italian lemons or bitter oranges from the Caribbean, liqueur specialties can be produced from as many different types of citrus fruits as there are in existence. The fruit peels especially, with their bittersweet flavor, provide a lovely basis for the taste. And it is no coincidence that some big names are to be found among the orange and citrus liqueurs: after all, in colonial times citrus fruit was seen as a luxury item, and eating them conjured up delicious visions of warmer climes.

Liqueurs made from oranges and citrus fruits are therefore found not just in Mediterranean regions like Italy or Spain. They have become a much sought-after specialty in the cool climate of The Netherlands, thanks to skillfully fostered trade relations with its colonies. What is more, the Dutch became the pioneers of this type of liqueur with curaçao.

Orange and citrus liqueurs belong to the category of fruit zest liqueurs, which means that the acidic juices of the fruits do not usually play any part in their production. These liqueurs are often clear, and this is why added blue coloring is seen to best advantage—curaçao blue, the trademark of what must be the most famous representative of this category, brought international status to the Lucas Bols company.

The flavor bearing peels come from a rich variety of different fruits, from the Mediterranean lemon to the exotic bitter orange, which defines the character of all curaçao and triple sec liqueurs. The peels are usually dried before being processed, but fresh peels are also used as the base for liqueurs. In order to obtain the desired flavors, the peels are macerated in alcohol. The strength of the alcohol and the maceration period are meticulously adjusted to extract the best possible flavors. The process is all about perfectly balancing the sweet and bitter flavors that make these liqueurs so fascinating.

## A bitter balance

Fresh peels are steeped in alcohol, which is the best way to release the essential oils they contain. Dried peels are macerated in spirits with an alcohol content of 40–60% vol. or less. The length of time for which the peels are macerated also affects the taste of the extract. After just a few hours, the easily

For liqueurs made with citrus fruits, it is not the juice but the peel that is important.

The peels are macerated in alcohol to extract their essential oils.

soluble substances are released, and with them the delicate flavors. As with fresh herbs, fresh lemon peels are only macerated for a short time. If they are left in alcohol too long, they begin to release the bitter parts as well. Depending on the liqueur, these may be desirable, or dreaded.

Many liqueur producers are not just content with a single maceration, so they distill the extracts additionally. During the distillation process, not all substances evaporate at the same temperature; instead, they do so at various points throughout the process, which gives the master distiller the chance to remove the unwanted ones. Citrus peels can also be directly distilled in rising alcohol vapors in special pot stills. The flavor structure of the extracted spirit can be precisely determined even using this method.

The finished liqueur base is now ready for further processing. Liqueur producers are more relaxed about telling us that it is then sweetened and adjusted to the correct drinking strength with water and alcohol, than they are about giving away details about additional ingredients—particularly the secret combination of spices that accounts for the individual character of each liqueur. High-quality brands are also granted a final aging period that allows the mixture of ingredients time to marry. If this takes place in an oak cask, it adds another distinctive note to the plethora of flavors and, not least, it also gives it a lovely color.

At De Kuyper in Schiedam they are proud of the old pot stills clad in brick, in which the macerate is refined.

# Selected fruit liqueurs II

### France

**Cointreau**
**L'Esprit d'Orange**
This world famous, crystal clear, orange liqueur has been around for over 150 years. It was created by Edouard Cointreau in a distillery in Angers that had been founded by his father, Edouard-Jean, and his brother Adolphe (both of whom were confectioners) in 1849. The aroma and taste of this liqueur come from the peels of bitter and sweet oranges. It is characterized by a perfect balance of complex sweet and bitter fragrances, accompanied by a slight hint of spice. Cointreau grow the oranges on their own plantations in Spain and on Haiti. Cointreau is an ingredient of classic cocktails like the Sidecar, Original Margarita, and Long Island Iced Tea.

### France

**Monin**
**Original**
In the heart of France in 1912 Georges Monin began to produce a liqueur made from sweet limes, which he recommended specially as an ingredient in mixed drinks. Monin had learned to appreciate cocktails in Manhattan but, as they were quite unfamiliar to the French at that time, his new liqueur faded into oblivion again. It was only in the early 1990s, when fancy drinks and refreshing cocktails flavored with lime became popular, that people remembered it. As it was produced more or less exactly according to the original recipe, the lime liqueur in its unmistakable bottle became known as "Monin Original." It is best drunk neat, with ice and a slice of lime, or with champagne.

### Italy

**Limoncé**
**Liquore di Limoni**
Liquore di Limoni, or lemon liqueurs, also known as limoncello, are among the most popular spirits in Italy. Plenty of stories circulate about the origins of these liqueurs. Many regions have their own specialties, from the Gulf of Naples to Sicily, and just one example is Limoncé. This traditional Italian limoncello is made from the aromatic peels of lemons from the south of Italy, which are left to soak for several weeks in neutral alcohol. A water and sugar mixture is poured onto the macerate, which is then filtered after a further rest period. Limoncello is usually served in Italy as a digestif after coffee. It tastes really good when served ice cold.

### Italy

**Villa Massa**
**Limoncello**
This limoncello from the famous Campania house of Villa Massa comes from Sorrento. The large, aromatic lemons that thrive on the fertile volcanic soils of the Campanian coast are used to make it. The liqueur does not contain any additives, coloring, or preservatives. It is enjoyed as an aperitif or digestif, neat and ice cold. In Italy limoncello is even served in ice-cold glasses. It is used as an ingredient for cocktails and long drinks, for the classic Italian drink *granita limoni*, and also as the finishing touch for special coffees and desserts. The typically Neapolitan variation of rum baba, made with lemons, is usually soaked in limoncello as well.

# Fruit zest liqueurs

**Netherlands**

### Bols
### Curaçao

This classic was created by Dutch liqueur producer Lucas Bols, who started making distinctive liqueurs in Amsterdam in 1575 and founded what must be the oldest distillery brand in the world. The first stone distillery building was built by his son Jacob Bols in 1612, and still stands on Rozengracht in Amsterdam to this day. Lucas Bols used bitter oranges from Curaçao, imported into the city's harbor, for his liqueurs. The pleasantly tangy taste of Bols Blue stems from the oil contained in the peel of green bitter oranges. The flavor of the liqueur (with an alcohol content of 21% vol.) is reminiscent of mandarins. Curaçao is popular in mixed drinks, not least because of its deep blue color, but it is also good neat or on ice.

**Netherlands**

### De Kuyper
### Triple Sec

With this elegant orange liqueur you basically get the prototype of curaçao in clear form. This triple sec comes from the well-established Dutch house of De Kuyper, which was founded back in 1695. All of the members of the curaçao family were developed from this clear version, though triple sec is different not only because it is colorless, but also because of its distinctly higher alcohol content of 40% vol. By comparison, De Kuyper Dry Orange, the orange-colored version of curaçao, is 30% ABV, and blue curaçao only manages 24% vol. Triple sec, with its pleasant, fragrantly sweet taste, is the classic component of countless cocktails and is part of the basic stock of every bar.

**Spain**

### Angel d'Or
### Licor de Orange

This fruity liqueur based on orange distillates comes from the Finca Can Posteta in Sóller on Majorca. The fruits grow in the valley around Sóller, a port nestling under the Tramuntana mountains in the northwest of the holiday island. They were brought over by Moorish seafarers to the island over 600 years ago. Plenty of water and a favorable climate allow over 120,000 orange trees to thrive in the Sóller valley, and they produce particularly aromatic fruits. Only fully ripe oranges are used to make Angel d'Or. The smooth, orange-colored liqueur, with an alcohol content of 31% vol., is mostly drunk neat on ice, but it can also be mixed with cava or orange juice.

**Spain**

### Ponche Caballero

*Ponche* sounds much like "punch," which in Andalusia means a spicy mixture based mainly on brandy and oranges. Of all the representatives of this category, this rates as the most popular. The striking silver bottle is designed as a reminder of the silver punch bowls from which ponche used to be drunk. Ponche Caballero comes from the Spanish spirits and wine house of Luis Caballero and is one of the best-selling liqueurs in Europe. As well as selected brandies and Andalusian oranges, its recipe contains macerates of raisin and other dried fruit, and spices—especially cinnamon. Delicious: espresso with a dash of Ponche Caballero.

# Wanderlust in bottles

Expertise and creativity are needed to coax the full flavor out of exotic fruits, which often have strange textures. Whether it is coconut, marula, or litchi, their liqueurs ensure variety and enrich mixed drinks with their unusual flavors.

Coconuts are prized for their unmistakable, fragrantly sweet flavor. Actually not nuts at all, but single seeded drupes or stonefruit, coconuts grow on palms as high as 100 feet (30 m). They are picked not only by people, but by specially trained monkeys called pig-tailed macaques, which twist the fruits until they drop from the trees.

Coconut milk is the basis for coconut liqueurs. It is made by straining grated coconut meat that has been soaked in warm water, or alternatively by directly squeezing the fresh coconut meat. The refreshing drink that can now be obtained in well-stocked grocery stores is also ideal for adding to all sorts of coconut liqueur mixes.

Caribbean rum and cachaça from Brazil lend themselves readily as the alcoholic base for coconut liqueurs—each brings out the striking coconut flavors to best advantage—and are also popular in traditional mixed drinks with fruit.

Flavors of Asia, for instance melon liqueur from Japan, also find their way into exotic liqueurs. With the penchant for Far Eastern specialties, highly perfumed litchis have claimed their place among liqueurs as well. They come from China and are grown in subtropical regions. Litchi liqueurs are popular among the younger clientele.

More recently African fruits have been attracting more attention, especially the tart, apricot-size fruit of the marula tree. An aura of mystery is used to market it, for in its home country of South Africa magical healing powers are attributed to it. Its fragrance attracts wild animals in summer, sometimes even whole herds of elephants. So it is hardly surprising that this plant inspired a delicious new liqueur.

Cane sugar from the Caribbean contributes to the exotic liqueurs in the form of rum.

# Selected fruit liqueurs III

### Barbados

**Malibu**

This coconut liqueur is made with white rum from the Caribbean island of Barbados, using different rums from the West Indies Rum Distillery. Molasses, a byproduct of processing sugar cane from its own fields, is fermented with water and yeast, and then triple distilled. This rum is refined with coconut flavoring and sugar. The final liqueur has a fresh, sweetish aroma, with a slight note of rum and vanilla on the palate. The favorite way to serve Malibu is mixed with fruit juices or sodas.

### Brazil

**Batida de Côco**

This coconut liqueur is a permanent feature of the gastronomic culture of Brazil. "Batida" is the term used there for refreshing mixed drinks that are low in alcohol, made mostly with cachaça, sugar, and fruit juices. Batida de côco is also homemade in Brazil, by mixing coconut milk, sugar, and cachaça. Rum can be used instead as the base spirit. Premixed drinks are available—such as Mangaroca Batida de Côco, which also contains milk in the recipe. A new version is Black Batida, a blend of batida de côco and a cream made from hazelnuts and Theobroma cocoa. It is enjoyed neat, with plenty of ice.

### France

**Soho Lychee**

This litchi liqueur has been specially developed for young consumers, and is distinguished by its fruity taste and exotic fragrance. Soho Lychee commends itself especially as a versatile addition to mixed drinks such as a White Pepper—with vodka, lime juice, lemon juice, sugar syrup, litchi juice, and a pinch of pepper. Soho's range of liqueurs has been expanded with new versions using Asian fruits. Soho Guave tastes refreshingly tart, while Soho Starfruit is similarly fresh, with a lovely subtle flavor of honey, citrus fruits, and spices. Both types are perfect for mixing with vodka, rum, and juices.

### Japan

**Midori Melon**

This famous melon liqueur from Japan was developed by Suntory, the large company also known for its whiskies. Outside Japan it is only produced in Mexico. Some time ago Suntory had produced a melon liqueur under the label Hermes, but it attracted little attention. It only really began to take off when it was adapted to the tastes of the US market. The high profile launch in New York's famous Studio 54 in 1978 was a contributory factor. Midori has won numerous awards in cocktail competitions, and is now one of the biggest selling liqueurs in the world. Classic cocktails like Margaritas, Piña Colada, and Sours are given a fresh twist with Midori. Adding sparkling wine makes an exotic aperitif.

### South Africa

**Amarula Cream**

The basis for this South African liqueur is marula spirit that has been aged for three years in oak casks and then finally blended with fresh cream. The golden yellow marula fruit grows wild on trees in the plains of South Africa. With a fairly moderate alcohol content of 17% vol., this spirit is consumed ice cold and neat, over ice, as a digestif with coffee, or in desserts. At the IWSC (International Wine and Spirit Competition) in London in 2007, it was awarded the gold trophy (Best in Class). The judges praised its fawn color, tropical fragrance, and excellent consistency, and the smooth, fruity taste of this extraordinary alcoholic drink with its long finish.

# Selected fruit liqueurs IV

### Germany

**Berentzen**
**Apfel**

Apple liqueur, which is very fruity with just a hint of sweetness, has been well established in Germany for decades. Introduced to the Berentzen range in 1976, it rapidly became a huge hit—it even ranks as the most successful new spirit to come on the market since 1945. This liqueur is the start of a completely new genre of fruit liqueurs that are based on wheat spirit. The flavor is defined by the high proportion of fruit juice, leaving the alcohol content at just 15% vol., or 20% at most. New versions have now been introduced. As well as apple, the spectrum of Berentzen fruit liqueurs includes sour apple, wild cherry, fruits of the forest, green pear, sour plum, cherry, redcurrant, and plum.

### Germany

**Marder**
**Holunderblüten Likör**

Edmund Marder has now attained cult status with the fruit spirits he has produced in the south of the Black Forest. Always prepared to seek out new challenges and capture nature's most delightful flavors, he has created this flower-based liqueur. To make it the umbels of the elder plant are picked when in full bloom and at their most fragrant. The tiny white flowers are painstakingly removed from the stalks and stems, which would yield only bitter constituents. The flowers are soaked in neutral alcohol to extract their aroma. After pressing and being adjusted to drinking strength, sugar is added. This liqueur is a dream, imbued with the fragrant scent of blossoms.

### France

**Rémy Cointreau**
**Passõa**

The name and flavor of this well-known exotic product derive from the passion fruit—the very name "Passõa" promises powerful emotions. This liqueur was introduced in the Benelux countries in 1986 and has been available internationally since 1994. It is now consumed in over 40 countries. Nowhere has it won the approval of liqueur lovers as in Puerto Rico, where it is by far the most important liqueur brand. It is also especially popular in The Netherlands and Belgium. A light liqueur at 20% ABV, it mixes well with apple and orange juice. Passõa is now sold in mango, pineapple, and coconut versions as well.

### France

**Gabriel Boudier**
**Guignolet de Dijon**

The experiments of Benedictine monks in the 18th century in Angers led to the development of this cherry liqueur. After the French Revolution the Anjou region became the center for it, and it rapidly became popular throughout the Loire. Its name comes from *guigne*, a type of sour cherry. When Gabriel Boudier began to make liqueurs in Dijon in 1874, Guignolet was one of his first products, alongside crème de cassis. Four different types of cherry combine to give it its high quality: two sweet and two sour varieties are macerated in alcohol. This liqueur is characterized by a strong cherry flavor and subtle sweetness, and it is served chilled and neat, or with a little kirsch or gin.

### Italy

**Luxardo**
**Maraschino**

Maraschino was originally a specialty of Dalmatia, so this liqueur represents the Dalmatian roots of the Italian liqueur company Luxardo. The fruity, sour marasca cherries in Maraschino, which is made by distillation, are grown by Luxardo themselves. The cherry spirits are then aged for two years in Finnish oak casks, which do not impart any color to the contents, even after years of use. After storage the spirits are adjusted to drinking strength and sugar is added. The clear liqueur has the characteristically intense, yet delicate, flavor of maraschino. The taste is surprising as the cherry spirit adds a distinctive almond-like note, and it lingers on the palate.

# Classics and oddballs

**Croatia**

**Nim**
**Julischka**
The combination of slivovitz (plum brandy) with the pear liqueur kruskovac is a traditional specialty of Croatia. Croatian pears and plums are renowned for their special flavor, and only fully ripe fruit are used to make the golden liqueur. The pleasure of julischka begins with a smooth, slightly sweet flavor, which slowly gives way to a lovely warm mouthfeel. The liqueur tastes best neat or on ice. It is popular on cold days as "hot julischka," and is also very good in coffee.

**Netherlands**

**Bols**
**Apricot Brandy**
It is a must in every bar, of course, as it is a real classic, regarded as the mixing ingredient *par excellence*. The term "brandy" is misleading, as usually no brandy, wine spirit, or cognac of any kind is used in this category of liqueur. Bols' apricot brandy, however, is an exception to the rule as it is refined with old brandy and apricot spirit. The amber colored liqueur exudes a gentle aroma of juicy apricots. Apricots dominate the flavor, followed closely by brandy notes. Almonds can be subtly discerned, adding to the character of this liqueur.

**Netherlands**

**De Kuyper**
**Bessen**
Liqueurs produced by simple soaking have a special history. They have been made at home since time immemorial. In many countries families hold dear their own secret liqueur recipes, which contain just alcohol, sugar, and all the fresh fruits that gardens and nature can supply. A version of this is Bessen-Jenever. This blackcurrant liqueur made with jenever is one of the most popular spirits in The Netherlands. It comes in many forms in its homeland, and Belgians are also fond of it. The one shown here is from De Kuyper, the famous Dutch liqueur house, which was founded in 1695 in Rotterdam and is still family owned to this day.

**Netherlands**

**De Kuyper**
**Crème de Menthe**
According to spirits regulations, the term "creme" may be used only for very sweet liqueurs with a sugar content of at least 37 oz per gallon (250 g per liter). Crème de menthe—which De Kuyper produces from peppermint oil and lime distillates they make exclusively themselves—comes in green and white versions. The raw material consists of nothing but fresh mint leaves, which gives a very clean taste. Crème de menthe is mainly used for mixing, especially with neutral tasting base spirits like white rum or gin. The white, or clear, version of crème de menthe is produced in the same way and simply contains a little more sugar. It is the choice for drinks that should not be tainted by additional coloring.

**USA**

**Heaven Hill**
**Pama**
Numerous myths and legends surround the pomegranate, which is said to have originated in Persia. This unusual ruby-red liqueur is made with Californian pomegranates. The ripe fruits are distilled with fine tequila and vodka, giving this very light liqueur (at 17% vol.) its fresh, fruity flavor, tinged with a hint of red berries. It is enjoyed neat, well chilled over ice, or in cocktails or long drinks. Pama hails from Kentucky, from the Heaven Hill Distilleries Inc., which were founded in 1934 shortly after the end of Prohibition. They are the last independent distillery in Kentucky.

# Drinks with orange and bitter liqueurs

Curaçao and triple sec gave bartenders their first real glimpse of liqueurs. Orange-based liqueurs owe their lovely intense aroma for the most part to Laraha oranges from Curaçao. This variety of bitter oranges originated from the sweet orange trees brought over and planted by the Spanish on the island. The peels are rich in essen-tial aromatic oils and the liqueur produced from them is crystal clear (unless blue, green, or orange food coloring is added). If the liqueurs have an alcohol content of at least 38% vol., they may be called "triple sec," which actu-ally means "triple distilled," not "three times as dry," as the name might suggest.

## Frozen Cointreaurita

3 tbsp (4 cl) tequila
4 bsp (2 cl) Toschi Fragoli
4 bsp (2 cl) lemon juice
4 bsp (2 cl) Cointreau
3 strawberries
1 slice of star fruit

Mix the first four ingredients in a blender with lots of crushed ice to a smooth consistency. Garnish with fresh strawber-ries and a slice of star fruit to taste.

## Cointreauversial

3 tbsp (4 cl) Cointreau
2 bsp (1 cl) cranberry juice
4 bsp (2 cl) lime juice

Stir the Cointreau and cran-berry juice in a mixing glass half full of ice, then strain into a tumbler filled with ice and add the juice of a quarter lime.

They only emerged as brilliant cocktail ingredients in the early 20th century, and now it is impossible to imagine dozens of recipes without them, from the legendary Margarita to Between the Sheets. Cointreau, one of the best-known triple sec brands, managed a very successful change of image in 2000 with its advertising campaign "Be Cointreauversial." Liqueurs in general, and fruit liqueurs (and syrups) in particular, are central to the bartender's creative mixtures at the moment as their dis-tinctive flavors work well in drinks that are nice and light, and good to look at. As soon as something refreshing with a sharp kick is the order of the day, however, then nothing less than bitters and herbal liqueurs will do. Campari is as popular for long drinks as it ever was, but it is now joined by another spirit with a long and rich tradition that is attracting more attention—gentian bitters, with distinctly bitter notes that give a sharp boost to juices and sodas.

## Suze Couture

6 tbsp (10 cl) Suze
6 tbsp (10 cl) mineral water
2 dashes violet syrup

Stir well in a hi-ball glass (dip edge in sugar, colored with the syrup), add 2–3 ice cubes and garnish with a slice of lemon.

## Suze Caliente

3 tbsp (5 cl) Suze
3 tbsp (5 cl) banana nectar
1 dash Grenadine
1 dash lemon juice

Stir together in a hi-ball glass, add 2–3 ice cubes, and garnish with a slice of lime.

# Precious fire: spirit-based liqueurs

In most liqueurs alcohol plays a subservient role as a flavor carrier. It emphasizes the flavors of the ingredients, helping them to marry and harmonize with each other, while remaining in the background itself. This is not the case with spirit-based liqueurs, where the recipes intend the fine cognac, aged whisky, top-quality fruit spirits, vodka, or grappa to form the confident, powerfully flavored base. These spirits are strong characters in themselves. We have the liqueur maker's sure touch to thank for making them get along well with all the other ingredients in spite of their muscle. When they succeed, they outstrip most other liqueurs in both style and class.

It is not without good reason that these liqueurs are reckoned to be the finest that the art has to offer. To taste the way the tangy orange notes accentuate the smooth cognac, or how the sweetly mellifluous honey takes the edge off whisky, is to grasp intuitively that the whole is indeed more than the sum of its parts.

These specialties are an exceptional case within the whole range of liqueurs. They are considerably more expensive to produce than ordinary liqueurs, so anyone wanting to taste them has to be able to afford them. And as anything that can be presented as a status symbol has an irresistible attraction in certain circles, you find the premium liqueurs in every situation where they can be seen as the perfect accessories of the elegant lifestyle of countless stars and minor celebrities—and where they find themselves in good company with their base spirits, for cognac, whisky, and vodka have long since claimed a permanent place in trendy bars. Catchy names and cosmopolitan designer bottles do their bit to showcase the cult status of these liqueurs on the outside as well.

However liqueurs made from fine spirits are presented these days, the contents of the bottles are what matters, and these are often superb. To produce them, their creators have to seek out the character and qualities of the spirit in question, so that they can then combine them with a selected choice of natural flavors, whether from fruits, herbs, spices, or honey. This is where the boundary with cocktails becomes blurred, especially when there are already two different spirits in the bottle, blended harmoniously with juices and other ingredients.

The most famous spirit-based cocktail is without a doubt Grand Marnier, that brilliant combination of finest cognac and tangy sweet oranges; a taste so perfectly matched to the spirit of its age that it occupies a place of honor in liqueur history to this day and has inspired generations of liqueur producers.

Anyone wishing to get an idea of the expressive power of spirit-based liqueurs should become acquainted with the group of whisky liqueurs, which have retained their regional character in spite of often international fame. Scarcely any other spirit has a taste so powerfully imprinted with the stamp of its particular homeland than whisk(e)y, which tastes quite differently in Scotland from in Ireland or the United States. These marked differences are carried over into the making of the liqueurs, and are discernible in every sip. As the whisky's austere flavors are so carefully blended with honey and herbs, however, these liqueurs can be enjoyed even by those who have yet to discover the pure whisky experience for themselves.

Another quite distinctive category is liqueurs made with fruit spirits and distillates. They are produced in small, high-grade distilleries and reflect the individuality of their creators as much as that of the region involved and its fruit varieties. These fine delicacies encapsulate all the richness of the fruits—their natural freshness as well as their finely distilled essence—and prove that the natural flavors of pears, cherries, or plums can be reproduced by this painstaking, artisan method.

Like all liqueurs, those made with fine spirits are eminently suited to all sorts of mixed drinks, and add the final touch to many a dessert. Yet if you have never before tried these liqueurs neat, you have surely missed out on the best part.

# Greatness is sealed

Page 616: Many spirit-based liqueurs improve when the base spirits are aged in toasted oak casks.

Grand Marnier concentrated on exports from early on, and nine tenths of its sales are now conducted abroad.

Louis-Alexandre Marnier developed the fruity, full-flavored cognac liqueur that bears his name.

Most stories end with the marriage, but this one begins with it. In 1876 the granddaughter of the fruit liqueur manufacturer Jean-Batiste Lapostolle married Louis-Alexandre Marnier, the son of a wine grower. Lapostolle had built a distillery at Neauphle-le-Château, not far from Versailles, in 1827, and it was here that Marnier developed his famous cognac liqueur in 1880, for he knew all about cognac. Louis-Alexandre's combination of smooth cognac and exotic, fruity orange spirit was a perfect match for contemporary tastes. When he introduced the liqueur to his friend César Ritz as "Curaçao Marnier," Ritz observed critically that the name was not grand enough for such an outstanding drink, and suggested "Grand Marnier" instead. Emperor Franz Joseph I is reputed to have immediately ordered 12 crates on tasting it, and Georges-Auguste Escoffier, the father of modern French cuisine, created what must be the most famous Grand Marnier recipe, Crepe Suzette.

The production of Grand Marnier has remained a family concern to this day. To make it, the best cognacs are selected each year and allowed to age for five years in the family's cellars at Château de Bourg-Charente. The cellar master creates a blend from them that is designed to marry harmoniously with the flavor of the tropical bitter orange *Citrus aurantium*.

These oranges come from a plantation in the Caribbean. They are still green when carefully hand picked, as this is when they are at their most aromatic. The fruits are quartered and the flesh is removed; the peels are then dried in the sun for several weeks until they undertake their journey to France.

In Neauphle-le-Château the peels are macerated in neutral alcohol and then the extract is distilled. The essence obtained is mixed together with the cognac blend, and then aged in casks made from French oak, which gives it a very smooth taste.

Grand Marnier is bottled in Aubevoye in

Normandy. The seal and red band are still attached to the classic brown bottles by hand even now, and these are then exported to 150 countries. Over 100,000 bottles leave the factory every day.

Grand Marnier Cordon Rouge has a rich aroma of orange blossom, with notes of candied orange peel and caramel. The palate is characterized by marmalade and hazelnuts, as well as oranges. The liqueur is offered as an accompaniment to desserts like lemon zabaglione and creme caramel, and also to Roquefort and other blue veined cheeses.

Even though Grand Marnier is seen as peerless, it is not completely unique. In addition to the famous Cordon Rouge the liqueur house offers three more excellent qualities that live up to the great name. Grand Marnier Louis Alexandre is a reference to the creator of the liqueur and his habit of adding an extra shot of cognac to his Grand Marnier. It has a powerful taste, and is less sweet, with notes of pine, sandalwood, and Earl Grey.

Grand Marnier Cuvée de Cent Cinquantenaire was developed in 1977 to mark the 150th anniversary of the house of Grand Marnier. It contains very old, high-quality cognacs from the best cognac crus. The bottle's snappy art nouveau design is very eye catching. The nose is distinguished by cocoa, cinnamon, and other spices, and the

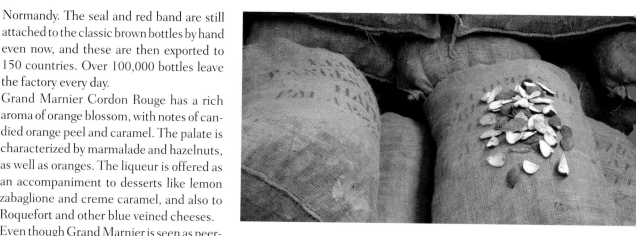

taste of bitter oranges is skillfully supplemented by notes of coffee, honey, and bitter almonds. This liqueur is good with hard cheeses like Cheddar and mature Gouda.

Since as far back as 1927 Grand Marnier Cuvée du Centenaire has reminded us of the centenary celebrations of this well-established house. The liqueur combines the essence of oranges with rare fine cognacs from Petite and Grande Champagne. It presents a perfect balance between oranges and cognac, with flavors of nuts, dried fruits, gingerbread, and nutmeg on the palate.

Dried bitter orange peels and their in-house cognac give Grand Marnier its base flavor.

Left: The final liqueur is rounded off by barrel storage.

Right: Tasting is the decisive factor in the final assemblage, or blending, of Grand Marnier.

# Extravaganzas

Using cognac instead of neutral alcohol modulates the pitch of a liqueur to a certain extent. Antoine-François de Fourcroy, Comte d'Empire and apothecary to Napoleon Bonaparte, recognized this long before Louis-Alexandre Marnier. He prepared a palatable digestive potion for his emperor from mandarins—which were imported to Europe for the first time in the early 18th century—by macerating the fruits in cognac with herbs. Fourcroy's heirs settled in Belgium as merchants, taking their recipe with them. There, they produced Mandarine Napoléon for general consumption, to lasting success, even to this day.

In terms of success, the Fourcroys were outstripped by the Marnier-Lapostolles, whose bitter orange and cognac liqueurs triumphed not only in bars, but in the kitchens of elegant restaurants. Their anniversary cuvées maintain their top position in the art of liqueur making unchallenged, if you disregard the most recent liqueur creations brought out as special editions by a few fine fruit distillers.

A sudden halt was brought to the dignified calm in the fine liqueurs segment of the market when cognac hit the hip-hop scene in the USA. For on the back of this, liqueurs (partly) based on cognac, Alizé and Hpnotiq, found undreamt-of success and have since assumed the role of primary flavor in numerous cocktails.

Underlying all this, however, is brandy from the Charente, the high quality of which rests—as it has always done—on the cultivation of the vineyards, the right soils and conditions, careful batch distillation, and years of elaboration in casks made from Limousin oak. These factors alone provide the liqueurs with that special dimension that their cheaper competitors can never match.

Ugni Blanc, the main grape variety used for cognac.

Left: The cellar master takes a sample in the Cognac Marnier cellar.

Right: New casks for the young cognac.

# Selected cognac-based liqueurs

## Belgium

### Mandarine Napoléon Grand Liqueur Impériale

Napoleon Bonaparte is said to have adored the cognac with mandarins prepared for him by the apothecary Antoine-François de Fourcroy. The Belgian heirs of the apothecary, now important wine and spirits merchants, follow the same recipe to produce a liqueur that they have sold since 1862, now worldwide. It is made by macerating dried mandarin peels and then distilling them. A blend of 27 herbs and spices is also distilled three times. Then the spirits are aged separately in casks for two years, before the cellar master puts together the final liqueur from both batches and adds Cognac Napoléon (aged at least six years), water, and sugar.

## France

### Alizé

These new, contemporary cognac liqueurs have been a hit in the hip-hop scene and glamour world since Tupac Shakur immortalized them in a song. The French cognac house L & L Lafragette in Boé developed Alizé in 1984 to boost the marketing of the stagnating cognac sector. It is now available in an eye-catching range: Alizé Bleu is a blend of cognac and French premium vodka with passion fruit, cherries, ginger, and other exotic fruits; Alizé Gold Passion combines cognac with passion fruit juice; and Alizé Rose is the latest creation, containing vodka, cognac, passion fruit, strawberry juice, litchi, and rose petals.

## France

### Navan

Cognac is cool. The golden spirit has long since gone from being an old man's drink to the incarnation of a modern lifestyle. Navan is capitalizing on this change too—it is the latest creation of the venerable house of Marnier-Lapostolle, which has achieved international fame with its cognac liqueur Grand Marnier. Navan is a harmonious blend of premium cognac and natural vanilla from Madagascar: the smooth aroma of the spice marries extremely well with the complexity of the cognac. With an alcohol content of 40% vol., it is one of the stronger liqueurs. Navan is enjoyed neat, or on ice, and in cocktails. It is named for a village in Madagascar called Navana, one of the well-known cultivation areas for vanilla. Navan is only available in North America.

## France

### Orange Boudier

This liqueur is the latest in the exclusive Paradoxales range by Destillerie Gabriel Boudier, founded in Dijon in 1874. It is made from a harmonious blend of citrus fruits and Fine Champagne, one of the finest cognac crus. This sophisticated liqueur takes account of the rising demand for super-premium spirits. Its intense aroma of juicy oranges and orange zest is immediately pleasing on the nose, giving way to a finely tuned orange flavor that blends very smoothly with the cognac and has a long finish. Gabriel Boudier's Paradoxales range offers four unique liqueurs to date, which are served in the very best restaurants in France.

## United States of America

### Hpnotiq

Premium vodka, cognac, and exotic fruit juices are the basis for this blue, spirit-based liqueur that has become the must-have accessory of the trendsetting scene, in America especially. It has also been a success in Canada, Japan, the UK, and Latin America. In the space of just two years, it rocketed into the coveted group of the 100 bestselling spirits in the world. It exudes an intense aroma of exotic fruits. On the palate it reveals citrus fruits, pineapple, and passion fruit, enveloped harmoniously by the alcohol. Sweet and sour flavors are perfectly balanced. This French-made liqueur (with an alcohol content of 17%) is owned, imported, marketed, and distributed by Heaven Hill Distilleries in Kentucky. The eye-catching bottle design has also contributed to its success.

# Selected whisk(e)y liqueurs

**Ireland**

### Celtic Crossing

This luxurious combination of Irish whiskey, French cognac, and a hint of honey is dedicated to all Irish emigrants. So it comes as no surprise that this liqueur, though produced in Ireland, is distributed by a New York company and is even available in Australia. The amber liqueur is subtly sweet and has a velvety texture. Its aroma has honey, vanilla, and smoked oak notes, and the taste is dominated by honey, spices, and whiskey, with a long, warm, powerful finish. With an alcohol content of 30% vol., Celtic Crossing can be drunk neat or with ice, or it makes an extravagant Martini when combined with vodka. It also goes well with lemon soda or coffee.

**Ireland**

### Irish Mist

With its gentle aroma, this liqueur professes to be made from an age-old recipe for heather wine, involving old Irish whiskey, exotic herbs, and a little honey. The recipe was rediscovered in 1947, making Irish Mist the oldest commercial Irish liqueur. It was first launched by the distillery in Tullamore. The carafe-shape bottle is modeled on expensive Waterford crystal, and the label bears the royal Tara Brooch design. The amber liqueur (35% vol.) is drunk as a digestif. It can be enjoyed neat, on ice, or with soda, and is often used as the finishing touch for desserts.

**Netherlands**

### Zuidam Honey Whisky Liqueur

The Netherlands has joined the whisky-producing nations, at least since its Zuidam distillery developed its Dutch Single Malt Whisky, Millstone. In the family distillery, founded over 50 years ago, they make this whisky in small, copper, hand-made pot stills from barley that is milled in traditional windmills. This has not only helped to preserve the historic mills, but also prevents the barley from being heated, which affects the taste. Using this high-quality, fruity whisky (aged in new casks made from American white oak) as a base, they have produced a honey and whisky liqueur that is well balanced in terms of sweetness.

**Scotland**

### Bruadar

The Scottish Liqueur Centre in Bankfoot, Perthshire, has once more demonstrated its expertise in whisky liqueurs with this astonishing new product. On the heels of the success of Columba Cream Liqueur, this family firm developed a light, subtly sweet liqueur called Bruadar, the Gaelic for "dream." It is characterized by the sloe berries that go to make it, as with traditional sloe gin, only Bruadar is made with malt whisky. It is sweetened with honey, which is skillfully balanced by the tartness of the sloes. Their pleasantly fruity taste comes to the fore without any hint of bitterness.

## Scotland

### Drambuie

Drambuie, from the Scottish Gaelic *an dram buidheach*, means "the drink that satisfies." This Scottish liqueur is said to have been the invigorating cordial used by Prince Charles Edward Stuart, "Bonnie Prince Charlie," who embodied Scotland's hopes for independence in the 18th century. This harmonious blend—made from single malts as old as 17 years from famous distilleries, Scottish heather honey, herbs, and spices—tastes good straight up, especially with ice, as well as in cocktails and mixed drinks, including what must be the best known, the Rusty Nail (Drambuie and Scotch in equal parts, served on ice). Drambuie is enjoyed in many countries, and in Buckingham Palace.

## Scotland

### Glayva

*Glè mhath* means "very good" in Gaelic, so it is the perfect name for this Scottish whisky liqueur. The story of its origins goes back to the mid 19th century, when a certain Ronald Morrison owned a distillery in Leith, a port to the east of Edinburgh. The exotic cargoes that ships brought in inspired him to make a rich liqueur with fruits, herbs, and spices from an old whisky recipe. This golden red spirit with an alcohol content of 35% vol. is initially sweet to the nose, with notes of herbs and citrus, and then the whisky appears. In the mouth, flavors of sweet mandarins and honey develop, with a spicy taste that reveals remarkable complexity.

## Scotland

### S Bramble Liqueur

The Scottish region of Perthshire is famous for its delicious berry fruits. Inspired by this plentiful natural resource, the Scottish Liqueur Centre developed three very fruity liqueurs made from Scottish malt whisky, under the "S" brand: bramble, cranberry, and raspberry and blaeberry. Each version has its own distinctively fruity flavor, which comes to the fore especially after the bottle has been opened and left to stand for some time. To make the bramble liqueur, they macerate large quantities of the fruit carefully in malt whisky and honey, which gives intense expression to the characteristic flavor of the berries.

## United States of America

### Southern Comfort

Whisky liqueur does not necessarily have to come from Ireland or Scotland, as this specialty from New Orleans, Southern Comfort, shows. Made from fruit and herbal essences which are fine tuned with American whiskey, this sweet amber liqueur has a very smooth, mild taste, in spite of an alcohol content of 35% vol. It was invented by a bartender from New Orleans. M. W. Heron, who worked in the famous Bourbon Street, and created a new cocktail in 1874 that he later bottled and sold commercially. Southern Comfort is drunk neat or on ice, and is a favorite ingredient in numerous cocktails and long drinks. The 6-year-old Southern Comfort Reserve is also available, but it is a specialty that is hard to find.

# Fruits, all ways

Vineyard peaches, with their distinctive flavor, are great for making fine liqueurs.

Clear Creek Distillery in Portland produces highly aromatic fruit spirits, as well as the finest liqueurs.

When fine spirits or aromatic fruit spirit specialties meet the fresh juices of the same fruits, their delicious flavors manifest themselves in different ways. On the one hand, the fresh fruity cherry notes can feed the gentle fire of the cherry spirit, while the subtle yet persistent aroma of pears can carry the warm taste of Williams pear eau-de-vie. It is not high-percentage neutral alcohol that forms the base for these liqueurs, as is usually the case, but instead the finest spirits and distillates that are produced by specialist regional distillers. Here, they know exactly where the fruits for the fine distillates come from, as they often grow right on their doorstep and always reflect the characteristics of the region: firstly the climate, then the soil type, and finally the whole landscape. So the well-known, international brands of liqueur are found less frequently in this category than the rugged individualists that are deliberately unconventional, and therefore always surprising.

In saying that, the majority of high-end distillers only make liqueurs if they are truly convinced about the compatibility of the juice and the spirit, and this is usually the exception. While they take great care to use high-grade fruit for their spirits, the requirements for the juice they use are even more stringent. Not a single wrong note can be allowed to enter the mix, or the expensive spirit would be wasted. Great care is also taken to prevent the fine spirit from overpowering the fresh fruit, or letting its fiery side disturb the fine balance: they prefer to let it age long enough to enrich the blend with only gentle warmth. And as these are special creations, they are destined for special occasions, whether neat, with champagne, or—and this is where their qualities are most surprisingly revealed—as accompaniments to sophisticated dishes, especially game and poultry.

# Liqueurs by fruit distillers

### Germany

**Lantenhammer**
**Williamsfruchtbrand-Liqueur**
The Lantenhammer distillery in Schliersee, Upper Bavaria, can look back on almost 80 years' experience in producing fine fruit spirits and liqueurs. Its range of high-quality fruit liqueurs includes wild raspberry, sloe berry, sour cherry, yellow plum, and quince versions, as well as the Williams pear spirit liqueur. All the liqueurs have a moderate alcohol content of 25% vol., and are extremely fruity and only subtly sweet. Distiller Florian Stetter does not add any neutral alcohol to these liqueurs, as all the alcohol comes from the spirit or distillate of the fruit in question. Until they are to be used, the distillates are stored in old stoneware containers, for varying lengths of time depending on the vintage, quality, and type.

### Germany

**Schladerer**
**Himbeerlikör**
The Alfred Schladerer Alte Schwarzwälder Hausbrennerei is renowned for its high-quality fruit spirits. This aromatic liqueur is made from the best fruit juice, fine crystal sugar, and fine raspberry spirit. It has no added colorings or preservatives, like the other fruit spirit liqueurs made by the company: cherry and pear. The liqueurs have a lovely consistency, combined with a rather restrained sweetness. At the same time, with an alcohol content of 28% vol., the intensity of flavors comes into its own, so these liqueurs should be tasted neat to begin with, before making contemporary cocktails with them, for which Schladerer lays on some imaginative recipes.

### Germany

**Vallendar**
**Roter Weinbergpfirsichlikör**
The Hubertus Vallendar distillery calls this product "The Original." The base is a highly aromatic fruit concentrate made from carefully pitted peaches. A spirit of red vineyard peaches is blended together with the extract of the fruit and a special sugar mixture. All the flavors can develop to the full at an alcohol content of 25% vol. This liqueur is drunk neat and chilled, or with a little dry Riesling sparkling wine. The jury of the World Spirits Award 2007 gave it a gold medal, highlighting its exotic, slightly plummy fragrance with notes of mango, papaya, and fresh peach, as well as the taste of sweetish peach juice, slightly tart and marmaladey, with faint hints of almonds.

### Austria

**Guglhof**
**Weichsellikör**
The family firm of Guglhof (based in the old saltworks town of Hallein to the south of Salzburg) has been making fine spirits for generations. Distiller Anton Vogl is also dedicated to the production of high-quality specialty liqueurs. The historic estate produces fruit liqueurs predominantly, but also a type of bitters and a liqueur made from green walnuts. Guglhof's sour cherry liqueur is dark and fruity on the nose, with a hint of chocolate. It is expressive and well rounded on the palate, and notes of marzipan accompany the fruit. The liqueur is pleasantly acidic, with a well-balanced sweetness in the finish. Guglhof makes other fruit liqueurs from wild raspberry, blackcurrant, yellow plum, damson, and sour cherry.

### United States of America

**Clear Creek Distillery**
**Loganberry Liqueur**
The New World makes fine liqueurs as well. For over 20 years the Clear Creek Distillery in Portland, Oregon, has been using artisan methods to produce spirits. The highlight of the fruit liqueurs from this distillery is one made from loganberries, a cross between raspberries and blackberries, which is named for its creator, the American lawyer and garden enthusiast James Harvey Logan. For this liqueur they are macerated in clear fruit spirit produced in house. The fragrance of ripe berries dominates the aroma, while the taste is defined by a subtle, fruity sweetness. The lovely tartness of the berries is more pronounced in the finish. Loganberry liqueur tastes great over vanilla ice cream or with champagne, or neat as well, of course.

# The smooth effect: cream liqueurs

Smooth, sweet, and satisfying—cream liqueurs can quite happily substitute for a full dessert. Other particularly sweet liqueur specialties are equally as good as a congenial finish to a good meal, without broadcasting the image of being a traditional digestif. Because sugar and fat act as flavor enhancers, these cream liqueurs have a distinctive taste that can hit the spot even after a rich celebratory feast. Such liqueurs are frequently found as a follow-up to coffee and cake as well, and may even replace them. Coffee- and cocoa-based liqueurs have been just the thing for sweetening many an afternoon chat.

Cream, or emulsion, liqueurs represent perfection in the art of liqueur making. Cream and eggs in particular prove to be tricky components in a combination, and in many cases painstaking tests and countless failed attempts are involved before all the ingredients can be amalgamated successfully and permanently. When all the elaborate work does finally pay off, every producer protects the processes that have been so hard to perfect, especially if they work without the help of any artificial additives. One classic example of this category is egg liqueur, or advocaat, which has far less to do with the law that its name might suggest.

Seductive liqueurs made with cream are in a class of their own. And this type of delicious creation does not only originate in the cool northern climes—countries in the south are also enthusiastic about these creamy delicacies. So Spain and Cuba, of all places, broaden the palette of cream liqueurs with some memorable taste experiences. And it is immaterial whether the recipes are inspired by the top products in the category or by local traditions, cream goes perfectly with a wide range of ingredients, enhancing their flavors and smoothing their sharper edges.

No one with an interest in liqueurs can bypass cream liqueurs—quite the opposite in fact. For it is often these that make the treasures of the liqueur world accessible to the beginner, because their sweetness and creaminess are remind-ers of already familiar things like candy and desserts. They begin by arousing mild curiosity, and then a desire to find out more. With more experience the creamy masterpieces can be appreciated in a quite different way, and discovered anew.

The seductive skills of this spirits family are by no means exhausted by cream liqueurs, however. Nuts, almonds, and fruit kernels are also used to make delicacies that aficionados adore for their lovely balance between sweetness and bitter notes. The latter come from the extracts of almond or cherry pits that provide the spicy zing that makes these liqueurs the perfect accompaniment for, or flavoring in, a cup of strong coffee.

As well as cream, eggs, and nuts, there is another ingredient that deserves individual attention: honey. It all started with traditional mead, the ancient drink that went down in history as the legendary strengthening potion of Germanic tribes. Much later, spicy honey and vodka liqueurs became part of the rich tradition of eastern European countries. The fact that honey had such an inspiring influence on liqueur makers was not just down to its versatile sweetness, but also because, for a long time in Europe, it was traditionally, and out of necessity, the first and only choice. Sugar was an acquisition from faraway lands yet to be discovered, and only spread to Europe with colonialization— even then it remained a luxury product for many years. Now, at a time when industrial sugar is available in huge quantities, gourmets prize all the more the delicate flavor of honey that defines the character of special liqueurs.

The Irish whiskey cream liqueur Baileys wins the undisputed title as the most famous cream liqueur. This tempting delicacy from the Emerald Isle has become an essential item in professional and personal bars all over the world, and has managed to boost the prosperity of its home country as hardly any other liqueur has done.

# First and foremost, cream

Page 626: Baileys Original Irish Cream makes a lovely Martini with vodka and ice from a shaker.

Mr. Baileys? A broad smile appears on Peter O'Connor's face: "If you like..." Since 1980 this jolly Irishman has been working tirelessly to ensure that Baileys Original Irish Cream Liqueur keeps on breaking successive records. Baileys is the best-selling liqueur in the world and seventh in the international list of top spirits. Today 73 million gallons (275 million liters) of milk are needed each year to produce Baileys: this comes from 1,500 farms on the Emerald Isle, with 45,000 dairy cows. Baileys is still a 100% Irish product, and comes from the two factories in Dublin and Belfast.

The story of this global success begins in 1971, when the managers of the long-established gin and wine company in Dublin, Gilbey's, put their heads together to create a typically Irish product. "What about combining the two most Irish things imaginable—milk and whiskey?" mused director David I. Dand. Enthused by the idea, they were soon

Left: Irish whiskey is one of the two classic ingredients.

Right: The latest technology is required to blend and stabilize the whiskey and cream.

sobered by the first attempt as cream and whiskey do not mix happily. But they were not easily put off. Matt Gluckman and Matt McPherson developed the greatest technical innovation in the history of spirits in decades. Baileys' director, Peter O'Connor, reveals the technical *pièce de résistance*: "When you make cream from milk, the milk protein is removed, but we put it back into the cream. No other cream liqueur is made in this way." This meant that what was previously incompatible became compatible: the mixture of triple distilled Irish whiskey, neutral alcohol, and cream stuck together, and stayed that way. The shelf life is guaranteed as being 24 months, but in reality it is more like 30 months or more, even once it has been opened.

And that is the name of the game for all cream liqueurs. In addition the alcohol preserves the cream so that Baileys needs no artificial preservatives whatsoever. Other added ingredients are cocoa, vanilla, sugar, and caramel.

## "Whiskey milk shake, how funny"

The Baileys team hit a bull's-eye with the fine, creamy toffee taste. The rest was down to marketing. David Dand was unfazed by the sector's skepticism at the launch in 1974, and brought Ireland its first international brand after Guinness. Five years later sales had risen to 12 million bottles.

Back home in Dublin, this would have wide-reaching consequences as they had to organize the supply of cream. Working in partnership with a cooperative, dairy farmers began to specialize in cream, breeding Holstein-Friesian cows, growing four nutritious types of grass, building stress-free stalls, and setting up their creameries to produce only top-quality cream all year round.

"The technical innovation was amazing," explains O'Connor. "If you make soup for ten people, it's a lot of work. Making it for 10 million people is quite another matter. We were able to keep the ingredients, but had to change the process." The company experienced its next big push when an advertising campaign was launched—"Baileys over ice"—as this suddenly appealed to young consumers as well. Baileys now comes in different versions: Mint Chocolate, with a hint of dark chocolate and fresh mint; and Crème Caramel with a lovely toffee note. Fresh cream and Irish whiskey define the taste experience nonetheless.

Baileys is usually drunk neat on ice. It also goes well with coffee, latte macchiato, or hot chocolate. On hot days go for Frozen Baileys: blend 3 tbsp (4 cl) Baileys and three ice cubes in a mixer for 30 seconds, strain, and garnish.

Peter O'Connor has good reason to laugh: Baileys is the best-selling liqueur in the world.

# Selected cream liqueurs

**Barbados**

**Ponche Kuba**

Throughout Latin America and the Caribbean, they love home-made cream liqueurs called *ponche*, and every family has its own recipe. In 1942 Don Jaime Sprock, a Caribbean merchant, came to Cuba and began to try out and study the different ponche recipes. He finally developed a new recipe from all this work, a quintessential version he called Ponche Kuba. With an alcohol content of just 9% vol. this creamy drink is, strictly speaking, not a liqueur at all: it is made on Barbados from milk, sugar, alcohol, and eggs, and flavored with rum and hints of spice. It is best served chilled and neat, or on ice. It goes particularly well with cognac, brandy, or rum.

**Germany**

**Behn**
**Dooley's Original Toffee & Vodka**

This cream liqueur proved to be a worldwide success for the medium-size Behn distillery in Eckernförde on the Baltic. Dooley's Original Toffee & Vodka regularly wins awards in international competitions and is sold in over 60 countries. Its light taste (for a cream liqueur) can be attributed to the comparatively low fat content and the moderate ABV of just 17%. A special feature is the base alcohol, vodka, which subtly flavors the liqueur while giving precedence to the cream and toffee constituents. Dooley's is excellent for mixing because it does not separate. It is good in cocktails as well as in hot drinks or desserts.

**Germany**

**Dirker**
**Sahnelikör Haselnuss**

This smooth liqueur is proof of the inventiveness of the Franconian distiller Arno Josef Dirker. The base is a high-quality nut distillate, which is made from freshly roasted hazelnuts, cocoa, and vanilla pods: it is one of Edelbrennerei Dirker's specialties. As well as cream and sugar, three other nut spirits are added to the distillate. This gives the liqueur its unusually intense, nutty flavor. It can be drunk neat, warm, or chilled. With an alcohol content of 20% vol. it also tastes good on vanilla ice cream or in cappuccino. Its shelf life is limited by the cream content. An opened bottle should be stored in the refrigerator and consumed fairly quickly.

**Germany**

**Vallendar**
**Orange Cremelikör**

Distillates from organic oranges and cream from highland milk form the basis of this liqueur from Hubertus Vallendar's distillery overlooking the Mosel river: it is regarded as one of the best distilleries in Germany. This orange cream liqueur won a gold medal at the World Spirits Awards as recently as 2006. The panel praised the fresh, fruity aroma with its tangy fragrance of peel and hints of orange-flavored frozen yogurt. Its intense, persistent taste reveals flavors of essential oils of orange, subtly tart peel, creamy sweetness, and a lovely melt-in-the-mouth quality. The house of Vallendar also produces a hazelnut cream liqueur made with cream and hazelnut spirit.

### Germany

**Wilthener**
**Di Crema Choco Latte**
Hardenberg-Wilthen, a family-owned company from Lower Saxony (which produces among other things the famous "Der Lachs" brand of Danziger Goldwasser), has developed this latest specialty. The Hardenberg dynasty dates back to 1100, and the familiar boar has been its heraldic animal since 1330. This modern, creamy liqueur with the Wilthener label has a moderate alcohol content and a rich chocolate flavor, though it is not overly sweet. This light drink with the Italian name was designed specifically for a female audience, which is also meant to find the sculpted bottle shape appealing. Di Crema Choco Latte is best drunk chilled and can also be served on ice.

### Ireland

**Carolans**
**Irish Cream**
Fresh cream and honey from Ireland give this Irish cream liqueur, developed in 1978, its lovely creamy consistency. It is made in Clonmel, the "vale of honey" in County Tipperary, Ireland. Like the honey, the cream comes from the surrounding countryside. To produce it, Irish whiskey and neutral alcohol are blended and mixed with cream. The mixture is then heated and homogenized using a special process and it is finished off with heather honey and other flavors. The liqueur is named in honor of Turlough O'Carolan, the greatest Irish composer, who traversed the land as a blind minstrel in the 17th century.

### Netherlands

**Zuidam**
**Caramel Dream**
The Dutch distillery Zuidam, which is still family owned today, produces this creamy, low-alcohol liqueur the traditional way and with natural ingredients. The rich caramel taste of this specialty reveals the bitter notes of the caramelized sugar that forms the basis of the liqueur along with fresh cream. Various spices are also added, including bourbon vanilla, which skillfully enhance the caramel taste. In spite of its full flavor, the liqueur is not heavy thanks to its relatively low sugar content and low fat cream. A tasting reveals notes of vanilla, coffee, and chocolate.

### Spain

**Gran Duque d'Alba**
**Crema de Alba**
Crema de Alba is the only cream liqueur in the world made from Solera Gran Reserva Spanish brandy. It comes from the sherry and brandy house Williams & Humbert, founded in Jerez de la Frontera in 1877. There the Gran Duque D'Alba Solera Gran Reserva brandy is aged for some 12 years in the solera system, where the casks have previously been used to age sherry for at least three years, thus soaking the oak wood. When the elaboration period is complete, cream, milk, cocoa, vanilla, and plenty of sugar are added to the brandy. Light in color, and with a creamy, velvety texture, it has an elegant note of chocolate and subtle flavors of raisins and other dried fruits from the south.

# Egg-ceptional

It is actually pure chance that egg liqueur is made of eggs, for its recipe originally included other ingredients. The story of this liqueur begins in 1624, when the Dutch conquered Bahia, the capital of what was then the Portuguese colony of Brazil. There they discovered an alcoholic drink that the native Indians made from the soft flesh of the avocado fruit, to which the Portuguese added cane sugar and its distillate. The Dutch liked it, and when they were in turn driven out of the colony, they took not only the recipe but also young avocado plants to their own lands, so that they would not be deprived of their favorite new drink. The avocado trees did not take, however, so the plan did not work out. The dry spell did not last long, though, as a dedicated liqueur lover managed to re-create the creamy drink with eggs. He mixed egg yolks, brandy, and sugar together in such a way that the end result was equal in appearance and taste to the Brazilian avocado drink. Advocaat was born.

"Advocaat" is not a protected name, nor does it indicate a level of quality: it is simply a synonym for "egg liqueur." The EU spirits regulation for egg liqueur stipulates that the minimum egg yolk content must be 21 oz per gallon (140 grams per liter) of the final product. Egg white may also be included. If the spirit has a lower egg yolk content, it must be labeled "liqueur with egg."

Liqueurs made with egg, despite the ingenious invention of advocaat, are not an achievement restricted to The Netherlands. Other places also know how to mix egg yolks and alcohol. Aficionados in Latin America and the Caribbean are fond of a glass of ponche crema, an egg liqueur based on rum, or a rompompe, its Mexican counterpart. They adore coquito, a rum and egg drink with coconut milk, in Puerto Rico, and in the USA and elsewhere they make eggnogs. At Christmas time especially, these egg-based delicacies are very popular.

Eggs naturally play the starring role in egg liqueur. At Verpoorten they are cracked open perfectly by machine.

# Selected egg liqueurs

### Germany

**Behn Spiegelei**

"Without words" is the motto of this premium egg liqueur. After all, the unmistakable bottle with its sculpted fried egg and witty eggshell top says it all. It is a mouth-watering invitation to try the contents, which include sugar syrup, alcohol, water, and vanilla as well as egg. This product has cracked open the egg liqueur market to young consumers, who have been more difficult to reach with these creamy sweet specialties in the past. Spiegelei is just one example of all the great ideas from Behn, the family business based in Eckernförde, north Germany, which was founded back in 1892 and has gained a worldwide reputation with its cream liqueur, Dooley's.

### Germany

**Verpoorten Original**

This egg liqueur deliberately does not call itself "advocaat," to differentiate it from other companies' products. The recipe was created by the founder of the company, Eugen Verpoorten, in 1876. With ten egg yolks per bottle and an alcohol content of 20% vol., Verpoorten Original far exceeds the minimum EU requirements for egg liqueur. The firm maintains a discreet silence, however, when it comes to revealing what else it contains apart from fresh egg yolks and fine spirits. The ingredients are emulsified by regulated heating in special pasteurization machines. Once opened, bottles should be kept in the refrigerator and be used within six months. Anyhow, this liqueur ought not to last this long with most aficionados.

### Germany

**Weis Advocaat**

Made with local kirschwasser, this egg liqueur is produced by the Elztalbrennerei Georg Weis in Gutach, Breisgau, in the heart of the Black Forest. This fruit distillery can look back on a long tradition: the family has been distilling the region's fruits on its farm since back in 1786. In 1924 Georg Weis went on to found his own company for the production of fine spirits and liqueurs. The distillery's specialties are also enjoyed abroad. The Elztalbrennerei scored a big hit with its hand-finished advocaat (20% ABV) that skillfully combines the flavors of fresh eggs with those of fine Black Forest kirschwasser.

### Netherlands

**Bols Advocaat**

This advocaat is rooted in the Dutch tradition of the original avocado drink from South America. It is produced by Lucas Bols, one of the oldest and most famous liqueur houses in the world. Bols Advocaat is made according to a recipe that has been fiercely guarded for centuries, using fresh egg yolk, sugar, and alcohol. It is drunk neat or mixed in cocktails, poured over ice cream and cakes, or used to finish off desserts. As a luxurious treat Bols recommends mixing it with triple sec, gin, orange juice, and mineral water. If you prefer it the more classical way, mix the advocaat with cherry liqueur, and then top it all with some orange juice.

### Switzerland

**Eiercognac Emile E.**

This Swiss premium version of egg liqueur is made from French cognac and eggs. It is produced by Appenzeller Alpenbitter AG, which stresses the fact that it only uses Swiss free-range eggs for its egg cognac liqueur. The name of the liqueur is a reference to the founder of the company, Emile Ebneter, who opened a spirits store in 1902 at the age of 20. It did not take long for his bitters to make it a real commercial success, and to this day the popular Appenzeller Alpenbitter is still the flagship spirit of the company. The company name was only changed from Emil Ebneter & Co. AG to Appenzeller Alpenbitter AG in 2006.

# Romantic almonds

Almond blossom heralds spring in Italy; the kernels are responsible for the fine flavor of most amaretti.

Many regional liqueur specialties come from Italy. A famous one is amaretto, which is made from sweet and bitter almonds, various herbs, and spices, and is produced by different companies. Its origins date back to the Renaissance, at least according to the story surrounding the most famous amaretto, Disaronno. At that time a young woman ran a tavern in Saronno, near Milan, where pilgrims to the town would spend the night. One of her guests, Bernardino Luini, was painting frescoes in the Santa Maria delle Grazie church in Milan. The young innkeeper sat as a model for him, and they fell in love. To capture his heart she prepared a pure, flavorsome liqueur from brandy, apricot kernels, and a secret aromatic blend, and called it Disaronno. She then gave the recipe of this original amaretto to the painter as a present.

The recipe from 1525 was safeguarded in his family. The heirs, the Reina family, did not decide to produce it commercially until the 18th century, and even to this day its production has stayed in the hands of this Saronno family. The 17 different spices, herbs, and fruits that are extracted by a special process grow on the Adriatic coast of Italy. These extracts are combined with neutral alcohol and sweetened with caramel. Apricot kernel oil gives it the smooth flavor of almonds and apricots, which distinguishes Disaronno from most of its competitors. It can be enjoyed neat, on ice, with a little lemon juice even, in coffee, in cocoa, or with orange juice. It is a component of famous cocktails like Almond Kiss, Amaretto Sour, and Mai Tai. Disaronno is one of the most important liqueur brands in the world and is sold in over 150 countries.

# Selected almond liqueurs

### Germany

**TABU**
**Volume 33 rpm Persico**
In recent years peach kernel spirit has experienced something of a renaissance. Part of its attraction is down to the fact that it was banned for a time because of its prussic acid content. Now you can devote yourself to enjoying this ancient specialty without worrying, as the modern version is made without prussic acid and quite legal. A few years ago the German distillery Felix Rauter dug up an old, original recipe from the 19th century. This spirit, with an alcohol content of 33% vol., contains distillates of peach kernel, bitter almonds, and peach blossom, as well as extracts of sandalwood and essential oils of roses, carnations, and other plants. Sauern mit Persico is a mixture of persico and cherry juice, bottled by several companies.

### France

**Gabriel Boudier · Prunelle**
**Liqueur de Bourgogne**
This specialty of Burgundy is based on the pits of sloe berries. The berries are shaken from the trees after the first frost. The flesh is then gently removed; the pits are washed and dried, then macerated for several weeks in alcohol. It is vital that they are not broken, so that only the fine flavorings are released, while the coarse ones are contained within the heart of the kernel. Mixed with a balanced measure of sugar and adjusted to drinking strength, this makes a lovely liqueur with a delicate flavor, reminiscent of almonds. It is consumed neat or used for fine pastries.

### Italy

**Barbero**
**Frangelico**
Frangelico, a liqueur made from wild hazelnuts, berries, and other fruits, is a specialty of Piedmont. The recipe is said to originate from a monk called Frangelico, who lived in Piedmont around 300 years ago. The ingredients are distilled and made into a liqueur, which is then aged in oak casks. Frangelico is drunk neat, with coffee or espresso, and even on ice. It is popular served as a long drink with orange juice. One specialty is Frangelico Barbero with butterscotch liqueur, grapefruit, and orange juice. The original bottle in the shape of a monk's habit reminds us of the creator of this specialty.

### Italy

**Toschi**
**Nocello**
This is the sweeter, lighter version (with 24% ABV) of the famous nut liqueur nocino. It has walnuts and hazelnuts in the recipe, and goes well with desserts or in coffee. Nocino is the inspiration behind it, with its rich, predominant flavor of green walnuts. The nuts are either fermented before they are ripe and distilled, or first macerated, in which case the extracts can also be distilled afterward. The Toschi distillery in Emilia Romagna prefers the maceration method, and rounds off the flavor of its liqueur with caramel and vanilla.

### Netherlands

**Wenneker**
**Amaretto**
The popular almond liqueur has long since ceased to be a strictly Italian specialty. They know all about how to produce it in The Netherlands as well, for instance at Wenneker, one of the largest Dutch liqueur manufacturers, which offers a wide and varied range of liqueur classics. Wenneker's amaretto is based on an old family recipe, dating back to Italy in the 16th century. It is made from almonds, caramelized sugar, and 17 different herbs and fruits, which are mixed with apricot oil. It has a lovely almond flavor and an elegant bitter-sweet note in the finish.

# Catching bears with honey

Page 638: Cocoa liqueur is an essential ingredient in Brandy Alexander, which tastes great with espresso.

Mead is one of the oldest alcoholic drinks known to humans, for honey begins to ferment slightly, provided it is thinned down sufficiently with water. Germanic tribes are reputed to have done ample justice to it: for one thing they had plenty of it, thanks to all the honey in the vast forests of northern Europe; and on the other hand they were smart enough to believe it was a gift of the gods, thus justifying the prolonged carousing as sacrificial rituals in religious services. Perhaps they also just drank it because it was a healthy, clean, and tasty thirst quencher, which only faded into oblivion when beer brewing was perfected.

The combination of alcohol and honey was to go hand in hand with the spread of alcoholic spirits, for nothing is more obvious. So the origins of Bärenfang (the name for honey liqueur in east Prussia, meaning "bear trap") dates back to the 15th century, when the art of distillation was presumably just being developed there. In some areas of east Prussia, Masuria, and Lithuania, they called their homemade liqueur Meschkinnes, from the Lithuanian word *meska*, meaning "bear," while in Russia, where it is now made by Stolichnaya, the term used is Okhotnichya, hunter's vodka.

Bärenfang is still a common home brew to this day as it is easy to produce; the main thing you need is patience. It is best to use mild blossom honey, which is dissolved in a mixture of alcohol and water (it can be gently heated to do this). The batch must be sealed so it is airtight, and then it takes a few months for the constituents to marry into a tasty, harmonious blend. The liqueur was rounded off early on by adding all sorts of herbs and spices; the favorites these days are cinnamon, cloves, vanilla, and citrus peel.

The first commercially produced honey liqueur, produced by the Königsberg company Teucke & König, came onto the market as late as 1945. Its Bärenjäger was an export success, not least due to the bottle with the beehive design.

Nowadays boxes containing frames are used as beehives. The bees fill them up with their honeycombs, where they deposit the honey.

# Honey liqueurs and Swedish punch

**Germany**

**Dirker**
**Tannenspitzenhoniglikör**
This unique liqueur comes from Edelbrennerei Dirker in Franconia. With his unconventional spirits Arno Josef Dirker, one of the most successful distillers in Germany, wanted to produce a fir honey liqueur, which proved impractical because of the expensive base material. So in spring the distiller gathers the fresh shoots of fir trees from the Baltic coast and macerates them in alcohol. This extract is then distilled and mixed at a specific temperature with selected honey. A maturation period then follows. As well as being enjoyed neat, this liqueur is also good as a finishing touch for unusual desserts.

**Germany**

**Teucke & König**
**Bärenjäger**
To this day this honey liqueur, with an alcohol content of 35% vol., is made according to the east Prussian recipe handed down over the years. The only thing that has changed is the honey. They now use pure highland honey from Yucatan in Mexico, renowned for its powerful flavor. Bärenjäger, which is made only from natural ingredients, is blended with neutral alcohol and stored in tanks for several months to clarify it and intensify the flavors. It is drunk neat or in hot tea, as honey grog or with milk. It is frequently served poured over ice cream as well. The Teucke & König brand is made in Steinhagen in Westphalia.

**Poland**

**Destylarnia Sobieski S. A.**
**Krupnik**
As far back as the Middle Ages the Polish aristocracy regaled themselves with sweet honey and vodka liqueur. According to the 18th-century recipe still used today, selected natural honey is processed with the root and leaf extracts of herbs. Krupnik may be described as a liqueur, but many regard it as a vodka, if not a separate category of spirit altogether. It is drunk cold, warm, and even in beer. The liqueur, with an alcohol content of 38% vol., is produced in the long-established Destylarnia Sobieski S.A. in Starogard Gdanski, which is now owned by Belvedere.

**Poland**

**Miodula**
**Presidential Blend**
This cask-aged, Polish honey vodka liqueur is based on a recipe from the 18th century. Miodula is one of the most important Polish spirits and was prized for generations by the Polish monarchy. Today Miodula Presidential Blend is served to visiting foreign statesmen at official occasions. Each bottle of the limited edition is signed and numbered by hand. With an ABV of 40%, the liqueur is produced by Toorak Polska. As well as Polish premium vodka, its ingredients include wild honey, spring water from the Wisla mountains, and a secret blend of herbs and spices. It is served neat on ice, but can also be drunk hot.

**Sweden**

**Carlshamns**
**Flaggpunsch Original**
This punch does not actually contain any honey, but it belongs to a similar cultural tradition to the honey liqueurs. At the same time it is inextricably linked to Swedish culture. The mixture—originally made from arrack, neutral alcohol, sugar, water, and wine—has been produced in Sweden since the first arrack reached its shores in 1773. Sweden's oldest brand of punch, registered back in 1885, was first produced by Destillerie Karlshamns Bryggerie and is part of the V & S group's range. The liqueur (26% ABV) distinguishes itself by its fresh arrack notes and well-balanced sweetness. It is drunk chilled from punch glasses, but in Sweden it is also consumed hot with pea soup.

# Stimulating liqueurs

It is no accident that spicy coffee flavors and liqueur make a very good combination. Unsurprisingly, one of the methods of producing coffee liqueur is very similar to a classic way of making coffee. What is meant by this is percolation, the constant dripping of the base material with alcohol, gently releasing and gathering the flavors.

Correspondingly, a piece of equipment traditionally used to make coffee is called a percolator. Water is heated in it, and then rises through a funnel and runs up and over the ground coffee, which sits in a sieve. Depending on the make, the liquid continues to circulate until the coffee has reached the desired strength, or else the coffee is ready after just one cycle of the process.

Of all the liqueurs, the coffee ones are characterized in particular by a subtle differentiation in range: one might be based on high grown Arabica beans from Mexico, another on the famous Jamaican Blue Mountain beans, or yet another on the classically brewed espresso.

If these liqueurs are often grouped together in one category, this relates to the affinity between coffee and cocoa beans and to their full-bodied flavor, rather than to a liqueur type. For depending on the production method and ingredients, they may be either cream based or spicy liqueurs.

They are also used in different ways. Coffee liqueurs taste good in, with, and of course instead of, coffee. While brown cocoa liqueur can be substituted, clear cocoa liqueurs (which are usually obtained by distillation and have a higher sugar content) are only used for mixing and are part of the basic stock of every cocktail bar. Coffee liqueurs have earned their place there too: you only need to think of the Black or White Russian.

# Coffee and cocoa liqueurs

## Ireland

### Sheridan's
Even the bottle of this coffee cream liqueur catches the eye. Divided into two parts, a third of it is a light liqueur made from fresh Irish cream and vanilla, with a moderate alcohol content of 15.5% vol. The other side of the bottle contains the other two thirds of dark coffee liqueur with chocolate flavoring, which proudly indicates its 37.6% ABV. If you pour this extraordinary liqueur with a steady hand out of both bottle openings into a glass simultaneously, you get an attractively layered drink: the coffee liqueur lies at the bottom, with the vanilla cream spread on top. Sheridan's is always served chilled on ice. The liqueur comes from the same Dublin firm as the world famous whiskey cream liqueur, Baileys.

## Italy

### Borghetti
Espresso has formed the basis of this very dark liqueur since 1860. Ugo Borghetti from Ancona, who at one time created this specialty (now produced in Milan by Fratelli Branca), stipulated a mixture of freshly roasted and ground arabica and robusta coffee beans. The typical feature of this liqueur is therefore its authentic espresso taste combined with subtle sweetness. Borghetti (25% ABV) is consumed neat at room temperature, or chilled, often with ice. It is particularly popular in hot drinks like espresso or coffee, or it tastes wonderful with cola and a dash of lime juice.

## Jamaica

### Tia Maria
The story goes that a faithful maidservant, Tia Maria (Spanish, meaning "Aunt Mary") was fleeing during the slaves' revolt in the mid 18th century in Jamaica. She was quick witted enough to save her mistress's old family recipe that was hidden in a casket along with a pair of black pearl earrings. To this day the liqueur is made from fine Jamaican Blue Mountain coffee. The cleaned and dried beans are lightly roasted, coarsely ground, and mixed with other ingredients, and then the flavors are extracted using the double percolation method. With an alcohol content of 20% vol., the liqueur has a subtly sweet flavor of roasted coffee, with hints of chocolate and caramel. It is served neat on ice, or with cola and ice.

## Mexico

### Kahlúa
This Mexican liqueur with an alcohol content of 20% vol. has been produced since 1936. Kahlúa is the most consumed coffee liqueur in the world and is now exported to over 120 countries. The base is freshly roasted, coarsely ground arabica coffee from the mountains of Mexico. The ground beans are heated to almost boiling point in water, and the prepared coffee must first cool down, before rum, vanilla, and caramel are added. Kahlúa is good over ice, with milk, or with hot and iced coffee specialties. The vodka cocktails White and Black Russian, with or without cream, are famous. The very brave can try the fierce Kahlúa B52.

## Netherlands

### Wenneker
### Crème de Cacao Brown
This powerful chocolate liqueur is made from the extract of selected cocoa beans. Its medium sweet taste is accompanied by the flavor of pure, dark chocolate and a hint of vanilla. Wenneker Crème de Cacao Brown tastes good in coffee and cocktails, and neat or on ice as well, of course—it is also a treat poured over ice cream. It has an alcohol content of 27% vol. Like all the house of Wenneker liqueurs, it contains only natural flavorings and colorings. As well as the cocoa liqueur, Wenneker has a white chocolate liqueur and a mint chocolate liqueur in the range.

# Unusual liqueurs

**Germany**

### Asbach
**A&A · Asbach und Auslese**

With this interesting riesling-based liqueur the house of Asbach in Rüdesheim on the Rhine has managed to combine two of its products successfully: "Auslese" (high-quality) riesling and the original Asbach Uralt, a specialty brandy that is double distilled and then aged for at least two years in small casks made of Limousin oak. The restrained sweetness of the golden riesling liqueur has notes of honey and fresh grapes. It tastes good as a change from the usual aperitifs, neat or over ice. For a special touch combine the liqueur with dry, sparkling wine. As a long drink it goes well with ginger ale, soda, or tonic, and it is lovely poured over ice cream, fruits, and cakes, as well as in sauces and marinades.

**Germany**

### Dirker
**Apfelstrudellikör**

All that was preventing the Franconian distiller Arno Josef Dirker from distilling an apple strudel were customs related technicalities. So he created an apple strudel liqueur instead. It is based on freshly pressed apple juice with apple brandy and sugar. Dirker achieved the typical notes of apple strudel using hazelnut spirit, rum, cinnamon, raisins, almonds, yeast, and more besides. The recipe contains a total of almost 20 ingredients, and is the result of a great deal of experimenting. This apple strudel liqueur tastes good neat and in desserts. For a Christmas aperitif cider is added, making a special variation of kir. Dirker makes his apple strudel liqueur available only during the winter months.

**England**

### Pimm's
**No. 1**

A genuine piece of British culture flows into the glass with this refreshing drink. Pimm's is based on London dry gin and is a favorite in mixed drinks. It owes its refreshing, fruity taste to a well-balanced mixture of liqueurs, fruit nectars, and herbs. James Pimm, the owner of a 19th-century oyster bar in London, invented this gleaming, reddish-brown drink. Of the countless cocktails and long drinks that Pimm's invests with distinctive character, Pimm's No. 1 with ginger ale or lemonade stands out as the most famous example.

**Finland**

### Altia
**Koskenkorva Salmiakki**

This typically Finnish liqueur, with an alcohol content of 32% vol., is made from salty licorice and vodka. As well as being available in 2- and 1-pint (1-liter and 0.5-liter) glass bottles, it is also sold in 1-pint (0.5-liter) plastic bottles, designed to highlight the contemporary, young character of this liqueur. Koskenkorva Salmiakki is best drunk neat. Koskenkorva is a Finnish spirit brand of the Altia group. In Finland, as throughout Scandinavia, salty licorice represents a candy that is as traditional as it is idiosyncratic.

**France**

### Boudier
**Liqueur de Roses**

Making a liqueur from roses may sound very exotic now, but the flavor of roses has been used in the kitchen since time immemorial. The Chinese were the first to use roses in cooking, a habit that spread via the Silk Road to Persia—in modern Iran confectionery is perfumed with them to this day. Rose flavors are also valued in the West for pastry making. Gabriel Boudier in Dijon produced this liqueur by macerating the petals of extremely fragrant roses in sugar and alcohol. Drinking it neat with ice cubes tempers its very sweet taste and leaves a lovely perfumed finish; you can also add a dash to champagne, enrich cocktails with it, or use it for oriental dishes.

## France

### Daucourt
### X-Rated Fusion Liqueur

This trendy liqueur is an exotic mixture of premium French vodka, Provençal blood oranges, mango, and passion fruit. The pure organic juices are fused with the vodka in a secret process. The liqueur was introduced in 2004 by Jean-Marc Daucourt, the award-winning spirits developer, and Todd Martin, the former president of Allied Domecq North America. Their aim was to create a pink, stylish liqueur. X-Rated Fusion experienced one of the highest growth rates of any spirit in the USA. X-Rated Fusion is enjoyed over ice, and the pink liqueur is also good in unusual cocktails.

## Italy

### Franciacorta
### Eclisse · Liquore di Liquirizia

Liquirizia, a licorice-based liqueur from Calabria, is one of the less well-known spirit specialties of the Mediterranean region. This spicy liqueur is made from the *Glycyrrhiza glabra* variety of licorice, which aids the digestion and is also valued for its detoxifying properties. Very dark in color, it has the unmistakable aroma and flavor of licorice, wrapped in a subtle sweetness. It is mainly enjoyed neat and well chilled as a digestif, and is also worth trying over ice cream and in long drinks. A special treat is hot licorice liqueur topped with cream. It is a product of the Franciacorta distillery, not far from Brescia.

## Netherlands

### De Kuyper
### Parfait Amour

De Kuyper in Schiedam, near Rotterdam, is one of the most important producers of fruit spirits. Its Parfait Amour is made from violets and a blend of oriental flower extracts. This liqueur is rounded off with distillates of lemon, coriander, and oranges, which are still obtained using pot stills from 1695. Its unusual, mysterious flavor adds to its popularity, as does its flamboyant violet color, which is outstanding in many cocktails.

## Netherlands

### Zuidam · Oud-Hollands
### Speculaas Liqueur

Zuidam is one of the last independent distilleries in The Netherlands, which still processes and produces all its distillates and extracts the traditional way in its family owned company. This old Dutch liqueur inspired by spicy speculatius cookies is made from lots of different oriental herbs and spices, familiar to The Netherlands since its merchants brought them home from their trade expeditions. Spices like cinnamon, cardamom, nutmeg, cloves, and bourbon vanilla are blended and soaked in alcohol. This base produces a pleasant, sweetly spicy liqueur.

## United States of America

### Bacmar International
### Voyant Chai

This tea-based liqueur is extravagantly presented in a red designer bottle. A cream liqueur with an alcohol content of 12.5% vol., it is produced in The Netherlands from four-year old Virgin Island rum, premium vodka, fresh Dutch cream, black tea, and classic chai spices—including cinnamon, aniseed, cloves, and vanilla. Only genuine spices are used, and even the coloring of this modern liqueur comes from the spices and tea. Voyant Chai tastes good chilled over ice, or in tea or coffee. In the USA this flamboyant new product has become the ultimate bestseller, as "chai" is the very latest trend in terms of flavor. Its low alcohol content allows the fine flavors of tea and spice to predominate.

# Sweet dreams

Liqueurs are a fascinating and colorful chapter, in terms of their ingredients, colors, and indeed their use. The old, frumpy image of liqueurs is long gone—you used to imagine hen parties of tight-lipped women guiltily sipping out of small crystal glasses. The classics are still going strong, and are served not just for enjoyment, but also for their health-promoting properties—examples are green Chartreuse, Benedictine, Ettaler Klosterlikör, Becherovka, and Elixier d'Anvers. Others proffer themselves for pure pleasure, thanks to their mastery in terms of taste, especially spirit-based liqueurs like Grand Marnier, whisk(e)y liqueurs, and the sweet inventions of the artisan distillers.

That isn't to say that they could not be drunk over ice, or used for cocktails as well; some classic mixed drinks have become popular precisely because outstanding liqueurs give them that special touch. Take, for instance, Benedictine in Singapore Sling, Grand Marnier in Red Lion, Drambuie in Rusty Nail, and the latest, Alizé in Thug Passion, and Hpnotiq in its own version of the Martini with coconut rum and pineapple juice.

Those drunk on their own as a digestif include, of course, the stomach bitters. Now they are penetrating the long drinks sector, however, and seem to be in tune with the tastes of the young generation when mixed with different ingredients, like cola or tonic. The custom of sipping a glass of liqueur at room temperature after a meal is a thing of the past. Many liqueurs make a spectacular entrance on ice: you only need to think of the

Top left:
Tequila Smash

Top right:
Starfish Cooler

Bottom left:
Beach at Night

Bottom right:
Nine Mile

second international breakthrough on the market of Baileys over ice. Adding ice tempers the sweetness, giving the flavors a fresh kickoff, before they gradually unfold on the palate with a persistent warm glow.

But the real strength of liqueurs lies elsewhere nowadays. They have attained unprecedented importance since the cocktail culture of the 1990s took on a totally new dynamic. They became the salt and pepper, chili and curry, oil and vinegar of the bar. The range of liqueurs on offer has never been as diverse as it is today, and they have never been used in such a wide ranging and imaginative way. The classics among them, like the orange and bitter liqueurs, have benefited from this trend as well, and some brands that had gone very quiet managed to achieve an astonishing turnround, especially Jägermeister. At the same time there has been a plethora of new liqueur creations, allowing

professional and amateur bartenders to launch new cocktails with new flavors, time and time again.

The cocktails on this double-page spread (all the recipes are in the cocktail section) reflect this fascinating diversity, in which Tequila Smash gets its extra something from maraschino, Starfish Cooler from limoncello, and Beach at Night from blue curaçao. Nine Mile is made special by banana liqueur, as is Midnight Moon by amaretto, which also combines with cocoa liqueur to define Kahlúa Frappé. Crème de cassis gives us the very special Cassis Margarita, and apricot brandy the delicious Apricot Colada, to name just a few examples of the delightful sphere of influence of liqueurs.

Top, left:
Kahlúa Frappé

Top, right:
Apricot Colada

Bottom, left:
Midnight Moon

Bottom, right:
Cassis Margarita

# Fortified wines

The Quinta do Castro lies on the right bank of the Douro between Régua and Pinhão, where the grapes for the best port wines grow.

Page 644: A sherry sample with *flor*, the yeast cells that form a protective layer on the wine in the barrel.

# Stylish eccentrics

Sherry and port are set features in any bar, both being components in a variety of cocktails as well as being served as an aperitif—as a dry, well-chilled fino, for example, or a white port with tonic. If the bar belongs to a good restaurant, then the selection of fortified wines will be more extensive because, as an aperitif, they have the advantage of not compromising the palate ahead of the subsequent enjoyment of fine wines. Oxidative sherries, ports, or banyuls are also ideal as digestifs, their complex aromas forming a pleasant conclusion to a good meal or a long evening.

Wines by origin, their quality is inseparably linked to their grapes and their terroir. What's more, be it banyuls or samos, sherry or port, madeira or marsala—they are among the world's greatest wines. This does not mean, however, that every bottle bearing these famous names on the label does justice to their reputation—far from it. All of these wines have been exposed to the madness of mass production and mass marketing in the past. They initially faced increased interest after World War II, their sweetness being the attraction at a time when nobody saw the need the need to keep an eye on the calories. At that time top-quality fortified wines existed in very small quantities only—such as in Jerez de la Frontera, for example—and these were seldom bottled because there was no market for them.

Sherry provides the most glaring example of this development. In 1940 export volumes amounted to 6 million gallons (24 million liters), reaching 19 million gallons (72.5 million liters) 30 years later before peaking in 1979 at 40 million gallons (150 million liters) or 200 million bottles (a further 4 million gallons / 16 million liters were consumed in Spain). The key markets were and remain England, The Netherlands, and Germany, where primarily sweetened medium or sweet sherries were sold. The somewhat short-sighted approach focused on quantity only, with the unremitting stocking of further vineyards once the prized, chalky Albariza soils had all been planted.

The inevitable then followed: demand collapsed, other drinks were considered to be more modern, sweetness fell into disrepute because the beauty ideal was suddenly much slimmer than in the past. This meant that sherry, as well as other sweet wines and not least the French *vins doux naturels*, were put on a drastic reducing diet.

Sherry vineyards have today shrunk to about 25,000 acres (10,000 ha) from around 44,000 acres (18,000 acres), with production having fallen to 15 million gallons (56 million liters). A change in thinking took place at the same time and while, in 1980, more than 60% of sherry was transported in tanks, it is today sold almost exclusively in bottles. This has been the result of a radical return to quality in the vineyards and wineries, and the range on offer today can no longer be compared with that of 30 years ago. The introduction in 2000 of vintage certification for sherries matured for more than 20 and/or 30 years in *soleras* provided a clear signal. These wines are sought-after rarities providing outstanding digestifs and have played a decisive role in the renewed growth of the sherry reputation. Even thought the price gap today is a wide one with the entry level bottle prices and those of the prestige wines from all producing regions being worlds apart, there is now a middle segment for all fortified wines providing outstanding value for money, whether it be finos or dry amontillados, late bottled vintage ports or reserve rubies, 10-year-old madeiras, mavrodaphnes, or maurys.

The wines from Andalusia and the Douro valley have an advantage in that they are usually mostly distributed by the large retailers with the best export connections, making them easily available. Fortified wines from other regions in Spain and Portugal, as well as from France and Italy, can be more difficult to find, however. These are often true specialties usually only found in the most specialist of wine shops—unless you seek them out yourself in their regions of origin.

# Sweet, strong, and durable

The sweet wines of the Mediterranean region enjoyed great popularity early on. The abundant sunshine made the grapes sweet while the wine makers lent a helping hand by allowing the grapes to raisin, either while still on the vine or spread out on straw mats. The highly concentrated sugar is too much for the yeasts once they have converted

The Alcazar of Jerez de la Frontera, whose wine trade enjoyed its first boom in the 16th century.

around 43 oz of sugar per gallon of must (285 g per liter) into alcohol, equating to an alcohol content of about 17% vol., this being the quantity at which the yeasts become inactive. The wines often retained a considerable amount of residual sugar. Sweet and aromatic, they were highly prized by all of those that could afford such an indulgence.

It was merchants from Genoa and Venice that took charge of the lucrative trade in these luxury goods. They were largely sweet wines from Malvasie and Muscat grapes, with Chios and Santorini, Cyprus and Candia—as Crete used to be called—Corfu and Kefalonia being sought-after origins. However, these wines were also made in southern Italy and southern Spain, as well as in the Setúbal region, these remaining rare and expensive, irrespective of quality fluctuations. The discovery that later led to the production principle behind sherry, port, madeira, marsala, and all fortified wines was made in the 13th century by Arnaldus de Villanova, alchemist and physician, personal physician to kings and popes, as well as later the head of the University of Montpellier. It was while experimenting with self-distilled spirits at Mas Deu, the headquarters of the Knights Templar near Perpignan in 1285, that he discovered that he could halt the fermentation of must by adding alcohol. This meant that the time consuming raisining process was no longer necessary in order to make wines sweet as well as durable.

The wines produced according to Arnaldus' method in the kingdom of Majorca, which also encompassed Roussillon, Montpellier, and the Balearics, soon became famous due to the promotional support of the Knights Templar. King Jacob 1 of Majorca protected this *vins doux naturels* method by means of customs duties as early as 1299. Joan of Evreux, wife of Peter IV of Aragon, scorned any other wine. Jacques Coeur, the French Fugger, exported these noble wines to Flanders and England. Louis XIV, who conquered Roussillon for France in 1659, served

it at Versailles. Voltaire sang the praises of the muscat de rivesaltes in particular, which was also a favorite of the gourmet Grimod de la Reynière.

## Fortified fortification

Once the Catholic monarchs Ferdinand and Isabella had expelled not only the Moors but also the Jews from Spain at the end of the 15th century, the deck of trading cards was dealt anew.

In Andalusia the duke of Medina-Sidonia seized the opportunity to promote his province as the source of the sought-after sweet wines, then known as *Romania*, abolishing the taxes on wine in 1491. In 1517 his successor in Sanlúcar de Barrameda, at the mouth of the Guadalquivir, went a step further and allowed "all persons, be they Spaniards or foreigners, residents of the town or non-residents, to transport their Romania wines... tax free...." The only condition he required was that the goods be labeled as products of Jerez. English merchants took up the offer as it saved their ships having to sail to the Mediterranean. Despite the complex political circumstances, 50 years later the wine trade had reached a volume of 40,000 barrels annually.

Port initially originated in the 17th century when England helped the Portuguese to rid themselves of Spanish rule. Using their sherry experience, the merchants fortified the wines of the Douro valley and brought them by river to Oporto with its good harbor. Port enjoyed its first significant boom when Lord Methuen concluded an agreement with Portugal in 1703 for the supply of wine and raw materials, imposing a tax five times higher on the Bordeaux wines popular in England.

The *azulejos* on the Pinhão train station building depict the famous port regions of the Douro.

Madeiras such as the magnificent Terrantes 1795 from Barbeito can age for a very long time.

# The silencing principle

Fortified wines largely originate from wine regions with a Mediterranean climate. It is only here that the sunshine is intensive enough to endow the grapes with sugar levels of 38 oz per gallon and more per gallon of must (250 g per liter). The production of such wines is largely focused on retaining part of this natural grape sugar by halting fermentation ahead of time. While sulfur dioxide is used for this with quality sweet wines such as sauternes, tokaji, Austrian ausbruch, or German beerenauslesen, with fortified wines it is done by adding spirits. The yeasts in the wine die off at an alcohol content of about 17% vol, making the wine durable. This technique is known as *mutage* in French, while in German the term for it means "silencing." Internationally such wines are known as fortified wines.

Usually 96% neutral-flavored alcohol distilled from wine is used for the *mutage*, younger brandy with an alcohol content of 77% vol. being used for port.

Each fortified wine-producing region has developed its own special features and individual style when it comes to production, and each of these is presented here. They range from dry, meaning with no or only very little residual sugar, through to wines with 19 oz or more residual sugar per gallon (125 g per liter). In the first instance the wine maker or cellar master allows the wine to ferment completely, only adding the spirits to stabilize the wine, as is the case with fino or amontillado, for example.

## Worthwhile sweetness

If residual sugar is to remain in the wine, it is up to the wine maker to decide how high the remaining level will be, in accordance with the legislative requirements. He monitors the fermentation process very closely and when the specific weight has reached the required level, he adds the spirits which are then carefully stirred in either by transferring or surging with nitrogen. The quan-

Left: An old photo at Graham shows how the harvest used to be brought in.

Right: At the Quinta Santa Eufemia, famous for its white ports, the pomace is added to the must by hand.

tity depends on the sugar already fermented and therefore the amount of alcohol already produced: the more residual sugar the wine is to contain, the more spirits need to be added. In a Muscatel with 19 oz residual sugar per gallon (125 g per liter) the wine maker lets the fermentation continue to an alcohol content of about 7% vol. before adding 8% vol. spirits. A manzanilla, on the other hand, is fermented completely and its natural alcohol content of 13% vol. then increased by 2% vol.

While the majority of sweet wines are made from white wine varieties, red grapes play the main role in both port and in some *vins doux naturels*. Top quality requires the optimal extraction of color and aroma. As with red wine, the crushing is the key factor and two different techniques have developed. In the Douro valley the crushed grapes are agitated in must for two to three days, either by means of muscle or machine power. In Roussillon, on the other hand, spirits are added to the mash and the skins, juice, and alcohol are left to macerate for three, four, or five weeks in a process known as *mutage sur grains* or *marc*.

Port is usually darker in color, but this is also dependent on the grapes. The principal distinction is made between two categories of fortified wines: non-oxidative and oxidative. While with the former category contact with atmospheric oxygen is prevented or kept to a minimum, such contact is required in the latter category. Non-oxidative wines are usually kept in full tanks or barrels while with the sherry types

fino and manzanilla, it is the famous *flor* that functions as protection against oxidation. In order to achieve the opposite effect and oxidize the wines they are either left to age in barrels that are not quite full in non-air-conditioned cellars, heated in *estufas* as is the case with madeira, or—in extreme cases—matured in glass demijohns out in the open, a process that only fortified wines are able to sustain, and this to their advantage.

Malvasia, madeira's sweetest grape variety.

Left: With *mutage* fermentation is halted by the addition of spirits.

Right: Fortified madeiras mature in old wooden tanks.

# The sweetness of Roussillon

The *vins doux naturels* deserve to be rediscovered. In the Middle Ages they were among the most highly prized and most expensive wines, in the 1950s they benefited from the success of vermouth with their astoundingly similar labels, and survived as an aperitif for the masses—until interest faded completely in the 1980s. Committed wine makers have since rediscovered these gems: as fortified wines that either display their intriguing young fruit or that, after years of oxidative maturation, are able to hold their own with old olorosos or tawnys.

Even in ancient times the majestic Canigou and its iron ore attracted the Ligurians, the Iberians, the Greeks, and the Romans to Roussillon. The Greeks, who landed on its coasts in around 600 B.C., introduced wine growing. The shale slopes of the Cote Vermeille were ideally suited to wine growing and yielded robust, sugary wines that were also prized by the Romans. Pliny the Elder sang the praises of the fiery liquor from Roussillon in his *Naturalis historia* in the 1st century.

The scholar and politician François Arago, born in Roussillon, used the fascinating history of these wines to introduce a law in 1872 protecting the special features of the *vins doux naturels*. Their vinification method was laid down in 1936, as were vineyard allotments, grape varieties, harvest, and aging, making them the most extensively controlled *Appellation d'Origine Contrôlée* after champagne.

The most appealing Roussillon fortified wines are based on the Grenache Noir grape variety. It originates in Spain where it is the most widely grown red variety, but is mainly used in blends or for young red and rosé wines. Grenache Noir shows its class as a dry wine in Priorat as well as in Châteauneuf-du-Pape and other southern Rhône appellations where it yields wonderfully velvety, full-bodied red wines. Heat and aridity are no obstacle, neither are poor soils, so it grows well on the shale slopes of Banyuls and Maury, develops plenty of sweetness, and easily achieves the prescribed 38 oz of sugar per gallon of must (252 g per liter), equal to 14.4% vol. of potential alcohol. The ripe grapes are carefully harvested by hand, stripped, and placed in the mash tank. The wine maker or cellar master then carefully monitors the conversion of the sugar into alcohol in order to be able to add the spirits at the right time. The prescribed residual sugar level is between 8 and 19 oz per gallon (50–125 g per liter), and the overall alcohol content (alcohol and residual sugar) in the finished wine is 21.5% vol. The amount of spirits added therefore varies between 5 and 10%, the alcohol content between 16 and 18.5% vol. For quality wines the "silencing," a simple process by which the spirits are added to the must, is carried out by pouring the spirits over the mashed grapes. In the case of *mutage sur grains* or *marc*, the alcohol is left to dissolve the color, aroma, and tannins out of the grape skins for two to five weeks, resulting in darker, more complex wines.

Traditional banyuls, maury, and rivesaltes age in wooden barrels and are oxidized deliberately. In order to accelerate this process, the wines are sometimes stored in *demi-muids*, half-size barrels, or even glass demijohns for up to a year out in the open, exposed to the wind and the weather, to the heat and the cold, before being matured further in the cellar.

The trend inspired by Portuguese vintages whereby the wines are protected from oxidation and bottled early on so that they retain their youthful fruit has been in evidence since 1975.

Such wines are called rimage, vendange, or grenat, and always indicate their vintage on the label.

# Banyuls, Maury, Rivesaltes

Rivesaltes and Maury were recognized as *Appellation d'Origine Contrôlées* as early as 1936 with the establishment of the legally protected geographic origins; banyuls and banyuls grand cru followed three years later and muscat de rivesaltes, which we will cover in more detail later, was added in 1956. Rivesaltes encompasses the largest region comprising vineyards in 86 Roussillon communes. What they all have in common is the hot, dry, windy climate and the grape varieties used, whereas the soils are very heterogeneous. Only the lower vineyards, where the grapes are able to ripen fully, are included. Maury, on the other hand, has a homogenous terroir made up of shale and extending to altitudes of 500–660 feet (150–200 m), dominated by the Cathar fortress of Queribus. The ground, heated during the day, releases its warmth during the night and as such is beneficial for the ripening of the grapes. Although the wine makers are also allowed to use other grape varieties, and these up to a proportion of 50%, the majority of maurys are based solely on Grenache Noir.

Banyuls is one of the most spectacular wine regions in the world as its laboriously laid out vineyard terraces extend along the furthest foothills of the Pyrenees where they descend into the Mediterranean. The brown slate cliffs take on a carmine red color in the morning and evening sun, which is why the coast is known as the Cote Vermeille. The grapes are exposed to the humidity rising from the ocean, allowing them to ripen fully. Here, too, Grenache Noir is king, and is required to make up half of the banyuls and three quarters of the banyuls grand cru.

## Prime Mediterranean

Only traditional grape varieties are considered for *vins doux naturels*. Apart from Muscat, which plays a special role and is largely processed separately, it is Grenache Noir that characterizes the best banyuls and maurys, sometimes supplemented by its white and/or rosé versions Grenache Blanc and/or Grenache Gris, as well as by the white varieties Macabeu and the rare Malvoisie. Up to 10% of the red varieties Carignan, Syrah, and Mourvèdre are permitted. Either way, Grenache Noir has to make up the main proportion, and at least 50% if used in a blend, irrespective of its rarer white versions added later.

With rivesaltes the wine makers restrict themselves to the six main varieties Grenache Noir, Blanc, Gris, Macabeu, Malvasie, and Muscat, but offer a wider range of styles, with the white varieties often setting the tone. Alternatively, if the wines are composed of Grenache Blanc, Grenache Gris, Macabeu, Malvoisie, and Muscat and then matured oxidatively, they are referred to as *amber* due to their amber color. Today the best cuvées are left to age in barriques. Typical ambré aromas include quince, candied oranges, dried apricots, and raisins, as well as nuts—often roasted. Cocoa and caramel develop with increasing age, as well as vanilla and cinnamon from barrique aging. Wines based on Grenache Noir and matured oxidatively are known as *tuilé* due to their brick-like color. Their aroma is usually characterized by red berry, cherry, figs, or plum nuances, cooked, candied, or preserved in alcohol.

Banyuls, banyuls grand cru, and maury exhibit a similarly aromatic spectrum. With

Domaine Puig-Parahy is famous for ancient *vins doux naturels*.

Page 652: The old Grenache vines on shale soils are what give maury its class.

Page 653: Wines mature on the Mas Amiel in glass demijohns, exposed to the wind and the weather.

Roussillon Vins Doux Naturels (VDNs)

- Maury
- Rivesaltes
- Banyuls
- Vins Doux Naturels (VDNs)

increasing age the traditional, oxidatively matured wines develop more intense dried or candied fruit aromas, then roasted nuts and almonds, cocoa, coffee, later also tobacco, until, after 15 or 20 years, the *rancio* nuance so prized by connoisseurs develops—one that is reminiscent of green walnut shells and that is also present in old cognacs and armagnacs. Wines that have aged for longer than five years are entitled to bear the predicate "Hors d'Age."

In Maury in particular, but also in Banyuls or with those rivesaltes known as grenat, wines made from Grenache Noir are often bottled young, usually after the copious *mutage sur grains* or *marc* has been completed. They are then fascinating with their especially deep color, much more intense, fresh or ripe cherry or berry fruit, and a fruity sweetness that initially masks their often concentrated tannin structure which gives these wines above-average aging potential.

Collioure in the Banyuls appellation.

In traditional vins doux cellars the wines age oxidatively in barrels.

# Sweet wines in Roussillon

This selection of Roussillon *vins doux naturels* demonstrates the full spectrum of its fascinating fortified wines, for which neutral flavored alcohol is used for the *mutage* so that the astounding diversity of aromas derives solely from the grape varieties, terroir, and maturation method. To start with (from the left) there is the Domaine des Schistes with its rivesaltes made from the Grenache Gris grape. The wine ages in 130 gallon (500 liter) barrels from which, according to the solera method, only small quantities are ever drawn and which Jacques and Mickaël Sire supplement with new wine. Full and round with a pleasant sweetness, this dessert wine is characterized by dried fruit, nut, and caramel aromas.

The Cuvée Aimé Cazes from the Domaine Cazes has a legendary reputation and rightly so. Comprising four fifths Grenache Blanc and one fifth Grenache Noir, it matures for at least 20 years in old barrels impregnated with sweet wines for decades. Elegance and length as well as nuances of candied orange, a touch of pine resin, and honey are what characterize this wine.

No other wine-making couple has dedicated themselves to the rivesaltes made from white grape varieties with the same commitment as Brigitte and Jean-Hubert Verdaguer from Domaine de Rancy, whose cellar—reminiscent of Ali Baba's cave—houses real treasures such as this extremely intense, sweet and complex 1982 vintage with subtle *rancio* nuances. These three wines are wonderfully suited to indulgent reflection

Whether with a strong, fruity emphasis or complex and sophisticated, the *vins doux naturels* offer an intriguing choice of styles.

following a meal or to turning nut desserts into an unforgettable experience.

Following a long break, top wine makers Gérard and Lionel Gauby produced a new rivesaltes made from Grenache Noir in 2005, one that combines ripe, dark fruit with a racy structure. It has a lot in common with the following four wines that show that the Maury wine makers know how to distinguish themselves with the non-oxidized Grenache Noir, be it the Domaine du Dernier Bastion with its delectable Premier Printemps, rich in the finest berry jam aromas, or the Preceptorie de Centernach, its cuvée exhibiting rust nuances and spices in addition to intense, sweet berries. The Cuvée Charles Dupuy from Mas Amiel shows how effortlessly a concentrated maury integrates new oak with tremendous finesse, while Robert Pouderoux's young bottled wine is a classic example of concentrated fruit and magnificent

tannins. All five of these young, Grenache Noir based wines can be enjoyed as an aperitif but are even better suited to dark chocolate and desserts containing the same.

The Cuvée Henri Vidal from Celliers des Templiers is a monumental wine with plenty of residual sugar, but also intense candied cherry and fig, cocoa, and coffee nuances. Just as monumental is the Extra Vieux from the Cooperative L'Etoile, famous for their unflinchingly traditional style that develops fruit, nut, and *rancio* nuances. The banyuls from Domaine La Tour Vieille, bottled after a short maturation period, is all about harmony with its red berry jam, orange peel, and cocoa nuances.

Al Tracou from Bernard Saperas, on the other hand, is the most characterful of the old banyuls on the market and is worth taking your time over in order to savor the diversity of is aromas.

# Voltaire's muscatel

Muscats with small fruit are what give the muscatels of the Midi their finesse.

Opposite: In Rasteau the Grenache grapes produce the sweet wine.

Exemplary muscatels between the Pyrenees and Dentelles de Montmirail.

Who doesn't know Muscat, the delicious table grape with the large fruit and the characteristic sweet and spicy flavor? That is the Muscat d'Alexandrie, one of the oldest cultivated plants in the world, which the Romans are said to have introduced to Roussillon. There it may be used for the Muscat de Rivesaltes, while all of southern France's other five fortified wines are only permitted to be made using *Muscat blanc à petits grains*, known as Muscat de Frontignan, and must have a residual sugar content of at least 19 oz/gallon (125 g/liter). It is considered to be the higher quality version, the fruit are somewhat smaller and round, and with its naturally lower yields it produces sweeter and more aromatic wines.

Wines made from Muscat grapes are to be found almost all over the world, and in the Mediterranean region the overripe and raisined fruit were used even in antiquity to make sweet delicacies. Between the 17th and 19th centuries sweet muscatel wines were considered to be among the most valuable wines available. In southern France they were produced as fortified wines, the most famous of which was the Muscat de Frontignan, praised by the English philosopher John Locke as early as 1676, whereas Voltaire enthused over the Muscat de Rivesaltes decades later.

While muscatel wines, which have outstanding aging capacity, often used to be matured oxidatively, exhibiting a brown color and heavy boiled fruit and caramel aromas, the style changed in the 1980s with the arrival of modern cellar technology. Today they are produced like white wines at a lower temperature, thus retaining their intriguing fruit that combines the Muscat nuances with citrus fruit and blossoms, maintaining a freshness on the palate despite the sweetness. Today they are enjoyed as an aperitif, with desserts, and with sorbets made from pale and citrus fruit, as well as with blue mold cheese.

## Muscat stronghold

There are six Muscat growing regions in southern France. In Languedoc the fame of the Muscat de Frontignan led to its being awarded the coveted *Appellation d'Origine Contrôlée* in 1936. It flourishes in the chalky clay soils of the Frontignan and Vic-la-Gardiole communes close to the sea and is characterized by the intensity and complexity of its aromas. Recommended: Château Stony. Muscat de Lunel, recognized in 1943, derives from the deep, stony soils of the four communes of Lunel, Lunel-Vieil, Vérargues, and Saturargues. Here the Muscat grape develops especially intense, overripe fruit and elegance. Recommended: Grès Saint Paul Rosanna.

The smallest muscatel appellation is that of Saint-Jean de Minervois, recognized in 1949, that extends over 250 acres (100 ha) to the south of the wine-growing area. The terroir is unique: a plateau at 660 feet (200 m), littered with white limestone on top of chalky clay soils. Here the Muscat grape

often develops an apricot aroma and tremendous finesse. Recommended: Domaine de Barroubio.

Muscat de Mireval, adjoining Frontignan, was recognized in 1959 and has the same natural conditions as its well-known neighbor. Recommended: Château d'Exindre Cuvée Vent d'Anges.

Further to the south the Muscat de Rivesaltes appellation, granted in 1956, covers widespread areas at the same latitude as Roussillon. Here the fruitier Muscat d'Alexandrie is also allowed in addition to the Frontignan, and the residual sugar content may only amount to 15 oz/gallon (100 g/liter). The majority of wine makers use this to produce a very fresh, lemony style. Recommended: Domaine Boudau.

Finally there is the famous Muscat de Beaume-de-Vénise, recognized in 1943, which ripens on the southern slopes of the Dentelles de Montmirail, may not have more than 17 oz/gallon (110 g/liter) of residual sugar and, depending on the harvest time, can be dominated by exotic or candied fruit aromas. Recommended: Vignerons de Beaumes-de-Vénise Carte d'Or.

## Rasteau

The only *vin doux naturel* north of the Rivesaltes A.O.C. not based on Muscat is made from Grenache Noir here in this famous Cotes-du-Rhone Villages wine-making location. It was a wine maker from Frontignan, working for the Cave Coopérative de Rasteau, that produced it for the first time in 1935. After production had reached its peak in the 1950s, the Rasteau A.O.C. maintained its position as a specialty of the commune. It is available as a *doré* when it is produced as a white wine, but it finds its most appealing expression as a red wine, characterized by cherry aromas and a touch of cocoa. It is enjoyed as an aperitif, with desserts made from red fruit, or with chocolate, to which the Cave de Rasteau's signature wine is especially suited.

# Sherry and other Spanish wines

When two people sing the praises of sherry, there is nothing to say that they are referring to the same thing because one of sherry's very strengths lies in the diversity of its many facets, which only increases its appeal to connoisseurs. The same also applies to its cousins from Málaga, Montilla-Moriles, and Condado de Huelva, only the diversity is baffling even to the Spanish. However, there is still one way to top the unbelievable wealth of magnificent flavor experiences provided by these fortified wines: with tapas.

Everyone knows tapas. What began as a lid on top of a glass of sherry to protect the contents from suicidal flies has developed internationally into a culinary art. The Andalusians remain the masters of this art both in terms of the ingredients—their seafood is unrivaled—and their preparation that can be traditional, modern, or avant garde. It is astounding how the light finos and the even lighter manzanillas stand the test of these changeable taste bud challenges time and again, while more substantial tapas are on hand for dry amontillados, palo cortados, or olorosos.

The dry sherries, málagas, montilla-moriles, and condados de huelva are unsurpassed as aperitifs, whereby the finos or manzanillas with their more moderate alcohol content are the more salubrious simply because you are far too easily tempted to drink more than one or two glasses. In Andalusia they are served in half bottles and an evening with friends is measured by the number of (empty) bottles. It is astounding how few side effects such evenings have, a phenomenon that remains unresearched to date…

Andalusia's fortified wines experienced an unequalled boom. Huge amounts were shipped to northern Europe, with Sir Francis Drake being said to be responsible for the marketing. When the Catholic Philip II and the Anglican Elizabeth I stood in war-like opposition to one another, the former buccaneer turned vice admiral supplied the era's only sherry imports. He attacked Cádiz in 1587 with 24 ships, razing it to the ground—but not before he had "saved" all the sherry barrels he could find—there were some 3,000 of them. What initially seemed to be a fiasco for the Spanish proved to be an effective advertising promotion. This liquid booty gave the English, who had known sherry for almost a century already, a real taste for it and they went on to become the best sherry customers, remaining as such today. Although sherry has been exported since the end of the 15th century—with interruptions—the sherry trade only started to take shape in the 18th century. It was partly the Spanish, in the case of Pedro Domecq it was a Frenchman, but especially the Irish, Scots, and the English who founded the *bodegas*. The first to start out in this foreign land was the Irishman Timothy O'Neale in 1724 whose company continued to exist up until the start of the 1980s. Many of the big names such as Delgado Zuleta (1719), Juan Haurie, later Pedro Domecq (1730), Garvey (1780), Sanchez Romate (1781), Osborne (1781), and Hidalgo (1792) date back to this era.

The first half of the 19th century saw an unbelievable upsurge among the sherry producers, with the British being responsible for nine out of ten barrels. This was followed by a major downturn, attributable not only to the phylloxera catastrophe that reached Málaga in 1875 and Jerez in 1894. The poor quality, numerous sherry imitations from other countries, and a certain degree of weariness in Britain were also responsible for the drastic slowdown in sales. It was only in the 1920s that sales picked up again, only to decline again dramatically following a new peak in 1979.

Sherry has today consolidated its position due to the quality and the autonomy of its wines. It has the advantage that, in contrast to other fortified wines, it has dry styles with manzanilla and fino, while offering "sweetness" at the same time with the cream sherries, as well as now also being able to serve the super premium segment with its decades old vintages.

# Andalusian specialties

Andalusia is one of the oldest wine-growing regions in the world. The Phoenicians landed in present day Cádiz 3,000 years ago and, 20 miles (30 km) away, founded Xera, now Jerez. Barely 200 years later they had built Málaga up into a further base and they introduced vines to both places. Although they later went on to develop wine growing in the Montilla-Moriles region near Córdoba as well as Condado de Huelva in the Costa de la Luz hinterland, Jerez and Málaga remained the driving forces in the wine trade. In earlier times of high demand it was the sherry producers in particular that marketed the produce of the two unknown regions, sometimes under their own name, a practice that came to an end with the creation of the Consejo Regulador in 1933.

All four regions focused on the production of fortified sweet wines. Málaga, which had achieved an almost legendary reputation back in the 13th century with its dark, viscous, and sweet wines, experienced its golden age in the 19th century. At that time the vineyards extended over a total of over 247,000 acres (100,000 ha). Badly affected by the phylloxera catastrophe, it was never able to repeat the successes of the past, gambling away its reputation with cheap wines and losing vast areas of vineyards to building industry speculators. Truly great málagas are an absolute rarity today. All four of the regions recognized as Denominación de Origen have suffered significant losses as a result of the dramatic decline in interest in fortified sweet wines.

## Jerez Xérèz sherry & Manzanilla de Sanlúcar de Barrameda

The best locations with the white chalky soils, the *albarizas*, are to be found in the sherry region between the towns of Sanlúcar de Barrameda, Jerez de la Frontera, and Puerto de Santa Maria. Today the growing area amounts to little more than about 2,500 (10,000 ha), with the Palomino Fino variety making up 95% of the vines and the rest being a combination of Pedro Ximénex and Moscatel that are used for sweet wines. Three quarters of the production (it used to be up to 90%) is exported.

## Málaga

Today the famous sweet wine D.O. region in the Costa del Sol hinterland has shrunk to less than 250 acres (900 ha). Only Pero Ximén (Pedro Ximénez) and Moscatel are permitted as the main grape varieties. The many styles and designations vary greatly depending on the production methods—the spectrum ranges from dry to exceptionally sweet, from 15% vol. to 22% vol. alcohol content. The great, old wines of the region have high residual sugar levels, however.

---

Perez Barquero and Alvéar are the leading names in Montilla-Moriles.

Page 660: vineyard work in the sherry region.

Opposite top: the best locations in Jerez consist of *albarizas*.

Below: clay *tinajas* are the usual wine tanks in Andalusian bodegas.

**Andalusia's wine regions**

- Condado de Huelva
- Jerez-Xérèz-sherry & Manzanilla de Sanlúcar de Barrameda
- Montilla-Moriles
- Málaga
- Wine centers

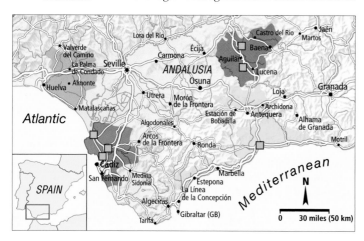

## Montilla-Moriles

The D.O. named after two towns in the Córdoba province extends over 24,500 acres (10,000 ha) planted primarily with Pedro Ximénez. The wines produced are finos, amontillados, olorosos, and palo cortados, matured according to the solera method. The grapes are so sweet that the wine does not require additional fortification. This method is used only for the sugary dessert wines or sometimes for stabilizing ready for export. Perez Barquero and Alvéar are the leading producers with outstanding wines and famous *soleras*.

## Condado de Huelva

The least well known of the four regions lies to the west of the Guadalquivir, bordering on the Atlantic and approaching the Portuguese border in the west. With the relatively high rainfall the vines produce largely dry white wines. The Zalema variety, however, is still used as it was in the past to produce fortified wines, matured in soleras until they resemble olorosos. Palomino, Pedro Ximénez (PX), and Moscatel are also grown, even though the vineyards have shrunk to about 15,000 acres (6,000 ha).

## Alicante and Catalonia

Mistela or liqueur wines, in which spirits are added to the must, have a long tradition in Levante and Catalonia, as does the *vino generoso*, in which the partly fermented wine is fortified. Sometimes, as with the magnificent Fondillón from Alicante, the fortification is unnecessary as the wine's natural alcohol content is sufficient. The company De Muller in Tarragona is famous for its fortified wines sold as dry *rancios* or *dulces*, its best soleras containing wine from Priorat.

# Floral magic

The sherry-growing area with its flat, gently undulating hills appears somewhat unspectacular when compared with the shale terraces of Banyuls or those of the Douro. Anyone who has traveled through this region in the summer, however, will be familiar with its full force, even if it does mean having to look away at times: the *albarizas*, the blinding white chalk soils that reflect the radiant sunlight during the more than 3,000 hours of sunshine annually so that you have to keep closing your eyes against the painful glare. The soils are a miracle of nature, storing the rain that falls during the cooler seasons to then make it available to the vines during the long, hot, dry summers.

Today 95% of the vines that benefit from this phenomenon are Palomino Fino, and the albarizas are almost the only soils in the world where this grape variety produces interesting, even great, wines. The vines are kept low in order to protect the grapes from the wind and heat. The wind blows almost unremittingly— either the dry, hot, at times strong Levante or the fresh, humid west Poniente wind from the Atlantic. With the proximity to the Atlantic the climate is relatively mild and it is only seldom that the mercury rises above 95 °F (35 °C)—in the shade, that is.

The wine harvest takes place in September but the week-long fiesta is celebrated before that, and then the harvest starts. In Andalusia, known for its diligent harvest helpers, the harvesting is done by hand. The grapes are transported to the bodegas in plastic crates and processed immediately, before being fermented at controlled, low temperatures. Modern technology has long since arrived in Andalusian wineries as well, with Palomino producing a clean, more neutral but always dry white wine. The Consejo Regulador has achieved the highest yields at 860 gallons/acre (8,000 liters/ha).

The alcoholic fermentation, which lasts a maximum of seven days, is followed by the second, malolactic fermentation when the acids are broken down biologically, which

Left: Palomino Fino is the most dominant grape variety for sherry.

Right: Old wooden fermentation vats that have long since been replaced by stainless steel tanks.

happens automatically thanks to the climate. Although this reduces the acid content, the wines gain in stability. They are then drawn off and placed in *botas*, old barrels with 130 gallon (500 liter) capacity.

## Sherry bar code

This is when things start to get serious for the *capataz*, the cellar master, who now has to taste and assess all of the wines. Those from the best albarizas have already been preselected as they are intended for manzanilla and fino, the finest sherry varieties. These barrels are then marked. If the wines have more structure, perhaps because they come from the somewhat heavier soils, then the barrels are marked with a line and a dot; these will be made into olorosos. With some wines it is not clear at this stage which type they will develop into and they are marked with two lines on the top of the barrel. If the cellar master is unhappy with the quality, he marks the wood with three lines and the wines will be distilled. The wines are now fortified according to the markings on the top of the barrel: manzanillas and finos up to 15% vol. alcohol content, olorosos up to about 17.5% vol., and this is where they go their separate ways. Manzanillas and finos are subjected to a phenomenon known as biological maturing, which plays a key role in the development, quality, and character of the wines.

The *flor*, literally the flower, develops on the surface of the wine provided that the barrels are not completely full. This is the work of the local yeasts that form a layer like cotton wool on the wine. They need three things for their optimal development: air, the appropriate alcoholic strength, and the special humid and warm climate found only in Poniente. That is why the *flor* flourishes especially well in the bodegas of Sanlúcar de Barrameda on the Guadalquivir and close to the Atlantic. Here it forms a thick, closed layer on the wine, providing effective protection against oxidation and turning it into manzanilla, the lightest and freshest of all sherries, with characteristic yeast and iodine nuances. The conditions in Jerez de la Frontera and Puerto de Santa Maria are often less suited to *flor*, which is why the finos there are often somewhat more robust.

Left: In the barrel the *flor* forms a thick layer protecting the wine from oxidation.

Right: Today it is seldom that pitchers are used to add the spirits to the barrels or to fill the soleras; pumps have also become widespread in Jerez.

# Ripe performance

In the old parts of the three sherry towns in Andalusia the alleyways are lined with whitewashed, windowless walls that appear bleak and repellent. Behind these walls are high, spacious rooms. In the semidarkness you can make out hundreds, if not thousands, of barrels stacked on top of one another in seemingly endless rows. These buildings, which are specific to Jerez, are known as *bodegas*, like the wineries. Most of them were built from sandstone in around 1900, their floors comprising yellow sand. The high walls have no openings except for those right at the top, just under the roof, often hung with bast mats in order to keep light exposure to a minimum. This is where the rising warmth is able to escape when the Poniente, the humid wind from the Atlantic, blows in. The hard floors are regularly sprayed with water in order to keep the temperature at an average of 64 °F (18 °C) and to keep the air humidity high. This moderate greenhouse climate is ideal for the formation and growth of the valued *flor*. In principle sherry is matured in barrels but,

depending on the type, this can also take place in their own solera. Named after the lowest row of barrels that used to rest on the ground——*suelo* in Spanish—this system needs to be seen as several rows of 300-gallon (500-liter) barrels or *criaderas* resting on top of one another. The solera contains the oldest wine and is the only barrel used for bottling, up to a maximum of one third of its contents. The rest is supplemented from the next highest criadera, which is filled from the one above it. Depending on the type of wine, finos and/or manzanillas for a specific vintage (usually 8–16 months old) are pumped from the topmost level, or olorosos and/or amontillados as vintage wines that may have been aged for a decade already.

The principle behind this aging system introduced in the 19th century is that the younger wines are "brought up" in such a manner that their passage through the individual criaderas enables them to take on the character of the solera gradually, so that they fully resemble the bottled wines. The sherries are

Surprisingly light and airy: the Las Copas bodega near Gonzalez Byass where the wines are produced.

named after the soleras. These also include some that were begun 100 years ago or even earlier and whose names cause a flutter in a connoisseur's heart.

## Oloroso and cream sherry

In addition to the biological maturing of the manzanillas and finos, there is also the oxidative maturing of the olorosos and amontillados. Amontillados start out as manzanillas or finos, but once they develop more robust aromas the capataz adds additional spirits to them after two or three years, which kills off the *flor*, allowing them to mature oxidatively. Olorosos follow their destiny from the moment when they are so fortified (up to 17.5% vol. alcohol content) that the yeasts kill off the *flor*. During their storage in the barrel the surface is in constant contact with the air, the wine oxidizes, and its color darkens, ranging from amber to mahogany.

Always full bodied but dry, olorosos—sweetened with Moscatel or Pedro Ximénez—become medium or cream sherries.

Moscatel and Pedro Ximénez, the other two grape varieties in the sherry region, make up just 5% of the vineyards together. They are processed separately and then later added to the olorosos or amontillados. The Pedro Ximénez, PX for short—a traditional and yet temperamental grape variety, which is why it is becoming ever rarer in the Jerez region—is famous and is used for the best cream sherries. It is spread out on straw mats in the sun for a few days after harvesting in order to concentrate its sugar content further. It is also sweetened with Moscatel, but the Muscat grape aroma is much too headstrong for it to be really suited to sherry. The varietal matured PX is a rarity.

Fino La Ina matures in Pedro Domecq's Moorish bodega La Mezquita.

# Sherry types

## Manzanilla

Benefiting from the location on the Guadalquivir and the proximity to the Atlantic, nowhere does a more consistent and thick *flor* develop as in Sanlúcar de Barrameda. This produces an especially light, pale fino, which proudly displays its identity. It is frequently characterized by intense, peppery yeast, iodine, and salt nuances, often together with a mineral undertone. Served chilled, it is an ideal aperitif and accompaniment for tapas, especially that containing seafood. A manzanilla pasada is very similar to amontillado.

## Fino

As the dry sherry *per se*, fino retains its freshness under the *flor* that forms in the barrels in Jerez de la Frontera and Puerto de Santa Maria. Fresh almonds and yeasts are the characteristic aromas, sometimes also nuts, pepper, and iodine, always followed by a very dry, often piquant aftertaste. Served well chilled, it is a classic aperitif and goes especially well with tapas. Once opened it should be stored chilled and drunk quickly. Fino is available with an alcohol content of 15–15.5% vol.

## Amontillado

If a fino remains in the barrel longer or has additional spirits added to it, it then becomes amontillado because, either way, the *flor* dies off and the wine matures in contact with the air. It develops a bright, amber color as well as dried fruit aromas such as apricot and fig, as well as nuts and tobacco. Strong and dry in flavor (mediums are a concession to the average customer's taste), with an alcohol content of 18–22% vol., it is suited to substantial tapas as well as to ripe cheeses, for example an aged Manchego.

## Oloroso

Also known as the "odorous one," in its original state it is always a dry sherry, usually appearing darker than an amontillado. Matured in contact with the air right from the start and over many years, it nevertheless develops a complex bouquet with sweet raisin, dried fig, and date aromas, as well as nuts, old wood, and tobacco. Often similarly complex on the palate but with strength, bite, a dry aftertaste, and an alcohol content of 17–20% vol., it goes well with beef ragout and makes a pleasant digestif.

## Palo Cortado

Rare and unique, this dry sherry initially tried to become an amontillado before it suddenly made the spontaneous decision to become an oloroso instead. It therefore combines the best properties of both types and almost always proves to be a very complex and an especially elegant wine that often has a very subtle, fine sweetness on the palate and significant length. It should be kept at 60 °F (16 °C) as this is the temperature at which its full diversity develops best.

## Cream

The velvety soft, full-bodied, sweet, and dark ruby red cream sherry has created a furor because it uses the complex aromas of an oloroso, but overlaps the latter's demanding aftertaste with additional sweetness. The top-quality wines are made from Pedro Ximénez, fermented separately, and otherwise from concentrated grape must. Almost a dessert in itself, it is an effortless accompaniment if not a sophisticated refinement for the last course, and should be served slightly chilled.

## PX

PX or Pedro Ximénez is not based on Palomino and is processed into a sweet wine only by leaving the grapes to dry in the sun on straw mats for two weeks, so that the sugar content increases to 60 oz per gallon (400 g per liter) of must. Fortified to an alcohol content of 15% vol., the viscous wine is then matured oxidatively. If given 15, 20, and more years it takes on a black-green color and exhibits heavy, sweet raisin, date, and cocoa aromas. It is magic served on top of quality vanilla ice cream.

## VOS and VORS

These two back labels, awarded only after detailed testing by the Consejo Regulador, provide an official guarantee. VOS (very old sherry) is awarded to sherries that have been aged for at least 20 years, while VORS (very old rare sherry) is for those that have been aged for 30 years and more. In most cases the veteran amontillados, olorosos, palo cortados, and PX exhibit a great deal of strength, usually with a firm texture as well as substantial aromatic diversity and a lingering aftertaste. These are wines for meditating over.

# The finest sherry

Sherry presents itself in a variety of styles and qualities. First of all there is the fresh, dry, fortified fino or manzanilla wine. The residents of the sherry triangle have their ancestral brand that they swear by, this often being dictated less by taste and quality and more by sentimental attachment. Ultimately almost everyone has relatives or friends working for one of the sherry producers. The size of a brand is no indication of its quality, smaller producers in principle not being any better than a worldwide distributor, and vice versa. However, Osborne's Fino Quinta, Domecq's La Ina, and Gonzalez Byass' Tio Pepe—three of the most well-known and most successful brands—are among the most reliable. The Puerto Fino from Lustau is one of the most complex, with intense almond and yeast aromas, as well as nutty and mineral flavors.

Manzanillas are less well known abroad, which is due not least to the fact that they are the main aperitif among the residents of Seville. The classics include La Goya and Las Medallas de Argüeso, both with yeast nuances and the peppery bite you expect. En Rama from Barbadillo is a more robust vintage wine with plenty of volume. Pastrana, a pasada originating from just one vineyard, has nut aromas and substantial length.

Well-aged amontillados, palo cortados, and olorosos are a matter for connoisseurs

Finos and manzanillas, the lightest of the dry sherries, are as popular as aperitifs and ideal tapas wines in Andalusia as they are abroad.

because you need to take your time in order to be able to appreciate fully their world of aromas and structure. The selection presented here comprises some of the most fascinating wines bottled in Jerez, Puerto, and Sanlúcar today, once they have spent years and decades in soleras that themselves were often set up 100 or more years ago.

Fernando de Castilla's Antique gives off the dry finesse of an old, nurtured amontillado. The 30-year-old vintages from the Bodegas Tradición, which are specialized solely in VOS and VORS, exhibit convincing complexity and volume in addition to sensational length. The Palo Cortado Viejo from the family concern Vinícola Hidalgo in Sanlúcar, founded in 1792, is a monument to elegance with a fine sweetness as well as cocoa and tobacco nuances, while Privilegio from the Jerez producer of the same name appears thick and velvety with candied almond and raisin aromas.

A somewhat older, sweeter oloroso is often added to very old wines to round off the otherwise very dry tannins, and this is how the Capuchino from Domecq acquired its magical harmony. The Oloroso 1730 from Alvaro Domecq has significant strength, structure, and length, while the appeal of the Sacristia de Romate lies in the fine *rancio*, nut, and pale tobacco aromas. Matusalem from Gonzalez Byass stands up to its sweetness that combines with the aromas of dried fruit, fine old wood, and the finesse to produce an extraordinary experience.

Amontillados, palo cortados, and olorosos that have aged over many years are today being granted the attention they deserve from wine connoisseurs and collectors.

# Port: ritual and sacrilege

The English have had a sustained influence on the wine trade as well as on the development of a variety of wine regions: firstly Bordeaux, then Jerez, and later the Douro region. The fact that port has an unmistakably British touch is due not only to the fact that they "invented" it and that the most important port producers were founded by the British—for a long time they were also the most avid consumers of port. Even today, no one else in the world masters the related ritual as perfectly. Yet port's main customers have long since changed: the Portuguese themselves are now among the most important consumers.

The English gentlemen's clubs were and remain the port bastions. The ritual begins with the decanting because quality vintage port develops substantial sediment over the course of time. Authenticity then demands that it is held over a lit candle in order to be able to determine when the crust begins, while slowly emptying the bottle into the crystal carafe.

The host pours the first glass and hands it to the guest sitting to his right. The host then hands the carafe to the person on his left, who then does the same, and so the port goes round the table. If you want a second glass it is considered indecorous to ask for the carafe directly; instead you ask the person who last had the carafe: "Do you know the bishop of Norwich?" He so loved the sound of his own voice that he forgot to pass on the carafe: an unforgivable oversight. The carafe obviously has to be empty before anyone may leave the table. And so the evening draws to a close: with neat port and perhaps a truly good cigar. Vintage port enjoys the highest prestige and in the past only the best vintages were bottled. Following the harvest there is always a certain degree of suspense as to which port producer will be the first to declare the vintage—especially when the quality of the harvest is doubtful, because declaring an unworthy vintage would severely compromise their reputation.

The principle still applies, but today the reality is somewhat different because climate warming means that harvests suitable for vintages are becoming more frequent. The demand for these prestige wines is growing at the same time, particularly since the Americans have committed the sacrilege of opening vintages immediately, discovering that these wines are absolutely unique when they are young too: somewhat raw and unpolished with intense fruit, massive tannins, and alcoholic liveliness,

but nevertheless lusty and fascinating. Port's reductive style with the appealing fresh sweet cherry and berry fruit continues to attract more and more fans who prize the ruby reserve, late bottled vintage, single quinta vintage, and of course the vintage—the first two have the advantage of being more affordable and more accessible when young, of not needing to be decanted, and of being available in most bars.

Yet the tawnies, the wines matured oxidatively in old barrels, the *pipes*, are in no way a thing of the past, quite the contrary. The simple, soft, still berry fruity wines enjoy great popularity in France, the main market for good-value ports—which is in fact a paradox, because their own French *vins doux naturels*, which are in no way inferior in quality, are disdained. The strong, affordable ports are also popular in The Netherlands and Belgium. The tawnies are still very appealing wines that, with increasing age, often develop a fascinating diversity of aromas often exceeding that of the vintages. The 30- and 40-year-olds, in particular, exhibit a tempting elegance and sophistication seldom found in other wines and spirits. Even today port remains primarily an export product. In the past the Portuguese were not able to afford it, apart from the fact that it wasn't intended for them anyway. Happily this has changed and the Portuguese themselves have become the most important port producers, having long since developed the taste for port as well.

# The Douro valley

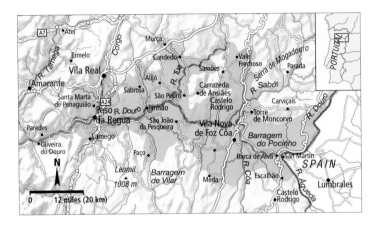

The wine-growing regions of the Douro valley.

Page 672: Typical terraced vineyards near Régua.

Niepoort's vineyards in the autumn.

Port wine or vinho do porto bears the name of the harbor from which it was shipped. The wine originates from the Douro valley and was brought up the river to Porto in barques. The first vines are planted about 60 miles (100 km) upriver and from there the wine-growing area extends about 90 miles (150 km) on both sides of the river as far as the Spanish border, measuring only about 15 miles (25 km) at its widest point. It encompasses a total of about 600,000 acres (250,000 ha), of which only about a fifth is planted with vines. It is divided into three regions: Baixo (lower) Corgo, Cima (upper) Corgo, and Douro Superior.

The westernmost region, the Lower Corgo, is the smallest but has the most fertile soils and the most vineyards. Close to half of all port wines come from here, albeit largely of a fairly basic quality. The region extends as far as the small town of Régua, where the Corgo and the Ribeiro de Temilobis flow into the Douro.

It is here that the Upper Corgo adjoins it, extending as far as the Cachão de Valeira gorge, which is far more expansive. It is the true home of the vintages and many of the most famous *quintas* with their steep vineyard slopes are situated around Pinhão. Extensive new plantings have been undertaken in recent years.

The third region, the Douro Superior, has the largest area but is the hottest and driest, contributing little more than one tenth of the port production.

## Terrace farming

You have to have seen the Douro valley to be able to understand what makes it so special. The steep mountain slopes have been terraced and made usable for centuries in Upper Corgo in particular. The Douro valley's great wealth is the barren shale that gives the wines their structure, their aging potential, and their finesse. The early farmers opened up the shale slopes, using the large blocks to build stone walls and layering the crumbly stone behind them. The work and fertilizing over generations has produced the top soil to which today's wines owe their quality. It is a unique terroir enjoying the combined effects of climate, topography, soils, and processing. Even though new estates are founded and existing ones are extended, the majority of the vineyard

The idyllic Quinta do Vesuvio directly on the Douro.

terraces are still worked by some 30,000 wine farmers, each of them owning an average of about 2½ acres (1 ha).

In the 1980s the view of the Douro valley was still breathtaking, the monumental efforts of the wine farmers remaining untouched. The valley has since changed entirely, the pressures of modern economics together with labor shortages having dictated the construction of new terraces capable of being worked by machines.

The revival of recent years, beginning with Portugal's entry into the EU and the subsequent subsidies, brought even more radical changes. It turned out that the valley was ideally suited not only to port, but also to outstanding red wines, drawing an army of investors to every suitable patch of land. The vineyards of the Douro valley are still spectacular today, but they no longer constitute the World Heritage Site that UNESCO intended to honor in 2001.

The distinction is now made in the three valley regions between which sites are better for port and which for both dry red and white douros. The two very different wine styles present very different challenges—the slopes could be used further up for dry wines in order to achieve more acid and elegance. Although it was known previously that the best wines derived from within earshot of the river, today's warmer climate is now forcing a change of thinking because with port, too, it is the balance that counts in addition to the strength.

Immortalized on *azulejos*: the old vineyard terraces near Pinhão.

# Better on foot

The English interest in wine from the Douro valley increased toward the end of the 17th century because their quarrels with France meant that there were problems with the claret supplies from Bordeaux. Yet the dark red wine, in those days still fermented dry and only stabilized afterward with a shot of brandy, was in no way as palatable as the later port and faced major competition. Demand fluctuated considerably, much to the distress of the Douro wine makers.

The prime minister, later the Marquês do Pombal, addressed these not unfounded concerns in 1756 with the founding of the Companhia Geral da Agricultura das Vinhas do Alto Douro, abbreviated by the English to the "Old Wine Company." The first "mountain boundary" was attributed to the company, a boundary recognizing only the best locations for port production. It was also the company's task to ensure quality, to prevent fraud, and to regulate supply and demand, so stabilizing prices.

Nowhere else in the world is there such a sophisticated system of classification, developed on the basis of vineyard and grape quality. Categories from A to F were allocated, whereby not only location, soils, and grape variety were taken into consideration, but also vine distances, the age of the vines, yield, and six other parameters. Points were then awarded and the quantity of port wine that could be produced was based on their sum—A indicating 160 gallons (600 liters) from 1,000 vines, while F is usually permitted only for dry table wines.

Portugal has a wealth of interesting grape varieties, some of which are endemic—originating from here only. Of these 90 are permitted in the Douro valley, but only about 30 are actually planted. Touriga Nacional, Touriga Francesa, Tinta Roriz (Tempranillo), Tinta Barroca, and the rare Tinta Cão are considered to be the best for red port wine. Viozinho, Rabigato, Arinto, Cedega, Gouveio (Verdelho), as well as Malvasia Fina are largely used for white port.

Left: In the Douro valley, too, the grapes are now selected for the top-quality wines.

Right: The open, stone *lagares* are still preferred for the brief but active mash fermentation.

# It's going to be port!

The grapes are harvested by hand and brought to the wineries, where they are stripped and crushed. In traditional processing they are placed in *lagares*, large, rectangular stone vats with a maximum height of 24 inches (60 cm), their large surface area ensuring good contact between the skins and the juice. The vats are filled with grapes during the day and these are then crushed by foot in the evening, which is not a case of simply treading as you like: the foreman's loud "left, right, left, right" sets the pace. In the lagares the selected few stand up to their knees in violet red must—in the large wineries in two rows opposite each other, young and old, men and women, who have been doing the harvesting during the day. Knees appear out of the juice only to sink in again. The rows approach each other step by step, extending up to the edge of the vat. The walking breaks the fruit open, the flesh gently separating from the skins in the perfect extraction method. The stamping goes on for hours, becoming more relaxed later with music and aguardente.

The valley's smart wine makers have long since come up with the idea of robots to take on this laborious task, and the latest versions are no longer inferior in quality to the human efforts. With the best vintages, however, the traditional tramping is still firmly adhered to. The extraction is complete after just 24–36 hours and the wine is half fermented. It is drawn off and the fermentation continues until the required residual sugar content is reached and it is silenced with 77% brandy. For the great ports special attention is paid to the use of first-class brandy quality. Today the majority of the wines are processed in modern wineries with temperature-controlled stainless steel tanks.

The wines are tasted and assessed after the first decanting in the winter following the harvest, and the port producers bring their wines to the lodges in Vila Nova de Gaia to mature further. In a good year the best wines are kept separate in order to declare them potentially a vintage. Depending on the category for which they are intended, the others then begin the maturation process in the large vats or tanks, or in the traditional, 145-gallon (550-liter) pipes, usually made from Portuguese oak and which are in use for years or decades.

Left: The traditional tramping by foot is still firmly adhered to for many of the great port wines.

Right: Vintages mature in large barrels with little air contact in order to retain their youthful fruit.

# Port types

### White Port

White port is drunk as an aperitif on ice as dry or extra dry with little residual sugar. The good grape varieties are Viozinho for body and aroma, Rabigato for freshness, and Arinto for elegance, but the majority of white ports tend to be more neutral in taste, the best of them having convincing candied citrus fruit aromas that are nutty and robust on the palate. Lágrima is the sweetest of all. The rarities are quality wines aged for a long time in barrels, developing great complexity and fine *rancio* nuances.

### Pink

This novelty from Croft is once again testimony to the creativity of the Fladgate Partnership; it also owns Taylors, which has repeatedly launched new port styles in the past: Dry White Port in 1934, the second run of the Late Bottled Vintage in 1970, and Organic Port in 2006. The red port grapes are pressed after brief mash contact and then fermented at a low temperature. With a light cherry color, its pleasantly fresh red berry aromas are appealing, their sweetness on the palate being offset by the alcohol.

### Ruby

Even a simple ruby fascinates, with its color much darker than ruby red. It is recommended as an introduction to the world of red port wines where the focus is on retaining the intense fruit of the grapes and the deep color. It should be juicy with sweet, candied, or cherry jam aromas, as well as red and blackberries. It is usually matured in the tank for two to three years and is pleasant without noticeable tannins. You should have no expectations of diversity and length.

### Reserve

There are two styles of reserve ports: ruby reserve and tawny reserve. Unfortunately, the explanatory categories are often not provided. Ruby reserves are a further step toward vintages, such as the Six Grapes with its distinctively sweet berry fruit, sometimes an additional spicy nuance on the palate, with tannins already present. Tawny reserves are matured in the barrel for at least seven years, and are paler, still with fresh fruit but mostly with dried fried and rust aromas.

## Late Bottled Vintage (LBV)

This high-quality vintage wine matures for four to six years in tanks or in barrels before being bottled. It therefore does not need to be decanted and is initially ready for drinking. Although it is less concentrated than a vintage, as a rule it does have—and this is independent of the vintage—full, balanced fruit aromas and a harmonious, albeit solid, tannin structure. Depending on the house style it can exhibit more young fruit or else nuances of developing wood flavors.

## Vintage

These deeply colored dark wines of outstanding quality made from a single vintage are matured reductively and bottled in the second or the third year following the harvest at the latest. Their durability in good years is legendary, becoming ever more harmonious, retaining their fruit for an astounding length of time, and developing intriguing aging aromas with complex rust and spice nuances, as well as a lot of sediment so that they do need to be decanted. As the name indicates, single quinta vintages come from individual estates.

## Colheita

In contrast to the vintage, colheita, also a vintage port, is matured oxidatively in the barrels as a tawny. It may be bottled after seven years at the earliest, but in many cases it is given significantly more time to develop its complex aromas that are then reminiscent of dried fruit, nuts, cocoa, fine old wood, and spices, and which exhibit ever greater elegance from year to year. In the 19th century, incidentally, the great vintages were left to mature in wood for years before they were bottled.

## Tawny

This category has two typical features: the oxidative maturation in wooden barrels and the blending of wines of different ages in order to achieve the relevant style. The simplest tawnies age within about three years into soft, harmonious, pale red wines. Always sold ready for drinking, it is the reserves or tawnies with an additional age category—10, 20, 30, and 40 years old—that guarantee more aromatic diversity. The older a tawny becomes, the more refined is its expression and the more lingering and multifaceted is its flavor.

# Great vintages

Vintages are not declared every year. Available a good two years after harvesting, batches of matured wines also sometimes appear on the market.

Drinking a vintage port is always an experience in itself. It is not simply a case of uncorking the bottle and pouring a glass. A vintage port is always celebrated. As it is bottled unfiltered it needs to be decanted in order to be able to exploit all of its true wealth of flavors and its aging potential fully, the decanting itself being a ritual. Once opened, a vintage is best drunk in one evening. Since it is both a strong and intense as well as a sweet and sophisticated wine, however, it does need a number of like-minded individuals once it has been opened. A vintage is therefore no everyday drink—happily enough, because each bottle of vintage is the result of the work of many people who have made every possible effort to obtain the best wine from the oldest vines on the first-class shale terraces of the Douro valley. This is not achieved every year and, when it is, it is only ever in very limited quantities. The quality and the rarity of a vintage ought to be savored when it is drunk. And you yourself should give it another few years before you drink it, enabling it to overcome its youthful coarseness.

While the very well-developed Ferreira 1978 may not derive from a particularly good year, it clearly demonstrates the finesse and the diversity that such a vintage is capable of achieving and its time has now come. On the other hand, the Sandeman 1980, from a great year, is fascinating in its appealingly youthful bouquet and very harmonious flavor. Both demonstrate how differently the vintages mature depending on the year.

The year 2000 is a great one and Graham's is an outstanding success with appealingly

complex ripe fruit and rust nuances, excellent concentration and tannins, multifaceted, elegant, and with great potential. Fonseca is hardly inferior, being voluminous, velvety, with exuberant berry fruit, licorice nuances, and an astounding accessibility. Ferreira and Offley, both brands belonging to the Portuguese Sogrape Group, are also testimony to the quality of the 2000 vintage. Ferreira has appealing sweet red fruit, a touch of cocoa, length, and balance; while Offley, whose vintage only ever comes from the top estate Boa Vista, has floral nuances, dark berries, and distinctive tannins with plenty of depth.

Heat and aridity also characterized the 2003 vintage in the Douro valley, resulting in a high degree of ripeness, plenty of sugar, and low acidity. Taylor's was very adept at coping with this, combining ripe berries and plenty of concentration with subtle acids to produce great elegance and sustainability. With Quinta do Noval the deliciously dark fruit predominate before the depth and the ripe tannins then develop; very long and harmonious. Croft made its entry in 2003 as the new addition to the Fladgate Partnership with sensational quality, very intense black berry fruit, great velvetiness, depth, structure, and a great future. Also part of the Taylor's group is Romariz, with a little less opulence and structure but with pleasantly sweet cherry and blackberry aromas.

Ramos Pinto made a courageous appearance with the 2004 vintage, exhibiting distinct dark, sweet fruit and spices, outstanding tannin structure, subtle acids, and very good aging potential. Niepoorts Vintage 2005 is no less inferior, displaying a sophisticated combination of blossoms, berries, and minerals, and exhibiting an appealing elegance despite its stable structure.

Even young vintages have their appeal, but they are intended to age for decades and there is nothing to beat the finesse that they develop with age.

# Selected single quintas

**Quinta de Ervamoira**
**Ramos Pinto**

The estate in Valle do Côa still retains its avant-garde flair, and all the more so since José António Ramos Pinto Rosas, whose forefathers founded the port company in 1880, and his nephew João Nicolau de Almeida redesigned it in 1976. At that time they departed from almost all of the Douro valley traditions, stocking 370 acres (150 ha) in the Douro Superior vertically on flat slopes for machine processing as well as large allotments separated according to variety for port and red wines. The high plateau they chose turned out to be ideally suited to this, yielding very fruity wines with spicy tannins and a distinct expression, as is clearly demonstrated by the 2004 vintage. Owned by the champagne company Roederer since 1990.

**Quinta dos Malvedos**
**Graham's**

In declared years the estate on the banks of the Douro near Tua provides the backbone of Graham's Vintage Port. The 168 acres (68 ha) of vineyards, now 25–50 years old, have been planted separately according to variety. The Scottish Grahams have been successful traders in Oporto since 1820, acquiring the estate in 1890. Graham's was taken over in 1970 by Symingtons, a family concern that has been involved in the port business for 350 years. In addition to three traditional stone vats, the Malvedos winery has been equipped with automatic lagares since 2000. The 1998 vintage with its very small harvest displays sweet red plums as well as candied orange and dark chocolate nuances. Average structure, well balanced, and harmonious.

**Quinta do Panascal**
**Fonseca**

Situated in the Tavora valley, this reputable estate has been supplying wines for the Fonseca Vintage Blend since the 1950s. It came up for sale in 1978 and since then Fonseca has renewed and expanded the vineyards to 109 acres (44 ha) with the purchase of the Quinta do Val dos Muros. The wines, whose grapes are trampled by foot, are made by David Guimaraens, successor to the company founder and the sixth generation wine maker in the family, irrespective of the fact that the company merged with Taylor's in 1948. The 2004 vintage exhibits juicy cassis and licorice aromas, with plenty of depth, a fine tannin structure, and a lingering, sweet, fruity aftertaste. Good potential.

**Quinta de Vargellas**
**Taylor's**

The idyllically situated estate in the upper Douro valley has the largest holding of old vines among all the quintas, 60% of the vines being over 75 years old. In declared years it provides the basis for Taylor's famous Vintage Port. Its wines have also been auctioned under its own name since 1820. Taylor's, a family company that has been established in the port business for more than 300 years and now operates as the Fladgate Partnership, acquired the estate in 1893 to 1896. The grapes are still crushed by foot. The 2005 vintage, which enjoyed ideal weather conditions, exhibits ripe, dark cherry and plum nuances, a touch of licorice, balanced sweetness, fine tannins, and an elegant aftertaste.

**Quinta do Vesuvio**
**Symington's**

With the imposing manor house directly on the river and 248 acres (100 ha) of steep vineyards, Vesuvio is one of the Douro's most impressive estates. It first achieved fame under the legendary Dona Antónia Adelaide Ferreira as of 1845, before gradually losing importance and finally being bought by Symington's in 1989. It has since been able to regain something of its former glory due to the fact that it is managed independently, with only vintages being bottled in its name, each of them comprising only a maximum of a quarter of the production. Still trampled by foot in *lagares*, the full-bodied 2003 Vintage is particularly impressive with its very intense, expressive fruit, stable tannins, and a long, distince aftertaste. Great potential.

# Selected tawnies

### Ferreira
#### Tawny 20 Years
This port company was founded in 1751 by a wine-growing family from the Douro valley. José and António Ferreira expanded both the property and the business substantially in the 19th century, the company then being consolidated and expanded further by Dona António Adelaide Ferreira, who married her cousin. She must have had a charismatic personality for she was committed to the ongoing modernization of the valley and to increasing the wine quality. Acquired by Sogrape Vinhos, Portugal's leading wine company, in 1987, Ferreira today provides a wide range of ports, including this very convincing, complex tawny that combines plenty of fruit with wood, cocoa, and tobacco nuances.

### Niepoort
#### 30 Years Old Tawny
There have been five generations of Van der Niepoorts, the fifth being especially significant because it is thanks to this generation that this small port and wine company today enjoys such an outstanding reputation. Dirk van der Niepoort has added new dimensions; after he took over in 1987 the basis was created through the purchase of their own vineyards in the Upper Corgo, in the best Douro region. Today no less famous for their dry wines than for their ports, the latter continuing the demanding family tradition, especially the garrafeira, colheitas, and tawnies, such as this outstanding 30 Year Old with wonderful complexity, dry fruit, roast nuts, dark chocolate, *rancio*, and tobacco, as well as lusty, dry aftertaste.

### Quinta do Noval
#### Colheita Tawny 1995
Designated as an estate since 1715, the quinta was acquired and restored by António José da Silva after the phylloxera catastrophe. His son-in-law Luiz Vasconcelos Porto built up Noval's reputation in England and the USA after having declared the legendary 1931 vintage. Noval was the first to provide tawnies with vintage details. Following a devastating fire in their lodges in Vila Nova de Gaia, they were the first large company to move their lodges to the Douro valley, in 1982. The heirs Van Zeller then sold the quinta to the AXA insurance company in 1993. Major investments have been made since then. Their colheita—processed by foot as befits a great vintage—is sweet and nutty, with dried fruit aromas, as well as being elegant and long.

### Sandeman
#### 40 Years Old Tawny
Who is not familiar with the don's black silhouette with the Spanish caballero hat and the Portuguese student's cape? Internationally the most well-known sherry and port brand, it was founded in London in 1790 by a young Scotsman named George Sandeman, and family members still work for the company today—even though it has belonged to Sogrape since 2002. Displaying convincing quality in their Vintage and Vau Vintage in recent years, the old tawnies from the House of Sandeman enjoy an outstanding reputation. These are some of the most magnificent old ports on the market, with great emphasis as well as length, and developing a whole range of aromas from dried fruit, nuts, cocoa, spices, and *rancio*.

### Warre's
#### Otima 10
The oldest British port company was initially founded in the Minho region by Clarke and Thornton about 1670. William Warre joined the company in 1729 and was the first Briton to buy land in the Vila Nova de Gaia. The Scotsman Andrew James Symington joined as a partner about 1892. The Warres and the Symingtons worked together until 1959 before the latter took over the company. Apart from the vintages and the Single Quinta da Cavadinha, Warre's unfiltered Late Bottled Vintage matured for five years in the bottle is as remarkable as the innovative Otima, a soft, ten-year-old tawny, lighter in style with more berry fruit, more lingering, and with fruity sweetness as well as raisins and nut nuances.

# Madeira forever

If madeira makes you think of sauces, then you had better think again because the truly noble madeira—to be found today in upmarket English and American hotel bars— is a legendary fortified wine with unbelievable durability. It is still possible to come across the odd bottle from the 19th-century vintages and you will be astounded at the fact that their contents have not only survived 100 or 150 years, but that they often display an astonishing freshness: a phenomenon worthy of respect. And because madeira has a lot more unusual features to offer, it is worth taking a detour to the Atlantic island.

João Gonçalves Zarco, a Portuguese captain in the service of Henry the Navigator, landed on the cloud-draped island 370 miles (600 km) from the Moroccan coast and 560 miles (900 km) from the Portuguese coast in 1420. He cleared large areas of the island and planted sugar cane as well as Malvasia, the sweet Cretan grape variety. Following the discovery of America, Madeira increased in importance as a supply station on the sea route over the Atlantic. English ships were only allowed to take on supplies there and it was not just water that they took on board. When sugar cane from the new colonies began to provide competition for the island in around 1570, the focus turned to wine growing and wine became the main export. Madeira's ideal location as a relay station on the important sea routes to North America, Brazil, Africa, and India made for easy trade in the island's own produce. It is alleged that July 4 has been toasted with madeira in the White House ever since the first celebration of Independence Day.

As a significant trading junction, the island's capital of Funchal became the base for an increasing number of British merchants who dispatched wine to the faraway colonies. The barrels were stored below deck, where the wine was not only in constant motion during the double crossing of the Equator en route to India, but also had to endure extreme temperatures. Strangely enough there were never any complaints from dissatisfied customers. When the first barrels were returned to Madeira in 1722 as undeliverable, it finally became evident why. The wine had altered completely en route: it had become denser and fuller in structure, as well as more diverse and intense in bouquet and flavor; it now resembled the *vinhos de canteiro* that had been aged for years in attics on the island. In the mid 18th century the merchants began deliberately loading barrels as ballast on the journey to India in order to sell them on their return to England or America, albeit not before they had fortified the wine with brandy. The *vinho de volta* or *vinho de roda da India*, in short *vinho de roda*, which meant the returned wine or the route wine, became famous and commanded top prices for a period of some 70 years.

There were markets with increasing demand; there were stable, high prices; but there wasn't enough wine. Consequently yields were increased and wine production became more haphazard. In times of political instability, when madeira was the only or one of the few types of alcohol available, the customers gritted their teeth and accepted the decline in quality accompanied by consistently high prices. However, once the peace treaties revived the market many customers looked elsewhere. This was accompanied by the two catastrophes that affected European wine production in the second half of the 19th century: powdery mildew and phylloxera. A mere fifth of the island's 6,000 acres (2,500 ha) of vineyards remained. What's more, phylloxera had all but exterminated the four noble wine grape varieties: Malvasia, Boal, Sercial, and Verdelho.

The new start at the beginning of the 20th century was also jinxed. Happy at being able to harvest grapes at all, the farmers planted those that promised the highest and the most reliable yields: hybrids and Negra Mole, which earned the dubious reputation as the "Whore of Madeira." These were made into cheap, quickly processed madeira-like cooking wines. There were hardly any top-quality wines. However, a renaissance in madeira has since taken hold, not least due to Portugal's entry into the EU and to the 1996 ban on hybrids.

# In the midst of the Atlantic

Page 684: Some of Madeira's best vineyards are to be found on the slopes above the picturesque fishing village of Câmara de Lobos.

Left: With the pergola method the grapes have to be harvested overhead.

Right: The wineries are now equipped with modern presses.

The soils on Madeira, a mountain in the eastern Atlantic, are largely of volcanic origin with basalt being predominant. The settlers who cultivated the island in the 15th century had to go to a great deal of effort to create space on the often steep slopes in order to plant fruit and vegetables, and more especially sugar cane and vines. They built terrace walls from the basalt rocks, filling the terraces with soil from the lower lying areas. They constructed an interlocking system of mountain terraces, *poios*, and built around 1,200 miles (2,000 km) of irrigation channels, *levadas*. They remodeled the island in the process, leaving their mark on its appearance.

The peasant farmers' reward was the fertility of the volcanic soils and the abundant rainfall in the subtropical climate where formerly sugar cane and now delicious small bananas flourish. As the soil was and is so precious, the vines were not kept low but were rather trained high up the pergolas in order to make space for other crops below. Many of the 4,000 small-scale farmers still use the 4,500 acres (1,800 ha) of vineyards in this dual manner. The grapes are harvested in a standing position with the arms held high, each of the grape baskets often having to be carried 700–1,000 feet (200–300 m) down to the road. The southern side of the island is preferred because here the grapes reach their optimal ripeness more easily, even in the case of the demanding Malvasia and Boal. The north side is more humid and cooler, but Verdelho and Sercial are happy with this location, provided the wine farmers protect their allotments from the moist, salty sea breezes with hedges of heather and fern.

The noble madeira varieties are the white grapes. Today Malvasia and Boal each comprise only 5%, while Sercial and Verdelho together amount to 2%, but this is increasing. Fortunately for the island, major port

companies are committed to ensuring a revival and are engaged in quality oriented wine growing, planting modern vineyards and restocking the famous varieties. The wine makers are also working on redeeming the Negra Mole's reputation, now referring to it as Tinta Negra—it makes up 85% of all vines. With conscientious work in the vineyards and modern processing they are producing respectable basic wines that can then be matured into good madeiras.

## Wine and warmth

Not too long ago the madeira producers claimed that careful wine production was not the most important factor; the only important issue was the long maturation period. They are now of an entirely different opinion. The leading companies have initiated an enological revolution and, like their colleagues on the mainland, have put their faith in precise, hygienic winery work with controlled temperatures. The best grapes delivered to the wineries are stripped, then pressed or mashed, and their fermentation is closely monitored. At the required point in time, which depends on the desired residual sugar content, 96% spirits are added in order to halt the fermentation. The maturation can then begin.

The special feature devised by the wine merchant Pantaleão Fernandes in 1794 has also been retained. While pondering the positive effects that the tropical sea voyage had on the wines, he came up with the idea of heating his wine cellar, a method that was soon also adopted by his colleagues. This led to the development of the *estufas*, tanks and cellars that can be heated to 113–122 °F (45–50 °C) with heating tubes and in which the wines "simmer" for three, preferably five months, accelerating their aging process. Today's enologists have now perfected this method and temperature controls are also used. The wines are then aged in barrels of differing sizes and begin what is at times a long maturation period. If they are not heated and are instead subjected to a protracted "madeirisation" in barrels, they are then referred to as *canteiro*.

Left: Today stainless steel tanks with temperature controls ensure problem-free processing.

Right: Non-air-conditioned rooms and attics are used for maturing the barrels of canteiro wines.

# Original madeiras

### The basics

The most noble of all madeiras come from the five historical white grape varieties and, after decades of aging, they constitute unique specialties:

Sercial prefers the cooler northern side of the island and produces the driest, very rare madeira displaying a complex, elegant bouquet after ten years of aging.

Verdelho is also well suited to the northern side; it ripens early and yields semisweet madeiras with subtle acids; headstrong iodine and rust nuances develop after longer aging.

Boal needs more warmth and does better on the southern side; it develops interesting aromas early on, including dried fruit, raisins, nuts, caramel, and later *rancio*; semisweet.

Malvasia requires the warmth of the southern side; the sweetest madeira, it has a high degree of balancing acids, plenty of depth and length, and with age it exhibits subtle cocoa and chocolate nuances.

Terrantez, the rarest variety, ages exceptionally well and almost forever, producing very expressive, semisweet wine of truly indescribable elegance.

However, the majority of madeiras today are based on Tinta Negra, also known as Negra Mole, from which all of the different styles can be produced, from dry through to sweet.

Madeiras are designated as follows, depending on age and type:

Seleccionado or finest is the lowest category for the drinkable, 3-year-old madeiras. Reserva designates the 5-year-old wines; reserva especial or velha have been matured for at least 10 years. Then there are also the age categories 5, 10, 15, 20, 30, and "over 40 years old." Frasqueira or garrafeira form the top of the quality pyramid with vintage wines that have been aged for a minimum of 20 years.

### Barbeito
#### Boal 1982 Frasqueira

Today "frasqueira" designates the vintages on Madeira. The requirement is that they are made from one noble grape variety only and that they have been matured for at least 20 years, for which Ricardo Freitas from Barbeito uses only used French oak barrels. Aided by their Japanese partners, the Kinoshita family, the focus is on high-quality wines. This amber colored Boal demonstrates the variety's astounding diversity. Its aromas range from dried figs and apricots to cooked bananas and candied oranges, roasted nuts, and dark chocolate. It has a great deal of expression and the freshness typical of Barbeito, as well as plenty of length. A truly great madeira.

### Barbeito
#### Malvasia 30 Anos

Mário Barbeito de Vasconcelos started Vinhos Barbeito in 1946 by acquiring the old madeiras, bottling them, and building up good contacts with customers all over the world. His daughter Manuela took over after his death in 1985, then handed over the reigns to her son Ricardo Freitas in the 1990s, who has been making Barbeito's wines since 1993, having developed a new wine range. Barbeito is famous not least for their great old wines. Small quantities are drawn off from the company's best Malvasia barrels for this outstanding, mahogany colored blend (1,550 bottles). Its appeal lies in its viscous texture, its nut, chocolate, and *rancio* aromas; and a subtle acidity ideally suited to balancing the sweetness. Exceptional length.

### Justino's
#### Colheita 1998

Juan Teixeira, Justino's committed wine maker, is among the champions of Tinta Negra and, with this wine, he shows that it is no way as bad as its reputation. He does handle it entirely differently from the way it is treated in mass wine production, however. The carefully stripped and crushed grapes are fermented as mash in the stainless steel tanks, being transferred repeatedly in order to extract as much color and aroma as possible before the fermentation is halted by the addition of alcohol. After at least five years in oak barrels, the wine has intense dried fruit and mandarin aromas, as well as nuts and spicy wood. As colheita it comes from a single year that may be indicated on the bottle's label.

### Justino's
#### Malvasia 10 Years Old

Based on a family company founded in 1870, Vinhos Justino took over a number of old bottlers (Henriques, Filhos, Lda.) in 1953, before the company was then bought by Sigfredo Costa Campos in 1981, taking on Gran Cruz Porto and La Martiniquaise as part owners in 1993. The winery in Cancela has developed into one of the leading madeira producers. This sweet Malvasia was placed in oak barrels immediately after being fortified and aged for a decade according to the canteiro system in a warm part of the building. With a bouquet of raisins, chocolate, and caramel—as well as the flavor of candied citrus fruit and chocolate, subtle acids, and plenty of length—it is a good accompaniment for desserts such as tiramisu and fruit puddings.

# Setúbals Moscatel

The third member of the league of Portugal's major fortified wines is Setúbal, a sweet muscatel wine from the peninsula of the same name south of Lisbon. Long known as Moscatel de Setúbal, only its main grape variety, Muscat d'Alexandrie, is now designated, while Setúbal belongs to the Terras do Sado wine region.

José Maria Fonseca founded what is today Portugal's second largest wine company in 1834, optimizing the production methods of the moscatel famous since the 17th century until he was able to produce truly quality wines. The wine has to contain a minimum of 70% Muscat grapes, usually Muscat d'Alexandrie, less often Moscatel do Douro or Roxo. Then there are also the white varieties Arinto, Boais, and Malvasia. A further contribution is made by the light, stony, and chalky soils of the Serra da Arrábida and the humidity from the Atlantic. The fermentation is halted by the addition of brandy, but—

and this is what sets it apart from Moscatel do Douro—the wine remains with the skins for another five months. The oxidative maturation takes place in used oak barrels, with the hot climate of the peninsula resulting in an especially distinctive concentration of the wine owing to evaporation. Silenced with at least 14 oz per gallon of sugar (90 g/liter), old moscatels can reach up to 30 oz per gallon (200 g/liter); the alcohol content is around 18% vol.

A variety of vintages are blended for the older quality wine so that Fonseca's magnificent 20 Year Old Alambre, for example, also contains wines that are up to 40 years old.

Characterized by fruity, sweet aromas as a young wine, with advancing age Setúbal develops dried fruit, nut, chocolate, and honey nuances, albeit always with an incomparable intensity. The port wine region is the origin of what is usually the younger, often somewhat lighter, but also less complex Moscatel do Douro.

Alambre shows how complex and sophisticated muscatel wines from Setúbal can be.

In addition to Setúbal, the Douro valley is also well known as the origin of good muscatel wines.

# Sweet wines worldwide

Plenty of sun makes the grapes sweet—and more perishable. Hence the tradition of fortified wines in the Mediterranean countries as well as in the wine regions of South Africa and Australia, initially for purely pragmatic reasons of durability. The non-fermented sugar was happily accepted as a "side effect." The sweet preference lasted until the 1960s: demand increased and quality fell by the wayside in the face of an astronomical number of bottles filled with mediocre ports, sherries, marsalas, muscats, and mavrodaphnes. It is thanks to modern enological techniques that quality has made a comeback.

Sweet wines have come back into fashion time and again ever since antiquity, and a variety of production processes developed in the warmer wine regions in order to convert what were already sweet grapes into even sweeter wines. Hence the grapes were deliberately left on the vines longer, for example, where they raisined. Or else they were spread out on straw mats in the sun, allowing the surplus water to evaporate. All of these methods had one thing in common: they were laborious, time consuming, and low yielding. As soon as it became possible to distill spirits in larger quantities, the fortification of wine proved to be the more affordable, quicker, and more productive option, apart from the fact that it made the wines more durable.

This fact was of interest to the merchants primarily because the sweet wine production areas were limited, the market for the sought-after luxury goods was therefore large, and the transportation correspondingly long. It was therefore no wonder that the development of fortified wines was usually driven by merchants because no decent sweet wine was worth anything once it had turned to vinegar en route. There was only one option: adding brandy to the wine.

The same also applied to mavrodaphne from the Peloponnese. Here it was a German, the Bavarian Gustav Clauss, who settled in Patras in 1854, attracted by the vineyards on the region's hills. The first wine that he produced in 1860 was made from the grape variety of the same name. In imitation of sherry, he had fortified it according to the solera system: it was matured in barrels. He began exporting this wine nine years later with tremendous success, creating not only the basis for the present day appellation, but also the framework for one of Greece's largest wineries.

In South Africa and Australia, too, the focus was on the fortification of wines in the 19th century, both countries producing—and diligently exporting—wines in both the sherry and the port styles, which is not to say, however, that there weren't a number of astounding muscatel wines produced as well. Then came the change in the 1960s: the luxury wines of the past were considered to be sickly sweet and full of calories. At the same time enology had progressed to the extent that clean, dry wines could be stored and dispatched without any problem. Only a few regions continued to be successful with fortified wines—one of these being Samos—the majority having converted almost entirely to dry wines. The sweet wines that did remain on offer were those that had established themselves as regional specialties.

Today fortified wines are enjoying renewed attention because, provided they are produced with due care and attention, they develop exceptionally intense and complex aromas. In order to savor them to the full these wines are often drunk as aperitifs or digestifs, but are also served with meals and desserts that can lead to truly intriguing taste experiences. As an aperitif they go well with nuts and dried fruit, these aromas also being present in the wines, but can also be served with savories such as olives, salted almonds, or salami. Savory and fatty food in general is unexpectedly well matched to these strong, aromatic wines, as is evidenced by the now famous combinations of port and Stilton, and muscat and Roquefort. Dry fortified wines such as a Marsala Vergine even go well with anchovies, while a tawny is excellent with venison dishes. Desserts are the source of many a happy combination, but the encounter between a vintage and quality dark chocolate remains a special experience.

# Marsala on heavy seas

Page 690: Yalumba in the Barossa valley in southern Australia is a bastion of fortified wines.

The Mediterranean may not have any tides but it does have heavy storms. It must have been just such a storm during which the English wine merchant John Woodhouse was forced to head for the harbor of Marsala in 1773—Marsah-el-Allah: God's gate. Seeking to recover from the horrors of his journey in a tavern, all of his tribulations were forgotten with the first sip of *perpetuo* and his journey was over: he had found the alternative to sherry and port wine he had been looking for. This amber colored wine matures and "madierises" for years in the same barrel; what is then drawn off is filled up with young wine after the next harvest. This most simple version of the solera system which is widespread throughout the Mediterranean region, fulfills its purpose but does not produce the finesse that distinguishes the finos, amontillados, and olorosos matured in Jerez.

Woodhouse immediately stocked up on the wine, mixing every 125 gallon barrel (476.5 liters) with 10 gallons (38.6 liters) of young spirits for preservation purposes, and dispatched his first cargo to England, where marsala received an enthusiastic reception. He opened his own winery in Marsala three years later and was then better able to adapt the wine to British tastes: either very dry or sweetened further with boiled must.

The advertising medium for Mr. Woodhouse's marsala was none less than Admiral Horatio Nelson himself, who was said to have found the wine to be "worthy of any gentleman's table," promptly placing a very generous order for the Royal Navy. Even during the famous battle of the Nile in 1798 Nelson had enough marsala supplies to be able afterward to give a toast to the major victory over the French with the newly christened "victory wine."

Even today only the best marsalas age in the Cantina Garibaldi, Florio's oldest cellars, just a stone's throw from the sea.

Driven by such marketing, marsala itself sailed from victory to victory, claiming its position next to sherry, port, madeira, and malaga, the other great fortified wines, within a short space of time. This encouraged another two Englishmen to settle in the harbor on the westernmost end of Sicily in 1812: Benjamin Ingham and his nephew Joseph Whitacker. Not only did the competition stimulate business, it also raised the quality of the wine as the two wineries now vied for the main British custom.

The era of the relaxed "home game" came to an end in 1832 when the first Italian entered the lucrative business. Vincenzo Florio was a successful merchant from Calabria; primarily specializing in the spice business, he had made his fortune in Palermo. He acquired a stretch of land on the coast directly next to the two English wineries, where he set up his company.

Florio made a name for marsala in Italy and abroad. The success of the Florio family continued to grow and, at the beginning of the

20th century, they took over the two British wineries. They had also acquired other marsala producers, including Rallo and Pellegrino as two of the largest. However, marsala was already past its peak in terms of quality, albeit not commercially.

Its outstanding suitability for use in the kitchen for cakes and desserts proved to be its undoing. The more popular a recipe with marsala became, the faster the production became and consequently the shorter the maturation times—and therefore the poorer the quality of the wine. On top of that, the willingness to experiment began to take on worrying dimensions with significant additions being made to the wine: coconut, almonds, strawberries, bananas, coffee, cream, even eggs. This brought a permanent end to its good reputation. Marsala disappeared from the wine shelves, only maintaining a position as a flavoring from then on: zabaglione had won. At least for a while.

Florio also focused on advertising early on, commissioning the famous poster artist Giorgio Muggiani from time to time.

The marsala winery boasts an impressive collection of 40,000 old bottles.

# Italy's hidden strength

**Fortified wine-growing regions in Italy**

- ▨ Lombardy
- ▨ Apulia
- ▨ Sicily
- ▨ Sardinia

- ☐ Wine centers

Contrary characters are to be found everywhere but their involvement has seldom been as positive as in Marsala, where they have implemented a radical cure for their wines. The relaxed conditions of their Denominazione di Origine Controllata were revised and made stricter in 1984. Today marsala is based solely on grapes, primarily Grillo—although Inzolia, Cataratto, and Damaschino are also permitted, as are the rare red versions Calabrese (Nero d'Avola), Nerello, and Perricone.

Without doubt it is the Grillo from the coastal plains that produces the greatest marsalas. Marco de Bartoli has dedicated himself to this grape variety. A descendant of the Pellegrino family who used to distribute simple marsalas on a large scale, he is determined to restore the reputation of what was once Sicily's greatest wine. This he does, together with his children, on the 50-acre (20 ha) Samperi estate adjacent to Mazara del Vallo, showing just what this old variety is capable of. In the dry, fresh Grappoli de Grillo it provides liveliness and plenty of minerals. In 1980, with the Vecchio Samperi, he "restored" the *perpetuo*, the high-proof but not fortified wine with which everything began. Finally, there is the full, 19.5% vol., robust Marsala Superiore 1986 with Balsamico, almond, tobacco, *rancio* nuances, a subtle sweetness on the palate, dried apricots, dates, and a degree of bite. They are all self-contained wines with distinctive characters.

Florio, Pellegrino, and Rallo also hark back to the golden age of the great wines, even though marsala is still supplied for culinary use. Florio has selected a range of top-quality wines that are ideally suited to reviving the former reputation. For example, the Vergine with its historically significant style is based on John Woodhouse's recipe: matured wine plus spirits. The Baglio Florio Vergine Riserva is made from Grillo grapes harvested at the end of September that are almost completely fermented together with the skins before the spirits are added and the wine is aged in 480-gallon (1,800-liter) barrels for at least ten years.

## Marsala vocabulary

**Colors**

Oro: (gold) from white grapes
Ambra: (amber) from white grapes
Rubino: (ruby red) from red grapes

**Residual sugar level**

Secco: less than 3 oz/gal. (40 g/l)
Semisecco/abboccato: 6 oz/gal. (40–100 g/l)
Dolce: more than 15 oz/gal. (100 g/l)

**Age categories (in barrel)**

Fine: less than 1 year
Superiore: 2 years
Superiore riserva: 4 years
Vergine/solera: 5 years (max. 1/2 oz/gal. or 4 g/l residual sugar)
Vergine stravecchio: at least 10 years

The result is an amber-gold wine with intriguing nut, spice, and tobacco nuances, a touch of sweetness and very impressive length ideally suited to drinking as an aperitif. Marsala Superiore Riserva Donna Franca is enriched with must and mistelle before being matured for 15 years and then attracting both cigar and dessert fans with its nut, raisin, date, and chestnut honey nuances, as well as a touch of iodine.

## Even more in the boot

Finding a good marsala today is not easy, and the *liquorosi*—Italy's other fortified wines—are seldom found outside the country's borders. They come in a pleasing variety and are highly prized within Italy. Here are a number of examples of *liquorosi*—there are always non-fortified versions as well. In Sicily and Sardinia these are largely wines based on Moscato or Malvasia, such as Pantelleria Moscato and Moscato di Noto, Moscato di Cagliari, and Moscato di Sorso-Sennori, Malvasia di Cagliari, and Malvasia di Bosa; the last two are also available as a secco version. Like Sardinia, Apulia also has a fortified wine tradition. The Primitivo di Mandaria and Moscato di Trani, Salice

Salentino (from Aleatico and Malvasia), and Gioia di Colle (from Aleatico) are considered to be *liquorosi*. In Campania the Aglianico is fortified in Irpinia, the Aleatico in Latium in Gradoli. The San Martino della Battaglia based on Tocai Friulano from lake Garda is rare, while in Oltrepo Pavese Moscato and Malvasia are enjoyed as *liquorosi*.

You can discover the changeability of the Grillo grape variety in the Cantina de Bartoli.

Apulia, its wine landscape characterized by Trulli, is known for its *liquorosi*.

# Samos and Mavrodaphne

**Main growing regions for fortified wines in Greece**

- ▨ Kefalonia
- ▨ Patras
- ▨ Limnos
- ▨ Samos
- ▨ Rhodes
- ▨ Santorini
- ▨ Crete

□ Sweet wine centers

The terraced vineyards are typical of Samos.

Samos, which is today the most well known of Greece's fortified wines, is more of a late-comer. Ankaios—an Argonaut and the island's first king—is said to have planted the first vines there 1,000 years before the Common Era, but the inhabitants did not seem to feel that wine growing was their calling. While the writers of antiquity could not praise the wines from the neighboring islands of Lesbos, Chios, and Kos—as well as Rhodes and Naxos— enough, they were silent in this regard when it came to Samos. There the focus was on olive oil, wool, and

cloth. There will certainly have been some wine growing, but the sweet wine from Samos was first mentioned by a 12th-century monk. In the mid 18th century the muscatel from Samos was mentioned by a scholar in the same context as the Cypriot commandaria.

In the second half of the 19th century it was the devastation caused by phylloxera in France that brought French wine makers to the island in search of new vineyards. Here they produced fortified muscatel, albeit not for long because phylloxera reached Samos in 1892, putting a definite end to production. It was only after 1934, when the cooperatives to which all wine farmers had to belong were set up, that muscatel wines gained in significance again. Clever, visionary management made the muscatel from Samos known internationally, turning the island's wine growers into the best paid in Greece. As with most Greek muscatels, samos is available in a variety of versions: as mistelle, fortified with spirits before fermentation; as *vin doux naturel*, its fermentation being halted by the addition of spirits; as nectar made from sun-dried grapes; and also as a late harvest.

Other reputable muscatel wines come from Rhodes and Limnos, as well as from Patras and from Kefalonia. The famous malvasia and muscat from Crete have lost their reputation and only the Daphne region still produces fortified wines.

In addition to the widespread muscatel, mavrodaphne from Patras on the Peloponnese and the Ionian island of Kefalonia is also considered a specialty. This dark variety produces a sweet wine similar to a tawny, the solera method also being used for its maturation. The wine's typical features include a brick and/or mahogany color, intense fruity sweet plum, fig, and caramel aromas, as well as plenty of sweetness, fruit, spices, and chocolate on the palate.

# Selected wines

### EOSS
### Samos Grand Cru
### Muscat Vin Doux Naturel

Today Greece's most famous appellation is produced solely by the Union of Wine Growers' Cooperatives on the island of Samos, which encompasses 25 smaller cooperatives with 4,000 members. In their two wineries 9,000 tons of grapes are processed annually. The vineyards, most of which are terraced on the higher slopes, extend up to 2,600 feet (800 m). With a strict selection process the union has managed to build up an outstanding reputation for its wines. Grapes from the higher slopes with deliberately low yields are preferred for the grand cru. They give the very pale, slightly green muscatel a wonderful freshness and elegance—as well as intense citrus aromas, which are joined by peach, aniseed, and honey nuances.

### Tsantali
### Moscato of Lemnos

The island, according to legend the seat of Hephaistos, the god of fire and of blacksmiths, known to the Romans as Vulcan, is known throughout the Aegean region for its muscatel. The Muscat d'Alexandrie grape grows on the typically volcanic soils and is harvested at the end of August. The Tsantali wine company produces its modern, white-gold wine by leaving the skins to macerate in the chilled must until the optimum aromas have been extracted, with the fermentation only then being carried out at low temperatures through to the silencing. The wine has a distinct muscatel bouquet, as well as hints of yellow plum, pear, and orange blossom. It is much sweeter on the palate with intense nutmeg, lemon, and lingering honey nuances.

### Nyx
### Mavrodaphne of Patras

"The after sunset wine," as it is called by the producer, has an elegant style and a convincingly intense bouquet combining sweet fruit aromas including plum, orange peel, figs, and currants with spices, caramel, and rust nuances. The sweetness dominates on the palate, combined with berry jam, dried fruit, cocoa, very intense spices, plenty of length, and the strength of the added spirits. BG Spiliopoulos SA in Patras is the company behind this stylish appearance, with one of the most modern distilleries in the country as well as an enormous cellar. They nevertheless retain their links to their own region and the 16,000 gallons (600,000 liters) of mavrodaphne are matured in oak barrels, the best of them being used for Nyx.

### Tsantali
### Cellar Reserve
### Mavrodaphne of Patras

The red Mavrodaphne grape and the fortified wine produced from it are a specialty of the Patras wine region, where the vines are planted up to 660 feet (200 m) in altitude. For the Cellar Reserve it is usually blended with 30% of the raisin variety Korinthiaki, which is harvested and fermented at the beginning of September, while the mavrodaphne follows three weeks later. The wine blend, fortified with spirits, is then given a five-year maturation period in oak barrels, where it develops its chestnut color and its raisin, dried fig, and plum aromas, as well as its balsamic nuances. In terms of flavor, the sweetness is followed by concentrated grapes and plums, dried fruit, and rust nuances, as well as a dry aftertaste of old wood.

### Commandaria

Cyprus is one of the world's oldest wine-growing regions. Grapes dried in the sun were apparently made into sweet wine as early as the 8th century B.C. The Crusaders, including the Order of St. John, settled on Cyprus following the island's conquest by Richard the Lionheart. They set up their headquarters in the Kolossi fortress, close to the present day town of Limassol. They planted the very fertile land near the fortress with vines, among other things, from which the knights of the order made a wine that soon became famous throughout the medieval world as "commandaria" (headquarters). Commandaria has been a recognized growing area since 1990, today comprising 14 villages. The wine is made from two varieties, the white Xynisteri—which is considered to be the better quality—and the red Mavro. Once harvested the grapes are left to dry in the sun for a week to concentrate their sugar content to 59–68 oz per gallon (390–450 g/liter). The fermentation stops as soon as the yeasts have produced 10–12% vol. The wine farmers then hand the wine over to the island's four large wine companies, where it is then fortified to an alcohol content of 15% vol. alcohol. The wines are matured in barrels according to a solera system for at least two years. When aged for a very long time the extremely sweet commandaria develops raisin, dried fruit, quince, cocoa, and coffee aromas.

# Fortification in South Africa

Philip Jonker from Weltvrede in Robertson has honored his grandmother with an outstanding muscatel wine.

The grapes from the first three vines planted in South Africa were crushed on February 2, 1659. These were one vine each of Palomino, Muscat de Frontignan, and Hanepoot, as Muscat d'Alexandrie is known at the Cape—the three varieties famous for fortified wines. The vin de Constance, a muscatel wine made from overripe and raisined grapes without fortification, was already creating a stir in Europe toward the end of the 17th century. Since the distillation of brandy in South Africa also began at about the same time, the production of fortified wines was an obvious next step. In the warmer wine regions such as Worcester, Paarl, Robertson, Olifants River, and Klein Karoo in particular, the fully fermented wines had only a limited storage life and the merchants will have welcomed the remedy. Hanepoot and muscadel, as well as jerepiko, a mistelle, and sherry and port became an ongoing export success and large quantities of sweet, cheap sherries were still being exported in the 1970s.

While South African sherry has become completely insignificant, the white and red muscadels—as well as hanepoot—have maintained their position as very sweet dessert wines. They are local specialties, especially in Robertson and the Klein Karoo. However, the production of fortified wines in general in South Africa is declining and at 300,000 gallons (1.2 million liters) between 2000 and 2006 it has reduced in scope by about one third, the white varieties having been the hardest hit. Only port is currently still on an upswing.

## Cape Vintage & Cape Tawny

The term "port" is still used at the Cape but it has been agreed with the EU that the designation has not been used for export products since 2007 and will be used only within South Africa until 2014. Port is South Africa's only fortified wine that continues to enjoy increasing sales. After the Cape region became a British crown colony in 1814 it was not long before the first wine makers came up with port and sherry style fortified wines. The Cape ports and sherries sold very well in the face of demand from England in the first half of the 20th century, but their

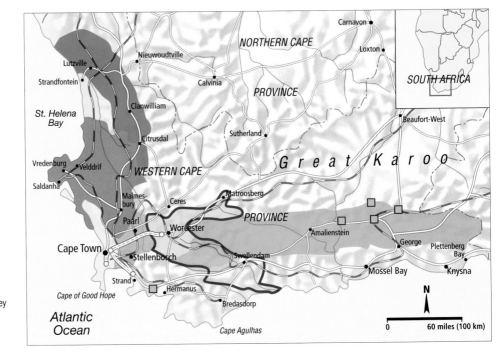

Fortified wine regions in South Africa

- Olifants River
- Swartland
- Stellenbosch
- Paarl
- Worcester
- Robertson
- Klein Karoo
- Breede River Valley

- Cape vintage centers

emphatically sweet style has been attracting less interest since the 1960s.

South African port owes its present day quality to Izak Perold, the pioneer of South African wine growing and father of the Pinotage grape, who began experimenting with port wines on Helderzicht Farm in Stellenbosch in 1942, producing the first promising results with Tinta Barocca (Portuguese Tinta Barroca), Tinta Roriz, and Souzão. Helderzicht was taken over by the Bredell family in 1965, who supplied the KWV cooperative with bulk port wine for three decades before Anton Bredell presented the first of their own bottlings.

Calitzdorp in the Klein Karoo is the center of South African port production. The hot, dry climate with summer temperatures reaching up to 104 °F (40 °C) was used for muscadel early on, but it was only in the 1970s that the first port was made there. The real upsurge began with the cousins Carel, Boets, and Stroebel Nel, with the first of the three running boplaas and the other two de krans. They share a passion for port and began to focus on top quality in 1982 by planting Tinta Barocca. Their vintages began collecting prizes just a few years later.

Encouraged by their progress, in the 1990s they planted Touriga Nacional, Tinta Roriz, and Souzão in specific arid, dry vineyards, far away from the Gamka river, the banks of which had been preferred by their forefathers for the growing of vines. And the poorer soils produced better quality.

In the meantime the 31-member South African Port Producers' Association had defined South Africa's port styles. At the top of the range was the Cape vintage reserve, declared only in truly great years, but the producers' focus is on top quality with the vintage as well. The late bottled vintage, which matures in barrels for three to six years, is ready to drink when it is released. Ruby is the most basic and most popular style, with a pleasant fruit emphasis. Tawny is matured oxidatively for a long time and is allowed to bear the year on the label. White port, for which Muscat grapes are prohibited, is the outsider where Chenin Blanc finds an intriguing, new expression.

In South Africa fortified wines are also made from Pinotage, but the Portuguese varieties are used for the Cape vintages.

# Cape vintages

The selection begins with an exception: the Pineau de Laborie from the top KWV estate in Paarl is made solely from Pinotage, which also includes the two-year-old brandy distilled from it and used for the fortification. It is softer than port but has more intensive plum and berry fruit nuances, as well as definite tannins.

Vergenoegd, the family estate founded in Stellenbosch in 1773, produces Old Cape Colony, a port with a lusty bite, strong tannins, and a balanced sweetness—it comprises two thirds Tinta Barocca, one third Touriga Nacional.

The mini-estate Axe Hill established by the late Cape wine master and wine writer Tony Mossop and his wife Lyn in Calitzdorp always produces one of South Africa's best vintages. Made using traditional methods and blended from Touriga Nacional, Tinta Barocca, and Souzão, it is complex with ripe elderberries, smoky, and has nut nuances as well as a great deal of elegance.

J. P. Bredell entered the wine scene only in 1995, but did so with style: the 1993 Vintage Reserve was the first South African wine to be awarded five stars by *Wine Magazine*. At Helderberg in Stellenbosch Anton Bredell initially processes all four grape varieties—Barocca, Souzão, Touriga Nacional, and Francesa—separately, fortifies them with 80% spirits, and blends them only after 18 months of maturation. The 1998 is a seamless continuation of the initial success with high density, concentration, and texture, plus dried fruit, mint, mocha, a great deal of freshness and potential. Further magnificent vintages include 2001, 1997, and 1991.

A selection of the best Cape vintages and fortified wines against the backdrop of Table Mountain.

Calitzdorp has risen to become the South African port capital. Carel Nel from Boplaas praises "the fantastic dry climate, the right grape varieties Touriga Nacional and Tinta Barocca, as well as the winemakers' dedication to producing world class wines." He adheres to the traditional Portuguese methods, and ferments the grapes in open vats for four days before they are matured in old, imported pipes. The result, the Boplaas Vintage Reserve, is a deep, dark port with fresh and dried dark berry and cherry, cocoa, and spice aromas, full bodied, rich in tannins, and very long.

"For a vintage the grapes need to be plump and fully ripened, they must not be allowed to start drying," explains Boets Nel from De Krans. The grapes are stripped and crushed, and the mash is macerated at a low temperature for up to 48 hours. For the vintage he uses all of the pressed juice. For the fortification he uses a mixture of pot still brandy and neutral alcohol, with maturation taking place in large, old barrels; only the tawny is aged in used 130-gallon (500-liter) barrels made from French oak. The vintage is bottled before the end of the second year, only becoming a vintage reserve port in really good years, when its appeal lies in the black berry fruit, dark chocolate, dense peppery tannins, and a great deal of potential.

At their Bergsig estate in the Breede river valley, the Lantegans fortify their Cape Vintage made from Tinta Barocca with a 67% vol. pot still brandy. The resulting wine has a great deal of fullness and length, a pleasant sweetness, and red berry jam, raisin, and cocoa aromas. Allesverloren, where it has been made for 200 years, is located in the Swartland near Riebeek.

For a long time the Malans have been making a convincing port with dense fruit, cocoa, nut, and pepper nuances, as well as a great deal of body.

# Stickies from down under

The Australians love nicknames and these are not limited to people: they apply them to wines as well. For example, they refer to any wines that are white and sweet as *stickies*. For them this term, with its associations of a pleasant stickiness, is a nickname for the wines of which they are particularly fond. Even though a number of late harvests with or without noble rot have joined their ranks over the last 30 years, it was originally only the fortified muscatels and tokays from Rutherglen and Glenrowan that were referred to as stickies.

Muscat blanc à petits grains and Muscadelle, the rare Sauternes variety (referred to as Tokay here), were planted in the northeast of the state of Victoria, where wine growing followed the gold rush of 1850, and have since been used to produce unique fortified wines. The grapes are allowed to raisin on the vines, concentrating the sugar but not the acids, before they are harvested and pressed. While some producers add brandy to the must right away, thus producing a mistelle, others wait for fermentation to start but then fortify early on in order to retain a high degree of residual sugar. The wines are aged in small oak barrels, often for many years, becoming more concentrated due to evaporation, taking on a brown color, and developing their unique character. While muscat retains its characteristic raisin-like aroma, the unique tokay develops tea, toffee, and malt nuances. The well-known producers all originate from the second half of the 19th century, and include Chambers Rosewood of 1858, Morris 1859, Mount Prior 1860, All Saints 1864, Campbells and Baileys 1870,

The Barossa Valley in southern Australia was and is the bastion of *liquid sunshine*, the Australian version of port.

and Stanton & Killeen 1875. Bullers Calliope came later in 1921, with Chris Pfeiffer adopting the tradition of fortified wines in the historic Glenrowan winery in 1984.

## Fortified History

Once wine growing in Australia developed into a very promising industry around the mid 19th century, the step was taken to fortify the wines with spirits in order to make them durable not only for shipping to England and other Commonwealth countries, but also in the hot climate at home. The best results were achieved with the Shiraz, Grenache, and Mataro (Mourvèdre) grape varieties—specifically in South Australia, which rose to become the leading wine-growing state. In the Barossa Valley, developed into a wine center by Silesian immigrants, the Seppelts were among the first to start developing port style wines in 1851, their 1878 Para Liqueur Port, aged in the barrel for a century, becoming a legend. Liquid sunshine, as the tawnies and sherries were referred to, remained in favor until the mid 1960s, making up six out of every ten empty bottles. In the 1970s interest diverted to dry wines, sales of which rose dramatically, while the fortified wines went out of fashion—especially Australian sherry.

Many wineries today produce fortified wines for the domestic market, including the very fruity, young white wines and tawnies aged for different periods, as well as vintages that are usually made from Shiraz only today. In the same way that the Aussies contributed to the rieslings coming back into favor, a number of companies are now actively involved in restoring well-deserved attention to fortified wines.

Such companies include d'Arenberg in McLaren Vale, who, until the 1950s used to make fortified wines exclusively from highly prized Shiraz, now also used for dry red wines. Today Chester d'Arenberg Osborn selects the smallest grapes from the oldest vineyards, which he then has trampled in open fermentation tanks, leaving them as mash for two weeks before pressing them and adding spirits. The exceptionally fruity

vintage is then bottled immediately, with wood maturation. When young its aromas and flavor are characterized by blackberries, mulberries, licorice, and aniseed, possessing plenty of potential.

Grant Burge in the Barossa Valley also feels himself obligated to the fortified wines that both his grandfather and his great-grandfather produced before him. He harvests Grenache, Shiraz, and Mataro by hand, matures the wines oxidatively in a modified solera system, and blends them with wines that are up to 40 years old to produce his 20 Year Old Tawny, rich in nuances and twice nominated as the world's best fortified wine by the specialist magazine *Decanter*.

The Brown Brothers in Milawa, Victoria, produce a variety of different wines, including stickies and other fortified wines.

# Cocktails and other drinks

- Ruffled feathers!
- From highball to pick me up
- Inspirational
- Classic
- Refreshing
- Fruity bowls
- Tropical
- Whimsical
- Invigorating
- Salubrious
- Heated
- Virgin

Measures, abbreviations
and symbols in the recipes
1 cl = 1 centiliter = 10 ml
1 bsp (bar spoon)
= ⅙ oz (0.5 cl)
1 tbsp (tablespoon)
= ½ oz (1.5 cl)
1 dash = 2–3 drops
◄    Far left
◄◄  Far right
▯    Top picture
▮    Bottom picture

French Champagne Cocktail 75
Opposite: Fancy Vanilla Sky
Page 704: Rum Sour

# Ruffled feathers!

Cocktails were around long before the first "American Bar" opened in Manhattan: ancient cultures are also known to have mixed alcoholic beverages. Cocktail culture itself, however, developed in the USA during the second half of the 19th century, made possible by America's melting pot of many immigrants, increasing prosperity, and the availability of products from all over the world. By the 1920s cocktail bars had become an American institution that was soon imitated in Europe and the rest of the world.

"Drank a glass of cocktail—excellent for the head," was the cheerful declaration by an author writing in the *Farmer's Cabinet* on April 28, 1803. This is considered to be the first written mention of the name "cocktail." Just three years later *The Balance and Columbian Repository*, in Hudson, New York, asserted that the cocktail was also ideally suited to election campaigns: "Anyone who can swallow a glass of that will swallow anything."

The origins of the word "cocktail," however, have been lost in the semiobscurity of bar history. It is alleged that feathers from a cock's tail were used as a stirrer or as a warning that the glass contained alcohol—a somewhat unlikely scenario, given the prevalence of spirits in everyday use at that time. Linguists consider the word "cocktail" to be a malapropism of the Latin *decoctus*, meaning watery. Or else, based on the observation that in New Orleans, being originally French, cocktails were enjoyed early on, probably served in very small glasses, it is alleged that the word *coquetier*, the French for egg cup, is the source. A linguistically plausible explanation, at least, is the story of the colonial barkeepers who liked to combine the dregs from their rum and brandy barrels. Since this compromised both the alcoholic content and the taste, such beverages were sold more cheaply. Price-conscious regulars used to request specifically the dregs (the tailings) from the stopcock.

Professor Jerry Thomas published the first book of cocktails in 1862, his legendary *Bartender's Guide or How to Mix Drinks*. This makes mention of Sours, Slings, Flips, and other categories of mixed drinks. More and more Americans were taking to the colorful mixtures on offer in the bars.

The Prohibition of 1920–33 banned the possession of alcohol in any form and so the owners of the speakeasies created mixtures as they saw fit in order to disguise it, but also to be able to make the best use of the hard to come by spirits. It was therefore the Prohibition that gave cocktail bars their first real boost.

Cocktails made more frequent appearances on the bar counters of Europe after World War II. It started with the bars in the grand hotels, but later every small town wanting to make a name for itself had to have a cocktail address. The often exaggerated glamor of the bars had become outdated by the end of the 1980s.

And hence the revival was all the more vibrant. The optimal ratio of tropical fruit juices, spirits, and syrups provides for almost unlimited options. This has long since been recognized by cocktail fans who often create imaginative combinations for themselves and their private audiences. There is no end in sight for the colorful cocktail.

# From highball to pick me up

Although cocktails and mixed drinks are (more or less) just pure pleasure and more especially fun, good bar-keepers take a very serious and precise approach to them. Recipes are laid down with exact quantities and ingredients as the barkeepers love to see their guests' eyes light up when presented with a creative drink, something that they would like to see repeated as often as possible. A successful recipe therefore soon becomes a bar's best-kept secret.

The drinks are divided into groups, the members of which share specific properties. Hence one drink might be a colada because it is dominated by coconut and pineapple juice, another is a fizz because it is always topped with soda or lemonade. The group can also be determined by the spirit upon which the drinks are based. Some of these groups themselves can be put together in categories based on a simple but useful criterion, namely quantity. Drinks that incorporate only a little liquid and fit into a small glass such as a martini glass are called short drinks, sensibly enough. Long drinks are therefore those combinations containing fruit juices or soda that are best suited to filling a voluminous glass. The occasion also determines the category and so various groups can be classified as aperitifs or after-dinner drinks. Of course, some drinks fit into several groups, with new ones being added all the time. What was all the rage in a Caribbean

## Cocktails and their "original recipes"

The first—and not the worst—mixed drinks were served more than 100 years ago.

History-conscious barkeepers proudly offer drinks such as these which have been ennobled by their history. The basis for these recipes is almost always the earliest known mention, but that does not necessarily mean it was the original. What's more, in those days almost all spirits were produced with significantly fewer technical resources and contained considerably more pollutants than those produced today. So anybody offering a classic based on the "original recipe" can never be entirely sure of being able to keep their promise.

bar five years ago has long since become history in a city club today. And so much the better, for every new mix makes it more interesting—even though, when you take a closer look, some of the new appearances are in fact the same as, or very similar to, that which went before. It is therefore worth getting to know a couple of the groups, and this book classifies drinks from classic to trendy, as well as from bitter predinner drinks through to sweet combinations that are ordered after a meal or in the bar adjourned to after the meal. There are several recipes for each group, including typical examples and, more especially, suggestions for trying out these drinks categories and developing them further according to your own taste.

# Inspirational ☖ bitter aperitifs

Talking of "bitter medicine" is hitting the nail right on the head when it comes to the raw ingredients for bitter aperitifs. Most of these herbs, roots, berries, and strips of peel were originally developed as medication. Ship's doctors used quinine to try to get sailors plagued with tropical infections back on their feet. In 1824 Dr. Johann Gottlieb Benjamin Siegert, the doctor with Simon Bolívar's army of freedom fighters in Venezuela, first tried out his bitter composition of 40 herbal extracts on soldiers with fever and stomach problems. The medication, which has become famous as a cocktail ingredient, was named after the town of Angostura where Siegert was stationed and not after the angostura bark, which is not included in the original recipe.

The sailors were quick to realize that they could make the bitter remedy much more pleasant to swallow by adding a little sugar and water and ensuring that they also had an alcoholic beverage to hand at the same time. Most bitters were very high proof but, nevertheless, a drink such as Pink Gin (gin in a glass that had first been wiped out with a few drops of angostura) gained official status in the British navy. Today the dry taste of this bitter aperitif has become a classic before a meal and is a timeless appetite stimulant that periodically reinvents itself. For example, the German Jägermeister brand, with its romantic associations of woodsmen and elderly gentlemen, recently underwent a revival within the heavy metal scene. It was American stars from this set, such as Metallica and Slayer, who discovered the herb liqueur as a party stimulant. The family-owned company from Wolfenbüttel in Germany that had originally developed the bitters recipe for medicinal purposes seized the opportunity and the biannual Jägermeister Music Tour promotes underground heavy metal bands, ensuring that "ice cold Jaeger" has since become an order often heard in American bars.

However, bitters appear much more frequently in mixed drinks. The intense bitter taste is ideal for combining with sweet flavors and sour citrus aromas. A simple Campari with orange juice is considered to be an accomplished aperitif or start to the evening. Many bitters have gone on to become legendary brand names since their invention in the 19th and early 20th centuries. Fernet Branca, Suze or Becherovka, Campari, Cynar, and angostura are known in many countries around the world.

## Negroni

1 oz (3 cl) vermouth rosso
1 oz (3 cl) Campari
1 oz (2–3 cl) gin
Organic lemon peel
Organic orange peel (optional)

Stir together in an aperitif glass with ice cubes. Flavor with 1 piece of lemon peel, garnish with 1 strip of lemon or orange peel.

Variations: False Negroni with spumante instead of gin; Negroski with vodka instead of gin; Straight Up without ice, optionally with lemon juice and soda, top up with cola.

## Columbo

1 oz (3 cl) Campari
4 bsp (2 cl) lime syrup
4 bsp (2 cl) lemon juice
3 tbsp (5 cl) orange juice

Shake together in a cold shaker, strain into a long glass over ice cubes, top up with tonic.

Where did this drink get its name? The inspector of the same name with the creased trench coat from the American TV series would perhaps be able to find out. He himself drank it very seldom.

## ◄◄ Buñueloni

1 oz (3 cl) Punt e Mes
1 oz (3 cl) vermouth bianco
4 bsp (2 cl) gin
Organic lemon and orange peel

Stir together in a small glass. Flavor with 1 piece each of lemon and orange peel. Garnish with zest.

The Spanish director Luis Buñuel swore that he had never spent a day without this aperitif.

## ◄ American Beauty

4 bsp (2 cl) dry vermouth
4 bsp (2 cl) vermouth rosso
3 tbsp (4 cl) brandy
1 dash grenadine
3 tbsp (4 cl) orange juice
Tawny port

Stir in a measuring jug and pour into a chilled cocktail glass, topping with a little tawny port.

The drink will stay cold longer if you place the cocktail glass in a wide glass filled with crushed ice.

# *Inspirational* ♼ *champagne cocktails*

### Champagne Cocktail

1 sugar cube or 1 tsp granulated sugar Angostura Champagne

Place sugar in a champagne glass and add a few drops of angostura. Top up with ice cold champagne.

There are some concoctions that must have been invented in heaven. A champagne cocktail is one of them.

### Kir Royal

2 bsp (1 cl) crème de cassis Ice cold champagne

Pour crème de cassis into a champagne glass. Fill it up with ice cold champagne.

As mayor of Dijon, Felix Kir was a keen advocate of town twinning after World War I. In addition to mending social bridges, he managed to promote a local product beyond his region.

## Bellini

White peaches
1–2 drops lemon juice
Pêche Mignon
Sparkling wine

Remove the skin and pits from the peaches, puree them and add lemon juice and Pêche Mignon according to taste, place in a chilled champagne glass and stir. Top up with ice cold sparkling wine.

This was a house specialty at the legendary Harry's Bar in Venice in the 1940s. Champagne is also extraordinarily good in a Bellini, even though it might cause Giuseppe Cipriani, the head barman, to raise an eyebrow.

## French 75

4 bsp (2 cl) gin
2 bsp (1 cl) lemon juice
1 dash grenadine
1 dash sugar syrup (optional)
Champagne

Shake the first four ingredients together in a shaker with ice cubes and filter into a champagne glass; top up with champagne. Optional: decorate with a Cape gooseberry.

The name French 75 almost certainly refers to a French artillery cannon, the firepower of which played an important role in the 1918 Ausonne offensive during World War I. Kaiser Wilhelm's empire became history a few months later.

# Inspirational ♼ Manhattan

The Manhattan is always to be found at the top of the menu in a classic cocktail bar. A loner, dry, bitter, puritan, timeless. It is likely that the majority of guests who ordered it were men. Orders have now become more infrequent with the increasing popularity of tropical drinks. The Manhattan recently underwent a revival as one of the favorite drinks of Carrie Bradshaw (Sarah Jessica Parker), star of the television series *Sex and the City*, symbolizing her love of Manhattan life. Drinks were already being prepared with the typical ingredients in the latter half of the 19th century in New York, where, on September 5, 1882, the *Democrat* newspaper stated that every barkeeper in town knew the recipe. Where exactly it was mixed for the first time remains a subject of debate among cocktail historians. Perhaps it was in 1874 in the Manhattan Club in New York, at a banquet attended by Jennie Churchill, later the mother of Winston Churchill. The former party girl is alleged to have been pregnant at the time. Does that explain Sir Winston's penchant for a good drink?

Either way, drinks containing the Manhattan ingredients first appeared in New York City and consequently later acquired the name Manhattan.

A number of other whiskey combinations also go back to the early days of cocktails. With their whiskey character they are often very bitter, this often being offset by sweet components, meaning it no longer fits in with current flavor trends. Many of the big names therefore slumber away in the "Classics" chapter of cocktail books, awaiting their renaissance.

The issue of the one and only true recipe soon leads to a clash with the purists. There was certainly more than one "original recipe," and it is highly likely that none of them is the historically correct one. Today there are numerous dry (with more or less vermouth) and sweet versions. The Manhattan has also been a source of inspiration for many new drinks, including Rob Roy with Scotch, Cuban Manhattan with dark rum, Florida Manhattan with lime juice instead of angostura, Latin Manhattan with white rum and Maraschino, and Sake Manhattan with sake instead of vermouth.

## New Orleans Sazerac

| | |
|---|---|
| 1 bsp granulated sugar | Place the sugar in a tumbler, |
| Angostura | add a couple of drops of |
| 2 oz (6 cl) bourbon | angostura and ice cubes. Pour |
| 2 bsp (1 cl) pastis | in bourbon and pastis, add |
| Organic lemon peel | lemon peel, stir, and top up |
| | with a shot of ice cold water. |

Sazeracs are among the oldest of cocktails, first served in 1859 at the opening of the Sazerac Coffee House in New Orleans.

## Old Fashioned

| | |
|---|---|
| 1 bsp granulated sugar | Place the first four ingredients |
| A few drops of angostura | in a large tumbler ("Old |
| 3 organic lemon wedges | Fashioned Glass") and press |
| 3 organic orange slices | down with a plunger. Add |
| 2 oz (6 cl) bourbon | some bourbon, stir, add ice |
| | cubes, top up with water, and |
| | garnish with 1 cocktail cherry. |

##  Manhattan

| | |
|---|---|
| 3 tbsp (5 cl) | Stir the first two ingredients |
| Canadian whiskey | together and add the angos- |
| 1 oz (2.5 cl) vermouth rosso | tura in a mixing glass with lots |
| 1–2 drops angostura | of ice cubes. Pour into a |
| | chilled cocktail glass and stir. |
| | Garnish with 1 cocktail cherry. |

This is the favorite drink of the International Bartenders Association (IBA).

##  Whiskey Sangaree

| | |
|---|---|
| 2 bsp (1 cl) granulated sugar | Dissolve the sugar in a tumb- |
| 2 oz (6 cl) rye or bourbon | ler of water, add the rye or |
| Soda | bourbon and ice cubes. Stir |
| 1 tbsp (1.5 cl) port | and top up with soda, float |
| | port on top, and sprinkle with |
| | a little grated nutmeg. |

# Classic ♼ sours

The question as to choice is answered by the barkeeper handing over a list the size of a small town telephone directory. Anyone who is unable to make decisions will have a hard time. Ordering a classic—i.e. a drink with a well-known name that you have heard or read somewhere—is therefore a good solution. It also makes it easy to tell whether the barkeeper knows what he is doing because a classic, which comprises only a few ingredients, has to be concocted and mixed with a great deal of precision. Light, dry drinks are usually best suited to the start of the evening or before a meal. The opulent sweet drinks put in an appearance later. If you stick to the drinks in this chapter you can't go wrong.

## Gin Sour

3 tbsp (4 cl) gin
4 bsp (2 cl) lemon juice
1 tbsp (1.5 cl) sugar syrup

Shake together in a shaker and filter into a small goblet with ice cubes. Garnish with 1 cocktail cherry.

## Whiskey Sour

3 tbsp (4 cl) bourbon
4 bsp (2 cl) lemon juice
1 tbsp (1.5 cl) sugar syrup

Shake in a shaker and filter into a small goblet with ice cubes. Garnish with 2 cocktail cherries.

## Rum Sour

| | |
|---|---|
| 3 tbsp (4 cl) dark rum | Shake in a shaker and filter |
| 4 bsp (2 cl) lemon juice | into a small goblet with ice |
| 4 bsp (2 cl) curaçao | cubes. Garnish with 1 cocktail |
| | cherry. |

## Pisco Sour

| | |
|---|---|
| 3 tbsp (4 cl) pisco | Shake together in a shaker |
| 4 bsp (2 cl) lemon juice | and filter into a small goblet |
| 1–2 drops angostura | with ice cubes. Garnish with 1 |
| according to taste | cocktail cherry. |
| 1 tbsp (1.5 cl) sugar syrup | |

A sour can be seen as the ancestor of many of today's well-known mixed drinks. Spirits, sugar, something sour—that's it. Famous drinks such as the Margarita, White Lady, Daiquiri, and Sidecar are basically sours and, apart from the fact that ice cubes were added later to give them a frosty touch, the ingredients remain the same today.

The sweet component can be provided by a syrup such as grenadine or by a liqueur such as triple sec. In terms of the "hard tack," there is hardly any high-proof spirit that is not suited to a sour. The list of recipes is therefore correspondingly long. About 2 oz (6 cl) of the basis spirit is mixed with 1 oz (3 cl) of the sweet component and 1 tbsp (1.5 cl) of lemon or lime juice. The propor-

tions vary with every drink. Gin has a different effect compared to rum, an American whiskey behaves differently from Scotch. The proportions are therefore best adjusted by tasting the concoction after mixing.

Despite the endless variations, some sours have managed to achieve lasting fame. A prime example is the sour made from pisco which goes especially well with fresh lemon juice and a few drops of bitters. The softness of brandy is used in a Brandy Daisy, for example. In tropical regions it is often sweetened with curaçao. The Whiskey Sour is a traditional southern states drink in the USA because the slight sweetness of the robust Tennessee whiskey is especially well suited to it.

# *Classic martinis and gin drinks*

Gin, vast amounts of which were consumed by 17th and 18th century Londoners, was not always the clean spirit with the juniper aroma that we know today. It was coarse hard liquor due to impurities and the inadequate separation of the pure distillate from the unusable elements. The addition of sweeteners and fruit was therefore needed to make the spirit drinkable and gave rise to the early combinations that later developed into classic cocktail recipes.

The martini is the most famous of all, and there is hardly any other name that is more closely associated with the sophisticated world of bars and luxury hotels. As is so often the case, its origins are obscure but the theory that the drink, which used to be somewhat sweeter, originated in the small town of Martinez is plausible. The citizens of this small Californian town seem to agree and they themselves have erected a commemorative plaque for the martini.

The martini appeared in a cocktail book as early as 1862 but it was during the American Prohibition that it really gained in popularity. During this crisis era whiskey, which needs to be matured for a number of years, became a lot more difficult to acquire than gin—which could be produced using primitive "bathtub" equipment. The gin/vodka concoction has been declared the favorite drink of American movie stars, as well as writers and politicians, time and again. The list extends from Franklin D. Roosevelt to Truman Capote and from Cary Grant to Robert Oppenheimer.

The martini has become so synonymous with the cocktail that the conical stemware cocktail glass is often simply referred to as a martini glass. The society critic Henry Louis Mencken once called the martini "the only American invention, the perfection of which is comparable to a sonnet."

**Alexander**

3 tbsp (4 cl) cream
1 oz (3 cl) gin
4 bsp (2 cl) crème de cacao

Thoroughly shake in a shaker, filter into a cocktail glass and sprinkle with a little nutmeg.

## Martini Cocktail

| | |
|---|---|
| 5 tbsp (8 cl) gin | Stir together in a mixing glass |
| 4 bsp (2 cl) dry vermouth | with ice cubes until the glass |
| | becomes frosted. Alternatively, |
| | place the cocktail glass in the |
| | refrigerator beforehand. |
| | Garnish with whole olives. |

Eccentrics allow themselves olives filled with almonds.

## Parisienne

| | |
|---|---|
| 4 bsp (2 cl) Noilly Prat | Stir together with ice and filter |
| 4 bsp (2 cl) gin | into a cocktail glass. Garnish |
| 1–2 drops crème de cassis | with an olive. |

For a more sophisticated version, pour the crème de cassis into the cocktail glass first, then add the clear ingredients. Guests are then able to mix the two layers themselves using a cocktail stick.

The British James Bond also had a significant input to the topic of martinis, always insisting that his martini be "shaken, not stirred." In the opinion of professional barkeepers that is precisely the wrong way round. In principle two clear spirits are always stirred. Shaking dilutes the drink and makes it unattractively cloudy. Nevertheless, the fictional figure ensured an ongoing discussion about the ratio of the ingredients and the technique. It achieved the status of scientific research a while ago. Biochemists at the University of Western Ontario claim to have established that a shaken martini contains significantly more antioxidants. These results might therefore be an explanation for James Bond's impressively robust state of health.

The correct ratio of vermouth to gin is the subject of endless debate, with the vermouth component having become smaller and smaller. Winston Churchill liked his gin to be ice cold and while drinking it he did no more than cast a glance at the bottle of vermouth. Our version is semidry but you can modify it to create your own recipe.

# Classic ❦ multitalents

### Earthquake

|   |   |
|---|---|
| 1 part absinthe<br>1 part brandy | Combine in a cold mixing glass. Serve in a large goblet with ice cubes. |

The drink stands up to its name. It is recommended that you temper it with a little water and sugar.

### Strawberry Margarita

| | |
|---|---|
| 3 tbsp (5 cl) tequila<br>3 tbsp (5 cl) triple sec<br>1 oz (2.5 cl) lime juice<br>2 oz (50 g) strawberries, fresh or deep frozen | Puree the ingredients with ice in a blender. Depending on the ripeness of the fruit, sweeten with confectioners' sugar or strawberry syrup. Pour into a cocktail glass. Garnish with 1 strawberry on the rim. |

## Bahía

| | |
|---|---|
| 1 oz (3 cl) white rum | Thoroughly shake in a shaker. |
| 3 tbsp (4 cl) pineapple juice | Filter into a tumbler of |
| 2 bsp (1 cl) coconut syrup | crushed ice, and garnish with |
| 1 oz (3 cl) coconut cream | a piece of pineapple and |
| 1 oz (3 cl) sweetened cream | cocktail cherries. |

## Thug Passion

| | |
|---|---|
| 2 oz (6 cl) Alizé | Stir Alizé in a cold mixing |
| 2 oz (6 cl) champagne | glass, filter into a narrow champagne flute, and top up with champagne. |

The concoction was the rapper 2Pac's favorite drink and he even dedicated one of his songs to it. The singer himself used Roederer Crystal for the sparkle and always had some available at home because he promoted it in his fan shop. If you find its retail price of € 250 for one bottle to be a bit much, you can of course use a different sparkling wine.

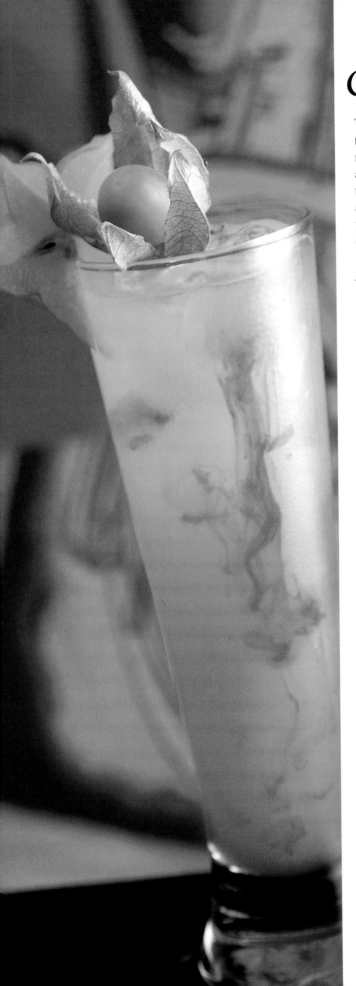

# Classic 🍸 vodka

The emergence of *mixed drinks* in the USA and England toward the middle of the 19th century brought with it numerous recipes using gin, rum, and whiskey. Bitters and vermouth, imported from Italy and France, were the trendy drinks of the time and included rare specialties among them. Vodka remained an outsider at first, the potato and grain liquor only asserting itself in the 20th century but then all the more dominantly. Its neutral taste meant it was the obvious choice for any kind of fruit juice, as well as for bitters, liqueur, and lemonade. Vodka, which is especially pure and mild due to activated carbon filtering, is a spirit that suits almost any ingredient used in a bar and is to be found in the proximity of any drink dominated by fruit and fruit juices. Its rise was so rapid that, following World War II, it soon overtook all other spirits on the American market. The United States remain the world's largest vodka consumers today. Even during the cold war it made no difference that vodka was popular in communist Russia. In order to make it clear that it was a US product—made from American grain—the later market leader Smirnov promptly changed its name to Smirnoff and used the advertising slogan: "Smirnoff White Whiskey. No Taste. No Smell."
Despite its late start, vodka still managed to have a number of classics make it on to bar menus around the world, often stealing ground from its older competitors in the process. Drinks that were originally made with gin have since become popular with vodka as well. Cocktails with names such as Vodkatini, Negroski, Caipirovka, and Vodka Gimlet speak volumes.

## Sea Breeze

| | |
|---|---|
| 2 oz (6 cl) vodka | Shake the vodka, cranberry |
| 3 tbsp (4 cl) cranberry juice | juice, and grapefruit juice |
| 2 oz (6 cl) grapefruit juice | together on ice. Filter into a |
| 1 Cape gooseberry | tall glass filled with ice, |
| 1 slice of star fruit | garnish with the fruit, and add |
| 1 shot of cranberry juice | the cranberry juice. |

## Gibson Vodka

3 tbsp (5 cl) vodka
1 dash of dry vermouth
Pearl onions

Stir the vodka and vermouth in a mixing glass with plenty of ice. Filter into a chilled cocktail glass. Pearl onions in the glass are the hallmark of this drink.

## White Russian

3 tbsp (4 cl) vodka
1 oz (2.5 cl) Kahlúa or another coffee liqueur
Lightly whipped cream
Coffee or cocoa for garnishing (optional)

Stir the vodka and Kahlúa well in a mixing glass with ice cubes. Filter into a cocktail glass and add cream. Garnish with a little coffee or cocoa according to taste.

## White Russian

The White Russian owes its name solely to the vodka element. Nevertheless, it is a very popular drink in the USA and is inextricably linked with pop culture. For example, the character The Dude played by Jeff Bridges "swims" through the cult movie *The Big Lebowski* with one. The British band Marillion dedicated a song to the drink in 1987. White Russian drinkers are experimenters and risk takers.

Here are just a few of the variations in existence:

Colorado Bulldog   with vanilla vodka and cola
White Trash        with whiskey instead of vodka
Gay Russian        with cherry brandy instead of Kahlúa
KGB                with high proof vodka
Anna Kournikova    with skimmed milk
Blonde Russian     with Irish Cream instead of cream
Cocaine Lady       with peppermint liqueur and milk
Colin Powell       with cocoa
Van Halen Special  with amaretto and rum

## Pimm's No 19

4 bsp (2 cl) vodka
4 bsp (2 cl) Pimm's
4 bsp (2 cl) Galliano
Ginger ale
Cucumber for garnishing

Pour the vodka, Pimm's, and Galliano into a tumbler with ice cubes, stir and top up with ginger ale. Garnish with cucumber.

# Classic ⅋ shooters and short drinks

Be it a conservative club or a wild techno location, even though the drinks served might be different, a shooter is drunk at every bar sooner or later. The quick kick is simply a must. Shooters are often ordered by groups and ensure a party atmosphere in next to no time. The names of the shooters are a graphic illustration of both the objective and the effect: Aftershock, Kamikaze, Gorilla Fart, Four Horsemen. The orders are as diverse as the guests, and some of them are very witty.

A shooter and a beer to wash it down is a popular order going by the name of Boilermaker or Car Bomb. A lot depends on the spirits used: the explosive mixture can become an Irish Car Bomb if there is Irish Whiskey in the liqueur glass. The different varieties possible have

had the real experimenters drinking two at a time. A tradition observed in many countries is the Submarine (photo left) that has a liqueur placed in a large filled beer mug. True fans empty the mug in one go and then wait to see what happens. Different spirits are used depending on the locality. Jägermeister (also known as Jäger-bomb) is popular, while vodka is more of a classic, allegedly from Poland. Modern versions have the shooter immersed into Red Bull (Flying Deer). The heaviest weapon, the Nuclear Submarine, goes to anyone who can down the quantities in the reverse ratio with a small beer immersed in a large liqueur.

## Tequila Slammer

part tequila
part tonic or lemonade
Seven Up, ginger ale)

ombine the tequila and tonic or lemo-
ade (Seven Up, ginger ale), cover with a
eer mat and slam down onto the table.

mple, but effective.

## Lemon Drop

Lemon juice for rim
Sugar
1 tbsp (1.5 cl) lemon vodka
1 tbsp (1.5 cl) lemon juice

Dip the rim of a liqueur glass in lemon juice first and then in sugar. Fill the glass with the lemon vodka and lemon juice.

As in many drinks, the alcohol is tamed by the sweetness or the fruity acid.

## Gold Rush

1 tbsp (1.5 cl) dark tequila
1 tbsp (1.5 cl) Danziger Goldwasser

Combine the ingredients to produce an upmarket shooter with a touch of glamour.

Still a shooter, but one with style.

# *Classic* 🍸 *legends*

## Pimm's No 1

3 tbsp (5 cl) Pimm's
Seven Up
Cucumber for garnishing

Fill a large tumbler with
crushed ice. Add the
Pimm's, top up with
Seven Up, and garnish
with cucumber.

## Ritz

4 bsp (2 cl) orange juice
4 bsp (2 cl) cognac
1 tbsp (1.5 cl) Cointreau
Champagne
Grape and orange for
garnishing

Shake the orange juice,
cognac, and Cointreau in
a shaker, filter into a
champagne glass, and
top up with champagne.
Garnish with a slice of
grape and a slice of
orange.

## Sidecar

3 tbsp (4 cl) cognac
4 bsp (2 cl) Cointreau
4 bsp (2 cl) lemon juice
Orange and lemon wedges
for garnishing

Shake the cognac,
Cointreau, and lemon
juice well in a shaker
and filter into a small
goblet with ice cubes.
Garnish with orange
and lemon wedges.

## Tipperary

3 tbsp (4.5 cl) Irish whiskey
1 oz (3 cl) vermouth bianco
1 tbsp (1.5 cl) Chartreuse
(green)
1 cocktail cherry for garnishing

Combine the Irish
whiskey, vermouth
bianco, and green
Chartreuse over ice
cubes and filter into a
cocktail glass. Garnish
with the cocktail cherry.

# Refreshing ♼ classic long drinks

A long drink has two obvious advantages that significantly reduce the risk of drinking too much alcohol at the bar too early in the evening. It contains less alcohol in relation to many short drinks and comprises a relatively large quantity of water or juice. Understandably, highballs soon became one of the most ordered drinks. Creating a highball itself is child's play as the simplest combinations are based on one part spirits with three to five parts lemonade or juice. It was this simple recipe that brought rapid fame to the Cuba Libre, the Screwdriver, and the like.

A *Time Magazine* reporter made an interesting observation in the bar of the New York Park Hotel on October 24, 1949. He saw Balkan refugees, American engineers, and Turkish secret service agents interacting peacefully with one another over a long drink, discreetly stirring the orange juice and vodka mixture with a screwdriver. In the 1970s the Screwdriver was considered the healthiest of alcoholic drinks due to its high Vitamin C content. The officers of the British East India Company praised the gin and tonic combination for its medicinal effects for their staff. Long drinks have continued their rise to fame in almost all inhabited areas, including those that have still to be explored—such as outer space in *The Hitchhiker's Guide to the Galaxy*, where gin and tonic puts in an infinite range of appearances. The classics in this category include the following four long drinks.

# Long Island Ice Tea

4 bsp (2 cl) white rum
4 bsp (2 cl) vodka
4 bsp (2 cl) tequila
4 bsp (2 cl) gin
4 bsp (2 cl) triple sec
2 drops lime juice
Cola
Slice of lemon

Shake the first six ingredients in a shaker. Filter into a tall glass with plenty of ice and top up with cola. The ingredients can vary. A sweet mix is often added in the USA, elsewhere a sour mix. A slice of lemon on the rim alludes to tea.

# Prince of Wales

1 sugar cube (or 1 bsp sugar)
1 dash of angostura
1 oz (2.5 cl) cognac
2 bsp (1 cl) Bénédictine
2 orange quarters
1 cocktail cherry
Champagne or sparkling wine

Soak the sugar cube in a dash of angostura in a large glass. Add the cognac and Bénédictine, top up with crushed ice, then add the orange quarters and cocktail cherry, finishing with champagne or sparkling wine.

The Prince of Wales is one of the few examples of a mixed drink with the perfect balance between bitter, sweet, and sour that retains the noble taste of its high-quality ingredients.

# Hurricane

4 bsp (2 cl) white rum
1 oz (3 cl) dark rum
2 bsp (1 cl) pineapple juice
2 bsp (1 cl) lemon juice
2 oz (6 cl) maracuja juice
2 bsp (1 cl) sugar-cane syrup
Citrus peel for garnishing

Thoroughly shake all of the ingredients in a shaker. Filter into a hurricane glass with crushed ice, and garnish with citrus peel.

The sailors in the French quarter of New Orleans knew how to cope with tropical cyclones. The regulars took the Hurricane so much to heart that today it is even available in instant powder form.

# Singapore Sling

3 tbsp (4 cl) gin
1 tbsp (1.5 cl) cherry liqueur
2 bsp (1 cl) Bénédictine
4 bsp (2 cl) lime juice
1 tbsp (1.5 cl) sugar syrup
Soda
Cocktail cherries

Stir the first five ingredients together in a cold mixing glass. Filter into a tall glass with crushed ice, top up with soda, and garnish with cocktail cherries.

After 1915 anyone who has not enjoyed a Singapore Sling at the Long Bar in the Raffles Hotel is regarded as not having been to Singapore.

# Refreshing ❦ highballs

### Horse's Neck

| | |
|---|---|
| 3 tbsp (4 cl) brandy | Pour the brandy into an Old |
| 7 tbsp (11 cl) ginger ale | Fashioned glass with ice cubes, |
| 1 dash of angostura | stir, and top up with ginger ale, |
| Lemon peel for | adding a dash of angostura |
| garnishing (optional) | according to taste. Garnish with |
| | lemon peel if liked. |

A drink with a name as unusual as its history, it first appeared in the 1890s as a soft drink. The first brandy versions had appeared by 1910, as had those with bourbon and rye, ultimately displacing the alcohol-free versions.

▼

### Harvey Wallbanger

▲

| | |
|---|---|
| 3 tbsp (5 cl) vodka | Pour the vodka and orange |
| 8 tbsp (12 cl) | juice into a tall glass with |
| orange juice | ice and stir. Add a shot of |
| 1 shot of Galliano | Galliano, stirring briefly. |

According to legend, Harvey was a Californian surfer. Following a lost competition he consoled himself in Duke's Blackwatch Bar in Hollywood with this sophisticated Screwdriver. Of course he did not stick to one, and Harvey banged into the walls on his way out. The rest is bar history. Whenever elections are held in the United States a significant proportion of spoiled votes are for a certain Harvey Wallbanger.

## Cuba Libre

| | |
|---|---|
| 3 tbsp (5 cl) white rum | Pour the white rum and cola |
| 3 oz (10 cl) cola | into a tall glass with ice. Stir |
| 1 dash of lime juice | and add a dash of lime juice. |
| Slices of lime | Add some lime slices to the |
| | glass and the most famous |
| | drink in the world is ready. |

The name does not derive from the socialist revolution of 1959, however. Legend has it that the drink was invented by soldiers in a bar in Havana drinking to the "liberation" of Cuba during the Spanish–American wars of the 1900s. Since both at that time and later original Coca-Cola was not available in Cuba, lemonade would have been an original component.

▼

▲

## Sex on the Beach

| | |
|---|---|
| 3 tbsp (4 cl) vodka | Stir the vodka, Pêche |
| 4 bsp (2 cl) Pêche Mignon | Mignon, and orange |
| 3 tbsp (4 cl) orange juice | juice together in a |
| 3 tbsp (4 cl) cranberry juice | Highball glass with |
| Cranberries | ice. Top up with the |
| | cranberry juice and |
| | garnish with the fruit. |

There is no need to ask which came first, the drink or the name. However, whether it is named after the famous scene in the movie *From Here to Eternity* (USA 1953), after the summer hit by the pop group T-Spoon, or after a leisure activity that is illegal in many countries remains open to debate.

# Refreshing fizzes & Collinses

A fizz has an extra portion of soda compared to a sour and is often served in bars with lemon or lime juice. It is the somewhat spiced-up version of the sour. The term "fizz" first appeared at the end of the 19th century when carbonated water became more readily available. The fizzing element makes the drink livelier and softer. The ingredients are easily available and it is merely a question of the mix ratio. A fizz is considered to be a refreshing drink during the day as well as later. Like sours, the fizzes' appeal derives from the clarity of their ingredients. There is one prominent spirit instead of an endless row of homogeneous forms of alcohol, which is then combined with the classic ingredients of sugar, citrus fruit, and water. There is no hiding anything behind a dominant ingredient here. A fizz made from cheap gin will taste cheap.

The Gin Fizz is the most well-known member of the family. This may be due to the fact that it goes exceptionally well with the lemon and soda combination, as is proved by the many variations such as the Silver Fizz with egg white, the Golden Fizz with egg yolk, and the Diamond Fizz with sparkling wine instead of soda.

## Gin Fizz

| | |
|---|---|
| 3 tbsp (5 cl) gin | Shake the gin, lemon |
| 1 oz (3 cl) lemon juice | juice, and sugar syrup in |
| 4 bsp (2 cl) sugar syrup | a shaker with ice. Filter |
| Soda | into a tall glass half |
| | filled with crushed ice |
| | and top up with soda. |

## Ramos Gin Fizz

| | |
|---|---|
| 3 tbsp (4 cl) gin | Thoroughly shake the |
| 1 tbsp (1.5 cl) sugar syrup | first five ingredients in a |
| 1 egg white | shaker. Filter into a tall |
| 4 bsp (2 cl) cream | glass with ice cubes and |
| Dash of fleur d'orange | top up with soda. |
| Soda | |

Collinses (also known as cobblers) are close relatives of the fizzes. Their ingredients are not shaken but are stirred in the glass and then usually topped up with a little more soda, making them ideally suited to hot summer afternoons. No family of drinks has as expansive a list of relatives as the Collinses.

Here is the family saga in brief:

| | |
|---|---|
| Jack Collins | with calvados |
| Tom Collins | with gin |
| Sandy / Jock Collins | with scotch |
| John Collins | with rye whiskey |
| Mike Collins | named after the Irish revolutionary leader and later Finance Minister, Michael Collins |
| Captain Collins | with Canadian whisky |
| Colonel Collins | with bourbon |
| Pedro Collins | with white rum |
| Ron Collins | with dark rum |
| Pisco Collins | with pisco |
| José Collins | with tequila |
| Comrade Collins | with vodka |
| Brandy Collins | with brandy |
| Pierre Collins | with cognac |
| Phil Collins | with tequila, Irish whisky, vodka, rum, and beer. |

## Jack Collins

3 tbsp (4 cl) calvados
4 bsp (2 cl) lemon juice
4 bsp (2 cl) sugar syrup
Soda
Lemon peel for garnishing
1 cocktail cherry for garnishing (optional)

Stir the calvados, lemon juice, and sugar syrup in a tall glass with ice cubes and top up with soda. Garnish with a strip of lemon peel and a cocktail cherry according to taste.

## Tom Collins

3 tbsp (4 cl) gin
4 bsp (2 cl) lemon juice
1 tbsp (1.5 cl) sugar syrup
Soda
Lemon peel for garnishing
1 cocktail cherry for garnishing (optional)

Stir the gin, lemon juice, and sugar syrup in a tall glass with ice cubes and top up with soda. Garnish with a strip of lemon peel and a cocktail cherry according to taste.

# Refreshing 🍸 fizzes

## Morning Glory Fizz

3 tbsp (5 cl) scotch
1 oz (2.5 cl) lemon juice
4 bsp (2 cl) sugar syrup
1 egg white
1 shot of pastis
Soda
Lemon or berries for garnishing

Thoroughly shake the first five ingredients in a shaker with ice. Filter into a tall glass with ice cubes and top up with soda. Garnish with lemon and/or berries.

## Chicago Fizz

1 oz (3 cl) white rum
1 oz (3 cl) port
4 bsp (2 cl) lemon juice
2 bsp (1 cl) sugar syrup
Soda
Lemon and/or berries for garnishing

Shake the first four ingredients in a shaker with ice. Filter into a tall glass with ice cubes and top up with soda. Garnish with lemon and/or berries.

## Sloe Gin Fizz

3 tbsp (4 cl) sloe gin
4 bsp (2 cl) lemon juice
1 tbsp (1.5 cl) sugar syrup
Soda
Lemon and/or berries for garnishing

Thoroughly shake the sloe gin, lemon juice, and sugar syrup in a shaker. Filter into a tumbler with ice cubes and top up with soda. Garnish with lemon and/or berries.

Sloe gin is a gin liqueur made with sloes.

## Green Fizz

3 tbsp (4 cl) gin
1 shot of crème de menthe
4 bsp (2 cl) lemon juice
4 bsp (2 cl) sugar syrup
Soda

Shake the first four ingredients in a shaker with ice. Filter into a tumbler with ice cubes and top up with soda.

The mint liqueur makes the drink all the more refreshing.

# Refreshing 🍸 daisies and crustas

Daisies and crustas are XXXL-size drinks. They need big glasses with lots of ice, lots of liquid, and lots of alcohol. These refreshments should not be underestimated, therefore. Traditionally, they are made with gin or brandy plus lemon juice and sugar. The crusta has a sugared rim as an additional feature.

## Gin Daisy

2 oz (6 cl) gin
4 bsp (2 cl) lemon juice
4 bsp (2 cl) grenadine
Soda
Preserved morello cherries for garnishing

Shake the gin, lemon juice, and grenadine in a shaker and filter into a large glass of crushed ice. Top up with soda and garnish with cherries.

## Applejack Daisy

3 tbsp (4.5 cl) calvados
1 oz (3 cl) brandy
3 tbsp (4.5 cl) lemon juice
2 bsp (1 cl) sugar syrup
1 tbsp (1.5 cl) grenadine
Cocktail cherries for garnishing

Thoroughly shake the first five ingredients in a shaker and pour over crushed ice cubes in an Old Fashioned glass. Garnish with cocktail cherries.

## Gin Crusta

Lemon juice and sugar
for the rim
2 oz (6 cl) gin
4 bsp (2 cl) lemon juice
4 bsp (2 cl) triple sec
2 bsp (1 cl) maraschino
1 strip lemon peel for
garnishing

Moisten the rim of a large
tumbler with lemon juice
and then dip in sugar.
Carefully shake off the
loose sugar. Fill the glass
two thirds full with crushed
ice.
Shake the gin, lemon juice,
triple sec, and maraschino
in a shaker with ice. Carefully pour into the glass.
Serve with a strip of lemon
peel and a straw.

## Whiskey Crusta

Lime juice and brown sugar
for the rim
1 cocktail cherry
2 oz (6 cl) bourbon
4 bsp (2 cl) lime juice
4 bsp (2 cl) sugar-cane syrup

Moisten the rim of a large
tumbler with lime juice, and
then dip in brown sugar. Place
a cocktail cherry in the glass
and fill it two thirds full with
crushed ice. Shake the bourbon, lime juice, and sugar-
cane syrup in a shaker with
ice. Carefully pour into the
glass and serve with a straw.

Bourbon is perhaps best suited to this drink, not least because the
first crustas were almost certainly stirred in the southern states.

# Refreshing ♼ juleps and smashes

Anybody serving a tray full of juleps at a party need not worry about creating a party atmosphere. Fresh mint and the exotic smoky sweetness of bourbon add a touch of *Gone with the Wind* and southern states romance to any summer party. The first julep was probably mixed in Virginia in the 18th century, becoming such a cultural asset that it was proudly presented in Washington in the 1850s by a senator named Henry Clay.

The word *julep* allegedly derives from the Arabic *julap* or the Persian *gulap*, and means rose water. How the term made its way from the Orient into American bar culture remains a mystery, however.

The Mint Julep is still a permanent feature of southern states culture today and is therefore one of the official drinks served at the sophisticated Kentucky Derby, where an astounding 120,000 glasses of the cocktail were ordered in 2007, using more than a ton/tonne of crushed fresh mint. In 2006 guests paid US $1,000 for the luxury version that comprised mint imported from Ireland, Australian sugar, ice from the Bavarian Alps, and a generous shot of Woodford Reserve bourbon. The profits were used to pay for the upkeep of retired race horses. The Mint Julep is featured in *The Great Gatsby*, the sociocritical novel by F. Scott Fitzgerald written in 1925, during the American Prohibition. Ray Charles, Homer Simpson, Bob Dylan, and the Beastie Boys have also paid homage to it. Goldfinger sang its praises to James Bond as "very palatable." A native of the southern states, Dr. Leonard Horatio McCoy, played by DeForest Kelly, surgeon on board the spaceship *Enterprise*, even mixed his favorite drink in space, despite Mister Spock's raising his flexible eyebrows in surprise.

Juleps are always made with freshly crushed mint leaves and then stirred in the glass together with crushed ice, while bourbon and cane sugar are also usually added. The garnish comprises not fruit but a sprig of mint.

A smash is very similar to a julep, but is prepared in a shaker and can be decorated with a lot of fruit. It also has a shot of soda added to it, making it even more refreshing and therefore all the more suited to daytime summer temperatures.

## Champagne Julep

3 tbsp (4 cl) brandy
1 bsp sugar
Mint leaves
Champagne
Sprig of mint as garnish

Place the first three ingredients in a tumbler and gently crush the mint leaves—the mint is only intended to emphasize the freshness of the champagne. Add some crushed ice, top up with champagne, stir briefly, and garnish with a sprig of mint.

## Mint Julep

Leaves from 1 sprig fresh mint
1 bsp demerara sugar
A little water or dark sugar syrup
2 oz (6 cl) bourbon
Mint leaves for garnish

Gently crush the mint leaves. Place the first three ingredients in a tumbler, top up with the bourbon and with crushed ice, stir, and garnish with a couple of mint leaves.

## Tequila Smash

3 kumquats, halved
3 tbsp (5 cl) tequila
1 tbsp (1.5 cl) lime juice
1 tbsp (1.5 cl) maraschino
Soda

Place the kumquats in a tall glass and crush gently with a pestle. Fill the glass half full with crushed ice. Shake the tequila, lime juice, and maraschino in a shaker and add to glass, topping up with soda.

A smash comprises a spirit, sugar, soda, and a flavoring ingredient that, due to its kinship with the julep, is usually mint. A sweet liqueur can be used instead of sugar and fruit instead of mint.

## Mojito

A few mint leaves
Juice of ½ lime
1 bsp sugar (or demerara sugar according to taste)
½ lime squeezed and cut into quarters
2 oz (6 cl) white rum
Soda

Crush the mint with a pestle. Place the first three ingredients in a tumbler. Add the squeezed lime quarters. Top up with the white rum and crushed ice. Stir and float with a shot of soda. Garnish with a sprig of mint.

The Mojito was invented in Cuba and is perhaps no more than a modification of the Mint Juleps ordered by US Prohibition refugees during their excursions to Havana.

# *Fruity* 🍸 *bowls*

Fruit is normally used to garnish cocktails and, ideally, it should be esthetic but not over the top, somewhat chic but a secondary detail in most cases. The drinks in this chapter, however, are among the key players. They vary according to the time of year and are ideally suited to summer parties, including those starting in the afternoon.

The term "bowl" came into use in the 18th century. In addition to an inexpensive sparkling wine, white wine—preferably a very dry one—is used as it offsets the sweetness of the fruit. The fruit is soaked in the white wine the day before and absorbs plenty of alcohol. One special variation is the May Wine Bowl—also known as a

### Balaclava

25 oz (75 cl) red Bordeaux
1 cucumber, thinly sliced
Juice of 2 lemons
5 bsp (2.5 cl) sugar syrup
½ organic lemon, thinly pared
A few lemon balm leaves
1 block of ice made from
about 2 pints (1 liter) water
25 oz (75 cl) mineral water
25 oz (75 cl) sparkling wine

Combine the first four ingredients in a bowl. Suspend a sieve containing the lemon peel and the lemon balm in the bowl and leave to infuse in the refrigerator for 1 hour. Remove the sieve. Add the block of ice to chill it, and add the mineral water and sparkling wine.

### Pineapple Cooler

25 oz (75 cl) Sauternes
or a similar sweet white wine
Juice of 1 lemon
8 oz (25 cl) pineapple juice
1 oz (3 cl) sugar syrup
9 oz (250 g) pineapple pieces
Dry sparkling wine

Combine the first five ingredients and leave to infuse in the refrigerator overnight. Top up with chilled dry sparkling wine the next day.

Woodruff Bowl, May Wine, or a May Bowl—and is dominated by an intense woodruff aroma. Infusing for half an hour is sufficient to extract the flavor from the leaves. The harmless aroma comes from the coumarin, which itself does need to be treated with caution, however: one or two leaves is enough, otherwise the toxic agent contained in them can cause headaches. The most popular bowls are those made with white wine. The quality ranges from cheap sparkling wine with tinned fruit to fresh fruits of the forest with the finest sparkling wine or champagne. The ingredients are served chilled in a round bowl. In order to keep the liquid cold the entire bowl is placed in a container of ice, or else a glass cylinder containing ice cubes is suspended in the bowl and the refreshing beverage is served on the terrace on summer afternoons.

## Rose Bowl

Petals of 5 scented roses
Sugar
25 oz (75 cl) dry Riesling
1 ice block made from
approx. 2 pints (1 liter) water
25 oz (75 cl) dry sparkling
wine, well chilled

Place the rose petals in a bowl, sprinkle with sugar, and crush gently. Add the Riesling. Leave to infuse at room temperature for 2 hours, add the block of ice to chill, and add the dry sparkling wine.

## Fruits of the Forest Bowl

2 lb (1 kg) fruits of the forest
(wild strawberries, blackberries,
raspberries, blueberries,
blackcurrants), small berries
pierced, large berries halved
2 white peaches, peeled, pits
removed, and finely diced
Sugar
50 oz (150 cl) dry Riesling
1 ice block made from approx.
2 pints (1 liter) water
25 oz (75 cl) sparkling wine

Layer the fruit in a bowl and sprinkle with sugar. Add 25 oz (75 cl) Riesling and leave to infuse in the refrigerator overnight. Chill the bowl with the ice block, add the remaining Riesling, and top up with the sparkling wine.

# *Fruity* ♼ *sangría and cold punches*

No Spanish holiday is complete without sangría. However, the high-proof versions that flow along the concrete beaches of the Balearics often do the name no justice. A sangría in Spain is like a *Feuerzangenbowle* in Germany. You either make it yourself or you don't bother. A Spaniard would never order a glass of sangría in a bar; that is something that only the tourists do.

Sangría was originally a soft drink. Wine, and there is plenty of it in Spain, was too much during the heat of the day, and fruit juices are not very popular. Combinations were therefore the answer and today they are available under a wide variety of names: *Calimocho* or *pitilingorri*, or else *caliguay* or *rebujito*, all of which are wine combinations with cola, juice, and lemonade.

A good sangría is by no means a sign of western decadence, however. Instead, it is a pleasant way of ending a hot summer day with a light drink.

Lemonade, sugar, and spirits, enjoyed by holidaymakers as a quick fix, are not among the original ingredients but, used in moderation, they can add an extra touch.

It is doubtful that the Spaniards brought their sangría with them during the colonial era, but there are comparable mixtures in South America as well as in many other countries, some of them made with beer or liqueur, depending on what is available.

# Sangría

1–2 tbsp honey according to taste
25 oz (75 cl) red wine (Rioja Crianza)
17 oz (50 cl) orange juice
17 oz (50 cl) red grape juice
1 oz (3 cl) Licor 43 or Spanish brandy
½ organic orange, thinly sliced
½ organic lemon, thinly sliced
½ organic apple, thinly sliced
1¼ lb (500 g) ice cubes

Dissolve the honey in the red wine, orange juice, and grape juice. Add the Licor 43 or Spanish brandy, together with the sliced fruit. Chill for 24 hours. Add the ice cubes before serving.

# Sangría Blanca

25 oz (75 cl) dry white wine
8 oz (25 cl) banana juice
8 oz (25 cl) peach juice
17 oz (50 cl) white grape juice
3 tbsp (5 cl) Cointreau
Sliced peaches, bananas, lemons, and kumquats
1¼ lb (500 g) ice cubes

Combine the first five ingredients and add the sliced fruit. Leave to infuse in the refrigerator for 24 hours. Add the ice cubes before serving in a large bowl.

# Afrococo Punch

Zest of 1 organic lime
2 oz (6 cl) vermouth rosso
17 oz (50 cl) cream
2 cans coconut milk
Ground cinnamon and nutmeg
2 pints (100 cl) light rum

Combine the first five ingredients in the list in a saucepan and slowly bring to the boil; allow to simmer gently for 10 minutes and then let it cool. Top up with the rum, check the taste, and chill for 2 days. Serve in brandy balloons sprinkled with a little cinnamon.

This recipe is alleged to have originated from north African oral tradition. This means that anyone can vary it according to their taste.

# Beer Punch

2 pints (100 cl) light beer
1 oz (3 cl) sherry
1 oz (3 cl) brandy
2 tbsp confectioner's sugar
Ground nutmeg
Zest of 1 lemon

Combine the first four ingredients in a bowl. Add some ice cubes. Garnish in the glass with nutmeg and lemon zest.

# *Fruity* ♼ *coolers and cobblers*

Many drinks, especially the classics, are mixed according to set rules, some of which boast an almost liturgical severity. This is undoubtedly necessary if the style of a drink that has since become timeless is to be retained.

On the other hand, colorful combinations and a basket full of fruit are all you need to create new ideas. If you like being inventive, then coolers and cobblers are the thing for you. Both come in large glasses with plenty of

## Starfish Cooler

3 orange slices
12 mint leaves
4 bsp (2 cl) Limoncello
4 bsp (2 cl) grenadine
4 bsp (2 cl) unsweetened iced tea
2 bsp (1 cl) sugar syrup
Champagne

Gently crush the orange slices and mint leaves in an Old Fashioned glass. Add the Limoncello, grenadine, iced tea, and sugar syrup, and top up with crushed ice. Stir and float with a generous splash of champagne.

In 2007 the bartender Stacy Smith won the annual *Tales of the Cocktail* bartenders' competition in New Orleans with this drink.

## Springtime Cooler

3 tbsp (4 cl) vodka
4 bsp (2 cl) triple sec
2 oz (6 cl) orange juice
1 oz (3 cl) lemon juice
2 bsp (1 cl) sugar syrup
Fruit for garnishing, e.g. star fruit, Cape gooseberries
Cocktail cherries for garnishing

Shake the first five ingredients in a shaker with ice and filter into a long glass of crushed ice. Garnish with fruit and cocktail cherries.

liquid, attractively decorated with elaborate garnishes. Coolers are among the most well known of cocktails. The basis spirit and/or a wine-based drink is poured into a tall or highball glass together with ginger ale—according to the original recipe at least—water, or lemonade. The cobbler is also a generous drink served with crushed ice, but is mixed with wine, liqueur, fruit, juice, or syrup in a highball glass. Cobblers are famous for their attractive, elaborate garnishes. There are those who say that cobblers are like a fruit salad, just with alcohol and for drinking. The cobbler is indeed similar to a bowl and can be a special treat.

## Coco Cobbler

3 tbsp (4 cl) dark rum
2 bsp (1 cl) dark tequila
1 oz (3 cl) Batida de Côco
2 bsp (1 cl) amaretto
2 oz (6 cl) orange juice
1 oz (3 cl) lime juice
3 tbsp (4 cl) apple juice
Fruit for garnishing

Fill a tall glass with shaved ice.
Shake all of the main ingredients together in a shaker. Filter into the tall glass and garnish generously with suitable fruit.

## Rum Cobbler

2 oz (6 cl) rum
4 bsp (2 cl) sugar syrup
Mixed fruit, e.g. pineapple, green grapes, strawberries, kiwi fruit, mango, orange, etc.

Prepare the fruit and cut into small pieces. Fill a large, tall glass with crushed ice. Add the rum and sugar syrup, followed by the fruit. Carefully mix a few pieces of fruit into the top layer of ice. Serve with a straw and a teaspoon.

# *Tropical* 🍸 *daiquiris*

Four out of five of the mixed drinks ordered at your average bar are tropicals. That was not always the case, however, with the drinks usually ordered being dry and strongly alcoholic. It was the bar renaissance of the 1990s that opened the way to the top of the menu for tropical drinks. Tropical drinks are precisely the opposite of their predecessors and cover a wide range of flavors.

They can be combined with many liqueurs and other modifiers, even cream (Piña Colada). And almost all of them are ideally suited to softening the taste of the high-

## Daiquiri Floridita

| | |
|---|---|
| 3 tbsp (4 cl) white rum<br>4 bsp (2 cl) lime juice<br>4 bsp (2 cl) maraschino<br>1 bsp sugar syrup | Thoroughly shake all of the ingredients in a shaker and filter into a cocktail glass. Ernest Hemingway's favorite bartender in Havana, Constante, mixed this drink for the writer in the El Floridita bar. A slight modification with a dash of grapefruit juices turns it into a Hemingway Special. |

## Illusion

| | |
|---|---|
| 3 tbsp (4 cl) rum<br>4 bsp (2 cl) melon liqueur<br>4 bsp (2 cl) orange liqueur<br>4 bsp (2 cl) lemon juice<br>3 tbsp (4 cl) maracuja juice | Thoroughly shake all of the ingredients in a shaker and filter into a cocktail glass. Serve with a toothpick and a piece of fruit. If you are clever with your hands you will be able to make an accomplished impression. |

## Mango Daiquiri

3 tbsp (4 cl) mango puree
4 bsp (2 cl) lime juice
4 bsp (2 cl) sugar syrup
3 tbsp (5 cl) white rum
Mango wedges for garnishing

Place the first four ingredients in an electric mixer together with some ice cubes. Puree and pour into a cocktail glass. Garnish with mango wedges.

## Strawberry Daiquiri

1 handful of strawberries
1 handful of ice cubes
Juice of ¼ lime
1 bsp sugar syrup
3 tbsp (5 cl) white rum
2 bsp (1 cl) strawberry syrup
½ a strawberry for garnishing

Place all the main ingredients in an electric mixer. Mix until smooth and serve in a large cocktail glass. Garnish with a half strawberry.

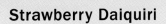

proof alcohol. They also harmonize well with lively local spirits such as rum, cachaça, and tequila. Tropical drinks are intensely flavored but seldom taste of alcohol. This is the secret of their success and, for those who neither want to taste nor to drink alcohol, there is the option of an alcohol-free mocktail.

One of the most popular tropical drinks is the daiquiri, allegedly invented by the American engineer Jennings Cox. The gin ran out prior to a reception at the place where he was working in Cuba, the Daiquirí mine, near Santiago de Cuba. Desperate, he used white rum and limes.

The daiquiri achieved international fame through Ernest Hemingway, who consumed vast quantities of the drink and sometimes tried out different versions. Some of these are still in existence, such as the Hemingway Special, for example, the Daiquiri Floridita, and the Papas Daiquiri with double the amount of rum for the hard drinking macho. This Caribbean drink went on to become truly American with John F. Kennedy declaring it his favorite aperitif. Marlene Dietrich used to order it when on tour in Europe, and John Cazale alias Fredo Corleone ordered it in *The Godfather*.

## Apple Sunrise

4 bsp (2 cl) cassis
5 tbsp (8 cl) orange juice
3 tbsp (4 cl) calvados
2 bsp (1 cl) lemon juice
Apple wedge and
blackcurrants for garnishing

Stir the cassis and orange juice with ice cubes individually in a separate mixing glass. Pour into a tall glass in layers. Using a pair of tongs, carefully add some more ice cubes. Top up with the calvados and the lemon juice. Garnish with an apple wedge and blackcurrants on the rim.

# *Tropical* ▼ *sunrises*

Like the sky at sunrise is how the colors change in a Tequila Sunrise. And not only the colors. Anyone who orders a Sunrise at the bar these days receives a mixture of tequila, orange juice, and grenadine.

Almost everyone knows the long, orange colored drink with the red streaks. The first version, however, is said to have been mixed in about 1940 in the Arizona Biltmore, using tequila, cassis, lime juice, and soda. A pineapple juice version came later.

The drink experienced the ultimate emotional kick in 1973 with the song of the same name by the country rock band The Eagles, as well as the movie of the same name in which the luckless drug dealer Mac Mckussic falls for the lively restaurant owner Jo Ann Vallenari, played by Michelle Pfeiffer.

## Tequila Sunrise

Juice of ½ lime
3 tbsp (5 cl) tequila
3 oz (10 cl) orange juice
1 shot grenadine

Fill a tall glass two thirds full with crushed ice. Add the lime juice, tequila, and orange juice and stir; then float with a shot of grenadine.

The mother of all sunrises has the advantage that it is in the glass in no time at all. The main thing is that the grenadine creates a few bright red streaks through the orange juice.

## Barbados Sunrise

2 oz (6 cl) dark rum—from
Barbados, of course
2 oz (6 cl) orange juice
3 tbsp (5 cl) maracuja juice
1 oz (3 cl) lime juice
4 bsp (2 cl) grenadine
Pineapple slices and mint
for garnishing

Thoroughly shake the first four
ingredients in a shaker with
ice and filter into a glass with
fresh ice cubes. Carefully add
the grenadine. Garnish with
pineapple slices and mint.

## Brazilian Sunrise

3 tbsp (4 cl) cachaça
2 bsp (1 cl) lemon juice
3 oz (10 cl) orange juice
4 bsp (2 cl) grenadine

Thoroughly shake the first
three ingredients in a shaker
with ice cubes and filter into a
tall glass with crushed ice.
Add the grenadine in a fine
stream. Ideally, the syrup
mixes with the upper half of
the drink, causing the colors
to run slightly: that's sunset
on the Copacabana Beach.

# Tropical ⍙ margaritas

Salt, citrus fruit, and the bitter sweet orange aroma—just a touch, mind you—and everything ice cold! More than almost any other drink, the margarita embodies the subtle magic that a mixed drink can create: complex but harmonious, cool and hot at the same time. The margarita is one of the best drinks in the world, as well as one of the most famous. It is therefore no wonder that the list of self-proclaimed originators resembles a small town telephone directory. There are as many myths about its founder as there are drinkers at the bars in Tijuana. Nevertheless, some of them are regulars when it comes to searching for the inventor.

The most well known must be the German, Danny Negrete, who roamed around Mexico as a restaurateur from 1936 to 1944, falling in love with a señorita named Margarita in the process. She had a penchant for salty drinks, which is why he invented the margarita just for her. A nice idea and a nice story that is told often but will probably never be proven.

A little further to the southwest of Tijuana is Rosario, where Carlos "Danny" Herrera claimed the honor of the drink's invention, even though he could never really say whether he had thought up the margarita in 1947 or 1948. He was able to remember his regular guest at the time, Marjorie King, however. He is said to have created the margarita for the showgirl who, allegedly, could only drink tequila.

## Margarita

| | |
|---|---|
| 1 lemon wedge | Moisten the rim of a |
| Fine salt | margarita glass with the |
| 2 oz (6 cl) tequila | lemon wedge and dip in |
| reposado | some fine salt. Carefully |
| 3 tbsp (4 cl) triple sec | shake off the loose salt |
| 4 bsp (2 cl) lemon juice | grains. Thoroughly shake |
| | the remaining ingre- |
| | dients in a shaker with |
| | crushed ice. Carefully |
| | filter into the glass. |

The salted rim is the hallmark of the margarita but is nevertheless a matter of dispute. Many bartenders will tell you on the side that the salt can conceal a lesser quality tequila.

## Cassis Margarita

| | |
|---|---|
| Blue curaçao | Dip the rim of the margarita |
| Sugar | glass in a saucer of blue |
| 2 oz (6 cl) tequila | curaçao and then in sugar. |
| 1–1½ oz (3–4 cl) cassis | Shake the rest of the ingre- |
| 4 bsp (2 cl) lemon juice | dients in a shaker with ice and |
| Fresh fruit for garnishing | carefully filter into the glass. |
| | Garnish with plenty of fresh |
| | fruit on a toothpick. |

The sugared rim is primarily for decoration and may be omitted.

## Frozen Mango Margarita

| | |
|---|---|
| 2 oz (6 cl) mango juice | Place all the main ingredients |
| 2 oz (6 cl) tequila | in an electric mixer. Half fill |
| 4 bsp (2 cl) lime juice | with ice cubes and mix until |
| 2 bsp (1 cl) mango syrup | you have a sorbet-like consis- |
| Star fruit and redcurrants for | tency. Pour into a margarita |
| garnishing | glass, and garnish with star |
| | fruit and redcurrants. |

## Banana Margarita

| | |
|---|---|
| 1 ripe banana, peeled | Place all the main ingredients |
| 2 oz (6 cl) tequila | in an electric mixer. Half fill |
| 1 oz (3 cl) Galliano | with ice cubes and mix until |
| 4 bsp (2 cl) lime juice | you have a smooth liquid. |
| Slices of citrus fruit for | Filter into a margarita glass |
| garnishing | and garnish with slices of |
| | citrus fruit, or other fruit. |

Francisco "Pancho" Morales hailed from Ciudad Juarez, the border town opposite the Texan El Paso, and dated the birth of the margarita as July 4, 1942. It's a shame that he forgot to patent his creation, spending 25 years of his professional life as a milkman, albeit he was far prouder of the margarita.
Enrique Bastante Gutierez was more successful with his story, claiming to have invented the margarita for the actress Margarita Carmen Cansino. In order to understand what makes this version so interesting, you need to know that the star's stage name was Rita Hayworth. Margaret Sames, an American demimondaine and John Wayne's neighbor, claimed to have invented the cactus liqueur mix at one of her legendary Christmas parties in Acapulco. The new drink was apparently so well received that the party went on for a full two weeks. That's also the reason why no credible testimonies that might have legitimated the legend have ever surfaced.

# Tropical ♀ coladas

The colada has virtually become a synonym for Caribbean drinks. Coconut, pineapple juice, and cream are the typical components, but these can vary as almost anything from raspberries to pineapple, from coffee to chocolate, goes with a colada.

Coconut cream is obtained from the first pressing of fresh coconut shavings and has a fat content of some 35%. Coconut milk, a combination of coconut cream and the liquid obtained from the second pressing of the same coconut shavings, thinned with a little water, contains

## Apricot Colada

3 tbsp (5 cl) white rum
2 bsp (1 cl) apricot brandy
2 oz (6 cl) apricot juice
4 bsp (2 cl) pineapple juice
3 tbsp (4 cl) coconut cream
2 bsp (1 cl) crème de cacao
Apricots and pineapples for garnishing

Thoroughly shake all the main ingredients in a shaker, and filter into a large beaker of crushed ice. Garnish with apricots and pineapple.

## Choco Colada

4 bsp (2 cl) dark rum
4 bsp (2 cl) white rum
1 tbsp (1.5 cl) Tia Maria
4 bsp (2 cl) crème de cacao
2 bsp (1 cl) coconut cream
3 tbsp (5 cl) cream
Dark chocolate and slices of banana for garnishing

Thoroughly shake all the main ingredients in a shaker, and filter into a large tumbler of crushed ice. Grate the dark chocolate over the top and garnish with slices of banana.

only 10–20% fat. The fat content is the deciding factor. The *Washington Post* made mention of a refreshing pineapple drink named Piña Fría as early as 1906. Rum and coconut were only added later. The title of inventor has many pretenders and the number of Caribbean bartenders claiming to have invented the colada has continued to grow since the 1950s. It goes without saying that a pineapple and coconut ice cream dessert named

Pina Colada Ice Cream, which was already being praised in American newspapers as early as the 1930s, remains a favorite today.

The moderately successful composer Rupert Holmes landed an evergreen hit with *Escape*, better known as the *Piña Colada Song*, which made it to the top of the charts when it was released in 1980.

## French Colada

4 bsp (2 cl) white rum
2 bsp (1 cl) cognac
2 bsp (1 cl) cassis
1 oz (3 cl) pineapple juice
2 bsp (1 cl) coconut cream
4 bsp (2 cl) cream
Cape gooseberries (for example) for garnishing

Thoroughly shake all the main ingredients in a shaker, and filter into a large cocktail glass of crushed ice. Garnish with a Cape gooseberry or other fruit.

## Piña Colada

3 tbsp (4 cl) coconut cream
2 oz (6 cl) fresh pineapple juice
1 oz (3 cl) dark rum
1 oz (3 cl) white rum
1 wedge of pineapple, 1 piece of coconut, 1 cocktail cherry for garnishing

Place the first four ingredients in an electric mixer and mix until you have a smooth liquid. Pour into a tall, wide glass and garnish with the pineapple wedge, coconut, and cocktail cherry.

# Tropical 🍸 Caribbean punches & swizzles

Punch can be both a hot drink and a tropical drink with lots of fruit. The word *punch* comes from the Hindi *panch* and means five, referring to the original ingredients: arrack, sugar, lemon, water, and tea. The sailors of the British East India Company brought the word to Europe, and the first mention of the word in British documents was in 1632. Initially they were largely hot winter punches, but the first Jamaica Punch had already become popular by 1655. Punch houses came into existence just 20 years later.

Cups are a subspecies of punch. Containing a little less alcohol, they were traditionally served in England before the hunt and also put in an appearance at picnics today. A well-known and very English cup is Pimm's No. 1, with Pimm's and cucumber or borage leaves. The most famous punch is most certainly the planter's punch, even though it does not constitute a specific mixture. It refers to a mixed drink with a rum base and diverse tropical fruits and fruit juices.

Just as well known is the mai tai, the invention of which is a matter of dispute between the American gastro-legends Trader Vic's and Donn Beach. The punch owes its name to Thai guests to whom it was served and who expressed their satisfaction with *mai tai*, meaning "tastes good." The mai tai and the Pacific bar culture that American GIs brought back home with them from their deployment in World War II have become deeply engrained in the American way of life. When the millionaire heiress Patty Hearst was released from prison on bail in 1976 following an interlude as an urban terrorist, the first thing she asked for was a mai tai.

The swizzle's namesake is the swizzle stick, the little mixing stick for mixed drinks that has acquired two teeth. Its history began in 1934. Shortly after the end of the Prohibition, Jack Sindler was sitting in Boston's Ritz Carlton Hotel, trying unsuccessfully to fish the olive out of his martini. The inventor immediately had the idea of perfecting the hunt with a small harpoon and had the swizzle stick patented.

There were some rum drinks known as swizzles in the 19th century, however, possibly relating to the colloquial meaning of swizzler: a swindler. The Swizzle Inn in the Bermuda Islands is famous for its swizzles, which it promotes with the fitting slogan "Swizzle Inn, swagger out."

# Zombie

1 oz (3 cl) white rum
2 oz (6 cl) dark rum
1 bsp sugar syrup
4 bsp (2 cl) lime juice
1 oz (3 cl) pineapple juice
1 bsp apricot brandy
1 dash pastis
1 dash angostura
Mint and fruit for garnishing

Shake all the main ingredients in a cold shaker and filter into a large glass of crushed ice. Garnish with mint and fruit.

# Rum Punch

3 tbsp (5 cl) white rum
2 bsp (1 cl) orange curaçao
3 tbsp (4 cl) maracuja juice
2 bsp (1 cl) amaretto
4 bsp (2 cl) lemon juice
1 bsp sugar syrup
Half passion fruit for garnishing (optional)

Thoroughly shake all the main ingredients in a shaker. Filter into a beaker of crushed ice. You can garnish the Rum Punch with a half passion fruit: fill the hollowed-out shell with high-proof rum and serve the drink aflame.

# Mai Tai

3 tbsp (5 cl) dark rum
1 oz (3 cl) white rum
Juice of 1 lime
1 oz (3 cl) grapefruit juice
2 bsp (1 cl) vanilla syrup
2 bsp (1 cl) orange curaçao
2 bsp (1 cl) cane-sugar syrup
2 dashes angostura
Mint and pineapple garnish

Thoroughly shake all the main ingredients in a shaker, and filter into a beaker of shaved ice. Garnish with mint and pineapple.

There are as many mai tai recipes as there is sand in the Pacific.

# Ti'Punch

Half lemon
2 bsp (1 cl) cane-sugar syrup
2 oz (6 cl) rum

Squeeze the lemon and place the zest in a beaker. Stir in the cane-sugar syrup and the rum.

Ti punch (short for *Petit Punch*) is served as an aperitif on the French-speaking islands of the Caribbean. The original version is made using rhum agricole only, the aroma of which is what gives the drink its appeal.

## Batida de Côco

1 small, ripe banana
3 tbsp (5 cl) pineapple juice
4 bsp (2 cl) cream
4 bsp (2 cl) coconut cream
3 tbsp (5 cl) cachaça
Pineapple for garnishing

Mix all the main ingredients in an electric mixer until the banana is pureed. Fill a tall glass three quarters full with crushed ice, pour in the Batida and stir. Garnish with pineapple.

# Tropical ▼ cachaça drinks

The raw material for Brazil's national drink is sugar cane. Unlike some rums, which are distilled from molasses, the byproduct of sugar refining, only fresh and then fermented cane-sugar syrup find their way into the tank for cachaça. Today Brazil produces mature cachaças of exceptional quality. However, these are not always the primary ingredients for caipirinhas, for which younger spirits are almost always used, the high quality of which also benefits the mixed drinks. The exotic salty taste of a cachaça is the perfect match for tropical fruit juices.

## Copacabana at Dawn

2 oz (6 cl) cachaça
3 tbsp (5 cl) maracuja juice
4 bsp (2 cl) chocolate syrup
1 oz (3 cl) cream
Slice of star fruit for garnishing

Thoroughly shake all the main ingredients in a shaker and filter into a tall glass containing ice cubes. Garnish with a slice of star fruit.

Chocolate and maracuja are ideal partners. In the right proportions they develop a sophisticated, bitter-exotic aroma.

## Brazilian Crush

4–5 kumquats
2 oz (6 cl) cachaça
1 tbsp (1.5 cl) grenadine
2 bsp (1 cl) lime juice
Sprig of mint and a straw for garnishing

Halve the kumquats and crush gently in a tumbler with a pestle. Add some crushed ice and mix well with the kumquats. Thoroughly shake the remaining ingredients in a shaker, filter into the glass, stir briefly, and garnish with a sprig of mint and a straw.

## Caipirinha

1 organic lime, cut into pieces
2 bsp demerara sugar
2 oz (6 cl) cachaça

Place the lime pieces and the sugar in a thick-bottomed tumbler. Squeeze the juice out of the lime pieces using a pestle. Add the cachaça, stir, and top up with crushed ice. Stir again briefly.

As a variation the drink can be prepared using organic mandarin oranges or with maracuja, mango, or fig puree. Other versions: with rum as Caipirissima, or with sake—then known as Caipisake.

# Tropical ♟ mocktails with a dash

## Aperol Starter

3 tsp (4 cl) Aperol
1 oz (3 cl) orange juice
2 bsp (1 cl) cane-sugar syrup
4 bsp (2 cl) lime cordial
2 bsp (1 cl) lime juice
1 cocktail cherry for garnishing

Shake all the main ingredients in a shaker and filter into a narrow goblet with ice cubes; garnish with a cocktail cherry.

A pleasant, straightforward, light, bitter aperitif.

## Golden Cadillac Convertible

4 bsp (2 cl) white crème de cacao
2 bsp (1 cl) vanilla syrup
3 tsp (4 cl) orange juice
4 bsp (2 cl) cream
1 kumquat for garnishing

Shake all the main ingredients together well in a shaker. Filter into a cocktail glass and garnish with a kumquat.

This mocktail is a clever modification of the Golden Cadillac, with the Galliano replaced with vanilla syrup.

## Mojito Mocktail

1 sprig of mint
1–2 bsp demerara sugar
2 drops angostura
Soda water
Sprig of mint for garnishing

Remove the leaves from the sprig of mint and place in a tumbler together with the demerara sugar and angostura. Crush the leaves gently using a pestle. Fill the glass with crushed ice, top up with soda water, stir briefly, and garnish with the second sprig of mint.

## Colada Linda

1 oz (3 cl) Batida de Côco
1 oz (3 cl) coconut cream
2 oz (6 cl) pineapple juice
4 bsp (2 cl) cream
2 bsp (1 cl) cane-sugar syrup
Piece of pineapple for garnishing

Place all the main ingredients in an electric mixer together with a handful of ice cubes. Mix until you have a smooth mixture and pour into a tall glass. Serve with a straw and garnished with a piece of pineapple on the rim of the glass.

# Whimsical ❦ spicy drinks

There are some cocktails whose histories sound like the family sagas of an American oil dynasty, with the family tree going back some 100 or 200 years. Some of them obviously landed in America with the first English ships. Many of those that followed were merely modifications of the earlier versions, with very few of them being truly new, and that includes spicy drinks. They have nothing to do with the usual character tests à la sangrita and Tabasco & Co. Spicy drinks combine typical cocktail ingredients such as spirits, fruit, and liqueurs with aromatic flavorings such as basil, black pepper, and ginger. Their exotic spiciness makes a surprising match for the classic partners. Spicy drinks are among the most interesting of what bar culture has produced this century.

# Basil Crush

| | |
|---|---|
| 1 sprig basil<br>1 oz (3 cl) lime juice<br>3 tbsp (5 cl) gin<br>1 tbsp (1.5 cl) cane-sugar<br>syrup<br>1 oz (3 cl) cloudy apple juice<br>Basil leaves and lime peel<br>for garnishing | Remove the basil leaves and carefully crush them with a pestle on the base of a tumbler. Thoroughly shake the remaining main ingredients in a shaker. Filter into the tumbler with crushed ice, stir, and garnish with basil leaves and lime peel. Serve with a straw. |

# Pepper Martini

| | |
|---|---|
| 3 tbsp (4 cl) pepper vodka<br>2 bsp (1 cl) Noilly Prat<br>1 tbsp (1.5 cl) Mangalore<br>Chili liqueur<br>2 red chilies for garnishing | Combine the first four ingredients in a mixing glass with ice cubes, and stir until the glass is frosted on the outside. Filter into a martini glass and garnish with the tips of 2 red chilies. |

# Green Cucumber

| | |
|---|---|
| 1 piece cucumber<br>1 piece chili<br>1 oz (3 cl) gin<br>1 tbsp (1.5 cl) melon liqueur<br>1 tbsp (1.5 cl) lime juice<br>1 tbsp (1.5 cl) cane-sugar<br>syrup<br>Fresh cucumber and chili<br>for garnishing | Crush the pieces of cucumber and chili in a shaker glass with a pestle. Add the remaining main ingredients, shake thoroughly in the shaker, and filter into a cocktail glass. Garnish with fresh cucumber and chili. |

# Ginger Cosmopolitan

| | |
|---|---|
| 1 oz (3 cl) vodka<br>2 bsp (1 cl) Cointreau<br>1 tbsp (1.5 cl) lime juice<br>3 tbsp (4 cl) cranberry juice<br>2 bsp (1 cl) ginger liqueur or<br>syrup, or a little freshly grated<br>ginger<br>Lime, a cocktail cherry, and<br>mint for garnishing | Thoroughly shake all the main ingredients in a shaker, filter into a cocktail glass, and garnish with lime, a cocktail cherry, and mint. |

# *Whimsical* 🍸 *fancies*

No set recipe, no rules, lots of fruit juice, and imagination, and the fancy drink is ready. Anything goes here. Fancy is everything that doesn't fit into any other category and is preferably bright and colorful. They can vacillate between a long drink and a milkshake, between a tropical cooler and fruit salad. Anything goes, including colored glasses and chunky fruit skewers. The bartender's favorites are therefore seldom missing from any good menu.

## Vanilla Sky

3 tbsp (4 cl) Vanilla Sky vodka
4 bsp (2 cl) strawberry liqueur
2 bsp (1 cl) vanilla syrup
4 bsp (2 cl) lime juice
3 tbsp (5 cl) cranberry juice
1 oz (3 cl) maracuja juice
1 pinch nutmeg
Fruit, citrus peel, vanilla pod, and 1 sprig of mint for garnishing

Thoroughly shake all the main ingredients in a shaker, filter into an Old Fashioned glass with crushed ice. Garnish generously.

### Pink Elephant

1 oz (3 cl) Baileys
1 oz (3 cl) strawberry syrup
3 tbsp (4 cl) pineapple juice
3 tbsp (4 cl) maracuja juice
3 tbsp (4 cl) cream
Strawberries and other fruit for
garnishing

Shake all the main ingredients in
a shaker with ice cubes. Filter into
a fancy glass with ice cubes.
Garnish with strawberries and
other fruit.

### Peppermint Petty

1 oz (3 cl) Captain Morgan
Spiced Rum
4 bsp (2 cl) Licor 43
3 oz (8 cl) stracciatella
(chocolate chip) yogurt
3 tbsp (4 cl) coconut cream
1 oz (3 cl) maracuja juice
Mint and fruit for garnishing

Thoroughly shake all the main ingredients in
a shaker. Pour into a large beaker. Garnish
with mint and fruit.

### Passione

1 oz (3 cl) Malibu
1 oz (3 cl) Passoa
Juice of ½ lime
2 oz (6 cl) pineapple juice
3 oz (8 cl) maracuja juice
Strips of orange peel and a half
passion fruit for garnishing

Shake all the main ingredients in a shaker
with ice cubes. Filter into a large brandy
balloon with crushed ice. Garnish with
generous strips of orange peel and
passion fruit.

# Whimsical ♗ molecular drinks

A little creativity in the combination of aromas and fruit should be invested in every drink. The cocktails on the following pages are for those that like experimenting and that can handle intelligently composed drinks with surprising ingredients.

Mocha foam and encapsulated pulpo pearls have created a stir in haute cuisine. Ferran Adrià, the Spanish protagonist of molecular cuisine, has managed to change foodstuffs through the addition of neutral chemicals to such an extent that they attain a completely new consistency. Algae turn into lollies and lobster into foam (*espuma*).

Resourceful bar mixers already have molecular cocktails in their repertoires. Whiskey Sour with *espuma de maracuya* and Bloody Mary with "celery pearls" are ideally suited to perplexing the evening's guests. Cocktails are broken down into gels and droplets that explode in the guest's mouth, ensuring surprised reactions. Anybody who wants to mix molecular drinks themselves needs to acquire an assortment of chemicals first of all. Gelling and thickening agents made from algae, seaweed, vegetable fibers, or seeds, in particular, are required. The calcium lactate required for making gel capsules is an organic mineral compound. These are therefore natural products, colorless and neutral in flavor, for which there are currently two main suppliers in Europe: *Texturas* by Ferran Adrià and the *texture* products from the Biozoon company, which were developed by the Technology Transfer Center. One or other of the ingredients may be somewhat pricey but, in general, they are not exorbitantly expensive.

That also applies to the hardware requirements: bowls and a high-speed mixer, perhaps a precision scale, and a couple of other utensils. The inexperienced will need to be prepared to undertake a number of test runs. It is all a question of the precise mixture and the timing. No one product is the same as the next. Even a syrup from two different manufacturers requires different quantities.

Quick success can be achieved with caviar made from Campari, for example. However, it will be a while before you can impress your guests with nitrogen ice creations. The recipes are intended as practice for beginners that can be elaborated upon as you wish once you have some experience. The precise quantities apply only when using exactly the same products, however.

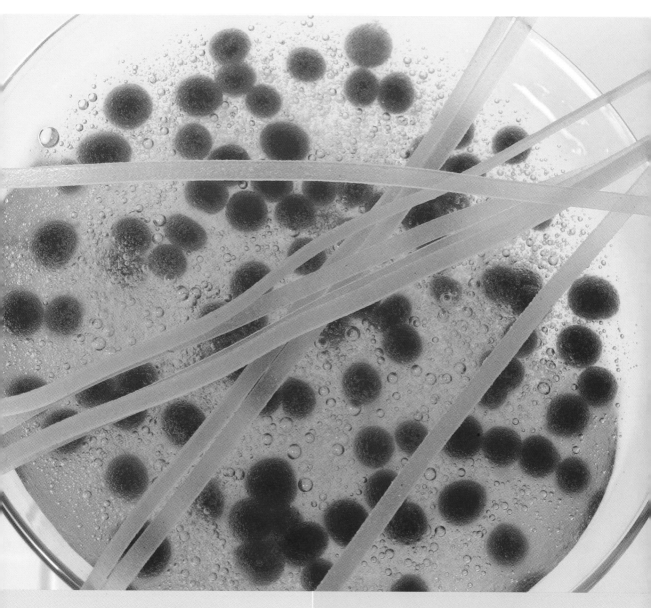

## False Cappuccino

3 level bsp xanthazoon, 17 oz (50 cl) Dooleys Cream Liqueur, 2 whipped cream chargers, 3 tbsp (4 cl) Kahlúa, 3 tbsp (4 cl) brandy, Chocolate for garnishing. Equipment: small cream whipper (iSi Whip). Dissolve the xanthazoon in the Dooleys Cream Liqueur, pour into a small cream whipper (iSi Whip), and screw on 2 whipped cream chargers. Leave to chill in the refrigerator for a couple of hours. Prior to serving, shake the Kahlúa with the brandy and some ice in a shaker, filter into a glass, and squirt the Cream Liqueur foam on top. Garnish with fancy chocolate decora-

## Kir Moleculaire

27 oz (80 cl) blackcurrant juice, 4 bsp (2 cl) crème de cassis, 4 bsp (2 cl) lime syrup, Small pinch (1 g) alginate, 5 level bsp calazoon, 13 cl (2.5 g) calcic in 17 oz (50 cl) cold water. Equipment: syringe. Combine the blackcurrant juice, crème de cassis, and lime syrup. Trickle in the alginate and stir until smooth, taking care to avoid bubbles forming. Leave to stand overnight. Dissolve the calazoon and calcic in 50 cl of cold water. Using a syringe, drizzle the juice and alginate solution into the calcium lactate solution so that caviar-like droplets are formed. Wait 30 seconds for the gel coating to form. Remove the droplets with a skimmer and neutralize them by dipping briefly in cold water. Add the cassis-caviar to a glass of champagne.

## Molecular Bloody Mary

6 level bsp guarzoon

7 oz (20 cl) tomato juice

7 oz (20 cl) vodka

Celery leaves or other kitchen herbs

1 bsp algizoon

Salt

5 level bsp calazoon

Equipment: syringe

Completely dissolve half the guarzoon in the tomato juice, and half in the vodka. Extract the juice from celery leaves or other kitchen herbs to obtain 3 oz (10 cl) juice. Stir the algizoon into the juice, season lightly with salt, and take care to avoid bubbles forming (best prepared the day before). To serve, fill a large cocktail glass half full with the tomato mixture and leave to set. Add the vodka mixture and again leave to set. Completely dissolve the calazoon in cold water and put aside in a bowl. Prepare a further bowl of water. Place the herb juice in a syringe and drizzle or slowly inject into the calazoon mixture so that long noodles or lentils are formed. Fish them out after 1 minute and rinse in cold water. Place the celery or herb lentils/noodles on the drink. When the guest stirs the drink with a straw, the tomato juice and vodka liquefy and combine. The lentils or noodles burst on the tongue, releasing the flavors.

## Piña Colada Espuma

6 leaves of gelatin (each ⅟₂₀ oz/1.7 g)
20 oz (60 cl) pineapple juice
12 oz (35 cl) coconut milk
3 tbsp (5 cl) dark rum (35% vol. alcohol content)
2 iSi whipped cream chargers
Candied fruit for garnishing
Equipment: cream whipper (iSi Whip)

Soften the gelatin in cold water, heat some of the pineapple juice, and dissolve the drained gelatin in it. Then combine with the rest of the pineapple juice, the coconut milk, and the rum. Place the liquid in a cream whipper (iSi Whip) and screw on two iSi whipped cream chargers. Leave to chill in the refrigerator for several hours. Before removing, turn the container upside down and shake thoroughly. Squirt into a goblet and garnish with pieces of candied fruit according to taste. Serve with a wide straw and a spoon.

# Invigorating 🍸 flips

Anybody that drinks a cocktail during the day usually has a good reason for doing so: perhaps a birthday, a promotion, or a hangover from the night before. All of these reasons are justified and each has the drink to match. Most of these drinks tend to have more moderate alcohol content, as well as ingredients such as cream or flavorings that bear some resemblance to the category "foodstuffs."

The reasons are obvious: not everyone wants to have to worry about the alcohol levels in their blood in the morning. Flips and eggnogs contain egg yolk, often cream, as well as winter ingredients such as almonds, sherry, and nutmeg. In the USA and other countries they have long been the drinks traditionally served in the winter and at Christmas. Many of them are alcohol free and therefore

## Brandy Flip

| 1 egg yolk | Thoroughly shake all the main |
| 3 tbsp (5 cl) brandy | ingredients in a shaker and |
| 1 oz (2.5 cl) cream | serve in a cocktail glass, |
| 2 bsp (1 cl) sugar syrup | sprinkled with ground nutmeg. |
| Ground nutmeg for decorating | |

## Broker's Flip

| 3 tbsp (5 cl) white port | Thoroughly shake the main |
| 1 tbsp (1.5 cl) gin | ingredients in a shaker and |
| 2 bsp (1 cl) vermouth bianco | serve in a cocktail glass, |
| 1 egg | sprinkled with ground nutmeg. |
| 1–2 dashes anisette | |
| Ground nutmeg for decorating | |

prepared in large quantities to be drunk by the whole family. The pick me ups, on the other hand, contain alcohol and are based on the hair of the dog theory, according to which a small dose of alcohol helps cure a hangover.

One thing that does belong in a flip is egg, together with the base spirit and sugar, and possibly a liqueur. Every-thing is thoroughly shaken so that the rather viscous ingredients mix well with one another and with the for-tified wines such as sherry and port. It also takes longer to chill everything. Nutmeg goes with most of the drinks as decoration. Many flips also contain milk and cream and are then called eggnogs, these having a somewhat higher nutritional value.

## Chocolate Flip

| | |
|---|---|
| 3 tbsp (5 cl) port | Thoroughly shake all the main |
| 1 bsp (0.5 cl) Chartreuse | ingredients in a shaker and |
| (yellow) | filter into a cocktail glass. |
| 2 bsp (1 cl) white crème | Sprinkle with a little grated |
| de cacao | dark chocolate. |
| 1 egg | |
| 1 bsp (0.5 cl) sugar syrup | |
| Dark chocolate for grating | |

## Sherry Flip

| | |
|---|---|
| 1 egg yolk | Thoroughly shake all the main |
| 3 tsp (4 cl) oloroso sherry | ingredients in a shaker and |
| (you can also add up to | filter into a cocktail glass; |
| 4 bsp/2 cl sugar syrup, | sprinkle with a little grated |
| depending how sweet the | nutmeg. |
| sherry is) | |
| 4 bsp (2 cl) cream | |
| Grated nutmeg for decorating | |

# *Invigorating ⟨image_ref⟩ eggnogs*

An eggnog is equal to half a breakfast: egg yolk, sugar, cream, and one or more spirits. The Americans drink eggnogs at Christmas, for breakfast with a hangover, or for brunch, without alcohol if preferred. George Washington, the first president of the United States, was a declared fan and treated his guests to eggnogs made according to his own recipes. When making eggnogs, be sure to use the freshest eggs from a reliable source. Do not use raw egg yolk unless you are satisfied that it is safe. Linguists have identified its origins in East Anglia, a

## Brandy Eggnog

1 egg yolk
1 bsp (0.5 cl) sugar
1 oz (3 cl) brandy
1 tbsp (1.5 cl) white rum
3 tbsp (5 cl) cream
Ground nutmeg and ground cinnamon, according to taste, for decorating

Using a whisk, beat the egg yolk and sugar together in a shaker glass until the mixture turns pale. Add the brandy, rum, cream, and lots of ice to the shaker and shake thoroughly. Filter into a goblet containing a few ice cubes; sprinkle with ground nutmeg and ground cinnamon according to taste.

## Breakfast Eggnog

1 egg yolk
2 oz (6 cl) brandy
1 tbsp (1.5 cl) orange curaçao
3 tbsp (5 cl) milk
3 tsp (4 cl) cream

Thoroughly shake all the ingredients in a shaker with ice. Filter into a large tumbler of crushed ice. This is a slightly milder but nevertheless well-flavored drink. Whether it is suitable for serving at breakfast, however, is a matter of personal opinion.

## Advokaat's Eggnog

| | |
|---|---|
| 1 egg yolk | Thoroughly shake all the main |
| 1 oz (3 cl) advocaat | ingredients in a shaker with |
| 2 oz (6 cl) tawny port | plenty of ice cubes, filter into |
| 3 tsp (4 cl) milk | a cocktail glass, and decorate |
| 4 bsp (2 cl) cream | with a little grated nutmeg. |
| Grated nutmeg for decorating | |

A recipe from Charles Schumann's bar in Munich.

## Mexican Eggnog

| | |
|---|---|
| 5 oz (15 cl) milk | Bring the milk, sugar, and |
| 1 oz (25 g) sugar | almonds to the boil and simmer |
| 1 oz (25 g) ground almonds | for about 15 minutes, stirring all |
| 1 egg yolk | the time until you have a smooth |
| 3 tsp (4 cl) dark rum | liquid. Leave to cool and place |
| 4 bsp (2 cl) dark tequila | in a shaker together with the egg |
| Flaked almonds for garnishing | yolk, rum, tequila, and plenty of |
| | ice. Shake well and filter into a |
| | chilled cocktail glass. Garnish |
| | with flaked almonds. |

rural area in the east of England. The word *nog* is said to have derived from the 17th-century *noggin*, meaning a strong ale that was often mixed with egg. In Scotland *old man's milk*, as eggnogs are called, is still served at Christmas and New Year. The Americans allege that the transformation of *egg* and *grog* —an earlier colloquial term for a mixture of rum, water, lemon juice, and sugar—into the commonly known *eggnog* is a genuine American invention. The eggnog has made its way round the world. It is drunk in the southern states of the USA with bourbon, in Puerto Rico as *coquito*, as *rompope* in Mexico, and the French enjoy a *lait de poule*. It is modified slightly in every country. The Peruvians celebrate the start of the holidays with *biblia con pisco*. A beer soup appeared on German tables a few decades ago that, ideally, was "refined" with egg yolk and cream. Today the eggnog has gone out of fashion somewhat, which is a pity because it has its very own style and is just the right drink for serving among good friends on a cold winter's day.

## Bloody Mary

◄◄

3 tbsp (5 cl) vodka
5 oz (15 cl) tomato juice
1 dash lemon juice
1 dash Worcestershire
sauce
1 dash Tabasco
Black pepper
Salt
Stick of celery for
garnishing

Shake all the main
ingredients well in
shaker and filter in
a large tall glass w
two ice cubes. Veg
etable fans will wa
to garnish the glas
with a stick of cele

## Bull Shot

◄

3 tbsp (5 cl) vodka
6 tbsp (10 cl) beef stock,
preferably fresh but
chilled

Combine the ingre
ents in a mixing gla
Season well. Filter
into a tall glass wit
ice cubes and stir.
strong beef stock w
help anyone in nee
of a little support t
get back on their fe

# *Invigorating* ♟ *pick me ups*

Pick me ups are intended to straighten up weary revelers with their throbbing heads and thick tongues the next morning. You are essentially on your own with your hangover as even scientists do not know for sure what happens in the head and what the best remedy for "alcoholic post intoxication syndrome" is. Up to now researchers have not considered it necessary to undertake a clinical investigation of one of the most frequent, albeit self-inflicted, of all headaches. The alcohol itself does not cause a hangover, however. It is the added ingre-

dients. The key suspects include acetaldehyde—the very word grates on your nerves—and fusel oils, an unpopular side-product of distilling that is especially prevalent in brown distillates such as brandy and whiskey. These are then often combined with colorants and sulfur, which does not help the situation. Sticking to clear spirits in the event of above-average consumption in order to be on the safe side when it comes to hangovers can backfire. As we know, however, to every rule there is an exception. As a chain-smoking cigar smoker, Winston Churchill

## Fallen Angel ▶▶

| | |
|---|---|
| 3 tsp (4 cl) gin | Shake all the ingredi- |
| dash crème de menthe | ents in a |
| 1 dash angostura | shaker with crushed |
| 1 dash lemon juice | ice and filter into a |
| | cocktail glass. |

Fallen Angel is the hair of the dog that bit you for
one that overindulged on gin the night before.
n in Shakespeare's day, it was common knowledge
t you can cure like with like—or, according to the
neopathic axiom, *Similia similibus curantur.*

## Prairie Oyster ▶

| | |
|---|---|
| Olive oil | Wipe out a margarita |
| 1–2 tbsp ketchup | glass with olive oil, |
| 1 egg yolk | place the ketchup in |
| Salt | the glass, position the |
| Freshly ground black | egg yolk on top, and |
| pepper | season with salt and |
| 1 drop Tabasco | freshly ground black |
| 1–2 dashes Worcester- | pepper, Tabasco, |
| shire sauce | Worcestershire sauce, |
| 1–2 dashes balsamic | and balsamic vinegar |
| vinegar or lemon juice | or lemon juice. You |
| Optional: | can add angostura |
| drop angostura and/or | and/or cognac |
| –4 bsp (1–2 cl) cognac | according to taste. |

used to consume large quantities of French cognac and
remained free of hangovers. Yet one sip of the late Queen
Mum's crystal clear gin and the prime minister looked
miserable the next day. Low quality fruit brandies can
also have disastrous consequences, even though they
are transparent.

In addition to fusel oils, further suspects include the so-
called *congeners* that are found more often in darker alcohols than in lighter ones and can cause nausea and
headaches. The most malicious of all the added ingredients, however, is methanol or methylated spirit. In contrast to ethanol, the drinking alcohol, its toxic brother is
broken down more slowly, forming formaldehyde and

formic acid, which cause excruciating headaches and,
in high doses, even blindness. Methanol therefore has
its greatest effect on the body once the alcohol has been
almost completely broken down. And this is where the
body has its chance to outwit the alcohol. The breaking
down of the ethanol is primarily the job of the liver, so if
you start the next day with a Bloody Mary, your liver stops
breaking down the methanol—according to the theory
anyway—therefore stopping the hangover, temporarily.
If you do not have any faith in this theory you can leave
out the alcohol. Most of the remaining ingredients should
help prevent hangovers.

# Salubrious ⟇ after dinner drinks

A good meal without a digestif used to be unthinkable. Nobody would have stood up from the table without ending the meal with a good cognac, a sweet cocktail, or a fine French liqueur. Each of these drinks has its own appeal after a generous meal. A cognac with coffee encourages relaxed contemplation. An ice-cold green Chartreuse calms the stomach. A simple sweet and creamy cocktail can be far better than many a dessert. Many of these treats have unfortunately become forgotten. Well-intentioned but exaggerated healthy eating means that more and more delicious meals are served and concluded with water. Happily enough, however, the after dinner drinks are still there, braving the storm, and they can also be drunk without a meal.

## BBC

3 tsp (4 cl) brandy
4 bsp (2 cl) Bénédictine
3 tsp (4 cl) cream

Thoroughly shake the ingredients in a shaker and filter into a tumbler with ice cubes.

Despite its name, the drink is not particularly newsworthy. The name is merely based on the combination of brandy, Bénédictine, and cream.

## Brandy Alexander

1 oz (3 cl) cognac
4 bsp (2 cl) crème de cacao
1 oz (3 cl) cream
Grated nutmeg for decorating

Thoroughly shake the main ingredients in a shaker. Filter into a cocktail glass and sprinkle with grated nutmeg.

Brandy Alexander is a classic with some high-profile relatives such as the Alexander, Alexandra (with gin and cream), and Alexander's Sister (with crème de menthe instead of crème de cacao).

 ## Alaska

3 tsp (4 cl) gin
4 bsp (2 cl) Chartreuse
Few dashes of bitter orange

Stir the ingredients together well in a mixing glass and filter into a small goblet. An Alaska is a good example of the almost forgotten positive effect of liqueurs after a meal.

## Angel's Delight

4 bsp (2 cl) gin
4 bsp (2 cl) Grand Marnier
2 dashes grenadine
3 tsp (4 cl) cream

Shake all the ingredients together well in a shaker and then pour into a cocktail glass. The color is enough to delight any angel.

# Salubrious ▼ sweet drinks

## Beach at Night

3 tsp (4 cl) rum
2 bsp (1 cl) almond syrup
3 tsp (4 cl) orange juice
4 bsp (2 cl) lemon juice
2 oz (6 cl) mango juice
4 bsp (2 cl) cream
4 bsp (2 cl) blue curaçao
Star fruit and lemon peel for garnishing

Shake all the ingredients except the last two in a shaker with ice. Filter into a tall glass with ice cubes, add the blue curaçao, and garnish with star fruit and lemon peel.

## Nine Mile

3 tbsp (5 cl) dark rum
4 bsp (2 cl) banana liqueur
2 bsp (1 cl) vanilla syrup
2 bsp (1 cl) cassis
2 bsp (1 cl) lime juice
2½ oz (7 cl) pineapple juice
2 oz (6 cl) cranberry juice
Fruit for garnishing

Shake all the main ingredients together well in a shaker and filter into a tall glass filled half full with crushed ice. Garnish with fruit.

## El Presidente

3 tsp (4 cl) white rum
2 bsp (1 cl) triple sec
2 bsp (1 cl) dry vermouth
2 bsp (1 cl) grenadine
2 bsp (1 cl) lime juice

Stir all the ingredients in a mixing glass with ice cubes and filter into a chilled cocktail glass.

El Presidente is a Cuban classic and needs no garnishing at all.

## Midnight Moon

2 bsp (1 cl) cognac
2 bsp (1 cl) amaretto
2 bsp (1 cl) Cacao Pico Champagne

Stir the first three ingredients together in an ice-cold mixing glass with ice cubes. Filter into a chilled cocktail glass and top up with ice-cold champagne.

Another cocktail that needs no garnishing.

# *Salubrious* ⅞ *cold coffee drinks*

◄

### Blackjack

2 bsp (1 cl) brandy
1 oz (3 cl) kirsch
1 oz (3 cl) cold espresso
4 bsp (2 cl) sugar syrup

Shake all the ingredients in a shaker with ice. Filter into a cocktail glass with crushed ice and serve with a straw.

### Black Prince

4 bsp (2 cl) white rum
2 bsp (1 cl) coconut syrup
1 oz (3 cl) cream
2 oz (6 cl) cold espresso
1 tbsp (1.5 cl) orgeat (almond syrup)
Dark chocolate for garnishing

Shake all the main ingredients together well in a shaker with ice. Filter into a chilled goblet with shaved ice. Sprinkle with grated dark chocolate.

### Kahlúa Frappé

4 bsp (2 cl) Kahlúa
4 bsp (2 cl) white crème de cacao
2 bsp (1 cl) amaretto
4 bsp (2 cl) coconut syrup
Lightly whipped cream
Cocoa powder for decoration

Shake the first four ingredients together well in a shaker. Filter into a tall goblet with shaved ice. Top up with about half to 1 inch (2 cm) lightly whipped cream and serve sprinkled with cocoa.

### Cappuccino Freddo

3 oz (8 cl) cold espresso
1 oz (3 cl) Kahlúa
1 oz (3 cl) brandy
Warm milk
Cocoa powder and ground cinnamon for decorating

Combine the first three ingredients in a glass with shaved ice and stir. Whip some warm milk and pour into the glass; sprinkle with cocoa powder and ground cinnamon.

# Salubrious ♼ pousse-cafés

Pousse-cafés are also known as rainbow drinks or scaffas and are labor intensive because they require a very complicated technique, but the optical effect is unbeatable. The ingredients must be of different colors and must not mix with one another when poured into the glass, instead remaining visible as clear layers one on top of the other. This is achieved using the physical densities of the ingredients. You start with a sugary syrup, and each of the following layers must contain less sugar but more alcohol than the layer beneath it. Most bartenders pour the ingredients carefully over the back of a bar spoon into the glass. Or, even better, you can pour the ingredients into the glass via a thin spout at one end of a bar spoon that has the spoon at the other end.

The quantities are measured so that equal or almost equal layers are created in either ascending or descending order. Ideally, you finish with a high-proof spirit but, in case that is too strong to be served to your guests as a drink, you can instead serve a pousse-café aflame: that gets rid of some of the alcohol and you create a spectacular effect with it.

## Rainbow Warrior

| | |
|---|---|
| Grenadine | A drink for gallant warriors. The |
| Blue curaçao | individual layers can be |
| Crème de banane | sucked up with a silver straw. |
| Maraschino | At least that way you know |
| Chartreuse (yellow) | what you are in for. |
| Brandy | |

### 4th of July

Grenadine
Blue curaçao
Batida de Côco

This is likely to please every
American. Whether it also tastes
good is another question.

### Flatliner

Sambuca
Tabasco
Tequila

This, too, is not a drink for gentle souls. It
does have some appeal as a strong digestif,
however.

### B-52

Tia Maria
Baileys
Grand Marnier

The B-52 is one of the few
pousse-cafés that is ordered
relatively often. Connoisseurs
order a Bifi.

# Heated ♼ hot punches

Heating alcohol is a delicate matter. It starts to evaporate at around 158 °F (70 °C) and anyone that allows a saucepan of Glühwein to boil away will be left with nothing more than an insipid, sticky, sweet mixture. On the other hand, warm alcohol enters the bloodstream more quickly, as will be confirmed by anyone who drinks a hot punch after skiing or warms their frozen soul with a hot grog at the water's edge. Hot punches are not only known in cold regions, even though they are usually drunk in winter and, of course, every country has their own punch. Ever since chilly carol singers were welcomed into English country houses with their halls decked with holly and mistletoe, flaming punch has become a part of Christmas tradition.

In contrast to their chilled, summery white wine relatives, hot punches are made with red wine spiced with the likes of cloves, cinnamon, and lemon and orange peel and heated. A cozy winter atmosphere develops as soon as the sugar is melted by the heat.

The world's largest bowl of flaming punch was prepared at Munich's Isartor in December 2005, when 2,380 gallons (9,000 liters) of punch were heated in a 10-foot (3 m) high copper kettle with a diameter of 8 feet (2.5 m). Of course, you can get away with making a smaller punch for what you need at home. However, the favorite recipes are almost always made for the whole family because they are best enjoyed in company. The quantities given here are sufficient for about six people. The other recipes are for four generous servings.

## Jean Gabin

| | |
|---|---|
| 8 oz (24 cl) dark rum | Place the rum, calvados, and |
| 4 oz (12 cl) calvados | maple syrup in a saucepan and |
| 6 tbsp (10 cl) maple syrup | make up to 2 pints (1 |
| Milk | liter) with milk before heating. |
| Ground nutmeg and a piece | Serve in fire-proof glasses |
| of apple for garnishing | sprinkled with ground nutmeg. |

## Rum Orange Punch

| | |
|---|---|
| 5 oz (16 cl) orange juice | Place the first six ingredients |
| 3 tsp (4 cl) Southern Comfort | in a saucepan and heat with- |
| 7 oz (20 cl) dark rum | out allowing to boil. Pour into |
| 3 oz (8 cl) lemon juice | fire-proof glasses, sprinkle |
| 3 oz (8 cl) lime juice | with the citrus zest, and serve. |
| 4 bsp (2 cl) sugar syrup | |
| Zest of 1 lemon (organic) | |
| Zest of 1 orange (organic) | |

## Amsterdam Punch

| | |
|---|---|
| 5 oz (16 cl) dark rum | Gently heat all the main ingre- |
| 27 oz (80 cl) black tea | dients, leave to infuse, and |
| 4 bsp (2 cl) sugar syrup | pour into fire-proof glasses. |
| 1 pinch ground nutmeg | |
| 1 pinch cinnamon | You can stir some hot milk |
| 1 clove | into the punch if you like. |
| Optional: hot milk | |

## Feuerzangenbowle

| | |
|---|---|
| Zest of 1 organic orange | Zest the orange and lemon |
| Zest of 1 organic lemon | thinly so that none of the |
| Juice of the organic orange | white pith adheres to the zest. |
| 1 dash lemon juice | Then squeeze the citrus fruit, |
| 50 oz (150 cl) red wine | and slowly heat the juice of |
| 6 tbsp (10 cl) orange juice | the orange and a dash of the |
| 1 cinnamon stick | lemon juice with the red wine |
| 2 cloves | and the 6 tbsp (10 cl) of |
| Sugar loaf | orange juice. Add the zest to |
| Dark rum (at least 54% vol.) | the saucepan. Flavor with the |
| Optional: | cinnamon stick, cloves, and |
| Vanilla pod, halved | (according to taste) the |
| A little star anise | halved vanilla pod and the |

star anise. Warm the mixture only—do not boil. Leave to infuse on the stove for a good 15 minutes. Shortly before serving pour into a fireproof bowl on a burner. Some specialist bowls have a perforated surface for the sugar loaf. Otherwise use a long pair of tongs. The sugar loaf is soaked in a small ladle of dark rum and then set alight. The heat melts and caramelizes the sugar so that it drips into the bowl, forming little floating islands of fire. The *Feuerzangenbowle* is then ready.

## Heated ♏ slings and toddies

A toddy is traditionally a kind of grog, heated alcohol with spices and hot water, often also with tea. Due to its climatic conditions Scotland is considered

### Apple Toddy

| | |
|---|---|
| 1 bsp (0.5 cl) cane-sugar syrup | Combine the cane-sugar syrup and calvados, and then top up with warm cider. |
| 3 tbsp (5 cl) calvados | |
| Warm cider | |

### Hot Dram

| | |
|---|---|
| 3 tbsp (5 cl) Drambuie | Combine the Drambuie and lemon juice in a fire-proof glass and add a few dashes of orange juice. Top up with hot water and stir with a cinnamon stick. |
| 1 tbsp (1.5 cl) lemon juice | |
| A few dashes of orange juice | |
| Cinnamon stick for stirring | |

to be the home of the hot toddy. Slings have similar basic ingredients but were first mixed on the other side of the Atlantic.

Today even cold drinks with the same basic ingredients are also referred to as a sling or a toddy, but the old recipes still have their appeal. In principle, a base spirit is combined with a hot liquid such as tea and an aromatic ingredient. Honey or cane-sugar syrup provides the sweetness.

## Hot Toddy

1 tbsp honey
4 bsp (2 cl) lemon juice
1 oz (3 cl) whiskey

Combine the honey and lemon juice in a fire-proof glass beaker, top up with hot water, and stir before adding the whiskey.

## Vodka Sling

2 oz (6 cl) vodka
2 bsp forest honey
4 bsp (2 cl) orange juice

Combine all the ingredients and top up with hot water.

# Heated ♼ hot coffee drinks

### Irish Coffee

◄

| | |
|---|---|
| 1 double espresso (approx. 2½ oz /7 cl strong black coffee)<br>1 oz (3 cl) Irish whiskey<br>2 bsp sugar<br>Lightly whipped cream | Place a spoon in an Irish Coffee glass so that the glass doesn't crack. Combine the first three ingredients in the glass and stir. Carefully fill the top quarter of the glass with whipped cream up to the rim. The more sugar there is dissolved in the coffee, the easier it is. It should look like a freshly poured Guinness. |

As with so many popular drinks, the Irish Coffee has been imitated in many countries: Scotch Coffee (with Scotch whisky), French Coffee (with cognac), Spanish Coffee (sherry), Russian Coffee (vodka), Jamaican Coffee (dark rum), Mexican Coffee (Tia Maria). The Coffee Advocaat with egg liqueur is also very similar.

### Russian Nuts

| | |
|---|---|
| 1 tbsp (1.5 cl) vodka<br>4 bsp (2 cl) Kahlúa<br>2 bsp (1 cl) macadamia syrup<br>1 double espresso<br>Lightly whipped cream | Combine the first three ingredients and heat, ideally in a microwave. Place a bar spoon in a liqueur glass to prevent it cracking. Pour in the mixture, add the double espresso, stir, and top up to the rim with the lightly whipped cream. |

### Banana Coffee

| | |
|---|---|
| 4 bsp (2 cl) cognac<br>4 bsp (2 cl) Baileys<br>2 bsp (1 cl) Kahlúa<br>2 bsp (1 cl) crème de banane<br>1 espresso<br>1 pinch cinnamon for garnishing | Combine all the main ingredients and garnish with a pinch of cinnamon. It is important that all the liquids are hot. |

# Virgin ♸ sherbets and freezes

Alcohol, its abuse, its mind-enhancing effects, and its influence on social connections are a significant component of bar history. However, there have also always been guests who, for different reasons, do not drink alcohol. Instead of ordering water and fruit juice they wanted accomplished drinks without alcohol and they got them. Many of these drinks compensate for the lack of alcohol with elaborate ingredients and garnishes. Sherbets usually feature a floating ball of half-frozen sorbet. Sodas shine with exotic ingredients such as ginger and basil, while cream and ice cream spruce up mixed milk drinks. Legend has it that the upper classes of ancient Greece and Rome had discovered ice for their revelries in order to chill their wine and honey mixture. Runners collected the snow from the mountains by working in relays with the filled containers. There are also reports of early ice consumption in China, and later in France as well. Catherine de Medici, born in Tuscany, is said to have brought ice cream recipes from her homeland with her to Paris, as well as a number of other things that also influenced French cuisine. The recipes spread from there to western Europe. Icy concoctions with rose petals, cherries, and a variety of spices had long been bestsellers in Turkey. The belief in the healthy properties of sorbets was common in the gardens of the Ottoman empire, where apothecaries and physicians monitored the quality of the plants and where a sherbet is still served at childbirth today, being considered an aid to stimulating milk production.

At the bar sherbets are drinks made partly of sorbet. Either the sorbet can be bought readymade or you can go to the trouble of making it yourself—which will probably result in a much more sophisticated version.

# Raspberry Grape Sherbet

2½ oz (7 cl) white grape juice
2 bsp (1 cl) sugar syrup
1 dash lime juice
1 scoop raspberry sorbet
Indian tonic
1 strip of lemon peel for garnishing

Shake the first three ingredients well in a shaker. Filter into a large cocktail glass and add a scoop of raspberry sorbet. Top up with Indian tonic and garnish with a strip of lemon peel.

# Peach Freeze

1 ripe peach, peeled, halved, and pitted
4 bsp (2 cl) cream
2 bsp (1 cl) sugar syrup
4 bsp (2 cl) coconut cream
1 scoop vanilla ice cream
1 glass of ice cubes
4 bsp (2 cl) redcurrant liqueur
Fresh raspberries for garnishing

Puree the first six ingredients in an electric mixer. Place the redcurrant liqueur in a large goblet. Add the mixture from the mixer, stirring briefly so that both liquids are mixed together slightly. Garnish with fresh raspberries.

# Coco Yogurt Sherbet

4 oz (12 cl) organic yogurt
3 tbsp (5 cl) coconut cream
1 oz (3 cl) acacia honey
2 bsp (1 cl) vanilla syrup
1 scoop blue curaçao sorbet

Mix the first four ingredients in an electric mixer with ice for a few minutes until the mixture has a creamy, foamy texture. Filter into a large tumbler and add a scoop of blue curaçao sorbet.

# Strawberry Choc Freeze

1 oz (3 cl) strawberry syrup
4 bsp (2 cl) chocolate syrup
2 oz (6 cl) cranberry juice
1 bsp raspberry jam
Grated dark chocolate and fruit for garnishing

Mix all the main ingredients with lots of crushed ice in an electric mixer. The mixture should be cold and thick but not so thick that a spoon can stand up in it. The crystalline consistency is the secret of this drink. Garnish with a little grated dark chocolate and fruit on the rim of the glass.

## Virgin 🍸 mocktails

Mocktails, a combination of the words "cocktail" and "mock," have become a standard bar feature despite their disparaging name. Initially they were existing drinks with the alcoholic components left out and cleverly replaced with other flavorings. False cocktails

### Hurricane Mocktail

2 oz (6 cl) orange juice
2 oz (6 cl) cranberry juice
1 oz (3 cl) grapefruit juice
1 oz (3 cl) apple juice
Kumquat, lime, and star fruit
for garnishing

Shake all the main ingredients together well in a shaker. Filter into a hurricane glass with crushed ice, garnish with a kumquat, a piece of lime, and a slice of star fruit, and serve with a straw.

### Mai Tai Mocktail

4 bsp (2 cl) orange juice
4 bsp (2 cl) almond syrup
4 bsp (2 cl) lime cordial
2 bsp (1 cl) lime juice
2 bsp (1 cl) cane-sugar syrup
3 drops angostura
Slice of lime for garnishing

Shake all the main ingredients together in a shaker. Filter into a large cocktail glass of crushed ice, garnish the rim with a slice of lime, and serve with a straw.

have long been a species in their own right, with their own competitions being staged among bartenders. The latter do not have to be asked twice and come up with one exotic creation after the other. Alcohol-free drinks have become a very dynamic category among bar drinks. And for those who do not want to go completely without, there are always the mocktails with a dash of something extra. Not really an alcoholic drink, but not a party pooper either.

## Shirley Temple

1 oz (3 cl) grenadine
2 oz (6 cl) orange juice
Ginger ale or another soda
Star fruit, orange, and kiwi fruit
(for example) for garnishing

Place the grenadine in a large goblet and fill with crushed ice. Carefully add the orange juice and top up with ginger ale or another soda. Garnish generously with fruit.

Originally a drink served to children so that they could take part in celebratory toasts, this has since become a standard feature in any classic bar.

## Champagne faut

6 tbsp (10 cl) white grape
juice
2 bsp (1 cl) chaï syrup
(green tea concentrate)
Tonic
Grape slices for garnishing

Combine the grape juice and chaï syrup and shake well. Filter into a champagne flute, top up with tonic, and garnish with paper-thin grape slices.

# Virgin ❢ exotic lemonades

### Cranberry Lemonade

1 oz (3 cl) lemon juice
4 bsp (2 cl) cane-sugar syrup
3 tsp (4 cl) cranberry juice
6 tbsp (10 cl) soda water
Lemon and strawberry for garnishing

Shake the first three ingredients together in a shaker. Filter into an Old Fashioned glass with ice cubes. Top up with soda water and garnish with a piece of lemon and strawberry.

### Ginger & Mint Lemonade

3 thin slices of fresh ginger
1 sprig of mint
1 oz (3 cl) lemon juice
4 bsp (2 cl) cane-sugar syrup
4 oz (12 cl) soda water
1 sprig of mint for garnishing

Place the fresh ginger and the leaves from a sprig of mint in an Old Fashioned glass. Crush gently with a pestle. Shake the lemon juice and cane-sugar syrup together in a shaker and filter into the glass with ice cubes. Top up with soda water and place a sprig of mint in the glass.

### Grapefruit Lemonade

1 oz (3 cl) lemon juice
4 bsp (2 cl) cane-sugar syrup
3 tsp (4 cl) pink grapefruit juice
4 oz (12 cl) soda water
1 piece of grapefruit peel for garnishing

Shake the first three ingredients together in a shaker. Filter into an Old Fashioned glass with ice cubes. Top up with soda water and garnish with a piece of grapefruit peel. The recipe could hardly be simpler—the classic lemonade concept: citrus juice, sugar, soda. Simply great.

### Basil and Grape Lemonade

Basil leaves
1 oz (3 cl) lemon juice
4 bsp (2 cl) cane sugar
3 tsp (4 cl) white grape juice
3 red grapes
4 oz (12 cl) soda water
2 basil leaves for garnishing

Place the first three ingredients in a large Old Fashioned glass and crush gently with a pestle. Add the white grape juice together with the red grapes and an ice cube. Top up with soda water. Stir briefly and garnish with basil leaves. Serve with a straw.

# Virgin ¶ smoothies

Fresh, ripe fruit tastes better than a readymade juice—an obvious fact that has been forgotten because the constantly growing range of new fruit juices provides an easy alternative. However, the intensive flavor and the velvety consistency of pureed fruit in a smoothie are hard to beat. The pureed fruit is of course the most important ingredient. You can be sure that smoothies bought at the supermarket contain more than just fruit. Many of the commercially produced "all fruit" smoothies contain sugar (some of them have even more sugar than cola), are expensive, and are pasteurized, but—because of their fiber content—they are still better than most fruit juices. Just not as good as homemade ones. Pureeing fruit is not difficult—you simply remove everything that is not meant to end up in the glass, such as pits. The skin is peeled or else the fruit is dipped briefly into boiling water and the skin then removed. Fruit needing hardly any cleaning, such as strawberries or raspberries, can be used deep frozen. That means you don't need the cubes when mixing. The fruit then has to be pureed in an electric mixer. This normally requires a certain amount of liquid, preferably a bought fruit juice from the same fruit or another liquid component of the drink-to-be. Any skin or pit residues can be filtered out at this stage.

Almost any kind of fruit can be mixed with another sort. Three almost always work, but with more fruit the flavor becomes somewhat uniform. Suitable ingredients include milk, creamy yogurt, and ice cream, as well as boosters such as soya milk and green tea. The individual quantities do not have to be strictly adhered to. What is important is that the finished drink feels soft and creamy—smooth—to the tongue.

## Banana Berry Mix

| | |
|---|---|
| 1 banana | Puree all the main ingredients |
| 2 tbsp blackberries | in a mixer. Add some crushed |
| 3 apricots | ice and briefly mix again. |
| 4 bsp (2 cl) cream | |
| 2 bsp (1 cl) sugar syrup | |
| 2 bsp (1 cl) coconut cream | |
| 1 oz (3 cl) milk | |
| Fruit for garnishing | |

If you want a more colorful effect, then mix the fruit separately. Filter everything into a tall glass and garnish with fruits.

## Kiwi Cranberry Smoothie

| | |
|---|---|
| 2 peeled kiwi fruit | Place the first five ingredients |
| 4 bsp (2 cl) milk | in an electric mixer and puree |
| 4 bsp (2 cl) cream | them. While the motor is still |
| 2 bsp acacia honey | running, add cranberry juice |
| Approx. 3 tbsp cranberries | through the opening in the top |
| Cranberry juice | until the drink has a smooth |
| Kiwi fruit and Cape | consistency. Add some |
| gooseberries for garnishing | crushed ice to chill the drink. |

Filter directly into a tall, narrow glass (so that you can see the kiwi seeds clearly) and garnish with kiwi fruit and Cape gooseberries.

## ◄◄ Blackcurrant Smoothie

| | |
|---|---|
| 2 tbsp pineapple puree | Shake the first four ingredients |
| 2 tbsp maracuja puree | together in a shaker and place |
| 2 bsp (1 cl) sugar syrup | in a hurricane glass. Shake |
| 4 bsp (2 cl) pineapple juice | the blackcurrants with the |
| 3 tbsp blackcurrants | sugar syrup in a shaker. Pour |
| 2 bsp (1 cl) sugar syrup | the creamy yogurt into the |
| 1 oz (3 cl) creamy yogurt | pineapple–maracuja mixture |
| 1 bsp maracuja puree | and then add the blackcurrant |
| Pieces of fruit for garnishing | puree. Stir the liquids a little |
| | so that the colors run, and |
| | then top with maracuja puree. |
| | Garnish with pieces of fruit. |

## ◄ Mango Smoothie

| | |
|---|---|
| ½ mango, peeled, flesh | Cut the mango into pieces |
| removed from the pit | against the grain of the flesh, |
| 4 yellow plums, ripe, peeled, | otherwise the long fibers will |
| pits removed | jam the mixer. Place in a mixer |
| 6 strawberries | together with the plums, |
| 3 tsp (4 cl) cream | strawberries, cream, yogurt, |
| 3 tbsp yogurt | and green tea, adding some |
| 3 tsp (4 cl) green tea | maracuja juice if necessary to |
| Maracuja juice | reach the right consistency. |
| Wedge of fruit and sprig of | Add some crushed ice. Leave |
| mint for garnishing | the mixer running until every- |
| | thing is thoroughly mixed. |
| | Serve in a brandy balloon gar- |
| | nished with a wedge of fruit |
| | and a sprig of mint. |

# Virgin ♼ mixed milk drinks

There was a time when milk bars were among the trendiest places. In the 1950s there was hardly anything more "in" than a pastel-colored milkshake served at a kidney-shape table. A mix with fresh organic milk is still a healthy treat today, however, and adding fruit makes it a real vitamin bomb.

### Strawberry Dream

5 oz (150 g) yogurt
4 bsp (2 cl) strawberry syrup
4 bsp (2 cl) lemon juice
2 oz (6 cl) maracuja juice
Strawberries and mint for garnishing

Mix all the main ingredients together in an electric mixer with some crushed ice. Fill a fancy glass with crushed ice and add the liquid. Garnish with strawberries and mint, not forgetting a straw.

### Virgin Swimming Pool

3 tbsp (5 cl) coconut cream
6 tbsp (10 cl) pineapple juice
1 bsp blue curaçao syrup
Pineapple for garnishing

Mix all the main ingredients together in an electric mixer with crushed ice until the mixture is smooth. Pour into a fancy glass, garnish with pineapple, and serve with a straw.

## Pink Peach Smoothie

3 oz (8 cl) white peach puree
5 oz (150 g) yogurt
1 tbsp white cane sugar
1 bsp lemon juice
1 cocktail cherry for
garnishing

Mix all the main ingredients in an electric mixer until you have a smooth mixture (the sugar needs to dissolve). Add some crushed ice through the opening in the top and leave the motor running until the drink is chilled. Place in an Old Fashioned glass, garnish with a cocktail cherry, and serve with a straw.

## Vanilla Passion

5 oz (150 g) yogurt
4 bsp (2 cl) vanilla syrup
4 bsp (2 cl) lemon juice
2 oz (6 cl) maracuja juice
Mint and a piece of vanilla pod
for garnishing

Mix all the main ingredients with some crushed ice in an electric mixer. Fill a fancy glass with 1 bar scoop full of crushed ice and pour in the mixture. Garnish with mint and a piece of vanilla pod.

Yogurt makes up the milk component in many milkshakes. It contains little fat but is still creamy. It all depends on the quality: a cheap version from a discount supermarket will always have the corresponding taste.

# Glossary

**A.O.C.** *Appellation d'Origine Contrôlée*; designation of origin of French wines and spirits, etc.

**aficionado Span.:** connoisseur and enthusiast/lover of bullfights (here, of spirits).

**alembic** Arabic word for pot still adopted into many other languages.

**amontillado** Amber colored dry sherry, derived from →fino.

**aperitif** Stimulating drink before meals; also the term used for the occasion (before lunch or dinner).

**assemblage** Blending; mixing together the contents of different tanks or casks.

**blend, blended** Term used for whisk(e)y made up of several different components.

**bodega Span.:** cellar.

**bonded distillery** Commercial distillery in which the alcohol produced is subject to spirits tax; the distilling equipment is therefore sealed by customs.

**Boston shaker** Two part shaker made of a stirring glass and a steel beaker; a separate sieve is used for straining.

**botanicals** Plants and parts of plants from which aromas and flavors are extracted.

**bottled in bond** Nowadays an American whiskey from one single distillation that has been aged for at least 4 years.

**built in glass** Drink mixed in the glass in which it is served.

**canteiro** Originally the beam on which madeira casks were aged in lofts; now a warm storage room; preference for use of →estufa. Also a type of wine.

**cask aging** Aging of wines and brandies in wood casks, mainly made of oak, in the course of which flavors are transferred to the → distillate and alcohol evaporates.

**cask strength** Whisk(e)y, or any other spirit aged in wood casks, the alcohol content of which is adjusted to →drinking strength not by adding water but instead by bottling it with its natural alcoholic content, which often amounts to 60% vol.

**centiliter (cl)** One hundredth of a liter; standard measure for cocktail ingredients, unless measured in *fluid ounces* (1 cl = 0.34 fl oz).

**chai** Term used in southwest France for an above ground maturation cellar.

**charge** Filling the pot still with one batch.

**chill filtering** Type of cold filtering process used for most whiskies that clarifies but also reduces the flavors; whisk(e)y with an alcohol content of 46% vol. and above is not usually chill filtered.

**chip ice** Ice broken into pieces smaller than an ice cube.

**cocktail** Small mixed drink which (nearly always) contains strong alcoholic ingredients and is served in a goblet-shape glass.

**Coffey still** Column still used for continuous distillation; perfected by Irishman Aeneas Coffey (1780–1852).

**cold stabilization** Chilling wines and spirits to below freezing in order to remove particles and prevent clouding; reduces the flavor intensity.

**colheita** Port or madeira aged for a minimum of 7 years in casks and bottled with vintage stated on label.

**column still** Distillation equipment in which distilling takes place without interruption (continuous process); as opposed to batch distillation in which the alcohol is concentrated during sequential passes.

**cooling coil** Component of distilling equipment; alcohol vapors are passed through it and condensed by cold liquid.

**crushed ice** Ice broken down into small pieces.

**curaçao** Liqueur the blue colored version of which has become famous, made with bitter oranges from the eponymous island in the Dutch Antilles.

**decanting** Pouring contents of a bottle into a carafe; essential in the case of vintage port, which develops a lot of sediment.

**dephlegmator** Attachment to column still; provides added concentration.

**digestif** Spirits, often made with herbal extracts, designed to aid digestion.

**distillate** High percentage product of distillation.

**double chauffe Fr.:** double distilled.

**drinking strength** Alcohol content of spirits reaching the market; fine spirit or spirits that have been cask aged contain too much alcohol and have to be broken down with water or →*petites eaux*; hurrying the process leads to cloudiness.

**eau-de-vie Fr.:** water of life, spirit, →distillate.

**eggnog** Type of punch made with eggs, also with cream.

**elaboration** Aging, maturation, of wines and spirits.

**estufa** Heating tank for madeiras.

**ethanol** Scientific term for alcohol used in drinks.

**etheric (or essential) oils** Extracts from plants, or parts of plants, that have a distinctive aroma.

**fillers** Fruit juices and sodas that often form the largest part of mixed drinks.

**fine Fr.:** brandy.

**fine spirit** Second distillation, from which the →distillate proper is obtained from the →raw spirit.

**fino** Light sherry type, aged using →*flor* yeast rather than by oxidation.

**flavoring parts** Ingredients in mixed drinks that influence the taste of the final product significantly; e.g. angostura bitters, grenadine.

**flip** Mixed drink made with egg; the best known are →eggnogs.

**flor** Film of yeast essential to the elaboration of →manzanilla and →fino in the sherry producing region.

**fluid ounce (fl oz)** Measure for cocktail ingredients in many English-speaking countries; divided into units such as ½ fl. oz, ¾ fl. oz; 1 fl. oz = 2.93 cl.

**fortify** Strengthening must with alcohol, to halt fermentation and increase the alcohol content of wines, especially port, sherry, madeira (→*mutage*).

**fruit brandy, fruit "wasser" (e.g. kirschwasser)** Distillate obtained from fermented fruits as indicated on the label.

**fruit juice concentrate** Fruit juice reduced in volume by steam extraction.

**fruit juice drink** Fruit component is 6–40% (depending on fruit type).

**fruit nectar** Fruit component is 25–50%.

**fruit spirit, eau-de-vie** Distillate of fruits macerated in neutral alcohol.

**fusel oils** Byproducts of fermentation, substances that may or may not be desirable, e.g. glycerine, succinic acid, higher alcohols; they are separated off in the →heads and →tails. Palatable fusel oils can be added by distillers to give character to a spirit.

**garrafeira Portug.:** bottle store; in port a term for wines aged initially in casks, then for years in bottles.

**grain whisky** Unlike malt, this whisky is made from any type of distilled grain.

**grape phylloxera** Catastrophic insect plague that devastated European vineyards in late 19th century.

**heads** Condensation of easily volatile substances during distillation pass; contains undesirable substances and is separated off.

**heart** The middle part of the distillation pass, which is collected separately from the → heads and →tails (*têtes* and *seconds*).

**highball** Long drink made with a base spirit, juice, or soda and often a third ingredient; one of the oldest types of drink.

**hybrids** Crossing of European and phylloxera resistant American grapes.

**invert sugar** Syrup made from sugar, water, and an acidic component (e.g. citric or ascorbic acid). When the mixture is heated the acid causes the sugar (sucrose) to break down into simple sugar, which does not crystallize as readily when cooled down. The syrup can therefore be far sweeter and yet remain liquid.

**jigger** Small beaker with calibrated measures used to measure liquids for cocktails. Calculated in →*fluid ounces* in the English-speaking world, and by →*centiliter* in continental Europe.

**late bottled vintage** Port from a vintage aged in casks for 4–6 years before bottling; when filtered

it can be drunk immediately; unfiltered it can age later; not a universally defined legal term.

**liqueur** Spirit with minimum of 15% vol. alcohol and minimum sugar content of 15 oz per gallon / 100 g per liter (12 oz / 80 g for gentian liqueur; 11 oz / 70 g for cherry liqueur). liquoroso Italian fortified wine.

**maceration** Steeping fruits in alcohol or wine to release their flavors and aromas.

**madeirization** Intensification of oxidized (produced in combination with oxygen) flavors in wine.

**maître de chai Fr.:** cellar master.

**malt** Grain brought to germination, mostly barley, the special enzymes of which can be used to convert the starch in the grain into sugar, a prerequisite for fermentation.

**malt or malt whisky** Whisky distilled from malted barley.

**manzanilla** Lightest sherry type from Sanlúcar de Barrameda.

**maraschino, maraschino cherry** Cherry liqueur from north Italy, ingredient in recipes (Singapore Sling, Sidecar); also very sweet candied cherries.

**marc Fr.:** pomace.

**martini glass** Classic cocktail glass with long stem and flat goblet shape; often used for martini cocktails.

**mash** Lightly crushed fruits fermented with the must.

**methanol** Alcohol not desirable in spirits as its metabolic products—formaldehyde and formic acid—are toxic.

**microdistillery** Production of spirits in distillation equipment that is not customs sealed (→bonded distillery); only a limited amount may therefore be produced.

**millésime Fr.:** vintage, year.

**minimum alcohol content** Alcohol content laid down by law for any traded spirit; also a criterion in spirit regulations used in defining specific types of spirit.

**mise-en-place** Work preparation for bartenders and chefs: everything must be in the correct position within reach.

**mistelle** Grape must in which fermentation is

halted with alcohol; used as ingredient or sold as liqueur wine.

**modifier** Ingredient in mixed drinks that alters the taste of the base spirit; classic example: vermouth in martini.

**mutage Fr.:** "silencing," also fortifying; stopping fermentation of alcohol by adding neutral alcohol or spirit; the yeasts responsible for fermentation die when the mash has an alcohol content of 17.5% vol.

**neutral alcohol** Ethyl alcohol of agricultural origin, with no discernible taste, and a minimum alcohol content of 96% vol.

**new spirit, new make** Colorless young whisky spirit before aging.

**nosing** Testing the quality of a whisky by its smell; for professionals the only sensory test for a malt or blend.

**Old fashioned glass** Large, wide rimmed tumbler.

**oloroso** Dry sherry fortified immediately after fermentation to an alcohol content of 17.5% vol., and then aged in old casks by oxidization.

**orgeat** Syrup made from almonds and other ingredients.

**palo cortado** Unusual type of sherry, a cross between amontillado and oloroso in taste and style.

**Pedro Ximénez (PX)** Grape variety used for sweet sherry wines; also the sweet wines produced from it.

**percentage volume (% vol.)** One hundredth unit of volume measurement.

**percolation** (Lat. *percolare* = to sieve through); method of extraction for plant substances.

**perpetuo** Classic marsala style wine; only a small amount is drawn from a cask each year and is then replaced by a young wine after the harvest.

**petites eaux** Mixture of distilled water and cognac, armagnac, or other spirit; used to adjust the alcohol content to drinking strength.

**plates** Component of distilling equipment: horizontal punched tray in a column still; the holes are extended upward with pipes that have bell-shape caps. The plates provide a larger contact surface for the gas mixture and liquid during the continuous process.

**pomace** Solids remaining after the grapes have been pressed; also known as marc.

**pot still** Traditional alembic still used for batch distillation—that is, sequential distilling (fractional process).

**Prohibition** Ban on sales, production, and transport of alcohol in the USA, law passed on January 29, 1919, came into force on January 1, 1920; repealed on December 5, 1933.

**pure pot still** Whisky made exclusively in pot stills.

**rancio** Walnut shell-like flavor produced during aging of brandies and fortified wines; generic term for heavily oxidized wines.

**raw spirit** Product of the first distillation run, which contains all the alcohol and most of the volatile substances. The weak →distillate is concentrated into →fine spirit, and unwanted components (→fusel oils) are separated in the →heads and →tails.

**rectification** Making alcohol more neutral tasting, and giving it a higher alcohol percentage, through repeated distillation.

**residual sugar** Sugar not converted to alcohol during fermentation, giving a wine its natural sweetness.

**ruby** Fruity, young, ready-to-drink port or similar wine with deep red color.

**rye whiskey** American whiskey made up of at least 51% rye spirit.

**secondes Fr.:** →tails.

**single cask** Bottling from a single cask of whisk(e)y, usually →malt; rarely used for other spirits till recently.

**single grain** Whisky from a single distillery, mainly unmalted and from an unspecified grain type.

**single malt** Malt whisky from a single distillery.

**snifter** Ideal glass for whisky and other cask aged spirits.

**solera** System used to produce sherry in particular, in order to achieve the same quality every year.

**spent mash** Residue of fermented mash after distillation; used as high-quality animal feed.

**spirits regulation** EU regulation NL 110/2008 of the European Parliament and Council of January 15, 2008, covering the definitions, descriptions, presentation, and labeling of spirits, as well as protecting the geographic details for spirits and replacing EU regulation NL 1576/89; published in European Union gazette of February 2, 2008.

**still** Part of the distillery's equipment, used to heat mash or wines; now the established term for traditional equipment used for batch distillation.

**straight whiskey** American whiskeys not blended with any other spirit.

**sugar syrup** Syrup made by heating sugar and water (→invert sugar).

**swan's neck** Component of distilling equipment; copper pipe through which the rising alcohol vapors are led from the still to the condensing coil, or condenser.

**tails** Last part of the distillation pass, in which non-volatile, undesirable, and partially harmful substances condense and are separated off.

**tawny** Style of port wine in which the port ages through oxidization by contact with air.

**triple sec** Colorless orange liqueur with alcohol content of over 25% vol.

**tumbler** Small cylindrical glass traditionally used for whisk(e)y neat or on ice, also suitable for short drinks with ice.

**unrectified spirit** →Raw spirit.

**V.S.** Very Special; term used to describe cognac aged for at least 2 years.

**V.S.O.P.** Very Superior Old Pale; term used to describe spirits, especially cognac, aged at least 4 years.

**vatted malt** →Blend of →malts from more than one distillery.

**vintage** Year of production; also type of port with specified year.

**vintage malt or bourbon** whiskies from a specific year.

**wash** "Beer" with 7–9% alcohol by volume, initial substance used in whisky production.

**wash back** fermentation tank for whisky production.

**wash still** Distillation equipment for the first distillation run for malt whisky.

**wine prewarmer** Additional tank in distillation equipment, in which wine is used as a coolant for the spirit and is itself warmed up in the process before it flows into the still; reduces energy consumption of the plant.

**wine spirit** Specialist term for fermented, fortified wine that is distilled to produce (bulk) brandies.

**X.O.** Extra Old; term used to describe spirits, especially cognac; at least 6 years old; most are much older.

# Bars of the world

## Bars that are illustrated

Absolut Icebar, Tokyo, Japan

B018, Beirut, Lebanon

Campbell Apartment, New York, USA

Club Camellia, Hiroshima, Japan

Club Embryo, Bucharest, Romania, www.embryo.ro

Green Door Bar, Berlin

Harry's New York Bar im Esplanade
Berlin, www.esplanade.de

Harry's Bar, Venice, Italy, www.cipriani.com

King Kamehameha Club, Frankfurt, Germany,
www.king-kamehameha.de

La Floridita, Havana, Cuba
www.floridita-cuba.com

LAN Club Oyster Bar, Beijing, China
www.lanbeijing.com

Loos Bar, A-1010 Vienna, Austria, www.loosbar.at

Morimoto, New York, USA

NASA, Copenhagen, Denmark, www.nasa.dk

Pat Club, Bucharest, Romania, www.inpat.ro

Peninsula Hotel Oyster Bar, Hong Kong

Raffles Hotel, Dubai, www.raffles.com

Raffles Hotel, Long Bar, Singapore
www.raffles.com

S Bar, Los Angeles

Supperclub, Bangkok, Thailand
www.bedsupperclub.com

Taj Tashi, Thimphu, Buthan, www.tajhotels.com

The Berkeley, London, UK
www.the-berkeley.co.uk

The Cuckoo Club, London, UK
www.thecuckooclub.com

T-o12, D-Stuttgart, www.t-o12.com

Volar, Shanghai, China

## Also recommended

Antidote, Hong Kong, China

Apartment, Belfast, Northern Ireland
www.apartmentbelfast.com

Aqua, Honkong, China, www.aqua.com.hk

Bamboo Bar, Bangkok, Thailand
www.mandarinoriental.com/bangkok

Bar Bacca, Belfast, Northern Ireland,
www.barbacca.com

Bar on the Orient Express
Orient Express, www.orient-express.com

Boadas, Barcelona, Spain, www.afuegolento.
com/secciones/boadas/texto.html

Bond Lounge Bar, Melbourne, Australia
www.bondlounge.com.au

Carpe Diem, Barcelona, Spain

Cloud 9, Shanghai, China
www.shanghai.grand.hyatt.com

Crow Bar, Auckland, New Zealand
www.crowbar.co.nz

Crystal, Beirut, Lebanon

Delano, Miami, USA
www.morganshotelgroup.com

Eight Lounge, Dallas, USA
www.eightlounge.com

Harry's New York Bar, Paris, France, www.harrysbar.fr

Hudson Bar, New York, USA
www.hudsonhotel.com

Mo Bar, Hong Kong, China

New Asia Bar, Singapore
www.swissotel.com/singapore-stamford

Orbit, Sydney, Australia
www.summitrestaurant.com.au

Planet Bar, Mount Nelson Hotel
Cape Town, South Africa
www.mountnelson.co.za

Purdy Lounge, Miami, USA
www.purdylounge.com/main.html

Purple Bar, Sanderson Hotel, London, UK

Rain In The Desert, Las Vegas, USA

Rainbow Room, New York, USA
www.cipriani.com

Schumann's Bar, Munich, Germany

Sketch, London, UK, www.sketch.uk.com

Sky Bar, Los Angeles, USA

Solar, Berlin, Germany, www.solarberlin.com

St Pancras Champagne Bar, London, UK,
www.searcystpancras.co.uk

Star Lounge, New York, USA

Teatriz, Madrid, Spain

The Dome, Bangkok, Thailand
www.thedomebkk.com

The Dorchester, London, UK
www.thedorchester.com

The Hemingway Bar
In the Hôtel Ritz
Paris, France, www.ritzparis.com

The Loft, Sydney, Australia
www.theloftsydney.com/home.html

Tou Ming Si Kao (TMSK)
Shanghai, China
www.tmsk.com/tmsk_sc.html

Vertigo 42, London, UK
www.vertigo42.co.uk

Vertigo, Bangkok, Thailand

Vu's Bar, Dubai
www.jumeirahemiratestowers.com/
dining/vus_bar/

## Bars that helped us

Bar Alexander, Dusseldorf, Germany
www.bar-alexander.com

Bogletti, Dusseldorf, Germany, www.bogletti.com

Meerbar, Dusseldorf, Germany, www.meerbar.de

Mojito's, Dusseldorf, Germany, www.mojitos.net

# Bibliography

Armogathe, Daniel: La légende dorée du Pastis, Geneva 2005

Arntz, Helmut: Weinbrenner · Die Geschichte vom Geist des Weins, Stuttgart 1975

Arthur, Helen: The Single Malt Whisky Companion, London 2005

Barnaby, Conrad III.: Absinthe · History in a Bottle, San Francisco 1977

Bathon, Roland: Russischer Wodka, Norderstedt 2007

Behrendt, Bibiana: Grappa: Der Guide für Kenner und Genießer, Munich 2003

Behrendt, Bibiana: Grappa-Lexikon, Weil der Stadt, 2004

Behrendt, Bibiana & Axel: Trester, Munich 1997

Behrendt, Bibiana & Axel: Sherry, Munich 1997

Bohrmann, Peter: Falken Mixbuch, Niederhausen/Ts. 1993

Bolsmann, Eric H.: Lexikon der Bar, Stuttgart 2003

Brandl, Franz: Liköre der Welt, Munich 2000

Brandl, Franz: Mix Guide, Munich 2006

Brennereizeitung: Geschichte der deutschen Kornbrennerei, Erfurt 1936

Broom, Dave: Spirits & Cocktails, 1998

Broom, Dave: Distilling Knowledge: A Professional Guide to Spirits and Liqueurs, London 2006

Camard-Hayot, Florette; de Laguarigue, Jean-Luc: Martinique · Terre de Rhum, 1997

Clade, Jean-Louis; Jollès, Charles: La Gentiane · L'aventure de la fée jaune, Yves sur Morges 2006

Cousteaux, Fernand; Casamayor, Pierre: Le Guide de l'amateur d'Armagnac, Toulouse 1985

Cowdery, Charles K.: Bourbon Straight · The Uncut and Unfiltered Story of American Whiskey, Chicago 2004

Curtis, Wayne: And a Bottle of Rum, New York 2006

Deibel, Jürgen; Obalski, Werner: Sherry: Kultur und Genuss, Weil der Stadt 2008

Dominé, André: Die Kunst des Aperitif, Weingarten 1989

Dominé, André (Ed.): Culinaria · Französische Spezialitäten, Königswinter 2007

Dominé, André (Ed.): Wine, Königswinter 2008

Euler, Barbara E.: Whisky: Kleines Lexikon von A–Z, München 1999

Faith, Nicholas: Cognac, London 2004

Fernandez de Bobadilla, Vicente: Brandy de Jerez, Madrid 1990

Fielden, Christopher; WSET (Ed.): Exploring the World of Wines and Spirits, London 2005

Foley, Ray: Das Bar Handbuch, Munich 2000

Gabányi, Stefan: Schumann's Whisk(e)y Lexikon, Munich 2007

Gage, Allan: Around the World in 80 Bars, London 2004

Gatti, Florisa (Ed.): Mondo Martini · A Journey Through a Unique Style, Piobesi d'Alba 2006

Gergely, Anikó: Culinaria · Ungarische Spezialitäten, Königswinter 2007

Givens, Ron: Bourbon at its Best · The Lore and Allure of America's Finest Spirit, Cincinnati 2008

Glüsing, Jutta/Flensburger Schiffahrtsmuseum: Das Flensburger Rum-Museum · Eine kleine Flensburger Rum-Fibel, Flensburg n.y.

Gölles, Alois: Edelbrände, Graz 2000

Gööck, Roland: Hochprozentiges aus aller Welt, Gütersloh 1963

Goodwin, Donald W.: Alkohol & Autor, Frankfurt/M. 2000

Hamilton, Edward: Das Rum-Buch, Munich 1998

Hartmann, G.: Cognac, Armagnac, Weinbrand (Weindestillat – Weinbrand-Verschnitt), Berlin 1955

Havana Club: Heart & Soul Book, Ciudad de La Habana n.y.

Hills, Phillip: Appreciating Whisky: The Connoisseur's Guide to Nosing, Tasting and Enjoying Scotch, Glasgow 2002

Hofer, Andreas: Schottland für Whiskyfreunde, Munich 2005

Huetz de Lemps, Alain: Histoire du Rhum, Paris 1997

Hume, John R.; Moss, Michael S.: The Making of Scotch Whisky, Edinburgh 2000

Italienisches Institut für Außenhandel (Ed.): Grappa aus Italien, Dusseldorf 1988

Jackson, Michael: Malt Whisky Companion, London 2004

Jackson, Michael: Whiskey · The Definitive World Guide, London 2006

Jarrard, Kyle: Cognac · The Seductive Saga of the World's Most Coveted Spirit, Hoboken 2005

Jeffers, H. Paul: High Spirits · A Celebration of Scotch, Bourbon, Cognac and More, New York 1997

Jeffs, Julian: Sherry, London 2004

Joseph, Robert; Protz, Roger; Broom, Dave: The Complete Encyclopedia of Wine, Beer and Spirits, 2000

Koch, Patrick; Meyer, Fabien: Des Alambics et des Hommes, Hayange 2005

Kolb, Erich (Ed.): Spirituosen-Technologie, Hamburg 2002

Kreipe, Heinrich: Getreide- und Kartoffelbrennerei, Stuttgart 1981

Kruck, Peter: Alcohol · Alles, was Sie darüber wissen sollten, Munich 2006

Lamond, John D.; Tucek, Robert: The Malt Whisky File, London 2007

Le Paulmier, Julien: Le premier traité du sidre 1589, Bricqueboscq 2003

Límon, Enrique Martínez: Tequila!, Munich n.y.

Lucas, E.: Auswahl werthvoller Obstsorten nebst kurzer Angabe ihrer Merkmale und Cultur, Ravensburg 1871/72

MacLean, Charles; Lowe, Jason: Malt Whisky, London 2006

MacLean, Charles: Scotch Whisky: A Liquid History, London 2005

Maier, Vene: Große Schnäpse · Ein Guide zu den besten Obstbränden und den besten Schnapsbrennern in Österreich, Italien, Deutschland und der Schweiz, Vienna 2004

Mattson, Henrik: Calvados · The World's Premier Apple Brandy, 2004

Mayson, Richard: Port and the Douro, London 2005

McCreary, Alf: Spirit of the Age · The Story of Old Bushmills, Belfast 1983

Milona, Marianthi: Culinaria Greece, Königswinter 2007

Milroy, Wallace: Malt Whisky Almanac · A Taster's Guide, Glasgow 1992

Mulryan, Peter: The Whiskeys of Ireland, Dublin 2002

Murray, Jim: Die großen Whiskys der Welt, Munich 1998

Murray, Jim: Whisky Bible, 2006

Museums- und Heimatverein Hilden e.V. (Ed.): Die historische Kornbrennerei, Hilden 1995

Nouet, Martine; Muriot, Alain: Saveurs du terroir · Le Calvados, Paris 2002

Ortner, Wolfram: World Spirits Guide 2006 · Die neue Welt der Edelbrände & traditionellen Spirituosen, Bad Kleinkirchheim 2006

Paczensky, Gert v.: Cognac, Weil der Stadt 1984

Parker, Suzi: 1000 Best Bartender's Recipes, Naperville 2005

Pessey, Christian: L'ABCdaire du Cognac, Paris 2002

Piras, Claudio; Medagliani, Eugenio (Ed.): Culinaria Italy, Königswinter 2004

Pischl, Josef: Schnapsbrennen, Graz, Stuttgart 2004

Quidnovi: Cellars of Gold: The Port Wine Heritage, 2007

Read, Jan: Sherry and the Sherry Bodegas, London 1988

Regan, Gary; Regan, Mardee Haidin: The Book of Bourbon and Other Fine American Whiskeys, Shelburne 1995

Russell, Inge; Banford, Charles; Stewart, Graham (Ed.): Whisky · Technology, Production and Marketing, London, San Diego 2003

Ruy Sanchez, Alberto; de Orellana, Margarita: Tequila, Washington 2004

Ryan, John Clement: Irish Whiskey, Dublin 1992

Samalens, Jean & Georges; Scharfenberg, Horst: Armagnac, Weil der Stadt n.y.

Schobert, Walter: Das Whiskylexikon, Frankfurt/M. 2007

Schobert, Walter: Scotch Whisky · Wasser des Lebens, Weil der Stadt 2006

Schumann, Charles: American Bar, Munich 2004

Schumann's Barbuch · Drinks & Storys, Munich 2002

Schumann's Tropical Barbuch · Drinks & Storys, Munich 2000

Siegel, Simon et al: Handlexikon der Getränke, 3 vols., Linz 2003

Smith, Frederic H.: Caribbean Rum · A Social and Economic History, Gainesville 2005

Sora, Joseph W.: International Bartender's Guide, New York 2002

Spirituosen-Jahrbuch, Berlin 1957ff.

Steed, Tobias; Reed, Ben: Hollywood Cocktails, Munich 2005

Tanner, Hans; Brunner, Hans Rudolf: Obstbrennerei heute, Schwäbisch Hall 1998

The Scotch Whisky Association: Scotch Whisky · Question and Answers, Edinburgh 1992

Tikos, Bill: Signature Cocktails, London 2005

Trutter, Marion (Ed.): Culinaria Spain, Königswinter 2004

Trutter, Marion (Ed.): Culinaria Russia, Königswinter 2007

Valenzuela-Zapata, Ana G.; Nabhan, Gary Paul: Tequila · A Natural and Cultural History, Tucson 2004

»Wem der geprant wein nutz sey oder schad...«, Zur Kulturgeschichte des Branntweins, Wilhelm-Fabry-Museum, Historische Kornbrennerei, Hilden 1989

Wilfert, Adolf: Die Kartoffel- und Getreidebrennerei, Wien, Pest, Leipzig n.y.

Willems, Marlous (Ed.): Behind Bars, Berlin 2008

Wilson, Anne C.: Water of Life · A History of Wine-Distilling and Spirits 500 BC to AD 2000, Totnes 2006

Wilson, Neil: The Island Whisky Trail · An Illustrated Guide to the Hebredean Distilleries, Glasgow 2003

Wüstenfeld, Hermann; Haeseler, Georg: Trinkbranntweine und Liköre, Berlin und Hamburg 1964

# Indexes

## Index of people

# Index of places

## Subject index

# Picture credits

The editor and the publisher have made every effort throughout the production process to identify all owners of image rights. Persons and institutions that it may not have been possible to contact and who claim rights to images used are asked to contact the publisher retrospectively.

t. = top; b. = bottom; l. = left links; r. = right; c. = center

All images are by Armin Faber and Thomas Pothmann

with the exception of:

© Absolut/MaxXium (101 t.), © Agroindustria Colonia Nova with the kind permission of Pithoi Weinimporteur (466, 469 b.), © akg images, Berlin (12, 17 t., 17 b., 21, 35, 42, 43, 50/51, 51, 306 b.r., 308 t., 354 l., 389 b., 438, 439 b., 440, 526 t.; Bianconero 45 t., 50; British Library 306 r., 439 t.; Hervé Champollion 547 t.; Erich Lessing 44, 494; Joseph Martin 22; Nimatallah 552; Sotheby's 354 r.), © Artemisia Claude-Alain Bugnon (496, 497, 498, 499), © Bacardi GmbH (34, 100 r., 366 t., 367, 414, 417, 443, 448, 449 l., 570, 571, 574, 575), © Baileys (626), © Berentzen-Gruppe AG (386, 387, 424, 425, 441 t., 462), © The Berkeley, London (52), © Beylerbye (509 l.), © BNIArmagnac (106/107, 139; Images Michel Carossio/Michel Fainsilber 137, 138 b.l.), © BNIC (26; Stéphane Charbeau 119; Gérard Martron 180, 181), © BO18/Beirut, Libanon/www.b018.com/Bernard Koury/Photos by Bernard Koury, with the kind permission of Joachim Fischer (55), © Gabriel Boudier (564 r., 600/601), © Campari (531, 582, 583 b., 588 l., 588 r.), © Camus (130 b.r.), © Chartreuse Diffusion (572/573), © Château de Beaulon (117 t.), © Club Camellia/Hiroshima, Japan/Suppose Design Office/Photos by Nacása & Partners Inc., with the kind permission of Joachim Fischer (57 b.), © Club Embryo/RO-Bukarest/www.embryo.ro/Square One/Photos by Nicu Ilfoveanu, with the kind permission of Joachim Fischer (39), © Comercial, Munich/www.barcomercial.de/ Stadler + Partner Architects/Photos by Andreas Pohlmann, with the kind permission of Joachim Fischer (14), © Comité Interprofessionnel des Vins du Roussillon (651 b.l., 655 l.), © Comité National du Pineau des Charentes (555), © Consejo Regulador del Brandy de Jerez (152, 153; Carajillo 153 b.c.; Cepa 153 b.l; José A. Glez 152 b.; Vincente Moltó 153 t.c.; Outumuro 153 c.r.; Leche de Pantera 153 t.r.; Keka Raffo 152 t.; Gonzalo Tomé 153 c.), © Courvoisier (129 b.r.), © Cusenier – Caves Byrrh (32, 544), © De Kuyper (606 b., 607), © Diageo (100 l., 101; Bushmills GBT - Yves Coentino 355), © Distilleries et Domaines de Provence (505), © Domäne Wachau (178 l.), © André Dominé (204/205, 337 t.r., 342 t., 345), © Efe Alkollu Icecekler Ticaret A.S. (508, 509 r.), © Engenho Terra Vermelha with the kind permission of Pithoi Weinimporteur (467 l., 468), © EOSS (696 b.), © Ets Lemercier Frères (493), © with the kind permission of the Fabry Museum, Hilden (25 b., 394 r.), © Pierre Ferrand (131 b.l.), © Manfred Fischer, Dresden (232, 273, 290 r.), © Flensburger Schiffahrtsmuseum (441 b., 463 t.), © Florio – Duca di Salaparuta (33 b., 693 t.), © Fratelli Branca Distillerie (560, 588 c., 589), © Getty Images (476 b., 477 l., 479 r.; AFP 475, 479 l., 485 t.; Art Montes De Oca 481 l.; Warner Bros. 488), © Gölles (298 l.), © Léopold Gourmet (151 b.r.), © Grand Hotel Esplanade Berlin (45 b.), © Grassl (584), © Ian Gray (364, 365, 368 b.l., 368 b.r., 369, 370), © Hardenberg-Wilthen AG (576 b.), © Havana Club (444, 445), © Herzog August Bibliothek Wolfenbüttel (25 t., 104), © Arnold Holstein Destillationstechnik (29), © Hospitality Holdings, Inc., New York (53), © Lorenz Humbel, Stetten (272 r., 278 l., 291 t.), © Informationsbüro Sherry/ICEX (664 l., 665 l.), © Jameson Archive Tony Hurst (308 b., 309, 356, 357), © Jenever Museum Hasselt (408, 409, 410 b.l., 410 b.r., 411), © Clem Johnson (449 l., 457 t.), © kamps markenberatung – Ice Bar (57 t.), © King Kamehameha Club/D-Frankfurt a.M./www.king-kamehameha.de/Mack+Co/Photos courtesy of King Kamehameha PR, with the kind permission of Joachim Fischer (38), © Kittling Ridge Distillery (376), © Krombacher (83 t.), © laif (Gonzalez 486, 487 t.; Heeb 472; Hemis 249; Hemisphères 483 c.t.; Heuer 480 r.; IML 461 t.r.; Krinitz 340 b.; Meyer 477 r., 478, 480 l., 481 r., 483 t., 483 c.b., 483 b.; Modrow 517; Anna Neumann 278 c.; Raach 270; REA 558; Schliack 516; Ulutuntcok 546; Wernet 292 b.), © Magyar Távirati Iroda Fotóarchivuma (591 r.), © Marie Brizard (520 l.), © Marnier-Lapostolle (618, 619, 620), © Martini & Rossi Historical Archives/Bacardi GmbH (33 b., 522, 528, 529, 530), © Mast-Jägermeister AG (592 b., 593 t.l.), © Ingo Maurer GmbH/Photo: Tom Vack, Munich (583 t.), © Steve McCarthy, Clear Creek Distillery, USA (266 r.), © Ditta Silvio Meletti srl (492, 520 r.), © G. Miclo (201), © Morimoto/New York, USA/www.morimotonyc.com/Tadao Ando, Ross Lovegrove/Photos courtesy of Morimoto, with the kind permission of Joachim Fischer (54), © H. Mounier (131 t.r.), © NASA/DK-Kopenhagen/www.nasa.dk/ Johannes Torpe Studios ApS/Photos by Jens Stoltze, with the kind permission of Joachim Fischer (58 t.), © Noilly Prat/Treehouse Marketing (537; Marc Torres/L'Oeil du Sud 524, 536), © Nonino (196 t., 228), © Pernod Ricard Studio Photo (495), © Pat Club/RO-Bukarest/Square One/Photos by Fred Valesi, with the kind permission of Joachim Fischer (58 b.), © Pernod-Ricard-Suisse (615), © Pithoi Weinimporteur (95, 467 c., 467 r., 469 t.), © Michael Quack (764, 765, 766, 767), © Raffles, Singapore (46, 47 b.), © Remi Cointreau/MaxXium (614), © Rotkäppchen-Mumm Sektkellereien GmbH (561, 564 l., 598, 599), © Martin Rutkiewicz/Eastway Pictures (400), © David Saradjishvili & Eniseli JSC (167 b.), © Gregor M. Schmid (166 b., 398), © Sketch, London/www.sketch.uk.com/Mourad Mazouz, Gabban O'Keefe, Noe Duchaufour Lawrance, Marc Newson, Chris Levine & Vincent Le Roy/Photos courtesy of Sketch, photocase, with the kind permission of Joachim Fischer (37) © Société Hennessy Collection Historique (111, 112, 113 b., 114, 115, 116), © Société Libanaise pour les Métaux Building, Bernard Khoury (54), © Société Ricard (502 r., 503), © St. George Spirits (226 b.), © St. Raphael – Boisset (547 b.), © Starck Network (60; Patricia Bailer 61), © Matthias Stelzig (166 t., 167 t.), © Suntory/Schlumberger GmbH (378, 379 t.), © Taj Hotels (47 t.), © Tandem Verlag GmbH (Günter Beer 122 (small image), 123, 186, 221 t., 274 t., 399, 406, 420, 504, 518/519, 525, 562, 567; Christoph Büschel/Ruprecht Stempell 279, 285, 591 l.; Sa_a Fuis 298 c.; Werner Stapelfeldt 164, 294 l., 512, 513; Ruprecht Stempell 295 r.), © Supperclub/Bangkok, Thailand/www.bedsupperclub. com/Orbit Design Studio/Photos by Marcus Gortz, with the kind permission of Joachim Fischer (56), © T-O12/D-Stuttgart/www.t-o12.com/ippolito fl eitz group/ Photos by Zooey Braun, with the kind permission of Joachim Fischer (59), © Juan Teixeira (651 b.r., 686, 687), © Tequila Cuervo La Rojeña, S.A. (476 t.), © The Cuckoo Club/UK-London/www.thecuckooclub.com/Blacksheep/Photos by Edmund Sumner, with the kind permission of Joachim Fischer (40), © Miguel Torres SA (158), © Verpoorten GmbH & Co. KG, Bonn (632), © Walkerville Times (374, 375), © Weutz (384), © Zuidam (566)

# Acknowledgments

Many people, companies, and organizations helped to make this book a reality. We should like to extend our sincere thanks to them. Unfortunately we cannot mention everyone, but we have tried to name those who provided us with information, images, and samples. Special thanks go to:

Petra and Jürgen Dietrich, Kölner Rum Kontor, Cologne, www.koelnerrumkontor.de
Ian Gray, Düsseldorf, www.iangray.de
Eric Martin, Vinça, www.ecommercephotos.com
Julia Mundt, Borco-Marken-Import, Hamburg, www.borco.com
Werner Obalski, Munich
Ricardo Rebuelta, Consejo Regulador de Brandy de Jerez, Jerez de la Frontera, www.brandydejerez.es
Marlene Elvira Seitz, Pithoi Import, Bindlach, www.pithoi.com
Dora Simões, Vini Portugal, Torres Vedras, www.viniportugal.pt
Juan Teixeira, Justino's, Madeira, www.justinosmadeira.com
Agata Andrzejczak, IWSR, London, www.iswr.co.uk
Eric Aracil, Comité Interprofessionnel des Vins du Roussillon, Perpignan, www.vins-du-roussillon.com
Stefanie Arntz, Zuidam Distillers, Baarle Nassau, Netherlands
Yvan Auban, Les Alambic du Bas-Armagnac, Estang
Séverin Barioz and Augustin Chazal, Fédération Française des Spiritueux, Paris, www.spiritueux.fr
Oliver Bartelt, Berentzen-Gruppe AG, Haselünne, www.berentzen-gruppe.de
Marlies Baum, Schwarze & Schlichte, Oelde
Andrea Baumgartner, Dettling, Brunnen, Switzerland
Jean and Claire Battault, Gabriel Boudier, Dijon, www.boudier.com
Michael Ben-Joseph, Tel Aviv
Nathalie Bergès- Boisset and Mélina Condi, Boisset, Nuits-Saint-Georges, www.boisset.fr
Familie Berta, Distillerie Berta, Casalotto di Mombaruzzo, www.distillerieberta.it
Su Birch and Andre Morgenthal, Wines of South Africa, www.wosa.co.za
Josephine Blad, Cusenier – Caves Byrrh, Thuir
Olivier Blanc, Cognac Léopold Gourmel, Genté, www.leopold.goumel.com
BNIA: Marie-Claude Segur, Christophe Logeais, Sébastien Lacroix, Eauze, www.armagnac.fr
BNICPE – Bureau National Interprofessionnel du Calvados, du Pommeau et des Eaux-de-Vie de Cidre et de Poiré, Caen
Stella Bouchette, Drinks & Food, Zahna
Frédérique Brion, Distilleries & Domaines de Provence, Forcalquier, www.distilleries-proven-ce.com
Günter Brunner, Freihof, Lustenau, Austria
BSI – Bundesverband der Deutschen Spirituosen-Industrie und -Importeure e. V., Bonn, www.bsi-bonn.de
Claude-Alain Bugnon, Artemisia Distillerie Artisanale, Couvet, www.absinthe-suisse.com
Xavier Cartron, Joseph Cartron, Nuits-Saint-Georges, www.cartron.fr
Alberto Casas and Luis Trillo, Bodegas González Byass, Jerez de la Frontera
Celtic Whiskey Shop, Dublin, www.celticwhiskeyshop.com

Laurence Chesneau-Dupin, Musées de Cognac, Cognac, www.musees-cognac.fr
Apostolos Chorinopoulos, Evangelos Tsantalis AG, Thessaloniki, www.tsantali.gr
Claire Coates, BNIC, Cognac, www.bnic.fr
Max Cointreau, Olivier Paultes, Cognac Frapin, Segonzac, www.frapin.fr
Emilie Dieudonné, Distillerie Paul Devoille, Fougerolles
Arno-Josef Dirker, Mömbris
Beltrán Domecq, Bodega Pedro Domecq, Jerez de la Frontera, www.domecq.es
Sébastien Dormoy, Martinique
Guillaume Drouin, Calvados Christian Drouin, Coudray-Rabut, www.coeur-de-lion.com
Hubert Duchamp de Chastaigne, Rhum JM, Martinique
David Ecobichon, Alain Fion GmbH, Reutlingen, www.fion.de
Chris Edwards and Elaine Weeks, Walkerville Publishing, Walkerville
Graham Eunston, Glenmorangie, Tain
Marco N. Faes, Diageo Germany, Wiesbaden
Cristiana Fanciotto, Martini & Rossi SpA, Pessione, www.martini.com
Pascal and Monique Fillioux, Cognac Jean Fillioux, Julliac-le-Coq
Nadine Fischer, Meike Frers, Informationsbüro Sherry, Integra Communication GmbH, Ham-burg, www.sherry-info.de
Claire Floch, Comité National du Pineau des Charentes, Cognac, www.pineau.fr
Bernadette Galliker, Schweizerischer Obstverband, Zug, Switzerland
Sarah Miriam Gässler, Moët-Hennessy, Munich
Alois Gölles, Riegersburg, Steiermark, Austria
Jean-Pierre Groult, Calvados Roger Groult, 14290 Saint-Cyr du Ronceray, www.calvados-roger-groult.com
Lothar Hausstein, Rosenhut, Rimpar
Hubert Heydt, Haselünne
Markus Holstein, Innovative Destillationstechnik, Markdorf, www.a-holstein.de
Karl Holzapfel,Joching, Wachau, Austria
Lorenz Humbel, Humbel Spezialitätenbrennerei, Stet-ten, www.humbel.ch
Amra Husejnovic, Haromex Development GmbH, Brüggen
Marie Genevieve Jouannet and Tatiana Troubetzkoy, Hennessy, Cognac, www.hennessy-cognac.com
Ruedi Käser, Elfinge, Switzerland
Meike Kent, Türkischer-Weinversand, Bochum
Christoph Kössler, Landeck, Tirol, Austria
Nikos Kokozis, Coracas Importe, Wiesbaden
Shefali Kotnala, United Spirits Limited, Bangalore, www.clubmcdowell.com
KWV, House of Brandy, Worcester
Pierre Laberdolive, Armagnac Laberdolive, Labastide-d'Armagnac
Martine Lafitte, Domaine de Boignères, Le Frèche
Marcello La Monica, Duca di Salaparuta SpA, Florio, Marsala, www.cantineflorio.it
Jürgen Langerfeld, WortFreunde GmbH, Stuttgart
Tim Lockwood, Australian Wine and Brandy Corporation, The Hague, www.wineaustralia.com
Ian Logan, Chivas Brothers, Keith
Brigitte Lucas, Centre de Documentation et d'information, BNIC, Cognac
The Machrie Hotel & Golf Links, Port Ellen, Isle of Islay

Daniel de Manuel, Grupo Matarromera, S.L, Valbuena de Duero, www.matarromera.es
Edmund Marder, Albbruck-Unteralpfen
Nora Carrión Martinez, Rhum Dillon, Fort-de-France
Petra Mayer, PM- Kommunikation, South Africa Wein-information, www.suedafrika-wein.de
Stephen McCarthy, Clear Creek Distillery, Portland, www.clearcreekdistillery.com
Robin Mouatt, Blackwood Distillers, Shetland Islands, Scotland
Familie Moutard, Champagne Moutard and Distillerie, Buxeuil, www.champagne-moutard.fr
Yasunori Nakai, Suntory Limited, London, www.suntori.com
Nationales Genevermuseum, 3500 Hasselt, www.hasselt.be
Claudine Neisson-Vernant, Rhum Neisson, Martinique
Birgit Nummer, Bernard-Massard Sektkellerei GmbH, Trier
Verena Oberwieser, Martin Beierl, Enzianbrenne-rei Grassl, Berchtesgaden
Peter O'Connor, Baileys, Diageo, Dublin
Andrea Ostheer, Mast-Jägermeister AG, Wolfen-büttel
Mark Palacio, Miguel Torres SA, Villafranca del Pendés, www.torres.es
Yiannis Parassiris, EOSS, Samos
Patrick Peyrelongue, Cognac Delamain, Jarnac, www.le-cognac.com/delamain
Marco Ponzano, Centra Servizi Maria Branca, Milan
Michel Poulain, Calvados Père Magloire, Pont - l'Evêque, www.pere-magloire.com
David Quinn, Irish Distillers, Cork
François Rebel, Cognac Guy Lheraud, Angéac-Charente, www.cognaclheraud.com
Hans Reisetbauer, Thening, Linzland, Austria
Pietman Retief, SA Brand Foundation, Stellenbosch, www.sabrandy.co.za
Cécile Richards-Luisoni, Zurich
Jacques Rivière, Cognac A.E. Dor, Jarnac, www.aedor.com
Michaela Robinson, Moët Hennessy Germany, Munich
Günther Rochelt, Fritzens, Tirol, Austria
Adela Córdoba Ruz, Perez Barquero, Montilla, www.perezbarquero.com
John Clement Ryan, Dublin
Tonnellerie Sansaud, Segonzac, www.sansaud-france.fr
Marc Sassier, Rhum Saint-James, Martinique
Syndicat de Défense de l'Appellation D'origine "Rhum Agricole Martinique", Fort-de-France
Kieran Tobin, Irish Distillers, Dublin
Philippe Traber, Distillerie Metté, Ribeauville, France
Kostas Tsililis, Trikala, Greece
Christos Tziolis, Cava, Berlin
Hubertus and Aurelie Vallendar, Pommern/Mosel
Benoît Vettorel, Tariquet, Eauze, www.tariquet.com
Jean-Pierre Vidal and Renaud de Gironde, Hennessy, Cognac
Jean-Paul Vuilmet, Clos d'Orval, Amaye-sur-Seulles
Beth Warner, Kittling Ridge Estate Wines & Spirits, www.FortyCreekWhisky.com
Brigitte Weutz, St. Nikolai, Steiermark, Austria
Ielanda Willemse, The South African Brandy Foundation, Stellenbosch, www.sabrandy.co.za
Ulrike Zölzer, Maxxium Deutschland Pressestelle, Schöneck
Patrick Zuidam, Zuidam Distillers, Baarle Nassau, Netherlands